Electronic Publishing Construction Kit

*Creating Multimedia for Disk,
CD-ROM, and the Internet*

Electronic Publishing Construction Kit

*Creating Multimedia for Disk,
CD-ROM, and the Internet*

Scott Johnson

Wiley Computer Publishing

John Wiley & Sons, Inc.
New York • Chichester • Brisbane • Toronto • Singapore

Associate Publisher: Katherine Schowalter

Editor: Tim Ryan

Managing Editor: Robert S. Aronds

Text Design & Composition: SunCliff Graphic Productions

This text is printed on acid-free paper.

Library of Congress Cataloging-in-Publication Data

ISBN: 0-471-12854-6

Printed in the United States of America

10 9 8 7 6 5 4 3 2 1

Contents

Part 3   **Applying Digital Publishing**   **389**

Chapter 17   **Building an Interactive Catalog**   **391**

Chapter 18   **Building a Web Site**   **481**

Introduction

Welcome to *The Electronic Publishing Construction Kit*! Before we discuss what this book covers, let's first start with what it *doesn't* cover. To be specific, there are three areas that *The Electronic Publishing Construction Kit* doesn't cover:

- Desktop publishing
- Print publishing
- Using electronic publishing to produce printed works

What *The Electronic Publishing Construction Kit* covers is publishing for digital media. By digital media, I am referring to interactive publications distributed on floppy disc, CD-ROM, local area network, and even the Internet's World Wide Web. In other words, true electronic publishing (not electronic publishing from the perspective of simply producing a printed work).

Who Am I?

Before you read too far, you will probably be curious as to my background and credentials. My name is Scott Johnson, and over the course of the past nine years, I have been president of a digital publishing tools developer named NTERGAID, Inc. based in Connecticut. Since our founding in 1987, NTERGAID has published a popular line of digital publishing tools known as the HyperWriter family of products. These products are in use both nationally and internationally, and have been used to produce literally thousands of digital publications. Over the years that I have been involved with digital publishing, I have developed software tools for digital publishing, published articles, created CD-ROM titles, spoken at conferences, developed Web sites and more. In short, I have been deeply involved with digital publishing for virtually my entire professional life.

NTERGAID: The Company with the Funny Name

NTERGAID is a software development firm specializing in the HyperWriter product line. Along with selling HyperWriter, NTERGAID also offers full-fledged electronic publishing services focused on custom development of CD-ROM titles and Internet Web sites. NTERGAID is one of today's leaders in digital publishing technology. The name NTERGAID is not a conventional corporate name. As you may be wondering what this name means, I am going to digress a bit and tell you. Pronounced "ENTER GADE" (sounds like GatorAde), NTERGAID is an invented word that uses every letter in "Integrated" only once. When I cofounded NTERGAID in 1987, we wanted a name that used the word integrated because we felt that digital publications were actually integrated together. Like many things, while the concept was good, the reality was less so. We discovered this when we signed for our first computer trade show and discovered that not only were digital publications integrated, so was everything else! From this bit of information, the name NTERGAID was created.

Understanding This Book

As with many topics in the computer industry, truly understanding digital publishing means actually publishing digitally. In short, digital publishing is an applied task, not an abstract task. Although the skills needed are different, it is very similar to programming in that reading about programming does not make you a programmer—programming makes you a programmer. To allow this book to make you a digital publisher, this book is bundled with a fully functional evaluation of our HyperWriter digital publishing toolkit. Not only does this book discuss digital publishing, it also walks you through the steps of building digital publications. By the end of this book, you will have developed several very substantial digital publications including an Internet Web site.

This book is organized into three parts as shown in Table 1.

What Is HyperWriter?

HyperWriter is a Windows based authoring system used for creating digital publications (a DOS version is also available). Central to HyperWriter is its underlying hypertext engine. Hypertext is a technology for structuring information into individual chunks that are interconnected by links. This hypertext engine lets you easily assemble digital publications as collections of hypertext elements. In fact, as discussed further in Chapter 1, HyperWriter uses hypertext as the backbone of digital publications.

Table 1 Understanding How this Book Is Organized

Part	Description
Part I: Chapters 1 through 5	**Digital Publishing Basics** Cover the theory and issues behind digital publishing. This includes an extensive look at the World Wide Web.
Part II: Chapters 6 through 16	**Learning HyperWriter** Cover learning HyperWriter and focus on walking you through HyperWriter's features on a topic-by-topic basis. This part is best treated as a tutorial where you actually work through them on the computer as you read the book.
Part III: Chapters 17 and 18	**Advanced Tutorials** Cover the steps in building actual digital publications, you learn by doing. In the course of these two chapters, you build an interactive catalog and an Internet World Wide Web home page. As with Part II, this part is best treated as a tutorial.

Unlike many digital publishing tools that focus on a particular type of publication such as technical documentation or electronic catalogs, Hyper-Writer is a general purpose tool that can be applied to many different tasks. Among the standard features in HyperWriter are:

- Hypertext linking, including automatic linking
- Screen design tools
- Configuration tools
- A built-in word processor with stylesheets
- Full-text retrieval
- Navigation tools for browsing documents
- A royalty-free runtime for digital publishing without licensing fees

Conventions Used in This Book

The focus of this book is showing you how to create documents that you can publish electronically, so it is important to understand how I will refer to the commands/keystrokes that you will use. The named keys (**Enter**, **Alt**, etc.) on your keyboard are represented in bold face. An example is **Enter**, which references the **Enter** key. Whenever you see one of these keys, this means to touch that actual key on the keyboard. If you are to touch another key concurrently with that key then a "+" sign indicates this. An example is **Alt+L**, which refers to pressing the **Alt** key along with the letter **L**. If you need to touch a sequence of keys that begin with one of the named keys on the keyboard, then only the named key is shown in bold face. For example, **Alt+L T J** indicates that you should press **Alt** with the **L** key and then the **T** and **J** keystrokes respectively. The **Arrowkey** command indicates that you should simply touch any arrow key such as **Uparrow**, **Downarrow**, **Leftarrow**, or **Rightarrow**.

Where Do I Go From Here?

Now that you have read the Introduction, you probably are wondering where to go from here. If you want to read this book conventionally, then Chapter 1 is the best place to start. The other approach to reading this book is to start by getting your hands dirty and actually working with HyperWriter to do some digital publishing. If this appeals to you, then I would recommend starting with Part II. If you are already familiar with HyperWriter, or are well-versed in Digital Publishing, then I recommend starting with Chapter 6, which covers installing HyperWriter, and then moving on to Part III which features advanced tutorials using HyperWriter.

Digital Publishing Basics

Welcome to Part I of the Electronic Publishing Construction Kit. In this part, we cover the theory and issues found in Digital Publishing. This includes the following topics:

- An overall understanding of digital publishing
- A short history of digital publishing
- A discussion of applications for digital publishing
- Coverage of the Internet's World Wide Web
- A discussion of where digital publishing is headed

Unlike Part II and Part III, Part I is not tutorial driven or designed to be used with a computer. Part I is best read as a traditional printed work (Part II is actually extensively tutorial driven and best read with easy access to a computer so you can follow the tutorials). When you have completed Part I, you should have a solid overview of digital publishing.

CHAPTER 1

Understanding Digital Publishing

Welcome to the Electronic Publishing Construction Kit. This book covers publishing information on digital media, specifically floppy disc, CD-ROM, and the Internet. Among the topics discussed are:

- Hypertext
- The World Wide Web
- Full text searching
- User interface design

A key topic covered in this book is *hypertext*. Hypertext is a technology for splitting information into multiple chunks, or *topics* that are interconnected by links. The reason that hypertext is so significant for digital publishing is that, when you come down to it, most digital publishing is based on hypertext at one level or another. You should note that this book is really based on approaching digital publishing through a hypertext metaphor. Consider a simple digital publication consisting of nothing more than a table of contents and series of related documents. When the user selects an entry from the table of contents, this can be considered a hypertext jump to a related document. Technologically, the system might not consider this hypertext, but to the user, it appears as a hypertext element.

One of the nice aspects of hypertext as an approach to digital publishing is that hypertext not only offers powerful linking and navigation facilities, but also subsumes other approaches to digital publishing, such as databases. A discussion of different approaches to digital publishing and how hypertext can be used in their place is covered in Chapter 3.

Before we get into a technical discussion of what digital publishing is, let's first consider reasons that we might want to publish in digital form.

Why Publish Digitally?

One of the questions I have encountered over the years is why someone would want to publish information electronically. Although there are a number of reasons for digital publishing, let's look at some of the key reasons.

- **Making money.** A key reason for publishing in digital form today is simply the desire to make money. Most publishers of print-based works are looking to generate additional revenue streams through CD-ROM and Internet-based versions of their existing products.

- **Saving money.** For some digital publishers, their publications don't make any money, but they can certainly save money. Depending on the publications that you have, publishing them in electronic form (whatever the distribution media) can be dramatically less expensive. Additional benefits include the elimination of outdated, incorrect print publications.

- **Free navigation.** If you think about traditional publishing, one of the difficulties for a reader is that he or she follows a predefined path—the order of the information in the document. While this is fine for a novel or other linear work, for reference materials the reader really needs to be able to browse a publication in the order he or she is interested in. This type of browsing puts the reader, not the author, in charge. Properly constructed digital publications support this type of free navigation.

- **Hypertext linking.** One of the real limits of print publishing is the difficulty of following cross-references. Although print publications can include cross-references such as "See page 125," they generally aren't followed, simply because it's too much work for the reader. Digital publications let these references be converted to easy-to-follow hypertext links.

- **Too much paper.** For many publishers, publishing on paper simply isn't an option. Whenever you have literally volumes of information, such as that found in the legal field, digital publishing not only lets you deliver them more effectively, but also deliver them more cheaply.

- **Full-text searching.** Although not all publications need to be searchable, when a publication needs to be searchable, it generally needs it badly. Although not all digital publishing tools support full-text searching, the better tools do.

- **Organizing information differently.** Print publications are generally organized only through a table of contents or an index. Digital publications can let information be organized more effectively through different tools. While these include tables of contents and indices, they can also include thematic maps, topical guidelines, hierarchical outlines, timeline views, and more.

- **Doing things print can't.** Depending on the type of publications you want to create, there are digital publications that simply never could be created using print media. Good examples of these can be found in the different multimedia encyclopedias, where text is fully integrated with different media elements to provide a much richer learning environment.

Basic Digital Publishing Concepts

Now that we understand some of the reasons for digital publishing, we need to go over some basic concepts of digital publishing. As this book takes a hypertext-driven approach, these concepts come from the hypertext field.

What Is Hypertext?

As noted earlier, hypertext provides a way to publish documents broken into topics and interconnected by links. In a hypertext document, rather than turning pages to find more information or using an index to find a topic, it is structured so that wherever more information exists it is linked off a key word or phrase. An example of this is shown in Figure 1.1.

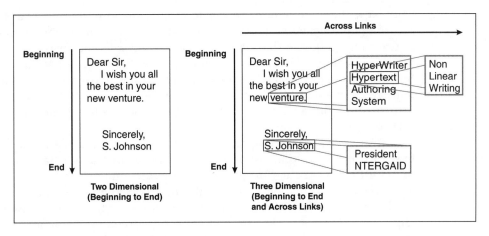

Figure 1.1 A sample hypertext.

As you can see, the document shown is nonlinear in nature. By definition, linear writing is two dimensional. Words go across the line and the lines flow down the page. Hypertext, on the other hand, is three dimensional; it gives writing depth. Every word in a document inherently has a meaning or a relationship to other words. But without hypertext, the people reading your document might have to look in a dictionary or encyclopedia to find an explanation of a difficult or obscure topic. Hypertext links allow any word or phrase to be linked to additional information, thus clarifying the original reference.

Although the idea of nonlinear writing on computers (hypertext) has only recently become popular (see the closing section for a history of hypertext), nonlinear writing has been in use for decades, if not longer. Any medium typically used for browsing instead of cover-to-cover reading is nonlinear. Common examples of this include encyclopedias, newspapers, and magazines.

Encyclopedias are an excellent example of nonlinear reading in action. Almost any article in an encyclopedia refers to other articles. In hypertext terminology, these references would be called *links*—electronic gateways to the article being referenced. Due to the extensive indexing and organization of most encyclopedias, almost any reference or link can be followed to more information. With encyclopedias, however, it is manually difficult to follow all the possible links. Accessing indexes and different volumes of the encyclopedia quickly takes the fun out of following links.

A normal session spent reading an encyclopedia might go something like this. You're interested in reading about Italian artwork of the High Renaissance. You go to an index volume, which directs you to Volume R of the encyclopedia. This gives you an overview essay and directs you to Volume A for more information. You take out Volume A and begin reading. Halfway through the article, you see a reference to the artwork of Michelangelo, and you're curious about that. So, you pull out the index volume again and look up Michelangelo. Now there are two references to Michelangelo to follow. After following the first reference, you discover it's not what you're looking for. From this, you return to the index to find out what the second reference was. Now you pull out the M volume. Here, you find an essay on the works of Michelangelo. By turning the pages you read the essay and see some of his artwork. After you're done reading about Michelangelo, you decide to return to the last article you were reading. But where was that? The A volume, the R volume, or somewhere else entirely?

Now, for contrast, compare this description of the same research using a hypertext encyclopedia. You're interested in reading about Italian artwork of the High Renaissance. You go to an index document with an entry for the Renaissance and click on it. This will jump you to an overview document of the Renaissance. From here, you can point to an entry for the artwork of the High Renaissance and click on it to jump right to that information. Here, there is reference to the works of Michelangelo. By clicking on Michelangelo, you can display pictures of his artwork right on screen. From any one of these points, alternative trails could be followed to more information. (Note: This session reflects an actual hypertext document called Culture 1.0.)

What Is Hypermedia?

Hypermedia is the modern offspring of hypertext. The focus of hypermedia is that any piece of information, not only text, should be accessible in a nonlinear fashion. Hypermedia extends the hypertext concept to pictures, video, animation, and audio. From this point on, the terms hypertext and hypermedia will be used interchangeably.

Hypermedia Terminology

Hypermedia, like many other disciplines, has evolved a set of semistandard terminology commonly used to describe it. For clarification of these terms, see Figure 1.2.

Link

The *link* is the basic element of a hypermedia document. Links form an instant relationship or connection between the link source and the destination. By pointing to a link and clicking on it, a reader or writer is brought to the destination of the link: a topic or node. Typically, links can be created to and from any of the media types (text, graphics, sound, etc.) present in the hypermedia document. The word *button* is commonly used for link. To HyperWriter, a button is just a more visual way of representing a link.

Link Anchor

The *link anchor* is the originator of the link. It serves as an activation point for accessing the contents of the link. In Figure 1.1, *venture* is the link anchor for *HyperWriter Hypermedia Authoring System*. Another term for link anchor is *link icon*. Link anchors are extremely important as links are created by first marking the link anchor.

Link End

The *link end*, also called the *destination* of the link, is the data that the link anchor accesses. In Figure 1.1, *President* is the link end for *S. Johnson*.

Topic or Node

Topics or nodes form the basic subunits or data elements of a hypermedia document. A topic may be viewed as a separate document or subdocument con-

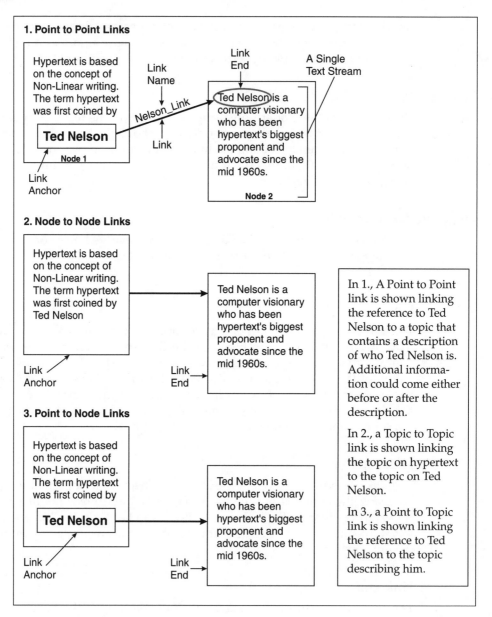

Figure 1.2 The anatomy of a hypertext document.

tained within one hypermedia file. In some hypertext systems, topics are called *cards*, *nodes*, or *pages*. The basic distinction between a link and a topic is that while a link connects information, a topic contains information.

Multimedia versus Digital Publishing

One of the topics often confused with digital publishing is multimedia. Multimedia, when you come right down to it, is just multiple media types. The common definition of multimedia is that of a presentation, something that is sequential in nature. This is very different from digital publishing, which puts the reader in control and lets the reader navigate freely. As a general rule of thumb, digital publishing is a superset of multimedia. Whereas digital publishing incorporates multimedia, multimedia does not necessarily incorporate digital publishing. Most digital publishing tools, such as our HyperWriter toolkit, include support for adding multimedia to digital publications. While the level of multimedia support differs from tool to tool, multimedia elements like video and audio can generally be integrated into digital publications.

SGML and Digital Publishing

SGML, Standard Generalized Markup Language, is a high-end text markup language that is often perceived as related to hypertext and digital publishing. While SGML can be related to hypertext, in and of itself there isn't a direct relationship between SGML and hypertext. SGML is an international standard (ISO 8879) for embedding markup in a document. By markup, SGML refers to explicit tags that indicate elements in documents. For example, a chapter might be indicated by **<CHAPTER>** and **</CHAPTER>** tags. There are two primary thrusts in SGML. The first is that it separates document content from document structure and the second is that it separates document formatting from document content. With all SGML documents, there is the concept of the DTD, or document type definition. The DTD is an SGML entity that defines the logical structure of a document. Because an SGML document has a logical structure (unlike a word processing document where anything can go anywhere), an SGML document can be automatically validated to determine if it is correct or not. This validation is a key feature in allowing SGML text to be used in applications where textual content needs to be automatically moved between different applications such as print manuals and electronic manuals. The second key thrust in SGML is that document formatting is separate from document content. Unlike a word processor where formatting is an integral part of a document, in SGML formatting is separate from the document. Let's consider how an SGML system treats a heading. In SGML, a heading might be tagged with **<HEAD1>** and **</HEAD1>** tags that indicate the start and end of a heading. Note that there is no formatting information stored with the **HEAD1** tags—this information resides separately and different sets of formatting information can be used for different purposes.

Note: People that have used the World Wide Web are probably recognizing similarities between HTML and SGML. This is correct, there are similarities between them. Please see Chapter 4 for more details on the World Wide Web.

Now that we have looked at some of the good features in SGML, the question becomes should one use SGML for digital publishing? Although I like SGML technology and feel it has a lot to offer, as a general rule the answer is no. While many SGML purists and advocates would disagree with me, there are a number of facts about SGML that lead me to conclude that it simply isn't ready for widespread digital publishing use. These include:

- **Price.** SGML-based tools are dramatically more expensive than non-SGML- based tools.
- **Selection.** There are relatively few SGML tools available, and really only one SGML-based digital publishing tool (DynaText from Electronic Book Technologies).
- **Conversion.** Standard digital publishing tools don't generally accept SGML data so special conversion tools need to be used.
- **Ease of use.** SGML is still a very technical standard and is difficult to use.
- **Training.** If you are trying to get started with SGML, you really need to invest in education and training.

Despite these drawbacks to SGML technology, there are situations where SGML should be of interest to you. If your organization has committed to SGML and your content is already in SGML format, then you should definitely consider an SGML-based digital publishing system. Other areas where SGML should be considered is when you are creating all new content and can avoid the issue of conversion all together. Although this still requires new software and training, it does skip one of the hardest aspects of moving to SGML. As noted, SGML technology can be difficult to understand. One thing that I hope is clear about SGML is that it is not required for digital publishing.

The History of Digital Publishing

To really understand any topic, look at its history. As noted in the beginning of this chapter, this book takes a hypertext driven perspective on digital publishing. Consequently, the history that follows is really a short history of hypertext. Like many technologies, hypertext was initially driven by a few key figures: Vannevar Bush, Douglas Engelbart, and Ted Nelson (who actually coined the term *hypertext*).

Vannevar Bush

Although hypertext and digital publishing have only recently (in the past few years) come to public attention, they are not new. Hypertext was first conceived of over 40 years ago, by Vannevar Bush—President Roosevelt's Science Advisor. In a ground-breaking article, first printed in the *Atlantic Monthly*, Vannevar Bush stated:

> *The human mind...operates by association. With one item in its grasp, it snaps instantly to the next that is suggested by the association of thoughts, in accordance with some intricate web of trails carried by the cells of the brain....*
>
> *Man cannot hope to fully duplicate this mental process artificially, but he certainly ought to be able to learn from it.... Selection by association, rather than by indexing, may yet be mechanized.*

The rest of this article focuses on Bush's description of such a machine to "mechanize the associations." His term for this machine was a memex, essentially a microfilm system with the ability to build trails between materials. Although the memex was never built, Vannevar Bush laid the framework from which all hypertext systems have descended.

It is important to note that Vannevar Bush's article was published in July of 1945, during World War II and before the modern era of computers ever began. Vannevar Bush's conception of the memex was a tool that a scientist could use to keep up with the vast amount of knowledge available. In 1945, before the information age had even been recognized, not only had Vannevar Bush recognized it, but created the intellectual foundation for an entire industry. Vannevar Bush revisited this topic in a book of essays issued twenty years later where he not only called again for a memex, but recognized that computer technology would be its core.

Douglas Engelbart

Douglas Engelbart is one of the unsung heroes of the computer age. In addition to pioneering cutting edge work in the hypertext community, he invented the mouse, outline processing, word processing, much of what is known today as groupware, multiple windows, and more. Douglas Engelbart first encountered the hypertext concept through Vannevar Bush's article while a radar technician in World War II. After the war, Douglas Engelbart entered the computer field, where he developed an initial hypertext system called NLS, which later evolved into an environment called Augment. The NLS research was initially done at the Stanford Research Institute (SRI) and then continued at McDonnell Douglas where the Augment system was developed.

Central to all of Douglas Engelbart's work has been the notion of augmenting a knowledge worker's intellect through software tools as expressed in his 1962 paper "A Conceptual Framework for the Augmentation of Man's Intellect." Rather than a specific focus on publishing information (though this is included), Douglas Engelbart's work has centered on how hypertext can allow a knowledge worker to perform better and accomplish more. A central guideline in the design of Augment is the absence of paper at all levels. With storage of everything a knowledge worker needs through a computer, there is no lost information, no missing notes. This promised an end to the ever present problem of losing productivity through missing information.

Today, some forty years later, Douglas Engelbart is still hard at work creating hypertext systems for augmenting knowledge workers. He has left McDonnell Douglas and has formed the Bootstrap Institute, a nonprofit organization focused on creating next generation hypertext and augmentation tools.

Ted Nelson

As the coiner of the term hypertext and the field's most flamboyant figure, Ted Nelson is the figure most commonly associated with hypertext. When describing Ted Nelson, I am really at a loss for words—Ted Nelson can't be described, he must be experienced. Whereas many figures in the computer industry tend to be solemn, introverted, and generally quiet, Ted Nelson is manic, colorful, extroverted, and possibly one of the most literate people I have ever met. I don't know how to describe Ted Nelson adequately, but I can tell a little bit of his story. (As a side note, if you ever have the opportunity to see Ted Nelson speak publicly, run, don't walk. It's well worth it.)

Like Douglas Engelbart, Ted Nelson was deeply influenced by Vannevar Bush. This influence has led Ted Nelson to carry the torch for hypertext through over thirty years of dedication, research, and commitment. From Vannevar Bush, Ted Nelson developed his conception of hypertext: "nonlinear writing or reading."

Working and attending a number of different academic institutions, Ted Nelson formed his own conception of the world's ideal hypertext system: Xanadu. Xanadu is a blueprint for a globally distributed, world-wide, hypertext-based information repository for all the world's publishing. Suffice it to say, Ted Nelson has never been accused of thinking small. Named for Coleridge's "magic place of literary memory," Xanadu was designed as a multi-user reading and writing system that included full accounting facilities, so a publisher could be compensated for someone reading information stored in the system. In addition, anyone could create links through material and even include material from another publisher in their own work through a transclusion mechanism which allowed for only a single copy of any piece of information to be stored in the system.

Over the course of time as Ted Nelson conceived of Xanadu, he has written, spoken, and generally preached the benefits of hypertext to all who would listen. Among his writings have been the books *Computer Lib/Dream Machines*, and *Literary Machines*, all of which served as direct or indirect inspiration for a great many of today's hypertext systems. With all this talk about Xanadu, you may be wondering how to use Xanadu. Unfortunately, you can't use Xanadu as it has never been completed and released. Xanadu was largely a labor of love by Ted Nelson and several associates. Never well funded, Xanadu was actually acquired by AutoDesk in the late 1980s, where the project was eventually disbanded due to financial difficulties. People familiar with the World Wide Web probably recognize more than a little bit of Xanadu in the Web, and, on the surface they are correct. The Web does provide a powerful, globally distributed hypertext system. However, the Web lacks most of the key features that Xanadu was to provide such as user billing, end-user linking, transclusion, and more. There is a very good possibility, however, that the Web will ultimately evolve towards what Xanadu was designed to be.

I should note here that neither Ted Nelson nor Xanadu have gone away. Ted Nelson is no longer with AutoDesk, but is still involved with hypertext and Xanadu. He is currently working in a Japanese research laboratory.

Tools for Digital Publishing: The Four Generations of Hypertext

Beyond the three central figures that really established the intellectual, practical, and ultimate goal of hypertext, hypertext technology has had a number of significant tools evolve that helped form today's digital publishing industry. When you look at how digital publishing and the tools digital publishing has evolved, you can really break it down into four separate generations of technology that have culminated in today's digital publishing environments:

- Early research tools
- Commercial hypertext architectures
- Windows help-based tools
- The World Wide Web

Each of these technology generations is covered below. I have also included a sidebar on page replacement tools like Adobe Acrobat which may constitute another generation of tools (it is still too early to tell).

Early Research Tools

In the 1960s, 1970s, and 1980s, hypertext was considered a very avant-garde topic among computer scientists. Consequently, a large number of early research systems were developed at different computer science departments, primarily in the United States and Europe. Typically minicomputer- or workstation/UNIX-based, these systems were the first hypertext systems to come into some sort of widespread use. Of the early research systems, three were particularly influential: ZOG, NoteCards, and Intermedia. For reasons of brevity, I am skipping over many notable systems.

ZOG was originally developed at Carnegie-Mellon University and really demonstrated that hypertext could scale up to large applications with the implementation of a shipwide hypertext-based information system for the USS Carl Vinson, a U.S. Navy aircraft carrier. ZOG focused on large textual frames that could be linked and hierarchically organized. ZOG still exists today as the KMS tool discussed in Chapter 3. NoteCards, developed at the Xerox Palo Alto Research Center, took the metaphor of hyperlinked index cards complete with specialized browsers and other navigation tools. Although Xerox ultimately did market NoteCards commercially, its reliance on special Xerox workstation hardware and implementation in a nonstandard programming language led to little commercial use. Of all the early hypertext systems, the Intermedia system, developed at Brown University, is the only one that would be recognizable to users of today's digital publishing tools, as it was based on the Macintosh user interface (although actually ran on a UNIX workstation). Intermedia was notable for its implementation of the Web concept whereby links were overlaid on existing documents and each user could have their own set of links. Other notable concepts in Intermedia were systemwide linking facilities as well as a series of robust applications including a word processor, image editor, three-dimensional modeling tools, and more. Using the systemwide linking facilities, any object from any application could be hyperlinked. Although Intermedia was eventually disbanded when it lost funding, it, like the other early research systems, paved the way for many of today's hypermedia products.

Commercial Hypertext Architectures: The PC Revolution

What came out of the early research tools was a number of different PC-based digital publishing tools. While some of these had direct ties to research systems, such as Guide, which was originally developed in Europe, others were all new creations, designed specifically for PCs, such as HyperWriter. Commercial digital publishing tools for PCs didn't really become available until the late 1980s. Among those initial products were our own HyperWriter (known at the time as Black Magic), Guide, and HyperCard. Although HyperCard is not really designed for digital publishing, it did dramatically raise interest in hypertext and digital publishing in general. One of the key factors in all the early hypertext systems was that developers of the systems had to develop everything, including the authoring and viewing environments. This is very different from the next two generations of technology: in Windows Help and the World Wide Web the viewing engines already exist.

Windows Help-based Tools

When Microsoft released Microsoft Windows version 3.0, they also released a little-noticed facility called the Microsoft Windows Help Engine or WINHELP. What WINHELP was designed to do was provide basic help system facilities for software programs through a hypertext approach. What WINHELP has become is an alternative platform for digital publishing, with many digital publications being published using its facilities. An active community of third-party developers also offer enhancement products and additional tools. The amount of interest in WINHELP seems unlikely given its humble beginnings. However, two key factors led to WINHELP's success. The first is that WIN-HELP is bundled with every copy of Microsoft Windows. This simple fact led to digital publishers not having to ship viewing software along with their publications. The net effect of this was that virtually anyone could read a document created in WINHELP, leading to rapid adoption as a popular tool for distributing information. The second factor was even more critical: WINHELP is royalty free and needs no runtime licensing. Although our HyperWriter software has never been royalty based, many digital publishing tools still are. This second factor also greatly led to widespread use of WINHELP. Although WIN-HELP is primarily a tool for help systems, it has become a popular alternative to other digital publishing tools.

The World Wide Web

The World Wide Web is today's fastest growing digital publishing environment. Originally developed at CERN, a European physics research laboratory, the World Wide Web or Web is a section of the Internet that has emerged as *the* place for electronic publishing and electronic commerce. Information published on the Web is presented to the end user in a graphical and textual format, making the information not only accessible but interesting to review. Not only can the Web present text and graphics, it can also let a user view video and audio clips as well as query databases, run programs, send mail, and more. In short, the Web offers an *information architecture* for presenting, viewing, and retrieving information. In just the few short years the Web has been in active use, it has really changed the face of digital publishing. What the Web has done is bring a new element to digital publishing, that of using the Internet as a distribution media. Whereas only a year ago, all a digital publisher might be concerned about was publishing on CD-ROM and (maybe) a commercial online service, now virtually all digital publishers expect to publish on the Web as well.

Note: Page Replacement Tools

One of the real deficiencies in terms of digital publishing has been the effort needed to author a digital publication. Although this depends on the tool used, no one can deny that creating digital publications can often be a time-consuming, difficult task. Given that most publications already exist in print format, one approach that can virtually eliminate this authoring effort entirely is to simply replicate the printed page on the computer screen. This is the approach taken by Adobe's Acrobat tool and others. Although the idea of replacing the page with the computer screen is not new, it has only recently been technologically viable for large-scale publishing with the introduction of Acrobat and its competitors which, rather than store the page as an image, store the page through a compact page rendering language such as PostScript. What storing a page as PostScript or another rendering language has done is dramatically reduce the storage size of each page as well as allow full-text searching of the publication. Although these page-replacement tools have been available for over two years now, the jury is still out as to whether they will really constitute a generation of technology or be just another digital publishing product. Adobe's Acrobat was initially unsuccessful and is now being repositioned as an adjunct to the World Wide Web, a strategic positioning that is too early to evaluate.

CHAPTER 2

Applications of Digital Publishing

Digital publishing, when you first consider it, seems to be a very specialized application of computers. How many people actually consider themselves publishers? This is a point with which I think most people would agree: most people aren't publishers. Or are they? All publishing is making information available to someone else. Yes, most people aren't involved in publishing per se, but an awful lot of people are involved in making information available to others. This ranges from people who write employee manuals to those who create catalogs, or even those who write newsletters intended only for internal corporate distribution. In an information-based society, something we're moving closer and closer to, publishing is really a fundamental act. This brings us to a fundamental reality: Although not everyone is a publisher, anyone who needs to retrieve information is a possible candidate for an application of digital publishing; that is to say, virtually anyone might need to read a digital publication. When you look at digital publishing from this perspective, it becomes much clearer that digital publishing can be applied to a large number of different applications.

This chapter will talk about different applications of digital publishing, as well as some of the constraints on digital publishing and when it should and shouldn't be used.

Understanding Constraints on Digital Publishing

Digital publishing is an incredibly powerful technology that can be applied to many areas where information is published. This isn't to say, however, that digital publishing is perfect. It certainly isn't and there are areas where it definitely suffers. Covered below are general situations where digital publishing can be used, as well as some of the constraints that apply to digital publishing.

Where Can Digital Publishing Be Used?

When you start to look at where digital publishing can be used, the first task is to look at the nature of digital publishing technology. What digital publishing technology does is make information more easily navigable, searchable, and retrievable. What this means is that natural applications of digital publishing technology are publications that follow an information-retrieval model as opposed to a reading in-depth model. A good example is an employee policy manual. Virtually every company has an employee manual, but who actually reads it? These manuals are used as retrieval tools—when you have a question about your vacation plan, you browse the publication to find this information and then read only that section. Another good example of a retrieval-oriented publication is computer software documentation. As we all know, no one reads the documentation. What people do is look up specific topics and then read only those topics. While strictly speaking there isn't anything that prevents you from applying digital publishing to information not oriented to information retrieval, you typically have the most luck with this type of information.

Another criteria for applying digital publishing technology is that you want to apply it to publications that will benefit from digital publishing technology, publications where digital publishing adds value. This point is further discussed in the next section.

Where Shouldn't Digital Publishing Be Used?

As noted above, one of the best applications of digital publishing technology is information retrieval applications where the reader needs to locate specific bits of information. The opposite of an information retrieval application is a publication that is designed to be read in full, such as a novel, which is a good example of an area where digital publishing just isn't applicable. This is partly due to the nature of a novel where the information retrieval aspects of digital publishing don't add any value to the work. This brings us to a good guideline for when to apply digital publishing technology: Use digital publishing technology when it adds value either for the publisher or the reader. Don't use digital publishing technology for the sake of using digital publishing technology.

Value in a digital publication can come either at the publisher or reader side. For a publisher, the added value might be that the digital version of a publication is less expensive to produce. For a reader, the value might be added navigation tools or the ability to search the content. The added value can be on either side of the publisher–reader relationship, but it needs to be there for a digital publication to be successful.

If we think a little bit more about novels and digital publishing, we realize how people read novels—they read them in a chair, in bed, in the tub, on a train. In short, they read them in areas where a computer just isn't available. We now have another guideline about when to use or not use digital publishing technology: As digital publishing requires a computer to be used as the retrieval device, digital publishing generally does best when the cost of a computer isn't an issue.

Until recently, with the dramatic drop in PC prices, this guideline often led to digital publishing being restricted to expensive, important publications where the cost or importance of the publication justified the cost of the hardware required to view the publication.

Another area where digital publishing has traditionally not done very well is with publications that are driven by their page layout. Consider a publication like a newspaper, with its multiple columns, embedded pictures, sidebars, and other design elements. A newspaper is a good example of a publication that is driven by its page layout. The size of a computer screen is so much smaller than a printed page, much less a newspaper page, that these types of page layout/design intensive publications often don't work well as a digital publication. You can get around this to some extent by picking a digital publishing tool that emulates a printed page. Still, this brings us to an additional guideline for when to use/not use digital publishing: Digital publishing generally doesn't do well when it has to emulate paper. When you come right down to it, a computer screen isn't paper and doesn't act like paper. Digital publications are best suited to taking advantage of this new medium, rather than replicating the old.

Traditionally, one of the real constraints on digital publishing was that it wasn't suited to publications that had to be frequently updated. This was due to the lead times associated with diskette or CD-ROM manufacturing. This limitation has largely gone away with the growth of the Internet's World Wide Web as a popular medium for digital publishing.

Applications of Digital Publishing

Digital publishing can be applied to a wide range of different areas for both internal corporate use and use by commercial publishers. The following sections cover selected applications of digital publishing. At the end of each application is an example that illustrates a real-world example of that digital publishing application, all of which are real-world applications of the Hyper-Writer digital publishing tool bundled with this book.

Electronic Documentation

From policy-and-procedure manuals to personnel manuals to technical documentation, electronic documentation is a proven approach. By delivering documentation electronically, not only can information access and retrieval be improved but publishing and distribution costs can be dramatically lessened. For electronic documentation, digital publishing offers many advantages over printed documentation including hypertext linking, full-text searching, and easy browsing of related topics.

Example: Mass Mutual has moved their guidelines to benefits plans (summary plan descriptions) for insurance agents in electronic form using HyperWriter. Not only is the information easier to retrieve, but it also is significantly less expensive to produce and distribute.

Computer-based Training

Although not often thought of as a digital publishing application, digital publishing offers a good approach to computer-based training. Digital publishing lets you create interactive applications where a user can learn at his or her own pace. Through hypertext links, students can even navigate to related information and then branch back to the topic they were originally viewing. Unlike traditional computer-based training tools, digital publishing applications let you make use of your existing text-based information for creating the computer-based training. This lets you easily repurpose your existing content for your computer-based training needs. Multimedia support lets training materials be rich and interactive.

Example: Sony Corporation (TM) has developed an extensive computer-based training application to train field sales people on video broadcasting equipment. This application draws from the printed workbooks Sony had originally used in print form.

Employee Performance Support Systems (EPSS)

An *employee performance support system* is a software system that aids in supporting an employee's performance on the job. Often fusing online documentation and computer-based training technologies, digital publishing applications are a key component of an EPSS. The hypertext linking and easy information retrieval are key attributes of an EPSS, which helps aid an employee's performance by rapidly retrieving needed information.

Example: Northern Telecom uses HyperWriter for an EPSS to assist sales people with the complex task of selling phone systems. This EPSS application fuses full-text documentation, a visual guide to the different phone systems produced by Northern Telecom, and selling tips for marketing to specific customer groups.

Electronic Publishing

Publishing on an electronic medium is one of the central applications of digital publishing technology. Publishing information in this fashion allows you to create interactive publications where the reader can more easily retrieve information. This includes elements like hypertext linking and full-text retrieval.

Example: John Wiley and Sons has used HyperWriter to produce a floppy disc version of "Litigation Services—Information Sources for Expert Witnesses."

Internal Document Distribution

A very powerful application of digital publishing technology is using it as a medium for internal document distribution. Under this approach, internal publications of a public nature (i.e., something that needs to be made available publicly, such as a policy guideline) are converted to digital publications and then posted on a central server. What this does is make these publications easily available to anyone with access to the server. By making this information more accessible, the organization has made it easier for their staff to locate and retrieve the information they need to perform their job tasks.

Example: BASF Corporation, one of the world's largest producers of industrial chemicals, uses HyperWriter for an internal document distribution system whereby virtually all internal corporate documents of a public nature are published electronically and distributed over an internal local-area network though hypertext links. This application is conceptually very similar to an Internet Web site, with the exception that it is purely for internal use.

CD-ROM Title Development

Digital publishing technology provides a powerful method for CD-ROM titles. This includes virtually any type of CD-ROM title where information publishing and distribution is the goal of the title. Among the organizations that we have seen use our HyperWriter as a digital publishing tool are WordPerfect, MicroAge, John Wiley & Sons, and many other publishers. The hypertext linking, information retrieval, and full-text searching elements of digital publishing make it a natural tool for CD-ROM title development.

Example: WordPerfect Corporation (TM) has developed the WordPerfect Magazine Five Year Collection CD-ROM disc containing the full text of all issues of WordPerfect Magazine.

Educational Courseware

Digital publishing can provide a very good avenue for educational institutions to build cutting edge educational courseware. For these institutions, the ability of digital publishing to work with text as well as multimedia is crucial.

Example: The University of Florida's nematology department has developed an extensive educational courseware application on insect control that has received national recognition.

Help Desk

Help desks are a much overlooked area of a corporation that can really benefit from digital publications. A help desk is a group of people that provide internal support to corporate employees, typically with respect to computer related problems. Given that what a help desk does is solve problems, digital publishing provides a powerful tool for not only documenting those problems, but also making them readily navigable so other help desks can easily find the solutions to problems that have already been documented.

Example: Lexmark International, one of the leading manufacturers of laser printers, uses HyperWriter as the help desk tool of choice for retrieving information on a constant basis.

CHAPTER

Digital Publishing Tools

3

With respect to choosing digital publishing tools, there are two perspectives as to how to approach digital publishing projects. One of these perspectives is to plan a particular digital publishing project in depth, figure out the requirements of the project, the features needed, and then search for a digital publishing tool that meets those requirements. The other perspective is to start by selecting a tool and then map the needs of a particular digital publishing project around that tool. I will not profess to tell you which is the better approach as there are pros and cons to both. However, selecting a digital publishing tool is, unquestionably, a key part of any digital publishing project. Just as a carpenter picks out tools to put in his toolbox when he begins a construction job, so does a digital publisher begin a project by choosing his tools. The goal of this chapter is to discuss several of the different leading digital publishing tools. Although this book ships with a full-featured digital publishing tool, HyperWriter, you may want to consider other tools as well.

Before I begin discussing the different tools covered in this chapter, you need to understand one basic point. The company that I run, NTERGAID, Inc., is a competitor of most of the products covered in this chapter. I am mentioning this up front as you should probably know this when I am evaluating tools that you may want to use. Although I am a competitor of most of these tools, I believe that you will find my analysis unbiased and accurate. One of the benefits of being a competitor of these tools is that it has forced me to truly analyze and learn them as our customers often ask us about other tools when they are considering HyperWriter for an application. Although this puts us in a good position to simply bash the competition, our business practice has always been to know the competition thoroughly so we could adequately compare and contrast ourselves to them.

Basics for Understanding Digital Publishing Tools

One of the hardest parts of digital publishing, often conceptually harder than the actual work of creating a digital publication, is choosing a digital publishing tool. The reason for this is that all digital publishing tools operate differently yet often create similar final applications. This means that looking at the end product isn't enough—you must evaluate the *process* needed to get to the end product. In short, you need to actually use the tool. This leads us to a bit of a conundrum—if you are choosing a digital publishing tool, you don't yet have the tool to use. I don't have a magic wand for helping you pick the digital publishing tools to use. One aspect of choosing tools that I have found extremely helpful is to understand the basic metaphor that digital publishing tools use, which helps you to understand how a particular tool would approach a specific digital publishing application. The benefit to this is that it gives you insight (although not hands-on experience) into the process you will use with the tool.

In addition to understanding the metaphors that digital publishing tools use, there are two other key aspects to choosing tools that you need to understand. These aspects are the degree of automation that the tool provides and the runtime or licensing policies of a particular tool. Although both of these are crucial, my advice is to pay particularly close attention to the section on runtime policies.

Different Metaphors that Tools Use

This chapter covers a number of different digital publishing tools. One of the hardest aspects of picking a digital publishing tool is understanding the basic approach to digital publishing that the tool uses. Unlike a technology area, such as spreadsheets, in which virtually all spreadsheets share a common metaphor, digital publishing tools are unusual in that they tend to take very different metaphors. Covered in the sections below are descriptions of some of the different metaphors used by digital publishing tools. As you read further in this chapter, you will note that not all of the metaphors are used by the tools described. Knowing all of these metaphors, however, will provide a better understanding of digital publishing technology.

Database

A tool using a *database metaphor* treats digital publishing as simply a database of content. When using a tool with a database metaphor, the task is to build a database of the content, separated into records and fields. When delivered to the user, the goal is typically to search specific fields of information to locate the desired records. The problem with database-metaphor–oriented tools is that much of the content that you want to publish in a digital fashion simply isn't well suited to this metaphor—documents just aren't databases. Where database metaphor tools have worked out well is in handling digital publications that are truly database-oriented, such as directories. In essence, publications that amount to databases are best treated with this type of tool. Database-metaphor tools are well suited to applications where complex reports need to be generated as database-metaphor tools lend themselves naturally to this.

Card

Card-based tools, as best represented by Apple's HyperCard, use a metaphor of splitting content across individual cards and then organizing the cards into either stacks or books. Card-based tools tend to rely on next-card and previous-card sequences for browsing, leaving them well suited to sequentially structured material. Chief among the limitations of card-based tools are poor searching abilities and poor abilities to handle document-structured information that isn't easily broken up between multiple cards.

Index

A metaphor similar to database metaphor is the *index metaphor*. Under the index metaphor, content in the form of documents is fed into an indexing engine where it is indexed for searching. Typically this is the extent of the development process using an index-metaphor–based tool—defining the content and then feeding it into an indexer. While this may make development easy, what it pays back with is a very limited digital publication that is generally usable only through full-text searching.

Time Line or Score

The *time-line* or *score metaphor* is used primarily for dedicated multimedia tools, not for digital publishing tools. Despite this, the time-line metaphor is important because as the dedicated multimedia tools add more features for digital publishing, this metaphor will become more widely used. Under the time-line metaphor, a time line or score is created along which media elements are synchronized.

Page

The *page-based metaphor* is based on the idea of displaying images of pages onscreen. Unlike most of the metaphors discussed thus far, I have extremely strong feelings about the page metaphor. By forcing the screen to emulate paper, the page metaphor really limits the power of digital publications. Whenever you force a new medium to emulate an older medium, you never use the full capabilities of the new medium. Additionally, there are some incredibly significant usability problems with the page-based metaphor. Current computer screens are approximately 1/4 the size of the printed page. What this means is that to use a page-based system to read information, the sequence is something like this:

- Scroll right (to keep reading the words onscreen)
- Scroll left (to get back to the start of the text)
- Scroll right (to keep reading the words onscreen)
- Scroll left (see above)
- Scroll right (see above)
- Scroll left (see above)
- Scroll right (see above)

All of the steps above are needed to read a single page from a page-based system. This clearly makes them difficult to use for actually reading digital publications onscreen. From what I have said, you would probably guess that I am against page-metaphor–based systems. This is both right and wrong. Whereas for general digital publishing I am against page-based systems, for certain applications I will admit that page-based systems are actually quite useful. Page-based systems are well suited for applications where there is a requirement for exactly replicating the printed page. For example, Adobe Acrobat has been used to create versions of IRS tax forms distributed as a digital publication. As there is clearly no point in recreating IRS forms in a fashion designed for digital publications, here page-based systems are quite valuable. Generally speaking the applications of page-based systems are those where a high degree of fidelity with the original printed page is required.

Hypertext

The hypertext metaphor for digital publishing takes the approach whereby information is divided into one or more *topics* (chunks of information) that are interconnected by hypertext *links* (connections between chunks). This is the metaphor used by HyperWriter and several other tools covered in this chapter. A key advantage of the hypertext metaphor is that it can often subsume other metaphors. For example, HyperWriter's hypertext metaphor incorporates much of the database, card, and index metaphors. You should note that this depends on the features of the particular hypertext system that you choose to use. Consider the list of metaphors in Table 3.1 and how HyperWriter approaches them.

Table 3.1 Digital Publishing Metaphors and the Equivalent in HyperWriter

Metaphor	*Equivalent in HyperWriter*
Database	Each HyperWriter topic holds a record, different paragraphs are fields and the indexer allows you to define fields for searches using a style sheet to define the fields to be indexed.
Card	Create topics that don't scroll for each card, assign a screen background for easy navigation, and use the next and previous relationships for card-to-card navigation.
Index or text database	Once your information is stored in a HyperWriter document and broken into topics, it can be indexed for full text retrieval.
Time line or score	In HyperWriter there is no time-line view or score, as an application consists of topics and links that a user chooses to move through. You can set up Auto Tours and Branch After actions to guide the user through a sequence of topics. You should note that this approach isn't as finely timed as when a toolkit with a time-line or score approach is used.

This brings us to the idea of hypertext as the *architecture* or framework for your digital publishing application. By using hypertext as a generalized architecture for building electronic publishing applications, hypertext tools can often allow almost any type of digital publishing application to be created.

The Text-compiler Metaphor

Accompanying the hypertext metaphor is the text-compiler metaphor. The text-compiler metaphor is generally used by hypertext systems that lack true authoring environments. When a hypertext system lacks a visual authoring tool that allows you to easily create hypertext relationships, what it substitutes is a markup language that allows you to define a hypertext document, and then a compiler which takes the marked-up documents and converts them to a viewable hypertext document. Hence the term text compiler, which refers to the compiling stage of making your text documents viewable. The best known example of a text-compiler metaphor is the Windows Help engine that accompanies Microsoft Windows. Although the Windows Help engine supports basic hypertext linking, it completely lacks authoring facilities. Microsoft instead provides a compiler and a specification for authoring documents in Rich Text Format (.RTF). While the text compiler approach is powerful, it tends to be very hard to use.

Automated Tools versus Manual Tools

One of the key areas that distinguishes between digital publishing tools is the degree of automation that a tool provides. What *automation* refers to is the ability to construct key elements of a digital publication without manual labor. Consider a policies-and-procedures manual to be published electronically. In automated systems, certain aspects of the publication could be automatically translated to a digital publication. For example, headings might represent hypertext topics. Similarly, word-processor cross-references could correspond to hypertext links. Even this type of very simple automatic linking goes a long way towards making digital publishing dramatically easier.

When Is Automation Important?

When picking a digital publishing tool, the need for automation is really determined by three factors:

- When documents are very large
- When documents change frequently
- When you are converting content, not authoring content

The first factor, large documents, is relatively easy to understand. If a document is large, then automation features are needed to effectively publish it in digital fashion. Without automation features, publishing large documents is extremely difficult and labor intensive.

With the second factor, when documents change frequently, the need for automation isn't as clear. Consider a short digital publication, approximately one printed page in length, that consists of daily news items. As this publication is very short, producing it wouldn't seem to require automation at all. When you consider that this publication needs to be produced over 365 times per year, all of a sudden it is a 365-page publication—not short at all. When you consider this as a 365-page work then automation can clearly be applied. This brings us to an important hypertext concept: Documents that change regularly, even if very short, can actually be quite long when the rate of change is accounted for.

The third factor, conversion, requires a bit of elaboration, although it is directly related to the first two factors. Digital publishing projects typically fall into two categories: authoring and converting. In an authoring project information is created specifically for the electronic environment. In a conversion project existing information is converted to the electronic environment. When you are converting existing works to an electronic environment, automation tools that can automatically convert existing publications to a hypertext form are a tremendous help, as they can reduce a large part of the manual labor that goes into creating digital publications. When authoring new publications for a digital environment, conversion tools are generally not needed as you can simply author documents within the digital publishing environment.

Automation: Programmable versus Nonprogrammable

When looking at digital publishing tools with automation features for automatically converting existing publications to digital publications, a key criteria to consider is whether the tool is *programmable*. By programmable, I am referring to whether or not the conversion tool can be adapted to meet the unique needs of your particular publications. To understand this, you need to understand one fundamental aspect about how people create publications: People are usually inconsistent when they create publications.

What I mean by this is that even with respect to very simple things like references, people are very inconsistent. Consider the simple task of referring to a chapter in a manual. Here are some of the ways that people do this:

- See Chapter 12
- Refer to Chapter 12
- Read Chapter 12
- This subject was covered in the previous chapter (when you are in Chapter 13)
- As you should note, this subject will be the focus of the next chapter
- As you may recall from an earlier chapter, ...

From the list above, you can see that these are all valid ways of referring to a chapter. Given that converting a reference such as this to a hypertext link is a key aspect of a conversion tool, the distinction between a programmable tool and a nonprogrammable tool is whether or not the tool can be adapted to recognize the particular style of referencing (and other publication specific behavior) found in your publications.

One approach in automation tools is to provide an actual programming or scripting language which you can use to write conversion routines specific to your publications. This type of language is called a text-processing language, as the language processes text instead of the type of numerical processing found in more conventional programming languages like C or Fortran. Our HyperWriter Professional product features an automation environment with a scripting language called HyperAwk (Awk is a standard UNIX-based text processing language, HyperAwk is our version). You should be aware that automation environments based on scripting languages offer both pros and cons. The advantages to a scripting-language–based approach is that it can accomplish virtually any tasks as it automatically builds your publication. We use our own HyperAwk, for example, to automatically reformat our print documentation into the correct formats for screen-based display as it also locates hypertext links and creates hypertext topics. The disadvantage to scripting-language–based environments is, of course, just that—they are scripting-language–based environments and they require learning a scripting language and doing some programming. Depending on your particular skills, this type of approach may or may not be for you.

Distribution and Runtime/Royalty Fees

One of the most distressing aspects of digital publishing comes when you have completed your digital publication and are ready to give it to a reader. While ideally this should be as simple as just copying a file or files onto a floppy, this isn't the case because of what is called *runtime licensing*. When you build a digital publication, what you create is displayed with what is called a *runtime program* (also called a viewer or browser). A runtime program lets a reader view your finished publication and generally supports navigation features like searching, following hypertext links, and more. The problem is that many digital publishing tools charge for the runtime tools. What this means is that you will pay a fee for every reader of your publication. To draw an analogy, this is equivalent to a publisher paying royalties on every book that is printed to the firm that made his or her printing press. This charging for runtime fees is generally referred to as the difference between a royalty-based system and a royalty-free system. Runtime fees can range from as little as $10 per reader (for digital publications that are widely distributed) to over $300 per reader, whereas royalty-based approaches can be something like 8 to 10 percent of your *gross* electronic publishing revenues.

Contrast digital publishing using a system with runtime fees with Hyper-Writer. Unlike many other digital publishing tools, HyperWriter is completely free of runtime or royalty fees. When you purchase HyperWriter, you get a full license of HyperReader, the runtime software it uses. Whether you are distributing an internal corporate application such as online documentation or commercial applications such as CD-ROM titles, there are no charges associated with HyperReader. Not only is HyperReader royalty free, but it is also fully functional with a wealth of powerful navigational tools including:

- Full-text searching
- Printing
- Export to ASCII and WordPerfect formats
- Annotation support

What Does Royalty Free Mean to You?

When digital publishing tools are royalty free, what happens is you gain tremendous flexibility for all of your digital publishing efforts. In short, it lets you treat your digital publications as if they were paper documents with all the advantages of digital publications. To illustrate this, consider one of NTER-GAID's actual customers, BASF Corporation. BASF Corporation is a 20-billion-dollar-a-year worldwide manufacturer of chemicals. Several years ago, BASF committed to using HyperWriter corporatewide and has since deployed digital publications to over 5,000 plus desktops across North America. Thanks to our royalty-free licensing structure, not only does BASF Corporation not have any licensing worries when distributing publications for their 5,000 internal desktops, they can also extend this information externally as well. When a supplier or subsidiary needs access to information stored in digital publications, that information can be moved onto a floppy disc or CD-ROM and freely distributed. This underscores what royalty-free licensing actually means: Digital publishers can treat the applications they create as if they were paper. Whether you are an internal developer of corporate digital publications or a developer of commercial applications for resale, the benefits of a royalty-free approach cannot be overestimated.

Calculating Runtime Costs

To help you understand the effect of runtime fees a little bit more clearly, consider the following two examples of how runtime pricing can work.

When considering royalty-based versus royalty-free digital publishing tools, your initial response may be that a royalty-fee–based approach doesn't matter all that much—I have only a few hundred users. Consider a digital publication distributed to only 200 users (which is not very many users) and a runtime fee of $100 per reader. What this means is that you will spend *$20,000* in runtime fees. When you add this cost onto your purchase cost of the digital publishing software itself, the cost of building the digital publication, the time involved with building the digital publication, the bookkeeping involved to make sure every time a new reader needs to read your publication, you purchase additional runtime licenses, you quickly find that this runtime licensing is not only incredibly expensive, but also incredibly difficult. With a royalty-free system, every bit of the runtime fees stays in your pocket.

Understanding Hidden Runtime Costs

One of the problems with runtime fees is that very often they are hidden from view. Consider the Guide digital publishing tool by InfoAccess. The Guide product literature makes certain to tell you that it has a free runtime engine.

What Guide's product literature doesn't make as clear is that the free runtime engine is actually limited and doesn't include full-text searching. To get full-text searching, you need to purchase the runtime software, which is approximately $99 per copy. Another example of hidden runtime costs can be found in the Acrobat software by Adobe. The first version of Acrobat released by Adobe featured per user runtime licensing. After the sales of the first version of Acrobat were only 10 percent of the official Adobe projections, Adobe released Acrobat version 2.0, with a free runtime. When we investigated this further, what we found out was that only the standard version of the Acrobat runtime software was free. If you wanted to encapsulate the display of Acrobat documents within another application or simply modify the look and feel of the standard runtime then you had to pay per copy fees to Adobe.

Another way that runtime fees can be hidden from view is for the vendor of your tools to discriminate between commercial and noncommercial uses of the tool. Typically this operates on the principle of "If you are making money with my tool then I should get some too." While many tool vendors have used this approach and argue that it is equitable and fair, the problem becomes determining what constitutes commercial use. Consider a demonstration version of your publication that you give away. Does this constitute commercial use? What about copies of your publication donated to nonprofit organizations? Simply put, the distinction between commercial and noncommercial use often isn't clear.

A Variant on Runtime Fees: Build Fees

A recent variant on runtime licensing is the idea of *build* fees. Build fees operate by allowing the user of the digital publishing tools to build only a certain number of publications. For example, you might purchase a license to build 10 publications using a particular tool. After you had built 10 publications, you would then return to the manufacturer of the tool and buy another license. This philosophy is used primarily by EBT's DynaText product. To be quite honest, I don't find this philosophy much better than the runtime-fee–based approach. Both are to be avoided if at all possible.

A Variant on Runtime Fees: Fixed-price Licenses

As digital publishers have grown more resistant to runtime fees in recent years, a new change is the advent of the fixed-price license. What this does is allow the developer of a tool to purchase a fixed-priced license for distributing publications. For example, a digital publishing tool might sell for $5,000 and then the runtime license for distribution might be $2,500 (bear in mind that actual pricing schemes vary). What this does is let a vendor of digital publishing tools claim to be royalty free while still charging distribution fees.

Although I don't like any form of distribution fee, my feeling is that this type of arrangement is significantly better than others.

Runtime Fees: A Summary

From this discussion of runtime fees, I hope you have gained a good understanding of the different issues surrounding them. What I also hope you have gained is a decision *not* to use digital publishing tools based on a runtime-fee–based strategy. For a discussion of where runtime fees are headed, please see Chapter 5, which discusses this in depth.

Overview of the Different Tools

In the following sections are descriptions of many of today's leading digital publishing tools. As noted earlier in this chapter, selecting digital publishing tools is a very difficult task. To help you sort through the different tools available, I have described all of the tools in a similar fashion. A basic description of each tool starts the coverage. This description is followed by three lists: key features, key weaknesses, and typical applications. The two remaining aspects covered for each tool are a screen capture (for a few of the tools, no screen capture may be available) and a standard table that describes each of the tools printed at the end of this chapter. All tools are covered in alphabetical order with the exception of HyperWriter, the tool bundled with this book, which is covered first. As our HyperWriter Professional tool is similar to HyperWriter it is covered directly after HyperWriter so you can more easily compare the two tools.

The Data Table

In order to help you choose a particular digital publishing tool, I have included a comparison table that compares the different tools along a series of standard metrics. This table doesn't try to assign a particular grade or score to a product (as I am a competitor of these tools, I did not feel that this was an appropriate or ethical approach). What the table does, rather, is gather together details on each tool and present them in a unified fashion. When you start evaluating digital publishing tools that aren't covered in this book, you may want to refer back to this data table and even use the same evaluation approach as this table covers some of the most important features found in a digital publishing tool.

HyperWriter by NTERGAID

HyperWriter, the digital publishing tool bundled with this book, is an interactive hypermedia and multimedia authoring system designed for creating interactive electronic documents that live on a computer screen and are specifically designed or converted for this medium. HyperWriter is a true hypertext authoring system complete with integrated editor and authoring system as well as spell checker and thesaurus. Unlike many other digital publishing tools, HyperWriter is a real-time authoring environment in that you can almost always be working with your application, creating links, formatting text, spell checking information. Many other tools tend to force you into separate authoring and viewing modes. HyperWriter is a very full-featured product including multiple-link types, multimedia support, automatic hypertext linking, full-text searching, a screen designer for configuring how documents are displayed, direct support for Internet publishing, a royalty-free runtime, and more.

Key features found in HyperWriter include:

- Native support for publishing on the Internet
- Screen designer for creating custom applications
- Full-text search engine
- Automatic linking
- Very configurable
- Powerful navigation tools
- Totally royalty-free runtime policy

Key weaknesses found in HyperWriter include:

- Only available for DOS and Windows, no other platforms currently available
- No scripting language

Typical applications for HyperWriter include:

- Online documentation
- CD-ROM titles
- Internet development
- Electronic magazines

A sample screen from HyperWriter is shown in Figure 3.1.

HyperWriter Professional by NTERGAID

HyperWriter Professional is a dramatically enhanced version of the basic HyperWriter product. HyperWriter Professional has all the features found in the basic HyperWriter product and adds a programmable automatic-linking engine, integral support for computer-based training applications, protection for your final applications to prevent them from being modified, a CD-ROM–specific runtime engine, and more.

Key features found in HyperWriter Professional include:

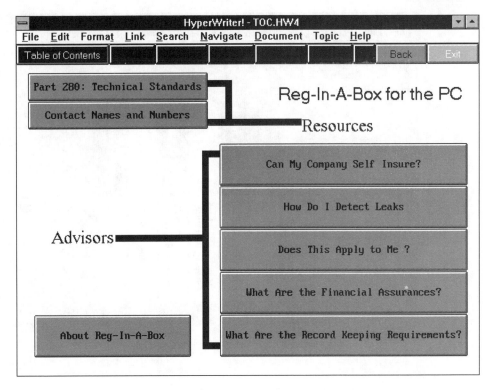

Figure 3.1 The HyperWriter product.

- Programmable automatic-linking engine
- Built in computer-based training support
- A CD-ROM–specific runtime
- Document maintenance tools for large-scale publishing efforts
- Runtime engines for both DOS and Windows
- Totally royalty-free runtime policy

Key weaknesses found in HyperWriter Professional include:

- Only available for DOS and Windows, no other platforms currently available
- No scripting language

Typical applications for HyperWriter Professional include:

- Online documentation
- CD-ROM titles

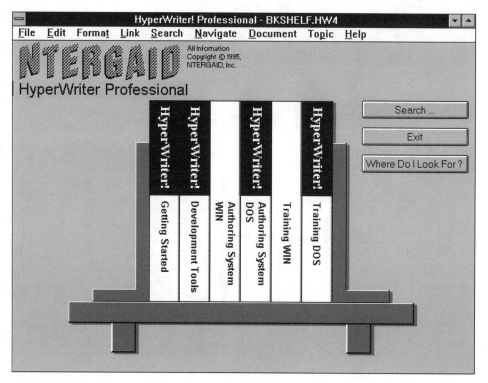

Figure 3.2 The HyperWriter Professional product.

- Internet development
- Large scale (tens of thousands of pages) digital publishing efforts

A sample screen from HyperWriter Professional is shown in Figure 3.2.

Acrobat by Adobe

Acrobat is a page viewing technology that is designed for the purposes of converting a PostScript (a page description language created when you print) file or files into a viewable onscreen document. A key difference between Acrobat documents and other forms of digital publishing is that Acrobat documents are simply print pages viewed on screen, leading to severe usability problems (reading an Acrobat document typically requires a dramatic amount of horizontal scrolling). Despite the usability problems, page-viewing approaches such as Acrobat can offer a number of advantages over other digital publishing technologies. Chief among these is ease of development. When using Acrobat, development generally consists of creating a PostScript document, something that can be done easily from virtually any application. This PostScript document is then fed into another program which distills an Acrobat document from the PostScript. As you can see, this circumvents most of the development found in other digital publishing tools. Another advantage to a page viewing application is that publications with complex page layouts such as headers, footers, tables, and sidebars are easily created—just process the PostScript.

In addition to the usability problems, Acrobat applications suffer from several other issues. Chief among these is taking the digital publication beyond the basic publication produced from the PostScript code. Specifically, Acrobat doesn't include any tools for automatically generating hypertext links or even tools for easily making links. What this means is that digital publications created with Acrobat tend to have a similar look and feel, with little room for a publisher to distinguish his or her digital publications.

Key features found in Acrobat include:

- Excellent printed output
- Excellent portability (DOS, Windows, Mac, and UNIX)
- Easy authoring (just create a PostScript file)
- Full-text searching

Key weaknesses found in Acrobat include:

- No control over screen design
- Integrating Acrobat into other applications requires licensing fees
- No support for automatic linking
- Internet support specific to Netscape browser
- Poor Internet performance (PostScript is slower than native HTML coding)
- Limited hypertext linking
- Difficult-to-use publications

Typical applications for Acrobat include:

- Document distribution (it reproduces pages exactly)
- Publications that have heavy page layout requirements

A sample screen from Acrobat is shown below in Figure 3.3.

Book Manager by IBM

Book Manager is a digital publishing system that functions along the lines of an indexing tool. What Book Manager allows you to do is import documents and then build electronic "books" from them. Book Manager is really notable for two reasons. First, it is a product of IBM and this fact lends Book Manager strength in IBM-specific environments. Additionally, Book Manager is avail-

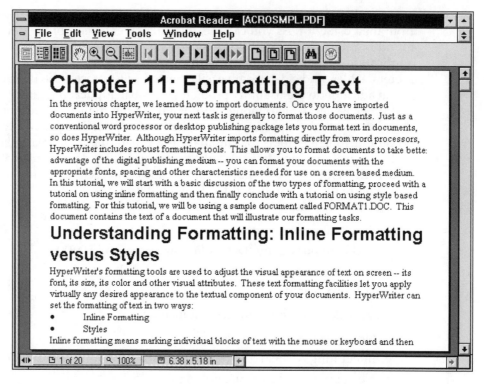

Figure 3.3 The Acrobat product.

able for IBM's OS/2 operating system, making it a logical choice if your digital publications need to run under OS/2. Despite Book Manager being an IBM product, it is not very widely used for commercial digital publishing; it is more often used for internal applications such as online documentation. Part of the reason for this is probably its royalty-based pricing model, which makes commercial publishing difficult. Another reason is definitely IBM's low focus on the product and its poor visibility.

Key features found in Book Manager include:

- Full-text searching
- Runs under OS/2
- Available for several platforms including character mode terminals

Key weaknesses found in Book Manager include:

- An inflexible tool
- Weak hypertext linking

- No control over screen layout or design
- Royalty-based pricing model

Typical applications for Book Manager include:

- Online documentation

No screen shot for Book Manager is available.

Doc-2-Help by WexTech

An interesting turn in the world of digital publishing is the shift to delivering digital publications through the Windows Help engine, WINHELP.EXE. Doc-2-Help is a digital publishing tool that uses this approach by providing an authoring environment for creating these Windows Help files. Unusually, Doc-2-Help is not even a true Windows application. Instead, Doc-2-Help is an add-in to Microsoft Word. The way that Doc-2-Help functions is it enables Microsoft Word with additional features for digital publishing such as hypertext linking. The drawback to this add-in approach is that you are not working in a true digital publishing system where the information is live. Doc-2-Help uses a compile-and-view metaphor, whereby to use your final digital publication, you must compile it to see your changes (for limited changes, Doc-2-Help has a preview mode). This tends to slow the authoring process as you are always one step away from your final goal.

Key features found in Doc-2-Help include:

- Good support for features in the Windows Help engine
- Create printed and online documents from a single source
- Tight integration with your word processor

Key weaknesses found in Doc-2-Help include:

- Depends on Windows Help (i.e., functions not explicitly supported by Windows Help are generally not available)
- Working in a nonlive authoring environment leads to a compile-and-view process
- Requires Microsoft Word to function
- No full-text searching
- Limited automatic linking

Typical applications for Doc-2-Help include:

- Windows Help systems
- Online manuals

No screen shot for Doc-2-Help is available.

DynaText by Electronic Book Technologies

DynaText is a very powerful digital publishing system that is available for a large number of platforms, ranging from Windows to the Macintosh and many different UNIX workstations. While a powerful tool, DynaText is deeply tied to SGML technology. SGML is a document markup technology that allows you to specify the logical structure of documents without reference to the document's appearance. While SGML is extremely powerful, it is not supported by most desktop applications, such as word processors. Using DynaText means that you have to convert your documents into SGML—not a trivial task. Another issue with DynaText are build fees/runtime licensing fees that can be quite steep. If you are committed to SGML then you definitely want to look at DynaText.

Key features found in DynaText include:

- SGML support
- Full-text searching
- Internet support
- Available for many different platforms

Key weaknesses found in DynaText include:

- Limited support for automatic linking
- Price (it is an expensive product)
- Runtime licensing
- Converting to SGML
- Customizing the screen display requires C-language programming

Typical applications for DynaText include:

- Online documentation
- Large maintenance and repair manuals

No screen shot for DynaText is available.

Envoy by Novell

Like Acrobat, Envoy is a page-viewing–based tool. As such, Envoy has many of the same features and limitations found in Acrobat. To start, Envoy shares the same usability problems imposed by displaying pages on screen (for more on this, see the description of Acrobat). Like Acrobat, developing with Envoy is quite simple, consisting of processing a file of print output through a program. One significant advantage of Envoy over Acrobat is that Envoy is bundled with the Novell WordPerfect office suite of programs. For companies committed to using WordPerfect, you may already have Envoy available to you. Other issues in using Envoy include problems with font handling

(Envoy's font technology doesn't seem to be as robust as Adobe's) and limited hypertext support. A nice feature in Envoy is the ability to embed the viewing software within the finished Envoy document. Envoy's position with respect to licensing fees has been confusing. Over time I have been told both that Envoy was royalty free and that it was not (and actually quite expensive—$30,000 for a commercial publisher). Given this opposing information, I would strongly encourage digital publishers to research this point in depth before committing to Envoy.

One concern that I have with respect to Envoy is the amount of corporate commitment that it will receive from Novell. Given that Adobe's Acrobat has virtually all the features of Envoy and that Adobe seems to be fully committed to it, it seems as if Envoy may well get lost at Novell as Novell focuses on its more core products. For this reason, if you are considering committing to Envoy, I would strongly encourage you to look at Acrobat as well.

Key features found in Envoy include:

- Excellent printed output
- Easy authoring (just create a print file)
- Full-text searching
- Embeds the viewing software within the final application
- Documents can be smaller than Acrobat

Key weaknesses found in Acrobat include:

- No control over screen design
- No portability—documents are viewable only under Windows
- Confusing royalty position
- No support for automatic linking
- No Internet support
- Limited hypertext linking
- Difficult to use publications

Typical applications for Envoy include:

- Document distribution (it reproduces pages exactly)
- Publications that have heavy page layout requirements

No screen shot for Envoy is available.

Folio Views by Folio Corporation

Unlike most of the digital publishing tools covered in this chapter, Folio Views takes the metaphor of an indexing engine where information is indexed for full-text searching. Working from the basic indexing metaphor, Folio Views has been enhanced with basic hypertext-linking abilities. Another key aspect of Folio Views is that Folio Views applications are merely sequential scrolls of information—Folio Views does not break documents into hypertext topics. Instead, a Folio document is always only a single scrolling topic. The problem with this approach is that it makes using a document very hard for a reader, as there is always only a single topic, moving the scroll bars even a 1/4" moves you the equivalent of *tens*, if not *hundreds*, of pages.

Central to Folio Views is its full-text search engine. Unlike a tool such as HyperWriter which makes indexing optional, in Folio Views indexing is required and can't be turned off. What this has done is give Folio Views a real orientation towards searching—if your application isn't well suited to searching or searching isn't a concern of yours, then Folio Views is not the right choice for you. Besides searching, Folio Views has several good features including multiple-user support (unusual for a digital publishing tool).

A key weakness of Folio Views lies in its runtime licensing structure. Folio is aggressively oriented around the idea that anyone who reads information from a Folio document should purchase a runtime license. What this means is that publishing with Folio Views is very expensive for publishers with large audiences.

Key features found in Folio Views include:

- Macintosh runtime
- Optional software development kit for customizing applications
- Powerful full-text searching
- Automatic linking
- Limited control over screen design
- Limited ability to configure the system

Key weaknesses found in Folio Views include:

- Internet support is extremely expensive and requires a special Web server
- Royalty-fee based publishing model
- Folio is owned by one of the world's largest publishers—Reed-Elsevier. Folio's royalty-based pricing model means you could be giving your sales data to a competitor
- Scroll-based orientation

Typical applications for Folio Views include:

- Legal text (Folio is widely used in the legal community)
- Online manuals
- CD-ROM titles

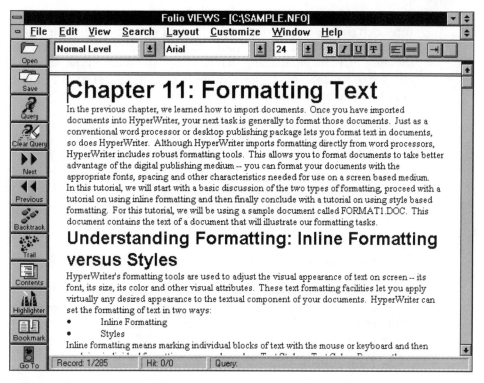

Figure 3.4 The Folio Views product.

A sample screen from Folio Views is shown in Figure 3.4.

HyperCard by Apple

To many people, HyperCard is the tool that started it all. While we know that this is not true, HyperCard does have a special place in the field of hypertext. HyperCard is a card-based development tool where information is structured across multiple cards and the cards are organized into *stacks* (a stack represents a file). Although HyperCard supports basic hypertext functionality, it really isn't a true digital publishing tool as much as it is a tool that can be adapted to digital publishing. HyperCard supports a very powerful language, HyperTalk. This language lets you control many of the very low-level aspects of Hyper-Card, allowing a skilled developer to adapt it to digital publishing applications.

Like other products in this chapter, HyperCard has suffered from an inconsistent strategy on the part of its developer, Apple Computer. When Apple first released HyperCard, it was treated incredibly well and a quick following sprung up. As people then realized that HyperCard had limitations, Apple

Computer let HyperCard fall by the wayside. Consequently, HyperCard's feature set hasn't been updated tremendously since its original release in 1987. An example of this is that in HyperCard's latest release, it still has poor support for color displays, something that has been standard on the Macintosh for literally years. Despite this lagging support from Apple, HyperCard is still a dominant tool for digital publishing on the Macintosh.

Key features found in HyperCard include:

- Good scripting language
- Great flexibility if you use the HyperTalk language
- Good control over look and feel of final application

Key weaknesses found in HyperCard include:

- No Internet support
- No full-text searching
- No automatic linking
- Only available for Macintosh platforms

Due to the nature of HyperCard as an application development tool, there isn't really a typical application for HyperCard. Over the years, HyperCard has been used for applications including:

- Help systems
- Interactive kiosks
- Electronic manuals
- Multimedia presentations

No screenshot for HyperCard is available.

Multimedia Viewer and MediaView by Microsoft

No aspect of computing today is complete without a mention of Microsoft. Despite Microsoft's prominence in the industry, Microsoft has taken a relatively low-key approach in this area. Both of Microsoft's tools are derived from the standard Windows Help engine with additional features. The Multimedia Viewer tool was Microsoft's first digital publishing system. This tool has been replaced by Microsoft's new MediaView toolkit. At this time it appears that Multimedia Viewer has been officially discontinued, but it is difficult to say for certain as Microsoft has released conflicting positions on this issue. As MediaView is the newer of these tools, you will find that most of the following comments are focused on MediaView.

Multimedia Viewer and MediaView are both text compilers for documents stored in **.RTF** format that create powerful hypertext documents. A key problem with using these tools is that Microsoft does not supply any type of authoring environment, only the syntax for the text compiler. In essence these tools operate with the philosophy of "if you can enter the right commands into the compiler, it will create what you want—but it won't do anything to help you enter the commands." What Microsoft recommends to ease development is to use Microsoft Word as a hypertext editor where creating a footnote indicates a topic. This is not an intuitive approach for creating digital publications. While both tools suffer from ease-of-use problems, they are powerful and can be used to create sophisticated applications. They also include good data compression and full-text searching.

Key features found in Multimedia Viewer/MediaView include:

- Full-text searching
- Royalty-free runtime
- Good multimedia support
- Integrate with traditional programming languages such as Visual Basic and Visual C++

Key weaknesses found in Multimedia Viewer/MediaView include:

- No Internet support
- Text compiler approach—no authoring tools at all
- No automatic linking
- No control over the look and feel of the final application without custom programming
- Limited configuration of the application without custom programming

The typical application for Multimedia Viewer/MediaView is creating CD-ROM titles.

A sample screen from Multimedia Viewer is shown in Figure 3.5.

SmarText by Lotus

Lotus Corp's SmarText is an electronic book-building tool with hypertext linking abilities. SmarText functions as a document compiler that takes information from document files and then compiles that information into finished electronic books. In SmarText there is no editor or authoring system. This lack of an editor/authoring system means that the developer of an electronic publication will always have to move back to the original source files for even the smallest change. Another key aspect of SmarText is that SmarText applications are merely sequential scrolls of information—SmarText does not break documents into hypertext topics. This means that users lack the modularity of information found in a topic-based system. SmarText is only available under

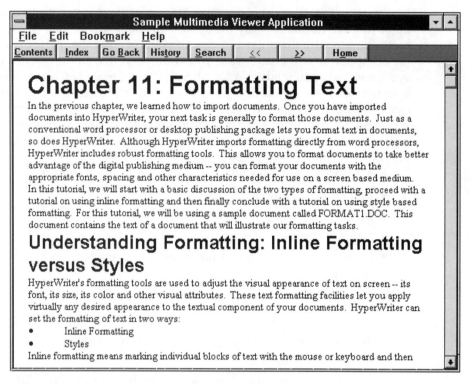

Figure 3.5 The Multimedia Viewer product.

Windows; it does not provide any cross-platform facilities. SmarText uses a runtime fee/royalty-based approach.

A real drawback to SmarText is not technological but that its manufacturer, Lotus, seems to lack direction with respect to SmarText. One very good example of this is that SmarText seems to be rarely marketed or advertised, seemingly relying on being a product from Lotus, instead of standing on its own feet. Long-time computer industry veterans will probably remember the similar treatment of products like Agenda, Symphony, and Manuscript, all of which were good products, but ignored by Lotus.

Despite the limitations that I have identified, SmarText does offer some key aspects. SmarText has powerful electronic linking features and really pioneered automatic linking in desktop hypertext products. Thanks to SmarText's automatic-build process, it creates powerful outline and index windows automatically.

Key features found in SmarText include:

- Good support for automatic linking
- Good support for Ami Pro

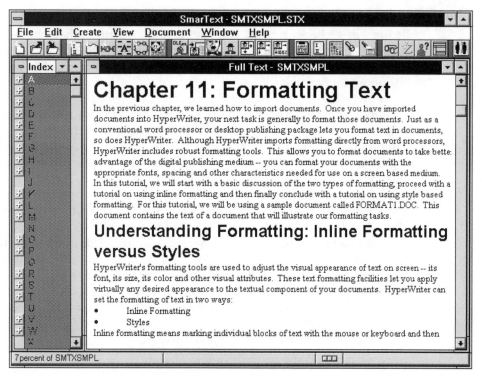

Figure 3.6 The SmarText product.

- Good support for publishing via Lotus Notes
- Powerful views facility for defining different views of documents

Key weaknesses found in SmarText include:

- No Internet support
- No ability to configure the user interface
- Keyword-based searching, not full-text retrieval
- Heavy overhead (i.e., size increases) in published documents
- General lack of flexibility
- No editor or authoring system
- Runtime fee/royalty based
- Scrolling-based orientation

The typical application for SmarText is electronic documentation.

A sample screen from SmarText is shown in Figure 3.6.

StorySpace by EastGate

Before I describe StorySpace for you, I should mention that I have known the author of StorySpace for as long as I have been involved in digital publishing and have great respect for his work. With that disclaimer out of the way, let's talk about StorySpace.

StorySpace, if for no other reason, is notable for being one of only two digital publishing tools that truly runs on the Macintosh (it is also available for Windows) as a native authoring tool that is covered in this chapter. While it is notable that it runs on the Macintosh, StorySpace is also notable for being a superb tool—if you understand what it is for. StorySpace is primarily a tool for creating hypertext based interactive fiction applications. As such a tool, Story-Space lacks many of the standard features that I have emphasized in this chapter, like full-text retrieval. In their place StorySpace includes unique features like guard fields which only allow a reader to view a section of a document if he or she has previously viewed a required section. This allows the structure of the digital publication to be dynamic and determined by what the reader has previously seen. Another unique aspect of StorySpace is that it has powerful document maps that allow you to visualize the structure of your publication. For this reason, StorySpace can also be viewed as a powerful hypertext-based writing environment.

Key features found in StorySpace include:

- Native support for publishing on the Internet
- Royalty-free runtime policy
- Excellent graphical mapping and browsing tools
- Guard fields

As a digital publishing tool intended for very different applications than the other tools in this chapter, I am not presenting a list of weaknesses for Sto-rySpace as it wouldn't be fair to the tool. What I would recommend is that you examine the data table for StorySpace.

Typical applications for StorySpace include:

- Interactive fiction
- Writing in a hypertext fashion

A sample screen from StorySpace is shown in Figure 3.7.

Toolbook by Asymetrix

Like HyperCard described earlier in this chapter, Asymetrix Toolbook takes a card-based metaphor to digital publishing. Toolbook differs from HyperCard with more features for digital publishing including better full-text searching and hypertext linking. Like HyperCard, Toolbook has a powerful scripting language called OpenScript. Thanks to the OpenScript language and the stronger features for digital publishing, Toolbook is more suitable for digital publishing than is HyperCard. This is not to say that Toolbook is a perfect tool for digital publishing; it isn't. Like HyperCard, Toolbook suffers from slow performance and large overhead. Toolbook also lacks automatic-linking features. Interestingly enough, Toolbook, like HyperCard, has a history of fragmented support from its developer, Asymetrix Corporation. When ToolBook first came out it received considerable support from Asymetrix, but this support soon faded. After a long period of neglect, ToolBook is now receiving considerably more support.

Key features found in ToolBook include:

- Good scripting language
- Great flexibility if you use the OpenScript language
- Good control over look and feel of final application
- Basic hypertext liking

Key weaknesses found in ToolBook include:

- No Internet support
- Limited full-text searching
- No automatic linking
- Only available for Windows platforms

Like HyperCard, ToolBook can be considered more of an application development tool than a true digital publishing tool. Over the years, ToolBook has been used for applications including:

- Interactive kiosks
- Simple digital publishing
- Multimedia presentations
- Digital publishing where a powerful scripting language is required

No screenshot for ToolBook is available.

The World Wide Web

Although not a specific digital publishing system, the World Wide Web needs to be considered in any discussion of digital publishing systems, as the Web can be considered an alternative to specific digital publishing systems. Although the World Wide Web can be described in many different ways, one of the best definitions is that the World Wide Web provides a distributed hypertext publishing system. What the World Wide Web provides for a digital publisher is basic hypertext facilities using a simple markup language (Hypertext Markup Language or HTML). When viewed in the context of other digital publishing systems, in some respects the World Wide Web can seem crude. For example, the World Wide Web lacks basic document-formatting facilities, such as control over fonts and justification. Other elements lacking in the World Wide Web include full-text searching, automatic linking, control over document presentation, and more. Despite these missing elements, what the World Wide Web provides is a powerful architecture for implementing digital publishing that spans virtually every computer system that currently exists. Thanks to the powerful architecture that the World Wide Web provides, virtually all of the limitations that I mentioned can be addressed—admittedly with the loss of some compatibility between systems. Since the World Wide Web has grown to become a major part of today's computing environments, all digital publishers should factor the Web into their digital publishing strategies. For more information on the World Wide Web, please see Chapter 4.

Windows Help by Microsoft

Like the World Wide Web, the Windows Help engine is more a basic digital publishing technology than a specific product (you can't purchase the Windows Help engine, it is just a part of Windows that you get when you purchase a computer). What the Windows Help engine provides is basic hypertext functionality together with limited navigational tools. Like Microsoft's Multimedia Viewer and MediaView, Windows Help takes a text-compiler approach where authoring consists of creating a marked-up document file using Microsoft Word. This document file is then fed into a compiler, which produces a help file that can be viewed using Windows Help. When you consider using Windows Help as a basic digital publishing system, you quickly realize that using Windows Help in its raw form is very difficult. This brings you to tools like Doc-2-Help and ForeHelp, which provide more powerful authoring environments and create the needed input files for Windows Help. One of the very powerful advantages of the Windows Help engine is simply that it is shipped with every copy of Microsoft Windows. Not only does this make it royalty free, but it also guarantees that the audience for your electronic documents already has the tools to view your digital publishing application. Despite the benefits to Windows Help, it hasn't been hugely successful as a digital publishing environment. This is primarily due to the limited nature of Windows Help, which supports only basic hypertext linking, very limited searching, and lacks an authoring environment.

Key features found in the Windows Help engine include:

- Support for content sensitivity
- Basic hypertext linking

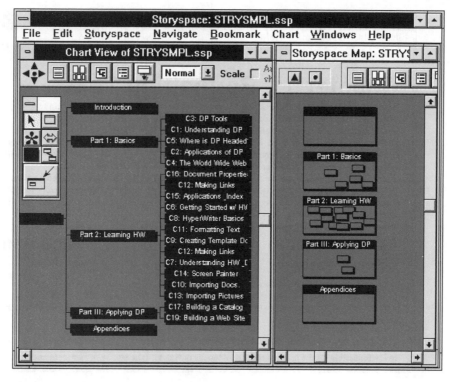

Figure 3.7 The StorySpace product.

- Extensibility through the macros facility
- The viewing engine, WINHELP.EXE, is shipped on every machine that runs Windows
- Royalty free, it ships with Windows itself

Key weaknesses found in the Windows Help engine include:

- Limited searching abilities
- No authoring environment
- No automatic linking
- Limited control over screen layout and design
- No Internet support

Typical applications for Windows Help include:

- Help systems
- Online manuals

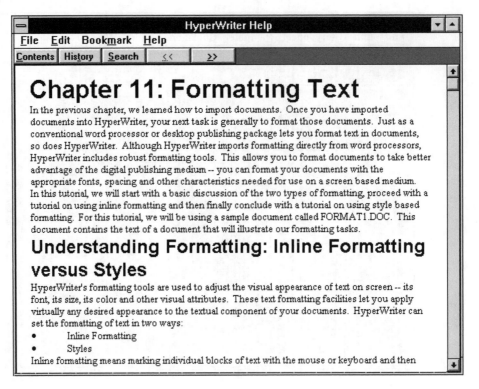

Figure 3.8 The Windows Help system.

A sample screen from Windows Help is shown in Figure 3.8.

CHAPTER

The World Wide Web 4

No authors professing to cover digital publishing today could even consider their books to be complete without discussing the Internet's World Wide Web (generally referred to just as "the Web"). First devised in the early 1990s, the Web really only came to prominence in 1994. Although the World Wide Web is defined differently by virtually everyone, I favor a very simple, technical definition: The Web is a distributed hypertext system available on a global basis through the Internet.

This is a very straightforward, technical definition of the World Wide Web. This is what the Web is; however, it is a little like defining the Empire State Building as a structure. True, it is a structure, but that doesn't really convey what it is. Similarly, describing the Web as a distributed hypertext system, doesn't convey the true nature of the Web. To clarify our definition of the Web, consider this:

The World Wide Web, or Web is a section of the Internet that has emerged as the place for electronic publishing and electronic commerce. Information published on the Web is presented to the end user in a graphical and textual format, making the information not only accessible but interesting to review. Not only can the Web present text and graphics, but it can also let a user view video and audio clips as well as query databases, run programs, send mail, and more. In short, the Web offers an information architecture for presenting, viewing, and retrieving information.

Whenever I describe the Web to someone, I am reminded of the response that my wife had I first described our HyperWriter product for her. Hyper-

Writer is a hypertext tool that allows you to create information in a hypertext fashion so it can be easily browsed, navigated, and retrieved. When I described it for her, her initial response was "This is how I always expected a computer to work." To a very large degree, the Web can be viewed in much the same way. By making information easily accessible, attractive, and navigable, the Web allows us to retrieve information that literally spans the globe. In short, the Web turns computers into what we always expected them to be.

The Web is based on a metaphor of hypertext or interconnected documents. This hypertext metaphor allows readers to easily navigate the Web in a point-and-click fashion without having to know much if anything about the Internet. The hypertext format that documents on the World Wide Web use is HTML or HyperText Markup Language. In order for information to be accessible on the Web it first must be converted to HTML. Once information is in HTML format it can be accessed by anyone on the Internet using a Web browser like Mosaic or Netscape. Web browsers are what give people the ability to interact with a Web site by supporting the graphical and hypertext formats of the Web.

As far as how the Web and digital publishing are related, the Web offers another choice of distribution media. Just as digital publications can be published on floppy discs and CD-ROM discs, they can also be published on the Web. For digital publishing, the Web offers a very compelling platform with some unique attributes. To start, the Web offers digital publications with a truly worldwide audience, as the Internet is global in nature. Another unique attribute is that the Web is truly platform independent, with Web browsers available for virtually any platform from PC to workstation. Another unique element to the Web is that it is dynamic in nature. As the Web doesn't require periodic distribution of CD-ROM discs or other media, the digital publications on the Web can be updated on a daily or even hourly basis. The final aspect to digital publishing on the Web is that because it doesn't require an investment in physical media production, publishing on the Web can have lower cost structures than other types of digital publishing. A real drawback to digital publishing through the Web is that while the Web is getting a tremendous amount of attention, it isn't actually making very much money for publishers. In fact, the publishers doing the best with the Web often seem to do so by selling advertising space in the publications instead of selling their content. Part of this seems to lie in the lack of standards for billing, encryption, and transaction processing on the Web, while the rest of it seems to lie in the relatively new nature of the Web.

You should be aware that this chapter is not intended to be an exhaustive discussion of the World Wide Web. The Web is rich enough that entire books can be written about it and still fail to capture all its elements. The goal of this chapter is to provide a basic overview of the World Wide Web so that you understand enough about the Web to understand its role in digital publishing.

Understanding World Wide Web Basics

For an information provider, the World Wide Web has some unique characteristics. One of those characteristics is that unlike most many other forms of publishing, the reader bears a large portion of the costs. Consider a high-tech firm such as Hewlett Packard. Hewlett Packard has a large (and well-constructed) Web site that features product information about its entire line of products. In the past, Hewlett Packard would print expensive product literature and physically mail it to customers. Now those same customers will navigate to Hewlett Packard's Web site and retrieve information on their own. Not only does Hewlett Packard not have to print this information, but the reader actually bears the cost of the connect time to retrieve it. This very simple fact is a basic concept that needs to be kept in mind with respect to the Web.

A Short Web Glossary

Like many areas of technology, the Web has evolved its own specialized terminology. Defined in Appendix A at the end of the book are several of the most common terms used with respect to the Web. I have also enclosed references to people and companies heavily involved with the Web. It is important to read through this glossary before continuing as the rest of this chapter relies on these terms.

Two Approaches to Web Servers

The Web server program is the software that sits between a physical Web page and the Web browsers that are used to view that page. A Web server responds to requests through the Internet for Web pages to view and sends out copies of the Web page as requested. There are two basic approaches to Web servers: the conventional or static Web page server and dynamic content servers.

A conventional Web server or *static web page server* is the type of Web server that the bulk of the World Wide Web is based on. This type of server sends out Web pages stored in ASCII files on the server's hard disc. With this type of server, Web pages are prebuilt and stored as physical files. The problem with this type of server is that it is poorly suited to applications composed of thousands of pages. This limitation is primarily due to overhead and problems with managing thousands of files on a hard disc. The second approach to Web servers is what I call a *dynamic content server*. Under this approach, content is stored in a central database of some sort and HTML pages are generated dynamically on request. This type of approach typically works with a conventional Web server to pass the HTML pages on to the Web browser. For a good example of this, consider putting the Oxford Dictionary & Thesaurus onto the Web. With dictionary type content, the typical approach is to make each term a single Web page. But, with over 190,000 words in the Oxford dictionary, this is an incredible quantity of individual Web pages to manage. Additionally, the disc space overhead for this large a number of physical files is huge and will have severe performance overhead. The solution is a dynamic content database whereby when the user looks up an individual word, an HTML page is generated on the fly and sent to the user's browser through a conventional Web server.

NOTE: The terms *static Web page server* and *dynamic content server* are my own, because there does not seem to be any type of consensus as to how these terms are used.

Appearance of HTML

One of the aspects of the Web that, to put it lightly, gives traditional publishers fits is its limitations in formatting documents. For a publisher that is used to the power, flexibility, and formatting options of programs like PageMaker and Quark Express, the Web can seem almost unbearably crude. When you come right down to it, HTML gives you very little control over formatting—basic headers, bold facing, and italicizing are it. There is no font control, no table support, and none of the myriad other elements typically relied on by publishers for formatting. What the Web does, however, is separate the appearance of content from its structure. By this I am referring to the fact that rather than define how a heading is to appear in a Web document, a publisher simply formats that element as a heading. The actual presentation of the element is left to the reader's Web browser software. What this enables is that the reader is placed in control of the document and can adjust its appearance to suit his or her own tastes. Although formatting content has traditionally been the role of publishers, HTML allows the reader to take part in this. This is similar to how other traditional broadcast media have been growing more customized over the past several years. It can even be analogized to the growth in television remote controls. Just as a remote control lets a viewer customize the television appearance (i.e., its channel, volume, and more), HTML's emphasis on document structure over presentation allows a reader to adjust how HTML documents are presented to them.

NOTE: Publishers should bear in mind that future versions of HTML will offer dramatically improved formatting abilities, but the nature of HTML will still let readers adjust the appearance of publications to suit their needs.

Understanding HyperWriter and the Web

HyperWriter, the digital publishing tool bundled with this book, has a close relationship with the World Wide Web. As a digital publishing tool centered around a hypertext model, constructs in HyperWriter have a very close conceptual similarity to the underlying structure of the Web. HyperWriter supports developing for the World Wide Web with a **Save As HTML** command which takes your HyperWriter applications and saves them to HTML format. This command transforms HyperWriter topics into HTML pages, converts HyperWriter links into HTML links, and allows you to map styles created in HyperWriter to specific HTML tags. Also supported is creating HTML image maps, which allow hot spots to be created on images. Unlike a traditional HTML editor where the focus is on creating individual pages, in using Hyper-Writer the focus is on creating hypertext where an application typically has many pages. Thus, using HyperWriter lets you focus on the information in your Web site and the hypertext links, rather than on specific HTML syntax. When thinking of HyperWriter with respect to the Web, it is usually helpful to think of HyperReader, the runtime module that ships with HyperWriter, as an equivalent to a Web browser—it lets you browse a HyperWriter document just as a Web browser lets you browse an HTML document.

Basic HTML Syntax

When you come right down to it, the core elements of the World Wide Web can really be reduced to just two: the Hypertext Transport Protocol (HTTP) Servers that make information available on the Web and the Hypertext Markup Language (HTML) that formats documents for use on the Web. With some exceptions, an HTTP server is really just like any type of server program; it does what it is supposed to do and really just functions. Due to this basic functional nature of a Web server, there really isn't much to understand about a Web server. HTML, however, is different. As a markup language designed to be used by the author of a Web page, HTML is complex and really requires a good understanding of the different HTML tags. The rest of this section focuses on basic HTML syntax along with a discussion of three variants on HTML syntax.

HTML v1.2:

HTML is a very simple markup language for creating Web pages. Before we move into specific HTML concepts, let's talk briefly about what a markup language is. A markup language is a way of formatting text by marking up different elements in the text. A markup language differs from a word processor where the focus is on the appearance of the information. When a markup language is used, the general approach is one of describing the different elements in a document instead of describing how they appear. For example, a basic HTML tag is the **<H1>** tag, which indicates a first level heading tag. You note that the **<H1>** tag doesn't indicate anything about how the heading appears—it simply indicates it is a heading. The Web browser that actually displays a document handles how a heading appears.

Tags

The HTML markup language is very simple and composed of what are called *tags*. A tag is an HTML formatting element that defines both how information is structured and how it is presented. HTML tags are surrounded by < and > characters. A very simple HTML tag is the **<EM>** tag which presents text in an emphasized appearance (such as boldface). An example is:

```
This text is <EM>Boldface</EM>
```

As you can see, the **<EM>** tag is part of a pair of tags. The **<EM>** tag starts the markup and the **</EM>** tag ends the markup. HTML tags can be used both in pairs and by themselves (this depends on what tag it is, some tags require pairing, some don't). Another example of a tag, the **H1** tag, is shown here.

```
<H1>
This Is A Heading
</H1>
```

The **H1** tag indicates a first level heading. Unlike many markup languages, HTML is not picky with respect to carriage returns

```
<H1>This Is A Heading</H1>
```

As noted, HTML isn't very picky with respect to carriage returns. In fact, HTML doesn't actually display carriage returns unless you tell it to using the **<P>** tag. If you want two lines of blank space to appear after your **<H1>** tag, you need to include the **<P>** tag explicitly:

```
<H1>A Heading</H1>
<P>
<P>
Some text that follows the two blank lines
```

To really understand HTML tags, you need to understand tag *attributes*. A tag attribute is a property of a tag that adds additional information that the tag needs to function. Consider the **<IMG>** tag which embeds an image into a page. This tag takes two attributes, one for the image file and one for the alignment of the image with the text.

```
<IMG SRC="NTLOGO.GIF" ALIGN=BOTTOM>
```

In HTML tags, some attributes are considered optional. For the **<IMG>** tag, the ALIGN attribute is optional (a default alignment of bottom is assumed). Thus, the **<IMG>** tag shown below has the same effect as the **<IMG>** tag shown here.

```
<IMG SRC="NTLOGO.GIF">
```

HTML tags can be nested within one another. For example, the **<OL>** tag defines an ordered list, but it contains one or more **<LI>** tags, which are the actual items in the list. When tags are nested like this (see below), the **<OL>** tag is said to be a container tag in that it "contains" the **<LI>** tag but doesn't actually have any data of its own.

```
The Web is:<P>
<OL>
<LI>Powerful
<LI>Easy to use
</OL>
```

The **<OL>** and **<LI>** tags would produce a list similar to that shown here.

The Web is:
1. Powerful
2. Easy to Use.

Although our **<LI>** tags didn't include numbering, HTML tags generate the numbers automatically when they display list items within an **<OL>** tag (OL stands for an ordered list, one that has numbers).

Now that we have looked at HTML tags a little bit, let's see how they are put together into an actual HTML document.

Looking at a Sample Document

With a basic understanding of a markup language and HTML tags, let's take a quick look at a sample HTML page.

```
<HTML>
<TITLE>
A Simple HTML Document
</TITLE>
<H1>
A First Level Heading: An Example of Structure
</H1>
A paragraph of text with a <A HREF="SCOTT.HTM">hypertext
link</A>
<P>
```

```
<UL>
<LI>Item 1 has an <A NAME="anchor">anchor</A>
<LI>Item 2
</UL>
</HTML>
```

What this document defines is a simple HTML page. It begins and ends with the **<HTML>** tag which is required for all HTML documents. The **<TITLE>** tag indicates the title of the page. A first-level heading, the **<H1>** tag is the first thing a reader sees when viewing this page in a Web browser. The **<H1>** tag is followed by a paragraph of text with a hypertext link to the Web page "**SCOTT.HTM**." This paragraph is then ended by the **<P>** tag and an unordered list starts. An unordered list is a list with bullet items. This list has two items, one of which has a destination for some other hypertext links to jump to.

As you are looking at raw HTML coding for the first time, you may find this a little bit confusing. Don't be concerned by this because HTML is actually very simple and only requires a little bit of getting used to.

Understanding HTML Tags

Listed here are a full set of the standard HTML tags.

<HTML>...</HTML>.   The required beginning for all HTML documents. This tag designates a text file as an HTML document.

<A HREF="URL" NAME="TEXT">...</A>.   The basic format for a hypertext link. Also defines an anchor within a page (when no **</A>** end tag is present, and it has only a NAME attribute, it acts as an anchor).

Example for Link: <A HREF = "/WELCOME.HTM">View Welcome Page</A>.

Example for Anchor: <A NAME="0001_0001">. This is the destination for a link.

<TITLE>...</TITLE>.   The title of a Web page. This is not the same as the H1 tag and typically isn't displayed on the screen. It is often used for hot lists and may be displayed in a status bar, field or window title.

<P>.   A paragraph break. Equivalent to pressing **ENTER** in a word processor.

Example: <P>.

<HR>.   A horizontal rule that runs across the screen of a Web browser.

Example: <HR>.

&lt.   A literal < character. Used because the < character indicates the start of an HTML tag.
Example: 4 &lt 5.

&gt.   A literal > character. Used because the > character indicates the end of an HTML tag.
Example: 5 &gt 4.

&amp.   A literal & character.
Example: &amp.

&quot.   A double quote character.
Example: &quotScott Johnson&quot would produce "Scott Johnson."

<H1>.   A first-level heading. Typically displayed at the top of a Web page.
Example: <H1>HyperWriter</H1>.

<H2>...</H2> - <H6>...<H6>.   Second- through sixth-level headings. Headings should generally be used in their correct (i.e., numerical) order, not in an order selected for they appear.
Example: <H2>Hypertext Linking</H2>.

<IMG ALIGN="option" SRC="filename">.   An inline image embedded within a Web browser. Alignment options include TOP, MIDDLE, BOTTOM. The alignment attribute can be omitted. SRC indicates a drive and path to an image file to display.
Example: <IMG ALIGN="BOTTOM" SRC="PRODS.GIF">.

<OL>...</OL>.   An ordered (numbered) list.
Example: See "Looking at a Sample Document."

<UL>...</UL>.   An unordered list (bulleted) list.
Example: See "Looking at a Sample Document."

<LI>...</LI>.   An item within a list.
Example: <LI>HyperWriter</LI>. See "Looking at a Sample Document."

<DL>...</DL>.   A definition list, a list with two columns of a definition on the right and a term on the left.

<DT>...</DT>.   A definition term.
Example: <DT>Hypertext</DT>.

<DD>...</DD>.   A definition of a term.
Example: <DD>A method for linking documents.</DD>.

<EM>...</EM>.   Emphasized text.
Example: <EM>HyperWriter is powerful</EM>.

<STRONG>...</STRONG>.   Strongly emphasized text.
Example: <STRONG>HyperWriter is powerful</STRONG>.

<B>...</B>.   Boldfaced text.
Example: The Web is a <B>powerful</B> concept.

<I>...<I>.   Italicized text.
Example: The Web is a <I>powerful</I> concept.

<U>...<U>.   Underlined text.
Example: The Web is a <U>powerful</U> concept.

<PRE>...</PRE>.   Preformatted text, text that is displayed in a mono-spaced, typically Courier font.
Example: <PRE>12345679</PRE>.

HTML and Hypertext.   When authoring HTML pages, it is important to really understand the **<A>** tag, which anchors hypertext links. To clarify this tag further, please examine the following samples.

A Sample Web Page: HTML0001.HTM

```
<HTML>
<HEAD>
<TITLE>Hypertext Example Page Number 1</TITLE></HEAD>
<BODY>
<H1>A Sample Page to Indicate HTML Linking</H1><P>
<P>
Link 1: <A HREF="html0002.htm">This is a link to another
page</A>.<P>
<P>
```

```
Link 2: <A HREF="html0001.htm#0001_0001">This is a link
to text on this page</A>.<P>
<P>
<P>
<A NAME="0001_0001">This is the destination of link 2.<P>
</BODY>
</HTML>
```

A Sample Web Page: HTML0002.HTM

```
<HTML>
<HEAD>
<TITLE>Hypertext Example Page Number Two</TITLE></HEAD>
<BODY>
This is the page the first link referenced.<P>
</BODY>
</HTML>
```

The first page, HTML0001.HTM, has two hypertext links. The first link, **<A HREF="html0002.htm">** is a link to another page **</A>**, linked to a different HTML page. As this link is going to the top of the page, it uses only an HREF attribute which tells the link which file to reference. It omits the NAME attribute which tells an HTML link where in the page the link should go to. The second link, **<A HREF="html0001.htm#0001_0001">** is a link to text on this page **</A>**, a link to a destination on the current page. This link indicates both the file to link to (the HREF attribute) and the destination within that file (the # sign indicates the name to jump to). The **<A>** tag within the first page, **<A NAME="0001_0001">**, indicates the unique destination within the page.

In addition to hypertext links within pages in your Web page, the **<A>** tag can also be used to reference Web pages at other Web sites as well. This is handled by including an "**http**" designator within the HREF attribute. An example:

```
<A HREF="http://www.ntergaid.com/">Go To NTERGAID</A>
```

By changing the HREF attribute to a "mailto," the **<A>** tag can be used to create links that actually send email messages when they are clicked on.

```
<A href="mailto:webmaster@ntergaid.com">Send email to
webmaster@ntergaid.com</A>
```

This concludes our discussion of the **<A>** tag, which provides the core of the Web's hypertext facilities. As you can see, the **<A>** tag offers very powerful hypertext facilities using a very simple syntax.

Standards: Take Your Pick

There is an old saying in the computer industry with respect to standards that goes something like this: "Standards are a good thing. I'm glad I have so many to choose from." In the early days of constructing Web sites, there wasn't really much choice in terms of standards. You authored a Web site using HTML v1.2 and that was it. Now, however, there are three basic flavors of HTML that you need to be aware of:

- HTML version 2
- HTML version 3
- Netscape HTML

The following sections discuss some of the changes in the HTML specification.

HTML Version 2 and HTML Version 3

The current state of HTML is that HTML version 1.2 is what is commonly considered to be standard HTML, in that all browsers will display HTML version 1.2. The Web standards organizations are currently considering two new HTML specifications, HTML version 2 and HTML version 3. Neither of these standards has been officially ratified yet and I wouldn't expect regular use of them until mid-1996 at best.

HTML version 2 is a mid-sized revision of HTML version 1.2. Although it adds several new tags, it doesn't really change HTML dramatically except for one addition: forms. HTML version 2 has extended HTML 1.2 with the ability to create data entry and selection forms as part of HTML documents. This is a dramatic change to HTML as it brings it into the interactive world by allowing interaction with an HTML document that isn't limited to clicking on hypertext links. Other changes in HTML version 2 include the addition of additional tags that improve document appearance such as the **<CITE>** and **
** tags (citations and line breaks) as well as a more SGML-like orientation. HTML forms are an element of HTML version 2 that have moved into widespread usage, despite the HTML version 2 standard not being official. As a general rule of thumb, most browsers now support HTML forms.

HTML version 3 is a much larger set of changes to the HTML version 1.2 specification. HTML version 3 adds many things, most notably a full-table model so tables can be displayed. Other changes include support for better text layout including font control, tabs, better user controls such as toolbars, and entirely new tags such as NOTE, which lets you embed notes in your documents, including footnotes. Overall, HTML version 3 offers much to look forward to and will dramatically improve the functionality of the Web.

Netscape HTML

Netscape has a special perspective on the World Wide Web. Cofounded by one of the primary authors of the original Mosaic browser, and with many of the original Mosaic programmers currently on their staff, Netscape has, to some extent, a belief that they can set the technical direction that the Web should follow. Along with this, Netscape has released its own set of HTML tags that enhance HTML v1.2 with additional facilities such as fonts and tables. The Netscape Navigator Web browser allows full display of these tags, which are partially derived from Netscape's own ideas on the direction that HTML should take and partially derived from advance versions of HTML specifications such as HTML version 2 and HTML version 3. There are two perspectives on using Netscape HTML tags. The first is really a pure, standards-driven perspective that says that using proprietary standards is bad and shouldn't be done. A more pragmatic perspective recognizes this, but also recognizes that HTML currently has limitations and that Netscape HTML provides a way around those limitations. Personally, I take a middle-of-the-road position with respect to Netscape HTML. My perspective is that ideally I wouldn't use it, but then, ideally, HTML wouldn't be limited—I lean more towards the pragmatist than the idealist.

The downside to using Netscape HTML tags is that not all browsers understand these HTML tags and this can lead to problems. Although technically when a browser encounters a tag it doesn't understand it should just display it as basic text, this is not always the case. You should be aware that using Netscape tags it is possible to create Web pages that are basically unreadable in anything other than a Netscape browser. However, Netscape, as of 1995 does have what is generally regarded as the best browser and has approximately a 70 percent market share for their browser. What this means is that 70 percent of all Internet users should be able to view your Web pages that use Netscape HTML. The only problem here is that the online world is changing very fast and Netscape may not retain their market share. The reason that I state this is that Microsoft has brought its Web browser and it doesn't support most Netscape HTML tags as it is a derivative of the original Mosaic, not Netscape. For this reason, use Netscape-specific HTML tags with caution and an awareness that you may later have to revise your site to eliminate them.

Learning More About the HTML Standards

To make it easier to learn more about the different HTML standards, on the CD-ROM accompanying this book I have included the draft versions of the following specifications:

- HTML 1.2 (HTML1_2.TXT)
- HTML 2.0 (HTML2.TXT)
- HTML 3.0 (HTML3.TXT)

These specifications are located in the \HTML directory. Please bear in mind that these specifications may be obsolete by the time you look at them, as they are currently only in draft status (which means that revisions are possible). When you look at the formal specifications, it is always interesting to look at what is changing. A good indication can be found in the size of the specification documents. The HTML 1.2 specification is only 81K in size. The HTML 2 specification is 145K in size (slightly under twice as long), but the HTML 3 specification is almost 400K in size (392K to be exact)—over four times larger than the original HTML specification.

Learning More About the Web

There are a number of sources you can turn to to learn more about the Web. To start, the Web is a popular topic—articles have been published in many different computer magazines. Along with articles, you can also turn to different books on the market—interest in the Internet has led to an absolute profusion of books on the Web. John Wiley & Sons, the publisher of this book, publishes several good books covering the Web. In addition to printed references, the definitive reference to Web is really the Internet itself. There are two good areas on the Internet to learn more about the World Wide Web. The first is the series of UseNet newsgroups that cover the World Wide Web. Although there is a huge amount of information in these newsgroups (which does make them hard to follow), the different newsgroups that discuss the Web are one of the best places to learn about it. The newsgroups I refer to are the COMP.INFOS-YSTEMS.WWW.xxx newsgroups where "xxx" indicates the focus of the newsgroup. The other major source of information about the Web is the literally thousands of Web home pages. A good place to start with the Web home pages is http://WWW.W3.ORG, the home page for the World Wide Web standards organization. Please see the Appendix for references to additional Internet Web sites that discuss HTML in greater depth.

Where Is Digital Publishing Headed?

Having been intimately involved in digital publishing for over nine years, I have often been asked where I see the field heading. Given that the past several chapters have covered not only where digital publishing came from as well as the current state-of-the-art of digital publishing tools, it is certainly appropriate that we look to the future. To make understanding this chapter easier, I have broken it into two major topics: technology changes and business changes.

Technology Changes

One of the most exciting aspects of working in the technology field is the constant rate of change. Over the past ten years, digital publishing tools have improved dramatically. Despite these improvements, there are a number of areas in which digital publishing technology will continue to get better.

Capacity Improvements

One of the short-term technology improvements in digital publishing tools will be the ability to handle significantly more information. This reflects the nature of publishing, where every year a publisher either gathers or creates more information to publish. What will happen in the next two years time is that digital publishing tools that currently lack CD-ROM support will scale up to CD-ROM–size applications, and the digital publishing tools that already support CD-ROM–size applications will gain the ability to handle applications that span multiple CD-ROM titles.

Internet Support: A Required Feature

The greatest technology shift in digital publishing's recent history has been the growth of the Internet's World Wide Web. What originated as a small experiment in hypertext-based document distribution at a European physics laboratory (CERN) has now become a key part of today's computing environment. The effect of the World Wide Web with respect to digital publishing tools is pretty simple: Every digital publishing tool either already has or will have the ability to output finished digital publications to the World Wide Web.

Producing Good Printed Output

One of the real limitations of most digital publishing tools today is that they generally have very poor facilities for generating printed output. A good way to see this is to take some content and print it from your word processor or page layout program. If you take the same content and place it into a digital publishing system you will find that the printed output is almost always of lower quality. One of the technology changes that we will see in digital publishing tools over the next few years is the ability to print out pages that look quite similar to the original printed documents. While this may seem like a small change, I suspect that the implications of it will be quite large, as it will go a long way towards lessening the absolute reliance on paper that many users have.

Better Link-generating Technologies

Automatic linking technology available today is generally oriented around two approaches:

- Translating word processor markup commands such as cross references, Goto buttons, and bookmarks to hypertext links
- Converting text patterns such as "See Figure 1" into hypertext links

The first approach is only automatic linking in that it automatically makes the link for you, but you still have to insert the markup commands yourself. Inserting the markup commands is tantamount to actually making links by hand. The second approach relies on what is called *pattern-matching* technology. This technology allows documents to be processed by digital publishing tools and hypertext links, connecting entities such as figures and figure references to be created. This type of automatic linking is extremely powerful, although it suffers from a number of drawbacks. The first of these drawbacks is that this pattern-matching technology does not take context into account, thus leading to incorrect links. Consider the phrase "See Figure 1 in my previous article." If the current article contained a figure named "Figure 1," then this reference to Figure 1 would end up linked to the incorrect version of Figure 1 (it would be linked to the current Figure 1, not the previous version). Another problem with pattern-matching technology is that people write in many different ways, such as:

- Figure 1
- Figure One
- See the first figure
- See the previous figure

While pattern-matching technology can account for all of these approaches, it requires special programming for each variation. This programming, while not terribly difficult, tends to be unique for each application, leading to expensive development.

Over the past several years, my firm, NTERGAID, and I have been heavily involved in both approaches to automatic linking. One thing that has become clear is that these approaches to automatic linking, while not running out of steam, are not as powerful as are needed. What is needed for better automatic linking is more of a linguistic approach to hypertext linking that takes into account the elements of the text and uses a more intelligent approach to create links.

What a linguistic approach to linking can do is create links between documents that are related not through explicit relationships (such as "See Chapter 10"), but through implicit, content-based relationships. Consider a digital publishing application that contains press releases about software products. Entries in the digital publishing application might contain press releases from Microsoft for the Microsoft Word word processor and the Novell WordPerfect word processor. If a talented human author was creating this application, he or she might cross reference these two press releases, as they are obviously related. What a pattern-matching approach would not do is create cross references of this type as there isn't an explicit pattern to match. A linguistic approach would allow recognizing that both documents contain related content and that a link should be created.

The need for better link-generating technologies ties into one of the first items covered in this section, that of capacity. Simply put, as the amount of material published in digital form increases each year, the ability of human authors to effectively create useful hypertext links diminishes. Without better link-generation technologies, authors of digital publications will find making links harder and harder.

While I can easily see the need for better link-generating technologies, I am hard-pressed to come up with a specific date prediction for its arrival. Unlike implementing the mechanics of a hypertext system which is fundamentally rooted in computer science and engineering, this type of linguistic technology is much fuzzier in nature. Today there are some very basic approaches to this type of linguistic-linking technology on the market. If I apply traditional software-development scheduling curves to them then I would assume that within the next few years, this would be a mature technology and ready for real use. My reservations stem from the nature of this technology, which is really an application of artificial intelligence—a technology that is extremely difficult to implement and really has never lived up to its promises.

Licensing Technology and CD-ROMs

One of the paradoxes of CD-ROM is that the size of a CD-ROM disc (approximately 600 megabytes) is actually larger than many of the digital publications that are distributed on CD-ROM. From the publisher's perspective this means that there is actually unused space on the disc. If a publisher has multiple publications, then what can be done is to deliver multiple publications on the same CD-ROM disc. Your thought may be that the publisher would then need to charge more for the disc to account for these extra publications. To address this, new licensing technology allows multiple publications to be stored on a CD-ROM disc and then selectively installed by the user of the disc with an encryption key. The way that this works is that the user receives a CD-ROM disc and after a phone call to the producer of the CD-ROM receives a software key that can be used to install one or more of the publications on the CD-ROM. As far as the time frame for this technology goes, it is already available in limited form but only in a few digital publishing tools. What will happen over the next year is the incorporation of this licensing technology into most digital publishing tools.

Updatable Publications

A trend that is just starting now is that of updatable publications. This technology lets a CD-ROM–based publication be updated with additional data either through the Internet or a commercial online service. This addresses one of the real problems of CD-ROM technology—that it is static and unchanging. Consider a publisher selling a monthly newsletter as a digital publication. If the publisher was using CD-ROM and wanted to keep subscribers up-to-date, then the publisher would have to press a new CD-ROM every month. Of course just pressing the CD-ROMs every month isn't enough—the publisher also has to distribute them as well. If the publisher was using an updatable publication technology then the publisher could have a single CD-ROM title that could be updated monthly through a communications line. This is not to say that updatable publications are a cure for all digital publishing problems with respect to updates; they aren't. What updatable publications will provide is an important technology that addresses some updating concerns.

Better Searching

When digital publishing tools first became available, one of the expectations from several software companies producing the tools was that hypertext linking would eliminate the need for full-text searching (we were *not* among those companies). As you almost certainly know, hypertext linking did not in any way eliminate full-text searching. What has occurred instead is that full-text searching has become an almost required component of digital publishing. Part of the reason for this is tied into our earlier discussion of capacity—when you have only a few documents, there isn't much need for full-text searching and hypertext linking can suffice. However, as the number of documents grows, hypertext links simply can't fill all the needs for information retrieval. Consequently, full-text searching becomes essential.

A specific prediction with respect to searching is actually easy. Virtually all digital publishing systems will include full-text searching within the next year's time. Additionally, search features previously found only in very high full-text searching systems will become standard in the same time frame. These features include relevancy ranking and natural language searching. Relevancy ranking is a search technology that finds only the search results that are most relevant to what you are looking for. Natural language searching allows you to search with more Englishlike queries than the traditional Boolean queries used in full-text searching.

Standard Scripting Languages

A real limitation in many of today's digital publishing tools is the lack of a programming or scripting language. While this is not a problem for simple digital publications, as publications grow more complex, a scripting language provides a crucial tool for extending the standard facilities available in the digital publishing tool. Additionally, a scripting language makes creating truly interactive, customized publications dramatically easier. Common applications of scripting languages within digital publications include creating custom dialog boxes and menu options, controlling multimedia devices, and creating custom navigation aids. Due to the growing trend of Visual Basic-compatible scripting languages being embedded into applications software such as Microsoft Word, it is easy to see that the standard scripting language will either be Visual Basic or some derivative. To make a specific prediction, what will happen in the short term (the next one to two years) is that a scripting language embedded into digital publishing systems will become a standard feature.

A Portable Delivery Device

Much, if not all, of the focus in this book has been on digital publishing for what may seem like commonplace, prosaic applications such as electronic manuals, interactive catalogs, and similar reference-oriented publications. One of the key reasons that digital publishing has focused on these business-oriented applications is actually quite simple: digital publishing requires a personal computer and most computers are currently in the workplace. Given that fact, the applications for digital publishing are more likely to be those that appeal to the workplace. One of the things that will change this is the advent of a true portable delivery device for digital publications. Although the computer world has seen laptop/notebook computers and limited function personal digital assistants (PDAs), neither of these have been really adequate for delivering digital publications in a portable fashion. What is really needed is a true portable delivery device on which digital publications can be viewed. A true portable delivery device would open entirely new markets to digital publications. When you consider some of the attributes that a portable delivery device should have, you quickly realize that such a device will end up competing with books, so it should have booklike qualities such as being lightweight, incredibly portable, and easy to use.

You should bear in mind that I am not predicting a release of a portable delivery device for digital publications any time soon. My personal expectation is that we are at least 10 years away from a really satisfactory device. The reason for this is that any portable delivery device really requires breakthroughs in several basic areas including:

- Screen technology (we need LCD screens capable of greater than 72dpi)

- Battery technology (a book doesn't run out of battery power so a portable device shouldn't either)

- Inexpensive, reliable distribution media (current floppy discs are too unreliable, CD-ROMs are too large physically)

- Encryption technology (to prevent piracy of digital publications)

Despite these problems with delivering a portable delivery device, such a device will come—the need for it is too compelling.

Business Changes

Unlike the technology changes just discussed, changes in the business of digital publishing are actually broader and more sweeping. This reflects the nature of the digital publishing business. While digital publishing technology has been available for almost ten years now, the actual digital publishing business is still very young and growing. As with all new businesses, the broadest and most sweeping changes come as the business matures.

The New Publisher: CD-ROM, Online, and the Internet

Over the past ten years, much has been made of the role of publishers as content providers or content owners. The first point that has to be made about publishers is that print publishing is not going away. For certain types of publishing, such as reference material, the role of print is being definitely lessened, but print publishing will be with us for a long time to come. What is changing, however, is that business pressures are forcing publishers to deliver content over as many different delivery media as the customer desires. What this means in practical terms is that all publishers interested in digital publishing need to consider three different media for all their publications:

- CD-ROM
- Commercial online service
- The Internet

The first option, CD-ROM publishing, is the best understood of all the options. CD-ROM media provides a large capacity (600+ megabytes) for delivering information that doesn't change. What this means is that CD-ROM is an excellent medium for delivering archives of data. An easy example that comes to mind is that of a technical magazine. CD-ROM technology lets a magazine publisher deliver a database of even hundreds or thousands of issues on a single disc. In short, CD-ROM provides a powerful medium for delivering large amounts of content inexpensively for the publisher. Due to the static nature of CD-ROM, what it doesn't do is address the needs of current information. For this the publisher needs to turn to either a commercial online service or the Internet.

Given that CD-ROM media will generally be used for archival media, the question becomes how content will be distributed between the commercial online services and the Internet. Unless a publisher sets up a secure transaction server on the Internet (such as a Netscape Web server), the general way that content will be distributed is that content the publisher wants to sell will be placed on the commercial online services. This provides a billing and transaction environment for selling digital publications on an incremental basis. What the publisher places on the Internet's World Wide Web will generally be promotional information, even sampler content that the publisher uses as a marketing aid. If publishers do set up a secure transaction server then they can take advantage of offering their digital publications for sale directly over the Internet.

While many analysts have predicted that the current online service providers such as CompuServe and America Online will ultimately lose out to widespread usage of the Internet, I personally don't believe this. My expectation is that both will coexist for the foreseeable future. The reason is that what the commercial online services provide, essentially a controlled, secure environment, is not available at all on the Internet. This type of controlled environment is very attractive to a large number of computer users that simply aren't ready for the free-ranging, uncontrolled nature of the Internet. Another reason for the continued existence of the commercial online services is that they provide a secure billing and transaction environment for electronic commerce. While this type of secure environment can be created on the Internet, currently it works only with particular Web server-and-browser pairs.

A Move to Electronic Commerce

With the exception of specialized, fielded reference databases, the bulk of digital publishing to date has been done on CD-ROM. Although CD-ROM has a number of very powerful features, with respect to pricing, publishing on CD-ROM can be described as an all-or-nothing medium. This means that when you purchase a digital publication on CD-ROM, you purchase the entire CD-ROM, not just the specific information that you need. For inexpensive digital publications this generally isn't an issue. When you consider more expensive digital publications, those costing several hundred dollars to a few thousand dollars per publication, then it really does become an issue. As noted in the previous section, most publishers will be moving to a threefold strategy of publishing via CD-ROM, online services, and the Internet. What distribution via online services and the Internet brings to digital publishing is the ability to sell information piecemeal—people may purchase only the exact information that they need. The implication for publishers is that they need to become ready to sell information.

NOTE: The licensing technology described earlier in this chapter really doesn't affect this move to electronic commerce, as this licensing technology is oriented to individual works, not specific pieces of information.

A Move to Anthologies

One of the paradoxes of publishing books on CD-ROM is that a single CD-ROM disc can hold literally hundreds of different books but is typically used to hold only one book. This will change in the coming years with a move towards publishing anthologies on CD-ROM. Consider how much easier it would be for scholarly tasks to have all works for a particular author (James Joyce, perhaps) available on a single CD-ROM within the context of a single digital publishing system. Another example can be found in the world of technical books where it would be incredibly useful to have a selection of leading books on the technical topic you were researching.

There are also advantages from the perspective of the publisher—rather than publishing literally hundreds, if not thousands, of CD-ROM titles, the publisher might move to publishing a dramatically fewer number of titles that contain collections of works. This trend of moving to anthologies couples nicely with the trend towards licensing technology and CD-ROM that was covered in the first section of this chapter. Given that publishers can place multiple works on a CD-ROM, they need a way to be compensated for each work. Licensing technology allows a publisher to place multiple works on a CD-ROM and then selectively license each publication on a per user basis.

It is important to note that the real obstacle in a true move towards anthologies lies in the nature of publishing, not in technology. The first obstacle lies in copyright permissions, where different publishers own the rights to works by the same author. This makes it very hard to produce definitive anthologies (not *All Works by James Joyce*, but *Some Works by James Joyce*). Another copyright-related issue is that many publishers even today don't have full rights to the electronic versions of the works they publish. Of course if you don't have the electronic rights to works that you publish then you can't publish them on CD-ROM. Fortunately, this obstacle is going away as negotiating in advance for electronic rights is becoming standard. A final issue with respect to CD-ROM–based anthologies concerns the marketing, pricing, and distribution of such anthologies. What price should be charged for an anthology of works? How should it be distributed? If distribution is through traditional book stores, then what is the incentive to distribute a product that essentially competes with yourself?

Advertising

Just as traditional print media is often oriented around an advertising-driven model, over the next few years you will see digital publications in many cases adopting an advertising-driven model. The reasons for this are twofold. The first reason is pretty simple: As digital publications have become widespread for the first time with large audience bases, there are finally enough users to make advertising in a digital publication worthwhile. Another reason that digital publications are moving to advertising models is that traditional print publishers are finally realizing that digital publications will soon become a key part of their revenue stream. For publishers that depend on advertising revenue unless they move advertising into their digital publications they run the risk of losing their advertising revenue unless they integrate advertising into their digital publications.

A good early example of advertising in a digital publication has been the recent growth in advertising on leading sites on the World Wide Web. Sites as diverse as Netscape and Global Network Navigator (GNN) have all introduced advertising plans in the past year. A major event that validated this advertising-driven approach occurred recently when A.C. Neilsen and company, the firm that rates viewership on television shows, introduced rating plans for the World Wide Web. What it has done is make advertising in digital publications real by providing a trusted authority with which advertising agencies are accustomed to dealing.

Runtime Fees/Royalties No More

As you may remember from Chapter 3, one of my most emphatic points was to avoid tools that use a basis of your paying royalties to distribute your digital publications. What I have observed recently is a definite trend away from runtime or royalty fees. My expectation is that over the next five to ten years you will not see runtime fees at all. A very good example of this is Adobe's dropping of runtime fees from Acrobat. When the first version of Acrobat was released, Adobe charged expensive per-user fees. When Acrobat 1.0 failed in the marketplace, Adobe recognized that the runtime strategy was at least partly at fault. Adobe then released Acrobat 2.0 without runtime fees. Part of the reason for the switch away from runtime fees has been the success of the World Wide Web which basically lacks runtime fees. Another part of the reason for this is that as people move more and more into digital publishing, runtime fees are less acceptable and many publishers are taking a hard line on time.

Digital Publishing: Both Easier and Harder

Given all the changes that I have forecast in the technology behind digital publishing and specifically in the improved tools that will be available, a real issue for digital publishers is what to expect in the area of production tasks. Specifically, will digital publishing become easier or harder? The answer, unfortunately, is that it will be both easier *and* harder. From the sense of working with better tools, digital publishing will be easier. However, tools are only part of the issue. From the aspect of what the user expects from a digital publication, digital publishing will be harder—significantly so. The real problem is that the user's expectations for digital publishing are getting higher all the time. If you are at all familiar with the world of software development, consider an analogy. Creating a program for MS-Windows is now easier than ever—development tools such as Visual Basic, Visual C++, and others can make the development process dramatically easier. The problem is that the user's expectations for that program are now higher than they ever have been. This is exactly the same problem faced by digital publishing.

Another reason that digital publishing will become a harder task is what I discussed earlier with respect to publishers moving to distribution via CD-ROM, online services, and the Internet. The implication of this for publishers is that they are faced with developing content for three different platforms. While advancement in digital publishing tools will make this easier, it is still more difficult to develop for three platforms than it is for a single platform.

Lower Manufacturing Costs

As noted in the technology section of this chapter, a growing trend in digital publishing is the integration of CD-ROM and the Internet/online services to create self-updating publications. While self-updating publications are of interest technologically, from a business perspective they are of even more interest. The reason for this is very simple: Self-updating publications go a long way towards decreasing manufacturing costs on digital publications. This point is generally only of significance to digital publishers with projects that have distribution in the thousands to tens of thousands of units.

The Shift to Electronic Reference Material

One change that is almost here is the conversion of virtually all types of reference material to digital publishing. Whether distributed on CD-ROM, online services, or the Internet, from encyclopedias to technical journals virtually any type of information will become available in digital form. If you are a publisher of reference information, then the expectation is that your information will be available in electronic form.

A Shift to Content Authored for an Electronic Medium

One of the characteristics of digital publications over the past ten years has been that they are invariably *conversion* projects, not authoring projects. In a conversion project, existing content, typically used for print publications, is converted for use in electronic media. This differs from an authoring project where content is written specifically for electronic media. The reason for using a conversion approach was that the size of the audience for digital publications until recently was too small to justify an authoring effort of its own. Consequently, existing print publications had to be converted to electronic media rather than being authored specifically for electronic media. Thanks to the advent of both truly inexpensive personal computers with CD-ROM drives standard and easy Internet access, there is finally starting to be content that is authored specifically for electronic media. The most common examples of this are on the Internet's World Wide Web, but CD-ROM–based examples are also available, such as Medio magazine, a CD-ROM–based magazine.

Some of the most exciting examples of content written for an electronic media can be found in the world of interactive fiction. Most visibly pioneered by Mark Bernstein's StorySpace authoring system and his company, EastGate Systems, interactive fiction is really cutting new ground in terms of publishing content that truly takes advantage of an electronic media. His firm currently publishes a number of works that nicely illustrate how content can be authored for digital publications. (If you are interested in exploring this further, please contact EastGate Systems at the address given in the Appendix.)

Learning HyperWriter

Welcome to Part II. In Part I, we covered the theory and issues found in digital publishing, in Part II, we cover how to use the digital publishing tool supplied with this book. Topics covered in this part range from basic tasks like formatting text to advanced tasks like designing screens and creating hypertext links. Please bear in mind that most of Part II, specifically Chapter 9 through Chapter 16, is actually tutorial oriented and is best done with easy access to a personal computer. This allows you to work through the different tutorials and become more comfortable in using HyperWriter. Although technically you will find that these tutorials can be done in any order, you will have better luck working through them in the order presented as they build on the details covered in the previous tutorials. Additionally, it is recommended that you complete each tutorial in a single session; this tends to help the learning process. Generally speaking, you should budget between half an hour to an hour for working through each tutorial. When you have completed Part II, Part III covers three advanced digital publishing tasks—building a Web site and building an interactive catalog.

When working through the tutorials covered in Chapter 9 to Chapter 16, an important point to understand is the idea of exploring HyperWriter. As these chapters compose a series of tutorials on using HyperWriter, but not a complete user's manual for HyperWriter, by definition there will be features that are not covered in these chapters. However, these chapters should give you the foundation or background necessary to learn virtually any aspect of HyperWriter provided that you are willing to explore a bit on your own. In the situation where you find this exploration difficult, you can always turn to either HyperWriter's online help or to the full online user's guide.

Getting Started with HyperWriter

As mentioned in the Introduction, this book includes a fully functional demo or evaluation version of the HyperWriter digital publishing toolkit. Hyper-Writer is a full-featured digital publishing toolset that supports many different features including:

- Hypertext linking
- HTML development for building Internet web sites
- Full-text searching
- User interface design tools
- Easy import and conversion from common word-processor documents
- Extensive hypertext navigation tools including bookmarks, history, annotation, and more

This chapter guides you through the following topics:

- Installing the HyperWriter software
- Understanding the HyperWriter digital publishing toolset
- Understanding the limits of the demo version of HyperWriter
- Understanding the documentation for HyperWriter
- Basic concepts and other important issues

While all of the topics in this chapter are important (this chapter lays a necessary framework for the rest of this book), the final major section "Basic

Concepts and Other Important Issues," is probably the most important as it defines many of the concepts that will be used repeatedly throughout the remainder of this book. After you have worked through this section, these concepts are further discussed in Chapter 7.

Installation

In the back of this book you will find a CD-ROM disc. Once you have removed it from the packaging (be careful not to bend or crack the disc as you remove it from the back of the book), you can begin using HyperWriter by running the SETUP.EXE program in the root directory of this CD-ROM. To install Hyper-Writer, you first need to be in the Windows Program Manager. Place the CD-ROM disk into your CD-ROM drive and follow the instructions that follow:

Installing the CD-ROM

1. Go to the Windows Program Manager.
2. Select the **Run** command from the **File** menu.
3. Use the **Browse** button to select the CD-ROM drive.
4. Select the SETUP.EXE program on the CD-ROM and then select the **OK** button to run the setup program.

This starts an automated installation program that questions you about your system and then installs HyperWriter and its sample files onto your hard disk. After installation, you will notice that a standard Microsoft Windows Program Group has been created with icons for several programs including HyperWriter, HyperIndexer, the electronic version of this book, the online documentation for HyperWriter, a guide to the sample applications supplied with HyperWriter, and other tools/documents. There are also several icons that represent different sample applications supplied with HyperWriter, such as the HyperWriter online manuals and a guide to the different HyperWriter demonstration applications. The Program Group installed by HyperWriter is shown in Figure 6.1.

Running and Exiting HyperWriter

HyperWriter is a standard MS-Windows application that is run from its MS-Windows icon like any other Windows application.

This chapter is *not* a tutorial on how to use HyperWriter. Using Hyper-Writer is covered from Chapter 6 through the end of the book. However, as this chapter covers installing HyperWriter, you are probably curious as to how to run HyperWriter and what HyperWriter looks like. The steps below cover running and exiting HyperWriter.

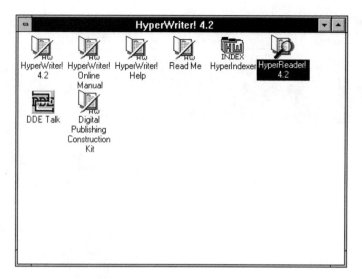

Figure 6.1 HyperWriter's Program Group.

Running HyperWriter

From the HyperWriter Program Group, double-click on the HyperWriter icon. This runs HyperWriter, displaying its opening logo and placing you in the HyperWriter startup document. This is shown in Figure 6.2.

When you run HyperWriter, it automatically opens a HyperWriter document, _STARTUP, which you may find useful. This document is called a *startup* document. Startup documents are automatically opened when you run Hyper-Writer.

To exit HyperWriter, select the **Exit** command from the **File** menu.

Exiting HyperWriter

Select the **Exit** command from the **File** menu. Depending on what you did, HyperWriter may ask you if your document needs to be saved. Answer Yes or No as needed. If HyperWriter prompts you to leave a bookmark, select Yes or No as needed. You will exit from HyperWriter and return to the Program Manager.

Getting Technical Support

If you have any problems installing HyperWriter or need other technical support for HyperWriter, please contact me or John Wiley & Sons through the e-mail addresses in the front of this book. As this book is low-priced (relatively speaking), but includes powerful development tools, all technical support is available solely by electronic mail.

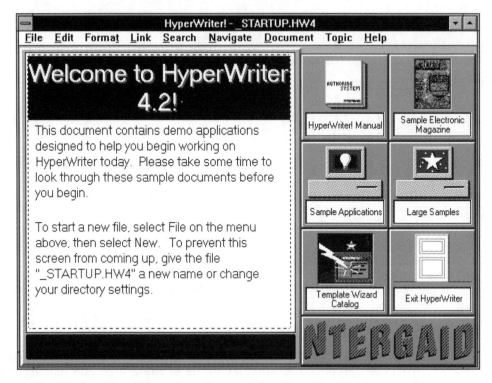

Figure 6.2 What you see when you run HyperWriter.

NOTE: A question that I am often asked when the matter of technical support comes up is "I don't have electronic mail so how do I get support?" Unfortunately, there isn't an easy answer to this question. Due to the need to keep costs down, I don't really have an alternative to electronic mail for technical support. My one comment to you is that if you want to be involved in digital publishing, electronic mail isn't a luxury, it is a *requirement*. If you don't currently have electronic mail, you should. As far as what electronic-mail provider to use, it really doesn't matter. The safest route is generally a commercial online service (such as CompuServe), but Internet access providers also provide quality electronic mail facilities.

What about Windows 95?

Given that this book will arrive on the market after Microsoft's new version of Windows, Windows 95, has shipped, you are probably curious about using HyperWriter on Windows 95. You should be aware that HyperWriter is not yet a Windows 95 application, so I can't say that it has been optimized for the Windows 95 environment. Despite this, you should have no problems using HyperWriter under Windows 95. Given that HyperWriter will function under both Windows 3.x and Windows 95, this has the added benefit that your digital publications can be distributed to an even wider base than just Windows 95—your digital publications will be accessible to all users of Windows.

Getting Printed Documentation

HyperWriter, the digital publishing toolkit supplied with this book, is a commercial product that has a current list price of $695.00 per copy. If you want full printed documentation for HyperWriter that goes beyond what is covered in this book, you need to purchase the full HyperWriter product from NTERGAID. We don't sell printed documentation separately from our products.

Getting More Information on HyperWriter

NTERGAID has a full line of digital publishing tools that include HyperWriter, HyperWriter for Training, and HyperWriter Professional. We also offer a full line of digital publishing services such as the development of CD-ROM titles and Internet World Wide Web sites. (For more information from NTERGAID, please contact us at the address listed in the appendix.)

If you are at all interested in learning more about HyperWriter, please feel free to contact us. Full literature and even demonstration CD-ROM titles are only a call away.

Understanding the HyperWriter Digital Publishing Toolset

HyperWriter is a powerful digital publishing toolkit used for both publishing information in digital form. Electronic publications created with HyperWriter are called *applications* and are generally content rich, including full-text data, pictures, a search-and-retrieval engine, and even multimedia information.

Among the different components you will find in HyperWriter are:

- The HyperWriter authoring system, generally referred to as HyperWriter. Among the many features in the HyperWriter authoring system are document import, full-text searching, manual and automatic hypertext linking, multimedia support, an interactive screen designer, configuration tools, and many other features.

- The HyperIndexer full-text indexer for indexing every word in your application for full-text searching.

- Over 10 megabytes of sample files: HyperWriter applications, text and graphics files, screen designs, and multimedia clips.

The HyperWriter Authoring Environment

The HyperWriter authoring environment is the entire HyperWriter authoring program itself. It is an integrated editing environment for creating hypertext documents. The HyperWriter program supports full word-processing functions including:

- Cut, copy, and paste
- Printing
- Search and replace
- Spell checking
- Style sheets

In addition, HyperWriter provides easy-to-use menu-driven facilities for creating the hypertext links that form the core of HyperWriter documents. HyperWriter has many different features for authoring your documents. These features include those listed in Table 6.1.

The HyperIndexer Full-text Indexer

One of the most powerful facilities in HyperWriter is its full-text or indexed-search facilities. The indexed-search facility allows you to conduct searches including such elements as fields, Boolean operators, wild cards, and more. Indexed searches in HyperWriter require that your HyperWriter application be indexed with the HyperIndexer program. HyperIndexer is an application indexing program that builds a full-text index of the text in your HyperWriter application so that the application can be searched very rapidly.

Table 6.1 Features in HyperWriter

Feature	Description
Multimedia	The ability to integrate text, graphics, audio, video, and animation in a single document.
Hypertext linking	Multiple-link types including jumps, replacements, comments, and actions.
Stylesheets	A full-featured stylesheet system (also called paragraph tags) allows easy presentation and management of your document's text formatting.
Screen painter	A powerful, object-oriented Screen Painter allows you to design a custom user interface for your application.

Understanding the Tools

From the list of development tools covered, you can see that HyperWriter contains many different development tools. This can be slightly overwhelming initially because it brings up the question of what the tools do and when they are used. To make understanding the different development tools easier, Table 6.2 lists each of the tools, gives a brief description, indicates the platform of the tool and its executable program, and when the tool is used.

The Version of HyperWriter Included with This Book

Included with this book on the CD-ROM is a special version of HyperWriter created just for this book (see Appendix A for more details). Our goal in bundling HyperWriter with this book was to provide you with one of today's most powerful digital publishing tools in such a fashion that it allowed you to not only understand digital publishing, but also get a real handle on how to best apply HyperWriter. We also hope that you will like using HyperWriter and consider upgrading to the most recent commercial version.

Understanding the Documentation for HyperWriter

Given that HyperWriter is a commercially available, tried-and-true software product, one of your questions might be whether this book is the only documentation for HyperWriter. The answer to this is of course not. As a commercially available product, HyperWriter is shipped standard with two detailed manuals totaling over 700 pages (yes, longer than this book). Just judging from length, this book is obviously not the full documentation for HyperWriter.

Table 6.2 HyperWriter Tools and When They Are Used

Tool	Description
HyperWriter Authoring System (HWW.EXE)	Interactive authoring system for creating or modifying HyperWriter applications.
	When to Use: The authoring system is used throughout the whole development process, as it supports the interactive design, testing, and modification of your application.
HyperIndexer (HWWINDEX.EXE)	Indexing software for making applications searchable.
	When to Use: When the text in your application is complete and won't be changed further.

What I have done in creating this book is gather together the most important features in HyperWriter as they pertain to digital publishing. The implication of this is that there will, of course, be features in HyperWriter that are not documented in this book. What you need to understand is that you have multiple sources of documentation including the following:

- **This book itself**. You should be aware that this book is available in electronic form (as a digital publication) as well as the print form you are currently reading. If you can't find particular information in the printed book, you should probably check the electronic version, as it might be easier to find.

- **HyperWriter's online manual**. Although HyperWriter's documentation isn't available in printed form, we did supply the documentation in electronic form. This manual is broken into two parts, a Getting Started manual and an Authoring System manual. The Getting Started manual covers how to begin using HyperWriter and new features in HyperWriter. The HyperWriter Authoring System manual covers all the features in Hyper-Writer. HyperWriter's online manual is shown in Figure 6.3.

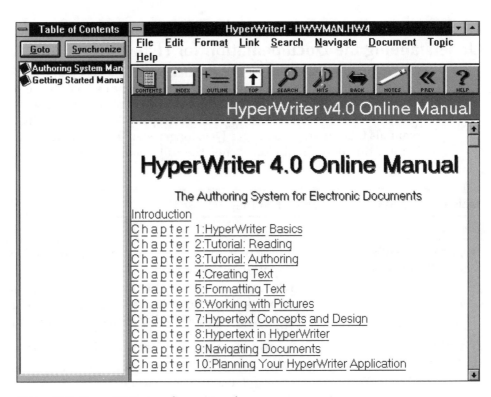

Figure 6.3 HyperWriter's online manual.

- **HyperWriter's README file.** As with many software products, any last minute changes made to HyperWriter are documented in a README file supplied with HyperWriter. Unlike most other products, HyperWriter's README file is actually a digital publication created with HyperWriter. This allows much easier access to information. HyperWriter's README file is shown in Figure 6.4.

Basic Concepts and Other Important Issues

To use HyperWriter effectively requires understanding certain basic concepts. In this book these basic topics are primarily covered in two places, in the following section and in the next chapter. These basic topics include:

- Things you should know before running HyperWriter
- Authors versus readers
- Links and topics

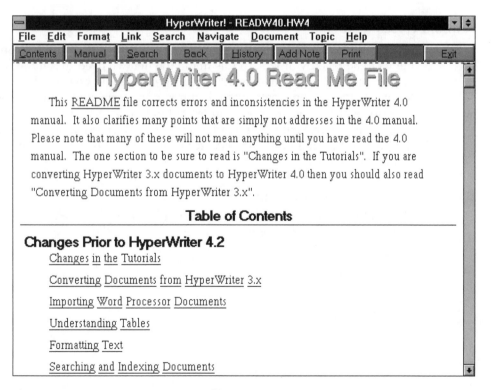

Figure 6.4 HyperWriter's README file.

Things You Should Know Before Running HyperWriter

HyperWriter is an MS-Windows application that uses the normal conventions of the MS-Windows environment. As a Windows application, HyperWriter is oriented around an easy-to-use graphical user interface—the graphical user interface that MS-Windows is based on. In this book, our assumption is that you understand the basics of using Microsoft Windows. These basics include:

- Understanding what a window is
- How to use the Control menu (displayed by pressing **Alt+Spacebar**)
- How to mark blocks using the mouse
- How to select and edit text
- How to use a dialog box including moving within the dialog and choosing an option
- How to move and size a window

If you are unfamiliar with MS-Windows, we strongly recommend that you refer now to the manuals supplied with MS-Windows. This book is not designed to be a guide to using MS-Windows.

Authors versus Readers

HyperWriter is a hypertext system often used for creating electronic documents to be read by others. In this manual when we need to refer to the person or persons reading the document, the term *readers* will be used. When we need to refer to the person creating the document, the term *author* will be used. If we need to refer to those who are either authors or readers, the term *user* will be employed. HyperWriter has reader software, HyperReader, which although not part of the version of HyperWriter included in this book, will be discussed from time to time.

Basic Concepts: Topics, Links, and More

HyperWriter uses several basic concepts repeatedly throughout all aspects of HyperWriter. These concepts are:

- Applications
- Document
- Topic
- Link
- Property
- Action list
- Paragraph tag or style
- Block

Although these concepts are clarified further in Chapter 8, learning them now provides a head start in becoming comfortable with HyperWriter. We strongly recommend that you read the rest of this section.

Applications and Documents

All HyperWriter applications are composed of at least one HyperWriter .HW4 file. These HyperWriter files are also called *documents*. HyperWriter .HW4 files can be up to 136 gigabytes in size, which effectively eliminates any worries about the size of a document. However, despite the ability to create documents up to 136 gigabytes in size, most HyperWriter authors opt to create documents that are much smaller. The typical HyperWriter document ranges from a few kilobytes in size to ten to twenty megabytes. Building a document in a single file that is larger than a few megabytes can often lead to distribution problems as this file simply can't fit on a floppy disc, a common method of distribution. This is one reason to keep the size of individual HyperWriter files below 2 megabytes (which with compression will fit on a single floppy disc). However, when you are planning to distribute your application on CD-ROM media or via a network server, this restriction should not apply to you.

Links and Topics

When you are getting started with HyperWriter, the distinction between a *link* and a *topic* can initially be confusing. The key to understanding links and topics is that topics contain information while links connect information. A document in HyperWriter will always have at least one topic but it may not have any links. As in other programs such as word processors or page layout applications, a document is what you create when you use HyperWriter. The term *file* is used interchangeably with document. The term *application* typically refers to a collection of related HyperWriter documents.

Properties

Used with links and topics are the concepts of properties. A property is a collection of attributes of an object, typically a link or a topic. For example, a topic can have properties of type, security, nonindexable, and so forth. A link can have properties of author, date, link name, and so on. This concept of properties is used throughout HyperWriter to simplify and organize attributes of objects.

Action Lists

Used with links and topics are the *action lists*. An action list is a collection of actions that are executed when either a topic is entered or a link is activated. For example, an action list might contain animations, video controls, digital audio files, among others. Action lists can be reused between links and topics to minimize the number of different action lists that need to be created. As properties and action lists both apply to links and topics, their difference may initially seem confusing. However, the difference between properties and action lists can be clearly stated. Properties are on or off settings while action lists contain actions that can be performed in an author defined order.

Paragraph Tags or Styles

HyperWriter uses the concept of *paragraph tags* or *styles*, generally referred to as just tags for text formatting. A style or tag is a collection of formatting attributes that can be applied to a paragraph or paragraphs. In HyperWriter, as in most word processors, a paragraph is the text between two successive uses of the **Enter** key. Tags are both author defined and author named and can contain any number of formatting attributes including font, font size, color, and margins. When you format text in HyperWriter, you rarely format the actual text itself. Instead, you define a tag that contains the needed formatting attributes and then apply this tag to the needed paragraph or paragraphs. The reason for this approach is that once paragraphs are tagged, their appearance can be changed globally by manipulating the characteristics of their tags instead of modifying each paragraph. Paragraph tags are often referred to in other programs as *styles* or *stylesheets*.

Blocks

Blocks are another concept used repeatedly throughout HyperWriter. As in other programs, a *block* is a piece of text on which operations pertain to the block as a whole, not to any single character of the block. Blocks allow you to perform an operation on a whole region of text instead of a single character. Before block operations can be used, a block must be marked. HyperWriter uses standard MS-Windows block-marking methods—the **Shift** key held down along with the **Arrow** keys as well as dragging the mouse with the **Left Mouse** button held down.

What Is a HyperWriter Document?

Unlike many other software programs, a HyperWriter document is not just a single file. Instead, a HyperWriter document is composed of several different files. The main HyperWriter document file has a file extension of .HW4. This file contains all the text, links, topics, properties, and actions contained in your document. The next file that makes up your HyperWriter document has an extension of .HWN. This file contains HyperWriter topic names. These names are stored externally to the HyperWriter document for fast access. The final required file that makes up your document has an extension of .HWT. The

.HWT file contains the HyperWriter paragraph tags that format the text of the application. This file can be named FILENAME.HWT where FILENAME is the same name as the .HW4 file or it can be named differently, as it may be shared across many different HyperWriter documents. For example, if you had a HyperWriter document named README, this would consist of the following files:

- README.HW4
- README.HWN
- README.HWT

These three file extensions are the three required files that make up a HyperWriter document file. Optional files that also are associated with your HyperWriter documents have similar file extensions (beginning with .HW).

NOTE: As a rule of thumb, all HyperWriter files that are associated with your document can be examined by looking at files ending with .HW? using the **DOS DIR** command.

Naming Conventions

As the majority of this book is actually a detailed tutorial in how to use Hyper-Writer, it is important that you understand how I will refer to the commands/keystrokes that you are to use. This book refers to the named keys (**Enter**, **Alt**, etc.) on your keyboard by representing them in upper- and lower-case letters and boldface. An example is **Enter** which refers to the **Enter** key. Whenever you see one of these keys, this means to touch that actual key on the keyboard. If you are to touch another key concurrently with that key then a "+" sign indicates this. An example is **Alt+L** which refers to pressing the **Alt** key with the letter **L**. If you need to touch a sequence of keys that begin with one of the named keys on the keyboard, then only the named key is shown in boldface. For example, **Alt+L T J** indicates that you should press **Alt** with the **L** key and then the **T** and **J** keystrokes respectively. The **Arrowkey** command indicates that you should simply touch any arrow key such as **Up arrow**, **Down arrow**, **Left arrow**, or **Right arrow**.

Understanding Tutorials

To make following the steps in the tutorials easier, I have used a consistent format for all tutorials. When a tutorial is explaining a particular point or discussing the goals of the tutorial, plain text such as what you are currently reading is used. When you are actually supposed to follow steps in a tutorial, a format such as that shown is used:

1. This is the first step in a tutorial.
2. This is another step in a tutorial.

As you can see, this offers a clear break between the information that you need to read and the steps that you need to follow. This should make using the tutorials in this book easy.

Where Do I Go Next?

After reading this chapter, we strongly encourage you to move to Chapter 7 which covers basic concepts for HyperWriter. This chapter clearly explains HyperWriter's basic approach to electronic publishing and discusses the development process for basic and complex applications. If you are eager to begin getting your hands dirty then I would recommend moving to Chapter 8. You should be aware, however, that reading Chapter 8 before Chapter 7 is not recommended.

NOTE: If you don't want to read any further at this time, you might want to start by examining some of the different HyperWriter sample applications so that you become aware of HyperWriter's capabilities.

Understanding HyperWriter and Digital Publishing

This chapter takes the background that you now have in digital publishing and applies it to the HyperWriter digital publishing toolset. To make reading this chapter easy, it has been broken into five basic sections:

- **HyperWriter and Digital Publishing.** Discusses HyperWriter as a digital publishing toolset and how HyperWriter is scalable to different applications.
- **Basic Concepts.** A short review of the different basic concepts found in HyperWriter.
- **Planning Your HyperWriter Application.** A detailed look at the different objects that make up a HyperWriter application and how they affect planning your HyperWriter application.
- **The HyperWriter Development Process.** A look at the development process.
- **Practical Development.** Notes on practical aspects of development.

HyperWriter and Digital Publishing

As discussed in Chapter 3, there are a number of different approaches that tools for digital publishing take. This section explains HyperWriter's basic approach to electronic publishing. To effectively use any digital publishing toolkit, you have to understand how that toolkit functions and its approach to electronic publications. To review from Chapter 3, some of the basic approaches found in different electronic publishing tools are listed here.

- **Database.** Build a database of the content, separated by record and field, and search across the different fields in the information.
- **Card.** Break the content across multiple cards and establish next card and previous card sequences for browsing.
- **Index.** Feed information into an indexer so that it can be freely searched.
- **Time line or score.** Create a time line or score along which media elements are synchronized.
- **Page.** Display page images onscreen.

HyperWriter takes a different approach to electronic publishing: Hypertext. Fundamentally, HyperWriter is a hypertext system where information is divided into one or more *topics* (chunks of information) that are interconnected by hypertext *links* (connections between chunks). From this simple hypertext architecture, all HyperWriter applications are created. Consider the sophisticated electronic documentation application shown in Figure 7.1.

As you can see from these captions, despite the sophistication of the application the whole application is collection of hypertext links and topics. This includes:

- The main text viewing area, shown in the background of the picture (a hypertext topic)
- Cross-references to different chapters (hypertext links)
- Navigation or user interface buttons (hypertext links)
- Pop-up index browser (a topic containing links to the destinations of the index entries)
- Outline view of the chapter, a topic containing a structural view of the entire chapter (a collection of hypertext links displayed in a floating or comment topic)

This very flexible approach even allows HyperWriter to address most of the different approaches to electronic publishing listed earlier in this chapter. If you are familiar with other electronic publishing environments, then this list may help you better understand HyperWriter by putting HyperWriter into a perspective you are familiar with.

- **Database.** Each HyperWriter topic holds a *record*, different paragraphs are *fields* and the indexer allows you to define fields for searches using a stylesheet to define the fields to be indexed.

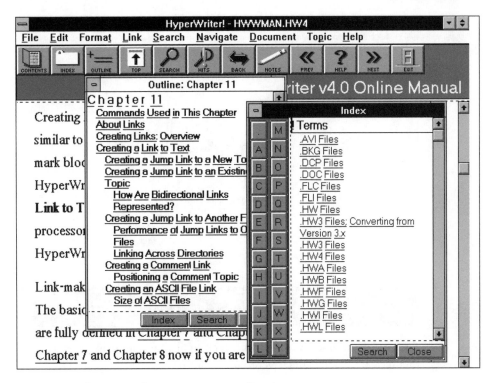

Figure 7.1 Electronic documentation application.

- **Card.** Create topics that don't scroll for each card, assign a screen background for easy navigation and use the next and previous relationships for card to card navigation.

- **Index or text database.** Once your information is stored in a HyperWriter document and broken into topics, it can be indexed for full-text retrieval.

- **Time line or score.** In HyperWriter there is no time line view or score as an application consists of topics and links that a user chooses to move through. You can set up Auto Tours and Branch After actions to guide the user through a sequence of topics. You should note that this approach isn't as finely timed as when a toolkit with a time line or score approach is used.

This brings us to the idea of hypertext as the *architecture* or framework of your electronic publishing application. By using hypertext as a generalized architecture for building electronic publishing applications, HyperWriter allows almost any type of electronic publishing application to be created. Consider the following different real-world electronic publishing and interactive applications that are currently being handled in HyperWriter. (See Figures 7.2 through 7.6.)

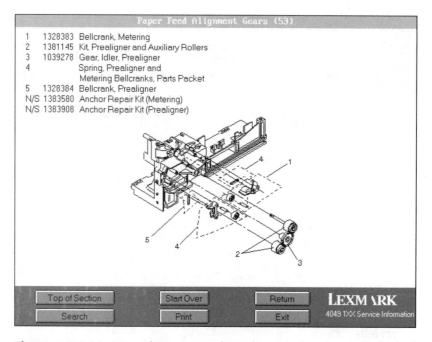

Figure 7.2 Interactive electronic technical manuals using hyperlinked graphics and an integrated parts catalog for use by field service technicians.

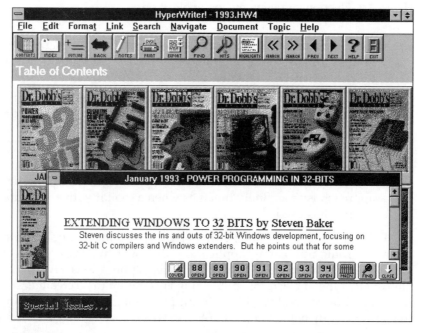

Figure 7.3 Monthly computer programming journal published on CD-ROM.

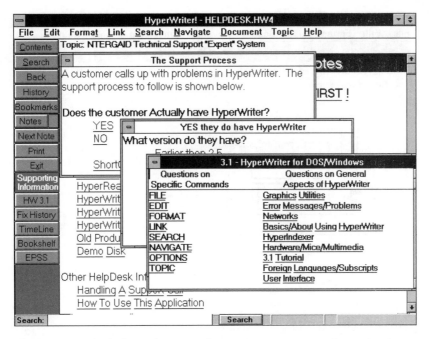

Figure 7.4 Helpdesk applications for storing customer information in an indexed, searchable environment.

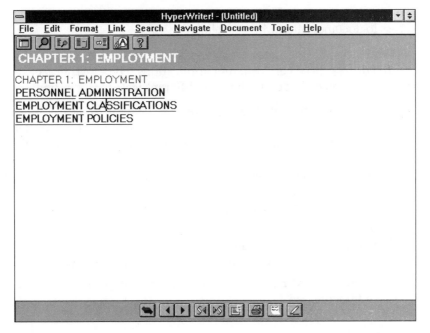

Figure 7.5 Online policy-and-procedure manuals.

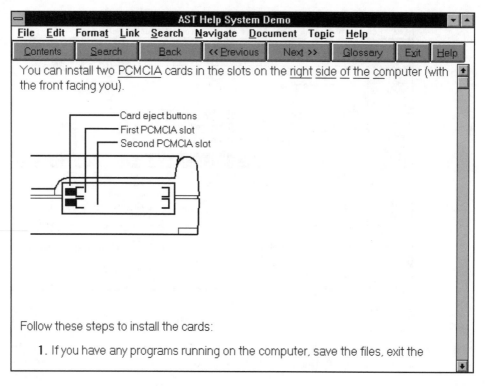

Figure 7.6 Electronic documentation to accompany laptop computers for easy access to documentation when traveling.

To address these very different applications, HyperWriter's basic hypertext model has been extended with many different features including:

- **Full-text Retrieval.** Search the entire contents of your application; even hundreds of megabytes of data can be searched. HyperWriter's full-text retrieval is extremely powerful and includes Boolean searching; full-text and fielded searching; word, phrase, and proximity searching; and automatic word stemming for fuzzy searching. How the user uses the search engine, its user interface is also configurable.

- **Multimedia.** Any HyperWriter link or topic can activate a multimedia clip.

- **Action lists.** Collections of different actions used to generate reports, run other programs, build menus, goto topics, and more.

- **Properties.** Attributes used to configure objects such as links, topics, and documents.

While HyperWriter has many different features, there are two main features that allow HyperWriter to be applied to these very diverse applications: hypertext linking and the Screen Painter.

Both the hypertext-linking features and the Screen Painter are found within the HyperWriter authoring system itself. To make learning the HyperWriter authoring system easy, it has an orientation as a graphical word processor. As most people are familiar with word processors, this makes learning to use the authoring system quite easy. When you are in the HyperWriter authoring system, you can always manipulate the textual content of your application using the built-in editor, use stylesheets to display the information, and even use a thesaurus and spell checker to make sure your information is correct. Although HyperWriter is not designed or intended to replace your word processor, the editing capabilities in HyperWriter make any text-oriented changes extremely easy. In addition to functioning as a graphical word processor, the HyperWriter authoring system incorporates features such as hypertext linking, an interactive screen designer, multimedia object support, and document configuration. How the HyperWriter authoring system functions both as a graphical word processor and a hypermedia system is covered in the section below on the development process.

With a better understanding of HyperWriter as a digital publishing toolset, we are now ready to move onto a discussion of the different basic concepts used in HyperWriter. This includes links, topics, and more.

Basic Concepts

HyperWriter uses several basic concepts repeatedly throughout all its aspects. These concepts are:

- Application
- Document
- Topic
- Link
- Property
- Action list
- Tags
- Backgrounds
- Index
- Block

It is quite important that you be comfortable with these concepts. To ensure this, this chapter covers them in two different sections. In the remainder of this section are short descriptions of each concept. In the section following, "Planning Your HyperWriter Application," are longer descriptions that feature more detailed and practical explanations.

Application

A HyperWriter application is what you are creating with HyperWriter. An application is the highest-level object within HyperWriter.

Document

All HyperWriter applications are composed of at least one HyperWriter .HW4 file or document. HyperWriter .HW4 files can be up to 136 gigabytes in size, which effectively eliminates any worries about the size of a document. However, despite the ability to create documents up to 136 gigabytes in size, most HyperWriter authors opt to create documents that are much smaller. The typical HyperWriter document ranges from a few kilobytes in size to over twenty megabytes.

NOTE: The HyperWriter Publisher can move your HyperWriter applications onto floppy discs despite the size of the file.

Topics and Links

When you are getting started with HyperWriter, the distinction between a link and a topic can initially be confusing. The key to understanding links and topics is that topics contain information while links connect information. A document in HyperWriter will always have at least one topic but it may not have any links. As in other programs such as word processors or page layout applications, a document is what you create when you use HyperWriter. The term *file* is used interchangeably with document. The term *application* typically refers to a collection of related HyperWriter documents.

Properties

A *property* is a collection of attributes of an object, typically a link, topic, or document. For example, a topic can have properties of type, security, nonindexable, and so forth. A link can have properties of author, date, link name, and so on. This concept of properties is used throughout HyperWriter to simplify and organize attributes of objects.

Action List

An *action list* is a collection of actions that are executed when either a topic is entered or a link is activated. For example, an action list might include animations, video controls, and digital audio files. Action lists can be reused between links and topics to minimize the number of different action lists that need to be created. As properties and action lists both apply to links and topics, their difference may initially seem confusing. However, the difference between properties and action lists can be clearly stated. Properties are on or off settings while action lists contain actions that can be performed in an author-defined order.

Tags

HyperWriter uses the concept of paragraph tags (or tags) for text formatting. A tag is a collection of formatting attributes that can be applied to a paragraph or paragraphs. In HyperWriter, a paragraph is the text between two successive uses of the **Enter** key. Tags are both author defined and author named and can contain any number of formatting attributes such as font, font size, color, and margins. When you format text in HyperWriter, you rarely format the actual text itself. Instead, you define a tag that contains the needed formatting attributes and then apply this tag to the needed paragraph or paragraphs. The reason for this approach is that once paragraphs are tagged, their appearance can be changed globally by manipulating the characteristics of their tags instead of modifying each paragraph. Paragraph tags are often referred to in other programs as styles or stylesheets.

Backgrounds

Background screens (or backgrounds) are the mechanism in HyperWriter for constructing visual user interface elements. These elements can contain buttons, pictures, text prompts, database fields, and margin regions. Backgrounds can be assigned to any topic in a HyperWriter document, allowing you to completely customize the look and feel of HyperWriter documents.

Index

An index is a separate file created by the HyperIndexer program to allow full-text searching of HyperWriter .HW4 documents. Index files allow Boolean searches including AND, OR, NOT, XOR, and wildcard operators. Without an index file being created for your HyperWriter .HW4 files, searching is nonindexed, which limits the speed of the search and prevents searching across multiple documents.

Blocks

Blocks are another concept used repeatedly throughout HyperWriter. As in other programs, a block is a piece of text on which operations pertain to the block as a whole, not to any single character of the block. Blocks allow you to perform an operation on a whole region of text instead of a single character. Before block operations can be used, a block must be marked.

Planning Your HyperWriter Application

Now that we understand the basics of digital publishing as they relate to HyperWriter, we are ready to discuss how HyperWriter turns basic hypertext into a platform for sophisticated digital publishing. One of HyperWriter's most unique characteristics is that it offers a platform for creating many different types of applications including:

- Electronic manuals
- Performance support systems
- Training tools
- Online documentation
- Help systems
- Electronic directories
- Multimedia applications

The HyperWriter's Ten Objects

All projects that you create with HyperWriter are composed of only 10 different types of objects:

- **Applications.** A collection of HyperWriter .HW4 files
- **Documents.** A physical HyperWriter .HW4 file
- **Groups.** A named collection of topics. All topics can belong to zero or more groups. Groups allow "meta-operations" on topics
- **Topics.** The underlying containers of information in a document
- **Links.** The connections between topics
- **Properties.** The attributes of a link, topic, or document
- **Action lists.** Actions that are associated with a link or topic and executed when the link is activated or the topic is entered
- **Tags.** Stylesheet entries for formatting the text in a document
- **Backgrounds.** A collection of screen objects that can be applied to a topic
- **Index.** An index file to allow Boolean searching of a document

Each different object will be further discussed. Where applicable, I have included screen shots from HyperWriter that show the features in HyperWriter for working with the different objects.

Applications

A HyperWriter application is a collection of HyperWriter .HW4 document files that make up what you are trying to create with HyperWriter. For example, if you are trying to create an electronic manual using HyperWriter, these Hyper-Writer .HW4 files would be considered a HyperWriter application. Applications are defined by a file named with the name of the application and an extension of .HWA (for HyperWriter application file). Our earlier example might have an application file named MANUAL.HWA. HyperWriter application files can be opened, as can HyperWriter document files. When a Hyper-Writer application file is opened, HyperWriter automatically opens the first file in the application. This brings up an important point: What value does an application file have for the author? First, an application provides a way to logically group all of the documents you have created together. Second, Hyper-Indexer, the indexing engine for HyperWriter document, indexes HyperWriter applications instead of HyperWriter document files. This makes indexing your application significantly easier, as you only need to tell HyperIndexer to index your application instead of telling it all the .HW4 files that comprise your application. Third, HyperReader's .INI file can restrict HyperReader's Open command to only opening application files. When you distribute Hyper-Reader, you might distribute only a handful of application files as opposed to the hundreds or even thousands of .HW4 files that you might distribute. This is obviously easier for the reader. Finally, an application defines the logical order of documents. This is extremely important for cross-document operations such as printing. All HyperWriter documents belong to only a single application.

Applications in HyperWriter are manipulated with the Application command. Shown in Figure 7.7, is the Application command being used with an application file. As you can see, an application file can reference exact drive and directory paths if needed.

Documents

All HyperWriter applications are composed of at least one HyperWriter .HW4 file. These HyperWriter files are also called *documents*. However, despite the ability to create documents up to 136 gigabytes in size, most HyperWriter authors opt to create documents that are much smaller. The typical Hyper-Writer document ranges from a few kilobytes in size to ten to twenty megabytes. Building applications stored in a single file that are larger than a few megabytes can often lead to distribution problems, as these files simply can't fit on a floppy disc. This is one reason to keep the size of individual HyperWriter files below 2 megabytes (which with compression will fit on a single floppy disc). However, when you are planning to distribute your appli-

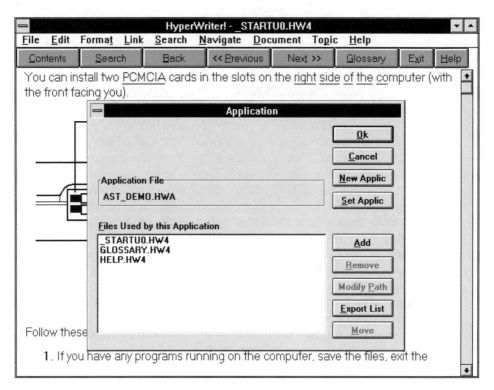

Figure 7.7 An Application file in HyperWriter.

cation on CD-ROM media or via a network server, this restriction should not apply to you.

There is one aspect of how the HyperWriter term *documents* can be confusing. The **Abstract** command located on the Topic menu allows you to define a logical name for a document. For example, a document might have the name "Online Manual, Version 4.0" as opposed to its DOS filename, MANC1V40. HyperWriter's indexed-search facilities are designed to look for logical document names and then display a list of documents to search. However, each document in the list is only listed a single time if multiple documents have the same logical name. Thus, you might have three documents with the same logical name that would only be listed once in the Documents field of the indexed-search dialog box. While this is a minor point, you should be aware of it.

When building a HyperWriter application that is based on information that originally resided in another file or files such as those of a word processor, this brings up the question of the file structure of the application that you are going to create. A file structure is just the number, arrangement, and names of the different file(s) that compose your application. Applications built from multiple files typically take one of two approaches—the correspondence approach or the archival approach. Under the correspondence approach, a HyperWriter .HW4 file that contains the contents of each original file is created. For example, if you had a policy-and-procedure manual that was originally made up of WordPerfect files named CHAP01.WP, CHAP02.WP, and CHAP03.WP, you would create CHAP01.HW4, CHAP02.HW4, and CHAP03.HW4. Under the archival approach, a single HyperWriter .HW4 file would be created that might be named POLICY.HW4. This file will contain an *archive* of all files in your application. Determining whether to use a correspondence or archival approach is generally determined by four primary factors:

- Desired modularity
- Update considerations
- How the application is built
- Tracking original file structure

The modularity of a HyperWriter application is generally tied to its file structure and how closely one module of the application can be replaced without affecting the other modules of the application. If each module corresponds to a HyperWriter document file, then this is relatively easy. However, when multiple modules are contained in a single file, then the application is less modular. Overall, the degree of modularity in your file structure helps to determine whether multiple authors can work on your application simultaneously, allowing concurrent development on your application.

The update considerations of your HyperWriter application are tied directly to the archival/correspondence approach decision for your application. For example, when your application will only be updated in full, then it really doesn't matter whether an archival or a correspondence approach is taken. In the situation where only a small module of your application will be updated at a time, then a correspondence approach can have significant advantages. With this approach only the files in the application that had changed would need to be distributed to your readers. Obviously this point is only valid when your application will have this type of interim distribution (many applications do not necessarily fall into this category).

How your application is constructed has quite a bit to do with the decision between a correspondence and archival approach. A key problem with an archival approach is not the approach itself, but the time that it takes a human author to build the large files characteristic of an archival approach. In addition, when a human author has to work with these large files, the requirement of frequently saving files takes too much time out of the working process (these large files take longer to save than standard-sized files). However, when the HyperWriter AutoLinker component of HyperWriter Professional is used to build an application, an archival approach to applications is much more easily constructed.

The need to track the original file structure in your application can be one factor that argues strongly for a correspondence approach. When a correspondence approach is used, there is a one-to-one relationship between the source files and the resulting HyperWriter documents. This makes it extremely easy to track the original file structure of the application. However, this depends on a consistent file extension being used in the original source files for the application. For example, when there are source files named CHAP1.ABS and CHAP1.SUM then the correspondence approach does not allow exact tracking of the original file structure, because HyperWriter files must have the extension HW4.

As you can see from the descriptions of the primary factors involved in choosing between a correspondence and archival approach, these factors are closely tied together. Determining which approach to use for your application is generally determined by performing a detailed analysis of your application. This should include all of the factors discussed and any other information that you may have about your application. You may well find that there is not a perfect answer for your application, as some applications seem to have attributes of both correspondence and archival applications. One possibility is to fuse both approaches within a single application.

A special file to the HyperWriter or HyperReader programs is the file named _STARTUP.HW4. This file is automatically loaded by HyperWriter or HyperReader whenever they first run. Therefore, the file _STARTUP.HW4 is often used as a table of contents document or cover screen document. In cases where your application consists of only a single file, this file might be named _STARTUP.HW4, as this would allow your application to be loaded automatically.

Groups

Topics, defined in the next section, are the primary chunks of information in a document. Any document can contain one or more topics. Groups provide the ability to associate topics that are related. Once groups are created, they can be searched. For a way to understand groups, consider the HyperWriter online manual supplied with all copies of HyperWriter. This manual is composed of 20 chapters, each chapter broken into multiple topics (one topic per heading level). While this approach provides excellent navigational functionality, it would not allow us to search all of Chapter 11 unless groups are used. As groups were used in this application, our search dialog boxes will allow us to select a single chapter for searching.

As a second example for understanding groups, consider a HyperWriter application composed of a single document that is used to support an attorney in a trial case. This single document would have multiple topics. Each topic would contain information such as a legal brief, a set of notes, information downloaded from an online legal database, and other similar information. Groups would allow you to classify this information into such categories as "Supporting Argument," "Dissenting Argument," "Possible Problems," "Insurance Settlement," and others. As you can see from this example, it is very important that a topic be contained in multiple groups as a topic in "Possible Problems" might also be found in "Insurance Settlement."

One thing that you should understand about groups is that they are similar to other aspects of HyperWriter, such as Guided Tours and a list of links to a group of associated topics. However, they have distinct advantages. First, groups are more dynamic than either of these concepts as groups are dynamically gathered by the search engine for display in its groups field. Second, groups are tightly coupled with HyperWriter's search engine, allowing you to logically restrict how a search is performed. This allows these operations that would otherwise work on only a single topic to function on multiple topics.

Groups are manipulated with the **Groups** command on the Topic menu. This command is located on the Topic menu as Groups apply to topics. Groups that the current topic belongs to are shown with a checkmark. The **Groups** command is shown in Figure 7.8.

Topics

Topics, also often called **nodes**, are the primary chunks of information within a document. All documents must contain at least one topic. Topics contain information allowing documents to be structured along their natural hierarchical or nonhierarchical structure. Topics can contain approximately 200k of text—equivalent to about 100 typed pages of text. In HyperWriter, most topics are full screen and can have a topic name and a scroll bar. Although the display of topic names can be configured, by default they are displayed at the top of the screen. Scroll bars appear automatically in any topic when the con-

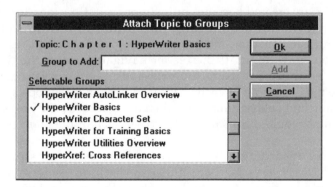

Figure 7.8 The **Groups** command.

tents of the topic are longer than the screen size of the topic itself. The only topics in HyperWriter that are not full screen are comment topics and picture topics. These topics can be sized and positioned as desired. Sizing a topic does not necessarily mean that the picture will match the size of the topic; you can size the topic larger to create white space around the picture or smaller to clip the picture.

A key question that faces HyperWriter authors is determining how the information for their application is mapped into one or more topics. This is a serious question that should consider the following factors:

- Original structure of the information
- Use of next-and-previous relationships
- Whether scrolling is allowed
- Searching requirements of the final application
- Desire to enforce the information's context

The first and one of the strongest factors in determining where topics are created is decided by the original structure of the information. When the original information is structured with headings and subheadings, these are generally good indicators of where topics might be created. For example, when NTERGAID builds the hypertext version of the HyperWriter manual, each first-, second-, and third-level heading indicates where topics are created. Fourth- and fifth-level headings are stored in topics with the third-level headings. The reason for this choice for fourth- and fifth-level headings is that these are generally quite short. In addition, these generally contain tangential information not as important as those indicated by a first-, second-, or third-level heading.

HyperWriter's next-and-previous relationships allow creating an ordered sequence of topics within a HyperWriter document. If you plan that your readers make use of this HyperWriter feature when navigating your documents, then where topics are created becomes quite important. Consider, for example, the HyperWriter online manual. Although this could have been structured into 21 topics, one for each chapter, this would have given very bad results with next-and-previous navigation. If the reader navigated across the document with this topic arrangement using the next-and-previous relationships, he would only see the beginning of each chapter. However, if the topics had been created at heading and subheading levels then navigation by the next-and-previous relationships would allow the reader to see each of the main sections of this document.

A controversy regarding how hypertext documents are structured is known as the *article versus card* debate. This issue basically centers on whether information should be allowed to scroll. As HyperWriter topics automatically have a scroll bar when information extends past the border of the topic, if you don't want your applications to scroll then each topic will be very limited in size. Under this approach, topics would be created not where headings or sub-headings indicated but where the information caused a scroll bar to appear.

HyperWriter's indexed-search facility is designed to locate topics of information within HyperWriter documents. Indexed searching generally operates by highlighting all occurrences of the search terms found for each topic. Thus, if your topics are large, approaching the 200K maximum, then you will have to scroll often to see all occurrences of the search terms. As a rule of thumb, the best topic size for searching purposes is to create topics the size of the information or documents that you want to retrieve with a search query.

The final method for determining where topics should be created is determined by a desire to enforce the *context* of the information. An objection that is sometimes made against hypertext is that it is random access. This allows people to navigate only to the topics that they wish to see—not seeing the topics that precede them. A common example of this is a manual of employee guidelines. A common desire of management is that employees see all items related to a particular guideline. Although there really isn't a way to truly ensure that this occurs inside HyperWriter, a way to partially ensure it is to have a single topic that contains all related information for a guideline—regardless of the length or heading structure of the information. This guarantees that all related information is stored in the same topic, thus ensuring that the context for each guideline is the same. Another example of this might be an online README file for a software product. This is an application that might be kept in a single topic to ensure that its readers might see all the information in the document without having to go to other topics. Therefore, keeping the information in the README as a single topic would ensure that all of the information in the document can be printed or exported with a single command. Although maintaining the context of information is limited to the maximum size limit of a topic (200K of text), this is rarely a problem—200K is a considerable amount of continuous text.

NOTE: Two other approaches to ensuring the context of how information is presented is to offer next-and-previous buttons that provide browsing sequences through the preceding information and to offer hypertext links out to the preceding information.

Links

Links are the component of a HyperWriter document that interconnect information inside a HyperWriter document. Links provide a dynamic gateway between any two pieces of information in a document or documents. For people unfamiliar with hypertext, the distinction between topics and links can often be difficult to understand. However, the distinction can be easily expressed: Topics contain information and links connect information that is contained in topics. HyperWriter documents can contain a variety of link types. Links are divided into three basic types or classes of links: links with a destination of text, links with a destination of graphics, and links with a destination of an action to be performed when the link is selected.

HyperWriter has a wealth of different linking commands. These are best illustrated by looking at HyperWriter's **Link** menu, which shows all of these commands, shown in Figure 7.9.

Properties

Properties are the attributes of objects. For example, a link might have a property of a link name or a security setting. Three different types of HyperWriter objects are considered to have properties: topics, links, and documents. The properties that topics and links have are quite similar, with only a few differ-

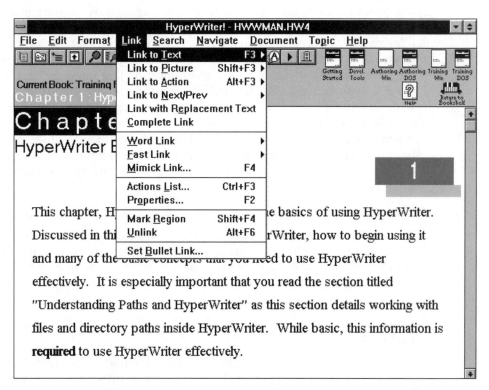

Figure 7.9 The **Link** menu.

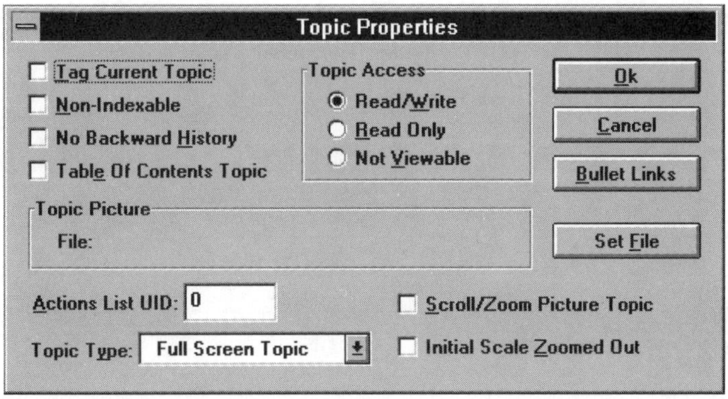

Figure 7.10 Setting topic properties in HyperWriter.

ences between them. However, the properties of a document are quite different from links and topics. Unlike link and topic properties, document properties generally affect aspects of an entire HyperWriter document. For example, document properties determine how links are represented in an entire document. Another example is that document properties set whether a cursor is present in a document. Thus, modifying document properties is quite different from topic and link properties. Modifying document properties uses the **Properties** command on the **Document** menu.

To get a good feel for properties in HyperWriter, we really need to look at three different types of objects: topic properties, link properties, and document properties. Topic properties are shown in Figure 7.10.

Using HyperWriter's Link Properties is shown in Figure 7.11.

Using HyperWriter's Document Properties is shown in Figure 7.12.

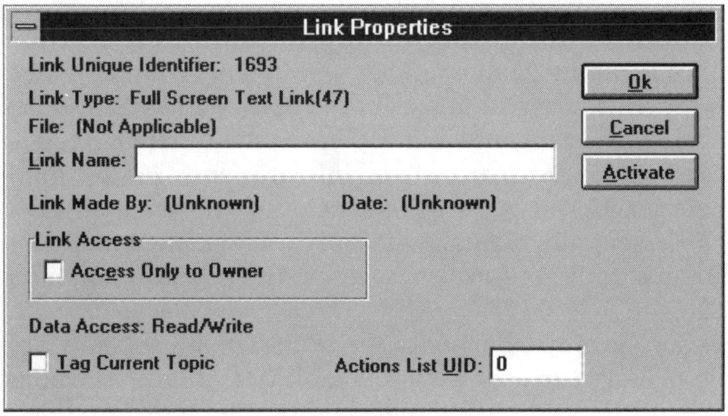

Figure 7.11 Setting link properties in HyperWriter.

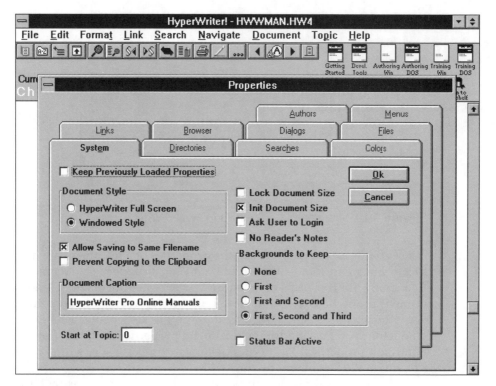

Figure 7.12 Setting document properties in HyperWriter.

Action Lists

An *action list* is a collection of actions that are executed when either a topic is entered or a link is activated. For example, an action list might contain animations, video controls, and digital audio files. Action lists can be reused between links and topics to minimize the number of different action lists that need to be created. As properties and action lists both apply to links and topics, their difference may initially seem confusing. However, the difference between properties and action lists can be clearly stated in that properties are simply on or off settings, whereas action lists perform actions when executed. Link and topic action lists are essentially similar with only a few differences between them. Common link and topic action lists include video, audio, animation, delays, and others.

As topics and links have many of the same action lists, how do you determine whether to assign an action list to a topic or to a link? The question to ask yourself is when the action list should be executed. For example, consider a multimedia action list that played back an audio file to accompany some text displayed onscreen. This action list could be either added to the link to the topic where the text is displayed or to the topic that contained the text. While either approach will work, the better approach is to add the action list to the topic containing the text. The reason for this is that it ensures that the reader of the document will always hear the audio. Adding the audio to the link to the topic only allows the audio to be heard when the reader follows that specific link. Always remember that readers can get to information in many different ways. For example, the reader might get to the text of the document by searching or other navigational tools.

Although both links and topics can have action lists, shown in Figure 7.13, is the command for creating action lists attached to topics.

Tags

Paragraph tags are the HyperWriter equivalent of stylesheets. A paragraph tag allows you to name many different formatting attributes such as font size, font name, margins, and ruling lines. Paragraph tags allow you to format the tex-

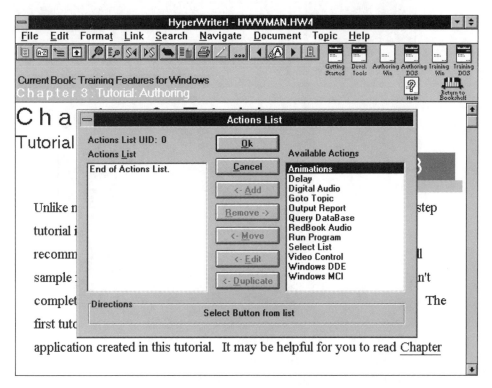

Figure 7.13 Action lists in HyperWriter.

tual component of an application easily by applying the paragraph tag to particular paragraphs. Common paragraph tag names are **HEAD1**, **HEAD2**, **CENTER**, **ABSTRACT**, **BULLET**, and **LIST_ENTRY**. Paragraph tags in source documents often indicate where hypertext topics are to be created. For example, **HEADING 1** paragraph tags from Microsoft Word documents are common indicators of where you might want to create hypertext topics.

Backgrounds

Background screens are the mechanism in HyperWriter for constructing visual user interface elements. These elements can contain buttons, pictures, text prompts, database fields, and margin regions. Backgrounds can be assigned to any topic in a HyperWriter document, allowing you to completely customize the look and feel of HyperWriter documents. Up to three backgrounds can be assigned per topic. Any HyperWriter document can have up to 256 separate backgrounds.

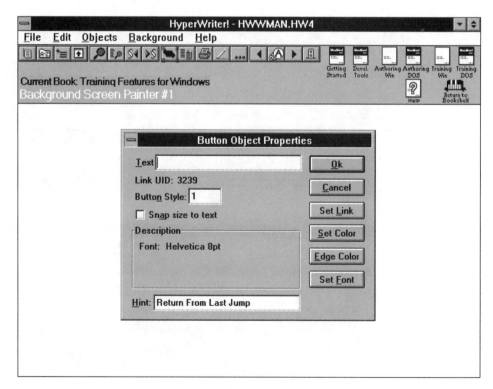

Figure 7.14 Backgrounds in HyperWriter.

To get a better feel for backgrounds in HyperWriter, examine the screen shot shown in Figure 7.14 from HyperWriter's Screen Painter. This illustrates the Screen Painter as well as setting the properties for a button.

Index

An index is a separate file created by the HyperIndexer program to allow full-text searching of HyperWriter .HW4 documents. Index files allow Boolean searches including AND, OR, NOT, XOR, and wildcard operators. Without an index file being created for your HyperWriter .HW4 files, searching is nonindexed, which limits the speed of the search and prevents searching across multiple documents. Index files always have an extension of .HWI and have a default filename of INDEX.HWI. Index files are assigned as a property of a particular HyperWriter document.

Once a HyperWriter application is created, the index file is typically viewed in two contexts: the indexing tool that creates it and the search command where it is searched. Shown in Figure 7.15 is the HyperIndexer options screen that controls how a document is indexed.

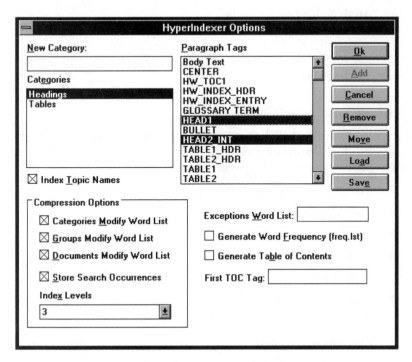

Figure 7.15 The HyperIndexer indexing program.

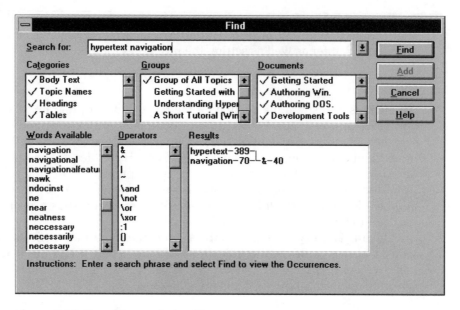

Figure 7.16 Searching an index file.

Shown in Figure 7.16 is a sample search screen generated from these HyperIndexer options.

The HyperWriter's Ten Questions

When we at NTERGAID begin building an application, what we generally do is ask ourselves ten basic questions. The following questions address the ten basic types of objects in a HyperWriter document:

- What is the application?
- What documents are needed?
- What groups are needed?
- Where are the topics?
- Where are the links?
- What properties are needed?
- What action lists are needed?
- What tags are needed?
- What backgrounds are needed?
- How should the application be indexed?

By answering the above questions, the HyperWriter developer can generally formulate the basic aspects of his or her application. From these ten simple questions, an entire HyperWriter application is designed.

The HyperWriter Development Process

When using HyperWriter to develop applications, you may be curious as to the nature of the development process or steps that go into developing an electronic publication. To address this, we have put together an example of the typical development process for a simple electronic publication. Please note that the development process for your particular applications will probably differ slightly from that shown. What we have done is to focus on automated development using HyperWriter's Import Text Wizard. This isn't the only way that development can be handled, as HyperWriter provides a full interactive authoring environment, but it is one of the faster ways to handle development.

Developing a Simple Application

To gain a better understanding of the development process for a simple Hyper-Writer application, let us consider a common electronic publication: the policy-and-procedure manual. Policy-and-procedure manuals are typically large manuals that cover the policies and procedures of a company. The first step is to consider what basic features you would want in an electronic version of a policy-and-procedure manual that was implemented in HyperWriter:

- Use a simple file structure of a single HyperWriter document file for the entire policy-and-procedure manual. This approach means that we have only one document file to manage and distribute.

- Hypertext links to connect related information.

- An attractive user interface for easy retrieval and quick access.

- Full-text searching so that every word is indexed and instantaneously searchable.

The simple development process for this application to meet the basic features listed above is covered in the following list. Please keep in mind that you haven't used these features in HyperWriter yet. At this point, we only want to acquaint you with the development process, not all the development details. In order to get you familiar with the different facilities in HyperWriter, some of the commands that you will use are shown below each step.

1. Use the Template Wizard to choose a user interface template that defines the user interface for your application. Save this template out to a new file. Use of the Template Wizard is shown in Figure 7.17.

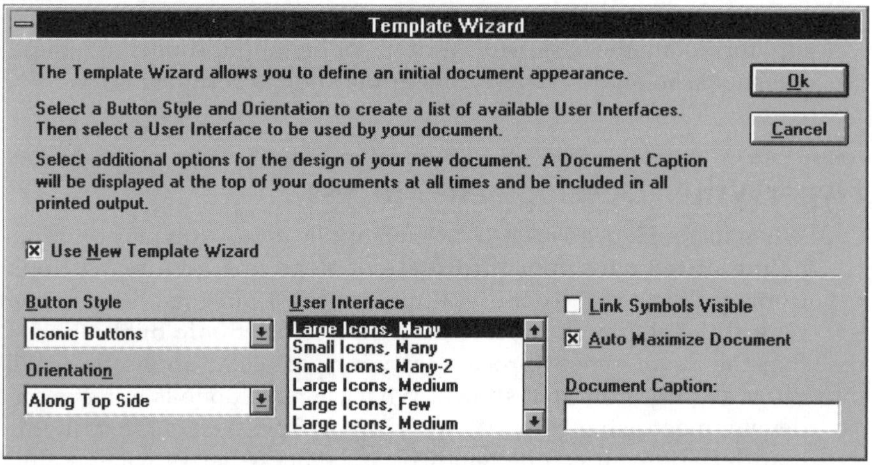

Figure 7.17 The Template Wizard.

2. Import the text for the policy-and-procedure manual into HyperWriter. Use the Import Text Wizard to automatically structure the information to a hypertext format and convert any existing cross references to a hypertext format. Use of the Import Text Wizard is shown in Figure 7.18.

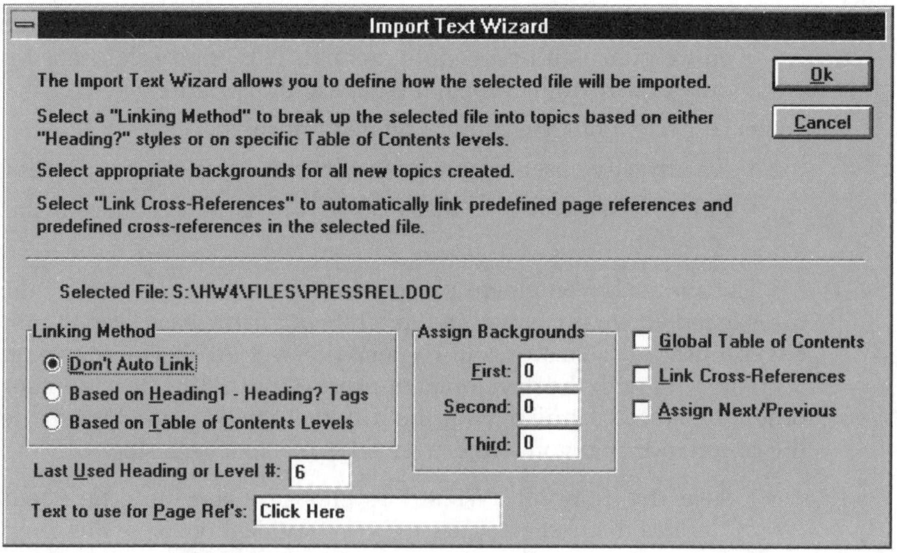

Figure 7.18 The Import Text Wizard.

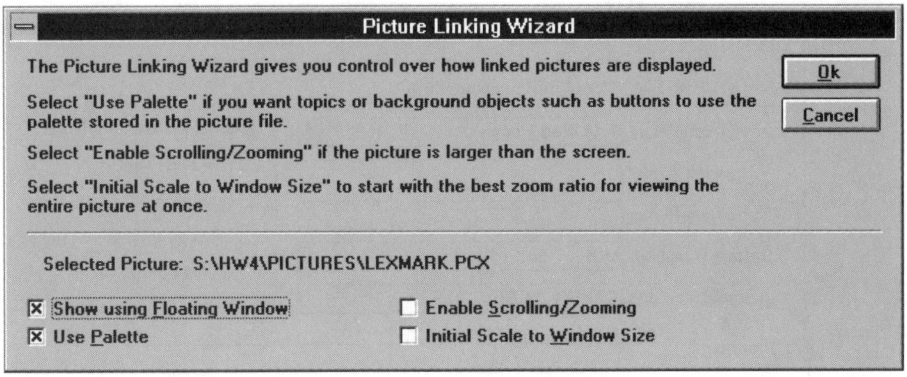

Figure 7.19 Linking to a figure with the Picture Linking Wizard.

3. Add any desired pictures that weren't imported with your application. This can be done by importing pictures or linking to pictures. Use of the Picture Linking Wizard is shown in Figure 7.19.

4. Make any additional hypertext links as needed. Good links to create are conceptual links that cross-reference information by major concept.

5. Name your document so that it has a logical name (this is used for searching). Naming your document is shown in Figure 7.20.

6. Define a HyperWriter Application file so that your application can be published onto a disc set using the HyperWriter Publisher tool and indexed for full-text searching.

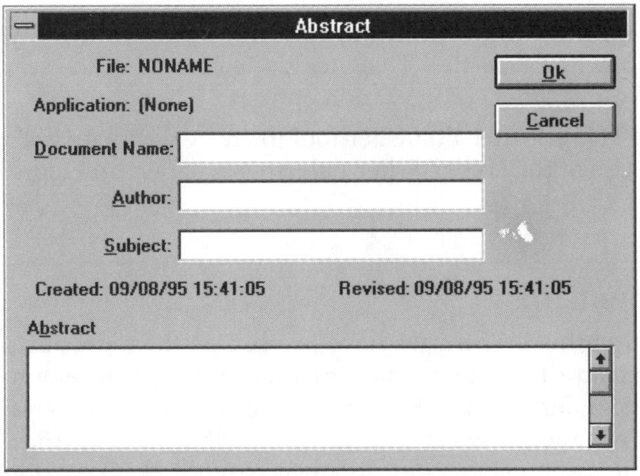

Figure 7.20 Setting the document name.

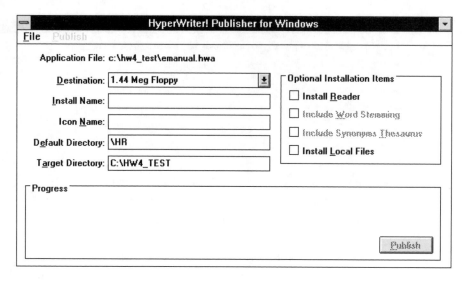

Figure 7.21 Using the HyperWriter Publisher.

7. Index your application using HyperIndexer. This makes your application fully searchable with every word indexed. Use the Exception List option in HyperIndexer so that noise words such as *the* and *of* are not indexed (if desired). You can also define searchable fields.

8. Check your application using the authoring system to make sure that the searching operates as desired. HyperWriter has all the document viewing and searching functions found in HyperReader, so checking your application in HyperWriter is very simple.

9. Configure your application's appearance and functionality by setting its Document Properties. This includes colors, how the searching is to function, and other configuration options.

10. Use the HyperWriter Publisher tool to create a disc set for your application. Use of the HyperWriter Publisher is shown in Figure 7.21.

Practical Development Tips

Up to this point in this chapter, we have focused on the more abstract aspects of HyperWriter and digital publishing than on practical development. While our discussion of planning your HyperWriter application was certainly practical, it still was abstract. It wasn't the type of in-the-trenches knowledge that makes the difference in using a development tool. What I have done is gather several different thoughts on this type of practical development and grouped them into the remainder of this chapter. None of these sections are particularly long, however, the recommendations (if followed) should prove to be quite valuable.

Using HyperWriter Productively

As someone who uses HyperWriter on a daily basis, I am continually asked, "How can I be more productive in HyperWriter?" The answer is threefold:

- Use the Template Wizard to automatically build a template document for your application.
- Use the Import Text Wizard to automatically link documents on import.
- Take advantage of development resources supplied with HyperWriter.

The first way to be more productive in HyperWriter is to start your applications with the Template Wizard. The Template Wizard allows you to quickly and easily generate a template document for your application, complete with user interface and configuration options based on over 50 professionally designed user interface screens. Even if you need to experiment with the Template Wizard several times to make the exact template document that you desire, this still makes you substantially more productive than starting in HyperWriter's Screen Painter and designing an application from scratch. Of course, even with the Template Wizard, you have the option of editing the template document that it created to your exact specifications. This gives you the best of all worlds—great productivity and powerful flexibility. To take advantage of the Template Wizard, please see Chapter 9 where it is used extensively.

As covered in the beginning of this chapter, the electronic publications produced by HyperWriter are really hypertext documents. When your electronic publications have a large amount of text, the Import Text Wizard can be used to automatically link the text and establish the majority of the hypertext relationships. This feature is extremely useful and can greatly enhance your productivity. The Import Text Wizard is documented in a tutorial in Chapter 12.

The third way to be more productive in HyperWriter is to take advantage of the different resources that accompany HyperWriter. Among these resources are:

- Sample applications
- Sample pictures
- Sample screen designs

By examining the sample applications and screen designs, you can see different authoring techniques and get a better feel for the capabilities of HyperWriter. Even if you need to customize these resources for your application, starting from these resources can dramatically reduce the time needed to design your application.

Naming Conventions

As a digital publisher, one of the greatest hassles that you face is dealing with naming conventions. What I mean by naming conventions is how you name files—whether they are picture files, document files, or your HyperWriter documents themselves. For the vast majority of users, filenames are limited to 8 characters with a 3 character extension, or 8.3. While the next generation of Microsoft Windows, Windows 95, addresses this, until it becomes the dominant standard in desktop computing, naming will be limited to 8.3. Given that you only have 8 character names, how do you name files appropriately?

The answer is to adopt naming conventions so that your names are readily understandable. Consider a picture file for "Figure 1" in a computer magazine. The impulse is to name that picture file something like "Figure 1." While this is a good impulse, this is actually a bad name. The reason is, of course, that no magazine has just one Figure 1. A better approach is to develop a naming convention so that the picture file would have a unique name. One such naming convention might create a filename by combining different elements such as: YEARMONTHTYPEARTICLENUMBER.

Assuming that the year was 1995, the month was December, the type of article was a feature, and that this was the first article in the issue, you would have a name such as: 9512F01.

This name would also have the three character extension that indicates the type of the file. If the type was .PCX then you would have the following name: 9512F01.PCX. As you can see, this type of naming convention yields unique filenames that can be applied to virtually any type of development process.

To summarize with respect to naming conventions, they provide a powerful tool for managing your content. I will not tell you that these types of naming conventions are simple or easy to understand. However, when you have a large digital publishing project, this type of naming convention is virtually indispensable.

NOTE: These types of naming conventions also lend themselves quite well to batch manipulation of content using tools like the Windows File Manager. For example, you could tell File Manager to copy only the 1995 graphics files.

Enhancing Each Application

An aspect of HyperWriter that a serious developer needs to become aware of at the early stages of using HyperWriter is that no HyperWriter application is ever really finished. The nature of HyperWriter lends itself extremely well to fine-tuning and constant refinement of applications. Always bear in mind the one rule of developing an application: If the customer doesn't understand your application when he or she needs to use it then the features it has may not matter.

Storyboarding

Storyboarding is a technique for laying out the flow of an application created in HyperWriter. Generally, it consists of a picture showing the branching structure of an application. While HyperWriter's hypertext linking can theoretically make this impossible as each link can lead to other links that make the possibilities endless, storyboards for HyperWriter documents generally focus on the first few topics in a HyperWriter document(s) such as the cover screen, help screen, and table of contents. Finally, a storyboard can be helpful for illustrating the file structure of an application by drawing boxes around groups of topics to show what topics are contained in what file.

Testing

One characteristic of HyperWriter applications that many people do not realize is that a HyperWriter application is really a piece of software. And, like all software, your HyperWriter applications need testing before they are distributed to their users. This testing is designed to ensure that your HyperWriter application is fully functional prior to its distribution. Listed are general guidelines for testing HyperWriter applications:

- Test the actual application as distributed to a reader, not the files as you developed them (where they resided on your development system).
- Spell check the help system for your application if one exists (also spell check the content of your application).
- Verify that all files supposed to be distributed with your application are present.
- Test the HyperReader .INI file to verify that the desired options are set.
- Test all buttons in the user interface of the application in all documents in the application.
- Verify that the user interface of your application is consistent throughout if this is desired.
- If the application is installed across multiple directories, then test indexed searching of the application.
- Verify that any temporary data files such as tours, bookmarks, and reader notes files are present if they should be.
- Test the application on a different drive and directory setup if possible.

Developing on Time—Develop to End

As noted in the section on testing, a HyperWriter application is really a piece of software. One of the most notorious truths in the software industry is that software development is never ready on time. As someone with a ten-plus-year background in software development, this is something that I can personally attest to. I am certain that most readers will agree with me. Although HyperWriter isn't a traditional development tool like a programming language, HyperWriter is still a software development tool. Consequently, as using HyperWriter is really software development, there is a good chance that your development will take longer than you think. I don't want to get into a discussion of why software development almost invariably runs late, as a discussion of this very simple topic could easily fill the rest of this book. However, I have developed a very simple development approach that I find eliminates a large portion of the problems with development schedules slipping. I call this *Develop to End*. What the term develop to end really means is that when involved in a development project, your goal should be to develop the application through to the end before you get to the end of the development. Confused? I'm not surprised. By develop to end, what I mean is that before you complete your development, you shouldn't leave any task to the end of a project, even if it means doing a partial version of that task.

Consider developing an electronic manual using HyperWriter. The typical approach would be to write and implement all of the text for the electronic manual first, and at the end of the project, use HyperWriter's indexer to make the text searchable. The problem with this is that it leaves a major aspect of the project untouched until very late. If any problems crop up then the impact can range from minor to catastrophic. And given that you would be near the end of the project, this would (inevitably) translate to a late delivery. With a develop-to-end approach, you would index the electronic manual as soon as you had a sizable portion ready. What this should do is reveal any problems much earlier in the development process, rather than leaving them to the end. Is this develop-to-end approach perfect? Of course not. What it represents is a first step towards eliminating a common reason for development delays—tasks left to the last minute often aren't as simple as they were thought to be, yielding unexpected problems. With a develop-to-end approach, these issues are typically found sooner in the development process, leading to fewer delays.

CHAPTER 8

HyperWriter Basics

Now that you have reached this chapter, you should be ready to get your hands dirty and really learn HyperWriter. We begin with a section called "Understanding HyperWriter," and then move on to cover two tutorials, each one designed to make you comfortable with a different major area in Hyper-Writer. "Understanding HyperWriter" covers many basic topics that you need to know before you can use these tutorials. The tutorials in this chapter cover reading a HyperWriter document and understanding HyperWriter's built-in word processor.

Getting Started

Before we jump into the tutorials, there are a few things to do. The first is that you need to install HyperWriter if you haven't already done this. See Chapter 6 for installation instructions. The second is to make sure that you have enough disc space to work without interruption (few aspects of computers are as purely annoying as running out of disc space). To work through all these tutorials, you should have at least 10 megabytes of free space. The final task before beginning these tutorials is to read Chapter 7. While these chapters can technically be read in any order, Chapter 7 is particularly important as it lays the framework on which this chapter is based—without reading it, many constructs such as links, topics, and applications may not be clear. With these tasks accomplished, you are ready to begin.

Understanding HyperWriter

HyperWriter is a very powerful digital publishing toolkit. As with most powerful tools, using HyperWriter effectively requires a good grasp of some very basic topics. These basic topics are covered in the following subsections and are arranged in order of complexity from the simplest to the most complex. Among the topics covered are:

- Marking blocks
- HyperWriter's menu structure
- Getting online help
- Exiting HyperWriter
- Full-screen and windowed-style documents

Although all of these topics are important, it is especially important that you read the section titled "Understanding Paths and HyperWriter," as this section details working with files and directory paths inside HyperWriter. While basic, this information is required to use HyperWriter effectively.

Marking Blocks

HyperWriter is considered by many of its users to be an editor-centered software product. By editor-centered, I mean that in HyperWriter the editor is the central feature in the software. HyperWriter's default development environment is that of an editor or word processor. Many actions in HyperWriter, such as making links, revolve around marking blocks of text. While marking blocks of text is a very simple act under MS-Windows, I am covering it here to make sure that everyone can work through this chapter without problems.

Marking a Block of Text

Press **Shift+Arrowkey to** start marking the block. Continue marking the block with **Shift+Arrowkey** until the entire block is marked. In addition to using **Shift+Arrowkey**, you can also hold down the **Left Mouse** button and drag the mouse over the block of text to mark. Once the block is marked, any valid block operation can be used on the block.

HyperWriter's Menu Structure

The main menu structure used in HyperWriter consists of nine menus. The main menu entries are listed in Table 8.1.

Table 8.1 HyperWriter's Menu Structure

Menu	*Description*
File	Use the File menu for all operations involving files. Exiting HyperWriter is also accessed from the File menu.
Edit	Use the Edit menu for accessing all editing commands. Editing commands change the content of the text. Search and replace commands locate exact information within a document and replace it with new information if necessary.
Format	Use the Format menu to access all document formatting commands. Formatting commands change the appearance of the text, not its content.
Link	Use the Link menu to access all commands for creating hypertext links both within and across documents. Link commands are used to create the underlying structure of a hypertext document.
Search	Use the Search menu to access indexed search commands.
Navigate	Use the Navigate menu for moving within or across hypertext documents. Navigation commands are used for locating your way through a large body of information.
Document	Use the Document menu to access commands related to HyperWriter document files. This includes configuring HyperWriter documents.
Topic	Use the Topic menu to access commands specific to working with topics.
Help	Use the Help menu option to access a submenu, which accesses HyperWriter's online help file.

Getting Online Help

HyperWriter has an extensive online help system that you may find quite useful in learning HyperWriter. The online help system is actually a large hypertext document that can be browsed in the same fashion as any other hypertext document in HyperWriter.

Accessing HyperWriter's Help System

Press **Shift+F1**. This activates the online help system.

NOTE: Shift+F1 is not the standard keystroke to access help in an MS-Windows application. The standard keystroke is **F1**; however, HyperWriter uses **F1** to activate hypertext links, so **Shift+F1** is used instead.

After **Shift+F1** is pressed to activate the online help system, the screen will clear and display a topic of help information. From this initial help screen, any link can be selected with the arrow keys to move to the link, then pressing **Enter** to select the topic. Links in the help system for HyperWriter for Windows are shown as underlined, green text.

Once you press **Enter** on a link, the destination of the link is displayed. To return from the link, press the **Esc** key. This is the basic method of navigating a hypertext document in HyperWriter—**F1** to activate a link and **Esc** to return from a link. The mouse can also be used to read documents by using the **Left Mouse** button to activate links and the **Right Mouse** button to return from links. If the information in a particular help screen topic extends off the screen, a scroll bar will be displayed on the right-hand edge of the help topic. To scroll down to the rest of the help information, press **Page Down**.

NOTE: Although HyperWriter uses **F1** to activate links, HyperReader uses **Enter** (although **F1** is still supported).

For more information about navigating a hypertext document in Hyper-Writer, see the tutorials later in this chapter that document several of Hyper-Writer's navigational aids.

Exiting from the Help System

Click back on the HyperWriter window to return to your document.

Exiting HyperWriter

To exit HyperWriter, choose the **Exit** command from the File menu. This exits HyperWriter and returns you to the Program Manager. If changes have been made to the document, you will be asked if you want to save changes. Answer Yes or No as needed. If HyperWriter's bookmarks facility is turned on, you may be asked to leave a bookmark. Answer Yes or No as needed. This exits HyperWriter.

Documents: Full Screen and Windowed

Almost all Windows applications are displayed in a movable, resizable Window. While correct for many applications, there are many applications where this behavior is undesirable. For example, in a tutorial environment, you may not want the overhead of a windowing environment. To address this, Hyper-Writer supports two different styles of documents: full screen and Windowed. When the Document Style is set to Full Screen, HyperWriter documents are assumed to take over a full VGA screen, a 640x480 grid of pixels, when being read. If you are running Microsoft Windows in only 640x480 standard VGA mode, then the viewport buttons (discussed below) on the status bar can be used to scroll the HyperWriter viewport around the full 640x480 screen.

NOTE: Most of the applications that we will focus on in this book, and HyperWriter's default settings for creating documents, will be Windowed style. However, it is important to understand the distinction as full-screen–style documents are a powerful feature in HyperWriter.

When you are authoring a full-screen document in standard VGA resolution (640x480 pixels), then HyperWriter displays a viewport onto the screen. This viewport is controlled by the viewport arrows on HyperWriter's status bar. These arrows let you scroll the screen right, left, up, or down. This is illustrated, in Figure 8.1, where only the first 640 by approximately 420 pixels could be displayed due to the overhead of Windows' menu bars.

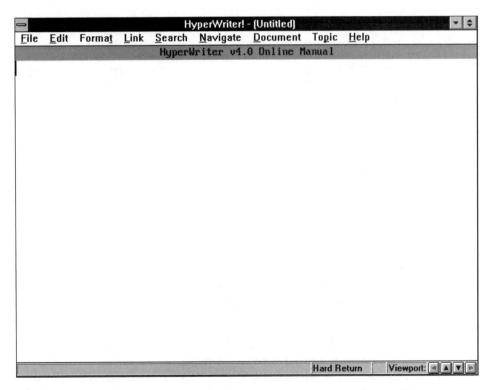

Figure 8.1 A full-screen document with a viewport.

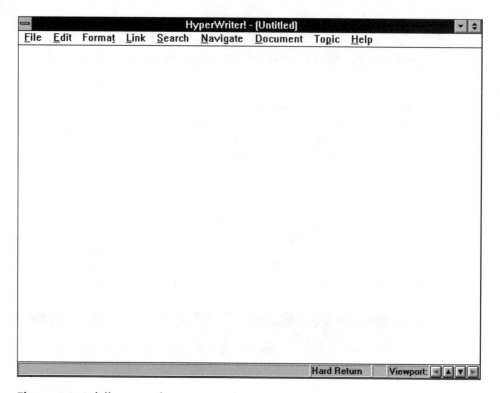

Figure 8.2 A full-screen document with the viewport scrolled (note the buttons at the bottom).

Shown in Figure 8.2, the viewport **Down** arrow has been used to scroll the viewport to reveal the remaining portion of the screen.

NOTE: If you intend to use the full-screen style, we strongly recommend that you install Microsoft Windows in greater than standard VGA resolution. Almost all SuperVGA graphics systems can be used to drive Microsoft Windows 3.1 at 800x600 resolution or 1024x768 resolution. Either of these choices will allow you to display a full 640x480 document without having to scroll the document using the viewport buttons.

When the document style is Windowed, HyperWriter documents appear in true scalable windows similar to those of the Windows help system, WIN-HELP.EXE. Windowed-style documents can be maximized to the maximum screen size that Microsoft Windows is installed for. In a Windowed-style docu-

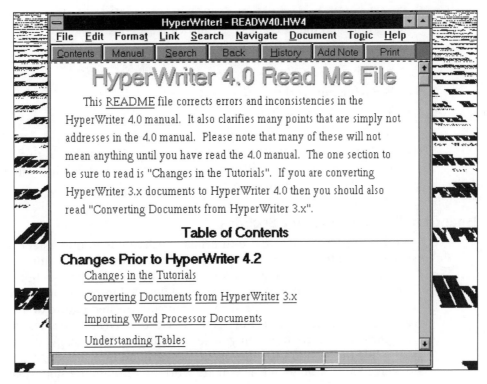

Figure 8.3 A windowed-style document in HyperWriter.

ment, the document is truly a part of the MS-Windows environment and is displayed in the same fashion as any other Windows application. It appears in a window where it can be resized as necessary (unless the Lock Size document property was used). In the following figures, a windowed-style document is shown in HyperWriter. Unlike full-screen–style documents, Windowed-style documents appear the same in HyperReader as they do in HyperWriter. A sample Windowed Style document is shown in Figure 8.3.

This concludes the background material that you need to know to feel comfortable using HyperWriter. At this point, you are ready to move onto the tutorials. The tutorials begin with a short introduction and then continue with a tutorial covering how to read digital publications using HyperWriter.

About These Tutorials

One of my goals in writing the tutorials in this chapter was to make it possible for you to sit down and simply work through each tutorial—even after not using HyperWriter for some time. To help accomplish this, every tutorial has a standard format that includes the following sections:

- Running HyperWriter
- Body of tutorial
- Saving our work
- Exiting HyperWriter

After the "Running HyperWriter" section in each tutorial, you will find the body of each tutorial. With this standard approach, you should find that working with the tutorials doesn't require you to memorize details such as how to run HyperWriter and how to exit.

Understanding the Reference Sections

Another aspect of using these tutorials effectively is to understand the difference between the tutorial and reference or background information that is relevant to, but not absolutely required, for each tutorial. These sections, typically at the end of each tutorial, give you more detailed information than could easily be covered when working through the step-by-step nature of a tutorial. To easily distinguish these sections, the keyword *Reference* precedes the heading that starts each section. When you see one of these sections, you should know that while the section provides useful background information, it doesn't have to be read at the same time as you are working through the step-by-step nature of a tutorial.

Tutorial 1: Reading a HyperWriter Document

In this tutorial we will examine a sample application created with HyperWriter to illustrate the nature of reading documents using HyperWriter.

As you should recall from Chapter 6, HyperWriter is the authoring environment for creating documents, while HyperReader is the reader or viewer program for browsing documents created with HyperWriter. Although an authoring environment, HyperWriter features all of the navigational tools found in HyperReader. As all HyperReader's navigational features are integrated into HyperWriter, using it to read documents is very easy and functions almost exactly like using HyperReader.

NOTE: The different steps in this chapter could be done in HyperReader as well as HyperWriter.

After working through this tutorial, you should understand:

- How to open a document
- How to activate a link or button
- How to search a document
- How to view your history
- How to add a note to a document

Before we begin this tutorial there is one important concept that you should grasp—HyperWriter applications look and feel how the author has designed them. Over the years, I have often been asked what a standard HyperWriter application looks like and my response is always, "it depends." Although in this tutorial we will examine a standard HyperWriter application, this does not mean that your applications must look and feel this way. While you could adopt this look and feel, more important, you can adopt a look and feel appropriate for your application and your audience. This point will be clarified in this tutorial and the succeeding tutorials as we examine different applications.

Running HyperWriter

Before we can open a sample document we must first run HyperWriter. Hyper-Writer is a standard MS-Windows application that can be run from the Program Manager. HyperWriter is run as follows:

1. Change to the Program Manager.
2. Double-click the HyperWriter icon in the digital publishing program group.

When HyperWriter runs you will notice that a HyperWriter document is loaded by default. This is HyperWriter's startup document feature. Any document named _STARTUP stored in HyperReader's or HyperWriter's Documents Directory will automatically be loaded whenever HyperWriter or HyperReader runs.

NOTE: The startup document feature is a great help when building applications, as you don't have to worry about configuring specific filenames at all. Just name the first document that makes up your application _STARTUP.HW4 and it will be automatically opened whenever your application is used.

If a startup document or another HyperWriter document is *not* loaded when you run HyperWriter, you would see a typical MS-Windows application with a menu bar, a blank screen, and a blinking cursor. It is important to understand that HyperWriter's basic orientation is that of a graphical word processor. Just as a word processor initially presents itself with a cursor and a blank screen, so does HyperWriter. However, unlike a word processor, when a HyperWriter document is loaded HyperWriter takes on the appearance of the current document. This can include elements such as pictures, onscreen buttons, and even the style of the window that is displayed.

Opening a Document in HyperWriter

With HyperWriter running we are ready to use the **Open** command to select the document we want to read.

1. Select the **Open** command from the **File** menu.
2. Select the document HWWCOVER from the list of available documents. If you are asked to leave a bookmark, answer No. This loads the document.

Turning Off Short Menus and the Toolbar

In order to make HyperWriter easier to use, HyperWriter's menu system can be used in two fashions. The default way that the menu system operates is called Short Menus. When Short Menus are turned on, many of the advanced commands in HyperWriter's menu system are hidden from view, thus shortening the menu system. As we are going to want access to all the commands in HyperWriter's menu system, we should turn this option off now before going any further.

Turn off the **Short Menus** command in the **File** menu. This will take away the checkmark next to the menu command that indicates that Short Menus are turned on. HyperWriter, like many Windows applications, has a floating toolbar of icons that access standard functions. This toolbar is turned on by default. HyperWriter's toolbar is shown in Figure 8.4.

Using a toolbar like this is really a matter of personal preference. However, in this book using the toolbar is not my preference and this book doesn't refer to it at all, allowing you to turn it off without concern. For this reason, the next step covers how to turn off HyperWriter's toolbar. If you do leave it on, then bear in mind that it will not be shown in any of the figures in this book.

Turning Off the Toolbar

1. Select the **Preferences** command from the **File** menu.
2. Select the **Toolbar** folder of options. This displays the dialog box shown in Figure 8.5.
3. Turn off the **Floating Toolbar Palette** option.
4. Select the **OK** button to close the **Preferences** dialog box.

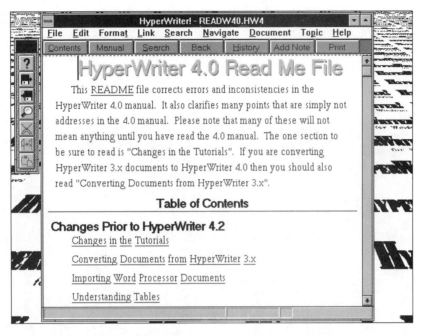

Figure 8.4 HyperWriter's toolbar.

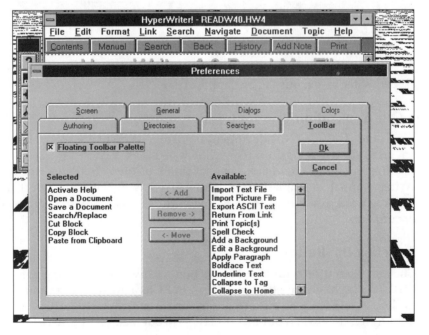

Figure 8.5 Turning off the toolbar.

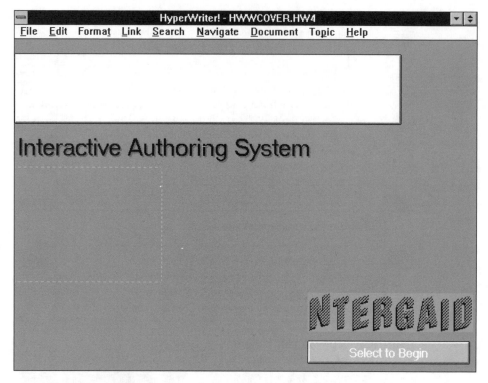

Figure 8.6 The opening screen.

With **Short Menus** and the **Toolbar** turned off, we are ready to begin using HyperWriter by examining our application.

Examining Our Application

When the HWWCOVER document is loaded, it displays an opening or cover screen as shown in Figure 8.6.

This opening screen is a close facsimile of the actual cover of the Hyper-Writer manual. A single button is displayed with the text "Select to Begin." We now need to select or activate this button so that we can begin reading our document.

Selecting the Button

Click on the button with **Left Mouse** button. If you aren't using a mouse, press **Ctrl+T** to highlight the button and press **F1** to activate the button. As you are in the HyperWriter authoring environment and not HyperReader, **Ctrl+T** is used to select between buttons (in HyperReader, **Tab** and **Shift+Tab** are used).

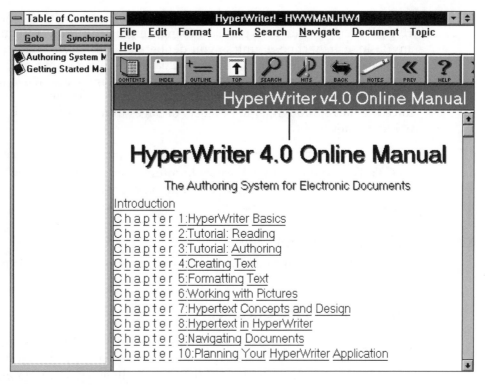

Figure 8.7 The HWWMAN document.

NOTE: This brings us to an important point about the nature of buttons. HyperWriter is a true hypertext system and all buttons are really hypertext links. A button is a different way to visually represent a link. Functionally, a button is identical to a link. Therefore, the terms *button* and *link* are often used interchangeably.

When the button is selected, a new HyperWriter document, HWWMAN, is opened. It is shown in Figure 8.7.

The HWWMAN document is an electronic version of the full printed HyperWriter documentation. This document is organized around the table of contents you see in Figure 8.6. A table of contents is a common way to organize an application because it provides a consistent structure for the reader with which they are familiar. In our online manual, entries in the table of contents are all hypertext links to their related section of the manual.

A great strength of documents created with HyperWriter is that due to HyperWriter's powerful hypertext linking, readers can browse documents in any fashion they choose, unless you deliberately design your documents so that the reader has to follow a particular path. This allows your readers to follow only the paths of information that interest them or are relevant to their task. This is very different from a paper document where a reader is typically forced to move through large numbers of pages to retrieve only a single piece of information.

NOTE: This type of random access to information is a key reason for digital publishing—it puts the reader, not the author, in charge.

Reading Information Electronically

We will now move through a sample trail of information in our electronic HyperWriter manual.

Moving Through the Document

1. Move the mouse over the Chapter 10 entry in the table of contents. Depending on your screen resolution, you may have to scroll the table of contents down to display the Chapter 10 entry. When your cursor is positioned over the Chapter 10 entry, you will notice that the cursor changes to a hand to indicate that you are over a link.

NOTE: As with almost every aspect of HyperWriter, how links are displayed is configurable—you can configure how links appear according to the needs of your application. This document has links displayed with green text on a white background, boldfaced, and underlined.

2. Activate the Chapter 10 link to move to this chapter.
3. If you scroll down you will notice several links. These links represent different main sections in Chapter 10.
4. Click on the **Forward Arrow** (it shows a right-facing arrow) button in the row of buttons at the top of the screen.

   Selecting the **Forward Arrow** moves you to the next topic of the hypertext document. All HyperWriter documents are composed of one or more topics—information containers that hold parts of documents or even entire documents. Although hypertext allows free browsing through documents, there can also be sequential relationships such as next and previous to support readers who want to see the entire document.

5. Select the **Index** button to display a list of terms. Choose a term that interests you and you will be taken to the location of that term.

A key concept in reading electronic documents is the notion of *backtracking*. When you activate a link or button in HyperWriter, you can almost always backtrack from the location that the link takes you to, returning you to your previous location. This allows you to roam freely through electronic documents, without fear of getting lost. In HyperWriter, backtracking is done with the **Esc** key (to escape, back up one level) or the **Right Mouse** button. As a rule of thumb, people invariably find backtracking in HyperWriter to be a natural, fluid method of reading documents. Although I am not going to illustrate backtracking here (it really is just that simple), consider what would happen if you tried to backtrack. The last instruction was to click on a term in the index. Backtracking would return you from the term to the index itself. Backtracking again would return you to the second topic in Chapter 10 (you had just selected the **forward** button). Finally, backtracking again would return you to the top of Chapter 10. If you continued backtracking, you could even return to the very first document that you started from (HWWCOVER in this case).

This concludes our brief example of how to move through a document. Feel free to continue browsing this document to become more familiar with HyperWriter documents and the options available to you as an author. At this point, we are ready to experiment with using some of the different navigation tools found in HyperWriter.

Using Navigation Tools

One of the most powerful aspects of digital publishing is the ability of the reader to apply different tools to the reading process. This is referred to as *navigation*—the idea that electronic information can be navigated through using tools just as you might use a compass for navigation through a forest. The difference is that instead of a compass, you might use tools such as full-text searching, annotation, bookmarks, and others. The concept behind HyperWriter's navigational tools is that the traditional reading process of reading a work in depth has been replaced with that of browsing a work to find what interests you. When you find what interests you, then and only then do you need to read in depth. In this sense, digital publishing is often more used like encyclopedias or other reference works than novels. This doesn't say that digital publishing cannot be used for applications that require reading in depth, but that this is not the general application of hypertext. HyperWriter's navigational tools allow you to read a work in a more powerful fashion by bringing additional control to the reading process.

Table 8.2 Navigational Tools in HyperWriter

Navigational Tool	*Description*
History	Display a popup list of all topics visited in this reading session. **Navigate** Menu.
Local Map	Display a graphic overview of the local linked structure of the document. **Navigate** Menu.
Bookmarks	Add or go to a named bookmark in the document. **Navigate** Menu.
Goto	Go directly to a particular topic. **Navigate** Menu.
Collapse to Home	Collapse to the beginning of the document. **Navigate** Menu.
Tag Topic	Tag a topic for later return. **Navigate** Menu.
Collapse to Tag	Collapse back to the last tagged topic. **Navigate** Menu.
Find	Search the index file for all documents. **Search** Menu.
View Saved Searches	View the different saved searches. **Search** Menu.
Topic Names	Search the topic names of the document(s) in the index. **Search** Menu.
Next Occurrence	Go to the next search occurrence. **Search** Menu.
Previous Occurrence	Go to the previous search occurrence. **Search** Menu.
Occurrences	Display a list of search occurrences. **Search** Menu.
Add/Read Notes	Add a reader's note. **Navigate** Menu.
Goto Next Note	Go to the next topic with a reader's note. **Navigate** Menu.
Guided Tours	Create a guided tour through the document. **Navigate** Menu.
Related Topics	Display a list of automatically generated links. **Navigate** Menu.

A full list of HyperWriter's different navigation tools is shown in Table 8.2 along with a reference to the menu in which they are located. All commands are located either on the **Navigate** or **Search** menu.

As you can see, HyperWriter has a large number of different navigational tools. The number of different tools reflects two aspects of HyperWriter. The first aspect is that HyperWriter is a publishing toolkit suitable for a variety of different projects. The large number of different navigation tools found in

HyperWriter make it applicable for these varied projects. When you create an application using HyperWriter, you can choose to selectively build in whichever navigational tools you need for your application. The second aspect is quite simple—HyperWriter is a feature-rich product and navigation tools are among some of its key features.

Now that you have an overview of the different navigational features found in HyperWriter, we will begin to use three of the navigational features: the **History** command, the **Add/Read Notes** command, and the **Find** command.

These commands will allow us to view where we have been in our document (this is called our *history*), to add/read notes in our document, and to search for information in our document. Before we move into our tutorials on these commands, you may want to consider the example listed below. If you are eager to move into the tutorials, you can also skip this example and move directly to them.

Reference: An Example of Using Navigational Tools

If you are at all uncertain of how HyperWriter's navigational tools are used, consider this example.

John, a personnel manager at ACME corporation is asked about company policies on childbirth leave time. He turns to the hypertext version of his personnel manual and activates a link from the table of contents titled "Child Birth and ACME Corp." As he arrives at the link end, there is too much information to read in depth, so he goes to the **Search** menu and chooses the **Find** command. He then specifies a search and presses **Enter**. This displays a list of search results. He selects the first result from the list. This brings him to the information he needs and he prints it out for further reading. He adds a note to the document indicating the question he was asked and his answer. This will aid him the next time the question is asked because he can always return to the document and use the **Goto Next Note** command to recall his note. Finally, he activates a link back to the table of contents where he looks for other related links. Finding one, he activates it and then activates a second link. Upon reading this information, he questions what he first found so he calls up his **History** to navigate back to "Child Birth and ACME Corp." At this point, he has all the information that he needs and he can answer the person's question.

John used three separate navigation functions—the **Find** command, the **History** command, and the **Add Reader's Note** command. These commands freed him from the drudgery of either reading the entire work in depth or manually backtracking his progress through the document. In addition, **Adding a Reader's Note** will make John's work significantly easier when the next question is asked. These are the three same commands that we will use in the tutorial sections below.

Viewing Your History

When a HyperWriter document is being read, the trail of topics that the reader has accessed by activating links without backtracking is referred to as the *history trail*. You can backtrack this history trail to the very first document and topic ever visited in a session. The **History** command allows you to access all topics in your history trail—even across multiple documents. This eliminates the problem of inadvertently backtracking from a topic and then not being able to return to it.

NOTE: Even if you create a new document with the **New** command on the **File** menu, you will note that the **History** command can still be used.

When the **History** command is accessed, it displays a dialog box with a scrolling list containing the names of all accessed topics. This dialog box has a menu bar that can be used to select the topic to visit. When the **History** command is displayed, topics that are a part of your history trail and topics that you have backtracked out of are distinguished with an asterisk ("*"). If an "*" appears next to a topic when displayed by the **History** command that topic could be returned to by pressing **Esc** or **Right Mouse**. If no "*" appears next to the topic then the only way to get back to that topic is through the **History** command.

Now that we understand the History command, we are ready to use it to look at the path that we have chosen in reading this document.

Using the History Command

Select the **History** command from the **Navigate** menu. This displays the dialog box shown in Figure 8.8. If you want to use the **History** command to jump back to a particular location, then select the topic to go to from the history list. Otherwise, you can select the **Cancel** button to close the dialog box.

NOTE: A unique aspect of HyperWriter's **History** command is that it tells you not only which topics you have visited but also the amount of time spent in each topic. This helps you to determine which sections of the document have been read in depth as opposed to merely browsed. This feature can be disabled if not needed or found confusing.

Using Annotation

HyperWriter's **Reader's Notes** function is the electronic equivalent to writing in the margin of a book. They provide a method to leave electronic notes attached to topics of documents. Reader's notes are created or viewed with the

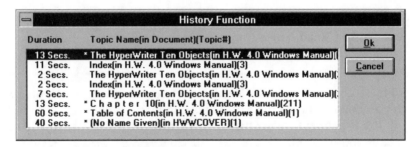

Figure 8.8 The **History** command.

Add/Read Notes command on the **Navigate** menu. Although reader's notes are typically used by the reader of the document when the document is distributed, they can also be used by the author of the document to aid in tasks such as document maintenance and quality control.

As discussed earlier, HyperWriter applications are composed of HyperWriter document files, which are in turn composed of one or more topics. Notes are added to documents on a per topic basis. Each topic in a document can have a single reader's note attached to it. As a reader navigates through a document, he or she can see that a note exists either by checking the Navigate menu (which displays a checkmark when a note exists) or by looking for an onscreen checkmark.

NOTE: You should note that if you want a checkmark onscreen to indicate reader's notes then you have to create a custom background screen.

Adding a reader's note is done with the **Add/Read Notes** command on the **Navigate** menu. When a reader's note is added, a dialog box is displayed where the note is entered. Reader's notes can be up to 32K in length, and all standard editing keys, including block marking, can be used in their creation.

Adding a Reader's Note

1. Select the **Add/Read Notes** command from the **Navigate** menu. This displays a dialog box for you to enter the reader's note.
2. Type the text of the note and select the **Save** button to save the note. This closes the dialog box, returning you to the original topic from which the note was created.

After a reader's note has been created, the **Add/Read Notes** command is also used to view that note.

Reading a Reader's Note

Select the **Add/Read Notes** command from the **Navigate** menu. Close the note by selecting the **Save** button.

NOTE: If you use the **Add/Read Notes** command to read notes and there aren't any notes, the **Add/Read Notes** command will add a note to the document. If this happens, select the **Cancel** button to cancel adding the note.

Once you have added reader's notes to a document, you can do several things with them, including deleting them, exporting them, and going to the next note. To delete a reader's note, display the note and then select the **Remove** button from the **Reader's Notes** dialog box. To export a reader's note, display the note, and then select the **Export** button on the **Reader's Notes** dialog box. This exports the current note to an ASCII text file. Once you have added multiple notes to a document, you can use the **Goto Next Note** command on the **Navigate** menu to jump between notes.

Using Full-text Searching

HyperWriter documents can contain large quantities of text stored in one or more HyperWriter documents. To help navigate, manage, and locate textual information within these HyperWriter documents, HyperWriter has a very sophisticated indexed or full-text search facility. If you are familiar with using a **Search** command in a word processor then you understand the concept of searching documents for information. HyperWriter's search facilities, however, extend far beyond simple word-processor searches. In HyperWriter, all search facilities rely on an index—a special data file thatcontains the exact position of every word in every document. This type of searching is called *indexed* or *full-text* searching (the actual index file is created by a tool called an *indexer*). Indexed searching allows almost instantaneous searches of even hundreds of megabytes of information and can include logical operators such as AND, OR, and NOT.

HyperWriter's indexed-search facility is accessed by the **Find** command located on the **Search** menu. When you select the **Find** command, it displays HyperWriter's **Find** dialog box where you enter search queries and select the range (where HyperWriter is to search) of the search. After you enter a search query and select the **OK** button, HyperWriter displays a list of search results (the **Search Occurrences** dialog box) that lists the topics that contain the search query. The desired topic can be selected from this dialog box. The **Search Occurrences** dialog box can be redisplayed to select additional topics as necessary.

One very different aspect of HyperWriter from other digital publishing tools is that HyperWriter's **Search** dialog box can be configured to the needs of

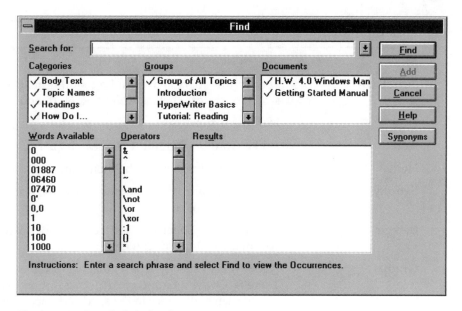

Figure 8.9 The **Find** dialog box.

particular applications. Depending on how you choose to configure the **Search** dialog box, it can offer the user a full-fledged set of options including word lists and search ranges to a very minimal, easy-to-use dialog box. When the **Find** command is selected from the **Search** menu, it generally displays the dialog box shown in Figure 8.9.

The different sections of the **Find** dialog box are covered in Table 8.3.

Using the **Find** command is covered in the next section. As with previous examples of navigation, this assumes that you have the HWWMAN document open.

Using the Find Command

1. Select the **Find** command from the **Search** menu, or click on magnifying glass icon on the toolbar.
2. Enter the search string **HYPERTEXT** into the **Search For** field of the dialog box. Search terms can be selected from the **Words Available** field and search operators can be selected from the **Operators** field. As you enter search terms into the **Search For** field, HyperWriter will search for each term and begin displaying results using **Search Results** field. If you just want to search *all* of the text in the application then skip to step 6, otherwise, continue reading. The results of entering **HYPERTEXT** into the **Search For** field are shown in Figure 8.10.

Table 8.3 The **Find** Dialog Box

Section	Description
Search For	Specify the query that is to be found. This can include search operators such as AND, OR, NOT, and XOR.
Find	Start the search.
Add	Add a word or operator to the search query.
Help	Display context-sensitive help on searching
Synonyms	Allow synonyms for common search terms to be created, viewed, or removed.
Categories	Allow you to specify a particular set of search fields within the text of a document.
Groups	Allow you to specify a particular set of topics to search. There is always a Group of All Topics option that allows you to search all topics in the specified documents.
Documents	Allow you to specify which HyperWriter document is searched.
Words Available	Display a list of words in the current search range.
Operators	Allow you to pick a search operator to use.
Results Summary	Display a graphic map of search results as you enter the search.

3. Move to the **Categories** field of the dialog box and select where you want HyperWriter to look within the text of the document. Use the **Left Mouse** button to turn on or off particular search categories.

4. Move to the **Groups** field of the dialog box and select what topic groups are to be searched.

5. Move to the **Documents** field of the dialog box and select what documents are to be searched.

6. Select the **Find** button to start the search. HyperWriter then locates the search string and returns a **Search Occurrences** dialog box of topics.

7. Select a search occurrence to view from the **Search Occurrences** dialog box. This loads the HyperWriter document (if necessary) and brings you to the correct topic.

A sample **Search Occurrences** dialog box is shown in Figure 8.11.

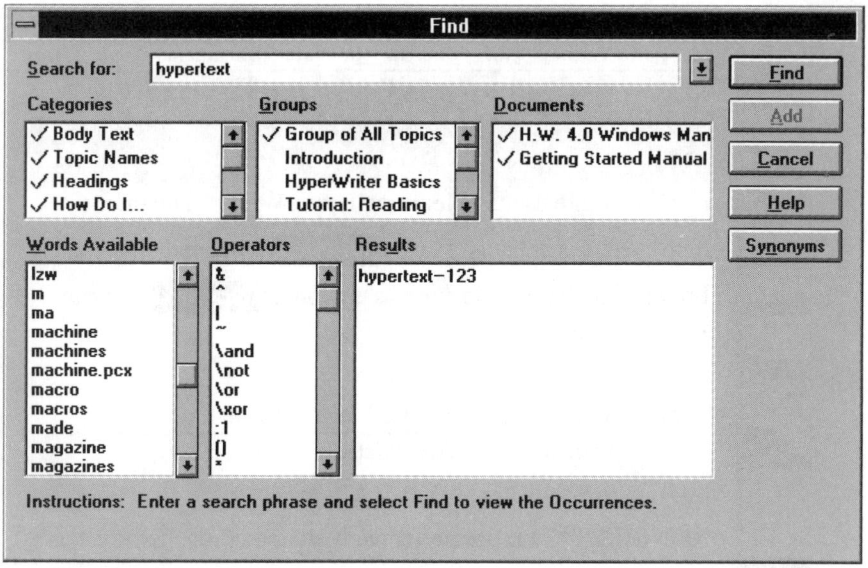

Figure 8.10 Searching for hypertext.

By selecting any of the topics listed in the **Search Occurrences** dialog box, you will be instantly taken to that topic. A sample topic is shown in Figure 8.12.

At this point you should understand the very basics of searching in Hyper-Writer—how to enter a search query and how to view the results of the search. This, however, is just that—the very basics of searching. HyperWriter's indexed searching includes Boolean operators such as AND, OR, NOT, and XOR; proximity searching; hypertext links that activate search queries; additional commands for using searching (**Next Occurrence** and **Previous Occur-**

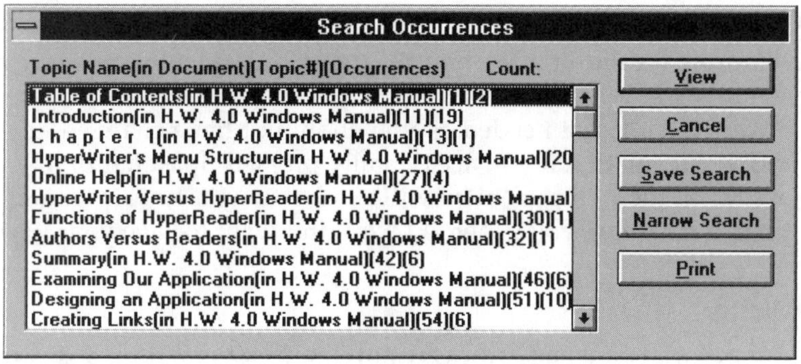

Figure 8.11 A **Search Occurrences** dialog box.

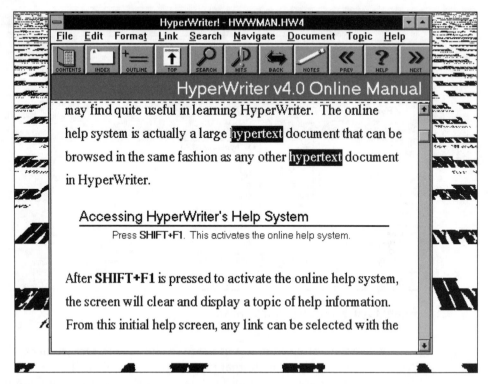

Figure 8.12 A topic located by searching.

rence); and more. Overall, searching is one of the richest areas in HyperWriter. This will become more apparent in later tutorials as we experiment further with indexing and searching.

Saving Our Work

In this tutorial, we didn't make any changes to our documents so we don't need to save our work. When HyperWriter is used purely as a reading environment, saving your work is not needed as you shouldn't have changed anything. You may find, however, that if you accidentally pressed **Spacebar** or any other editing keystrokes then HyperWriter will *think* that you have changed the document. In this situation, you generally wouldn't want to save your work.

Exiting HyperWriter

With our tutorial finished, you can now exit HyperWriter if desired. This is done with the **Exit** command on the **File** menu. Select the **Exit** command from the **File** menu. Depending on what you did, HyperWriter may ask you if your document needs to be saved. In this tutorial, you want to select No. If Hyper-Writer prompts you to leave a bookmark, select Yes or No as needed. You will exit from HyperWriter and return to the Program Manager.

Tutorial 2: Understanding HyperWriter's Word Processor

With our first tutorial completed, you should now have a good understanding of how to use a completed HyperWriter application including opening documents, searching text, activating links, and other common tasks. With this accomplished, we need to start by understanding HyperWriter's basic editor or word processor. HyperWriter has at its core an easy-to-use text editor or word processor used to create digital publications. You will often find that using HyperWriter is very similar to using a word processor. When you run HyperWriter, you are immediately in an editing window and you have a cursor that can be used to edit text. This is HyperWriter's word processor and is always available to you. Although you are not required to use Hyper-Writer's word processor to create documents (documents can be imported from a variety of sources), you should be familiar with it to use HyperWriter effectively.

This tutorial is different from the tutorial that you just completed. The nature of an editor is that it is difficult to write a tutorial for an editor without having the student/reader type in text—something that is clearly not needed. For this reason, I have oriented this tutorial more as a discussion of the editor with specific tasks that you should accomplish from time to time. If you are at all familiar with different MS-Windows based word processors, you shouldn't find HyperWriter's built-in word processor hard to learn.

Running HyperWriter

Before we can open a sample document we must first run HyperWriter. Hyper-Writer is a standard MS-Windows application that can be run from the Program Manager by double-clicking its icon.

Word Processor Basics

When you run HyperWriter, you are always in HyperWriter's word processor (the only exception to this is when you are in the screen designer, a feature discussed later in this chapter). You can always tell that you are in HyperWriter's word processor as there is a cursor onscreen. Even when you run HyperWriter and a document is automatically loaded through the startup document feature, you still have a cursor. In any HyperWriter document, if you just start typing what you type will be inserted into the document. This is the nature of HyperWriter's word processor—it is always there and you can

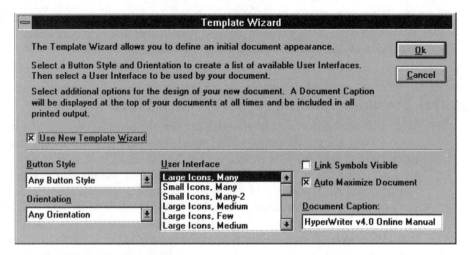

Figure 8.13 The Template Wizard.

always make changes to your documents. To get a better feel for HyperWriter's word processor, we will create a new document and enter some text.

Creating a New Document

1. Select the **New** command from the **File** menu. Save your current document if needed. If HyperWriter prompts you to leave a bookmark, select Yes or No as needed.

2. In the **Template Wizard** dialog box, turn off the **Use New Template Wizard** option. This prevents the Template Wizard from being used, shown in Figure 8.13.

3. Select the **OK** button. This creates a new document. As you can see, HyperWriter creates a new document named "Untitled" that appears onscreen with a blinking cursor in the upper-lefthand corner of the document. Now, we want to add some text to our document.

4. Type "This is a new document." This will appear as shown in Figure 8.14.

By entering some text, you have now used HyperWriter's built-in word processor. What we will now do is insert some additional text by importing a sample document by using the following method.

1. Select the **Import Text** command from the **File** menu.

2. Select WordPerfect as the format to import.

3. Select the file EDITOR01.WP as the file to import.

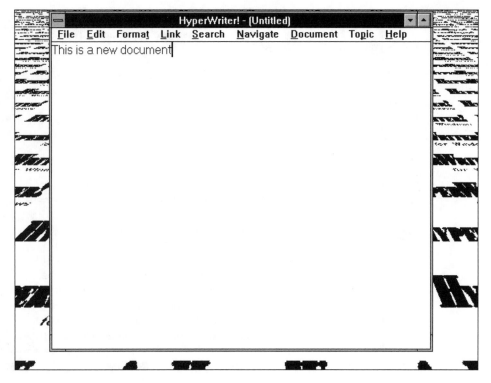

Figure 8.14 Sample text in our document.

4. Select **OK** from the **Import Text Wizard** dialog box to import the file. The imported document is shown in Figure 8.15.

With some basic text in our document, we can now use some of the different features in the word processor. The first editing command that we will use is **Convert Case**.

Using the Convert Case Command

The **Convert Case** command in HyperWriter's word processor lets you select a block of text and then choose whether that text should be presented in uppercase, lowercase, or capitalized. This is very useful in a hypertext tool as you often need to present information with consistently formatted headings and subheadings, and these headings and subheadings from source documents often aren't formatted consistently. Rather than force you to retype or edit headings, **Convert Case** can easily reformat the text.

In this tutorial, we will select the title of our document (the first paragraph of text in the document) and convert it to all uppercase.

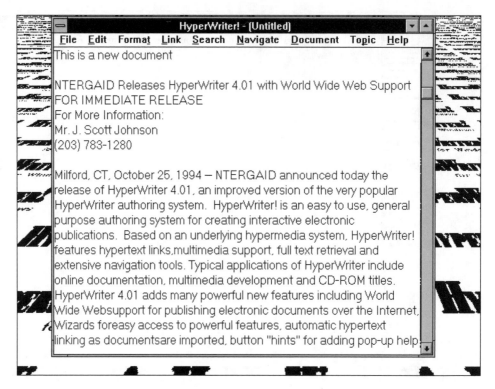

Figure 8.15 The imported document.

Importing Text

1. Move to the top of the document if you are not there. A useful keystroke for this is **Ctrl+Home**.

2. Select the first paragraph of text and mark it as a block by holding down the **Left Mouse** button and dragging the mouse over it.

3. Select the **Convert Case** command from the **Edit** menu. Select the **Uppercase** option from the submenu. The **Convert Case** command is shown in Figure 8.16.

Now that we have worked with a simple command, **Convert Case**, we are ready to move to a more complex command, HyperWriter's **Spell Check** command.

Spell Checking Documents

When producing digital publications from existing word processor documents such as WordPerfect or Microsoft Word, as a general rule of thumb you are bet-

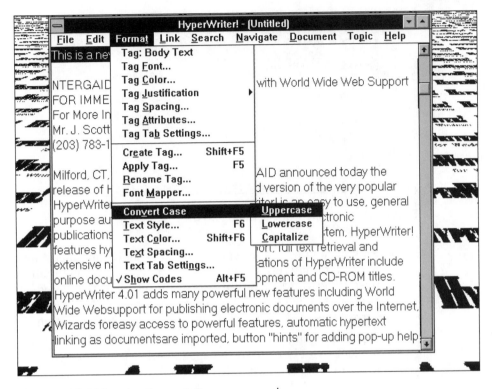

Figure 8.16 Using the **Convert Case** command.

ter off using the spell-checking facilities of your word processor. As WordPerfect and Microsoft Word both specialize in word processing, they have a better spell-checking facility than does HyperWriter. Despite this, HyperWriter offers a complete spell checker to handle digital publications that are written directly in HyperWriter as well as checking text that you add in HyperWriter to existing documents. The task that we are going to tackle now is to use the spell checker to check our document.

To Spell Check a Document

1. From the **Edit** menu select the **Spell Check** command. This displays a submenu for choosing between checking the current topic, all topics, or a selected block. Select the **Current Topic** option to check the spelling in the current topic. Currently, our HyperWriter document has just one topic to be checked. In HyperWriter, the topic that you are currently viewing is called the *current topic*. When HyperWriter finds a misspelled word, the dialog box shown in Figure 8.17 appears.

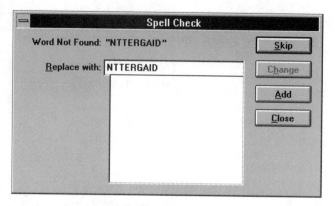

Figure 8.17 The **Spell Check** dialog box.

2. As you can see, the misspelled word is shown in an editing field and a list of alternatives is also shown. You can either manually correct the misspelled word by retyping it or by selecting a replacement word. As you can see, we have a sample misspelling of "NTTERGAID." You can correct this to "NTERGAID" and select the **Change** button.

3. After correcting this error, you can select **Close** if any other errors come up, since you have used the spell checker once, you probably wouldn't learn any more from simply continuing.

This concludes the tutorial exercises in using HyperWriter's word processor. What you should have now is a good feel for using the word processor as well as an understanding of some of the different commands. The remainder of this tutorial offers reference sections to some of the more useful types of commands in HyperWriter's word processor, which include:

- Moving within text
- Blocks
- Search and replace
- Understanding undo
- Creating and editing tables
- Understanding HyperWriter's character set

Reference: Moving within Text

HyperWriter supports several different methods for moving within text. For moving within a strictly linear or text-only document, scrolling and search functions are most often used. The keys listed in Table 8.4 can be used for moving within text in HyperWriter:

Table 8.4 Keystrokes for Moving within Text

Keystroke	Description
Page Up	Up one screen
Page Down	Down one screen
RightArrow	Right one character
LeftArrow	Left one character
UpArrow	Up one line
DownArrow	Down one line
Home	Beginning of line
End	End of line
Ctrl+Home	Beginning of topic
Ctrl+End	End of topic
Ctrl+Page Up	Top of screen
Ctrl+Page Down	Bottom of screen
Ctrl+UpArrow	Beginning of paragraph or previous paragraph if already at the beginning of a paragraph
Ctrl+DownArrow	Next paragraph
Ctrl+RightArrow	Move one word to the right
Ctrl+LeftArrow	Move one word to the left

Reference: Blocks

In HyperWriter, *blocks* are chunks of text treated as single characters. Generally, anything you can do to a single character, you can also do to a block of text (no matter how large the block). As in most MS-Windows programs, before you can use a block of text you must first define it. Blocks can be defined by dragging the mouse over text while holding down the **Left Mouse** button or by pressing **Shift+Arrowkey** and moving over the text with the keyboard. You will notice that any text you mark as a block is highlighted; this is how Hyper-Writer shows a block of text.

NOTE: The **Shift+Ctrl+DownArrow** and **Shift+Ctrl+UpArrow** commands allow for block marking by paragraph. This is very useful for creating macros that link entire paragraphs.

Table 8.5 Commands for Working with Blocks

Command	Description
Cut	Remove text from the document to the clipboard
Copy	Copy text from the document to the clipboard
Paste	Paste text from the clipboard to the document
Delete	Delete text without putting it in the clipboard
Append w/ Copy, Append w/ Cut	Block append allows an author to take marked blocks of text and add them to the clipboard when creating a document. Then, later in the authoring session, the entire block can be pasted into the document at its destination. This feature is very useful for gathering the elements of a table of contents from within a document or documents. Block append works with both **Copy with Append** and **Cut with Append**. The first copies the selected text and appends it to the clipboard while the second cuts the text and then appends it to the clipboard
View Clipboard	Used to look at the text contained in the Clipboard. The **View Clipboard** command activates the Microsoft Windows Clipboard Viewer and makes it the active Windows application

HyperWriter has six major commands for manipulating blocks as illustrated in Table 8.5.

Reference: Search and Replace and Find Commands

Search commands are used to locate text within a document. HyperWriter has two very different types of search commands: the **Search/Replace** command and the **Find** command.

The **Search/Replace** command is located on the **Edit** menu. The **Search/Replace** command supports both search and replace and is designed for use when editing a document. It is a traditional word-processorlike search-and-replace facility. Among its features are it allows you to specify exact or near exact search strings and then search for them or replace them with new text. The **Search/Replace** command is generally used for editing purposes only. The **Search/Replace** command searches either the current topic or all topics; it cannot search across documents. The **Search/Replace** command takes you to each instance of the search term one by one.

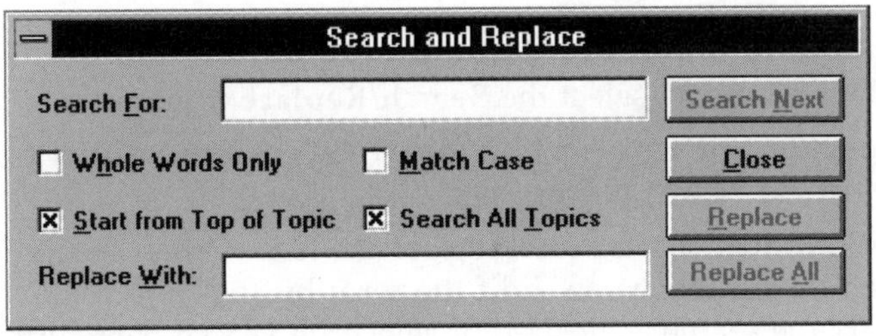

Figure 8.18 The **Search/Replace** dialog box.

The **Find** command, located on the **Search** menu, activates HyperWriter's indexed-search facilities. As the **Find** command uses HyperWriter's indexed search facilities, it offers access to advanced search facilities such as Boolean operators, word lists, search fields, groups, and more. The **Find** command does not search the current document. Instead, it searches a prebuilt index of one or more documents. Thus, use of the **Find** command requires preindexing of documents. Among the advantages to the **Find** command are:

- It is significantly faster than the **Search/Replace** command.
- It offers Boolean operators for search queries.
- The output of the **Search/Replace** command is a hit list of each occurrence of the search query.

When the **Search/Replace** command is chosen from the **Edit** menu, you should see the dialog box shown in Figure 8.18.

The primary commands in the **Search/Replace** dialog box are listed in Table 8.6.

Using the **Search/Replace** dialog box is covered in the following steps.

Table 8.6 Commands in the **Search/Replace** Dialog Box

Command	Description
Search Next	Find the next occurrence of the search term
Close	Close the search dialog box
Replace	Replace the found term with the text specified in the **Replace With** field
Replace All	Tell HyperWriter to replace all found terms with the text specified in the **Replace With** field
Search For	Specify a term to search for
Replace With	Specify a term to replace the text located

Finding a Term with Search/Replace

1. From the **Edit** menu, select the **Search/Replace** command.
2. Type the word or words to be found. Select any needed options and then select the **Search Next** button.
3. HyperWriter then starts searching for the term. When the term is found, it is highlighted on screen. Edit the term by selecting the **Close** button or modify the search as desired or select the **Search Next** button.

Reference: Understanding Undo

HyperWriter's **Undo** command acts to undo the effect of previous commands. The **Undo** command is not limited to a single **Undo** operation. It allows you to undo multiple operations, one after the other. The one exception to how **Undo** works is that it does not let you undo structural changes to your HyperWriter document. For example, if you create a link to a new topic (thus creating the new topic), this change cannot be undone as it has changed the structure of the document.

Undoing an Operation in HyperWriter

Select the **Undo** command from the **Edit** menu. This reverses the effect of the previous operation.

Reference: Creating and Editing Tables

HyperWriter's table editor allows you to build tables inside your HyperWriter document. A *table* is an arrangement of columns of text and numbers that is grouped together in a row-and-column matrix. All tables in HyperWriter are made up of one or more *rows* that run horizontally across the screen and two or more *columns* that run vertically up and down the screen. Each cell in a table acts as an editing window where text can be entered independently from the other cells in the table. If you have ever used a spreadsheet program then you should already be familiar with the basic concepts behind tables. Although HyperWriter's tables do not support math operations, the same basic table concepts are behind both tables in HyperWriter and a spreadsheet program.

In the following sections, there are full descriptions of how to create, edit, and format tables in HyperWriter. You should find working with tables to be quite similar to the rest of HyperWriter's editor covered in this chapter. For example, text can be cut or copied from one cell in a table and pasted into another cell. Similarly, you will find that the formatting techniques you learn in Chapter 11 are generally applicable to tables as well.

A sample table is shown in Figure 8.19.

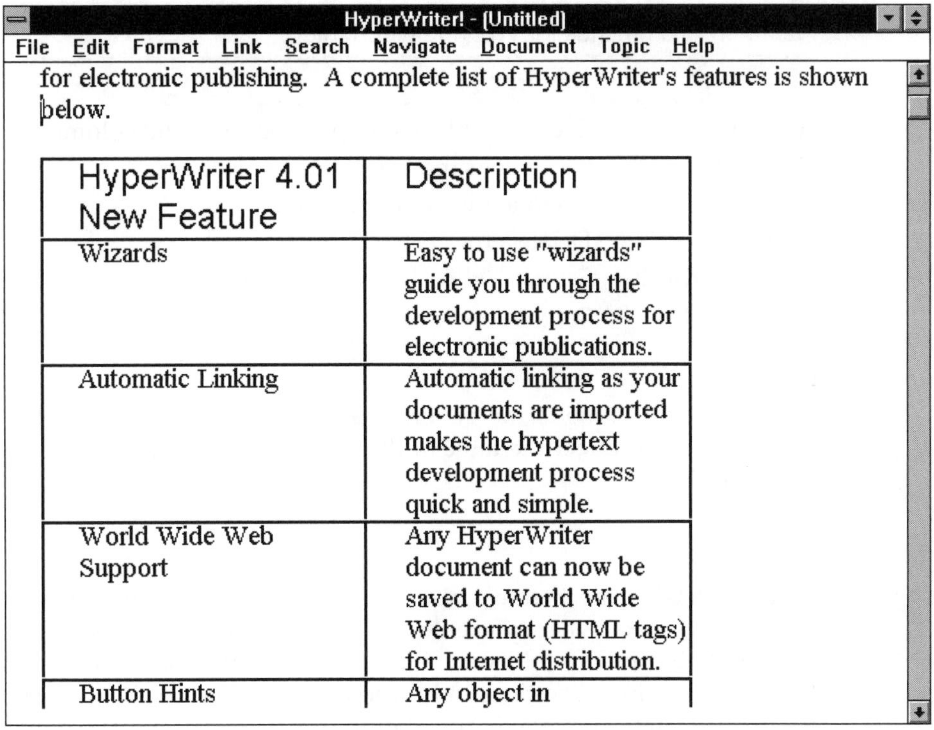

```
─                        HyperWriter! - [Untitled]                    ▼  ↕
File  Edit  Format  Link  Search  Navigate  Document  Topic  Help
```
for electronic publishing. A complete list of HyperWriter's features is shown
below.

HyperWriter 4.01 New Feature	Description
Wizards	Easy to use "wizards" guide you through the development process for electronic publications.
Automatic Linking	Automatic linking as your documents are imported makes the hypertext development process quick and simple.
World Wide Web Support	Any HyperWriter document can now be saved to World Wide Web format (HTML tags) for Internet distribution.
Button Hints	Any object in

Figure 8.19 A sample table.

As you can see, there is a columnar arrangement of text and numbers. Some of the columns of descriptions in the table are longer than the column is wide, causing the text to be wrapped down and making the cell larger. This is how tables operate in HyperWriter.

The remainder of this section is broken into three parts. "Creating Tables" describes how to create tables and the options available for creating tables. "Editing Tables" covers how to alter the structure of a table once it is created. Finally, "Formatting Tables" covers formatting options for tables, options that affect how the table is displayed. Table formatting is also covered in Chapter 11.

All tables in HyperWriter are created, edited, and formatted with the same basic set of commands. Each of these commands can be accessed from the **Table** command on the **Edit** menu. When the **Table** command on the **Edit** menu is selected, a submenu allows you to select the different table commands. When the **Table** command is chosen from the **Edit** menu, the commands listed in Table 8.7 are available.

As you can see from the command summary, many commands can be applied to an entire row (horizontally), an entire column (vertically), or to an

Table 8.7 Commands for Working with Tables

Command	Description
Create	Create a table of the specified rows and columns.
Options	Set options that affect the whole table.
Insert	Insert a row, column, or cell.
Delete	Delete a row, column, or cell.
Column Width	Set the width of a row, column, or cell.
Border	Set the border of a row, column, or cell.

individual cell. This is the general nature of working with tables in Hyper-Writer; you can affect the table at the row level, the column level, or the individual cell level.

Creating Tables

To create a table, the **Create** command is used from the **Table** submenu. This displays a dialog box where you enter the number of rows, number of columns, and whether the column widths are relative. The number of rows and columns that you enter are initial settings only. These can always be changed later with the **Insert** or **Delete** command. You should, however, specify the number of rows and columns that you need as closely as possible. All columns that you create are initially set to the same width. This width can be later adjusted on a per column or cell basis with the **Column Width** command. When you are creating tables, you will find that lines automatically border each cell to show where the *editing windows* are located. Although these lines can be turned off, you will find that they are helpful when creating a table and entering data into it.

The **Relative Column Widths** option defines whether changing one column of the table affects other columns and whether the table width stays the same. When this option is turned on, changing a column's width alters the width of other columns (they are relative to the column that is changed). Tables can be created anywhere in a document in HyperWriter, in any type of topic. The one exception to this is that tables cannot be created within a table itself.

Creating a Table

1. Place your cursor where you want the table inserted.
2. Select the **Table** command from the **Edit** menu. Choose the **Create** command from the submenu. A dialog box is displayed asking for the number of rows, columns, and if the column widths are relative.

3. Enter the number of rows into the **rows** field and move to the next field.

4. Enter the number of columns into the **columns** field and move to the next option.

5. Turn on or off the **Relative Column Widths** option and select the **OK** button. This creates the table.

Setting Table Options

Once you have created a table, you can use the **Options** command to adjust the **Relative Column Widths** setting for the table. The **Relative Column Widths** setting allows changing a column's width to affect the width of the other columns. Turning this option on or off prior to making changes to the table can be useful depending on how you want the width of other columns altered.

Setting Relative Column Widths

1. Select the **Table** command from the **Edit** menu. Select the **Options** command from the submenu.

2. Turn on the **Relative Column Widths** option and select the **OK** button to close the dialog box.

Editing Tables

After a table has been created, its structure can be modified in several different ways. Table 8.8 summarizes how tables can be modified and the command used.

Before covering these commands, we need to review block marking and tables. Tables can be marked in two ways. First, an entire table, from beginning to end, can be marked and then cut or copied. Second, within individual cells, text can be cut or copied. The one restriction on block marking and tables is that entire cells, rows, or columns cannot be cut or copied. HyperWriter's block marking and tables only support in-cell block operations or moving an entire table as a block.

Although you specify a table's row-and-column structure when it is created, this can always be modified with the **Insert** command. The **Insert** command can

Table 8.8 How Tables Can Be Modified

Command	Description
Insert	Insert rows, columns, or cells
Delete	Delete rows, columns, or cells

be used to insert rows, columns, or cells. Inserting columns functions differently depending on where the cursor is placed. When the cursor is placed at the beginning of the first cell, inserting a column inserts that column to the left of the cell. When the cursor is placed anywhere that is not the beginning of the first cell, inserting a column inserts that column to the right of the cell. Inserting rows functions differently depending on where the cursor is placed. When the cursor is placed at the beginning of the first cell, inserting a row inserts that row above the cell. When the cursor is placed anywhere that is not the beginning of the first cell, inserting a row inserts that row below the cell. Inserting cells functions similarly. When the cursor is placed at the beginning of the first cell, inserting a cell inserts that cell to the left. When the cursor is placed anywhere that is not the beginning of the first cell, inserting a cell inserts that cell to the right.

Inserting Table Elements

1. Place your cursor where you want the table element inserted.
2. Select the **Table** command from the **Edit** menu. Choose the **Insert** command from the submenu. A dialog box is displayed asking whether to insert a row, column, or cell.
3. Select the table element to insert and select the **OK** button. This inserts the table element and redisplays the modified table.

The **Delete** command allows you to delete a row, column, or cell from the table. When you delete an entire row or column from the table, HyperWriter prompts you before deleting the row or column in case you made an incorrect choice.

Deleting Table Elements

1. Place your cursor where you want the table element deleted or mark the table elements to delete as a block.
2. Select the **Table** command from the **Edit** menu. Choose the **Delete** command from the submenu. A dialog box is displayed asking whether to delete a row, column, or cell.
3. Select the table element to delete and select the **OK** button. If you choose to delete an entire row or column, a dialog box will ask you if you are sure you want to delete it. Select the **Yes** button to finish the delete. This deletes the table element and redisplays the modified table.

Formatting Tables

Once you have created a table, you can format the appearance of the table. Tables can be formatted in three different ways. First, the **Border** command can be used to adjust the appearance of the lines that surround each cell. As you may recall, there are lines that surround each cell by default, however, each line can be controlled individually. The second method of formatting a table is to mark the text in each cell as a block and then use the **Text Style** command to adjust the appearance of the text. The third method is to apply a paragraph tag to any or all cells in the table. This is the most powerful method as it allows formatting the entire contents of a cell with one action. Formatting a table by marking the text as a block or by applying a paragraph tag to a cell or cells is covered in Chapter 11. An additional method of formatting a cell is the **Join** command, which we covered in the previous section. Using the **Borders** command is covered in the next section.

Adjusting a Table's Borders

1. Place your cursor in the cell where the borders need to be adjusted.

2. Select the **Table** command from the **Edit** menu. Choose the **Border** command from the submenu. A dialog box is displayed asking whether to set the border for a row, column, or cell. Select the table element to format and select the **OK** button. A second dialog box is displayed for setting the thickness of each line that surrounds the table element.

3. Enter the thickness of each line in the dialog box. Fields are available for the top, left, right, and bottom lines. To turn off a line completely, set its width to 0. Select the **OK** button to close the dialog box and redisplay the modified table.

Reference: Understanding HyperWriter's Character Set

HyperWriter has an extensive character set that encompasses all of the extended ASCII character set as well as additional characters needed for using HyperWriter with foreign languages.

HyperWriter supports the extended ASCII character set. This means that all characters from character 32 to character 255 can be entered in a document. Some uses for these characters include line drawing, international characters, table creation, and mathematical equations.

Although the **Alt** key can be used to enter characters from HyperWriter's character set by pressing the **Alt** key plus numbers on the numeric keypad, this is not a reliable method to enter characters. The problem with using the **Alt** key is that its effect will vary depending on what code page is loaded for your computer. A better approach to entering characters from HyperWriter's character set is to use the **Ctrl+O** keystroke. When the **Ctrl+O** keystroke is pressed, HyperWriter displays a dialog box listing all characters in its character set. Selecting a character from the dialog box inserts that character into your document. The **Ctrl+O** dialog box is shown in Figure 8.20.

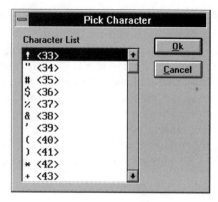

Figure 8.20 The **Ctrl+O** dialog box.

While **Ctrl+O** provides an easy way to enter special characters into a document, it does not allow you to enter special characters into a dialog box such as the **Search/Replace** dialog box. Instead, these characters can be entered into a dialog box by entering the character's number enclosed within < and > characters. For example, entering **<33>** into a dialog box is equivalent to the ! character.

NOTE: Although using the **Alt** key with numbers entered from the keyboard is not a recommended approach, if you do this and a character appears in a dialog box, then this character will be the character used. This would give the equivalent of entering **<number>** in the dialog box.

NOTE: The HyperWriter document ASCII.HW4 displays all the characters in HyperWriter's character set.

Saving Our Work

In this tutorial, as we didn't accomplish any real tasks, we don't need to save our work. In the next section, we will exit without saving our work.

Exiting HyperWriter

With our tutorial finished and our work saved, you can now exit HyperWriter if desired. This is done with the **Exit** command on the **File** menu.

CHAPTER

Creating a Template Document 9

With the tutorials in Chapter 8 completed, you should now have a good understanding of how to use a completed HyperWriter application including opening documents, searching text, activating links, and other common tasks. With this under our belt, we are now ready to tackle the first real step in building our own applications—creating a template document.

In HyperWriter, a template document is simply a starting point for an application. It is a HyperWriter document file (a file with the extension of .HW4) with a user interface that you want to use in your application. As you may recall from Chapter 8, in HyperWriter the user interface to an application is located within each of your HyperWriter documents. Given that a template is really just a HyperWriter document file, a template can be created just as you create any other document. However, HyperWriter offers a more powerful tool for creating a template—the Template Wizard. What the Template Wizard offers is a built-in command for creating polished HyperWriter documents complete with a user interface. To make creating these documents even easier, the Template Wizard includes over fifty different user interface options ranging from icons to text buttons and with screen positions for user interfaces that include across the top, bottom, left-, and right-hand edges of the screen. The overall goal of the Template Wizard is to enable you to generate professional-looking digital publications with a minimum of effort.

So that you can become more familiar with the Template Wizard, shown below are six screen shots of different documents created using the Template

Wizard. To make recreating the documents easier, each caption lists the exact text shown in the Template Wizard.

The "Large Icons, Many" screen design, shown in Figure 9.1, is a good general-purpose design, suited for users without extensive computer experience.

The "Small Icons, Many" screen design, shown in Figure 9.2, is often used for applications where the users have a good grasp of using Microsoft Windows (the style of icons is similar to the toolbars in many Windows applications).

The "WinHelp Modified" screen design, shown in Figure 9.3, is an attractive text-button–based design that is often used in applications where easy customization is important.

The "Small Icons, Many" screen design shown in Figure 9.4, can also be located across the bottom of a screen as well as the top.

The "Technical Documentation" screen design, shown in Figure 9.5, is a good design for when you want to present technical documentation organized into frames of information and support linking to the next and previous section as well as the next and previous document.

The "Large Icons, In Palettes" screen design, shown in Figure 9.6, is a good design that is very simple for readers to understand as it groups together related icons.

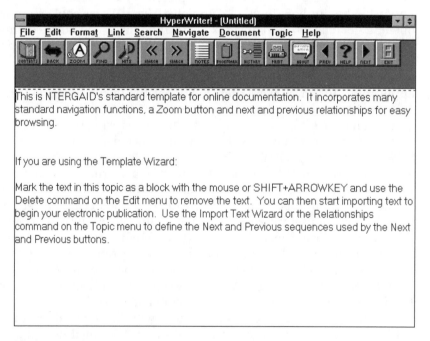

Figure 9.1 The "Large Icons, Many" screen design.

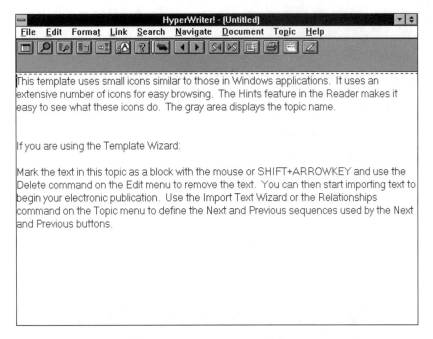

Figure 9.2 The "Small Icons, Many" screen design.

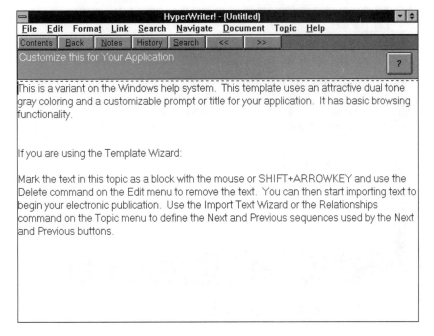

Figure 9.3 The "WinHelp Modified" screen design.

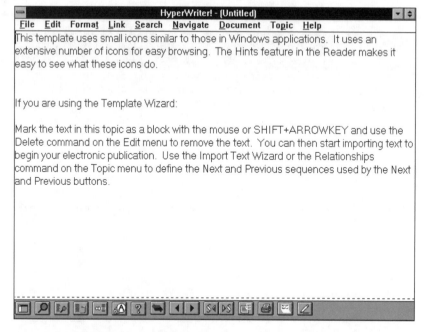

Figure 9.4 The "Small Icons, Many" screen design (along the bottom).

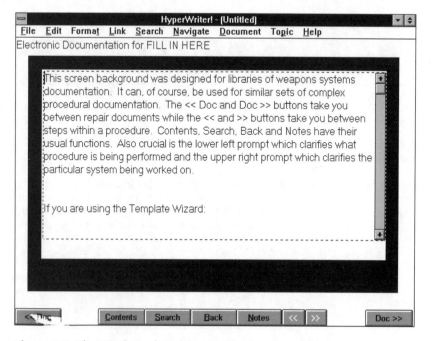

Figure 9.5 The "Technical Documentation" screen design.

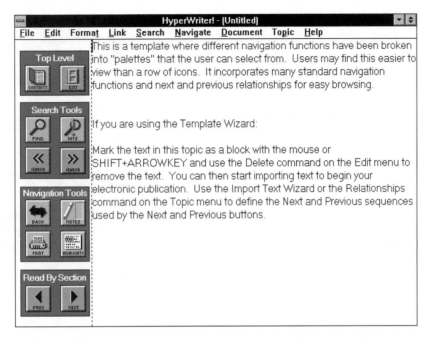

Figure 9.6 The "Large Icons, In Palettes" screen design.

As you can see, virtually any type of digital publishing user interface can be created using HyperWriter. In addition to using the Template Wizard, you can also use HyperWriter's Screen Painter to manually create your own custom user interfaces. The Screen Painter is a feature in HyperWriter for designing screens element-by-element including such design tools as text regions, buttons, pictures, and more. Now that you understand what the Template Wizard is, we are now ready to create our own document templates.

Before we can begin using the Template Wizard, we must first run Hyper-Writer. HyperWriter is a standard MS-Windows application that can be run from the Program Manager.

Using the Template Wizard

Our task is to create a particular template document using the Template Wizard. Rather than being an individual command in HyperWriter, the Template Wizard is tied to the **New** command on HyperWriter's **File** menu. Whenever you create a new document in HyperWriter, the Template Wizard is displayed so that you can select how to best create your document. You should note, however, that you don't have to use the Template Wizard if your application doesn't require it. The Template Wizard can be turned off if desired.

Before using the Template Wizard, it is generally a good idea to have an understanding of what you want to create. This should include:

- Whether your application is to use icons or buttons
- What orientation you want to use for your user interface (top, left, right, bottom, or top and bottom)
- Whether you want link symbols displayed or to use the default Windows method of representing links (green, underlined text)
- If your document should appear maximized
- What Document Caption should be displayed in the MS-Windows caption bar and the MS-Windows Task Manager

As we haven't defined what we want to create with the Template Wizard, we should start with this task. For this template document, we should use icons along the top and bottom of the screen, no link symbols displayed, a maximized Window and the caption "Electronic Press Kit."

The first step is for us to create a document template using the Template Wizard. This is done as follows.

Creating a Document Template

1. Select the **New** command from the **File** menu. Save your current document if needed. If HyperWriter prompts you to leave a bookmark, select Yes or No as needed.

2. If the **Use New Template Wizard** option is turned off (this option is not "checked"), turn it back on.

3. In the **Template Wizard** dialog box, select the **Button Style** field and set it to **Iconic Buttons**. This tells the Template Wizard that you only want to look at templates using icons.

4. Select the **Orientation** field and set it to **Along Top and Bottom**. This tells the Template Wizard that you only want to look at templates with buttons along the top and bottom of the screen.

5. In the **User Interface** field, you can now see that the number of available interfaces has been greatly reduced. As the option that we want, "Small Icons, Many," is at the top of the list, we don't need to select it. However, we have other options that we still need to select.

6. Make sure that the **Link Symbols Visible** option is not selected (the Template Wizard retains options from previous usages so if you had turned this option on previously, it could still be set and would thus need to be reset).

7. Turn on the **Auto Maximize Document** option if it isn't already turned on.

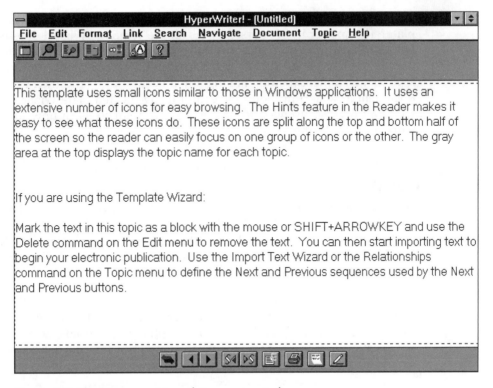

Figure 9.7 The Document template you created.

8. Move to the **Document Caption** field and enter the caption "Electronic Press Kit" into this field, and then select the **OK** button. This creates a document template using the selected interface.

After creating the interface, what should be displayed on your screen is shown in Figure 9.7.

As you can see, this document template has a button bar across the top with icons for functions including contents, back, notes search, previous and next, and a blank area below the icon bar. This blank area gives a location for the topic name of the current topic to be displayed (to review, each Hyper-Writer application is broken up into sections called *topics* and each topic has a name called the *topic name*). The topic currently has some message text giving you instructions as well. This text can be deleted at any time by marking it as a block (just drag the mouse over it) and selecting the **Delete** command from the **Edit** menu.

At this point we have created a template document and could begin working with it. This brings us to an interesting point: Given that using the Template Wizard requires a number of different options to be correctly set, do you have to use the Template Wizard every time that you want a particular template? The answer is, of course, no. As all the Template Wizard does is create a HyperWriter document, once you have used the Template Wizard to create a particular template document that you wish to use repeatedly, you can always save that document (before making any links or topics) and then use the saved document as a starting point instead of using the Template Wizard. Although we don't necessarily need to, this is a good point to learn how to save your work in HyperWriter.

Saving Our Work

With our tutorial finished, we are now ready to save our work. This is done with the **Save** command on the **File** menu.

Select the **Save** command from the **File** menu. HyperWriter will prompt you for the name of the file to save. While you can give any filename, the recommended name is TEMPL01.HW4.

NOTE: In HyperWriter (as in all other applications), it is always a good idea to save your work frequently. In all of the following tutorials, we will generally only remind you to save your work at the end of the tutorial. However, you should always save more frequently.

Exiting HyperWriter

With our tutorial finished and our work saved, you can now exit HyperWriter if desired. This is done with the **Exit** command on the **File** menu.

Importing Documents

One of the characteristics of digital publishing today is that it is generally based on content originally written for another medium, typically print. In fact, republishing existing printed works in electronic form has typically been the rule rather than the exception for digital publishing. While, as we discussed in Chapter 5, this is starting to change the fact remains that digitally publishing existing documents is still crucial. When your digital publishing task relies on publishing existing documents, powerful import facilities are a key requirement. For this reason, HyperWriter has a powerful import module that supports rich import including fonts, margins, tables, and more. Rather then wed itself to a particular word processor, HyperWriter supports all of today's leading word processor formats:

- Microsoft Word .DOC files for DOS and Windows
- Rich text format .RTF Files
- WordPerfect 4.x, 5.x, and 6.x document files
- Lotus Ami Pro .SAM files
- ASCII

The remainder of this tutorial covers how to import documents in Hyper-Writer. This includes how to import documents both one at a time and in batches. A key text-importing feature that will not be covered in this section is HyperWriter's Import Text Wizard, which automatically transforms imported document into hypertext form. The feature will be covered in Chapter 12 as we are not yet at the stage of working with hypertext.

Before we can begin importing documents, we must first run HyperWriter. HyperWriter is a standard MS-Windows application that can be run from the Program Manager.

Importing Documents into HyperWriter

Documents are imported into HyperWriter using the **Import Text** command on HyperWriter's **File** menu. This command allows you to select the document file or files to import and then bring them into HyperWriter, complete with formatting. In this tutorial, we will start by creating a new document and then import the sample documents IMPORT1.DOC and IMPORT2.DOC.

The first step in our tutorial is to create a new document. As we are only creating a new document to import other documents (i.e., only for the purpose of illustrating document import), we won't use the Template Wizard. Use the following steps to create a new document.

Creating a New Document

1. Select the **New** command from the **File** menu. Save your current document if needed. If HyperWriter prompts you to leave a bookmark, select Yes or No as needed.

2. In the **Template Wizard** dialog box, turn off the **Use New Template Wizard** option and then select the **OK** button. Turning this option off prevents the Template Wizard from being used. After creating this new document, your screen should appear similar to that shown in Figure 10.1.

As you can see, when you create a new document in HyperWriter without using the Template Wizard, HyperWriter presents this document to you literally as a blank slate. This reflects HyperWriter's nature as a design environment where you can implement virtually any type of electronic publication, as HyperWriter doesn't enforce unnecessary (or unwanted) elements on you. However, this is getting off the track of importing documents.

Now that we have created a new document, we are ready to use the Import Text feature. We'll start by importing the document IMPORT1.DOC. This file is a Microsoft Word .DOC file that contains a single press release issued by NTERGAID. As a cautionary note, don't think that this file is a Microsoft Word document because HyperWriter has special ties to Microsoft Word—it doesn't. Microsoft Word is used solely because Word seems to have a large, successful presence in the marketplace. With that point clarified, use the steps below to import IMPORT1.DOC.

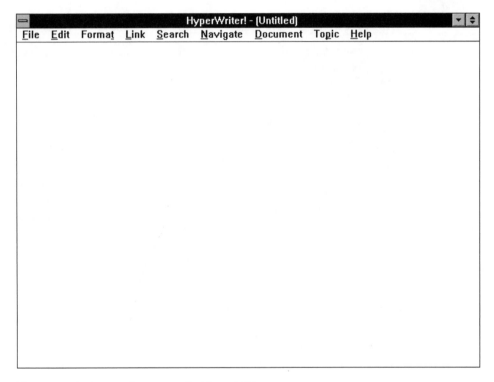

Figure 10.1 A new document in HyperWriter.

Importing a Document

1. Select the **Import Text** command from the **File** menu.
2. Select Word as the format to import.
3. Select the **Options** button. This displays the dialog box shown in Figure 10.2.
4. Turn on the **Use Tag Names** option. This allows tags or styles to be imported with the document.

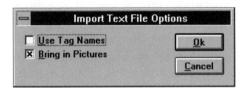

Figure 10.2 The **Import Text File Options** dialog box.

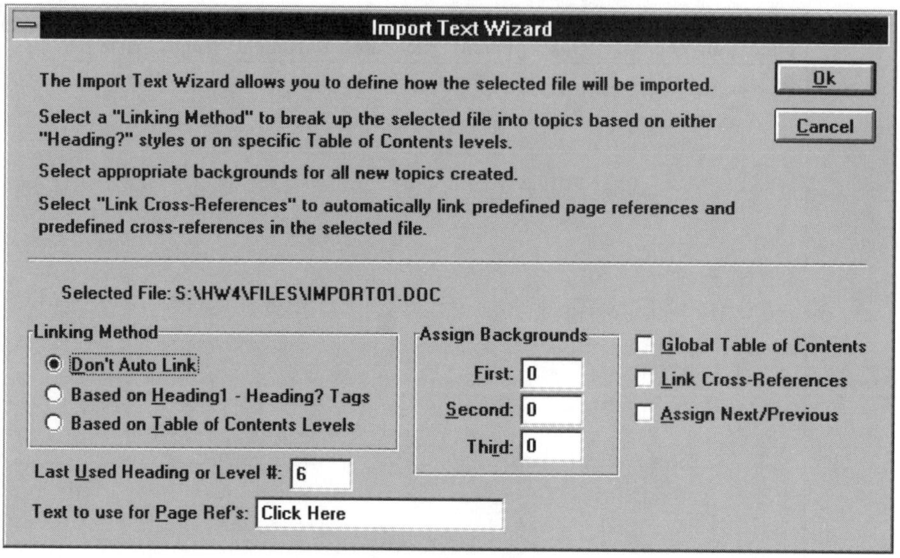

Figure 10.3 The **Import Text Wizard** dialog box.

5. Select the document IMPORT1.DOC from the list of .DOC files shown. This displays HyperWriter's **Import Text Wizard** dialog box as shown in Figure 10.3.

As discussed at the beginning of this tutorial, the Import Text Wizard provides tools for automatically converting documents to hypertext. However, at this point, we aren't yet ready to apply the Import Text Wizard features. For this reason, we will use the **Don't Auto Link** option to skip using it.

6. Leave the Import Text Wizard set to its default setting—**Don't Auto Link** and select the **OK** button to import the document. This will bring the document in and should display it as shown in Figure 10.4.

As you can see, HyperWriter has imported the contents of the IMPORT1.DOC document and loaded it into the HyperWriter document displayed onscreen. Having now imported a single document into HyperWriter, we are now ready to import multiple document files. Before we start, it would probably be easier to see the effect of importing our new documents if we first cleared out the document that we just imported. While this can be done by just creating a new file, we'll do it instead by using HyperWriter's built-in word processor.

Deleting Our Imported Document

1. Move to the top of the imported document if you have paged down to examine it. To jump to the top immediately, either use the **Scroll Bar**

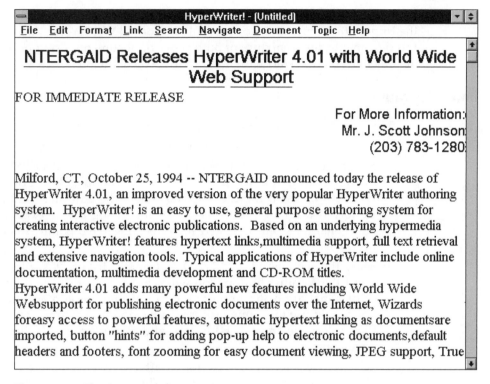

Figure 10.4 The imported document.

or press **Ctrl+Home** (a speed key for jumping to the top of a document).

2. Mark a block from the top of the document down to the end of the document. This can be done with the mouse (by dragging the mouse across the text with the **Left Mouse** button selected) or by pressing **Shift+Ctrl+End** (a speed key for marking to the end of a block). As HyperWriter's block marking isn't very fast when marking across screens, I recommend that you use the speed key.

3. Select the **Delete** command from the **Edit** menu. This will delete the text from the document so that you are ready to start importing documents. After the text is deleted, what you should see is a blank screen similar to what we started with after using the **New** command.

With the text for our last imported document deleted, we are now ready to import multiple documents with the **Import Text** command. This brings us to one restriction on importing multiple documents: When you import multiple documents using HyperWriter, you are restricted to all imported documents being in the same format. For example, although HyperWriter supports Word-

Perfect and Ami Pro format documents, when you import multiple files with the **Import Text** command, you can only import all WordPerfect files or all Ami Pro documents, not a mixture of both types of documents. To import multiple documents, you first start with the **Import Text** command.

Importing Multiple Documents

1. Select the **Import Text** command from the **File** menu.

2. Select Word as the format to import.

3. Select the document IMPORT1.DOC from the list of .DOC files shown by highlighting it in the list of files (do not double-click it or select the **OK** button). With the file selected, select the **Another** button on the **Import Text** dialog box. This causes the dialog box to expand so that additional files can be added for importing. This is illustrated in Figure 10.5.

4. Select the document IMPORT2.DOC from the list of .DOC files and then select the **Another** button. You will see that this adds the file to the list of files that are being imported. If you wanted to add additional files, you would use this same process. As we don't want to import any other files, select the **Import All** button and HyperWriter will import your documents.

5. As in our earlier import example, after selecting the files to import, HyperWriter will display the Import Text Wizard. Again, as in our ear-

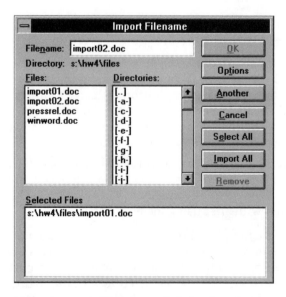

Figure 10.5 The **Import Text** dialog box for importing multiple documents.

lier import example, we don't want to use the Import Text Wizard so leave it set to **Don't Auto Link** and select the **OK** button to bypass the Wizard. HyperWriter will then import the IMPORT1.DOC files and IMPORT2.DOC files. After importing the IMPORT1.DOC and IMPORT2.DOC files, HyperWriter will display the contents of both files onscreen with the first file that you selected for import followed by the second file that you selected for import.

At this point, having used HyperWriter's **Import Text** command several times, you should have a good feel for how HyperWriter imports documents. However, HyperWriter's **Import Text** command is quite powerful and we haven't yet examined the options available with it. For this reason, we will wrap up the final steps to this tutorial and then continue by examining the different options that it has as well as a detailed look at how documents are imported.

Saving Our Work

In this tutorial, we really only explored how this feature works in Hyper-Writer—we didn't really accomplish anything substantial. Thus, you don't really need to save your work.

Exiting HyperWriter

With our tutorial finished, you can now exit HyperWriter if desired. This is done with the **Exit** command on the **File** menu. Ignore the prompts to save your document when you exit.

Reference: Understanding Import Options

When you used the **Import Text** command in the preceding examples, you may have noticed the **Options** button on the **Import Text** dialog box. This **Options** button allows you to control how documents are imported. When the **Options** button is selected, it displays the dialog box shown in Figure 10.6.

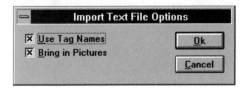

Figure 10.6 The **Import Text** options.

The **Use Tag Names** option tells HyperWriter to import any paragraph tags (more commonly referred to as *styles*) along with the document. When this option is turned on, HyperWriter will import the name and appearance of the style along with the document. Generally speaking, you would always want the **Use Tag Names** option turned on. The **Bring In Pictures** option tells HyperWriter to import pictures from the MS-Word file. Whether the **Bring in Pictures** option is turned on for your application really depends on your application. If you want to bring your pictures through into HyperWriter, then this is a very easy way to do it. However, please note that pictures from word processors often appear too large onscreen as they were usually designed for a printer, not a screen (a printer has over four times greater resolution than the screen). For this reason, you may often want to turn this option off.

Reference: Understanding How HyperWriter Imports Documents

As you import your documents into HyperWriter, you will probably notice that the majority of your formatting such as fonts, tables, and margins are imported into HyperWriter. However, you may notice different formatting elements that are not imported. This typically occurs when a word processor offers a feature that has no equivalent in HyperWriter. To make it easier to understand how HyperWriter imports documents and exactly what features are imported from each supported import format, I have included a comprehensive reference to HyperWriter's import features below. In case you aren't familiar with a particular formatting feature, you can look ahead to Tutorial 4 which discusses formatting in depth.

Microsoft Word Documents

Microsoft Word .DOC document files from Microsoft Word for Windows 1.0, Microsoft Word for Windows 2.0, Microsoft Word for Windows 6.0, and Microsoft Word for DOS .DOC document files can be directly imported into HyperWriter. The elements in Table 10.1 from Microsoft Word either are or aren't imported into HyperWriter.

Table 10.1 How HyperWriter Imports Microsoft Word Documents

Document Element	*HyperWriter Supports*
Paragraph styles	Fully supported.
Character styles	Fully supported.
Tables	Tables are fully supported. Table shading does not import. Landscape mode tables will not be displayed perfectly as the screen is smaller than the page.

Bullets	Paragraph styles with bullets are imported and mapped as closely as possible to the correct bullet character.
Pictures	Embedded pictures in .BMP and .WMF format are imported into HyperWriter as .WMF files (the .WMF file is automatically created). Use **the Text Spacing** or **Tag Spacing** commands to set the width of the .WMF files. .TIF pictures linked by their filename into the Word document are also imported into HyperWriter. Please note that pictures from word processors often appear too large on screen as they were usually designed for a printer, not a screen (a printer has over four times greater resolution than the screen). To prevent this problem when importing documents, picture import can be turned off with the **Options** button on the **Import Picture** dialog box.
Frames	HyperWriter does not have a frame construct so frames are not imported.
Headers/Footers	Headers and footers are different in HyperWriter, so these are not imported. The **Properties** command on the **Document** menu is used to define these for printing.
Alignment	Alignment as part of paragraph styles is imported into HyperWriter. Alignment on its own is not imported.
Soft returns	Soft returns are not imported from Microsoft Word as soft return characters. Soft returns are instead imported as "|ATTR 10|" text strings which can be searched for and replaced with a HyperWriter soft return (the **Ctrl+Enter** keystroke).

Rich Text Format Documents

The elements in Table 10.2 from Rich Text Format documents either are or aren't imported into HyperWriter.

Table 10.2 How HyperWriter Imports Rich Text Format Documents

Document Element	Description
Inline formatting	Fully supported (including font changes, boldfacing, italics, and underlining).
Paragraph styles	Fully supported.
Character styles	Fully supported.

(continues)

Table 10.2 *(Continued)*

Document Element	Description
Tables	Tables are fully supported. Table shading does not import. Landscape mode tables will not be displayed perfectly as the screen is smaller than the page.
Bullets	Paragraph styles with bullets are imported and mapped as closely as possible to the correct bullet character.
Pictures	Embedded pictures in .WMF or .BMP formats are imported into HyperWriter as .WMF files (the .WMF file is automatically created). Use the **Text Spacing** or **Tag Spacing** commands to set the width of the .WMF files. If a filename for a linked picture exists in the document then HyperWriter attempts to import it; this will not work for pictures in unsupported formats. Please note that pictures from word processors often appear too large on screen as they were usually designed for a printer, not a screen (a printer has over four times greater resolution than the screen). To prevent this problem when importing documents, picture import can be turned off with the **Options** button on the **Import Picture** dialog box.
Frames	HyperWriter does not have a frame construct, so frames are not imported.
Headers/Footers	Headers and footers are different in HyperWriter, so these are not imported. The **Properties** command on the **Document** menu is used to define these for printing.
Alignment	Alignment as part of paragraph styles is imported into HyperWriter. Alignment on its own is not imported.

WordPerfect Document

The elements in Table 10.3 from WordPerfect documents either are or aren't imported into HyperWriter.

Table 10.3 How HyperWriter Imports WordPerfect Documents

Document Element	Description
Inline formatting	Fully supported (including font changes, boldfacing, italics, and underlining).
Paragraph styles	Fully supported.

Character styles	Fully supported.
Tables	Tables are fully supported. Table shading does not import. Landscape mode tables will not be displayed perfectly as the screen is smaller than the page.
Bullets	Paragraph styles with bullets are imported and mapped as closely as possible to the correct bullet character.
Pictures	For WordPerfect 5.x documents, .EPS pictures are imported. For WordPerfect 6 documents, pictures are currently not imported.
Frames	HyperWriter does not have a frame construct, so frames are not imported.
Headers/Footers	Headers and footers are different in HyperWriter, so these are not imported. The **Properties** command on the **Document** menu is used to define these for printing.
Indents	WordPerfect indent characters are imported as tab characters. You may need to adjust the tab settings so they are displayed correctly.
Alignment	Alignment as part of paragraph styles is imported into HyperWriter. Alignment on its own is not imported.

Lotus Ami Pro Documents

The elements listed in Table 10.4 from Lotus Ami Pro documents either are or aren't imported into HyperWriter.

Table 10.4 How HyperWriter Imports Ami Pro Documents

Document Element	*Description*
Inline formatting	Fully supported (including font changes, boldfacing, italics, and underlining).
Paragraph styles	Fully supported.
Character styles	Fully supported.
Tables	Tables are fully supported. Table shading does not import. Landscape mode tables will not be displayed perfectly as the screen is smaller than the page.
Bullets	Paragraph styles with bullets are imported and mapped as closely as possible to the correct bullet character.
Pictures	Embedded pictures in .BMP, .WMF, and .TIF formats are imported into HyperWriter as .WMF files (the .WMF file is

(continues)

Table 10.4 (*Continued*)

Document Element	Description
Pictures (*continued*)	automatically created). Use the **Text Spacing** or **Tag Spacing** commands to set the width of the .WMF files. Please note that pictures from word processors often appear too large on screen as they were usually designed for a printer, not a screen (a printer has over four times greater resolution than the screen). To prevent this problem when importing documents, picture import can be turned off with the **Options** button on the **Import Picture** dialog box.
Frames	HyperWriter does not have a frame construct so frames are not imported.
Headers/Footers	Headers and footers are different in HyperWriter so these are not imported. The **Properties** command on the **Document** menu is used to define these for printing.
Alignment	Alignment as part of paragraph styles is imported into HyperWriter. Alignment on its own is not.

Reference: What About the Clipboard?

As most users of MS-Windows are aware, the Windows environment includes a sophisticated clipboard mechanism that allows cut, copy, and paste of information from one Windows application to another. Should the clipboard be used to import information instead of HyperWriter's **Import Text** command? Generally speaking, the answer is no. While the reasons for this aren't terribly important, you should be aware that when using HyperWriter, the clipboard is better used for transferring simple text data, not richly formatted documents. Overall, HyperWriter's **Import Text** command does a far superior job of importing documents than pasting from the clipboard.

CHAPTER 11

Formatting Text

In the previous chapter, we learned to import documents. Once you have imported documents into HyperWriter, your next task is generally to format those documents. Just as a conventional word processor or desktop-publishing package lets you format text in documents, so does HyperWriter. Although HyperWriter imports formatting directly from word processors, HyperWriter includes robust formatting tools. This allows you to format documents to take better advantage of the digital publishing medium—you can format your documents with the appropriate fonts, spacing, and other characteristics needed for use on a screen-based medium.

In this tutorial, we will start with a basic discussion of the two types of formatting, proceed with a tutorial on using inline formatting, and then finally conclude with a tutorial on using style-based formatting. For this tutorial, we will be using a sample document called FORMAT1.DOC. This document contains the text of a document that will illustrate our formatting tasks.

Understanding Formatting: Inline Formatting versus Styles

HyperWriter's formatting tools are used to adjust the visual appearance of text on screen: its font, size, color, and other visual attributes. These text-formatting facilities let you apply virtually any desired appearance to the textual component of your documents. HyperWriter can set the formatting of text in two ways: inline formatting and styles.

Inline formatting means marking individual blocks of text with the mouse or keyboard and then applying individual formatting commands such as **Text Style** or **Text Color**. Because these formatting commands are stored *inline* with the body of the document, this is referred to as inline formatting. The formatting commands that can be applied to blocks are a subset of the formatting commands that can be applied to styles. Available formatting commands that can be applied to a block of text include **Font**, **Size**, **Color**, **Bold Facing**, **Underlining**, and **Double Underlining**, among others.

Formatting text by style is identical to defining a style in a word processor. The one difference is that in HyperWriter, styles are called *tags* (different word, same meaning—in this book, both terms will be used). Styles or tags operate by defining one or more formatting commands as a tag or style with an author-defined name. For example, you might decide to format headings with a **HEAD** tag which is 24-point bold text. Once a tag is defined, tags can be used repeatedly throughout a document or documents. Styles have many advantages over inline formatting. Chief among these advantages are that styles are maintained globally throughout a document. This means that once tags are defined in a document, they can be changed globally just by modifying the tag, instead of having to modify each formatting command individually. In short, this allows global reformatting of documents that use styles with only a single command. An additional advantage is that a properly named style aids in understanding the structure of a document, because rather than wondering why a particular text element is boldfaced (or a different font), you can look at its style name and see that it is a heading.

Tags in HyperWriter can be applied either to a whole paragraph or paragraphs or to a marked block of text. In addition, multiple tags can be applied to each paragraph. When multiple tags are applied to each paragraph, the first tag can be applied to the paragraph as a whole; however, any additional tags must be applied to marked blocks. HyperWriter allows you to either create new sets of tags in every document that you create or to share sets of tags across multiple HyperWriter documents.

Before beginning to learn about formatting documents, we must first run HyperWriter. HyperWriter is a standard MS-Windows application that can be run from the Program Manager.

Using Inline Formatting

As described in the first part of this tutorial, inline formatting allows you to format blocks of text just the way you do with a word processor. To get started, we should open the sample document FORMAT1.HW4.

1. Select the **Open** command from the **File** menu.

2. Select the document FORMAT1.HW4 from the list of available documents. Save your current document if needed. If you are asked to leave a bookmark answer No. This loads the document. A picture of this document is shown in Figure 11.1.

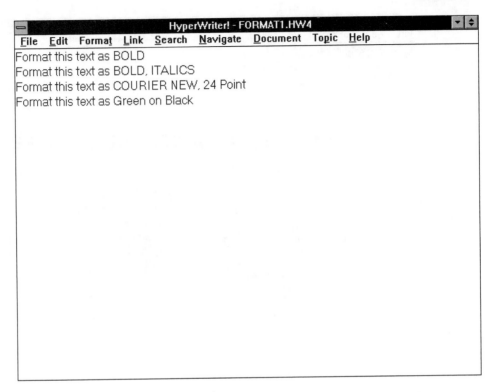

Figure 11.1 The FORMAT1.HW4 document.

As you can see, this document features several samples of text along with formatting instructions for each sample. With our document now open, we are ready to begin formatting the first sample, format this text as BOLD.

Formatting the First Sample

1. Use the mouse to mark the first sample as a block.
2. Select the **Text Style** command from the **Format** menu. This displays the **Text Style** dialog box shown in Figure 11.2.
3. Select the **Bold** option from the **Appearance** group of options on the dialog's right-hand side.
4. Select the **OK** button to close the dialog box.

As you can see, this has formatted the first sample of text using a bold font. With this sample formatted, we are ready to format the second sample, format this text as BOLD, ITALICS.

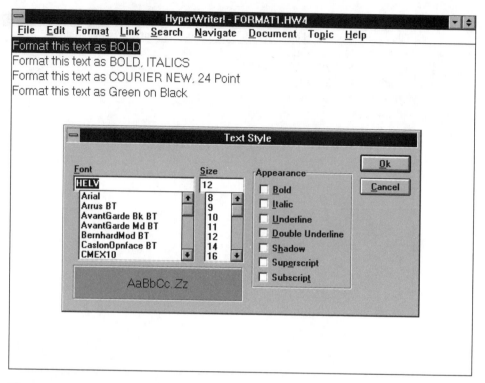

Figure 11.2 The **Text Style** dialog box.

Formatting the Second Sample

1. Use the mouse to mark the first second as a block.

2. Select the **Text Style** command from the **Format** menu. This displays the **Text Style** dialog box.

3. Select the **Bold** option from the **Appearance** group of options on the dialog's right-hand side.

4. Select the **Italic** option from the **Appearance** group of options on the dialog's right-hand side.

5. Select the **OK** button to close the dialog box.

As you can see, this has formatted the second sample of text using both the bold and italics attributes.

NOTE: A question that may have occurred to you when using the **Text Style** command is "Does HyperWriter store the font and size with the marked text when the **Text Style** command is used?" The answer to that is that as long as you don't modify the font or size, then HyperWriter doesn't store any changes to it with the marked text—only the attributes that you changed are saved. The reason that this is important is that due to HyperWriter's stylesheet features, if the font or size was stored every time that you boldfaced text, using a stylesheet for global changes would be quite difficult.

Now that we have used both the bold and italics attributes, we are ready to use the Font and Size attributes on the third sample, formatting this text as COURIER NEW, 24 Point.

Formatting the Third Sample

1. Use the mouse to mark the third sample as a block.
2. Select the **Text Style** command from the **Format** menu. This displays the **Text Style** dialog box.
3. Select the Courier New font from the list of fonts in the **Font** field.
4. Select or type in **24** as the font size in the **Size** field.
5. Select the **OK** button to close the dialog box.

As you can see, this has formatted our third sample of text as 24 point, Courier New. This brings up an interesting question—what if the reader of our documents doesn't have the fonts that we choose for our documents? For the font that we just selected, this wouldn't be a problem (Courier New is a standard MS-Windows font), but the question still remains. When you select a font for your documents, HyperWriter shows you all fonts that are available in your Windows system. When you give an electronic document to a reader, HyperWriter tries to match the fonts in the document with the fonts in his or her system. If a font you used isn't present in his or her system then Hyper-Writer will substitute another font, typically Arial.

To address this obvious problem, HyperWriter supports *font embedding*. Font embedding, a feature found in the TrueType font standard, allows supported TrueType fonts to be embedded within a particular document or stylesheet file (for HyperWriter, fonts are embedded in the .HWT stylesheet file used by the document). When documents with embedded fonts are moved between computers and displayed with HyperReader, the embedded fonts are first temporarily installed into the Windows system, used by the document as needed, and then removed when the application is terminated. The reason for this approach is that like any software, a font actually has a copyright and is owned by someone or some company. Consequently, you can't simply distribute a font along with your HyperWriter application. However, the TrueType font embedding standard, although only supported on certain fonts, provides a powerful method for distributing fonts without having to ship actual font files with your application that would violate the copyright of the font owner.

NOTE: The **Font Mapper** command is used to actually embed font files into your HyperWriter application. This command is not covered in this tutorial.

With a better understanding of fonts and font distribution, we will now continue our discussion of inline formatting. The sample of text that we want to format is the fourth sample, format this text as green on black. For this exercise, we will use the **Text Color** command as we want to set the formatting to a set of colors.

Formatting the Fourth Sample

1. Use the mouse to mark the fourth sample as a block.
2. Select the **Text Color** command from the **Format** menu. This displays the **Text Color** dialog box shown in Figure 11.3.
3. The **Text Color** dialog box is divided into two groups of colors: a foreground color (shown in the top half of the dialog) and a background color (shown in the bottom half of the dialog). The foreground color is the color of the text itself, while the background color is the color behind the text. Now that you understand how to use the **Text Color** dialog box, select dark green as the foreground color and black as the background color.
4. Select the **OK** button to close the dialog box.

With the fourth sample now formatted, your screen (showing the effect of formatting the four text samples) should appear similar to that shown in Figure 11.4.

Having covered **Text Style** and **Text Color**, there are still two inline formatting commands that we haven't covered yet: **Text Spacing** and **Text Tab Settings**. Both of these commands will simply be discussed, as we won't work through examples for each (these commands are very similar to **Tag Spacing** and **Tag Tab Settings** which will be covered further). The **Text Spacing** command inserts spacing values such as left-margin and right-margin space and paragraph spacing above and below. The **Text Tab Settings** command sets tab values on a per paragraph basis, allowing each paragraph to have its own set of tab settings.

Now that we have used inline formatting extensively, we are ready to move onto using styles.

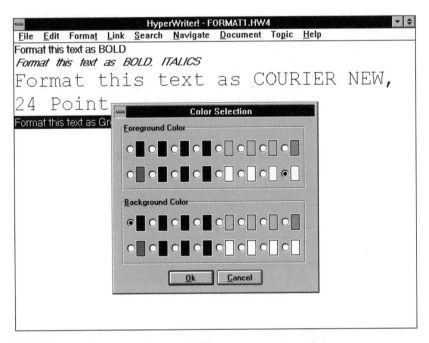

Figure 11.3 The **Text Color** dialog box.

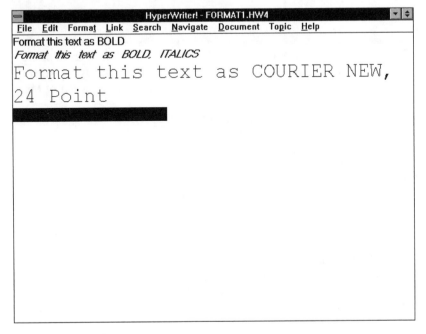

Figure 11.4 All four samples formatted.

Using Styles

As described in the first part of this tutorial, style-based formatting allows you to format text using tags or styles (named combinations of formatting attributes). To get started, we should open the sample document FORMAT2.HW4.

Opening FORMAT2.HW4

1. Select the **Open** command from the **File** menu.

2. Select the document FORMAT2.HW4 from the list of available documents. When HyperWriter asks if you want to save your work, select No (we really didn't accomplish anything in our last exercise). If you are asked to leave a bookmark, answer No. This loads the document. A picture of this document is shown in Figure 11.5.

As you can see, this document is a collection of different press releases arranged in a hypertext fashion. With our document now open, we are ready to begin formatting styles. Our first task is to move from our table of contents

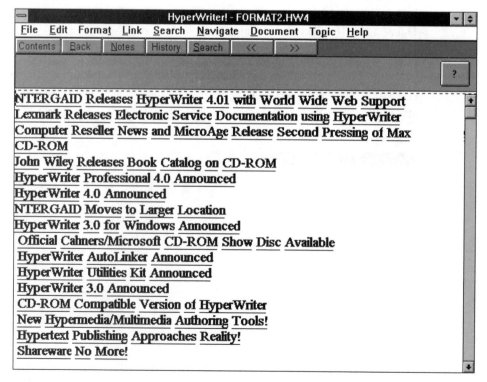

Figure 11.5 The FORMAT2.HW4 document.

(which is what is currently onscreen) to one of the press releases that we want to format.

Moving to a Press Release

Activate the first link displayed onscreen by clicking on it with the **Left Mouse** button. This should display the press release we want to format. This press release is shown in Figure 11.6.

With our press release shown, we are ready to format some of the different styles in the document. However, before we actually format any of the styles, we need to find out their names. The **Apply Tag** command both shows the name of the style applied to the paragraph where the cursor is located, and lets you select the style that should be applied to the paragraph.

Finding the Name of the Current Style

1. Place the cursor on the first paragraph of text in the press release (the title of the press release). As you can see, it is currently left-aligned text without any particular formatting attributes.

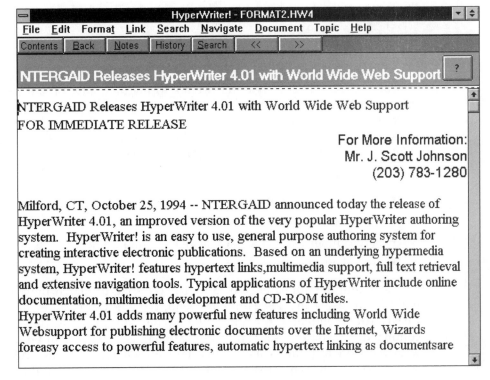

Figure 11.6 The press release to format.

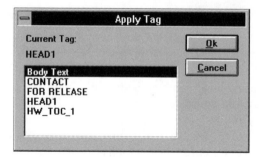

Figure 11.7 The **Apply Tag** dialog box.

2. Select the **Apply Tag** command from the **Format** menu. This displays the dialog box shown in Figure 11.7.

3. As you can see, the name of the style is **HEAD1**. Select the **Cancel** button to close the **Apply Tag** dialog box.

NOTE: The name of the current style is also shown in the **Format** menu as the first item in the menu (it has the description Tag: before the name of the style).

Now that we know which style we are formatting, we can define its appearance. As this is a style that we are formatting, any formatting changes that we make will be applied to all other paragraphs of text with the same style. Provided that our other press releases are similarly formatted with a **HEAD1** style, their appearance will be updated as well. The appearance changes we want to make to our **HEAD1** style are:

- 18-point, bold Arial font
- Blue text on a white background
- Centered alignment
- Large amount of blank space below the paragraph
- Special effect such as a wipe or fade

Changing the appearance of our **HEAD1** style to match the goals listed will require using the **Tag Font** command, the **Tag Color** command, the **Tag Justification** command, the **Tag Spacing** command, and the **Tag Attributes** command. As you can see, all of the commands that we will be using start with the keyword Tag. This is consistent within HyperWriter: Whenever a command modifies the attributes of a tag or style, the command name starts with Tag.

Formatting Our HEAD1 Style

The first item that we want to modify is the font of our **HEAD1** style. To do this, we need to use the **Tag Font** command. The **Tag Font** command is used to set the font, size, and formatting attributes that the current style is using. HyperWriter uses any standard fonts installed in your MS-Windows system. As with all **Tag** commands, you must first place your cursor on the paragraph whose style you want to modify before selecting the **Tag** command.

Setting Tag Font

1. Place the cursor on the paragraph with the **HEAD1** tag if it isn't already there.

2. Select the **Tag Font** command from the **Format** menu. This displays a dialog box that can be used to select the desired font. The **Tag Font** dialog box is shown below in Figure 11.8.

   As you can see, **Tag Font** is broken into four main sections. The first section is the Font list, which allows you to select the font to use for the text. The second section is the Size list, which allows you to select the size for the text. From the Size list, you can select an existing size or type in a new size of your choosing. If you type in a new size, the MS-Windows system will automatically scale a font as needed. The Appearance section of the **Tag Font** dialog box allows you to define an appearance attribute such as Bold or Underline that affects how the text is displayed. Finally, the sample field at the bottom of the **Tag Font** dialog box displays a sample of how the text will appear. As you modify the size or appearance, a new sample will be displayed.

3. Select Arial as the font to use. Select 18 point as the size to use. Select Bold as the attribute.

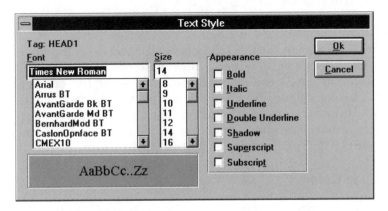

Figure 11.8 The **Tag Font** dialog box.

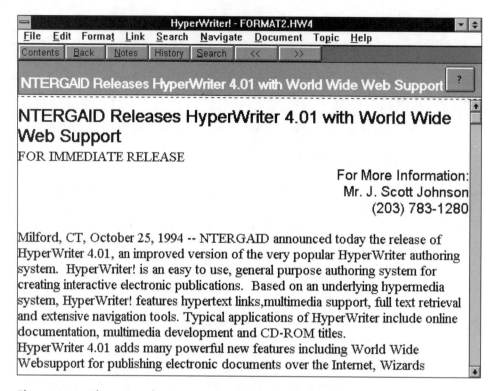

Figure 11.9 After using the **Tag Font** command.

4. Select **OK** to close the dialog box. This reformats the paragraph to the new font.

After formatting the **HEAD1** style as Arial, 18 point, bold text, this should appear on screen as shown in Figure 11.9.

As you can see, we have started to set the appearance of our heading as needed. If you remember our original list of goals, however, we aren't done yet. The next step is to use the **Tag Color** command to set the color of the text. The **Tag Color** command sets both a foreground or text color and a background or screen color. The available colors are those of the currently selected EGA/VGA color palette and are displayed in two separate palettes: the foreground and the background. The foreground determines the color of the text. The background determines the color of the screen behind the text. Each palette starts with black and ends with bright white.

Setting Tag Color

1. Place the cursor on the paragraph with the **HEAD1** tag if it isn't already there.

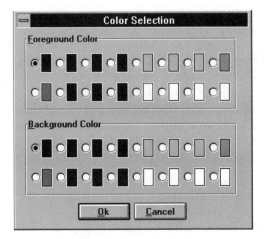

Figure 11.10 The **Tag Font** dialog box.

2. Select the **Tag Color** command from the **Format** menu. This displays a dialog box that can be used to select the colors of the text. The **Tag Color** dialog box is shown in Figure 11.10.

   As you can see, the **Tag Color** dialog box has two separate groups of colors. For this task, we need to set the color of the text to dark blue and the color of the background to white.

3. To set the color of the text to dark blue, click the mouse on the dark-blue color setting in the first group of colors.

4. To set the color of the text background to white, click the mouse on the white color setting in the second group of colors.

5. Select the **OK** button to close the **Tag Color** dialog box.

As you can see on your screen, the color of the text has changed onscreen and should now be dark blue on a white background. I haven't included a picture of this here as this book doesn't include color pictures (which is the only way that you could see the effect of using this command). Now that you have used the **Tag Color** command, this brings up an interesting question of whether or not to set the background color setting. When using **Tag Color**, we obviously wanted to set the dark-blue foreground color for our text, but as our background color was already white, did we need to set this option? The answer to this question is yes. Whenever you set any color setting in Hyper-Writer, you have to set both the foreground and background color settings. If you set only the foreground color then HyperWriter would have assumed that the background color should have been black—the default color setting.

Now that we know how to set the color for a particular style or tag, this brings us to the question of how to reset the colors for a style or tag when you want to remove its color settings. After a tag has its colors set, the default color setting can be restored by setting the tag's color to black on black. As you may recall, this was the default setting when we first used the **Tag Color** command.

Having used both **Tag Font** and **Tag Color**, we are halfway through this exercise. Our next task is to set the alignment of the paragraph using **Tag Justification**. **Tag Justification** controls the appearance of the left- and right-hand edges of the text with four options: Centered, Full Justified, Left Justified, and Right Justified. These options have the effect on text alignment that you would expect from their names. As you can see from looking at the text onscreen, our **HEAD1** style is currently set to Left Justified, the default option. We will now use **Tag Justification** to set the alignment to Centered.

Changing a Paragraph's Justification

1. Place the cursor on the paragraph with the **HEAD1** tag if it isn't already there.

2. Select the **Tag Justification** command from the **Format** menu. This displays a submenu for setting justification. The current justification setting is shown by a checkmark. The screen shot in Figure 11.11 illustrates this.

3. Select the **Centered** option from the submenu. HyperWriter will tell you that tabs only work with left-justified text. Select **OK** to close this message.

From the steps above, you can see that using **Tag Justification** is actually quite easy. Despite this, there are two elements of **Tag Justification** that you should understand. The first is that in HyperWriter, unlike in word processors, justification can *only* be set through a style or tag. Whereas in most word processors you can simply mark a block and then center it, in HyperWriter that block must have a style applied to it. As this is a significant difference from word-processing software, you should keep this in mind. The second aspect of **Tag Justification** to understand is that tab settings can only be used with left-justified text. When you set the justification to Right Justified, Full Justified, or Centered, HyperWriter informs you that tabs only function with left-justified text.

Now that we have centered our **HEAD1** style and almost completed its formatting, what does the sample press release that we have been formatting look like? This press release is shown in Figure 11.12.

We now have only two more attributes to set for our press release. The next one we want to set uses the **Tag Spacing** command. When you use a word processor and you want to insert some blank lines of space below text, you typically just press **Enter** a few times. When building an individual document this is a fine approach as it is easy, convenient, quick, and does the job. When working with digital publishing, this is not a good approach. The reason is that this approach leads to considerable inconsistencies (was that two times I need to press **Enter** or three times?) as well as dramatic problems in document

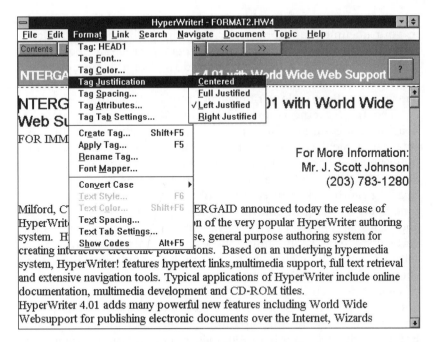

Figure 11.11 Using the **Tag Justification** command.

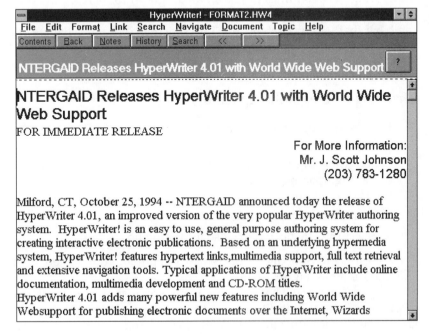

Figure 11.12 The **HEAD1** tag, mostly formatted.

maintenance (maintaining this situation would require going to every location in your document and physically deleting the blank lines added by pressing **Enter**). To address these problems, HyperWriter's **Tag Spacing** command lets you control spacing both to the left and right of a paragraph as well as above and below. As you set these values with a style, maintenance tasks become just a matter of setting style attributes, not physically editing text.

The **Tag Spacing** command controls the spacing of tagged paragraphs. Spacing is measured in increments of *pixels* (picture elements). A pixel is the smallest element your computer can display. Depending on the type of computer you have, your computer has a different amount of pixels. Typically, you have at least 640x480 pixels (pixels across x pixels down) on your screen. **Tag Spacing** can be set in three different ways: Margins, Paragraph Spacing, and Line Spacing. Margins control the indentation of the paragraph from the left- and right-hand edges of the screen. Paragraph Spacing controls the amount of vertical space between paragraphs with two settings, Above and Below. These settings control how close each paragraph is in relationship to the paragraphs above and below the current paragraph in pixels. Line Spacing controls the placement of each line in relation to the lines directly above and below each line. Line Spacing is based on the concept that paragraphs typically contain multiple lines. While the separator or delimiter between paragraphs is the **Enter** key, the delimiter between lines in a paragraph is either word-wrapping text or the soft-return keystroke—**Ctrl+Enter**. Line Spacing lets you increase the spacing between lines of text in a paragraph to increase the onscreen legibility of text.

Now that we understand the **Tag Spacing** command, we are ready to use it. For this exercise, we need to set the paragraph spacing above and below the HEAD1 style. This will nicely separate it from the body of the press release.

Changing a Paragraph's Spacing

1. Place the cursor on the paragraph with the **HEAD1** tag if it isn't already there.

2. Select the **Tag Spacing** command from the **Format** menu. This displays the **Tag Spacing** dialog box shown in Figure 11.13.

3. Move to the **Paragraph spacing** field and set the **Above** value to 15 and set the **Below** value to 30.

4. Select the **OK** button to close the dialog box.

With the **Tag Spacing** values set to 15 and 30, your screen should appear like that shown in Figure 11.14.

As you can see, we have a small blank space above the press release's title to prevent it from being too close to the top of the screen while we have a larger blank space after the title. With these changes made, you should now be

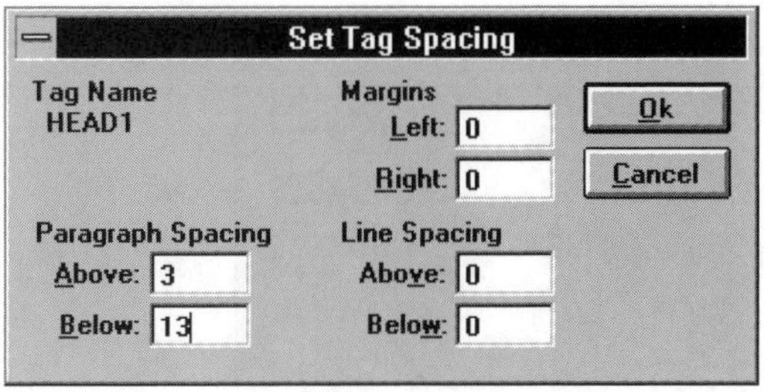

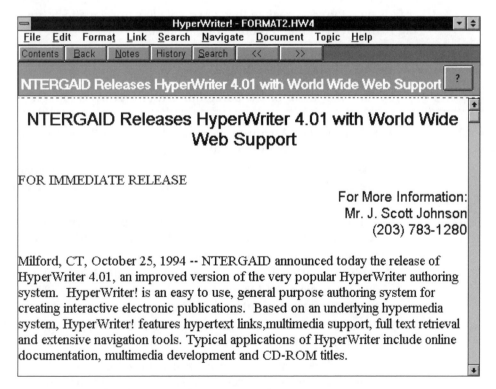

Figure 11.13 The **Tag Spacing** dialog box.

able to read the press release much more easily, as we definitely improved its legibility.

Our final task in formatting the **HEAD1** style is to add a special effect to the style, such as a fade or wipe. HyperWriter has several of these special effects that can be applied as part of any style. What a special effect does is to display a piece of text with that effect. For example, if you have a Slide Left

Figure 11.14 After formatting the **HEAD1** style's spacing.

Figure 11.15 The **Tag Attributes** dialog box.

effect set, then HyperWriter slides the text left whenever it is displayed. What we will do now is set a Fade In special effect so that our headings will dissolve or fade onto the screen when they are displayed. Special effects are set with the **Tag Attributes** command on the **Format** menu.

Changing a Paragraph's Special Effects

1. Place the cursor on the paragraph with the **HEAD1** tag if it isn't already there.

2. Select the **Tag Attributes** command from the **Format** menu. This displays the **Tag Attributes** dialog box shown in Figure 11.15.

3. Special Effects are considered a bullet effect, so now we need to select **the Set Bullet** button. This displays the **Set Bullet Attributes** dialog box shown in Figure 11.16.

4. Turning on special effects takes several steps. The first is to set the **Bullet** field to **Character**. Do this now. This tells HyperWriter that there will be a bullet effect for the paragraph.

5. With the **Bullet** field set to **Character**, set the **Effects** field to **Fade In** and then select the **OK** button to close the dialog box. This will return you to the **Tag Attributes** dialog box.

6. Select the **OK** button to close the **Tag Attributes** dialog box. This will return you to the text of your document.

As you can see, with the special effect turned on, the title of your press release now fades onto the screen. This is now a good time to examine other press releases in this document. What I recommend is that you return to the table of contents (easily done by pressing **Esc**), select a different press release,

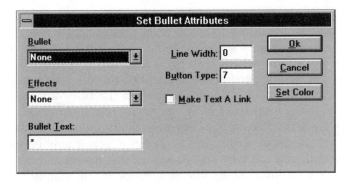

Figure 11.16 The **Set Bullet Attributes** dialog box.

and check out its appearance. You may want to do this with multiple press releases. What you should see is that all of the press releases have a similar appearance now that you have set all formatting attributes for the **HEAD1** style. To illustrate this, I have included a picture of a different press release shown in Figure 11.17.

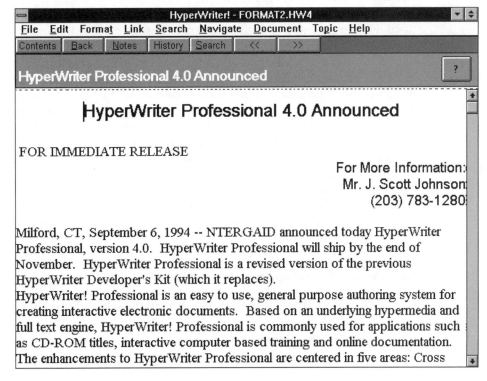

Figure 11.17 A sample press release.

Now that you have applied the special effect to the text, and we have navigated within this document and seen several press releases, we need to ask ourselves if this was actually a good effect to use. What we have done is to alter our stylesheet so that whenever a press release is displayed, it has a Fade In special effect. From our perspective as authors, this is good because it highlights our information and focuses the reader on the title—an important element of the press release that they chose to read. However, from our perspective as readers, these special effects actually aren't good at all. While the first time that a reader encounters a special effect, it may be regarded as (marginally) useful, you can virtually guarantee that the second time it will be less useful, and by the third and successive times, it will simply frustrate the reader. One of the main reasons that it will frustrate the reader is that you are slowing down the reader's progress and forcing he or she to wait unnecessarily. As a general digital publishing rule of thumb, slowing down the reader unnecessarily is bad.

If it's not advisable to use special effects when they slow the reader, why then does HyperWriter even have them? The answer to this is three fold. First, for the right type of electronic document, these types of special effects are crucial. Specifically, when your application isn't a reference-and-retrieval type of document, these special effects work well. Consider an interactive presentation built in HyperWriter. In such an application, special effects could be used for displaying lists slowly as well as for transitions between slides in the presentation. A second way these might be used, even in a reference-and-retrieval type of application, is to make sure a reader notices particularly important information. A good example is reference documentation for an oil refinery. Given the nature of the information, items such as caution warnings are crucial and could make the difference between successful use of the refinery and destroying it. A special effect could make sure that a caution warning was definitely noticed when it was slowly displayed onscreen. The third aspect as to why HyperWriter has special effects is actually quite simple—our users requested them when we surveyed them as to features that they wanted to see added to HyperWriter.

Now that we realize that we shouldn't have used a special effect, we need to remove it. This is done with the **Tag Attributes** command. To do this, you need to go to a sample press release as your cursor needs to be located on the style that you are modifying.

Removing a Paragraph's Special Effects

1. Place the cursor on the paragraph with the **HEAD1** tag if it isn't already there.
2. Select the **Tag Attributes** command from the **Format** menu.
3. Select the **Set Bullet** button to open the **Set Bullet Attributes** dialog box.

4. Set the **Bullet** field to **None**. This turns off the bullet effect (which correspondingly turns off the special effect).

5. Select the **OK** button to close the **Set Bullet Attributes** dialog box.

6. Select the **OK** button to close the **Tag Attributes** dialog box.

What you should now see is a press release onscreen without any special effects. We have now finished our exercise on formatting headings. At this point, you should be familiar with most of HyperWriter's tag formatting options. We are now ready for a discussion of **BODY TEXT**, the default style for all paragraphs.

Formatting Body Text

In HyperWriter, all documents start with one style or tag—**BODY TEXT**. If you use Microsoft Word, then the style **NORMAL** is used instead of the style **BODY TEXT**. The **BODY TEXT** tag is automatically applied to all paragraphs of text unless a different paragraph is specified. This **BODY TEXT** tag is very much tied into the nature of modifying tags. As you should recall, whenever you modify a tag, that change is made globally everywhere the tag is used. For example, if you have a tag named **HEAD1** formatted for 10-point text and you then change its font size to 14 points, everywhere that tag is used will now be formatted to 14 point text. Similarly, if you make a change to the **BODY TEXT** tag, it will apply to paragraphs that use this tag. In this exercise, we will rely on the **BODY TEXT** tag to quickly and easily improve the formatting of our document.

Before we start this exercise, let's look at the sample document that we need to improve. A picture of one of our press releases that make up our document is shown in Figure 11.18.

As you can see, the title to the press release is well formatted, but the rest of the press release is bunched together, stretched all the way to the margins and, generally, quite difficult to read. With these observations, it isn't hard to come up with goals for reformatting our press release. Specifically, we want to:

- Add left and right margins so that our text is not stretched the width of the screen

- Increase the spacing between paragraphs

- Increase the interline spacing

- Add a first line indent so that the first line of each paragraph will be indented for easier reading

People reading this book with any experience in desktop publishing or any type of document formatting will probably recognize that these are basic, simple formatting techniques for increasing the legibility of any document. Just as

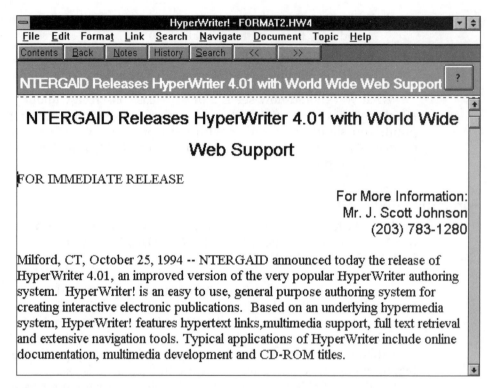

Figure 11.18 A sample press release.

you would never think of making a print publication where the text ran across the whole page without margins; you shouldn't do this for a digital publication. As a general rule of thumb, many of the same design and formatting conventions that you know for producing print publications can also be used for producing digital publications.

Making these changes to our document requires using the **Tag Spacing** and **Tag Attributes** commands. As we have already used these commands, I won't be including pictures of these commands in the following steps. Our first task is to use the **Tag Spacing** command.

Using the Tag Spacing Command

1. If you aren't viewing a press release now, select one from the table of contents.

2. Place your cursor anywhere in the body of the press release. Our first task is to make sure that we are on a paragraph with the **BODY TEXT** tag. Select the **Apply Tag** command from the **Format** menu and check

the **Current Tag** prompt to make sure that you are on a tag with the **BODY TEXT** tag. If you aren't, then scroll up or down and check again until you are on a paragraph with this tag.

3. Select the **Tag Spacing** command from the **Format** menu.

4. Move to the **Margins** group of fields and set the Left and Right fields to 50 pixels. This adds a fifty-pixel margin (slightly more than 1/2") to the left- and right-hand edges of the text.

5. Move to the **Paragraph Spacing** group of fields and set the Above field to 10. This adds a 10 pixel (slightly less than 1/4") margin between paragraphs.

6. Move to the **Line Spacing** group of fields and set the Above field to 5. This increases the interline spacing slightly within each paragraph, making it easier to read.

7. Select the **OK** button to close the **Tag Spacing** dialog box.

NOTE: Given that the **Paragraph Spacing** options have both above and below options, does it matter which one that you use? While technically the answer is no, HyperWriter tends to perform better when you use the above option, not the below option.

A picture of our reformatted document is shown in Figure 11.19.

As you would probably agree, the reformatted **BODY TEXT** style is definitely easier to read. Although we have done a good job of reformatting this text, we now have just one more task in this exercise. What we want to do is indent the first line of every paragraph. This, coupled with the paragraph spacing, will combine to make it easier to scan down each paragraph, looking for particular information. Setting a first-line indent is handled with the **Tag Attributes** command.

Setting a First Line Indent

1. Place the cursor on the paragraph with the **BODY TEXT** style if it isn't already there.

2. Select the **Tag Attributes** command from the **Format** menu.

3. Move to the **First Line Indent** group of options. Set the **Width** field to 25 pixels.

4. Set the **Indent/Outdent** option to **Indent** if it isn't set this way already.

5. Select the **OK** button to close the **Tag Attributes** dialog box.

A picture of our reformatted document, with its indented first line paragraph is shown in Figure 11.20.

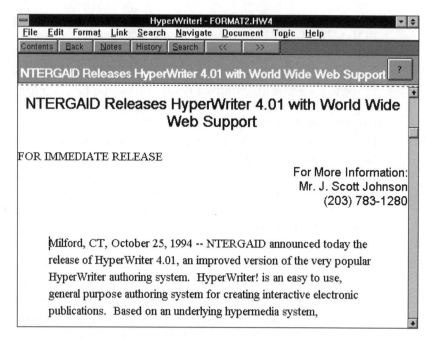

Figure 11.19 The reformatted **BODY TEXT** style.

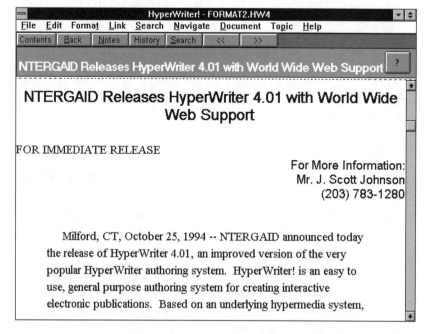

Figure 11.20 The reformatted **BODY TEXT** style with indent.

This completes our formatting of the **BODY TEXT** tag. We will now move onto formatting lists of information, both for bulleted lists and for numbered lists.

Formatting Bulleted Lists

A very common element in most documents is that of a list of items or **bulleted list**. A bulleted list is a list of items that places a special character or text string in front of a paragraph, generally for emphasis. The follow text is an example of a bulleted list that incorporates several levels:

- Digital Publishing

- Storage Mediums

  - CD-ROM

  - Floppy Disc

  - Internet

Bulleted lists can be created just by typing in the character needed for the list, pressing **Tab**, entering the rest of the list, pressing **Enter** and so on. But, as with the **Tag Spacing** command and adding spacing to documents, Hyper-Writer's stylesheet tools provide a better approach. The **Set Bullet** button in the **Tag Attributes** dialog box controls HyperWriter's text bullet features. HyperWriter's bullet features operate by allowing you to input the text for the bullet, a single character or more of text, and an indent setting. The indent setting specifies the horizontal space from the left side of the bullet character to the body of the paragraph. When these options are set for a tag, a bullet appears automatically in front of every paragraph with that tag. By setting these attributes as part of a style or tag, it is much easier to maintain and update documents.

An example of text in a document with bullet characters is shown in Figure 11.21.

As you can see from the figure, there are several different bullet types, including single characters, lines, and even text prompts. In the picture above, the Problem:, Cause:, and Solution: prompts are created with the **Bullet Character** option. This ability of bullet character to display these types of prompts starts to give HyperWriter a fielded approach to data.

For this exercise, we will take the document that we have been working with and make the table of contents into a bulleted list. Although tables of contents are not typical applications of bulleted lists, this will nicely illustrate how bulleted lists are used.

Defining bulleted lists is handled with the **Tag Attributes** command, a command we have previously used for setting special effects. As with modifying all other styles, we have to first place our cursor on a paragraph with the style that we want to modify. This is illustrated in the first step shown below.

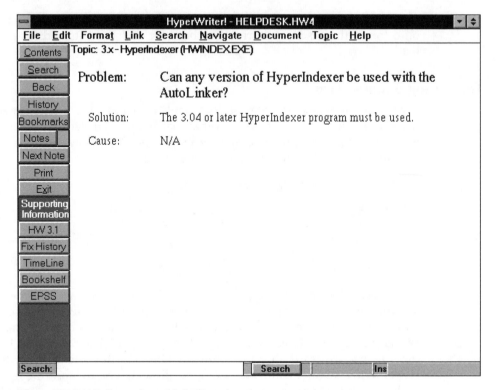

Figure 11.21 Paragraphs with bullet characters.

Setting a First Line Indent

1   Move to the table of contents by pressing **Esc** until you return to it (this has the effect of backtracking you through the document).

2. Place your cursor on one of the paragraphs with the HW_TOC_1 style if it isn't already there (this would be a paragraph that is a link from the table of contents).

3. Select the **Tag Attributes** command from the **Format** menu.

4. Move to the **First Line Indent** group of options. Set the **Width** field to 25 pixels.

5. Set the **Indent/Outdent** option to **Indent** option if it isn't set this way already. In steps 4 and 5, we told HyperWriter that the HW_TOC_1 style should have a character outdented by 25 pixels. The next step is to define the outdented character (the bullet character).

6. Select the **Set Bullet** button.

7. Set the **Bullet** field to **Character**.

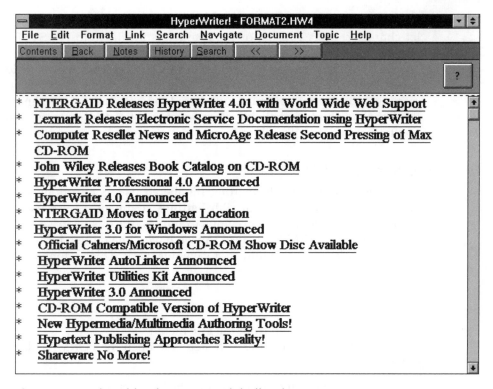

Figure 11.22 The table of contents with bullet characters.

8. Move to the **Bullet Text** field and enter an "*" into the text field.

9. Select the **OK** button to close the **Set Bullet Attributes** dialog box.

10. Select the **OK** button to close the **Set Tag Attributes** dialog box.

After setting the bullet character, your table of contents should appear as shown in Figure 11.22.

As you would imagine, since the bullet features in HyperWriter are stylesheet controlled, they can be controlled like any stylesheet. This allows global changing of bullet characters if needed. With an understanding of the bullet feature, we need to understand the difference between the **Character** and **System Character** options for bullets. The **Character** option, the one that we used for our bullet in step 7, takes a bullet character from the font that HyperWriter is using for the paragraph. **The System Character** option takes a character from HyperWriter's system font, HWSYSTEM. HWSYSTEM is a font supplied by HyperWriter that is identical to the characters in the standard DOS text font. It also is extended by NTERGAID for several additional useful characters such as those for bullets. For example, setting the **System Character** option and then setting **<315>** as the character to use inserts a true, round bullet character. For a full list of the characters available to HWSYSTEM, press **Ctrl+O**.

Bulleted lists are one of the features in HyperWriter that you do need to experiment with to get a real good feel for. You may want to do this now before moving onto the next exercise, numbered lists. If you do experiment, look at the **Set Color** button available after you select **Set Bullet**, as this button lets you format bullets with colors.

Formatting Numbered Lists

Like formatting bullets, formatting numbered lists is also done with the **Tag Attributes** command. The **Tag Tab Settings** command is also used to format numbered lists. Unlike our previous examples, for this exercise we will use a new document, FORMATLI.HW4. As we have done quite a bit of work on the previous exercises, we should first save our work. This is done with the **Save** command on the **File** menu.

Saving Our Work

Select the **Save** command from the **File** menu.

With our work saved, the next step is to open the FORMATLI.HW4 document.

1. Select the **Open** command from the **File** menu.
2. Select the document FORMATLI from the list of available documents. If you are asked to leave a bookmark answer No. This loads the document.

A picture of this document is shown in Figure 11.23.

As you can see, this document consists of several numbered lists. What we will do for this exercise is properly format the numbered elements. As in previous formatting tutorials, the first step is to place the cursor on a paragraph with the style that you want to format.

Formatting a Numbered List

1. Place the cursor on any of the list items that start with a number. If you use the **Apply Tag** command on the **Format** menu, it should display the tag name NUM_LIST.
2. Select the **Tag Attributes** command from the **Format** menu.

   Setting up a numbered list in HyperWriter consists of using the **Tag Attributes** command to set the outdent value and then using the **Tag**

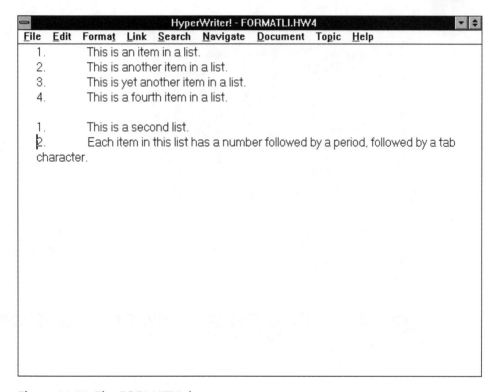

Figure 11.23 The FORMATLI document.

Tab Settings command to match the tag settings to the outdent value (most numbered lists consist of a number followed by a period, followed by a tab character and then the rest of the numbered list). We will set these two commands in the following steps.

3. Set the **Indent/Outdent** option to **Outdent**.

4. Set the **Indent Width** field to 35.

5. Select the **OK** button to close the dialog box.

With our outdent setting correct, we only need to set the **Tag Tab Settings** command to match it.

6. Select the **Tag Tab Settings** command from the **Format** menu. As we haven't used this command yet, it is shown in Figure 11.24.

7. Set the first tab setting to 35 and select the **OK** button.

Having set the needed options for numbered lists, your screen should now appear as shown in Figure 11.25.

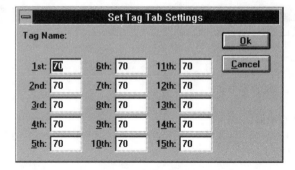

Figure 11.24 The **Tag Tab Settings** command.

This completes the exercises on formatting text. At this point you should be very comfortable with HyperWriter's different text formatting tools and able to work with them effectively. The final topic that we need to cover is Character Styles.

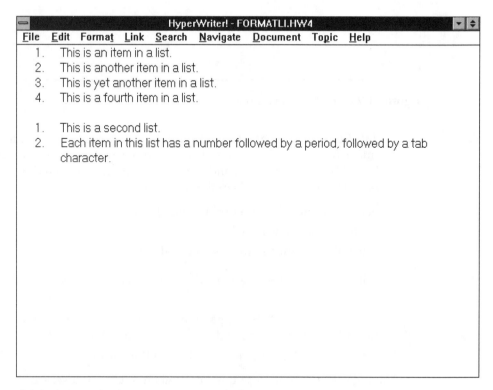

Figure 11.25 The formatted numbered lists.

Reference: Character Styles

Any style or tag can be used in one of two ways: to format a paragraph or to format a marked block. When a tag formats a paragraph, then it is applied to the entire paragraph. When a tag formats a marked block, then it is applied only to the marked block within the paragraph. In this situation, it is called a *character style* or *character tag.* Any paragraph that has text formatted with a tag applied to a marked block has two tags used within the paragraph. The first is the tag for the paragraph (every paragraph has at least the **BODY TEXT** tag). The second is the tag for the marked block. Unlike other programs that use different commands for working with character styles, HyperWriter uses the same set of commands that are used for paragraph tags. As with paragraph tags, to find out what tag a marked block is using, place your cursor within the marked block and select the **Apply Tag** command from the **Format** menu. This shows the tag applied specifically to only the marked block if a different tag applies to the block rather than the paragraph. You will find that most of the commands used for paragraph tags function correctly with character styles with the exception of the Tag Justification and bullet related features.

Saving Our Work

With our tutorial finished, we are ready to save our work. However, as we really did very little in this last exercise, we don't need to.

Exiting HyperWriter

With our tutorial finished and our work saved, you can now exit HyperWriter if desired. This is done with the **Exit** command on the **File** menu.

Reference: Understanding Styles

From time to time I have been asked what is the best way for individuals to make documents easy to publish digitally. My answer always has been (and remains) simple and to the point: Use styles in your documents. Styles, also referred to as stylesheets or as tags, are one of the least understood and rarely used features in modern software.

As discussed earlier, a stylesheet lets you store multiple formatting commands as a name (the style) and then apply the formatting commands to the text by applying the name. For example, every heading in your document could use a **HEADING1** style, which had attributes of 24-point, bold Helvetica font. By storing these attributes as a style, new headings can be formatted by clicking on the text to format and then clicking on the style. Need to revise the appearance of a heading? Simply modify the style and all headings will be revised instantly. As discussed earlier, styles can even ease document maintenance by adding a powerful level of structure to your documents. When the different elements that make up your documents have styles applied to them (such as all first-level headings having a **HEADING1** style, all second-level styles having a **HEADING2** style, all lists using a **List** style and so on), not only does understanding the document's structure become easier, but also so do tasks such as formatting and maintenance. Another point, as you will see in Chapter 12 when we cover the Import Text Wizard, HyperWriter is able to do very powerful things with styles, including creating hypertext links automatically based on styles. One final reason to use styles is that publishing to the Internet's World Wide Web basically requires that you use styles as the World Wide Web is itself driven by styles (like HyperWriter, the Internet calls them tags).

Given the many overwhelming advantages of styles, why have I found it necessary to stress their use as I have? There is a very simple answer for this—most people don't use styles in their documents. While the reasons for this can definitely be debated, I attribute it to the long-dominant position that WordPerfect version 5.1 had in the word-processing market prior to the release of Microsoft Windows version 3.0. Put simply, WordPerfect 5.1 defined word processing for a huge number of users, and while WordPerfect 5.1 was a great product in a number of ways, with respect to styles, it was utterly abysmal. What I have found is that for a great many people, their first and last encounter with styles was using WordPerfect 5.1 (and they simply haven't ever tried again). With this said, I would strongly encourage you to consider using styles if you haven't been using them. Most modern Windows-based word processors make using styles easy. By spending a few minutes learning to use a very simple feature, not only can you decrease the time spent for digital publishing, but also the time required for your traditional publishing.

Given my position on using styles to format and structure your documents, is there a wrong way to use styles? While I would generally argue that using styles is better than not using styles, there is a way to use styles that is not a perfect approach—naming styles for the appearance that the style represent. Consider a style used to format a heading with attributes of 24-point, bold text that is left justified. When this style is named as described earlier in this section, it might have a name such as **HEADING1** (for a first-level heading). If this same style was named for its appearance then it might be named something like **LEFT 24 Bold**. Naming this style for its appearance, rather than its function in the document, leads to three problems. The first problem is that the style name doesn't reflect the function that it serves in structuring the document. This makes it harder for document authors maintaining the document to understand how it is structured. Similarly, it makes it harder for digital publishers to understand the document structure (and consequently produce digital publications). The final problem with appearance oriented naming is that when the names are appearance oriented, document authors tend to reuse the style to produce a particular appearance, rather than for its intended purpose (i.e., as a heading). Given that different document elements can often have the same appearance, this is a very common problem with this type of style naming.

Reference: Understanding Fonts for Digital Publishing

Conceptually, the idea of a *font* is quite simple. A font provides a typeface with a unique look and feel. Simple, right? Unfortunately, fonts for digital publishing are one of the single thorniest issues that currently plague digital publishing. One of the little-known aspects of fonts concerns their copyright. A font belongs to the person or organization that created it. As you may well have paid for one or more fonts in the past, this probably doesn't come as a big surprise. Now, consider what happens when you give a document created with a particular font to another person. If it isn't a digital publication, then the answer is simple—print out the document and hand it to the person. The font is on the paper and the person has the document. For paper documents, fonts are pure simplicity. However, if you want to give that person a digital publication, what do you do? You can't just give the person the disk that you got from the font supplier (not without removing the font from your system as well). And, as the font's copyright is owned by someone else, you can't (legally) make a copy of the font and supply it to the person.

The real problem here is that once a font is installed on a computer system, it becomes accessible not only for viewing documents, but also for creating them. Given that fonts are generally sold for document creation, it seems that if there were a way to lock out font use for document creation, but preserve it for document viewing, that would be the answer. As you may recall, we discussed TrueType embeddable fonts earlier in this chapter. Font embedding, a feature found in the TrueType font standard, allows TrueType fonts to be embedded within a particular document or stylesheet file (for HyperWriter, fonts are embedded in the .HWT stylesheet file used by the document). When documents with embedded fonts are moved between computers and displayed with HyperReader, the embedded fonts are first temporarily installed into the Windows system, used by the document as needed, and then removed when the application is terminated. This approach satisfies the legal nature of embedded fonts—that they can only be used for document display, not to create new documents.

NOTE: While the description of how embedded fonts function is correct and knowledge of this function is required to prevent embedded fonts from becoming part of the Windows system, it has an interesting side effect when your documents with embedded fonts are modified in HyperWriter on systems without these embedded fonts. In this situation, to prevent the embedded fonts from becoming part of the user's Windows system, the embedded fonts will be removed from the .HWT stylesheet file. As a general rule of thumb, embedding fonts should always be your last development step before distributing your documents to prevent this from occurring.

In closing, it should be noted that despite font embedding, fonts remain a thorny issue for digital publishing. TrueType font embedding is not a perfect tool for digital publishing, nor do all font suppliers support it, nor even are all TrueType fonts embeddable. However, it is currently the best approach to moving fonts transparently with your documents. With this stated, there is an alternative to moving fonts along with your documents. That alternative is simply to rely on the existing standard fonts that are supplied with Microsoft Windows. I don't claim that this is a perfect approach, but it is a recommended one. To make this approach work, however, you need to know exactly which fonts are shipped standard with Microsoft Windows. Those fonts are:

- Arial
- Courier
- Courier New
- Symbol
- Terminal
- Times New Roman
- WingDings

As a general rule of thumb, if you aren't trying for absolute perfection in the area of fonts, you can usually get by using the fonts listed. These fonts provide a basic range of characters in both serif and sans serif faces as well as two specialized fonts, Symbol and WingDings. Provided that you aren't trying for perfection, the one additional font that you might need is a scientific or mathematical one.

Making Links

Up to this point several of our tutorials have covered tasks that you may have done in other software, such as work with an editor, import documents, and format text. In this tutorial we will move to something that is probably new to you—creating hypertext links. Creating links in HyperWriter is extremely easy and very similar to using a word processor. Just as in a word processor where you mark blocks and then choose commands such as **Cut, Copy,** and **Paste,** in HyperWriter, you first mark a block and then choose commands such as **Link to Text, Link to Picture,** and **Link to Action.** This word-processor–like approach to linking makes learning how to link information in HyperWriter very easy.

Before you begin this tutorial, you should be familiar with the basic concepts used in Chapter 7 as this tutorial does rely on them. For those who might have skipped Chapter 7, a brief summary follows. Hypertext documents in HyperWriter are composed of one or more topics interconnected by hypertext links. As you may recall from our earlier definition, topics *contain* information while links *connect* information. All links have two components, the *anchor* or selectable region of text or a picture that activates the link, and the *link end*, the information contained at the destination of the link.

In HyperWriter, when you create a link a corresponding topic is created when necessary. For example, a link to a comment topic creates a new comment topic. However, a jump link to an existing topic doesn't create a new topic; instead, you are linking to an existing topic. This integration of link making with topic creation eliminates the requirement for separate commands for link creation and topic creation.

NOTE: Topics can also be created independently from links with the **Relationships** command on the **Topic** menu.

In this tutorial, we will start with a discussion of the different type of links and then proceed to creating the different links. As we create links, we will discuss the type of document structure that you are creating. After we have created the different links, we will continue with a more practical tutorial.

Understanding Links in HyperWriter

Hypertext links are typically viewed as connections between two pieces of information. When activated, a hypertext link lets you jump to the link's destination, viewing the contents at the destination. HyperWriter extends this basic hypertext concept with the concept of different *classes* of links. Some of HyperWriter's links don't really provide destinations at all—they are simply objects within a HyperWriter document that do something when they are selected. HyperWriter's different link types are organized into three basic types or classes of links:

- Link to text
- Link to picture
- Link to action

The distinguishing factor among the different classes of links is the type of information contained at that link destination (where the link takes you). A Link to text has a text destination. A Link to picture has a picture destination. A Link to action has an action to execute as its destination. In this sense, a link to an action has a *virtual* destination.

Along with each class of link are several subclasses of links. These subclasses change how the destination of the link is displayed onscreen. HyperWriter's full-link hierarchy is shown in Table 12.1.

The table summarizes HyperWriter's various classes and subclasses of links. Discussed below are several aspects of using the different link types.

The first link-to-text class, Jump Link, physically jumps you from one point in the document to a new point, either in the current document or in another document. Jump Links have two major purposes. First, they form the basic structure of a hypertext document. Generally, almost every document that you will create with HyperWriter will have Jump Links at its core. Second, Jump Links are useful for cross-referencing information, allowing almost instant access to any piece of information in any document.

The Comment Link displays a popup topic containing text or imported pictures. This topic can be named, sized, or positioned as desired. Comment

Table 12.1 Types of Links in HyperWriter

Type of Link	Description
Link to Text	Create a link to text material.
Jump Link	Create a link for cross-referencing.
New Topic	Create a cross-referencing link for you to enter new information into.
Existing Topic	Create a cross-referencing link to an already existing topic. When creating this link, the document cannot be edited.
Another Document	Create a cross-referencing link to another document file stored on disc. When creating this link, the document cannot be edited.
Comment Link	Create a link that displays a popup topic overlapping the current topic.
ASCII File	Create a cross-referencing link to an ASCII file on disc. The ASCII file cannot be edited, although it can be browsed.
Link to Picture	Create a link to a picture. Links to pictures are displayed either in popup topics or in full screen topics depending on how the Picture Wizard is used.
Link to Action	Create a link to an action.
DOS Link	Create a link that activates external DOS programs.
Menu–Action	Create a link that activates one of HyperWriter's internal menu functions.
Action List	Create a link that activates an action list.
Link to Next/Previous	Create a link to the next or previous topic.
Next Topic	Create a cross-referencing link to the next topic. This is a relative link whose value changes if a different next topic is created.
Previous Topic	Create a cross-referencing link to the previous topic. This is a relative link whose value changes if a new previous topic is created.
Link with Replacement Text	Create an expansion, or outlining style text link.

Links are typically used for clarifying existing material through popup definitions or also lists. Comment Links are also useful for building user interface structures, such as dialog boxes.

ASCII file links are useful for creating links that display external ASCII files. They let external applications update a hypertext document. By using ASCII file links, the task of the hypertext author is easier because the document does not need to be updated as frequently—instead, the external ASCII files are updated.

The Link with Replacement Text class adds an outlining element to HyperWriter that allows for text expansion of either words or even whole linked hierarchies of information. This allows you to select on a link with replacement text titled "Chapter 1" and then have each subsection of Chapter 1 appear with an associated link.

The Link to Picture class displays pictures. The accepted picture formats are .PCX, .JPG, .TIF, .EPS, .WMF, and .BMP. Pictures can be displayed in either a full screen or an overlapping window as desired by the author of the hypertext.

The Link to Action class creates links that have actions to execute as their destination. DOS links create a link that executes a DOS application (there is a similar Run Program Action as part of the Action List link for running MS-Windows programs). Menu action links create links that activate functions on HyperWriter's menus. These links are generally used to build control buttons for your documents, such as buttons. Action List links activate HyperWriter action lists that contain actions such as branching and multimedia.

Creating Links: Overview

All links are created in the same fashion, no matter what type of link is being created or whether the link anchor is from text or from a picture. To create a link, first mark the link anchor as a block. The link anchor is the piece of text or graphics that you will select to activate the link. If the anchor is text, this is done with the block marking command, **Shift+Arrowkey** or with the **Left Mouse** button. The link anchor can be as large as you like—a character, a word, a paragraph, or more. For most purposes, a word or phrase is sufficient. If the link anchor is on a picture, this is done with the **Mark Region** command located on the **Link** menu. If your link anchor is part of a picture, then any rectangular area of the picture can be your link anchor. When using the **Mark Region** command either the **Arrowkeys** or the **Left Mouse** button can be used to expand the area to link.

Next, you must tell HyperWriter that you wish to create a link by selecting one of the five linking commands from the **Link** menu. These commands are:

- **Link to Text**
- **Link to Picture**

- **Link to Action**
- **Link to Next/Previous**
- **With Replacement Text**

After selecting the main linking command from the **Link** menu, a submenu appears to choose the subclass of link you want to create. Additional submenus are then displayed as necessary until the link is created. HyperWriter creates a topic (if needed) for you to either enter the destination of the link or select a destination to cross-reference. After entering the body of information composing the link end, choose the **Complete Link** command from the **Link** menu. HyperWriter returns you to the link anchor. The link is now completed and can be viewed by activating it with **F1**.

Creating Links—Summary

1. Mark the link anchor as a block. If marking a region of a graphic, use the **Mark Region** command.
2. Select a **Link...** or the **With Replacement Text** command from the **Link** menu.
3. Enter the destination for the link and choose **Complete Link** from the **Link** menu. This returns you to the anchor of the link.

Having covered the necessary background on HyperWriter's linking facilities, we are ready to begin our tutorial. The first task is, of course, to run HyperWriter. HyperWriter is a standard MS-Windows application that can be run from the Program Manager.

Creating Links to Text and Understanding Hypertext Structure

When creating applications with HyperWriter, one of the most important things always to keep in mind is that what you are actually doing with Hyper-Writer is creating hypertext structures. What we will do in the rest of this section is illustrate how hypertext links and topics create hypertext structure. To make these hypertext structures more apparent, we will illustrate the structures as we create them. In addition to learning about hypertext structures, this will also teach us how to make links.

NOTE: For reference, as we discussed earlier in this chapter, the distinction between links and topics is that links connect information and topics connect information.

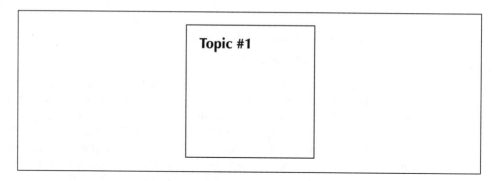

Figure 12.1 The hypertext structure with only one topic.

Our first step is to create a new document. We can do this with the **New** command on the **File** menu.

Creating a New Document

1. Select the **New** command on the **File** menu. This displays the **Template Wizard** dialog box. The Template Wizard creates an initial document structure and user interface. We don't want to use this, as all we want to do is create a blank document.

2. What we need to do is turn off the Template Wizard using the **Use New Template Wizard** option. Select this option so that no "x" is shown for this option.

3. Select the **OK** button to create our new document.

In creating our new document, what we have created is a document consisting of only one hypertext topic. All HyperWriter documents have at least one topic, topic number 1. A picture of the hypertext structure we have now is shown in Figure 12.1.

As you can see, the structure we have is very simple—only a single topic. What we are going to do now is add one link and one topic. The command that we'll use for this is the **Link to Text** command, used for creating the structure of a document. Specifically, we'll use the **New Topic** option which creates a new topic when it is used.

Creating a Link and Topic

1. Type in the text "**This is link number 1 to a new topic (number 2).**"

2. Mark this text as a block.

3. Select the **Link to Text** command from the **Link** menu.

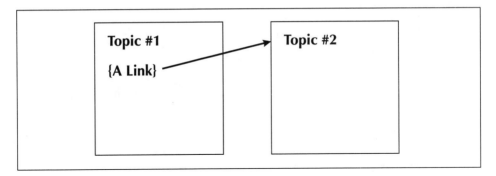

Figure 12.2 The hypertext structure with one link and two topics.

4. Select the **Jump Link** option.

5. Select the **New Topic** option. This creates a new topic and places you in it.

6. Type in the text "**This is the destination of link number 1.**" Press **Enter** twice and enter the text "**Another link will access this text.**"

7. Select the **Complete Link** command from the **Link** menu. This completes our link and returns us to the link we created.

In using the **Link to Text** command, we selected **Jump Link** and then **New Topic**. The **Link to Text** command creates the basic structure of a document and creates topics as are needed. The structure that we have created is shown in Figure 12.2.

As you can see, we now have two topics connected by a single link. What we'll do now is create another link to illustrate how links to existing topics work. When you create a link to an existing topic, what you are creating is a cross-reference to information that already exists.

Creating a Link to an Existing Topic

1. Press **End** to move to the end of the current line. Press **Enter** twice to add two blank lines.

2. Type in the text "**This is a link to an existing topic.**"

3. Mark this text as a block.

4. Select the **Link to Text** command from the **Link** menu.

5. Select the **Jump Link** option.

6. Select the **Existing Topic** option.

   This places link markers around the link and puts you into what is called *Point Mode*. In Point Mode, you navigate to the destination of a

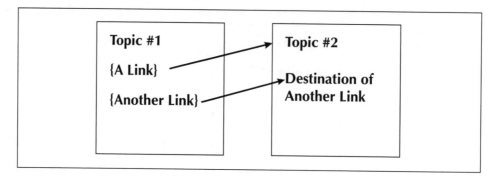

Figure 12.3 The hypertext structure with two links and two topics.

link (i.e., pointing to it), mark it as a block, and then use the **Complete Link** command to complete the link. When you enter Point Mode, HyperWriter tells you this with a dialog box. When you are in Point Mode, you cannot edit text or changes topics—you can only point to the destination of a link.

7. Select the **OK** button to close the dialog box telling you about Point Mode.
8. Activate the first link we created.
9. Mark the second paragraph of text as a block (the one that discusses a destination).
10. Select the **Complete Link** command from the **Link** menu. Because you have a block marked when you select Complete Link, HyperWriter will ask you if you want to make a *bidirectional link*—a link that can be accessed from either end. Select No and you will be returned to the link you created.

What we have done is created an additional link without creating a new topic. A picture of our hypertext structure is shown in Figure 12.3.

As you can see, our hypertext structure has grown more complex with the addition of another link. Our next exercise is to add an additional link and topic to see how this affects our application.

Creating Another Link and Topic

1. Type in the text "**This is link number 3 to a new topic (number 3).**"
2. Mark this text as a block.
3. Select the **Link to Text** command from the **Link** menu.
4. Select the **Jump Link** option.

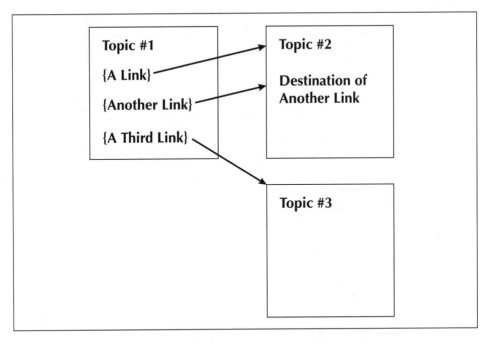

Figure 12.4 The hypertext structure with three links and three topics.

5. Select the **New Topic** option. This creates a new topic and places you in it.

6. Type in the text "**This is the destination of link number 3.**"

7. Select the **Complete Link** command from the **Link** menu. This completes our link and returns us to the link we created.

In using this command, we created a link from topic number one to a new topic. Our structure now appears as shown in Figure 12.4.

As you can see, this has created yet another topic and a link to interconnect it. This is the fundamental nature of working HyperWriter—what you are really doing is creating links and topics. As you add a link, you add a connection between topics, whereas when you add a topic, you add an additional information container to your application.

While our short tutorial we just worked through illustrated hypertext structure and how to use HyperWriter's linking commands, it was abstract and didn't offer a practical example. Let's think of this now in practical terms. You start HyperWriter and create a new document. You have a blank document with only one topic. Rather than create text from scratch, you decide to import a document. Using the **Import Text** command, you bring in a document. As this document is lengthy, you decide to break it into topics. The way to do this is to use the **Cut** command to cut the sections of text for each topic to the clipboard and then create a link to a new topic where the text can be pasted in. With this example, it is much easier to see how the hypertext structure affects our application.

Now that we have looked at one practical example, let's consider another. You create a new document for your HyperWriter application. You know that for this application you want to have an attractive cover screen—the first thing the user sees. This cover screen is to have a link to a table of contents. When you think about how to do this, a simple answer emerges. The way to do this is create a simple link to a new topic. This leaves topic number 1 as the topic for the cover screen and gives a link that the user can activate to go to the table of contents (which would go in the new topic we created).

This completes our first exercise on links to text. We should save our work so we can review it later if needed.

Saving Our Work

Select the **Save** command from the **File** menu. Enter the name "LINK01.HW4" and select the **OK** button.

Creating Hypertext Links: A Simple Tutorial

Now that we have a basic understanding of creating hypertext links and topics, we are ready to move onto a more advanced tutorial. In this tutorial, we will work on a simple digital publishing task—converting a chapter from a manual into hypertext form and then cross-linking it to a table of contents. Unlike our first tutorial on linking where we worked only in one document, in this tutorial we will work in two documents. The source files that we have are two WordPerfect files, one containing a table of contents and the other containing the text of Chapter 4 of our manual. Each of the WordPerfect files listed will be imported into HyperWriter to create a HyperWriter document that corresponds to the original WordPerfect file. For example, MAN_TOC.WP becomes MAN_TOC.HW4 and CHAPTER4.WP becomes CHAPTER4. This idea of a one-to-one correspondence between your source document and your HyperWriter documents can be a useful technique for authoring HyperWriter versions of print documents.

Basic Steps: Importing Text

Before we can start to create our links, we need to first create our HyperWriter documents and import our source files. The way we'll do this is by opening a template document, importing our text files, and then saving our template document to a new file. Although HyperWriter has a Template Wizard function which automatically creates template documents, any HyperWriter document can be a template. Before importing text, we need to open our template document.

Opening the Template Document

1. Select the **Open** command from the **File** menu.
2. Choose the file TEMPLATE from the **File** dialog box. This displays the template document.

Once our template document is opened, we can continue by importing the MAN_TOC.WP file into the template.

Importing the MAN_TOC.WP File

1. Select the **Import Text** command from the **File** menu.
2. Select WordPerfect as the format to import.
3. A list of all WordPerfect files is displayed. Select the file MAN_TOC.WP from the **File** dialog box.

When you import the MAN_TOC.WP file the template document should appear as shown in Figure 12.5.

Once the MAN_TOC.WP file has been imported, we need to save our document. We can't yet link the table of contents entries because the other documents haven't been created. To save our file we will use the **Save As** command from the **File** menu.

Saving our Document

1. Select the **Save As** command from the **File** menu.
2. Type the name MAN_TOC and select the **OK** button to save the document.

NOTE: If you try to save the template document to its original filename, you will find that you can't, because the **Allow Saving to Same Filename** document property has been turned off. This option prevents you from accidentally overwriting your template document.

With the table of contents document created we will now import the CHAPTER4.WP file. This requires opening the template document again and using the **Import Text** command again. The steps to do this are outlined here.

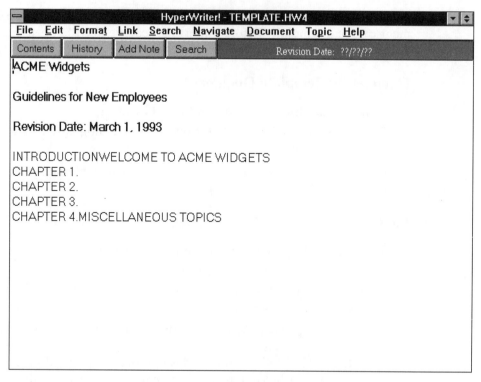

Figure 12.5 The template document with MAN_TOC.WP.

Opening the Template Document

1. Select the **Open** command from the **File** menu.
2. Choose the file TEMPLATE from the **File** dialog box. This displays the template document onscreen as shown earlier.

Importing the CHAPTER4.WP

1. Select the **Import Text** command from the **File** menu.
2. Select WordPerfect as the format to import.
3. A list of all WordPerfect files is displayed. Select the file CHAPTER4.WP from the **File** dialog box.

After you have imported CHAPTER4.WP your screen should appear as shown in Figure 12.6.

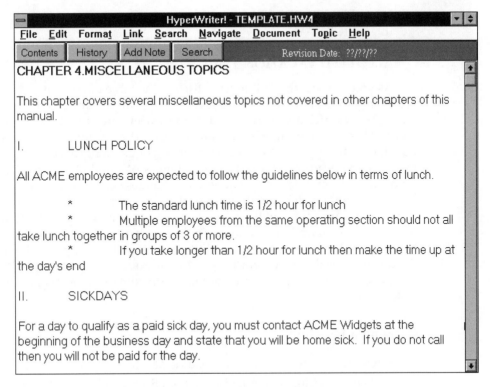

Figure 12.6 The template document with CHAPTER4.WP.

Saving our Document

1. Select the **Save As** command from the **File** menu.
2. Type the name CHAPTER4 and select the **OK** button to save the document.

We have now created both MAN_TOC and CHAPTER4. If our tutorial covered the additional chapter files, then we would import those files at this time. In the next section of this tutorial we will link the text of CHAPTER4 and MAN_TOC.

Creating Links

With the text imported and formatted, we are ready to begin building hypertext links. Like many hypertext documents, this one will be structured around a table of contents metaphor. For example, the first few entries in the table of contents for Chapter 4 would be as follows:

I.   LUNCH POLICY
II.   SICKDAYS
III.   VACATION DAYS
ALLOTTED VACATION TIME

As you can see, the first-level entries in the table of contents all begin with roman numerals and the second-level entries are all uppercase and in bold-face. These entries also correspond to the various heading levels in the document. This is a common situation in most documents. When converting documents from paper to electronic form, we generally recommend creating links and topics that follow the document's original structure. This makes revising the electronic document when it changes significantly easier.

To handle this document, we will place an entire first-level section and its subsections into a topic of their own. The way to begin is by creating an outline of these sections and subsections. To do this, we will first copy the different headings in the document to the clipboard. We will next paste them into the document after the document title and its introductory paragraph. Place your cursor on the first paragraph beginning with roman numerals and follow the instructions.

Copying a Heading

1. Use the mouse to mark the heading as a block.
2. Select the **Copy** command from the **Edit** menu.

After copying the heading, a copy of it is in the clipboard, where it can be pasted into the document. However, if we build our document by copying a heading, returning to the top of the document, pasting it in, and then going and finding the next heading and repeating this whole process, it will take some time. To address this, we can use the **Append w/ Copy** feature. **Append w/ Copy** copies a marked block and *appends* it to the end of the clipboard. This allows us to page through our document and gather all the headings and subheadings into the clipboard and then paste them in only once. Page down through the document until you find the next heading (all uppercase text beginning with a roman numeral) or subheading (all uppercase text in bold-face) and then use **Append w/ Copy** (as shown) to add that into the clipboard.

Appending a Heading/Subheading to the Clipboard

1. Mark the heading or subheading as a block.
2. Select the **Append w/ Copy** command from the **Edit** menu.

After you select **Append w/ Copy** to copy a heading or subheading to the clipboard, you can use the **View Clipboard** command to examine what is in the clipboard. Continue paging down through the document to copy all headings and subheadings to the clipboard. When you reach the end of the document, press **Ctrl+Home** or use the scroll bar to return to its beginning. Position your cursor after the introductory paragraph that follows the title of the document. Now you are ready to paste the headings and subheadings into the document to create links from them.

Pasting Text

1. Position the cursor after the introductory paragraph that follows the title of the document.
2. Select the **Paste** command from the **Edit** menu.

After the headings and subheadings have been pasted in, your screen should appear as shown in Figure 12.7.

With the headings and subheadings pasted in, we now have a table of contents to use as the anchors for the links we will create. Links have two compo-

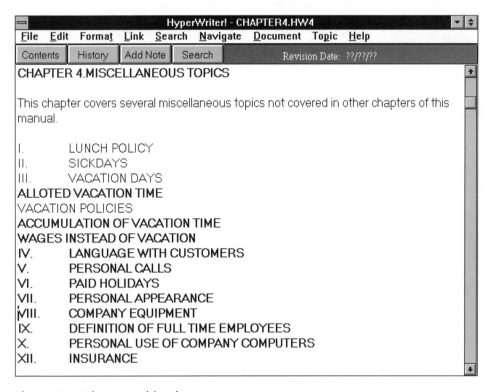

Figure 12.7 The new table of contents.

nents—the link anchor and the link end. The link anchor is the text surrounded by link symbols. The link end is the destination of the link. Link ends can either be an entire topic of information or a specific point within a topic. With the link anchors established, we need to begin creating links. The first step in creating the links is to cut all of the information associated with a first-level heading to the clipboard. This means marking a block from the beginning of the heading preceded by a roman numeral to the next heading with a roman numeral. Note that we want only one of the roman numeral headings and all its associated text in the clipboard at a time. Information in the clipboard will be pasted into a topic of its own. By moving this information into a single topic, the reader can pick or choose the topics that he or she wants to read without having to read or page through all topics in the document.

Cutting Text to the Clipboard

1. Press **Shift+Arrowkey** to mark text from the beginning of the heading to the next heading.
2. Select the **Cut** command from the **Edit** menu.

With the text of an entire section in the clipboard, we now need to set an option before making our link and topic. This option is the **Default Backgrounds** option. By setting this to the backgrounds that we want assigned for our topic, we don't have to do this later.

Setting Authoring Options

1. Select the **Preferences** command from the **File** menu.
2. Select the **Authoring** folder of options.
3. Enter a "**1**" into the **First Background** field of the **Default Backgrounds** group of options.
4. Enter a "**2**" into the **Second Background** field.
5. If the **Link Anchor as Topic Name** option isn't turned on then turn this option on now.
6. Select the **OK** button to close the dialog box.

Place your cursor on the first roman numeral heading that we pasted into the document earlier. This should be approximately the third paragraph in the document (not counting blank lines). We can now create the link from this paragraph to the text that is currently in the clipboard. The type of link that we will create is a Jump Link to a New Topic. Building this type of link creates a new topic for us to enter or paste information into.

Creating a Link

1. Press **Shift+End** to mark the heading as a block.

2. Select the **Link to Text** command from the **Link** menu.

3. Select the **Jump Link** option. Select the **New Topic** option. A new topic, complete with the screen backgrounds you specified as defaults, is created.

4. Select the **Paste** command from the **Edit** menu. This inserts the text for the first heading into your new topic.

5. Select the **Complete Link** command from the **Link** menu to complete the link. This returns you to the link you just created.

After building the link, you need to create the remaining links from the other headings that begin with roman numerals. To do this, repeat the process you just finished: cut the text of the entire section to the clipboard, mark the anchor, and create the link. After you have finished, the screen should appear as shown in Figure 12.8.

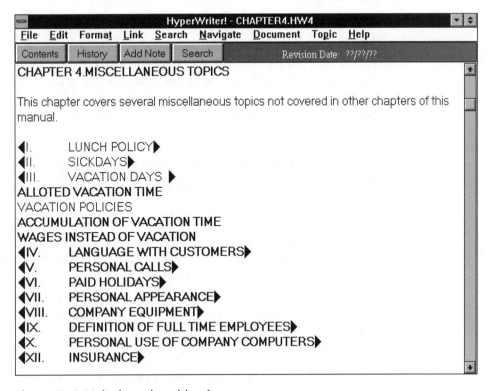

Figure 12.8 Links from the table of contents.

As you can see, we have not linked the subheadings in the table of contents—only the major, first-level headings. The links from the subheadings to their link end will be as links to existing topics. We chose not to put the subheadings and their associated text into a topic of their own because there isn't very much text with each subheading. In addition, this would force people into too much navigation. There are two guidelines to use when deciding how much information to put in a topic. The first is the amount of the information in the topic. Placing too much information in a topic forces the reader through unnecessary scrolling, while placing too little information in a topic forces the reader through unnecessary navigation. This brings us to the second guideline—put the amount of information in a topic that the reader wants to retrieve. By looking at how a reader uses a document, electronic or paper, you understand how it is read and, thus, where the topics should be created.

To begin creating the links from the subheadings to their destination, place your cursor at the first subheading's beginning in the table of contents. The link we will be creating now is a Jump Link to an existing topic.

Creating a Link to an Existing Topic

1. Mark the subheading as a block.
2. Select the **Link to Text** command from the **Link** menu.
3. Select the **Jump Link** option. Select the **Existing Topic** option. This places you in Point Mode—a mode in which you point to the destination of a link, mark it as a block, and select **Complete Link** from the **Link** menu. Select the **OK** button when HyperWriter tells you that you are in Point Mode, so you can begin making your link.
4. Activate the link surrounding the heading directly above your position. This brings you to the topic where the subheading appears.
5. **Page Down** or use the **Find** command to locate the subheading we want to link to.
6. Mark the subheading as a block with **Shift+Arrowkey**.
7. Select the **Complete Link** command from the **Link** menu to complete the link. A dialog box asks if you want to leave a bidirectional link symbol. Select No. This returns you to the link you just created.

After creating the initial subheading link, create links from the subheadings remaining in the table of contents to their respective topic. Once these links are complete, the first topic in your document should contain only the title of the document, an introductory paragraph, and a linked table of contents.

The links we have created to this point can be described as *structural*—they define the structure of the document. Besides structural links, there are also *cross-referencing* links—links that connect related topics or related information within topics. Although the structural links make your hypertext possible, the cross-referencing links make your hypertext valuable. These links are the added content that a hypertext author brings to the application. Cross-referencing links can be indicated in your printed document several ways. First, *See* or *See Also* references are clear indicators of cross references. Second, relationships that you become aware of can be translated into cross references. Third, indicators such as the name of a heading, subheading, or document often indicate possible links. For example, the sentence "Information on employee education is contained in Chapter 3," clearly indicates that this is a link to Chapter 3.

To create a cross-referencing link, you need to navigate to the anchor of the link, mark it as a block, and create a link to an existing topic, as we did previously. One sample cross-referencing link appears at the end of the topic "VIII. COMPANY EQUIPMENT." This is a *See Also* reference that should be linked to the topic "X. PERSONAL USE OF COMPANY COMPUTERS." Activate the link to the "VIII. COMPANY EQUIPMENT" topic. Press **Ctrl+End** or use the scroll bar to move to the end of the topic. Now you can create the cross-referencing link.

Creating a Link to an Existing Topic

1. Mark the entire *See Also* reference as a block.
2. Select the **Link to Text** command from the **Link** menu.
3. Select the **Jump Link** option. Select the **Existing Topic** option. This places you in Point Mode.
4. Press **Esc** to backtrack to the first topic with the table of contents.
5. Activate the link "**X. PERSONAL USE OF COMPANY COMPUTERS.**" This places you in the topic you want to link it to.
6. Mark the heading of the topic as a block.
7. Select the **Complete Link** command from the **Link** menu to complete the link. A dialog box asks if you want to leave a bidirectional link symbol. Select Yes. This returns you to the link you just created.

Since we wanted to reference a specific point within the topic, we left a bidirectional link symbol at the second *See Also* reference. An important point is that bidirectional link symbols are generally used only for point-to-point references within the body of a topic. If you are referencing the beginning of a topic, then you probably don't want a bidirectional link symbol. As this link is from one *See Also* reference to another, then leaving a bidirectional symbol is a good idea. With a bidirectional symbol at the other end of the link, we don't have to link both ends of the topics—a single link will suffice.

Although there are other possible cross-references both between and within topics, these are left as student exercises. All links in HyperWriter are made in the same fashion we have already used. First mark the anchor of the link, select a **Link to...** command from the **Link** menu and then select the **Complete Link** command from the **Link** menu. In the next section, we will build a link from the main table of contents document, MAN_TOC, to the CHAPTER4 file we finished in this chapter.

Linking the Contents File

As you can recall from the earlier description of our application, multiple HyperWriter document files compose the application. Although we have built the individual files, they are currently discrete or separate from one another. At this time, a reader could not begin with MAN_TOC and then follow links into CHAPTER4. Instead the reader would have to manually use the **Open** command and select CHAPTER4 from the dialog box. To integrate the two documents, we need to open MAN_TOC and make a link from it to CHAPTER4.

Opening MAN_TOC

1. Select the **Open** command from the **File** menu.

2. Choose the file MAN_TOC from the **File** dialog box. You will be asked to save your changes. Answer Yes. If you are asked to leave a bookmark, select No. This displays the table of contents document that we created earlier.

3. Place your cursor on the Chapter 4 entry in the table of contents. We can now build a link from this to the Chapter 4 document. This is a link to another HyperWriter document.

Creating a Link to Another Document

1. Mark the Chapter 4 entry as a block.

2. Select the **Link to Text** command from the **Link** menu.

3. Select the **Jump Link** option. Select the **Another Document** option. This places you in Point Mode.

4. Select the file CHAPTER4 from the dialog box.

5. Mark the first line of the topic as a block.

6. Select the **Complete Link** command from the **Link** menu to complete the link. A dialog box asks if you want to leave a bidirectional link symbol. Select No. This returns you to the link you just created.

We have now built a link from the table of contents to Chapter 4. A reader can begin with the table of contents and then follow links from there into Chapter 4. This process of building a link to another document would be used if Chapter 4 needed to reference Chapter 2, or to complete the other links from the main table of contents to their respective files.

This concludes our tutorial on creating links to text. As you have learned both in the first tutorial and in this tutorial, links to text really create the structure of a HyperWriter application. Creating the links that establish the structure of an application can really be a mechanical, tedious process. To make this easier, HyperWriter includes a powerful automated linking tool, the Import Text Wizard, which automatically places text into topics and creates links as it imports documents. The Import Text Wizard is covered later in this chapter.

Creating Links to Pictures

Creating links to pictures lets you create links in your HyperWriter documents that display pictures when they are activated. In this exercise we will create a simple link to a picture. Links to pictures are further covered in Chapter 13.

We need to start by opening the document LINK02.HW4.

Opening a Document in HyperWriter

1. Select the **Open** command from the **File** menu.

2. Select the document LINK02.HW4 from the list of available documents. If you are asked to leave a bookmark, answer No. This loads the document.

As with our starting document for creating links to text, this document has a button bar across the top and a piece of text to link to a picture. The picture file that we want to link to is NTSITE.PCX, and we want this picture linked to so that it comes up a popup window.

Linking to a Picture

1. Select the text Link to a Picture and mark it as a block.

2. Select the **Link to Picture** command from the **Link** menu.

3. Select .PCX as the format to link to.

4. Select the picture file NTSITE.PCX. This displays the Picture Linking Wizard shown in Figure 12.9.

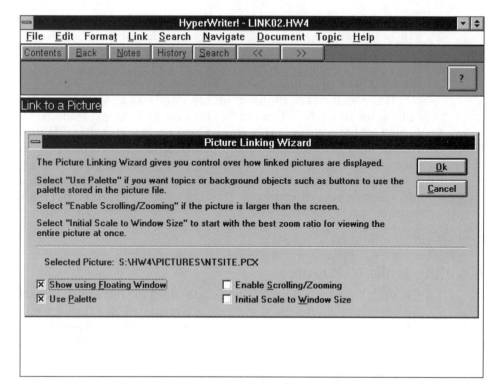

Figure 12.9 The Picture Linking Wizard.

The Picture Linking Wizard lets you set how a picture is displayed when it is linked to. Options include using a floating window (if you don't select this, then it comes up in a full-screen topic, like a Jump Link), using the palette from the image, turning on scrolling and zooming, and initially scaling the picture to the window size. For our purposes, just leaving the default options turned on, **Show Using Floating Window** and **Use Palette**, is sufficient.

5. Select the **OK** button to complete the link. What you will see is the picture file displayed onscreen in a window as shown below in Figure 12.10.

This concludes our exercise on linking to a picture. As noted at the beginning of this exercise, linking to pictures is covered in greater depth in Chapter 13. Before we move onto our next exercise, we should save our work.

Saving Our Work

Select the **Save** command from the **File** menu.

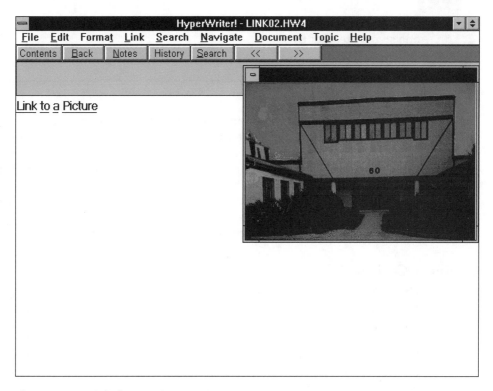

Figure 12.10 A link to a picture.

Reference: Links to Text versus Links to Pictures

Now that you understand linking to text and linking to pictures, you may be wondering if there really is a difference between links to text and links to pictures. Although we haven't illustrated it in a tutorial yet, HyperWriter can import pictures. Given that HyperWriter can import pictures and create links to text topics, couldn't a link to text actually display a picture? The answer, of course, is yes. Creating a link to text, either a new topic or a comment topic, and then importing a picture into the topic would create the same effect as a link to a picture. There are two primary differences between this approach and using the **Link to Picture** command. The first is that when HyperWriter links to a picture, it does so in such a way that allows background screens (the user interface component of HyperWriter documents) to be displayed over the picture, whereas in a normal imported picture, the picture is imported over the background. If your pictures will be displayed with backgrounds at all, this is a serious advantage. The second benefit of using the **Link to Picture** command is simple—it is just easier. Using the **Link to Picture** command requires only one step instead of two.

Creating Links to Actions

HyperWriter's Link to Action facilities let you create dynamic actions that can run other applications, execute functions from HyperWriter's menus and execute other types of actions—HyperWriter's powerful action list tool. In this tutorial, we will start with simple DOS links and continue through to the more powerful action list links. When creating digital publications, action links (specifically DOS links and action list links) provide a method for executing tasks outside the digital publishing environment. While for some digital publishing tasks this isn't necessary at all, for others it is crucial.

Creating DOS Links

HyperWriter's DOS link creates links that execute standard DOS programs, not Windows programs. If you are reading this book and using this software, then you are most probably using Microsoft Windows (you might also be using OS/2). Why then would you want to run DOS programs from HyperWriter? Well, even today, not all software is available for Windows. DOS links let you tie older or legacy applications into your digital publishing applications. One example might be an external communications package that allowed the reader of your publication to retrieve information from within your digital publication.

We need to start by opening the document LINK03.HW4.

Opening a Document in HyperWriter

1. Select the **Open** command from the **File** menu.
2. Select the document LINK03.HW4 from the list of available documents. If you are asked to leave a bookmark, answer No. This loads the document.

As with our starting document for creating links to text, this document has a button bar across the top and text to link to various actions. The text that we want to link starts Link to DOS Link.

Linking to a DOS Link

1. Select the text Link to DOS Link and mark it as a block.
2. Select the **Link to Action** command from the **Link** menu.

3. Select the **DOS Link** option. This displays HyperWriter's **DOS Link** dialog box shown in Figure 12.11.

   The DOS Link dialog box lets you enter the DOS commands for HyperWriter to execute. As we don't have a specific external program to run, we will have HyperWriter run a directory (**DIR**) command. The **@RESTART** command shown in the dialog box above must always be left in the DOS link, as this is what allows HyperWriter to return from the DOS link.

4. Add the link DIR on the line before the **@RESTART**. As the **@RESTART** will be selected when you start typing, press **Rightarrow** first to prevent wiping out this text.

5. Add the line PAUSE on the line after the **DIR** command.

6. Select the **OK** button to close the **DOS Link** dialog box. You will see that link symbols have been added to the link.

Unlike all other links in HyperWriter, DOS links do not activate immediately when they are selected. DOS links instead display the **DOS Link** dialog

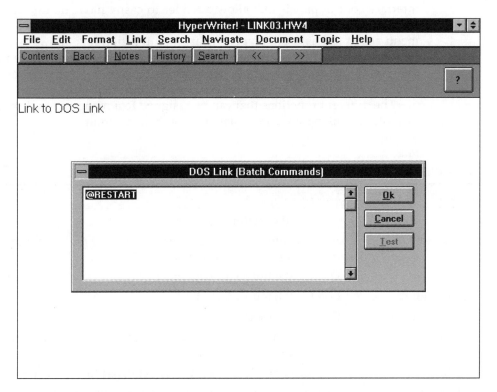

Figure 12.11 The **DOS Link** dialog box.

box so that they can be edited. To activate a DOS link once the dialog box is displayed, select the **Test** button. If you do this now then you will see your computer start a DOS session under Windows and then do a directory. At the end of the directory, it will pause, wait for you to press a key and then return to Windows.

This concludes our discussion of DOS links. We really don't want to spend too much time on DOS links, as the action list link that we cover below provides more powerful facilities, with the ability to run Windows programs instead of DOS programs.

Before we move onto our next exercise, we should save our work.

Saving Our Work

Select the **Save** command from the **File** menu.

Creating Menu Action Links

As you may recall from Chapter 7, in HyperWriter user interface buttons are actually links. These buttons, generally called *background screens*, provide user interface control panels that allow a reader to easily navigate through a document. To provide the functionality needed by these buttons, HyperWriter's menu action link is used. HyperWriter's menu action link allows any function found on HyperWriter's menu system to be assigned to a link (and consequently a button). For example, a button that linked to HyperWriter's search function would allow an application to search information.

The different functions that can be assigned to a menu action link are listed in Table 12.2, along with an explanation of their function.

Table 12.2 Menu Action Links in HyperWriter

Menu Action Link	Description
History	Activate the **History** command.
Add/Read Notes	Add a reader's note to the current topic. If the topic already has a reader's note then it displays the note.
Find	Display the **indexed search** dialog box.
Guided Tours	Display the **tours** dialog box.
Show Topic Name	Display the topic name.
Run Tour	Run a specific tour. When being created, it asks the author for the number of the tour to run.
Tag Topic	Tag current topic for use with the collapse to tag function.
Collapse to Tag	Activate the local collapse function to return the reader to either his or her last tagged topic or the first topic in the current document.

Menu Action Link	*Description*
Export Text	Export the current text to a file. It asks the reader for the filename.
Print	Print the contents of the current topic to the printer.
Search Text	Activate the in-memory text-search function of HyperWriter.
Collapse to Home	Return to the first topic in which you began the reading session.
Local Map	Display your current link map.
Log-in User	Log in the current author or reader. This can also be done with a document property.
Help/Contents	Activate the contents topic of HyperWriter's or HyperReader's internal help system.
Return from Link	Return from the last link activated; functions exactly like backtracking from a link.
TSR Wait State	Activate the TSR Wait State to run TSR software. Useful for compatibility with HyperWriter for DOS.
Page Setup (Printing)	Display the **Printer Options** dialog box (reserved). Kept for compatibility with older versions.
Page Up	Scroll the screen up as would the **Page Up** key.
Page Down	Scroll the screen down as would the **Page Down** key.
Edit Text File	Call up HyperWriter's editor for use to edit ASCII text files. When creating the link, a filename can either be specified for the editor always to edit or the editor can ask the reader for the name of the file to edit when it starts.
Exit	Exit HyperWriter and gives the typical bookmark prompt in the process if this is turned on (reserved). For compatibility with older versions.
Add Named Bookmark	Add a named bookmark to the current topic. It prompts the reader for the name of the bookmark (reserved). For compatibility with older versions.
View Saved Searches	Display all saved searches for you to create a link to a specific search. If you want to link to the **Saved Searches** dialog box then press **Esc** when this dialog box is displayed.
Redo Topic Action List	Reactivate the Actions List for the current topic. This allows you to replay audio, video, or other properties of the current topic.
Goto 1st Alternate Topic	Take you to the first alternate topic from the current topic.
Goto 2nd Alternate Topic	Take you to the second alternate topic from the current topic.

(continues)

Table 12.2 *(Continued)*

Menu Action Link	Description
Goto xth Alternate Topic	Take you to a specified alternate topic from the current topic. When creating the link, it asks you for the number of the alternate topic to use.
Goto Next Tour Point	Take you to the next point in the tour.
Set Tour Point (Query User)	Add the current topic to the tour presently being created.
Save Tour	End the tour and save it to disc.
Return from Tour	Abort tour and return to where the tour began.
Goto Next Note	Take you to the next reader's note.
Run Tour Without Prompts	Specify a tour number to run that uses the above Menu Action links for going between destinations. The tour is run without the usual tour prompt appearing.
Related Topics	Display the related topics for the current topic.
Next/Prev Database Search	Search for the next or previous database record to meet the search criteria.
Next/Prev Database Record	Search for the next or previous database record.
Stop Redbook Audio	Stop audio being played from a compact disc.
Jump to Tag	Jump to the previous tagged topic.
Jump to Home	Jump to the home topic (the first topic in the first document that you began reading).
Collapse to Previous TOC Topic	Collapse back to the previous TOC topic.
Jump to Previous TOC Topic	Jump to the last TOC topic.
Next Occurrence	Go to the next search hit.
Previous Occurrence	Go to the previous search hit.
Occurrences	Display the **Search Occurrences** dialog box.
Bookmarks	Display the HyperWriter **Bookmarks** dialog box.
Goto Named Bookmark	Link to a named bookmark. You will be prompted for the name of the bookmark to go to.
Document Abstract	Link to HyperWriter's **Abstract** dialog box which displays a summary of a document.

Menu Action Link	Description
Next Highlight	Go to the next highlight for a search query.
Toggle Highlighting	Turn on or off highlighting of all search terms found by the search engine.
Ctrl Home	Jump to the top of the current topic.
Ctrl End	Jump to the end of the current topic.
Printer Setup	Display HyperWriter's **Printer Setup** dialog box.
Font Zooming	Zoom the font for easy reading.
Print	Display HyperWriter's **Print** dialog box.
View TOC	Display HyperWriter's **TOC** browser.
Synchronize TOC	Synchronize HyperWriter's **TOC** browser with the current topic.

Although we haven't discussed HyperWriter's background screen facility in depth yet, from the range of different screens that you have seen in working through the tutorials in this chapter, you probably understand that Hyper-Writer can present whatever type of screen design you want for your application. Given the wide range of functions available through menu action links, it isn't hard to see that HyperWriter lets you build applications with virtually any type of functionality. This really reflects HyperWriter's nature as a *development environment* or *construction kit* for digital publications.

In the exercise below, we will create a sample menu action link. If you are curious about a particular menu action listed in the **Menu Action Link** dialog box, you may want to select it to see its functionality.

Creating a Menu Action Link

1. Mark the text that says "Create a Menu Action Link Here."
2. Select **Link to Action** from the **Link** menu.
3. Select the **Menu Action** link option. This displays the **Select Menu Action** dialog box shown in Figure 12.12.
4. Select the **Font Zooming** menu action link. This function is located at the end of the list.

After selecting the menu action, you will see that link symbols have been added to the link. Selecting on the menu action link that you just created displays a popup menu for setting the zoom ratio of the text, allowing a reader to control how text is sized when they are reading text. A picture of using the **Font Zooming** menu action link is shown in Figure 12.13.

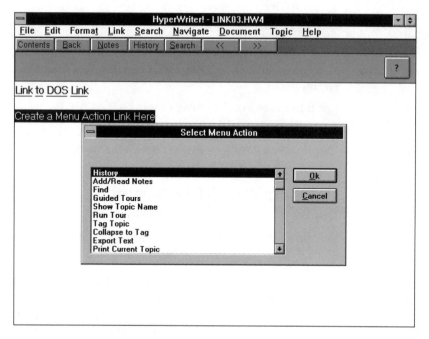

Figure 12.12 The **Select Menu Action** dialog box.

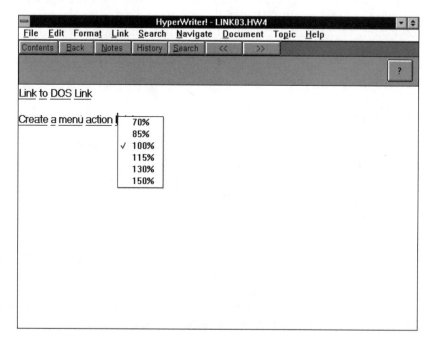

Figure 12.13 Using the **Font Zooming** menu action link.

The **Font Zooming** menu action link brings up an interesting point about menu action links. Many of the menu action links actually don't exist on HyperWriter's menu system! Despite the name, it isn't required that menu action links actually exist on HyperWriter's menu system. When we first created HyperWriter, all menu action links existed on HyperWriter's menu system, hence the name. Over time, however, our user base needed more and more features, often features that didn't make sense to put on the menu system. An example of this is the **Page Up** menu action link which just pages up one screen. While this is a needed feature for digital publishing, as many readers prefer to use the mouse exclusively for reading digital publications and this allows paging up one screen to be assigned to a mousable button, putting **Page Up** on a menu just isn't necessary. As we kept adding features, we opted to keep the term *menu action* as so many of our users already knew it. This completes our tutorial on menu action links. We are now ready to move onto action list links. Before we move onto our next exercise, we should save our work.

Saving Our Work

Select the **Save** command from the **File** menu.

Creating Action List Links

As with menu action links, action list links provide a dynamic link. In short, an action is something that occurs when a particular link is activated or a particular topic is entered. An action list is simply a *collection* of one or more actions listed in the order that they are executed. For example, an action list might contain animations, video controls, digital audio files, and so on. Actions lists can apply to both links and topics. When an action list is applied to a link, the action is performed when the link is activated. When an action list is applied to a topic, the action is performed when the user enters a topic. In the remainder of this section we will focus on action list links, although action lists and topics will be covered as well.

To make using HyperWriter more powerful, a number of standard actions are included. In Table 12.3 are all available actions for both links or topics.

As you can see, most of the actions are available for both links and topics. The notable exception is the **Fade Types** action, which is only available for links (assigning a fade type to a topic doesn't make much sense—the user would go to a topic, the topic would fade away, and then it would return).

Before we can begin using Actions Lists, we need to first understand HyperWriter's **Actions List** dialog box.

Understanding the Action Lists Dialog Box

All actions, either those attached to a link or a topic, are created with essentially the same tool—the **Actions List** dialog box. This dialog box allows creating and editing of the different actions contained in an action list. The differences

Table 12.3 Action Lists in HyperWriter

Action List	*Link or Topic?*
Animations	Both link and topic
Delay	Both link and topic
Digital Audio	Both link and topic
Fade Types	Link only
Goto Topic	Both link and topic
Output Report	Both link and topic
Query Database	Both link and topic
Redbook Audio	Both link and topic
Run Program	Both link and topic
Select List	Both link and topic
Video Control	Both link and topic
Windows DDE	Both link and topic
Windows MCI	Both link and topic

between the Actions List dialog box for links and topics lies only in the particular actions that are available. Certain actions are available only for links and certain actions are available only for topics as different actions are appropriate for each. However, most actions are available for both links or topics. The **Actions List** dialog box for actions attached to links is shown in Figure 12.14.

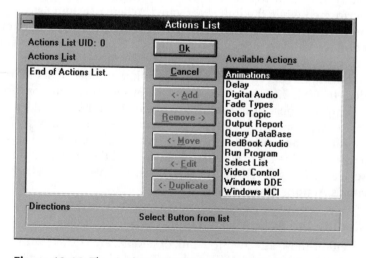

Figure 12.14 The **Actions List** dialog box for link actions.

As you can see from the previous picture, the **Actions List** dialog boxes are arranged into two lists, with a row of control buttons between them. The list at left is called the *Action List*. It lists the actions that have been created in the order that they will be executed when the action list is used. The list at right is called the list of *Available Actions*. It lists all available actions for the link or topic to which you are attaching an action list.

The different buttons in the **Action List** dialog box are described in Table 12.4.

Table 12.4 Using the **Action List** Dialog Boxes

Button	Description
OK	Close the **Actions List** dialog box and return to the link or topic that you came from. Select this button when you are through modifying the Action List.
Cancel	Cancel the **Action List** dialog box and return to the link or topic that you came from. It does not cancel your changes to the **Action List** dialog box; it will cancel moving the actions.
<- Add	Add new actions to the list. Select an action that you want to add from the Available Actions and then select the **Add** button to add it to the list. The arrow in the button title indicates that the action that you add is being added to the list at left, from the list at right. A shortcut for using this button is to double-click the action that you want to add to the list.
Remove ->	Remove actions from the Action List. Select an action that you want to remove from the Action List and then select the **Remove** button to remove it from the list. Be careful with this command as there is no confirmation before the delete occurs.
<- Move	Reposition an action within the Action List. Select an action in the Action List and then select the **Move** button. Select the new position in the list and then select the **Finish Move** button to place the action into its new position. Please note that the **Move** button becomes a **Finish Move** button when the **Move** button is selected.
<- Edit	Edit a particular action in the Action List. Select an action in the Action List and then select the **Edit** button to call up that particular action in a dialog box for editing. A shortcut to using the **Edit** button is to double-click an action in the Action List.
<- Duplicate	Duplicate an existing action shown in the Action List. Select an action in the Action List and then select the **Duplicate** button. This duplicates the action and places a copy of it below itself in the Action List.

An important aspect of the **Action List** dialog box that may not be obvious at first is that the **Action List** dialog box allows you to control the order in which actions are executed when you are creating the different actions that go into the action list. When there is more than one action in the action list you are creating, you can define where additional actions are created (i.e., above, below, or between existing actions). This is done by moving the selection bar to the correct place before adding additional actions.

NOTE: While the **Move** button can be used to change the position of an action in the **Actions List** dialog box, it is generally more efficient to set this up when creating the actions themselves.

Two special aspects of the **Action List** dialog box that we haven't discussed are the **Action List UID** field and the **Directions** field. The **Action List UID** Prompt lists a UID or unique identifier for the Action List, which allows you to reuse the Action List with another link or topic. The **Action List UID field** allows useful action lists to be reused when needed. The **Directions** field displays directions specific to what you are doing. For example, when moving an action it instructs you how to complete the move. While these instructions are not long, they serve as quick reminders in how to complete what you are currently doing.

Creating Action Lists

Now that we understand both the actions that are available and the dialog box used to create them, we are ready to begin working with action lists.

For working with action lists, we need to start with a new sample document, LINK03A.HW4.

Opening a Document in HyperWriter

1. Select the **Open** command from the **File** menu.
2. Select the document LINK03A.HW4 from the list of available documents. If you are asked to leave a bookmark, answer No. This loads the document.

With our document open, we need to start by deciding what type of action list link we want to make. While we could make any action list, let's start with a **Fade Types** action. The **Fade Types** action is used to create attractive transition effects between topics. It is often used when building interactive presentations, multimedia titles, or kiosklike applications.

As with creating any other type of link, creating an action list link requires selecting the anchor of the link and then choosing the **Link to...**command.

Creating an Action List Link

1. Mark the text that says "Create a Fade Type Link Here."
2. Select **Link to Action** from the **Link** menu.
3. Select the **Actions List** option. This displays the **Actions List** dialog box shown in Figure 12.15.
4. Select the **Fade Types** action and then select the **Add** button. This displays the **Set Fade Type** dialog box shown below in Figure 12.16.
5. Select a **Fade Type** that you want to see displayed and then select the **OK** button.
6. Select the **OK** button to close the **Actions List** dialog box. This returns you to your document.

Activating the action list link that you just created will display a fade effect that gradually wipes the screen blank. A picture of using the **Fade Types** link is shown (the Drop Out Blocks fade was selected) in Figure 12.17.

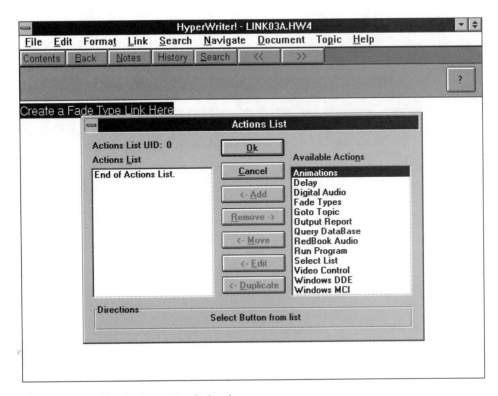

Figure 12.15 The Actions List dialog box.

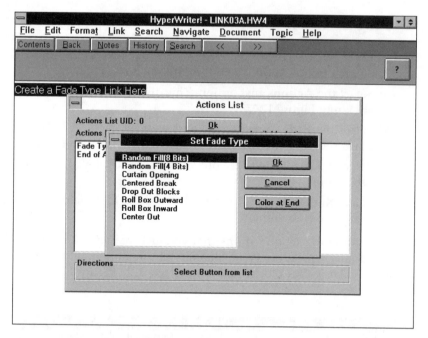

Figure 12.16 The **Set Fade Type** dialog box.

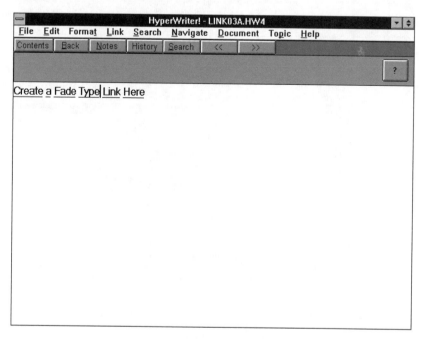

Figure 12.17 The Drop Out Blocks fade type.

Creating this action list link to a Fade Type brings up an interesting point—a **Fade Type** action list link by itself really doesn't do anything. It just fades the screen and returns the user to his or her original location. Where a **Fade Type** action list is really useful is when it is either attached to another link such as a **Jump** link, or when it is used before a **Goto Topic** action. When attached to a **Jump** link, the **Fade Type** is executed prior to the jump, thus providing a nice visual transition effect. When used before a **Goto Topic** action, the **Fade Type** first provides a transition which the **Goto Topic** action follows by moving the user to another topic. To add an action list to an existing **Jump** link, use the **Actions List** command on the **Link** menu. To use a Fade Type with a Goto Topic action, create the **Fade Type** action first and then add a **Goto Topic** action.

Now that we have created a very simple action list link, we are ready to move to a more complex action list link—a multimedia action that plays video. As in our previous example, we'll start by marking our link anchor.

Creating an Action List Link

1. Mark the text that says "Create a Video Link Here."

2. Select **Link to Action** from the **Link** menu.

3. Select the **Actions List** option.

4. Select the **Video Control** action and then select the **Add** button. This displays the **Video Controls** dialog box shown in Figure 12.18.

5. Select the **Add** button to add an individual video control. This displays the dialog box shown in Figure 12.19, used for selecting video controls.

6. Select the Load Digital Video filename control. This displays a standard file selection dialog box for selecting a video file. Select the file VIDEO.AVI. In HyperWriter selecting the video file is only the first part. Now we need to add additional video controls that tell Hyper-Writer what to do with the video file.

7. Move the selection bar down (so it appears after the video file) and select the **Add** button.

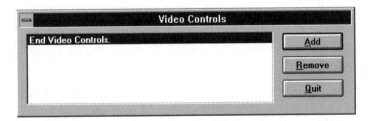

Figure 12.18 The **Video Controls** dialog box.

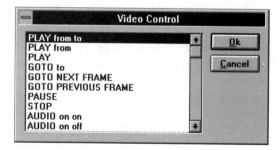

Figure 12.19 Selecting a video control.

8. Choose the **Play** option and enter a **1** into the **From Frame** dialog box. This tells HyperWriter to play the video file to its end from frame number 1.

9. Select the **Quit** button to close the **Video Controls** dialog box.

10. Select the **OK** button to close the **Actions List** dialog box.

Activating the action list link that you just created displays a popup video playback window as shown in Figure 12.20.

NOTE: Video clips in HyperWriter can also be played back in the main Hyper-Writer document window with a custom background screen.

This completes our tutorial on **Action List** links. Although we only created two **Action List** links, you should have a good feel for what **Action List** links bring to your digital publications. **Action List** links allow you to create powerful, dynamic links for tasks like playing back multimedia objects. They also extend to such complex tasks as running other Windows applications and allowing two applications to communicate (through Dynamic Data Exchange or DDE). Before we move onto our next exercise, we should save our work.

Saving Our Work

Select the **Save** command from the **File** menu.

Creating Links from Pictures

One of the most exciting aspects of HyperWriter's linking facilities is its ability to create links from areas on pictures. Links to text, other pictures, or actions can be created from rectangular regions on those pictures. This hot spot or

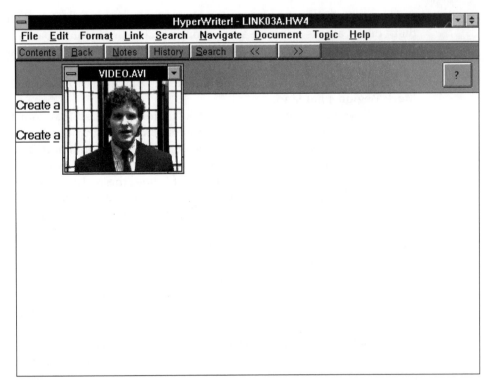

Figure 12.20 Playing back the video file.

hypergraphic ability frees you from solely text links, allowing any image to serve as a link source.

Link from a hot spot requires using the **Mark Region** command, which lets you mark blocks on a graphic and then choose one of HyperWriter's linking commands. Using the **Mark Region** command, however, requires understanding some low-level details about HyperWriter. I'd like to start by warning you that to use **Mark Region** effectively, you really need to understand the points that I am going to make. When you use **Mark Region**, it can be used in two basic situations: when the topic does not have a background and when the topic does have a background. The first point to understand about **Mark Region** is that the link it creates can be associated with the picture that you link from or with the background assigned to the topic where the picture that you link from is displayed. The difference between the two is that when the link is assigned to the picture, everything functions as you would expect— clicking on that picture activates that link. When the link is assigned to the background, then the link that you made from the picture ends up becoming part of the background. The implication of this is that the link you made from the picture will be accessible everywhere the background is displayed. Given that your goal was to create a link from a picture, not from a background, this is probably not the effect that you intended. Now that you know the possible effects of using the **Mark Region** command, how do you avoid this situation? The answer concerns where your cursor was positioned prior to selecting the **Mark Region** command.

When you create a link using **Mark Region**, provided that your topic has a background displayed (as it almost always does), your cursor can be positioned in two places before using the **Mark Region** command: at the start of the picture or not at the start of the picture. If your cursor is positioned at the start of the picture (slightly to the left of where the picture is first displayed) then the link that you create using **Mark Region** will be stored with the picture. The problem with this is that HyperWriter doesn't explicitly tell you when you are at the start of the picture, as the start of the picture is defined by an invisible object embedded in the document.

When you import a picture into a document, that picture's location is defined by an invisible object. When you are positioned at the start of the picture, you are positioned on the invisible object and this tells HyperWriter that you want to assign the link to the picture. Fortunately, HyperWriter provides a way to locate these invisible objects. If you turn on HyperWriter's status bar using the **Preferences** command on the **File** menu (it is located at the bottom of the Screen folder), and then turn on the **Show Codes** command on the **Format** menu, when you place the cursor near the picture you will see the invisible object displayed in the status bar as Picture or Object. If you don't see this, then you need to move the cursor with **Arrowkey** around the picture until this is displayed. When you see it you can then use the **Mark Region** command to make links, and know that the links that you create will be assigned to the picture. If your cursor is positioned anywhere in the topic that is not at the start of the picture, then HyperWriter will assign the link that you create with **Mark Region** to the background and not to the picture itself.

One aspect of using the **Mark Region** command that makes this issue with invisible objects simpler is the way that the **Mark Region** command behaves if your cursor is located at the picture's start. When the **Mark Region** command is used, it displays an onscreen sizing box that you use to define the region of the picture that you want to link. If your cursor is located at the start of the picture, then the onscreen sizing box appears at the start of the picture. If your cursor is not located at the start of the picture, then the sizing box will appear at the upper-left corner of your HyperWriter window. In short, if the sizing box doesn't appear at the start of the picture, then your link will be associated with the background, not the picture itself. In Figure 12.21, you can see the effect of using **Mark Region** when you were not positioned at the start of the picture— the **Mark Region** sizing box is not located at the start of the picture.

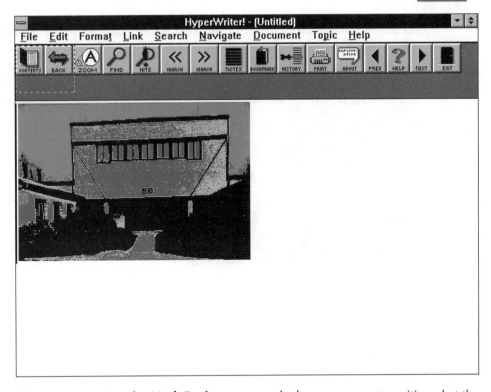

Figure 12.21 Using the **Mark Region** command when you are not positioned at the start of the picture.

In Figure 12.22 you can see the effect of using **Mark Region** when you are positioned at the start of the picture—the **Mark Region** sizing box is located at the start of the picture.

With our discussion on the **Mark Region** command, invisible objects, and positioning the cursor, we are ready to start our tutorial. In this tutorial we will start with a new HyperWriter document, LINKIMG.HW4. Open this document now.

Opening a Document in HyperWriter

1. Select the **Open** command from the **File** menu.

2. Select the document LINKIMG.HW4 from the list of available documents. If you are asked to leave a bookmark, answer No. This loads the document.

With the LINKIMG.HW4 document open, we can get started creating a link from a picture. As you can see, this document has a picture of NTER-

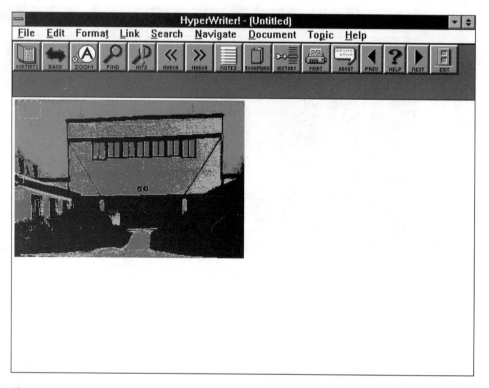

Figure 12.22 Using the **Mark Region** Command when you are at the start of the picture.

GAID's offices (which you have now seen several times before) displayed at the center of the screen, with a button bar above it. What we want to do is create a link around this picture. In order to locate our invisible objects, we need to turn on the status bar and HyperWriter's **Show Codes** command.

Turning on the Status Bar

1. Select the **Preferences** command from the **File** menu.
2. Select the **Screen** folder. This displays the dialog box shown below in Figure 12.23.
3. Select the **Status Bar Visible** option.
4. Select the **OK** button to close the **Preferences** dialog box.

When the Status Bar is turned on, you will see a rectangular bar across the bottom of the window. The Status Bar is shown in Figure 12.24.

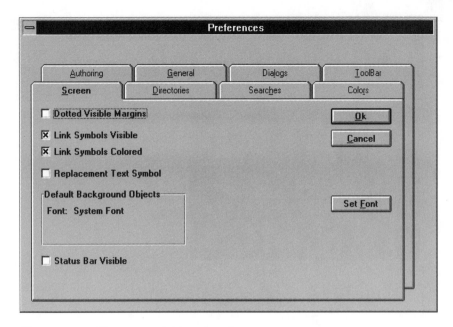

Figure 12.23 The screen folder of options.

The **Show Codes** command tells HyperWriter to display the invisible objects in the Status Bar.

Turning on Show Codes

Select the **Show Codes** command from the **Format** menu. This will place a checkmark next to the command. With the status bar visible and show codes turned on, we are ready to create a link from our picture. The goal is to create a link from an entire picture to a new topic where some text might be displayed.

Creating a Link from an Imported Picture

1. Position your cursor next to the picture at the picture's start. As the picture was inserted with the **Insert Picture** command, you will notice that the cursor becomes the height of the picture.

2. Turn on the **Show Codes** function from the **Format** menu. Move the cursor left or right until the word "Object" appears in the status bar. By placing your cursor at this point, the link from the picture will be associated with the picture.

3. Select the **Mark Region** function from the **Link** menu.

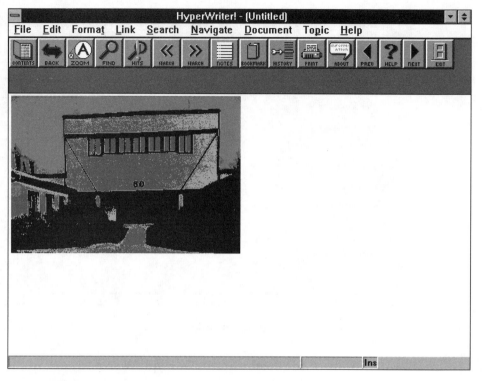

Figure 12.24 HyperWriter's Status Bar.

4. The normal text cursor now changes to a sizing region or box cursor. You will notice that this box cursor starts at the upper left hand edge of the picture. This box cursor is used to mark a rectangular link from the picture. Use the mouse to drag the sizing region out to the full size of the picture (we want to link the entire picture).

5. Select the **Link to Text** command from the **Link** menu.

6. Select the **Jump Link** option.

7. Select the **New Topic** option. This creates a new topic where we could display text associated with the link (we don't actually have any text that we want to use).

8. Select the **Complete Link** command from the **Link** menu. This completes the link and returns you to the picture.

This completes our exercise on using **Mark Region** to create links from pictures. As you can tell, with the exception of how we select the anchor of the link (the region of the picture), creating a link from a graphic functions in the exactly the same way as does creating a link from a piece of text.

Saving Our Work

With our tutorial finished, we are now ready to save our work. This is done with the **Save** command on the **File** menu.

Exiting HyperWriter

With our tutorial finished and our work saved, you can now exit HyperWriter if desired. This is done with the **Exit** command on the **File** menu.

Using the Import Text Wizard

The Import Text Wizard is a powerful hypertext linking tool that can automatically create links and topics for you when it imports your documents into HyperWriter. To continue learning about the Import Text Wizard, it is strongly recommended that you work through the tutorial "Creating Links to Text," covered earlier in this chapter. Completing this tutorial before using the Import Text Wizard should help you to understand the Import Text Wizard more thoroughly. Our discussion of the Import Text Wizard is broken into three parts. The beginning of this section covers how the Import Text Wizard functions. The second part walks you through using the Import Text Wizard and the third part is a reference section that covers how different word processing formats are treated by the Import Text Wizard.

Understanding the Import Text Wizard

By working through "Creating Links to Text" you got a good feeling for how HyperWriter's hypertext linking functions. One aspect of HyperWriter's hypertext linking is that for large applications, making links manually simply takes too long. If you consider a book-length work, creating links, importing files, and then breaking the files into topics, while not difficult isn't efficient. To tackle these larger projects, HyperWriter's Import Text Wizard is used. The Import Text Wizard offers an automated toolkit for automatically creating links as documents are imported. This reduces or eliminates the need to make links manually. The Import Text Wizard automatically converts stylesheet entries and table of contents marks to their hypertext equivalent, generates a table of contents, assigns screen backgrounds, establishes next and previous browsing sequences, and converts word-processor page references into hypertext links. As you can imagine, this can dramatically reduce the time needed to build your HyperWriter application.

The Import Text Wizard provides assistance when importing documents into HyperWriter. When you import a document into HyperWriter, the Import Text Wizard pops onscreen and helps you to import the document. The Import Text Wizard is shown in Figure 12.25.

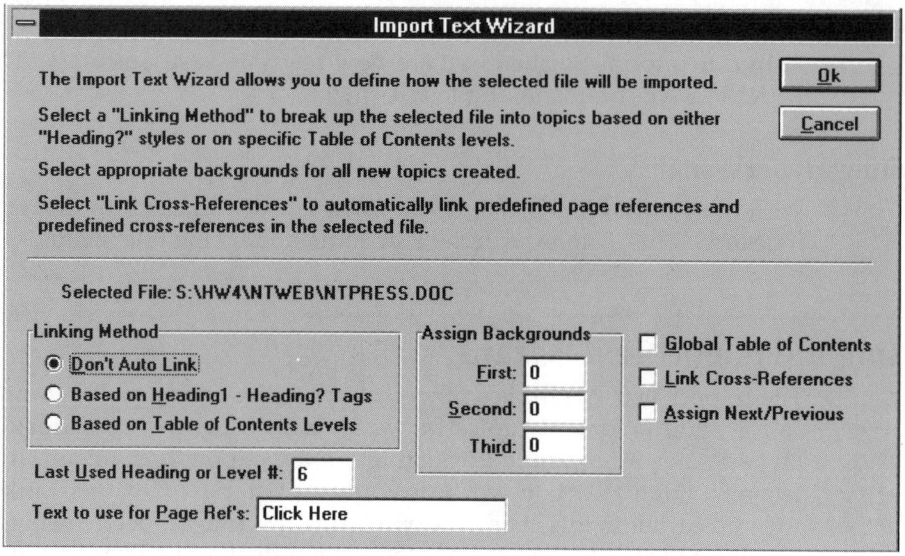

Figure 12.25 The Import Text Wizard.

Each of the options on the Import Text Wizard is described in Table 12.5. The steps to use the Import Text Wizard are described below.

Using the Import Text Wizard

1. Either open an existing HyperWriter document (such as a template document) or create a new document.
2. Select the **Import Text** command from the **File** menu.
3. Select the format of the text file to import.
4. Select the text file to import.
5. After selecting the text file, the Import Text Wizard is displayed.

Use the Import Text Wizard to configure how the text should be imported and if automatic linking should be used. Bear in mind that for large text documents, the Import Text Wizard will take some time to function. When building links automatically, the Import Text Wizard will display a table of contents, in topic number 1, to the information that it imported. To make formatting the table of contents generated by the Import Text Wizard easy, the Import Text Wizard automatically assigns the stylesheet tags HW_TOC_# to all table of contents entries that it creates. This allows you to format these table of contents entries one time and have all entries with that same stylesheet automatically formatted.

Table 12.5 Options for the Import Text Wizard

Option	Description
Linking Method	Set the method used to create automatic links. The **Don't Auto Link** option prevents any automatic links from being created and imports the document as a long text document. The **Based on Heading1-Heading?** option creates a hypertext topic and link at every place a stylesheet tag named HEADING# is located. The Based on **Table of Contents** option creates a hypertext topic and link at every occurrence of a table of contents mark. These *marks* are inserted using the Table of Contents feature in your word-processing software.
Last Used Heading or Level Number	Set the number of heading styles or table of contents levels to convert to links and topics. For example, enter a **3** in this field if you wanted to link heading styles HEADING1, HEADING2, and HEADING3.
Linking Method	Set the method used to create automatic links. The **Don't Auto Link** option turns off the Import Text Wizard and imports files into the current topic.
Assign Backgrounds	Assign the specified screen background to any topics created by the auto link. This option requires that the screen background already be created.
Global Table of Contents	Create a table of contents, located in topic number 1, to all topics created by the auto link. When this option is turned off, the table of contents generated is placed at each section level, with only the highest-level table of contents entries appearing in topic number 1.
Link Cross-References	Convert word processor cross references to hypertext links.
Assign Next/Previous	Assign next-and-previous relationships so documents can be browsed sequentially. When this option is used, documents should be imported in the correct order (Chapter 2 before Chapter 3, so the browsing is in the correct sequence).
Text to Use for Page Ref's	Set a text string to automatically insert when cross references are page number based. A page number-based cross-reference would be one that such as *See page 12* where the 12 is the reference being created. As the 12 is a page number that isn't relevant in the hypertext, a text string can be automatically inserted.

NOTE: If possible, you want to import documents into HyperWriter in the correct order. If you had three chapters then you would want to import the first chapter, the second chapter, and then the third chapter. The reason for this is that HyperWriter assigns next-and-previous browse sequences in the order the information was imported (Chapter 2 browses directly to Chapter 3, not some other chapter). While browsing sequences can be fixed with the **Relationships** command on the **Topic** menu, importing documents in order prevents the need for this.

One possible error you may find with the Import Text Wizard is that your documents may not be arranged how you expect them to be. Consider a document structure where the chapter number (Chapter 1) and the chapter title (Some Chapter) are two separate paragraphs. The chapter number might have a stylesheet tag of Chapter Num while the chapter title would have a **HEADING1** tag. This will cause the chapter number to be separated from the rest of the chapter (which would be linked). The solution to this problem is generally to move the **HEADING1** tag up to the chapter number, merging the two paragraphs into one.

If you find that using the Import Text Wizard does not create the type of hypertext document that you were expecting, you have two options. The first is to modify your original documents, your source documents, so that they import correctly into HyperWriter with the desired hypertext elements. The key to this approach is to better understand how the Import Text Wizard converts an imported document to hypertext. Modifying your original documents has the benefit of allowing you to use the word-processing software you understand and are comfortable with, instead of being required to learn how to use HyperWriter as a word processor. The second option is to create the hypertext elements of your document by hand, not using the Import Text Wizard to create hypertext automatically. This is done by selecting the **Don't Auto Link** option on the Import Text Wizard.

Understanding How Hypertext Links Are Created

When the Import Text wizard imports a document into HyperWriter, it automatically creates hypertext links in two cases:

- When stylesheet tags use the keyword "head" as part of the stylesheet tag name
- When table of contents levels are found

Understanding how the table of contents levels are converted to a hypertext format is relatively simple—the different table of contents levels indicate where topics are created. Understanding how stylesheet tags are converted to a hypertext format is slightly more difficult. Consider a document that has text formatted with **HEADING1, HEADING2,** and **HEADING3** stylesheet tags. HyperWriter will create hypertext topics where these stylesheet tags are applied to the text. In addition to just stylesheet tags named **HEADING1**, HyperWriter will create topics at any stylesheet tag that begins with the keyword **HEAD** and then a number (this is a common syntax used by Microsoft Word as its default).

If your documents are formatted with stylesheet tags that begin with **HEAD**, then this gives you an easy way to control how the Import Text Wizard functions. Consider, for example, a document with **HEAD1, HEAD2,** and **HEAD3** stylesheet tags. If you wanted the hypertext topics created only at the **HEAD2** and **HEAD3** stylesheet tags, then the easiest approach is to rename the **HEAD3** stylesheet tag (in your word-processing software) to _HEAD3. This will create the hypertext topics only at the **HEAD1** and **HEAD2** stylesheet tags. Changing the name of the **HEAD3** should have little to no effect on your word-processing files as it is only the name of a style.

This same approach, changing the name of a stylesheet tag, can be used very successfully in most cases where you want to change how the Import Text Wizard creates links and topics. Consider an electronic document structured around individual chapters, where you wanted each chapter to be an entire topic (perhaps so that the reader could scroll through the entire chapter). This could be accomplished with two steps. First, rename the **HEAD1** (or similar stylesheet tags that start with **HEAD** and a number) to _HEAD1 to prevent topics from being created at the different heading levels. Second, change the name of the stylesheet tag that indicates the title of the chapter to **HEAD1**. This creates a document with a first-level heading of the chapter title. When this document is imported into HyperWriter, the Import Text Wizard will structure it so that the entire chapter is a single topic in HyperWriter.

What If the Import Text Wizard Doesn't Work for My Documents?

If you find that the Import Text Wizard doesn't function for your documents, you have two options. The first option is to import your documents without making any links and create your links manually. While this approach is actually quite easy, it can be time-consuming as the Import Text Wizard not only creates links and topics but also names topics, assigns backgrounds, creates a table of contents, and assigns next-and-previous browsing sequences. In this situation, you may find it easier to revise your documents so that they meet the specifications the Import Text Wizard uses to automatically create links and topics. Revising your documents in this fashion can be done by:

1. Renaming existing stylesheet tags to the **HEAD#** syntax documented in the previous section.

2. Add stylesheet tags using the **HEAD#** syntax at the headings in your documents where hypertext topics and links are to be created.

3. Insert table of contents levels at the headings in your documents where hypertext topics and links are to be created.

A common question that NTERGAID receives about using the Import Text Wizard is "Do I need separate copies of my source documents for paper publishing and electronic publishing?" The answer to this is "Generally not." All of the changes we described that you might make to your source documents are generally changes that won't affect your paper publishing (changing a stylesheet tag name doesn't affect your printed output at all). This allows you to modify your original source files once (before you get ready for your Hyper-Writer application), and then use those same source files for both print and electronic publishing. This is a strong plus for HyperWriter, as it allows you to have only a single copy of your source files that you either print out or bring into HyperWriter to make your electronic publication.

Running HyperWriter

Now that we understand what the Import Text Wizard offers us, we need to start this tutorial by opening the document TXTWIZ1.HW4. Use the **Open** command from the **File** menu to open the document TXTWIZ1.HW4.

Opening a Document

1. Select the **Open** command from the **File** menu.
2. Select the document TXTWIZ1.HW4.

When the document is opened, you will see that it is just a HyperWriter template document complete with a user interface. With our document open, we are ready to use the Import Text Wizard. The first step in using the Import Text Wizard is to import a document into HyperWriter.

Importing a Document into HyperWriter

1. Select the **Import Text** command from the **File** menu.
2. Select Word as the format to import.
3. Select the document PRESSREL.DOC from the list of documents to import.
4. The Import Text Wizard is now displayed. This dialog box is shown in Figure 12.26.

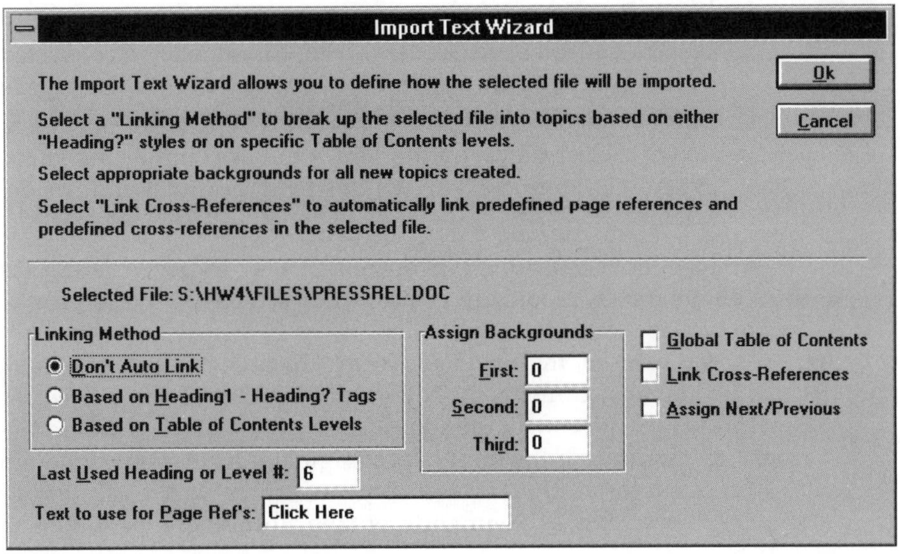

Figure 12.26 The Import Text Wizard.

5. Set the first option, the **Linking Method**, to **Based on Heading1-Heading? tags**. The document we are importing as a Word for Windows document uses the standard heading styles. This option creates a hypertext topic and link at every place a stylesheet tag named **HEADING#** is located. For our tutorial, we only need to set that the first two headings should be linked. Enter a **2** in the **Last Used Heading or Level Number** field.

6. Enter a **1** in the **First** field of the **Assign Backgrounds** option. The **Assign Backgrounds** option assigns a HyperWriter user interface (a background screen) to each topic created in the import process. You entered a **1** in the **First** field as the only background screen in your document is background number 1.

7. The **Global Table of Contents** option can be left in its off position as the document that we are importing has only one level of hierarchy.

8. Turn on the **Link Cross-References** option to convert any word-processor cross-references to hypertext links.

9. Turn on the **Assign Next/Previous** option so that the document we are importing can be browsed sequentially. Even though our electronic publication is a nonlinear hypertext, most readers still like to browse a publication in sequence.

10. Leave the **Text to Use for Page Ref's** option at its default setting. This option lets you specify a text string to use when a converted hypertext link has no text (i.e., the link was originally around a page number).

11. This completes setting the Import Text Wizard to function for our document. Select the **OK** button for it to begin importing your document. When it is complete, you will see the Word for Windows document on screen.

We have now imported our document into HyperWriter and created our links automatically. A picture of how your screen should appear is shown in Figure 12.27.

As you can see, the first topic in the document displays an automatically generated table of contents to the information that was imported. This table of contents is formatted with the stylesheet tags HW_TOC_# where # is a number from 1 to 9 indicating the level of the original information. Although we won't do it in our tutorial, this table of contents can be very easily formatted using HyperWriter's **Tag...** commands on the **Format** menu which manipulate

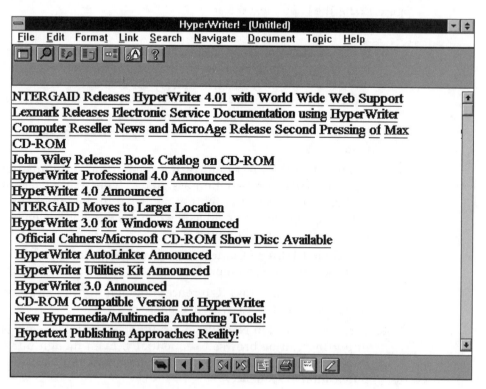

Figure 12.27 The results of the Import Text Wizard.

stylesheet tags. What I would recommend before reading further is that you explore this document and examine the features that the Import Text Wizard has created for us. I would recommend that you activate some of the different links, select the next button, and so on.

NOTE: Although we only had a single document to import, it is important to point out that you usually want to import documents into HyperWriter in the correct order as this ensures that the next and previous browse relationships function correctly (from Chapter 2 to Chapter 3, not to Chapter 10).

At this point you have used both the manual linking features and the Import Text Wizard. Clearly the Import Text Wizard, while reliant on documents being formatted a particular way, offers some huge advantages over the manual linking features. Essentially, the Import Text Wizard has built the entire structure of our application with one command, importing over 25 press releases and creating all the necessary links and topics. What this tends to argue for in your development is to focus (as much as possible) on using the Import Text Wizard to develop the structure (links, topics, table of contents) that you need while saving your manual linking for the situations where it is truly required.

Having applied the Import Text Wizard successfully, we are done with this tutorial and need to save our work and exit HyperWriter. Use the **Save** and **Exit** commands on the **File** menu for this.

Reference: The Import Text Wizard and Document Import

When the Import Text Wizard imports documents into HyperWriter, it takes advantage of formatting codes and markup in the imported documents to automatically create hypertext links and topics. For this reason, it is very important to understand how HyperWriter converts simple text formatting such as heading styles and table of contents entries to hypertext (see the preceding section). Each of the sections below covers a particular type of document and how different items in the document are imported into HyperWriter.

Microsoft Word Documents

Microsoft Word .DOC document files from Microsoft Word for Windows 1.0, Microsoft Word for Windows 2.0, Microsoft Word for Windows 6.0, and Microsoft Word for DOS .DOC document files can be directly imported into HyperWriter. The elements in Table 12.6 from Microsoft Word either are or aren't imported into HyperWriter.

Table 12.6 How the Import Text Wizard Handles Microsoft Word Documents

Document Element	Description
Table of contents levels for creating links and topics	Fully supported
Page references	Converted to hypertext links
Bookmarks	Used for hypertext link destinations
Goto button field	Converted to hypertext links

Rich Text Format Documents

The elements in Table 12.7 from Rich Text Format documents either are or aren't imported into HyperWriter.

Table 12.7 How the Import Text Wizard Handles Rich Text Format Documents

Document Element	Description
Paragraph styles for creating links and topics	Fully supported
Table of contents levels for creating links and topics	Fully supported
Page references	Converted to hypertext links
Bookmarks	Used for hypertext link destinations
Goto button field	Converted to hypertext links

WordPerfect Documents

The elements from WordPerfect documents in Table 12.8 either are or aren't imported into HyperWriter.

Table 12.8 How the Import Text Wizard Handles WordPerfect Documents

Document Element	Description
Paragraph styles for creating links and topics	Fully supported
Table of contents levels for creating links and topics	Fully supported
Page references	Converted to hypertext links
Bookmarks	Used for hypertext link destinations

Lotus Ami Pro Document

The following elements from Lotus Ami Pro documents in Table 12.9 either are or aren't imported into HyperWriter.

Table 12.9 How the Import Text Wizard Handles Ami Pro Documents

Document Element	*Description*
Paragraph styles for creating links and topics	Fully supported
Table of contents levels for creating links and topics	Fully supported
Page references	Converted to hypertext links
Bookmarks	Used for hypertext link destinations

ASCII Documents

Documents stored as ASCII text are just that—plain ASCII text. No formatting is imported from ASCII files (except for tab characters), as there is no formatting in an ASCII file. You might think that the Import Text Wizard wouldn't function for ASCII files, but it does. What the Import Text Wizard does for ASCII files is offer the option to break the ASCII files into hypertext topics at blank lines. When you use the Import Text Wizard for ASCII files, the options it gives you are shown in Figure 12.28.

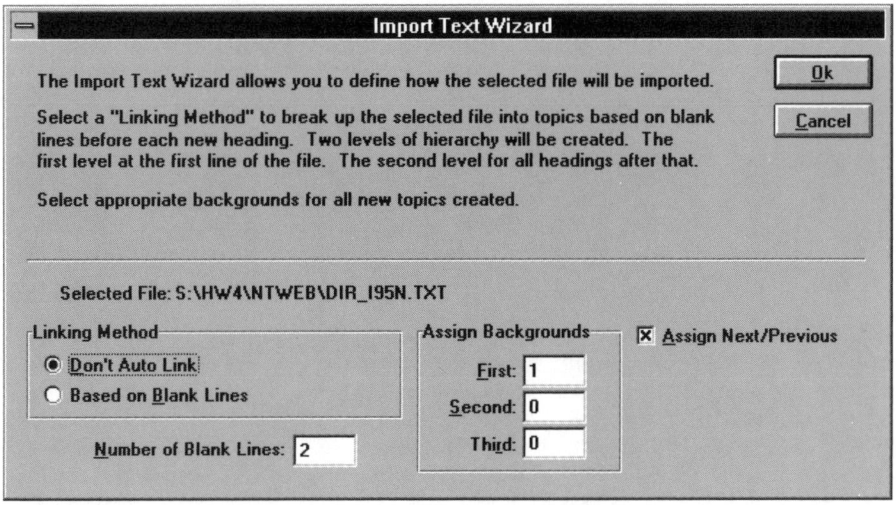

Figure 12.28 Using the Import Text Wizard with ASCII text.

By setting the **Number of Blank Lines** field to the number of blank lines between sections of text in your ASCII files, the Import Text Wizard can convert your ASCII files to a hypertext format. Although this is not a perfect approach, it often gives very good results (the results do vary based on your ASCII files). There are two additional points you should note about using the Import Text Wizard with ASCII files. The first is that if you have multiple ASCII files and all you want to do is start each file in a new topic, then set the **Number of Blank Lines** field to **9** (its maximum setting). As it is unlikely that you will have nine blank lines within a single file, this usually causes each file to be imported into a single topic.

The second point with respect to importing ASCII files into HyperWriter is to cheat. By telling HyperWriter that your ASCII files are WordPerfect, Hyper-Writer will look for embedded heading styles within the file. Although ASCII files do not support styles, HyperWriter does support a way to embed styles or tags within your files using Ventura Publisher format. This format is an @ sign followed by a tag name and then the = sign. If you embedded "" and "" before your first-level and second-level headings, then the Import Text Wizard can recognize these codes and create links and topics just as it does for a format like Microsoft Word. Thanks to HyperWriter's handling of the WordPerfect import filter, HyperWriter can import your ASCII files even when WordPerfect is specified, and this allows the Import Text Wizard to be displayed so you can select the **Based on Heading1 - Heading9 Tags** option that using the **@HEAD** approach requires.

Importing Pictures

There is an old saying that a picture is worth a thousand words. In a digital publishing sense, a single picture is perhaps worth even more than a thousand words, because a picture, like no other element, can add a real degree of vibrancy and engagement to your digital publications. Just as pictures can bring a printed work alive, they can have the same effect on digital publications. On a more pragmatic sense, pictures bring with them some serious problems. Even a small picture takes up more storage space and memory than a similar amount of text (a picture takes up a lot more storage space than a thousand words). Another problem with pictures is that creating them takes a set of skills that not all authors have.

Adding pictures to your documents is a very powerful way to improve their appearance. HyperWriter features four separate ways that pictures can be integrated into your documents:

- The **Import Picture** Command
- The **Insert Object** Command
- Creating Links to Pictures
- Using Background Screens

In HyperWriter, as in many other programs, there are often multiple ways of accomplishing the same or similar tasks. Nowhere is this more true in HyperWriter than with pictures where HyperWriter features four different methods for integrating pictures. The first of these is the **Import Picture** command, which allows you to import a picture or pictures into a topic. When the **Import Picture** command is used, the picture is treated as if it was a point, rather than as an object. The implication of this is that when **Import Picture** is used, the picture can't be easily integrated into the body of a document alongside text, as the text doesn't "know" the width of the picture, and consequently, where the text should be positioned next to the picture. Unlike the **Import Picture** command, the **Insert Object** command inserts pictures that are treated as true objects, allowing them to be easily integrated alongside text in documents. The **Link to Picture** command creates hypertext links that display pictures. Pictures displayed with the **Link to Picture** command are displayed in a separate topic of their own that can either be a full screen topic or a popup topic (a popup window). The final method of integrating pictures into documents is through background screens, a topic that we haven't yet discussed. A background screen provides a screen design environment where pictures and other types of objects can be displayed. Using a background screen, a picture or pictures can be dragged around the screen and dropped into position wherever desired. Overall, a background screen provides the highest degree of control for positioning pictures on the screen, however, a background screen is the hardest method to use for displaying pictures.

To make it easier to understand when to use each of the different features for working with pictures, please see Table 13.1.

In the sections that follow is a discussion of supported picture formats as well as tutorials for all the different methods of importing pictures except for background screens (covered separately in Chapter 14). This tutorial will use the sample documents IMPORTP1.HW4, IMPORTP2.HW4, and IMPORTP3.HW4.

Table 13.1 Working with Pictures in HyperWriter

Feature	*When to Use*
Import Picture	When you need to display pictures on their own—typically without text alongside of them.
Insert Object	When you need to insert pictures into the body of a document.
Link to Picture	When you want pictures accessed by a hypertext link.
Background Screen	When you need exact control over the positioning and placement of pictures. Another approach is for overlaying text over pictures.

Reference: Supported Picture Formats

Just as HyperWriter supports different formats for text documents, Hyper-Writer also supports several file formats for pictures. This allows you to choose the right picture file format for different types of digital publishing applications. HyperWriter supports the following file formats:

- .PCX
- .BMP
- .TIF
- .EPS
- .WMF
- .JPG

HyperWriter supports both *bitmapped* pictures and object-based pictures. A bitmapped picture, or simply a bitmap, is a picture that consists of thousands of tiny pixels (picture elements) or bits. These bits are arranged and colored to form distinct pictures. Of the picture formats supported, the majority are bitmapped formats. Also supported are object graphics formats. In an object-based format, pictures are represented by geometric objects such as points, lines, boxes, circles, and so on. Object-based pictures have several advantages over bitmapped pictures, including the ability to zoom the image in or out without losing resolution. However, displaying an object-based picture can take considerably longer than displaying an equivalent bitmapped picture. In HyperWriter, both bitmapped and object-based pictures can be imported, inserted as objects, linked to, and used in backgrounds screens.

Supported .PCX Files

The .PCX file format is a bitmapped picture format that was originally developed for a program known as PC-Paintbrush. Pictures in the .PCX format can be created with the Windows PaintBrush program that is supplied with every copy of Microsoft Windows. .PCX files can also be created by numerous other graphics programs. Unlike other formats, the .PCX format was originally intended more as an onscreen format than one for printed reproduction. For this reason, the .PCX format is well suited for online information applications like HyperWriter.

NOTE: If you use Windows 95, you can't create .PCX files as Microsoft has taken this feature out of Windows 95.

Supported .BMP Files

The .BMP file format was originated by Microsoft and intended as the standard file format for Microsoft Windows. However, as you probably realize, .BMP is only another graphics standard, not the only standard. Files in the .BMP format can be created by Microsoft Paint supplied with every copy of Microsoft Windows. Only noncompressed .BMP files are supported. Although Microsoft has provided the ability to compress .BMP files, no commonly available Windows program allows you to create compressed .BMP files.

Supported .WMF Files

The .WMF or Windows MetaFile file format is an object-based format allowing true object or vector graphics to be displayed. .WMF files can be created by most Windows-based illustration or drawing packages such as Corel Draw or Micrographx Designer. Only metafiles that conform to the Aldus Placeable Metafile Format are supported. Most applications that export or import metafiles support this format.

Supported .TIF Files

The .TIF file format was originated by Aldus and a collection of other manufacturers as a format for storing scanned images. Because of this, .TIF images typically share two attributes. First, .TIF images are often black and white. Second, .TIF images are generally created at printer resolution, not screen resolution. Screen resolution is only 72 dpi (dots per inch) while printer resolution is typically 300 dpi or greater. Therefore, .TIF files often appear oversized when brought into HyperWriter. If you find this to be the case, we recommend that you use these images as background objects or as linked pictures. Both background objects and linked pictures allow larger than screen pictures to be scrolled. Color .TIF pictures are supported as well as black-and-white pictures.

HyperWriter supports the following types of .TIF files: Uncompressed, LZW, Packbits, Modified Huffman Encoding, CCITT Group 3 1D, CCITT Group 3 2D, and CCITT Group 4.

Supported .EPS Files

The .EPS or Encapsulated PostScript file format is a bit of an anomaly. Developed by Adobe, the inventors of PostScript, .EPS files are generally perceived as a powerful way to display complex, object-based pictures. This is true—but only for PostScript printers or object-based graphics packages. When HyperWriter displays an .EPS format picture, it displays only an embedded, low resolution .TIF image or Windows Metafile stored in the file. This image is created by the program that saved the .EPS file and is not generally of high quality. Due to this your high-resolution .EPS pictures may not appear in HyperWriter as you might expect. For this reason, we don't recommend including .EPS files in your digital publication.

Supported .JPG Files

The .JPG or J-PEG format is a very powerful image format. Like .PCX, .BMP, and .TIF, .JPG files are considered bitmapped images. Unlike these formats, .JPG files provide extremely powerful data compression features that reduce the size of images. Designed for photographic-quality images (not for line art or computer graphics), .JPG files are extremely small. For example, a .JPG file containing a scanned picture might be only 20K in size, whereas the same image as a .PCX or .BMP file might be 250K or more in size. The very powerful compression that .JPG files offer does have a price; on slower computers, .JPG format images will be displayed more slowly than images in .PCX or .BMP formats. Given the move to fast 80486 and Pentium-class personal computers, this is less of an issue than it was just a year ago. As a general rule of thumb, consider using .JPG format images if your digital publishing projects are subject to disc space constraints or are distributed via a modem.

Understanding the Different Picture Formats

Given that HyperWriter supports six different picture formats, the question is what format should be used for digital publishing? Unfortunately, the answer is that it depends on your application. As a general rule, I tend to recommend .PCX as the overall image format for people to use, and have geared this book around .PCX format pictures for example files. In all honesty, this is probably as much due to habit as anything else. I suspect .BMP or .TIF format images could probably serve as well. With this in mind, you should consider that over the past nine years of digital publishing applications, I have been able to use .PCX files almost exclusively with only brief excursions into .WMF files (for object graphics) and .JPG files (for compression). Looked at objectively, .PCX format pictures have a number of good qualities including support for both 16-color and 256-color images, relatively small image size (most of the picture files supplied with HyperWriter for user interfaces are only 10K to 15K in size) and good performance both for image display and image scrolling. To make the issue easier to understand, Table 13.2 lists the different formats along with recommendations for when to use them.

Now that we understand the different picture formats, we are ready to begin working with pictures. Before we can begin working with pictures, we must first run HyperWriter. HyperWriter is a standard MS-Windows application that can be run from the Program Manager.

Table 13.2 When to Use Different Picture Formats

Format	*Description/When to Use*
.PCX	The recommended picture format. A powerful, all-around image format well-suited to most aspects of digital publishing.
.BMP	A powerful, all-around image format. Well-suited to digital publishing.
.WMF	Unlike the other supported formats, .WMF files are an object graphic format which makes it a good option for images such as line drawings. Well suited to digital publishing.
.TIF	A powerful, all-around image format. Well suited to digital publishing.
.EPS	Generally speaking, this format is geared solely for printing PostScript images; it does not reproduce well onscreen and is not recommended for digital publishing.
.JPG	Use for photorealistic images such as photographs as well as for images that are very small in disc space requirements. Also well suited for use in documents that will be moved to the Internet.

Using Import Picture

The **Import Picture** command is the easiest way to insert a picture into a document, as it offers virtually no options except for selecting the type of picture file and the picture file itself. To get started, we should open the sample document PICTURE1.HW4.

Opening PICTURE1.HW4

1. Select the **Open** command from the **File** menu.
2. Select the document PICTURE1.HW4 from the list of available documents. Save your current document if needed. If you are asked to leave a bookmark, answer No. This loads the document. This document is shown in Figure 13.1.

With the PICTURE1.HW4 document open, we are now ready to start working with the **Import Picture** command. As you can see from looking at the document, it shows a sample press release issued by NTERGAID. Our goal for this tutorial is to start by importing the graphics file NTLOGO1.PCX into the top of the document, so that readers will immediately recognize that this document was from NTERGAID. To start adding our picture to this document, we need

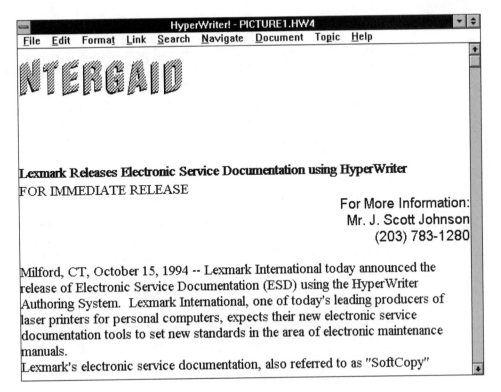

Figure 13.1 The PICTURE1.HW4 document.

to first add some blank space at the top of the document for our logo to be displayed. The reason for this is that we are using **Import Picture**, a command where the picture is considered as a point, not an object. When you use Import Picture, your pictures will overlap any text where they are imported if you don't add extra blank lines or spaces around the picture. Our solution will be to add four blank lines of space at the top of our document.

Adding Blank Lines Before Using Import Picture

1. Move to the top of the document if you aren't already there and position the cursor exactly at the left margin. A useful keyboard shortcut for this is **Ctrl+Home**.
2. Press **Enter** four times to insert four blank lines prior to the first few lines of text.

With the blank lines inserted, we are now ready to use **Import Picture** as detailed in the following steps.

Using Import Picture

1. Move to the top of the document and position the cursor exactly at the left margin. A useful keyboard shortcut for this is **Ctrl+Home**. This places the cursor where the picture will be imported.

2. Select the **Import Picture** command from the **File** menu. This displays a submenu for choosing the format of the picture to import.

3. Select .PCX as the format to import. A dialog box is then displayed for selecting the picture file to import.

4. Select the picture file NTLOGO1.PCX. This imports the picture and displays it onscreen. The imported picture is shown in Figure 13.2.

Although we have now used **Import Picture**, the distinction that a picture is treated as a point, not an object, has not really been made evident. To demonstrate this, we will create a style, applying it to our picture, and then try to center the picture using HyperWriter's **Tag Justification** command. The first step is to create the needed style.

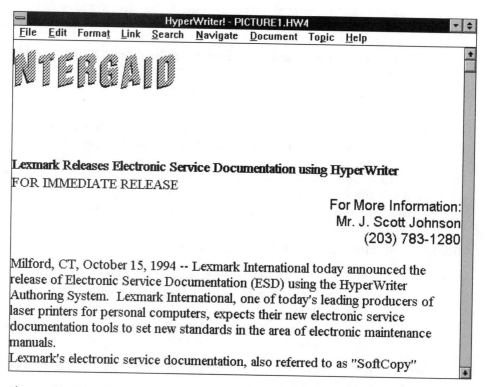

Figure 13.2 The imported picture.

Creating a Style

1. Having just imported a picture, your cursor should be on the same line as the picture. If not, place your cursor on this line. By placing the cursor on this line, the style that we will now create will be applied to the picture itself.
2. Select the **Create Tag** command from the **Format** menu.
3. Enter the name "Centered Picture" into the **Create New Tag** dialog box. This creates a new style and applies it to the picture.

With our style created, we are ready to begin formatting its justification using the **Tag Justification** command.

Setting Justification

Select the **Tag Justification** command from the **Format** menu and set its justification to **Centered**. As you can see, while the picture changes position, it does not appear correctly centered in the document. This is shown in Figure 13.3.

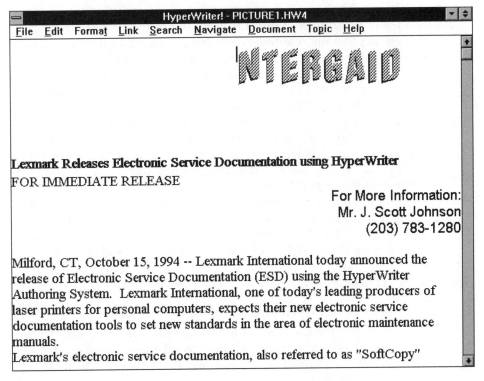

Figure 13.3 The "centered" picture.

As shown, the logo embedded at the top of our document is centered, but not correctly. This is due to how the **Import Picture** command treats pictures—as points, not as objects. If we had used the **Insert Object** command instead of **Import Picture**, we would have seen that our picture would have been properly centered.

Having now used the **Import Picture** command to bring in a logo displayed at the top of our document and experimented with formatting pictures with styles, we are now ready to move on to the next step in our tutorial—working with the **Insert Object** command.

Using Insert Object

As noted earlier in this tutorial, unlike **Import Picture**, the **Insert Object** command allows pictures to be treated as true objects. This allows HyperWriter to understand the dimensions of the picture so that text can be automatically wrapped to the right and left of them and formatting commands such as **Justification** function properly. This is quite different from the **Import Picture** command which treats pictures as if they are single characters and does not wrap text around them (the pictures are treated as if they are overlays onto the screen). When **Insert Object** is used, the picture that it places into your document is generally referred to as a *framed picture*, as it behaves as if the picture was in an invisible frame that describes the picture's size.

When a framed picture is inserted into a paragraph of text, the framed picture sets the height of the current line and the text appears along the bottom edge of the paragraph. Additional advantages to framed pictures include that they can be scaled, sized, and cropped right in the text where they are displayed. A final advantage is that stylesheets can be applied to framed objects and the framed objects will be properly handled (such as center justified or right justified). Generally speaking, framed pictures are significantly easier to use than the **Import Picture** command and offer many advantages.

With an understanding of the advantages of using **Insert Object**, we will begin using **Insert Object**. For this exercise, we want to start with the sample document PICTURE2.HW4. As we don't need the document that we created by modifying PICTURE1.HW4, we will not save those changes.

Opening PICTURE2.HW4

1. Select the **Open** command from the **File** menu.

2. Select the document PICTURE2.HW4 from the list of available documents. Select No when asked to save your changes. If you are asked to leave a bookmark, answer No. This loads the document, as shown in Figure 13.4.

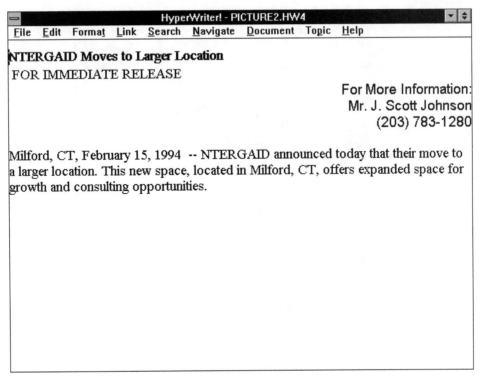

Figure 13.4 The PICTURE2.HW4 document.

As you can see, this document is a press release about NTERGAID moving into its new offices in Milford, Connecticut. What we will do is first insert our company logo at the top of the document, and then insert a picture of NTER-GAID's office building in the body of the document. Inserting the first picture will allow you to compare using **Insert Object** with using **Import Picture** while the second picture provides additional practice.

We are now ready to insert the picture file NTLOGO1.PCX into the top of our document. As we don't want our picture file inserted on the same line as the title of the press release, we will add start by adding a blank line to the top of our document. Unlike when we used **Import Picture**, we will only add one blank line.

Adding a Blank Line to our Document

1. Move to the top of the document if you aren't already there and position the cursor exactly at the left margin. A useful keyboard shortcut for this is **Ctrl+Home**.

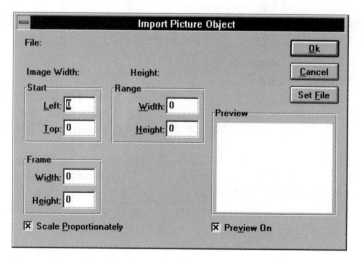

Figure 13.5 The **Import Picture Object** dialog box.

2. Press **Enter** one time to insert one blank line prior to the first few lines of text.

With the blank line inserted, we are now ready to use **Insert Object** as detailed in the following steps.

Using Insert Object

1. Move to the top of the document and position the cursor exactly at the left margin. A useful keyboard shortcut for this is **Ctrl+Home**. This places the cursor where the picture will be imported.

2. Select the **Insert Object** command from the **Edit** menu. This displays the **Import Picture Object** dialog box as shown in Figure 13.5. As you will note, the **Import Object** dialog box has a number of different options. We will only use the **Set File** option now (the other options will be covered later in this tutorial).

3. Select the **Set File** button and then select .PCX as the format to import. A dialog box is then displayed for selecting the picture file to import.

4. Select the picture file NTLOGO1.PCX. This imports the picture and sets various options in the dialog box. It will also display a preview of the picture in the Preview field.

5. Select the **OK** button to close the dialog box and display the picture onscreen. This displays the screen shown in Figure 13.6.

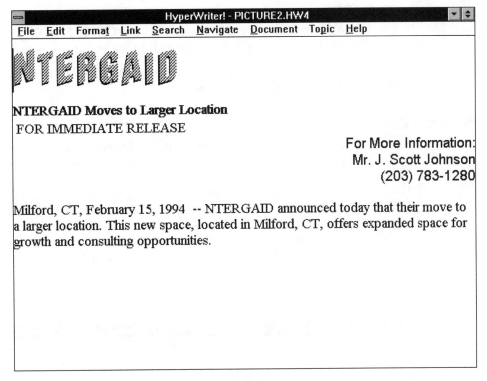

Figure 13.6 The picture we inserted using **Insert Object**.

As should be evident on your screen, the picture is now displayed at the top of the screen. As we used the **Insert Object** command not the **Import Picture** command, our picture was treated as a true object and we only had to insert a single blank line for it, not the four blank lines that we inserted earlier. In order to illustrate how **Insert Object** treats pictures as objects, our next task is to create a new style (as we did previously) and then use **Tag Justification** to center the picture. As you may recall, this is exactly the same task that we did previously when experimenting with **Import Picture**. The difference is that having used **Insert Object**, our picture will be correctly centered onscreen. As before, our first step is to create a new style.

Creating a Style

1. Having just inserted a picture object, your cursor should be on the same line as the picture. If not, place your cursor on this line. By placing the cursor on this line, the style that we will now create will be applied to the picture itself.

2. Select the **Create Tag** command from the **Format** menu.

3. Enter the name **Centered Picture** into the **Create New Tag** dialog box. This creates a new style and applies it to the picture.

With our style created, we are ready to begin formatting its justification using the **Tag Justification** command.

Setting Justification

Select the **Tag Justification** command from the **Format** menu and set its justification to **Centered**. As you can see, the picture's justification immediately changes to centered (shown in Figure 13.7).

As shown, the **Tag Justification** command allows true centering of picture objects—provided that the pictures are embedded using the **Import Picture** command.

In order to finish working with **Insert Object**, we have two tasks left. The first is that we should do another exercise using **Insert Object**, and the second is that we need to cover the options available to **Insert Object** that we haven't covered yet.

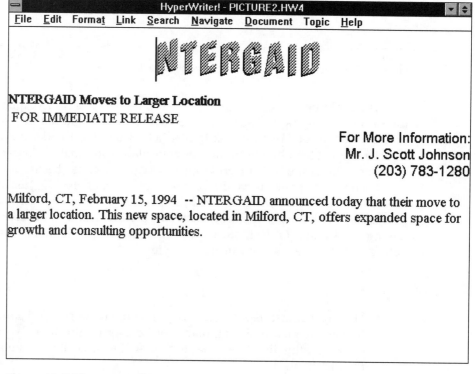

Figure 13.7 The centered picture.

For this exercise, we want to start with the sample document PICTURE3.HW4. As we don't need the document that we created by modifying PICTURE2.HW4, we will not save those changes.

Opening PICTURE3.HW4

1. Select the **Open** command from the **File** menu.
2. Select the document PICTURE3.HW4 from the list of available documents. Select No when asked to save your changes. If you are asked to leave a bookmark, answer No. This loads the document shown in Figure 13.8.

As you can see, this document is a press release about NTERGAID moving into its new offices in Milford, Connecticut. In this exercise, we will insert a picture of NTERGAID's actual office building into our text to illustrate using **Insert Object** with pictures inserted alongside text.

Having opened the document PICTURE3.HW4, we are ready to start inserting our picture.

Figure 13.8 The PICTURE3.HW4 document.

Using Insert Object

1. Place your cursor at the beginning of the first text paragraph in the body of the document, after the document title.

2. Select the **Insert Object** command from the **Edit** menu. This displays the **Import Picture Object** dialog box.

3. Select the **Set File** button and then select .PCX as the format to import. A dialog box is then displayed for selecting the picture file to import.

4. Select the picture file NTSITE.PCX. This imports the picture and sets various options in the dialog box. It will also display a preview of the picture in the **Preview** field.

5. Select the **OK** button to close the dialog box and display the picture onscreen. This displays the screen shown in Figure 13.9.

As you can see from using **Insert Object**, the picture that you inserted has been located at the left-hand margin with text from the paragraph where it was inserted positioned next to the picture, along the picture's bottom edge. This is

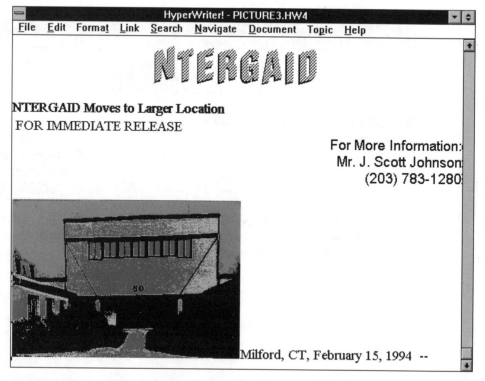

Figure 13.9 The picture we inserted using **Insert Object**.

how text is aligned with pictures added to documents using **Insert Object**. If you were to start editing this document, you would find that the picture would flow with the document, moving with and being repositioned as needed. This is quite different from **Import Picture** where editing with the picture would require hand alignment of pictures with the text.

NOTE: When you type on the same paragraph where a picture object has been imported, you may notice screen flicker as you are typing. If this proves to be a problem, press **Enter** (to create a new paragraph), continue typing, and then later delete the extra carriage return. Screen flicker is generally only noticeable with large pictures.

NOTE: When the cursor is on a line of a paragraph that contains a framed picture, the cursor will become as tall as the framed picture itself. This is how the cursor is designed to operate in this situation.

This concludes our usage of **Insert Object**. As you have seen, not only is **Insert Object** more flexible than **Import Picture**, it also gives a better final result. Although we have worked through our tutorials using **Insert Object**, we still need to go over the different options available when using it.

Reference: Understanding Insert Object

As you have seen, **Insert Object** has a number of different options. You have also seen that despite all these commands, you don't necessarily have to use all of them (in using **Insert Object** to this point, we have only used the **Set File** button). Table 13.3 covers the different options available to **Insert Object**.

Reference: Editing a Picture Object

Once you have inserted a picture object, you can edit that picture object by placing the text cursor next to the object and then selecting the **Edit Object** command from the **Edit** menu (when the cursor is next to a picture object, the **Insert Object** command becomes an **Edit Object** command). This redisplays the **Import Picture Object** dialog box for the selected picture and allows you to edit the settings for the picture object.

Editing a Picture Object

1. Place the cursor next to the picture object you want to edit and select the **Edit Object** command from the **Edit** menu.

Table 13.3 Options for Insert Object

Option	Description
Set File	Set the file to be imported. It displays a list of file types and then a file dialog box for setting the file to import.
Image Width and Image Height	Prompts tell you the size of the image. This information is helpful for setting the Start, Range, and Frame parameters.
Start	Set the upper left and top starting corner for the picture, allowing you to crop the image from the top and left edges. This is entered in pixels measured from the upper left corner of the image. The default setting is 0,0.
Range	Set how many pixels of the image are to be displayed. This is measured from the settings in the **Start** field. The default setting is the size of the image.
Frame	Set the visible size of the image displayed on screen. The default setting is the size of the image. With the default settings for Start, Range, and Frame, the picture object will display a picture in a frame the size of the picture. If the picture object is larger than the screen then HyperWriter will default to creating the picture to 75 percent of screen size.
Scale Proportionately	Set the picture so that it is proportionately scaled. You should note that Scale Proportionately is a property of the dialog box, not of the image (i.e., it will be turned on or off automatically based on how it was previously set).
Preview	Instantly see the effects of your changes.
Preview On	Turn on or off the Preview display. This may be helpful for performance reasons.

2. Select the options to change from the **Import Picture Object** dialog box and then select **OK** to close the dialog box and see the results of the editing.

Creating Links to Pictures

Up to this point, the types of pictures that we have been working with could well be described as embedded, in that the picture is embedded within the content of the document. We are now ready to move onto a new type of picture, the *linked* picture. With a linked picture, the author of the document creates a link that, when activated, displays a picture. Creating links to pictures is done with the **Link to Picture** command on the **Link** menu. For this exercise, we want to start with the sample document PICTURE4.HW4. As we don't need the document that we created by modifying PICTURE3.HW4, we will not save those changes.

Opening PICTURE4.HW4

1. Select the **Open** command from the **File** menu.
2. Select the document PICTURE4.HW4 from the list of available documents. Select No when asked to save your changes. If you are asked to leave a bookmark, answer No. This loads the document shown in Figure 13.10.

As you can see, this document is a press release about NTERGAID moving into its new offices in Milford, Connecticut. In this exercise, we will insert a

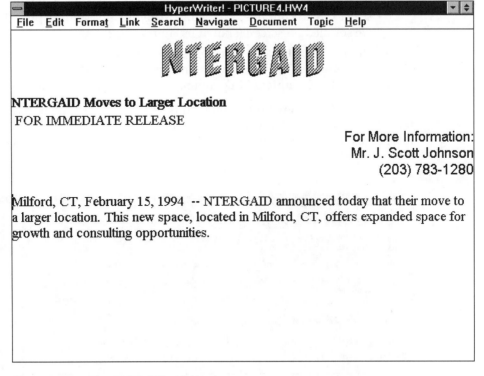

Figure 13.10 The PICTURE4.HW4 document.

link to a picture of NTERGAID's actual office building into our text to illustrate creating links to pictures. Having opened the document PICTURE4.HW4, we are ready to start inserting our picture.

Creating a Link to a Picture

1. Place your cursor at the beginning of the second text paragraph in the body of the document, after the document title.

2. Press **Enter** one time to insert a blank line and type the caption **NTER-GAID's New Location** onto this line.

3. Mark the caption that you just typed as a block and select the **Link to Picture** command from the **Link** menu.

4. Select .PCX as the picture format you want to link to.

5. Select the file NTSITE.PCX as the picture to link to. This brings up HyperWriter's **Picture Linking Wizard** dialog box (shown in Figure 13.11).

6. The **Picture Linking Wizard** dialog box helps you create links to pictures. For now, we can leave the options set at their defaults and just select **OK** to continue. This will create our link and display the picture we selected on screen (shown in Figure 13.12).

7. Having used **Link to Picture**, we have now created a link that displays a picture file. To return to the link anchor, we need to complete the link. Select the **Complete Link** command from the **Link** menu now.

After the **Complete Link** command is selected, HyperWriter returns you to the text that you originally marked as a link (the link anchor). This text is now marked as a link and when selected will display the picture of NTERGAID's offices.

Picture Linking Wizard

The Picture Linking Wizard gives you control over how linked pictures are displayed.

Select "Use Palette" if you want topics or background objects such as buttons to use the palette stored in the picture file.

Select "Enable Scrolling/Zooming" if the picture is larger than the screen.

Select "Initial Scale to Window Size" to start with the best zoom ratio for viewing the entire picture at once.

Selected Picture: S:\HW4\PICTURES\NTSITE.PCX

- [X] Show using Floating Window
- [X] Use Palette
- [ ] Enable Scrolling/Zooming
- [ ] Initial Scale to Window Size

[Ok] [Cancel]

Figure 13.11 The **Picture Linking Wizard** dialog box.

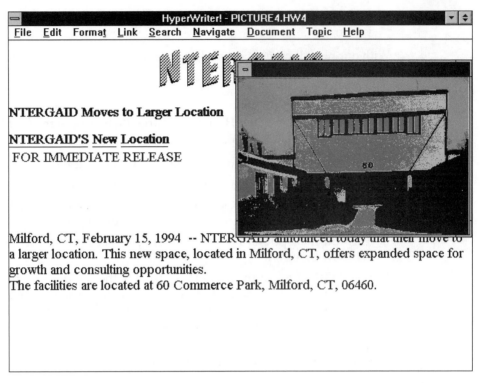

Figure 13.12 The picture we linked to.

One of the more powerful features in HyperWriter is the ability to handle pictures larger than screen size. Using the Picture Linking Wizard, when you link to pictures you can tell HyperWriter that the picture is to be displayed using scroll bars and even to display the picture so that it is initially scaled to the window size. This greatly facilitates using HyperWriter with large pictures such as charts, schematics, and engineering drawings. In our next exercise, we will create a link to a large picture and use these options. Unlike our previous tutorials, we will start not by using an existing HyperWriter document, but by creating a new document.

Creating a New Document

1. Select the **New** command from the **File** menu.
2. When HyperWriter asks if you want to save changes, select No. If HyperWriter asks if you want to leave a bookmark, select No.
3. Turn off the Use New Template Wizard feature so that no template is used.

4. Select the **OK** button. This creates a new blank document and places you in it.

With our new document created, we are ready to create a link to a picture.

Creating a Link to a Picture

1. Type the caption **Click Here for A Large Picture** onto the first line.
2. Mark the caption as a block.
3. Select the **Link to Picture** command from the **Link** menu.
4. Select .PCX as the picture format you want to link to.
5. Select the file SCROLZOOM.PCX as the picture to link to. This brings up HyperWriter's **Picture Linking Wizard** dialog box.
6. Turn on the options **Enable Scrolling/Zooming** and **Initial Scale to Window Size**.
7. Select **OK** to make the link. This displays the picture in a popup window, complete with scroll bars and a zoom box. The picture is also displayed so that the entire picture can be seen (HyperWriter has set the picture's initial scale to match the size of the window). The picture that we linked to is shown in Figure 13.13.
8. Select **Complete Link** to finish making the link.

NOTE: In the picture shown, the scroll bars allow *panning*, or scrolling across the picture while the zoom box located in the bottom right hand corner of the picture window supports zooming in or out on the picture. To zoom in or out on the image, click on the appropriate part of the zoom box. Clicking on the lower-right corner (pointing out of the picture) of the zoom box zooms out. Clicking on the upper-left corner of the zoom box (pointing into the picture) zooms in. In addition to the zoom box, HyperWriter also supports zooming in by marking a section of the picture by clicking with the mouse and dragging it around the region.

This exercise completes our hands-on work covering links to pictures. Our final task is to review the different options that the Picture Linking Wizard supports.

Reference: Using the Picture Linking Wizard

As shown in the previous section, the Picture Linking Wizard appears automatically when you link to a picture. Although we were able to use the Picture

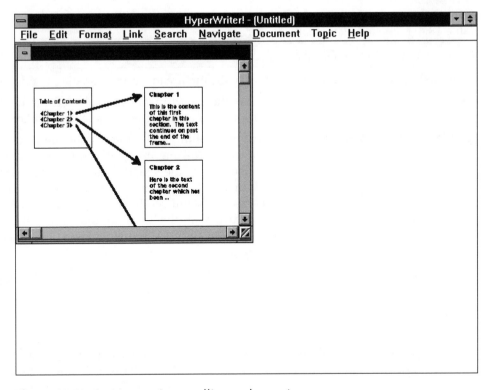

Figure 13.13 A picture using scrolling and zooming.

Linking Wizard without many changes to its options, the Picture Linking Wizard provides several options should we need them. Each of the options on the Picture Linking Wizard is described in Table 13.4.

Reference: Performance, A Real Advantage for Linking to Pictures

As you have probably noted by this point, the key difference between embedded pictures and linked pictures is that an embedded picture does not give the reader any control. By control, I am referring to whether or not the reader chooses to view that picture. When the reader navigates to a topic where an embedded picture is displayed, that picture is displayed no matter what the reader does. In contrast, a linked picture is displayed only when the reader wants that picture displayed. On the surface, this difference does not appear terribly significant. After all, the picture displays relatively quickly in both cases, correct? The answer, unfortunately, is that pictures don't always display quickly. While on a hard drive or even CD-ROM, pictures do display quickly, as soon as you move your application to the Internet's World Wide Web, you will find that the speed of picture display is a big issue. As the World Wide

Table 13.4 Using the Picture Linking Wizard

Picture Linking Wizard Option	*Description*
Show Using Floating Window	Display the picture in a popup floating window.
Use Palette	Import the palette from the selected picture into the topic or background screen where it is displayed.
Enable Scrolling/Zooming	Turn on scrolling and zooming for the picture so that users can scroll the image horizontally and vertically and zoom in on the image. This option is generally used with images larger than screen size. (If an image can fit on screen without scrollbars, why use them?) Zooming is handled with the zoom in/out icon in the corner of the scrollbars or by selecting a region of the picture with the mouse.
Initial Scale to Window Size	Tell HyperWriter to scale the picture to the window size when the picture is first displayed.

Web (for the vast majority of users) operates through a modem, when your documents have pictures embedded in them, the user is forced to view those pictures—even if he or she has slow hardware. Contrast this with linked pictures where the user can choose to display linked pictures, but doesn't have to display them if they are not required. As a general rule of thumb, use linked pictures if your application is to be used over the World Wide Web.

NOTE: As HyperWriter documents can be used over local area networks (as well as the World Wide Web), the same comments on linking to pictures applies to use over local area networks.

Reference: When Do I Use Links to Pictures?

Applications that will be published over the Internet are one area where linked pictures are preferable to embedded pictures. The following situations listed in Table 13.5 are other areas where linked pictures are preferable to embedded pictures.

Table 13.5 When to Use Linked Pictures

Situation	Description
Larger than screen pictures	HyperWriter supports scrolling of pictures when the picture is linked, not when the picture is embedded.
Progressive disclosure	When the type of application that you are creating requires the user to first read some information and then view the picture, linking to pictures can accomplish this as the information is progressively disclosed to the reader.
Picture zooming	HyperWriter supports zooming of pictures, but only for linked pictures not for embedded pictures.
Performance	When performance is critical (such as on the World Wide Web or on a local area network), linked pictures provide better performance than do embedded pictures.

Inserting Pictures through Background Screens

HyperWriter's Background Screen facility provides another powerful tool for inserting pictures into documents. As mentioned earlier in this tutorial, this facility will be covered in the next tutorial.

Saving Our Work

In this tutorial, we really focused on working with different picture features in HyperWriter—not on a particular application. For this reason, there is no need to save your work.

Exiting HyperWriter

With our tutorial finished, you can now exit HyperWriter if desired. This is done with the **Exit** command on the **File** menu.

Using the Screen Painter

One of HyperWriter's key features is unquestionably its object-oriented Screen Painter. The Screen Painter allows you to create a unique, engaging user interface or screen design geared to your particular application. By reaching this tutorial, you have seen a number of different applications created with Hyper-Writer. One characteristic of these applications is that they each had their own unique design. This is the power of HyperWriter's Screen Painter—it allows you to create a unique design for your application by simply dragging and dropping objects. In HyperWriter, these designs are called *backgrounds*. Even better, HyperWriter has a series of useful templates that can be used intact or to provide a starting point on which to base your design. In this tutorial, we will accomplish the following tasks:

- Learn to use the Screen Painter
- Modify an existing text-button–based design (using the Template Wizard)
- Modify an existing graphics-button–based design (using the Template Wizard)
- Create a screen design from scratch

Understanding Backgrounds

Until this tutorial, we have primarily focused on creating, formatting, and linking information. However, all of this information has always been manip-

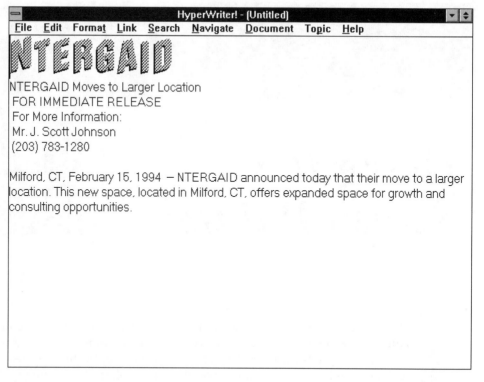

Figure 14.1 A topic without a background.

ulated in the *foreground* of a topic. When you are typing information, importing pictures, and creating links, you are working in the foreground of a topic. Information in HyperWriter can also be manipulated in the background of a topic by using a HyperWriter feature called *background screens* (generally just called *backgrounds*). Backgrounds add a powerful tool for adding a user interface to your HyperWriter documents. This can include such elements as buttons, pictures, and other user interface objects. Backgrounds can be attached to any type of topic—full screen, comment, or picture.

A background screen is a collection of fixed, unmoving objects displayed with any topic or topics in a document. Backgrounds appear behind any text, pictures, or video information onscreen in that topic, hence the term *background*. Backgrounds are used to create attractive, functional screens for information presentation and can be used in either card- or article-based hypertext documents. Background screens typically form the user interface to your documents. A topic without a background is shown in Figure 14.1.

A sample background is shown in Figure 14.2. This background is inside HyperWriter's Screen Painter. The Screen Painter is a special editor inside

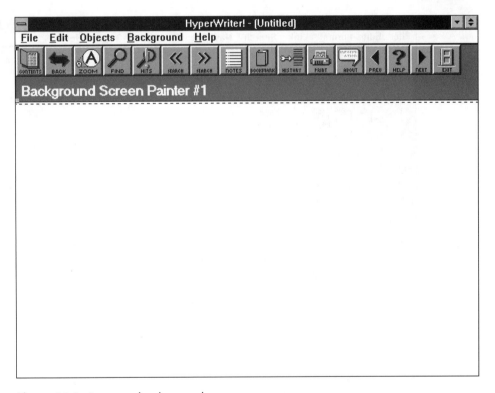

Figure 14.2 A screen background.

HyperWriter just for creating background objects. In the Screen Painter, Hyper-Writer's word processor is not available, instead there are a special set of only the commands used to create background objects. Because of this, when you are in the Screen Painter, the text of the topic is not displayed, only the background objects.

Shown in Figure 14.3 is this background assigned to the topic shown earlier. As you can see, a background screen provides a user interface to the information in the topic. This user interface allows the reader to select on a search button, add a note, and use other navigational functions.

A key concept for effectively applying HyperWriter's screen backgrounds is that of reusing backgrounds. Once a background is created, it can be used in an unlimited number of topics. Understanding this concept of reuse is very important, since it saves you from having to create a unique background for every topic. Instead, you can reuse backgrounds that you have previously created. This obviously saves a great deal of time and effort when creating a document.

HyperWriter supports up to three backgrounds per topic. These backgrounds are called First, Second, and Third. The name of the background refers

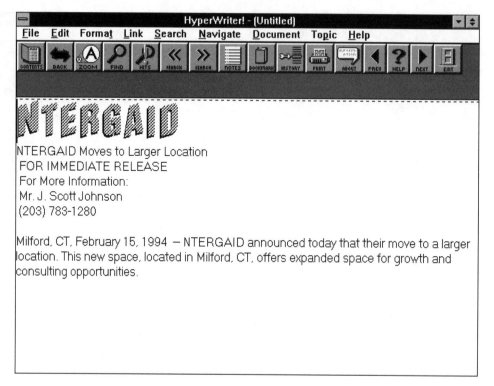

Figure 14.3 The screen background assigned to the topic.

to the order in which it is drawn. When a reader enters a topic, the First background is drawn first; the Second background is drawn second; the Third background is drawn third; finally the text in the topic is drawn within the margin area as defined by the background screens. Understanding the order in which backgrounds are drawn is important, because otherwise an object might be incorrectly drawn over another object. For example, if the Second background contained a screen color setting, this would **hide** all objects in the First background.

HyperWriter supports three backgrounds per topic—First, Second, and Third—for powerful screen design. Backgrounds common to all topics are generally used as the First background screen for all topics and screen backgrounds specific to only certain topics are generally used as the Second and Third background. With proper design, this prevents having to recreate common screen objects unnecessarily.

A key concept to understand with backgrounds is that when your background screen has a margin area where scrolling text is displayed, the objects in the background screen cannot extend into the margin area. If your background objects extend into the margin area when the text scrolls, there will be

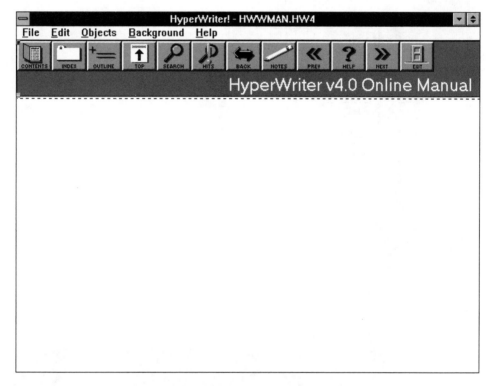

Figure 14.4 Backgrounds used for online documentation.

a color change. This results from the text picking up the color from the background objects. The solution to this is to have your background objects not be inside the margin area. However, if the text in your topic where the background is applied is not scrolling, then this will not occur and background objects can be in this area without problems.

What Can I Do with Backgrounds?

To illustrate the types of applications that can be constructed with backgrounds, consider the following applications, all created using HyperWriter's Screen Painter. Shown in Figure 14.4 is a background used to provide the user interface for online documentation.

In addition to backgrounds that are applied to full-screen topics, backgrounds can also be applied to comment topics. Shown in Figure 14.5 is a background used with a comment topic.

When creating a digital publication, a common task is to create an attractive opening screen for an application. Shown in Figure 14.6 is the opening screen that we will use for the tutorial in Chapter 18.

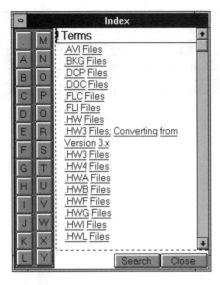

Figure 14.5 Backgrounds used in a comment topic.

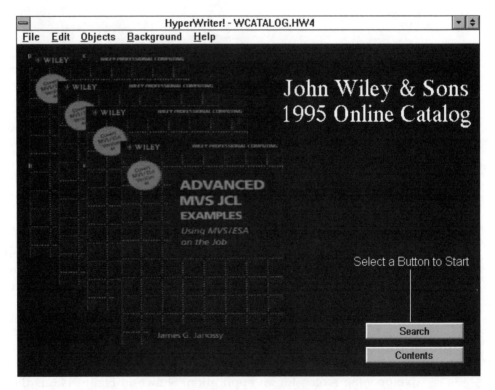

Figure 14.6 Backgrounds used for the opening screen of an application.

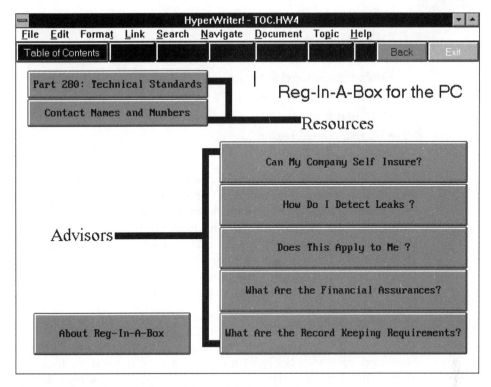

Figure 14.7 Backgrounds used for a visual table of contents.

Backgrounds can also be used to create a visual table of contents for an application. Shown in Figure 14.7 is the document TOC.HW4, which illustrates a visual table of contents.

Understanding the Screen Painter

The Screen Painter is a mode of operating HyperWriter used only for creating backgrounds. It has its own menu system and series of keystrokes. As the Screen Painter is a *mode* within HyperWriter, when you are in the Screen Painter you cannot use HyperWriter as you normally would. Instead, you can only make backgrounds. Within the Screen Painter, background objects can be created, positioned, and linked. The different objects that can be created with the Screen Painter are:

- Buttons
- Text
- Pictures
- Video overlay region

- Repeating characters such as lines
- Database fields
- Lines
- Reader's notes checkmark
- Active checkmark region
- Related icon
- Active related region
- Topic name locator

Besides creating these objects, backgrounds can also be used to set margins, define screen colors, and set or modify the palette for the background. Even if you do not need true background objects such as buttons, the Screen Painter can still be useful for setting margins and defining screen colors—as a background, these settings are reusable across topics. Once you define a background to set the margins or colors of a topic, it can be used repeatedly. This saves you from having to reset these values for every topic. Similarly, when you edit a background, it is updated everywhere it is used in the document.

Why Should I Use Backgrounds?

There are several advantages to working with information in the background. First, once created, a background can be reused in multiple topics. Second, it is easy to put together attractive, visually compelling screen designs with the Screen Painter. Third, creating visual user interface elements such as buttons can only be done with backgrounds. Fourth, creating video regions for use with digital video can only be done using background objects.

Learning to Use the Screen Painter

Using the Screen Painter is a little bit different from what we have covered up to this point, as with the Screen Painter you aren't working with text and documents, you are working in terms of objects. To make using the Screen Painter easier, this section is an overview of the concepts behind using background screens and steps to follow.

The first step in using a background is to create one with the **Add Background** command from the **Edit** menu. Documents initially have no backgrounds until the **Add Background** command is used.

NOTE: The one exception to this is when you use the Template Wizard which does add backgrounds to documents.

Choosing **Add Background** enters the Screen Painter. Displayed in the status bar is Background Screen Painter #? where the ? is the number of the background being created. As with links and topics, backgrounds are numbered sequentially in the order of creation. Thus, the first background you create is background number 1. The second is background number 2 and the third is background number 3. This continues until background 255, the last background in the document. To make understanding backgrounds easier, backgrounds can also be named as well as numbered.

When you add a background, HyperWriter's menu system changes to reflect that you are in the Screen Painter. The main menu choices are now **File**, **Edit**, **Objects**, **Background**, and **Help**. This reflects the object-based nature of the Screen Painter where you work in terms of objects rather than documents.

Backgrounds are created by first selecting the type of object from the **Objects** menu. This puts the object onscreen with dummy information instead of the actual information later entered with the **Properties** command. For example, all buttons are automatically given the text Button Text for their dummy information. When an object is first put onscreen, it is automatically selected for the author. Selected objects are shown by four colored blocks, one at each corner of the object. A selected object, a **Search** button, is shown in Figure 14.8.

Use the mouse to move the selected object to its destination. Once the object is positioned, the next step is to define the properties of the object with the **Properties** command from the **Objects** menu. A short cut for the **Properties** command is to select the Object and then press the **Right Mouse** button when the mouse pointer is over the object. A keyboard-oriented short cut for the **Properties** command is **Ctrl+F3**. This displays a dialog box specific to the selected object so that its functionality can be set. For example, a button would have properties of link number, color, and so on. A picture would have properties of the type of picture file, the picture file to be displayed, and how it is to be displayed. After the object's properties have been set, reposition the object if necessary or add additional objects. If you find that certain objects overlap other objects, preventing them from being displayed, you can select individual objects and use the **Bring to Front** or **Send to Back** commands on the **Edit** menu to change the order the objects are displayed in. Other commands in the Screen Painter let you:

- Create margins for foreground text and pictures
- Set background and foreground screen colors
- Set how background objects are drawn
- Set the palette for the background

After all the objects have been added to the background and you are pleased with the result, select the **Exit** command from the **File** menu to exit the

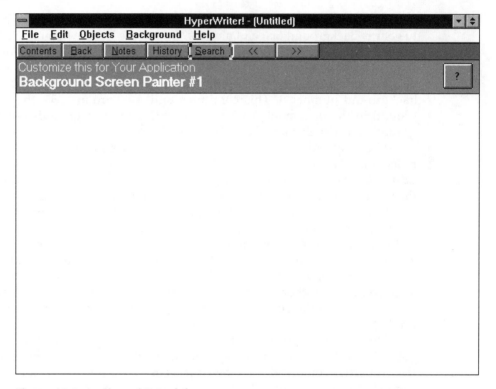

Figure 14.8 A selected **Search** button.

Screen Painter. This returns you to the topic from which you entered the Screen Painter. At this point, although you have created a background, the background is not displayed. This is because the background has not yet been applied to the topic with the **Apply Background** command on the **Edit** menu. To assign the background to the topic, select the **Apply Background** command from the **Edit** menu and enter the number of the background you just created. If you recall, this number was displayed in the status bar in the Screen Painter (if you had the status bar on). Any topic can have up to three backgrounds: First, Second, and Third. Once a background has been assigned to a topic, it will be displayed onscreen. If you watch the screen closely, you will see that the First background is drawn first, the Second background is drawn second, the Third background is then drawn and, finally, the text and/or pictures within the margin area are drawn.

To review, creating and assigning backgrounds is a six-step process:

1. Create the background with **Add Background**.
2. Background objects must be added to the background by selecting them from the **Objects** menu.

3. Each object's properties must be set by selecting the object and using the **Properties** command from the Objects menu.

4. Other background commands such as color, margins, and properties can be used.

5. Exit the painter by choosing the **Exit Painter** command from the **File** menu.

6. Assign the created background to the current topic with the **Apply Background** command from the **Edit** menu.

Now that we have a good conceptual understanding of backgrounds, we are ready to begin working with them in our tutorial. First, we need to run HyperWriter.

Running HyperWriter

Before we can open a sample document we must first run HyperWriter. HyperWriter is a standard MS-Windows application that can be run from the Program Manager.

Working with an Existing Design (Text Buttons)

Our first task using the Screen Painter is to create a particular document template using the Template Wizard, and then modify the background in that template to add additional functions. By modifying this background, we will get a better feel for how the Screen Painter functions. This will also give us valuable experience in using the Screen Painter.

The first step is for us to create a document template using the Template Wizard.

Creating a Document Template

1. Select the **New** command from the **File** menu. Save your current document if needed. If HyperWriter prompts you to leave a bookmark, select Yes or No as needed.

2. In the **Template Wizard** dialog box, select the **Button Style** field and set it to **Text Buttons**. This tells the Template Wizard that you only want to look at templates using buttons with text titles (not icons).

3. Select the **Orientation** field and set it to **Along Top Side**. This tells the Template Wizard that you only want to look at templates with buttons along the top of the screen.

4. In the **User Interface** field, you can now see that the number of available interfaces has been greatly reduced. Select the **Winhelp Modified** interface and then select the **OK** button. This creates a document template using the selected interface.

After creating the interface, what should be displayed on your screen is shown in Figure 14.9.

As you can see, this document template has a button bar across the top with buttons for contents, back, notes history, search, previous and next, a customizable text object, and a blank area below the text object. This blank area gives a location for the topic name of the current topic to be displayed (to review, each HyperWriter application is broken up into sections called *topics* and each topic has a name called the *topic name*). The topic currently has some message text giving you instructions as well. This text can be deleted at any time.

Our next step is to modify this template by customizing the text object. To do this, first move from HyperWriter's normal word-processing environment into the Screen Painter. The commands for entering the Screen Painter are

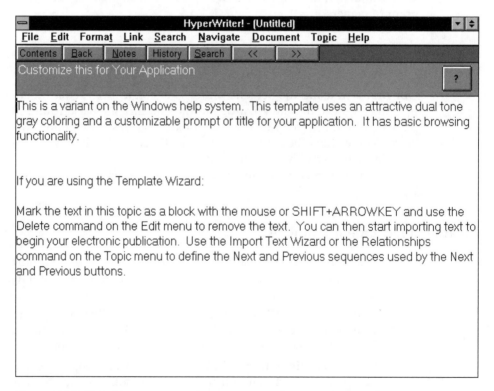

Figure 14.9 The document template you created.

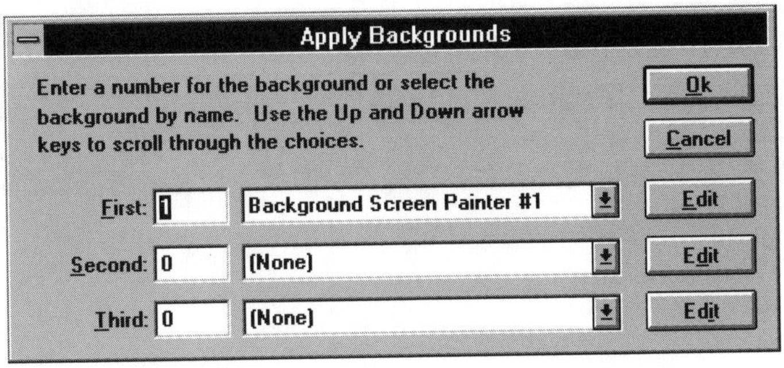

Figure 14.10 Using the **Apply Background** command.

located on the **Edit** menu. The specific command that we want to use is the **Apply Background** command. **Apply Background** lets you look at the backgrounds in use for the current topic and edit the backgrounds as needed. Every HyperWriter topic can have up to three backgrounds applied to it. These backgrounds are called the First background, the Second background, and the Third background. Whenever you use the Template Wizard, the background that it creates for you is always the First background applied to a topic. Hence, we want to modify the First background.

Editing a Background Using the Apply Background Command

1. Select the **Apply Background** command from the **Edit** menu.
2. Select the **Edit** button next to the **First** field. This will move you into the Screen Painter. In Figure 14.10, the first step, using the **Apply Background** command, is shown.

After you have selected the **Edit** button on the **Apply Background** dialog box, HyperWriter moves you into the Screen Painter. The Screen Painter is shown in Figure 14.11.

As you can see, when you are in the Screen Painter, HyperWriter's menu structure is reduced considerably—only **File**, **Edit**, **Objects**, **Background**, and **Help** menu are available. This reflects that the Screen Painter is a mode within HyperWriter; in the Screen Painter only commands needed for the Screen Painter are available. The different menus are used as shown in Table 14.1.

Within the Screen Painter, HyperWriter functions differently than you have seen to this point. One major difference is that you no longer have a text cursor. This reflects that in the Screen Painter you are editing objects, not text. What has replaced the text cursor is a series of four small handles shown at the corners of the currently selected object. These four handles indicate that any editing operations will affect this object. If you look back to the previous picture, you can see the handles if you look to the left of the **Contents** button. As

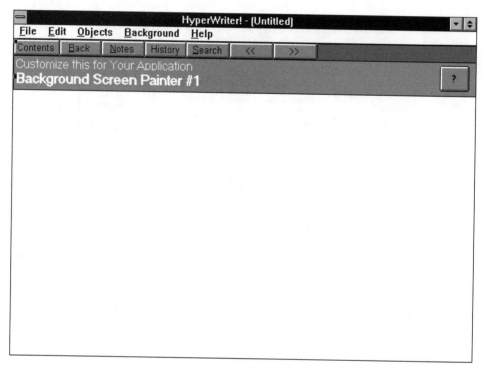

Figure 14.11 HyperWriter's Screen Painter.

you select different objects, the handles will be moved to that object. This brings us to our first real task—selecting an object and then changing its appearance.

Table 14.1 Menus in the Screen Painter

Menu	Description
File	Create/edit other backgrounds, import and export backgrounds, set preferences, and exit the Screen Painter.
Edit	Edit objects in the Screen Painter including cut, copy, paste, bring to front, send to back, and undo.
Objects	Create background objects including text, pictures, buttons; set object properties and anchor objects to corners of the screen.
Background	Set options that control the entire background as a whole including palette, margins, name, grid, and more.
Help	Get online help.

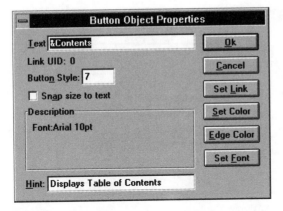

Figure 14.12 The **Object Properties** dialog box.

Selecting and Editing an Object

1. Using the mouse, select the **Contents** button by placing the pointer over the **Contents** button and clicking the **Left Mouse** button. You can also select objects in the Screen Painter by pressing the **Tab** and **Shift+Tab** keys (**Tab** moves forward one object and **Shift+Tab** moves backward one object).

2. With the **Contents** button selected, choose the **Properties** command from the **Objects** menu. This displays the **Object Properties** dialog box which allows you to configure how an object functions. The way to think of this is that you are altering the *properties* of the object. This dialog box is shown in Figure 14.12.

   NOTE: A shortcut for displaying the **Object Properties** dialog box is to place the mouse over the object and then press the **Right Mouse** button. Another shortcut is to press **Ctrl+F3**.

   Now, with the object selected, we are ready to modify it. Our task will be to adjust the object's formatting—to set the text of the button to a Bold font.

3. Select the **Set Font** button. This displays the **Button Object Font** dialog box. Select the **Bold** option and then the **OK** button. This will present the button with its text in a Bold font. The **Button Object Font** dialog box is shown in Figure 14.13.

You have now taken the first step in using HyperWriter's Screen Painter, having successfully modified an existing background. We will now take this to the next step by adding an additional button to the background.

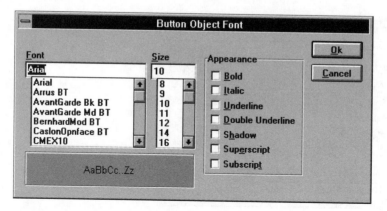

Figure 14.13 The **Button Object Font** dialog box.

Adding a Button to a Background

There are two ways to add a button to a background. The first method is to just select the **Button** command from the **Object** menu. This creates a brand new button object that can be altered as needed (such as its font, text that it displays, and its functionality). While this is an easy enough command to use, it is typically better suited to working with entirely new backgrounds, not existing ones. The reason for this is that this approach creates a button with Hyper-Writer's default settings, not the settings of the other buttons in the background. While HyperWriter's default settings for button font and button color can be altered to match that of the buttons in your background, often this isn't the case, thus giving a newly created button on which you also need to set the font and color. A better solution when adding a button that you want to match those in the current background, is to select a button with an appearance that you want to duplicate and use the **Copy** command. This process is illustrated below.

Copying and Pasting a Button

1. Select the **>>** button with either **Tab** and **Shift+Tab** or the **Left Mouse** button.

2. Select the **Copy** button from the **Edit** menu. This places a copy of the button in HyperWriter's Paste buffer.

3. Select the **Paste** command from the **Edit** menu. A second copy of the button will appear onscreen. Initially the button will appear below the **Contents** button, behind the text object that displays Customize this for your Application. What you need to do is drag it so that it is located

next to the original >> button. This will give the initial effect of showing two >> buttons onscreen next to each other (the next task fixes this).

With our button now copied and pasted, we have a button onscreen that we can modify to suit our needs. What we want to do is change the button to a **Print** button so that users of our application can print out what they are viewing. The **Set Link** button in the **Object Properties** dialog box is used to adjust how buttons function.

Making a Print Button

1. Select the second >> button with either **Tab** and **Shift+Tab** or the **Left Mouse** button.

2. Click the **Right Mouse** button over the >> button or use the **Properties** command from the **Objects** menu. This displays the **Button Object Properties** dialog box.

3. In the **Text** field, replace the >> characters with the word **Print**. This sets the text that the button will display when it is activated. If you want to make the button respond to a keystroke such as **Alt+P** then add a **&** character in the **Text** field before the **P** (or any other character you wanted to use).

4. Select the **Set Link** button. This displays the **Set Background Link** dialog box, which lets you create links for background objects. This dialog box is shown in Figure 14.14.

5. Select the **Make New Link** command (we don't currently have a Print link so we have to create an entirely new link).

6. Select the **Action** option.

7. Select the **Menu Action** option. As you may recall, a menu action is a link that accesses a function from HyperWriter's own internal menu functions. This displays a list of available functions.

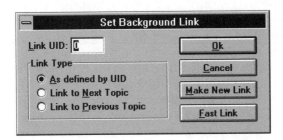

Figure 14.14 The **Set Background Link** dialog box.

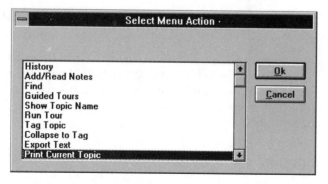

Figure 14.15 Setting the **Print Current Topic** function.

8. Select the **Print Current Topic** function by selecting it and then selecting the **OK** button (you can also just double-click on the function). Setting the **Print Current Topic** function is shown in Figure 14.15.

What we have just completed is adding a new button to our background that adds the ability to print text in the current topic. The next real task for us is to exit the Screen Painter and try out our new button, as in the Screen Painter buttons can be created, modified, and deleted, but they cannot be activated. Exiting the Screen Painter is done with the **Exit** command on the **File** menu.

Exiting the Screen Painter

Select the **Exit** command from the **File** menu. This returns you to the topic where you were before entering the Screen Painter. What should be displayed is shown in Figure 14.16.

In order to test our **Print** button, all that we need to do is select it and HyperWriter will print out the text in our topic. If you care to see this now, just click on the **Print** button (you need a printer hooked up to your machine and turned on for this to work).

With our background successfully modified, is there anything else that we need to do with this task? Technically there isn't, given that we have accomplished our goals. However, we can learn one trick for making editing backgrounds easier. As discussed earlier, editing backgrounds is a modal task—when you are editing backgrounds, you can't view the text topics where they are displayed. Similarly, while editing text, you can't also be editing a background. To make editing backgrounds more convenient, HyperWriter includes a command for always editing the last background that you were in. This command, the **Edit Last** command, is found on the **Edit** menu and makes editing backgrounds considerably easier. Keep this in mind when you are editing backgrounds and need to pop in and out of the background. For faster use, this command also has a keystroke equivalent (**Alt+F7**).

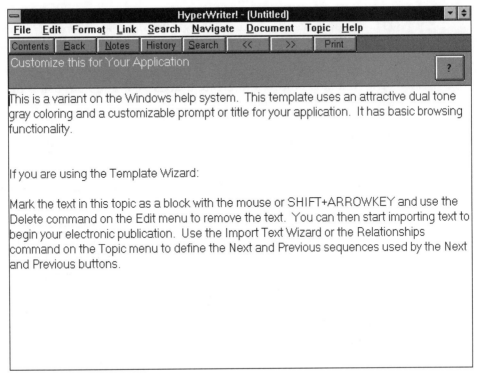

Figure 14.16 The completed background (not in the Screen Painter).

Saving Our Work

With the first exercise in our tutorial finished, we are now ready to save our work. This is done with the **Save** command on the **File** menu. HyperWriter will prompt you for the name of the file to save. Enter the name SCREEN01.HW4.

Working with an Existing Design (Graphic Buttons)

While the Screen Painter lets you create many different types of screen designs, fundamentally these types of designs can be broken into two types, *text based* and *graphics based*. A text-based design is similar to what we just did; it uses text-based buttons with descriptions such as Print, Search, and so on. The other type of design uses graphics or icons instead of text. In this exercise, we will use the Template Wizard to create a screen design based on graphic buttons, and then modify it. This tutorial will basically follow the model that we used in the previous exercise where we start with the Template Wizard and then move into the Screen Painter.

NOTE: If you haven't worked through the previous exercise, "Working with an Existing Design (Text Buttons)," you should do so before continuing.

The first step is for us to create a document template using the Template Wizard. This is done as follows.

Creating a Document Template

1. Select the **New** command from the **File** menu. Save your current document if needed. If HyperWriter prompts you to leave a bookmark, select Yes or No as needed.

2. In the **Template Wizard** dialog box, select the **Button Style** field and set it to **Iconic Buttons**. This tells the Template Wizard that you only want to look at templates using buttons with icons, not text buttons.

3. Select the **Orientation** field and set it to **Along Left Side**. This tells the Template Wizard that you only want to look at templates with buttons along the left-hand side of the screen.

4. In the **User Interface** field, you can now see that the number of available interfaces has been greatly reduced. Select the **Large Icons, In Palettes** interface and then select the **OK** button. This creates a document template using the selected interface.

   After creating the interface, what should be displayed on your screen is shown in Figure 14.17.

As you can see, this document template has a button bar along the left-hand edge of the screen with a series of icons arranged into different palettes of functions. Notice that although we chose the **Iconic Buttons** options, our icons can still have text labels to offer the best of both worlds. Grouping the icons into palettes organized by functions is quite a different approach from the background screen we just worked with previously. By grouping the icons together, this background aims to provide an easier to understand interface. This type of interface might be used for applications where the end user of the information is less familiar with digital publishing.

Given that our goal is to modify this template, we should start by deciding what we need to modify. Although technically we could implement any type of modification, we will focus on a very small and subtle change—simply replacing one of the buttons. With this decision, we have to decide what button to replace. When we look at this background, one inconsistency that becomes evident is that the **Highlights** icon, which turns off search highlighting is not grouped with the **Search Tools** palette. If our goal is to logically group functions together, then this isn't correct. Exploring this further naturally leads us to the idea that if we are to replace the **Highlights** icon, we need a function to

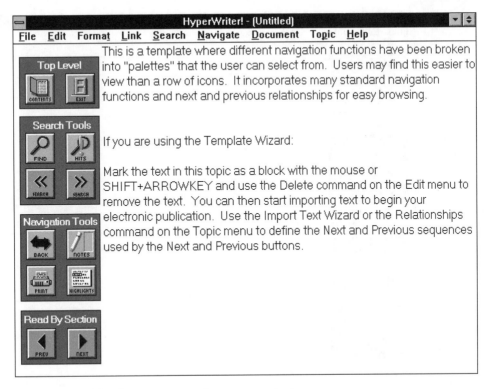

Figure 14.17 The document template you created.

replace it with. Given that the **Highlights** icon is next to the **Print** icon, the idea of replacing it with an **Export** icon seems natural, as both **Export** and **Print** serve similar functions. As you probably remember from the tutorial on linking, assigning this type of action to a button requires using a Menu Action link. And, yes, HyperWriter can assign to a button the ability to export text. With this decided, we know the goal for our exercise. We want to replace the existing **Highlights** icon with an **Export** icon tied to an Export menu action link.

Having used the Template Wizard, we are currently located in a Hyper-Writer document. To modify the icons in our background, we need to enter the Screen Painter using the **Apply Background** command to edit the First background in our document.

Editing a Background Using the Apply Background Command

1. Select the **Apply Background** command from the **Edit** menu.
2. Select the **Edit** button next to the **First** field. This will move you into the Screen Painter. HyperWriter's Screen Painter for this design is shown in Figure 14.18.

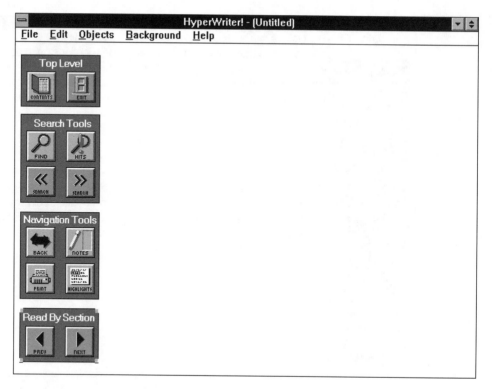

Figure 14.18 HyperWriter's Screen Painter.

As noted earlier in this tutorial, in the Screen Painter HyperWriter functions differently—it acts as an object editor for editing the objects that make up background screens. What we need to understand is how this background screen is put together. If you press the **Tab** key in the Screen Painter, Hyper-Writer will move from object to object (you can also just click on the object with the mouse, but using the **Tab** key better illustrates this point). As you press the **Tab** key, you can see the different objects being selected (you may want to do this now). If you press the **Tab** key until you have moved through all of the objects in the background then you will remain on the last object (the **Next** icon for this background).

The important point that can be understood by watching the different icons be selected is simply this: HyperWriter did not select any of the icons twice. The reason that this is significant is that there are two basic ways that icons can be made into a background screen. The first and simpler of the two ways is that individual picture files can be used for each icon with the individual graphics file having its own link to a menu action in HyperWriter. The background screen that we are currently working with uses this approach. The second method for making a background screen into an icon is to use one picture file for all icons with invisible buttons behind each icon in the picture file. You will find that different backgrounds shipped with HyperWriter or created with the Template Wizard use both approaches. For example, the Small Icons, Many Screen background from the Template Wizard uses the second approach. While there are pros and cons to both approaches, it is important to understand both of them as when you modify backgrounds, you will encounter each approach.

Given that our background screen uses multiple picture files, one for each icon, what are the steps involved in modifying our background?

- Select the icon to modify
- Replace it with a new icon
- Change the menu action link
- Update the hint for the icon

For our first task, we need to select the icon to modify. This is easily done with the mouse.

Selecting the Highlights Icon

Using the mouse, select the **Highlights** icon by placing the pointer over the **Highlights** icon and clicking the **Left Mouse** button. With the **Highlights** icon selected (you should see four small handles at the corners of the icon), we can replace it with a new icon.

Replacing Highlights with a New Icon

1. With the **Highlights** icon selected, choose the **Properties** command from the **Objects** menu. This displays the **Object Properties** dialog box, which allows you to configure how an object functions. The way to think of this is that you are altering the *properties* of the object. This dialog box is shown in Figure 14.19.

2. Select the **Set File** button. This lets us assign a new picture file in place of the existing one.

3. Select .PCX as the picture format to use.

4. Select _EXPORT as the picture file to use.

5. Select **OK** to close the **Picture Filename** dialog box. Leave the dialog box open as we will resume using it shortly. With the correct picture file displayed, we need to link to the **Export** function. For this, we will use the **Set Link** button on the **Object Properties** dialog box.

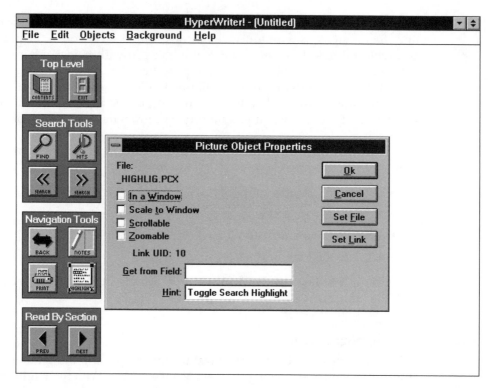

Figure 14.19 The **Object Properties** dialog box.

Linking to the Export Function

1. Select the **Set Link** button. This displays the **Set Background Link** dialog box.

2. Select the **Make New Link** button. This displays the **Link Type** dialog box.

3. Select **Action** as the type of link to create.

4. Select **Menu Action** as the type of link to create. This displays the **Select Menu Action** dialog box.

5. Scroll down the list and select the **Export Text** function and then select the **OK** button. This returns you to the **Object Properties** dialog box. Leave this dialog box open as we will return to it shortly.

With the picture file updated and the **Export Text** function assigned to it, we need to finish modifying this background by updating the *hint* for the button. HyperWriter allows all background objects to have an optional hint displayed whenever the mouse (in the HyperReader runtime software) passes over a background object. This helps a user understand what a particular icon does. While these icons do have text descriptions (so a hint technically isn't necessary), it is generally good form to assign hints to any icons used in your application. Additionally, as we started with hints on all our icons, our current hint is now *wrong* and we wouldn't want to leave it this way.

Updating the Hint for the Icon

1. Move to the **Hint** field.
2. Enter the text **Export Text to an ASCII File** into the **Hint** field.
3. Select the **OK** button to close the **Object Properties** dialog box.

We have now completed modifying our background screen. The next real task for us is to exit the Screen Painter and try out our new button, as in the Screen Painter buttons can be created, modified, and deleted, but they cannot be activated. Exiting the Screen Painter is done with the **Exit** command on the **File** menu.

Exiting the Screen Painter

1. Select the **Exit** command from the **File** menu. This returns you to the topic you were in before entering the Screen Painter. What should be displayed is shown in Figure 14.20.

In order to test our **Print** button, all that we need to do is select it and HyperWriter will export the text in our topic to a text file. If you care to see this now, just click on the **Export** icon. A picture of the **Export Text** dialog box is shown in Figure 14.21, as it would be displayed when you click on the **Export** icon.

With our background successfully modified, we have now completed this exercise. We should probably save our work as you may want to come back to it.

Saving Our Work

With the second exercise in our tutorial finished, we are now ready to save our work. This is done with the **Save** command on the **File** menu. Select the **Save** command from the **File** menu. HyperWriter will prompt you for the name of the file to save. Enter the name SCREEN02.HW4.

Creating a Screen Design From Scratch

Having now modified two very different screen designs, we are now ready to move into designing a screen from scratch. In this exercise, we will design a

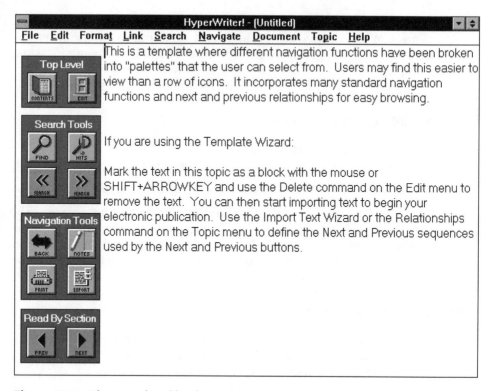

Figure 14.20 The completed background (not in the Screen Painter).

sample screen using only a few background objects such as pictures and buttons. The types of screens that we have worked with up to this point all focused on user interface type of screens. What we will do next is implement a

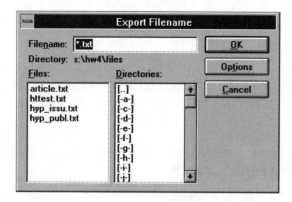

Figure 14.21 Clicking on the **Export Text** icon.

screen that uses a background to display a picture in an attractive fashion. You may recall a reference to this in our tutorial where we looked at ways of importing pictures into HyperWriter.

One of the great strengths of HyperWriter's Screen Painter is its ability to let you place objects anywhere on the screen. This allows you to create whatever type of screen is needed, in effect "painting" a screen from objects. In this exercise we will create a screen that has an NTERGAID logo across the top, a picture of NTERGAID's offices centered in the middle of the screen, and then a button for more information. This screen could be used for a HyperWriter application that was an interactive presentation about NTERGAID itself. This exercise shows us how to use the Screen Painter to display a picture, a topic we discussed in Chapter 13.

For this exercise, like our two previous exercises covering backgrounds, we will start by creating a new document. For this exercise, however, we will not use the Template Wizard, as we want to create a new background from scratch. The first step is to create a new document.

Creating a New Document

1. Select the **New** command from the **File** menu. Save your current document if needed. If HyperWriter prompts you to leave a bookmark, select Yes or No as needed.

2. In the **Template Wizard** dialog box, turn off the **Use New Template Wizard** option.

3. Select the **OK** button. This creates the new document without using the Template Wizard.

After creating the new document, what should be displayed on your screen is shown in Figure 14.22.

As you can see, when you create a new document without using the Template Wizard, what HyperWriter creates is just a blank document. There is no content and no background. Our first step is to add a background. As we don't have any backgrounds in our document, we need to use the **Add Background** command, not the **Apply Background** command.

Adding A Background

Select the **Add Background** command from the **Edit** menu. This adds a background and places you in the Screen Painter. What you should see onscreen is shown in Figure 14.23.

When you create a new background, just as when you create a new document, that background is empty, containing no objects when you enter it. Now that we are in the Screen Painter, we need to start by creating a picture object for our NTERGAID logo that we want displayed at the top of the screen.

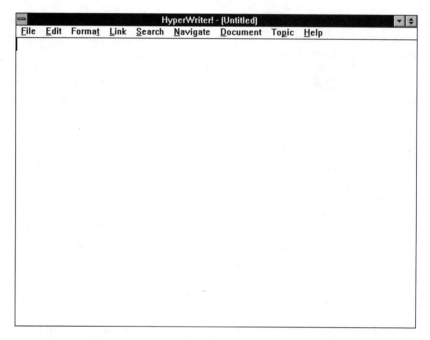

Figure 14.22 The document template you created.

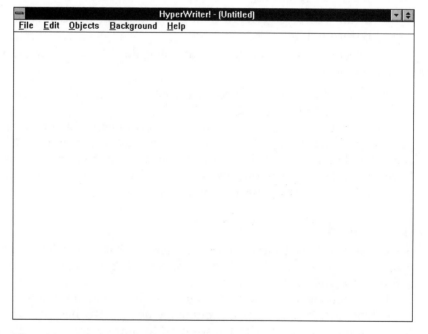

Figure 14.23 HyperWriter's Screen Painter.

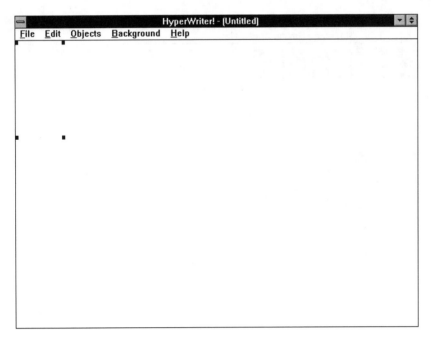

Figure 14.24 A "blank" picture object.

Adding a Picture Object

1. Select the **Picture** command from the **Object** menu. This places a blank picture object (one without any properties) in the background and indicates its position by selecting the object with handles at its corners. A picture of our blank picture object is shown in Figure 14.24.

2. Select the **Properties** command from the **Objects** menu. This displays the **Object Properties** dialog box, which allows you to configure how the picture object functions.

3. Select the **Set File** button. This lets us assign a new picture file in place of the existing one.

4. Select .PCX as the picture format to use.

5. Select NTLOGO1.PCX as the picture file to use.

6. Select **OK** to close the **Picture Filename** dialog box. Select the **OK** button to close the **Object Properties** dialog box. The completed picture object should appear as shown in Figure 14.25.

With our first picture completed, our next step is to add our second picture object—the picture of NTERGAID's offices.

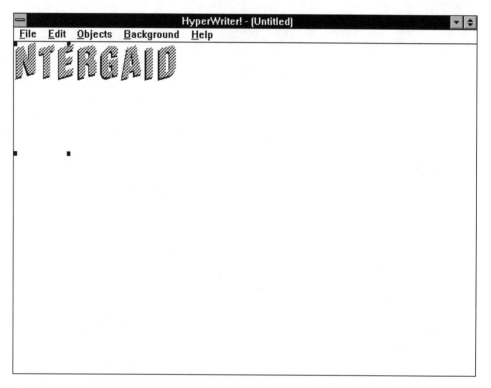

Figure 14.25 The completed picture object.

Adding a Second Picture Object

1. Select the **Picture** command from the **Object** menu. This places a blank picture object (one without any properties) in the background and indicates its position by selecting the object with handles at its corners. You will see that the picture object is initially created over the top of the first object. For right now, we want to leave the picture object in this position.

2. Select the **Properties** command from the **Objects** menu. This displays the **Object Properties** dialog box which allows you to configure how the picture object functions.

3. Select the **Set File** button. This lets us assign a new picture file in place of the existing one.

4. Select .PCX as the picture format to use.

5. Select NTSITE.PCX as the picture file to use.

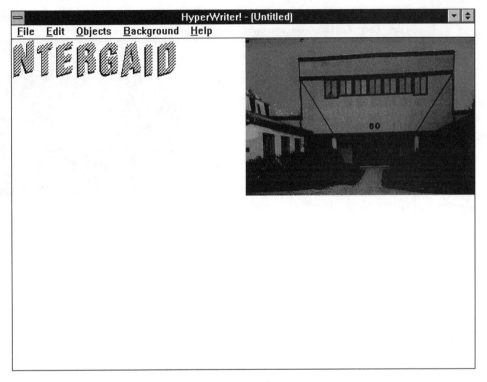

Figure 14.26 Our background with company logo and picture of offices.

6. Select **OK** to close the **Picture Filename** dialog box. Select the **OK** button to close the **Object Properties** dialog box.

7. Click the upper left-hand corner of the picture object that you have been modifying with the **Left Mouse** button and drag it to the right-hand edge of the screen as shown in Figure 14.26.

With both of our pictures placed in our background, we need to add a button to our background. This button will display a popup window where more information can be displayed.

Creating a Button Object

1. Select the **Button** command from the **Objects** menu. A button object will appear onscreen.

2. Drag the button object below the picture object with the picture of NTERGAID's offices. The approximate positioning that you want to use is shown in Figure 14.27.

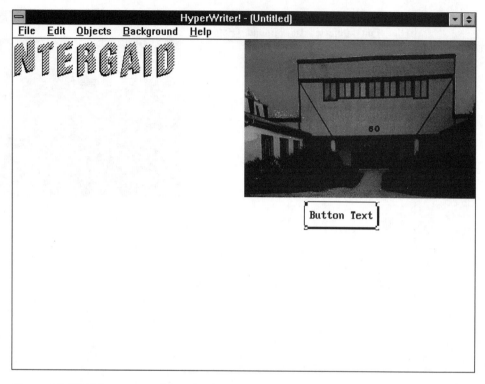

Figure 14.27 Where to position the button.

With the button object created, we can now modify it as needed. The properties of the button that we need to change are its font, its color, its link, and its snap-size setting.

Modifying a Button Object

1. Select the **Properties** command from the **Objects** menu.
2. Enter the text **Click Here for Details** into the **Text** field.
3. Select the **Set Font** button. This displays the **Button Object Font** dialog box shown in Figure 14.28.
4. Select Arial, 10 point, Bold as the font for the button.
5. Select **OK** to close the **Button Object Font** dialog box.
6. Turn off the **Snap Size to Text** option. This allows the button to be sized by dragging on the button's corners with the mouse.
7. Select the **Set Color** button. This displays the **Color Selection** dialog box shown in Figure 14.29.

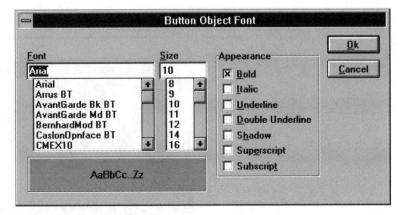

Figure 14.28 Setting the font of a button object.

8. Set the button's colors to black text on a gray background by clicking on the black color in the foreground group of colors and the light gray color in the background group of colors.

9. Select **OK** to close the **Color Selection** dialog box.

10. Select the **Set Link** button. This displays the **Set Background Link** dialog box.

11. Select the **Make New Link** button. This displays the **Link Type** dialog box.

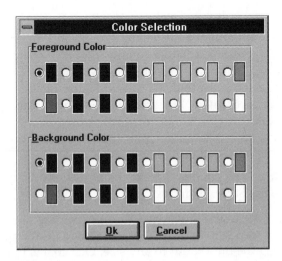

Figure 14.29 Setting the color of a button object.

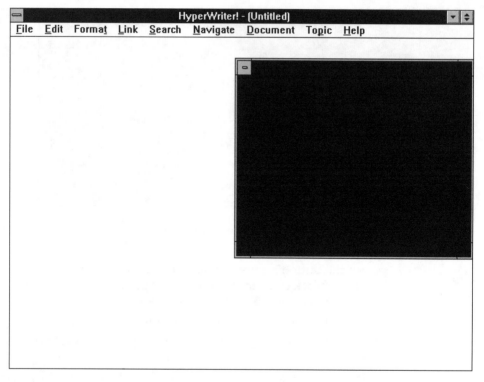

Figure 14.30 Creating a comment link.

12. Select **Text** as the type of link to create.

13. Select **Link to Text-Comment Link** as the type of link to create. This tells HyperWriter to create a link to a comment topic (a comment topic is really just a popup window). HyperWriter will then exit the Screen Painter and create a comment topic (shown in Figure 14.30).

    When creating a comment link from the Screen Painter, you can either enter text into the comment topic at that time or just complete the link and enter the text later. For this application, we really don't care about the text, so we will just complete the link.

14. Select the **Complete Link** command from the **Link** menu. HyperWriter will return you to the Screen Painter.

Having created, formatted, and linked our button, we are almost done with it. The one remaining step is to resize it. Having turned off the **Snap Size to Text** option, we can drag the button out to any size. Our goal is to make the button thinner and the width of the picture of NTERGAID's offices.

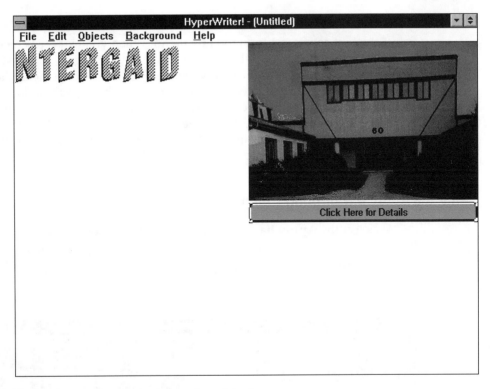

Figure 14.31 The approximate size of the button.

Sizing our Button

1. Click the **Left Mouse** button on the handle at the lower right-hand corner of the button.

2. Holding down the **Left Mouse** button, drag the corner of the button to the right and up. This will resize the button to the width of the picture. The approximate size of the button that you are looking for is shown in Figure 14.31.

NOTE: The **Shift+Arrowkey** keystroke is helpful for sizing buttons very finely.

With our picture files placed and our button created, we should probably exit the Screen Painter and take a look at our work. As backgrounds are part of our HyperWriter document, not a separate file, we don't need to save them at this time.

Exiting the Screen Painter

Select the **Exit** command from the **File** menu. When you exit the Screen Painter you may be surprised as what you will see is nothing at all—just a blank screen. You should remember that when we created this document, there were no backgrounds as we created it from scratch. If there were no backgrounds then no background could be applied to the topic that we are currently viewing. Consequently, we see nothing when we exit the Screen Painter. The solution is to apply the background to the topic we are viewing with the **Apply Background** command.

Using the Apply Background Command

1. Select the **Apply Background** command from the **Edit** menu.
2. Enter a **1** into the first field and select **OK**. This applies the background to your topic so that it can be displayed. What you should see onscreen is shown in Figure 14.32.

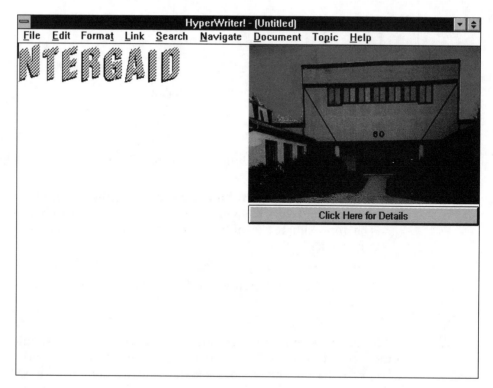

Figure 14.32 The background applied to the topic.

As you can see, our background screen is displayed complete with both pictures and our one button. One thing that you will notice if you look carefully at the screen is that there is a cursor in the upper left-hand corner of the screen. This reflects the fact that we didn't set our margins for the background screen. The implication of this is that HyperWriter would allow text to overwrite the background objects. The solution is to set the margins for the background. Before we do this, however, let's import a document and see what it looks like.

Importing a Document

1. Select the **Import Text** command from the **File** menu.
2. Select Word as the format to import.
3. Select the document PRESSREL.DOC as the file to import.
4. Select the method **Don't Auto Link** and select the **OK** button to import the document.

When HyperWriter is finished importing the document, what should appear onscreen is shown in Figure 14.33.

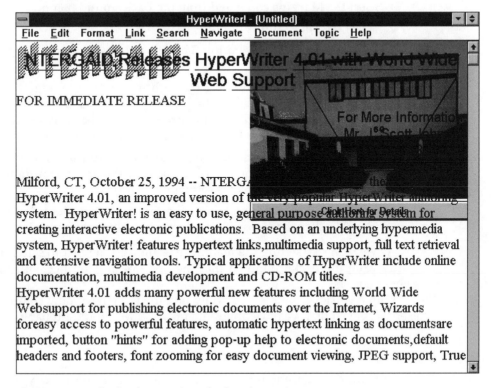

Figure 14.33 The background applied to the topic.

As you can see, when no margins are set in a background, text is free to overwrite the objects. While this doesn't matter for some types of backgrounds, for any background where text is displayed, this is definitely undesirable. To fix this, we need to go back into the Screen Painter. The **Edit Last** command will jump us back into the last background that we were editing.

Editing our Background

Select the **Edit Last** command from the **Edit** menu.

To fix the problem, we need to add a margin region to our background. Backgrounds in HyperWriter support a single margin region per background and are created with the **Margins** command on the **Background** menu. Unlike most of the commands in the Screen Painter, setting margins is done solely with the keyboard. You can either enter the coordinates of the background or use the **Arrowkeys** to position the margins onscreen.

Setting Margins

1 Select the **Margins** command from the **Background** menu.

2. Select the **Set Margins** option.

3. Select the **Set Visually** button. This lets you mark out the margin region using the **Arrowkeys**.

4. Press **Shift+Leftarrow** until the right-hand margin edge has moved past the left-hand edge of the picture of NTERGAID's offices. If you move too far, press **Shift+Rightarrow** to move back. When the margin is correct, press **Enter**. This is shown in Figure 14.34.

5. Set the top margin by pressing **Downarrow** until it moves past the NTERGAID logo at the top of the screen. When the margin is correct, press **Enter**. This completes setting the margins.

6. Select the **Exit** command from the **File** menu. A picture of the completed background, along with the text is shown in Figure 14.35.

As you can see, setting the margins has allowed the text to scroll independently from the background so that the text doesn't conflict with the background objects.

With our background successfully modified, we have now completed this exercise. Given that we have done a lot of work, we should probably save it.

Saving Our Work

With the third exercise in our tutorial finished, we are now ready to save our work. This is done with the **Save** command on the **File** menu. Select the **Save**

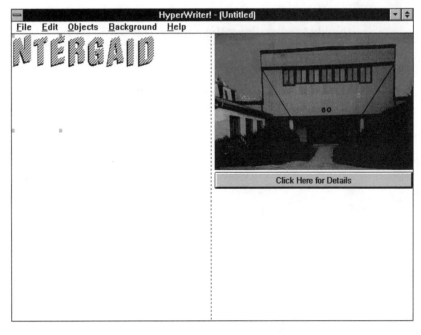

Figure 14.34 Setting margins.

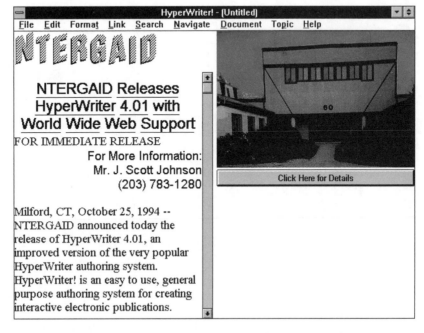

Figure 14.35 The completed background with margins and text.

command from the **File** menu. HyperWriter will prompt you for the name of the file to save. Enter the name SCREEN03.HW4.

Exiting HyperWriter

With our tutorial finished and our work saved, you can now exit HyperWriter if desired. This is done with the **Exit** command on the **File** menu.

Applications and Full-Text Indexing

Having now used many of the different features in HyperWriter, we are now ready to begin wrapping up some of the final details that concern Hyper-Writer. This chapter focuses on three of those details:

- Creating an application file
- Defining a document name
- Indexing an application

An application file defines the files that make up your digital publication using HyperWriter. Application files are quite important because they are required for certain tasks in HyperWriter, such as indexing documents. A document name defines the logical name for a document, so that a document is referred to by its logical name rather than its filename. Indexing a HyperWriter application makes it fully searchable. Each of these topics will be covered.

Building an Application File and Other Details

In this tutorial, we will start with a basic discussion of the application file and then continue with a tutorial on defining an application file. At the end of the tutorial on application files, we will explore the **Abstract** command. For this tutorial, we will be using a sample document called APPLIC1.HW4. This is a good document for illustrating application files.

What is an Application File?

A HyperWriter *application* is a collection of HyperWriter document files arranged in a particular order to perform a specific purpose. In essence, a HyperWriter application defines how particular documents are related to one another, and make up a single, logical collection of documents. Applications allow you to perform operations on groups of HyperWriter topics and documents. This includes HyperIndexer, which indexes a HyperWriter application for searching; HyperWriter's Groups feature which requires an application to function, HyperWriter's Group Printing features, which allow printing of groups of topics, and the HyperWriter Publisher, which copies HyperWriter applications onto floppy discs.

HyperWriter applications are defined by a HyperWriter application file. An *application file* is a binary file that lists all the HyperWriter documents in the application and has an extension of .HWA. All HyperWriter documents can belong to only one application at a time. HyperWriter application files can be opened by HyperWriter and HyperReader, as can HyperWriter document files. When a HyperWriter application file is opened, HyperWriter automatically opens the first file in the application, saving you from manually determining what is the first file in the application. Looking at the .HWA files in your directory instead of the .HW4 files in your directory can be considerably simpler as there are generally fewer .HWA files than .HW4 files.

With a basic understanding of applications, we are ready to move to the next step in exercise, which is to run HyperWriter, open our sample document and then define an application file.

Before we can open our sample document we must first run HyperWriter. HyperWriter is a standard MS-Windows application that can be run from the Program Manager.

Opening Our Sample Document

With HyperWriter running, we need to open our sample document, APPLIC1.HW4.

Opening our Sample Document

1. Select the **Open** command from the **File** menu.
2. Select the APPLIC1.HW4 document from the **Open** dialog box.

With our sample document open, we are ready to begin defining our application file.

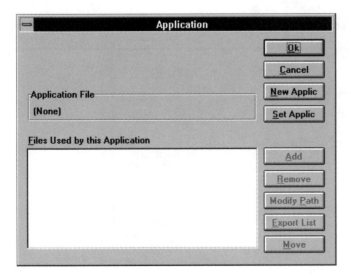

Figure 15.1 The **Application** command.

Defining an Application File

HyperWriter applications are defined with the **Application** command on the **Document** menu. The **Application** command displays a dialog box where documents can be selected and added to our application as well as removed from an existing application. The following steps let you define an application file.

Using the Application Command

1. Select the **Application** command from the **Document** menu. This displays the dialog box shown in Figure 15.1.

2. Select the **New Applic** button. This button defines that we want to create a new application.

3. Enter the name **SAMPAPP** into the dialog box and press **Enter**. This should update the **Application** dialog box so that the name of the current application is shown under the **Application File** group and the name of the current document (APPLIC1.HW4) is shown in the **Files Used By This Application** field. This is shown in Figure 15.2.

4. Select the **OK** button to close the dialog box.

At this point, we are essentially done with defining our application. As our application only had a single file in it, our task was very simple. If our application had multiple files in it, then we would have had to do this multiple times.

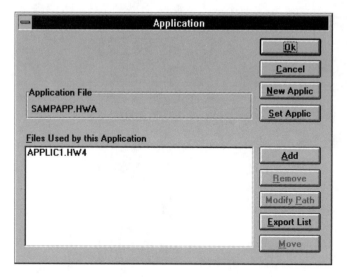

Figure 15.2 After using the **New Applic** button.

With our application file completed, we can now move onto some further background on the **Application** command. Before we do this, we should consider what some of the other buttons on the **Application** dialog box will let us do. (See Table 15.1.)

Reference: Details of the Application Command

Once you have created your HyperWriter document or documents, the **Application** command on the **Document** menu defines a single application file. This application file contains a list of all your HyperWriter documents in the order they are to be used. Once your application file is created, you can index your

Table 15.1 Buttons on the **Application** Dialog Box

Button	Description
Set Applic	Define an existing application file that the document belongs to.
Remove	Remove an .HW4 file from the application.
Modify Path	Modify the path to an .HW4 file in the application.
Export List	Export the list of .HW4 files in the application to the file FILE-NAME.LST.
Move	Move the position of an .HW4 file in the application.

application with HyperIndexer and assign any desired topic groups with the **Groups** command on the **Topic** menu. An important point to understand about the **Application** command is that it is affected by the **Use Paths with Linked Files** option. The **Use Paths with Linked Files** option instructs Hyper-Writer to store the full drive and directory structure to any linked files. This option is set with the **Authoring** folder of options accessed with the **Preferences** command on the **File** menu. If this option is turned on when you build your application, HyperWriter stores in the application file the drive and directory structure to each file in the application. There are no problems with this if you will be distributing your application to computers with the same drive and directory structure. However, if the drive and directory structure differ then there will be a problem. The solution is to use the **Application** command to remove the drive (and directory if necessary) from the application to create a relative directory structure.

Understanding the Document Abstract Command

While the **Application** command accomplishes many tasks, we were really using it in this tutorial for its purposes with respect to indexing documents, as our next tutorial focuses on document indexing. An important command related to document indexing is the **Abstract** command. The **Abstract** command on the **Document** menu allows you to define an abstract for the document. An *abstract* defines common information about the current HyperWriter document such as its name, its author, when it was created, and other information. The element of the **Abstract** command that is particularly important for us right now is the **Document Name** option, which allows you to specify a logical name for the document such as "HyperWriter 4.0 Online Manual." Before we can really understand the **Document Name** command, we need to better understand HyperWriter's search facilities.

When the **Find** command is chosen from the **Search** menu (and the document is indexed), the **Find** dialog box, as shown in Figure 15.3, is displayed.

As you can see, there is a documents list on the **Find** dialog box. This list allows you to select which documents are searched by the **Find** command. Documents are listed by their document name as defined on the **Abstract** dialog box. If there is no document name, then their DOS filename is displayed. The **Document Name** field on the **Abstract** dialog box allows you to provide a much more descriptive name than the default DOS 8 character filename.

However, while this functioning is apparent when the HyperWriter applications are composed of a single .HW4 document file, how does it function when the HyperWriter applications are composed of multiple .HW4 files? One approach would be to display the name of each .HW4 file in the documents list. However, you generally do not want the reader of your document to be required to understand how you structured the files inside your application.

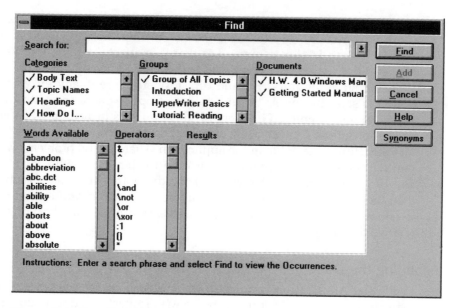

Figure 15.3 The **Find** dialog box.

This is confusing and unnecessary work for the reader. The solution is to define the same document name using the **Abstract** command for each related file contained in your application. HyperWriter automatically groups documents in an application by their name when the same name is used for multiple documents.

What Other Benefits Do I Get from the Abstract Command?

Although the **Abstract** command is of interest to us now for its relationship to searching, it does have relevance to other aspects of HyperWriter. Specifically, the **Abstract** command makes understanding a document's purpose and making changes simpler when maintaining a document.

Setting the Document Name with the Abstract Command

Now that we understand the **Abstract** command, what we need to do is use it to define our document name. The document name that we want to set with it is "Press Releases."

Using the Abstract Command

1. Select the **Abstract** command from the **Document** menu. This displays the dialog box shown in Figure 15.4.

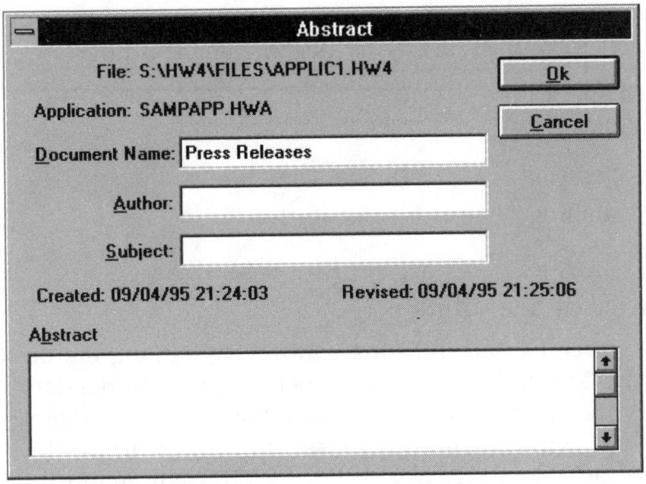

Figure 15.4 The **Abstract** command.

2. Enter the name "Press Releases" into the **Document Name** field. You can leave all other fields blank at this time.

3. Select the **OK** button to close the **Abstract** dialog box.

We are now finished using the **Abstract** command and are ready to save our work.

Saving Our Work

With our tutorial finished, we are now ready to save our work. This is done with the **Save** command on the File menu. Select the **Save** command from the **File** menu.

Exiting HyperWriter

With our tutorial finished and our work saved, you can now exit HyperWriter if desired. This is done with the **Exit** command on the **File** menu.

Full-text Indexing

As discussed in the first tutorial in this chapter, HyperWriter includes a full-text indexing tool, HyperIndexer, for creating the index files required for full-text searching. HyperIndexer functions by taking a HyperWriter application file and then indexing the content that the application file references. In this tutorial, we will take the documents that we prepared in the previous tutorial and index them using HyperIndexer. HyperIndexer adds many different searching features to your HyperWriter documents including:

- Wild card operators
- Proximity operators
- Boolean operators
- Fielded searching

Understanding the Basics of Searching

HyperWriter's searching and indexing features are among the most powerful features in HyperWriter. As such, using them requires understanding searching in HyperWriter. For a thorough understanding of searching in Hyper-Writer, let us start with HyperWriter's search user interface. HyperWriter's indexed-search facility is accessed from the **Find** command on the **Search** menu. When the **Find** command is selected from the **Search** menu, a dialog box similar to that shown in Figure 15.5 is generally displayed.

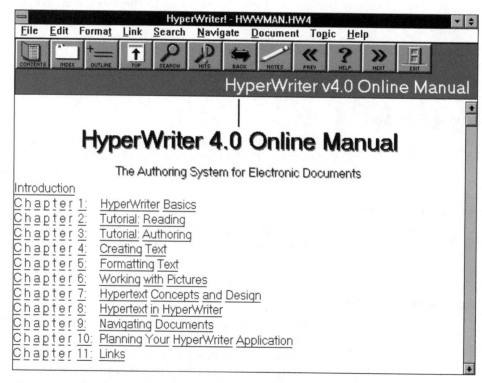

Figure 15.5 The **Find** dialog box.

NOTE: The word *generally* is used because HyperWriter's indexed-search facility is highly configurable, allowing you to adapt it to your specific needs. This includes modifying the dialog box displayed by the **Find** command.

The different sections of the **Find** dialog box are described in Table 15.2.

As you can see, HyperWriter's search engine offers great power and flexibility. This power and flexibility comes directly from three concepts: documents, groups, and categories. These three concepts let you modify the scope or range of your search. These three concepts can be thought of respectively as the *documents* to search in, the *topics* to search in, and the *paragraphs* (categories contain one or more paragraphs) to search in. By restricting the range of the search, searches are more precise and return fewer search occurrences. Each search concept has its own section of the **Find** dialog box used for indexed searches. As this dialog box can be configured (described under "Document

Table 15.2 Using the **Find** Dialog Box

Section	Description
Search For	Specify the query that is to be found. This can include search operators such as AND, OR, NOT, and XOR. Use the **Downarrow** button next to the **Search For** field accesses your previous search queries.
Find	Start the search.
Add	Add a word or operator to the search query.
Help	Display context-sensitive help on searching.
Synonyms	Allow synonyms for common search terms to be created, viewed, or removed.
Categories	Specify a particular set of search ranges within the text of a document. This is discussed further later.
Groups	Specify a particular set of topics to search. There is always a **Group of All Topics** option that allows you to search all topics in the specified group.
Documents	Specify which HyperWriter documents are searched.
Words Available	Display a list of words in the current search range.
Options	Pick a search operator to use.
Results Summary	Display a graphic map of search results as you enter the search.

Properties"), you do not need to use all of the concepts. However, when used together these concepts provide powerful and flexible searching of your HyperWriter application. In the **Find** dialog box, each of the fields that display these concepts uses checkmarks next to the elements listed in the field. These checkmarks define which options will be added or taken away from the search. Each of these concepts is explained.

The documents to search in are grouped by logical names. For instance, even though an online manual may have many .HW4 files, they might all fall under the logical document name, "Online Manual." An example of how the **Documents** field could be used is more apparent when a user has a bookshelf of manuals to search. Consider, for example, the HyperWriter Professional product which has manuals that include "HyperWriter Interactive Author," "Getting Started," "HyperWriter Professional," and "HyperWriter AutoLinker." These are all logical document names and could be shown in the **Documents** field of an indexed search that would encompass the HyperWriter Professional product. This would allow a user that was interested in features specific to HyperWriter Professional to select just the "HyperWriter Professional" entry and search only this information.

The groups to search in are defined on an individual topic basis. Any number of groups can exist for an application, and a topic can belong to any number of those groups. This allows a topic to consider two things at the same time. For example, there might be a group named "Step-by-Step Approach" and a group named "Topics with Video." Assume that additional groups exist for other concepts covered by the application you are searching. Some topics will have step-by-step approaches listing the steps required to perform a function. But sometimes the information on how to do something may be contained in a video presentation. By selecting "Step-by-Step Approach" before searching the application, a user would only get those topics that contained step-by-step approaches. By selecting both "Step-by-Step Approach" and "Topics with Video," the user is presented with a larger range for the search. One group is always present in the **Find** dialog box, the **Group of All Topics** group. By default this will allow you to search all topics in your application. Selecting on only those groups which closely fit your search criteria will greatly improve your searching ability.

The categories to search are defined on a paragraph basis. Categories use HyperWriter formatting tags (paragraph tags) for creating the different categories or fields that could be searched. As you can see, when HyperWriter displays the **Find** dialog box, all categories are initially selected. This allows you to search the full text in your HyperWriter application. One default category exists, named **Body Text**. The name **Body Text** for the default category has only a limited relationship to the paragraph tag named **BODY TEXT**. The use of the **Body Text** category can best be described with an example.

Consider a database of companies and the products they sell. A document would probably have categories for the Company Name, Address, and Product Descriptions. This would allow a person to search for HyperWriter and look for it among the Product Descriptions. To do this, a person would select the **Categories** field of the **Find** dialog box and select only the **Product Descriptions** category (i.e., only the **Product Descriptions** category should have a checkmark next to it). However, if you weren't sure if the Product Description was the only place it might be and there were no other categories that fit what you were looking for, then you could also select the **Body Text** category. By selecting the **Body Text** category, the indexed search would also look in any locations not defined by the other categories.

NOTE: Another common example of how categories are used is the equipment manual with a parts list. A **Parts List** category would allow searches of only the part numbers in the equipment.

In this situation, the product descriptions example, the **Body Text** default category can best be described as the remaining text of an application. When using the categories to search in field, your users of your application will not be familiar with the **Body Text** paragraph tag and hence will not have any preconceptions about its function. To your user, the **Body Text** category can be defined as the remaining body of your application that isn't in other specific categories (or fields).

An additional aspect of categories that will only become clear when you index your application is that categories are named not by the particular paragraph tag or tags they correspond to, but by a name defined by the author of the application. This allows you to rename and simplify the tag structure in your document to present an understandable set of categories to the reader of your document. For example, your document might have tags named **H1**, **H2**, and **H3** that indicated first-, second-, and third-level headings. If you wanted your reader to be able to restrict his search to headings only, then you might define a category named "Headings," that included the **H1**, **H2**, and **H3** tags.

NOTE: If there is no document name defined for each HyperWriter .HW4 file then documents are listed by their DOS filename.

A picture of several different HyperWriter .HW4 files that are defined as two documents, complete with topics, groups, and categories, is shown in Figure 15.6 to illustrate the different HyperWriter objects for searching.

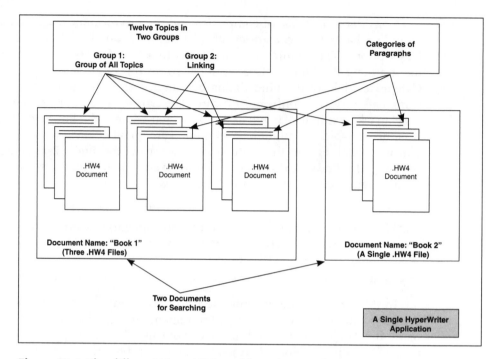

Figure 15.6 The different HyperWriter objects for searching.

With a thorough overview of searching completed, we are ready to begin our tutorial. In this tutorial, we will run HyperIndexer instead of HyperWriter and use it to index our documents.

Running HyperIndexer

Before we can begin to index our application, we must first run HyperIndexer. Like HyperWriter itself, HyperIndexer is a standard MS-Windows application that can be run from the Program Manager.

1. Change to the Program Manager.
2. Double-click the **HyperIndexer** icon in the digital publishing program group.

When HyperIndexer runs, it is displayed on your screen as shown in Figure 15.7.

Indexing an Application

With HyperIndexer now running, we are ready to index our application. The first step is to select the application file to index.

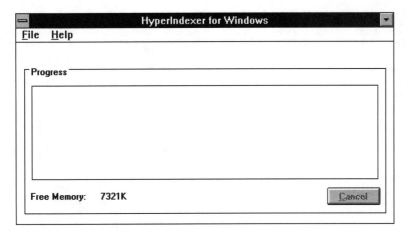

Figure 15.7 The HyperIndexer program.

Selecting an Application File

1. Select the **Set Application File** command from the **File** menu. This displays a file selection dialog box for selecting the application to index (this dialog box is shown in Figure 15.8).

2. Select the \HW4\FILES directory and then the application file SAMPAPP.HWA (if you don't have this file available, then you need to work through the beginning of this chapter, as we created this file in this chapter's first tutorial). With the application file selected, the title bar of the HyperIndexer application will display the name of the application file as shown in Figure 15.9.

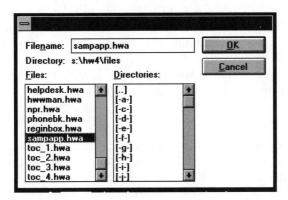

Figure 15.8 Selecting an application file.

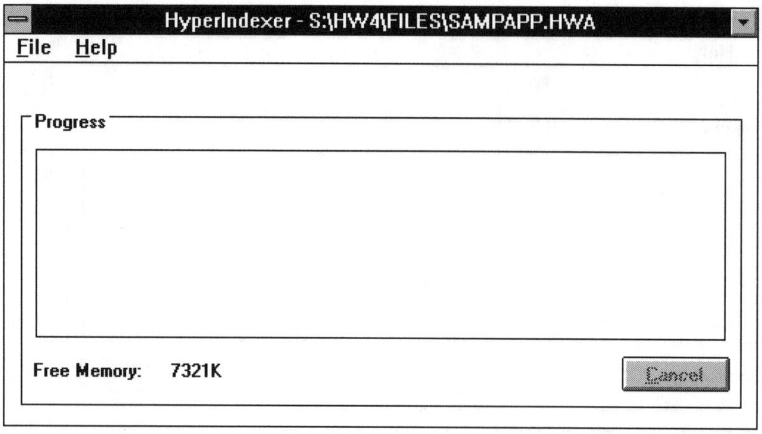

Figure 15.9 The selected application file.

Using HyperIndexer is basically a three-step process:

1. Set the application file (which we already did).
2. Set the different indexing options that define how to index the application. This uses the **Options** command on the **File** menu.
3. Start the indexing process with the **Create Index** command from the **File** menu.

We will now continue by setting the indexing options.

Setting Options for Indexing

With the application file that we want to index selected, we are ready to begin setting the options needed for indexing. As there are a number of different indexing options that we can set, we will review them in depth before setting them. To relate the different options that we want to set to the explanation of the indexing options, I have placed notes at the end of each section that indicate how this option will be set.

The dialog box for setting HyperIndexer Options is shown in Figure 15.10. Each HyperIndexer option is summarized in Table 15.3.

The Category Options

The category series of options are used to define the category fields available in the **Search** dialog box. A category can be thought of as a field within the text of your HyperWriter document. When you use a category in a search, what you are defining is what HyperWriter is to look in when searching. For example, if you select only a particular category or categories, then HyperWriter

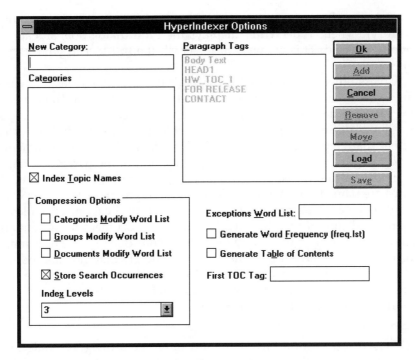

Figure 15.10 HyperIndexer options.

Table 15.3 HyperIndexer Options

Option	Description
Category	Define the category options for the index file.
Index Topic Names	Tell HyperIndexer to index topic names.
Compression	Specify options that compress the index file.
Exceptions Word List	Tell HyperIndexer to read an exception list of words not to include in the index file.
Generate Word Frequency List	Generate a word-frequency list of each word in the documents indexed and the number of times it occurs. Word-frequency lists are always stored in FREQ.LST.
Generate Table of Contents	Create a hierarchical table of contents.
First TOC Tag	Set the first table of contents tag.

will only search the contents of that category (looking into the contents of that category). When HyperWriter displays the **Find** dialog box, all categories are initially selected. This allows you to search the full text in your HyperWriter application.

Unless otherwise specified, by default the two categories that are defined when you index an application are **Body Text** and **Topic Names**. The **Body Text** category defines that HyperWriter is to search all the text in a document that is not defined as part of another category. The **Topic Names** category defines that HyperWriter is to search all topic names in the documents. Additional categories can be defined that correspond to the paragraph tags in your document, or to some combination of paragraph tags in your documents. Categories are named not by the particular paragraph tag or tags they correspond to but by a name defined by the author of the application. This allows you to rename and simplify the tag structure in your document to present an understandable set of categories to the reader of your document. For example, your document might have tags named H1, H2, and H3 that indicate first-, second-, and third-level headings. If you wanted your reader to be able to restrict his search to only headings then you might define a category named Headings that included the **H1**, **H2**, and **H3** tags.

NOTE: For our tutorial, we will want to define a category named titles that makes the titles of the press releases a searchable category. As a side note, you should be aware that this category will have the same effect as the **Topic Names** category because in this particular document, the only occurrences of the **HEAD1** tag are also the names of the topics. Despite this, setting this one category provides a good way to learn about categories.

The Index Topic Names Option

The **Index Topic Names** option tells HyperIndexer to index the topic names in the application so they are presented to the user as an available category. By turning this option on, the reader of an application can restrict the search of an application to only the topic names found in the application.

NOTE: For our tutorial, we will leave this option turned on so that topic names are searchable.

The Compression Options

To reduce the size of an index file created by HyperIndexer, there are several compression options that can be used to reduce the size of the index file created by HyperIndexer. The drawback to using the different compression options is that the different compressions tend to reduce the performance of an indexed search. You will note that some of the different compression options actually result in changing the user interface of the **Search Dialog** box. For example, the **Groups Modify Word List** option allows the selection of a particular group to adjust the available words shown in the words list. However, for this option to function, inside the index file there must be additional information stored for each word to indicate what group(s) the word is associated with. By giving up this aspect of the search user interface, the size of the index file can be reduced. However, the different word list compression options do not alter the functionality of the search. The different compression options in HyperIndexer are listed in Table 15.4.

As HyperIndexer gives you a variety of different compression options, it is sometimes difficult to determine which compression options should be used

Table 15.4 Compression Options in HyperIndexer

Compression Option	Description
Category Modifies Word List	Store additional information in the index file so that each category can dynamically modify the word list as it is selected.
Groups Modify Word List	Store additional information in the index file so that each group can dynamically modify the word list as it is selected.
Documents Modify Word List	Store additional information in the index file so that each document can dynamically modify the word list as it is selected.
Store Search Occurrences	Store the exact position of each search occurrence in the index file. This option must be turned on in order for an indexed search to highlight the results of search queries and to position the cursor at the first matching query term. Without this option turned on, a search query will result in being positioned only to the top of the topic where the search query is found. As a general rule of thumb, this option is usually turned on. Finally, unless this option is turned on, proximity searching is not supported.
Index Levels	Determine the degree of speed with which an index term is retrieved. Available index levels are 2, 3, 4, and 5. The greater number of index levels defined, the faster a particular search query can be retrieved. However, the fewer levels defined, the smaller the index file created.

for your application. The first point to understand about compression options is that the one option that has the most dramatic effect on the size of an index is the **Store Search Occurrences** option. This option records the position of every search term in the index file. However, this option is generally one that you want to leave turned on as without it there is no search highlighting. The one occasion when you could probably turn this option off without adversely affecting your application is if your application uses a card metaphor to present the text of the application. Here the text is generally short and locating the search terms visually is usually not a problem.

A second point to understand about compression options is that except for the **Store Search Occurrences** option, no single option greatly affects the size of the index file. However, the combination of these different compression options can greatly affect the size of your final index file. Therefore, you should always look at multiple compression options to cut down the size of your index file.

NOTE: As our tutorial has only a single category and no documents or groups, we will turn on the **Categories Modify Word List** option as well as the **Store Search Occurrences** option. The **Index Levels** option will be left at 3 and the **Groups and Documents** option will be turned off.

The Exceptions Word List

A common technique for indexing documents is to use an exceptions list. An exceptions list is a list of words that are not to be indexed. This prevents common words such as *a*, *of*, *an*, *the*, *not*, and others from being indexed. A benefit to using an exception file is a reduction in the size of the index file generated by HyperIndexer.

NOTE: As our application is quite small, we do not need to use an exceptions list.

The Generate Word Frequency List Option

The **Generate Word Frequency List** option tells HyperIndexer to create a word frequency list of each unique word in the application and the number of times it occurs. Word frequency lists are always stored in the file FREQ.LST. This file is located in the same directory where the index is created.

NOTE: As our application is quite small, we do not need to create a word frequency list.

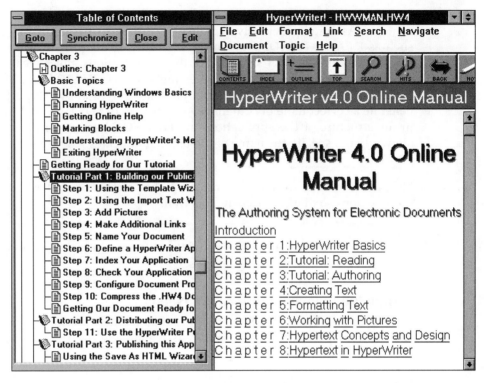

Figure 15.11 The table of contents created by HyperIndexer.

The Table of Contents Options

One of the unique features about HyperWriter's indexing module, Hyper-Indexer, is that in addition to indexing documents, it also creates a graphical, browsable table of contents for the documents that it indexes. This table of contents provides a powerful navigational aid that can be displayed side by side with your document. The table of contents created by HyperIndexer is shown in Figure 15.11. Please note that this table of contents is not for the document that we will be indexing, but from HyperWriter's own online documentation.

As you can see, the table of contents offers a powerful, hierarchical view of a document that can be contracted and expanded. This table of contents is based on styles found in the document that use names such as **HEAD1**, **HEAD2**, **HEAD3**, and so on. The same style names documented earlier for use with the Import Text Wizard are used by HyperIndexer to create the table of contents.

There are two **Table of Contents** options that need to be set for Hyper-Indexer to use: **Generate Table of Contents** and **First TOC Tag**. The **Generate Table of Contents** option tells HyperIndexer to create the table of contents.

The **First TOC Tag** option lets another tag provide the first level in the table of contents. As noted previously, the table of contents is based on stylesheet tags such as **HEAD1**, **HEAD2**, and so on. However, many people don't use these tags for the first level of structure in their applications, but instead use them for heading levels and have another tag such as **CHAPTER**, **CENTER**, or **TITLE**, that identifies the first level of structure. To allow HyperIndexer to generate a correct table of contents even when a **HEAD1** tag is not the first tag in the structure of the application, the **First TOC Tag** field in HyperIndexer allows you to specify the name of the tag that indicates where a section starts.

NOTE: Although our application already has a table of contents, we will set these options so that one is created as well.

This completes the discussion of the different indexing options. We can now set the different indexing options.

Setting the Indexing Options We Need

Setting the different indexing options that we need requires that we first selected the application file to index. As we already did this, we need to use the **Options** command.

Setting Indexing Options

1. Select the **Options** command from the **File** menu. This displays the HyperIndexer **Options** dialog box shown in Figure 15.12.

2. Our first step is to define a searchable category or field. Type the name **Title** into the **New Category** field and select the **Add** button. This adds a category named Title to the list of categories.

3. Select the **Title** category from the list of categories by clicking on it with the mouse. When the **Title** category is selected, the list of paragraph tags to its right will become enabled so that they can be selected.

4. Select the **HEAD1** style or tag from the list of paragraph tags and click on it with the mouse. What this does is to map the **Titles** category to **HEAD1** style so that any searches in the **Title** category search information is formatted with the **HEAD1** style. As we don't need to define any other categories, this completes the category definition.

5. Select the **Index Topic Names** option if it isn't already turned on.

6. Select the **Categories Modify Word List** option to turn it on. This makes our word lists for our categories dynamic so that only words in the category will be displayed when the category is selected.

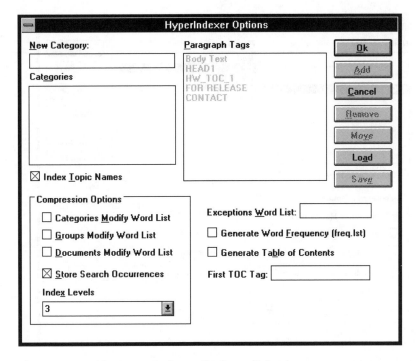

Figure 15.12 The HyperIndexer **Options** dialog box.

7. Leave the **Groups Modify Word List** and **Documents Modify Word List** options set to off as our document has no groups and only one document.

8. Leave the **Store Search Occurrences** option turned on and the **Index Levels** set to 3.

9. Select the **Generate Table of Contents** option so that a table of contents will be generated.

    To make sure that you have set the HyperIndexer options correctly, compare your screen with the picture shown in Figure 15.13 where the options are correctly set.

10. Select the **OK** button to close the dialog box. This will return you to HyperIndexer's main screen.

From setting the different HyperIndexer options, you probably understand why we went through all of the options in depth before setting them. Hyper-Indexer is a very powerful tool and setting these options can be a bit difficult and even intimidating the first time. Despite this, after you have used Hyper-Indexer a few times, setting these options becomes much easier. With all of our options set, we move to the final step, starting the indexing process.

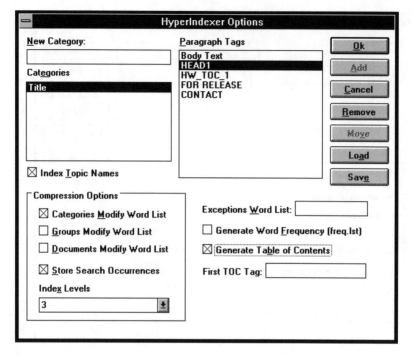

Figure 15.13 All the HyperIndexer options correctly set.

Starting the Indexing Process

Before we actually start indexing our document, you should first understand the name of the index file that this will produce. When HyperIndexer runs, it indexes all documents in the application and creates an index file named INDEX.HWI. If an INDEX.HWI file is in the current directory before files are indexed then it will be overwritten. The INDEX.HWI file is HyperWriter's default index file, which any HyperWriter application will default to when no other index file is specified as a document property. To allow multiple index files in a single directory, this index file can then be renamed as desired and configured for use with certain HyperWriter applications.

With our indexing options set, we can start the indexing process.

Starting the Indexing Process

1. Select the **Create Index** command from the **File** menu. HyperIndexer will begin indexing your application and display its progress onscreen. A picture of HyperIndexer illustrating its progress is shown in Figure 15.14.

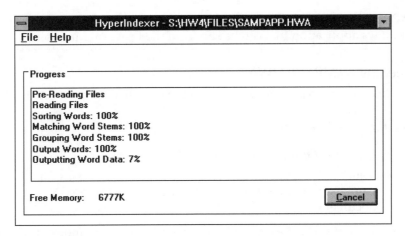

Figure 15.14 HyperIndexer showing its progress.

2. When HyperIndexer has completed indexing your application, it will display an **Index Complete** dialog box. Until this additional dialog box comes up onscreen, your index is not completed (I state this because you can misread the **HyperIndexer** dialog box and accidentally cancel its indexing). When this additional dialog box comes up onscreen, select the **OK** button.

Saving Our Work

Unlike working in HyperWriter itself, working in HyperIndexer doesn't require any work to be saved.

Exiting HyperIndexer

With our tutorial finished and our index file created, you can now exit Hyper-Indexer if desired. This is done with the **Exit** command on the **File** menu. Select the **Exit** command from the **File** menu. You will exit from HyperIndexer and return to the Program Manager.

Illustrating Searching

In the very first tutorial in this chapter, we demonstrated searching using a document that had been indexed by HyperIndexer. What I *don't* want to do right now is repeat that same tutorial on searching. However, it would be good to simply look at our indexed application and understand what the effects of some of our indexing options were. We will now open the application file SAMPAPP.HWA and go through a few options. Before we can open SAM-

PAPP.HWA, we must first run HyperWriter. HyperWriter is a standard MS-Windows application that can be run from the Program Manager.

Opening SAMPAPP.HWA

For this exercise, we want to start with the sample document SAMPAPP.HWA.

Opening SAMPAPP.HWA

1. Select the **Open** command from the **File** menu.
2. Select the document SAMPAPP.HWA from the list of available documents. If you are asked to leave a bookmark, answer No. This loads the document.

By opening SAMPAPP.HWA, the same file that we indexed, HyperWriter will automatically open the first .HW4 document file in the application. With this file open, we can look at the **Search Dialog** box.

Opening the Find Dialog Box

1. Select the **Find** command from the **Search** menu. This displays the dialog box shown in Figure 15.15.

    The primary aspect of the **Find** dialog box that you should notice is the categories list, which has a category named Title, that was defined

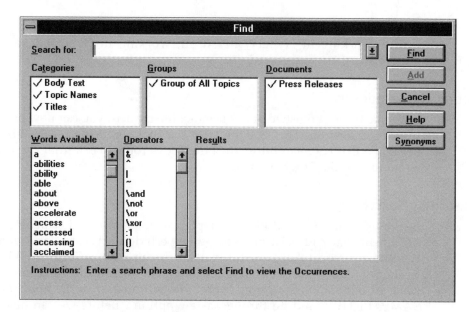

Figure 15.15 The **Find** dialog box.

as part of the indexing process. The other elements in this dialog box are standard for HyperWriter's search features.

Given that you have a better understanding of searching and indexing at this point as compared to the beginning of this chapter when you last used the search features, you may want to experiment with searching before going any further. If so, then enter some same queries and look at the results. If not, then continue with step 2.

2. Select the **Close** button to close the **Find** dialog box.

The one final aspect of this document that HyperIndexer affected was the table of contents. The **View TOC** command on the **Navigate** menu lets us view the table of contents.

Using the View TOC Command

1. Select the **View TOC** command from the **Navigate** menu. This displays the dialog box shown in Figure 15.16.

You may want to expand the size of the table of contents to view it more completely. As you can see, it illustrates the structure of the document graphically. For this document, the structure is only a one-level hierarchy. When you are done viewing the table of contents, continue with step 2.

2. Select the **Close** button to close the table of contents.

This completes our tutorial on indexing. By working through this tutorial, you should have a much better understanding of both searching and indexing.

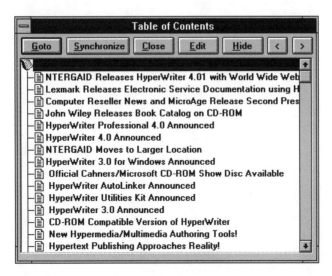

Figure 15.16 The **View TOC** dialog box.

Saving Our Work

We really didn't do any work in HyperWriter so we don't need to save anything.

Exiting HyperWriter

With our tutorial finished, you can now exit HyperWriter if desired. This is done with the **Exit** command on the **File** menu.

CHAPTER

Document Properties

16

One of the underlying characteristics of HyperWriter is that it is a very configurable tool. Unlike many other digital publishing tools, in HyperWriter you can invariably configure your application to function as needed. We saw this in Chapter 14 where we used custom backgrounds to configure how our application appeared to the user. In this tutorial, we will use HyperWriter's configuration facility for documents: document properties.

HyperWriter is a document-oriented tool in that what you are really doing with HyperWriter is building documents. In HyperWriter, these document can have *properties*. As noted in Chapter 7, a property is an attribute of an object. To be specific, a document property is a property that affects an entire HyperWriter document. Examples of document properties include how link symbols are displayed, how searches function, and what colors are used in a document. Document properties are modified with the **Properties** command on the **Document** menu. Unlike most other commands in HyperWriter, the **Document Properties** command groups different options into *folders* as shown in Figure 16.1.

Before we begin working with document properties, we need to understand the **Keep Previously Loaded Properties** option that appears in the **Document Properties** dialog box. As you may have noticed from the above screen shot of the **Document Properties** dialog box, the first option in the shown folder is **Keep Previously Loaded Properties**. This option, which is automatically turned on by default, instructs HyperWriter to retain all previous docu-

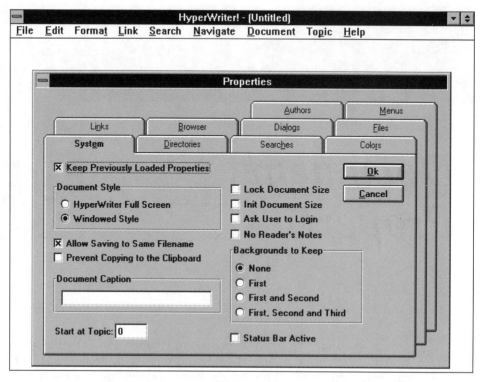

Figure 16.1 The **Document Properties** command.

ment properties. To change the options in a particular folder, this option must be turned off for that folder.

The reason for the **Keep Previously Loaded Properties** option is that in a HyperWriter application composed of multiple HyperWriter documents, if all document properties are supposed to be the same, needed document properties can be set only once—for the first document in the application. As long as all needed document properties are set in the first document in the application, the **Keep Previously Loaded Properties** setting allows all other documents to retain the previously set document properties. Each **Keep Previously Loaded Properties** option only affects options on the current folder. The reason that HyperWriter operates in this fashion is that this makes document maintenance in applications composed of multiple .HW4 documents significantly easier. Any document properties that need to be modified can be modified only for the first document in the application without having to modify them in multiple documents. The one situation where this is not so is when individual documents within the application need to have different document properties. Here, the document properties must be maintained separately.

Now that we understand **Keep Previously Loaded Properties**, we are ready to begin our tutorial. In this tutorial, we will open a document and set its document properties. We will also look at the different options for document properties (at the end of the tutorial).

Working with Document Properties

Before we can begin working with document properties, we must first run HyperWriter. HyperWriter is a standard MS-Windows application that can be run from the Program Manager.

For this tutorial, we want to start with the sample document DOCPROP1.HW4.

Opening DOCPROP1.HW4

1. Select the **Open** command from the **File** menu.
2. Select the document DOCPROP1.HW4 from the list of available documents. If you are asked to leave a bookmark, answer No. This loads the document. This document is shown in Figure 16.2.

As you can see, this document is a collection of NTERGAID press releases. In fact, this document is just a different version of the document that we worked with in the tutorial on indexing in Chapter 15. In this tutorial, we will configure the functioning of this application to match our needs. In specific, we will configure the following areas:

- Headers and footers for printing
- How searching functions

Configuring Headers and Footers

Although HyperWriter is a digital publishing toolkit, HyperWriter fully supports printed output. In fact, despite the power of digital publishing there are a large number of users who will always want to print out information. Although I can't tell you that HyperWriter will provide true desktop-publishing quality, HyperWriter can produce basic printed output complete with headers and footers. To prevent the end user from adding his or her own print headers and footers, HyperWriter supports document properties that define headers and footers that are used whenever HyperWriter prints information. These headers and footers allow you to add copyright statements, page numbers, and other notices whenever information is printed.

Setting headers and footers is done with the **Menus** folder of options.

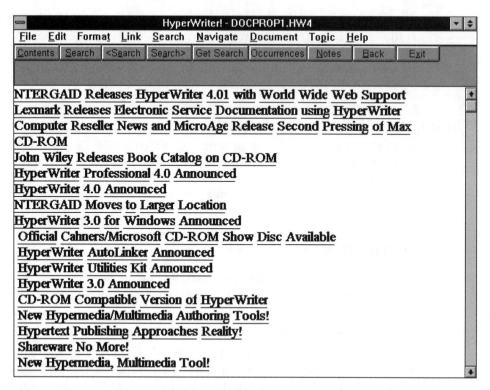

Figure 16.2 The DOCPROP1.HW4 document.

Setting Headers and Footers

1. Select the **Properties** command from the **Document** menu.
2. Select the **Menus** folder of options. This displays the dialog box shown in Figure 16.3.
3. Turn off the **Keep Previously Loaded Properties** option at the top of the dialog box.
4. In the **Header** field, enter **NTERGAID Press Releases**.
5. In the **Footer** field, enter **Copyright (C) NTERGAID, Inc. 1989-1995**.
6. Select **OK** to close the dialog box.

With the previous steps we have added both a header and a footer to our document that will be displayed at the top and bottom of the page whenever a printout is made from our document. HyperWriter's **Print** command is located on the **File** menu. If you want to see the headers and footers that you have just added, select the **Print** command from the **File** menu and examine the top and bottom of the page.

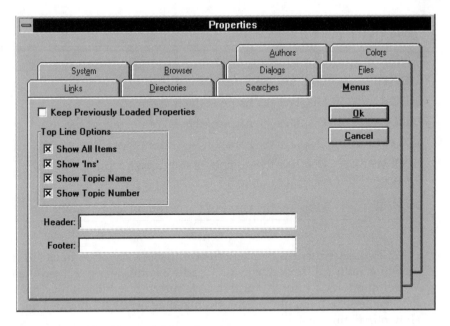

Figure 16.3 The **Menus** folder of options.

While setting print headers and footers was useful, the headers and footers that we set were very static in that the headers and footers couldn't change as the information was printed. This is addressed in the next section, "Understanding Print Codes."

Reference: Understanding Print Codes

To make print headers and footers more dynamic, HyperWriter supports a number of different **@Codes**. These are text codes that can be embedded in the header or footer field and will be replaced with the appropriate value when the contents of the field is printed. For example, a footer with the text **Printed on @DATE, only valid for 30 days past this date**, would insert the current date whenever a page was printed. A full list of **@Codes** is shown in Table 16.1.

Having configured our print headers and footers, we are now ready to configure searching in this document.

Configuring Searching

As discussed several times in this chapter, HyperWriter supports a very powerful full-text search engine. Full-text searching is a very interesting and very powerful technology. One of the real drawbacks to full-text searching is that as it gets more powerful, the user interface of the search engine tends to get more

Table 16.1 HyperWriter @Codes

Code	Description
@DATE	Displays the date.
@DOC	Displays the name of the document.
@FILE	Displays the name of the .HW4 document file.
@NAME	Displays the name of the current topic.
@NUMBER	Displays the number of the current topic.
@TIME	Displays the time.
@USER	Displays the name of the currently logged in reader.

complex. Consequently, less experienced users very often have a difficult time working with full-text retrieval. To address this very real problem, Hyper-Writer supports a unique, configurable interface which allows the user interface to the search engine to be customized as needed. Consider the dialog box shown in Figure 16.4.

As you can see, HyperWriter's default search dialog box offers a lot of powerful functionality. However, by definition, this functionality will be hard for less experienced people to use. Now, consider the dialog box shown in Figure 16.5.

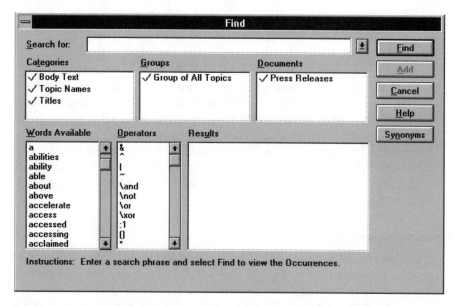

Figure 16.4 HyperWriter's default search user interface.

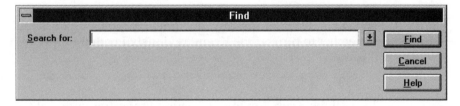

Figure 16.5 A customized search user interface.

As you can see, HyperWriter's default search dialog box has been replaced with a very simple dialog box consisting of only a search field. This nicely illustrates the power that customizing the search interface gives you—you can create an interface that is appropriate for the audience of your electronic publication.

Customizing the **Search** dialog box uses the **Searches** folder in the **Document Properties** dialog box.

Configuring Searching

1. Select the **Properties** command from the **Document** menu.
2. Select the **Searches** folder of options. This displays the dialog box shown in Figure 16.6.

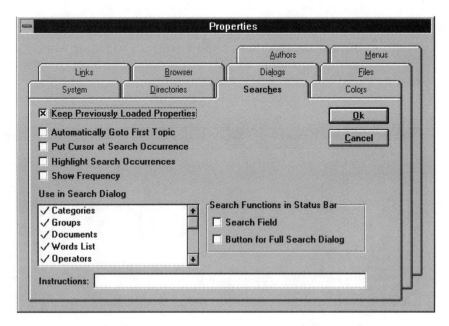

Figure 16.6 The **Searches** folder of options.

NOTE: Before setting any document property, you should always remember to turn off the **Keep Previously Loaded Properties** option (as illustrated in step 3).

3. Turn off the **Keep Previously Loaded Properties** option at the top of the dialog box.
4. Move to the **User in Search Dialog** group of options and turn off the following options: **Categories**, **Groups**, **Documents**, **Operators**, **Results**, **Instructions**, and **Synonyms**.
5. Select the **OK** button to close the **Document Properties** dialog box.

As you can see, setting document properties hasn't had an immediate effect on the appearance of our document. However, when you select the **Find** command from the **Search** menu, the dialog box shown in Figure 16.7 will be displayed.

As you can see, this dialog box is considerably simpler than HyperWriter's standard search dialog box (shown earlier in this tutorial), featuring only a search field and a word list of terms in the document.

Now that we have worked with document properties, we are ready to save our work and look at a discussion of document properties in HyperWriter.

Saving Our Work

With our tutorial finished, we are now ready to save our work. This is done with the **Save** command on the **File** menu. Select the **Save** command from the **File** menu. HyperWriter will save your work.

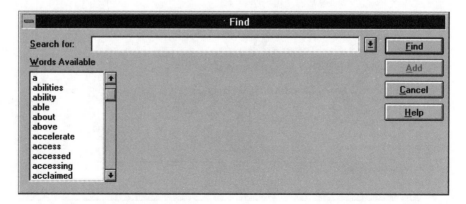

Figure 16.7 The **Modified Find** dialog box.

Exiting HyperWriter

With our tutorial finished and our work saved, you can now exit HyperWriter if desired. This is done with the **Exit** command on the **File** menu.

Reference: The Template Wizard and Document Properties

As covered in the first tutorial in this chapter, HyperWriter's Template Wizard offers a very powerful tool for creating a template or starting point for your HyperWriter documents. When the Template Wizard is used, depending on which options you pick, it can set the following document properties:

- Document caption
- Set the links folder to have links displayed in the MS-Windows style (green, underlined text)
- Print headers (the document caption is set to be the print header)
- Set the document size to be a maximized window

Reference: Document Properties

As you saw when setting document properties in this tutorial, all of Hyper-Writer's document properties are referenced through a folders metaphor. The **Document Properties** dialog box is composed of ten different folders of options. These folders are listed in Table 16.2.

Table 16.2 Folders of HyperWriter Document Properties

Folder	Description
System	Set the options in the document that modify all of the HyperWriter system.
Links	Set how links are displayed.
Menus	Set options that alter HyperWriter's menu system.
Directories	Set the documents, pictures, text, and local files directories in HyperWriter.
Browser	Set how the ASCII browser functions.
Files	Set how HyperWriter works with files.
Searches	Set how HyperWriter's indexed search command functions.
Dialogs	Set how HyperWriter's dialog boxes functions.
Colors	Set HyperWriter's default colors.
Authors	Set a document's authors list.

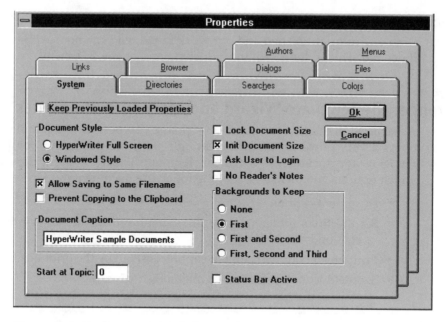

Figure 16.8 The **System** folder of options.

Reference: What Document Properties Do I Need?

HyperWriter has ten different folders of document properties. With an average of ten commands per folder, this amounts to over 100 different properties to set. To make understanding document properties easier, in the sections below are pictures of all of the different document properties folders along with a table of the most commonly used commands for each folder. This isn't to say that these are the only document properties that you will need, only that these are the ones that you are most likely to need.

The System Folder

The **System** folder of options on the **Document Properties** dialog box sets general options that apply to all of HyperWriter. Selecting the **System** folder displays the dialog box shown in Figure 16.8.

Commonly used options on the **System** folder are listed in Table 16.3.

Table 16.3 Commonly Used Options on the System Folder

Option	Description
Document Caption	Set the caption displayed at the top of your application in HyperReader.

Option	Description
Lock Document Size/ Init Document Size	Set the size of the window where your application is displayed.
Links Folder	Set the options that apply to how links are displayed as well as several other miscellaneous options that pertain to how the document functions in HyperReader (cursor presence and the like). Selecting the **Links** folder displays the dialog box shown in Figure 16.9.

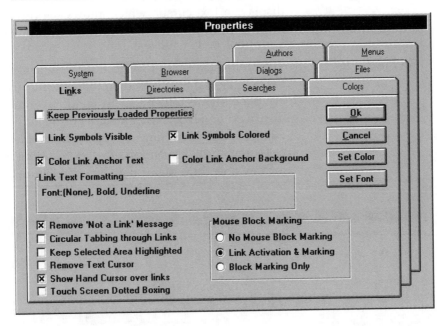

Figure 16.9 The **Links** folder of options.

Commonly used options on the **Links** folder are listed in Table 16.4.

Table 16.4 Commonly Used Options on the **Links** Folder

Option	Description
Link Symbols Visible	Set if HyperWriter's default link symbols are available. As most people prefer Windows-style link symbols, this is generally turned off.
Set Color	Set the color for link symbols. This is generally set to green on white.

(continued)

Table 16.4 (Continued)

Option	Description
Set Font	Set the font for link symbols; this is generally set only to underline.
Remove Not a Link Message	Tell the reader that they haven't selected a link when they click on an option that isn't linked. Many people don't want this function, so this option is generally turned off.
Remove Text Cursor	By default, even when reading documents, HyperWriter displays a text cursor, which allows the reader to copy blocks of text to the clipboard or export them to files. Turn this option on to remove the cursor if desired.
Menus Folder	The **Menus** folder isn't particularly well named—most of the options don't really pertain to the menu system at all. What the **Menus** folder actually controls is how items are displayed on HyperWriter's status or menu line when a Full Screen style document is open. This folder also controls preset print headers and footers. Selecting the **Menus** folder displays the dialog box shown in Figure 16.10.

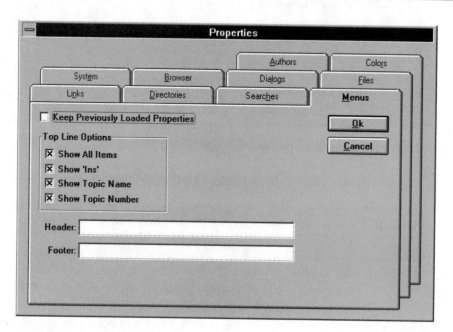

Figure 16.10 The **Menus** folder of options.

Commonly used options on the **Menus** folder are listed in Table 16.5.

Table 16.5 Commonly Used Options on the **Menus** Folder

Option	Description
Header	Set a header automatically added to the document when it is printed out.
Footer	Set a footer automatically added to the document when it is printed out.

The Directories Folder

The **Directories** folder of options on the **Document Properties** dialog box sets the drive and directory from which linked files should be referenced. Selecting the **Directories** folder displays the dialog box shown in Figure 16.11.

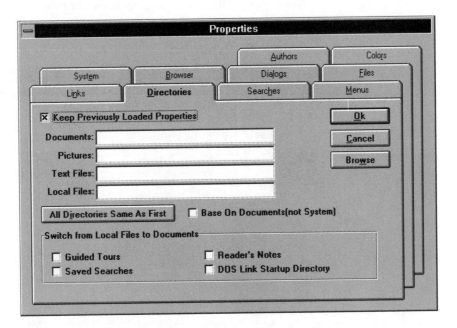

Figure 16.11 The **Directories** folder of options.

Commonly used options on the **Directories** folder are listed in Table 16.6.

Table 16.6 Commonly Used Options on the **Directories** Folder

Option	Description
Pictures	Set the default directory where the current document looks for picture files, allowing different documents to access pictures from different directories (useful if you have a large number of pictures).
Base on Document(s) Not System	Set the default drive to be used with the **Pictures** setting to be the drive where documents are accessed from, not where HyperReader is accessed from. This is useful with CD-ROM applications where the HyperReader software is commonly installed to the hard drive and the documents stay on the CD-ROM drive.
Browser Folder	Set the options that apply to HyperWriter's ASCII browser. HyperWriter's ASCII browser is the facility for linking to ASCII text files. The **Browser** folder of options allows you to define the margins and screen backgrounds displayed to browse ASCII files. Selecting the **Browser** folder displays the dialog box shown in Figure 16.12.

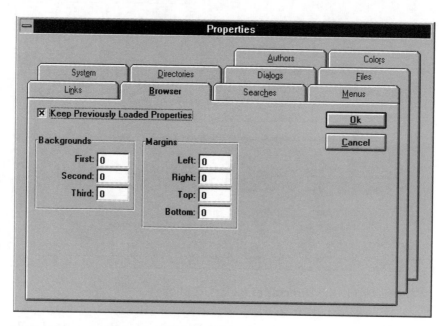

Figure 16.12 The **Browser** folder of options.

To be quite honest, there really aren't commonly used commands in this folder of options, as this is not a commonly used feature in HyperWriter.

The Files Folder

The **Files** folder of options on the **Document Properties** dialog box sets the options that apply to how HyperWriter works with files. Selecting the **Files** folder displays the dialog box shown in Figure 16.13.

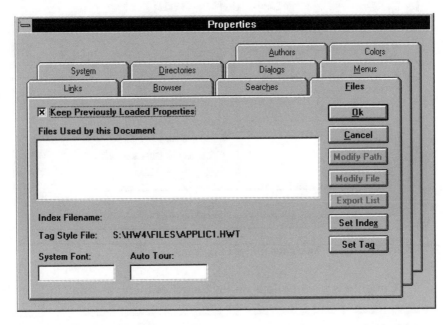

Figure 16.13 The **Files** folder of options.

Commonly used options on the **Files** folder are listed in Table 16.7.

Table 16.7 Commonly Used Options on the **Files** Folder

Option	Description
Files Used by this Document	List all files referenced from the current document.
Modify Path	Modify the drive and path from which a file is referenced.

The Searches Folder

The **Searches** folder of options on the **Document Properties** dialog box sets the options that apply to how HyperWriter's indexed search command functions. Selecting the **Searches** folder displays the dialog box shown in Figure 16.14.

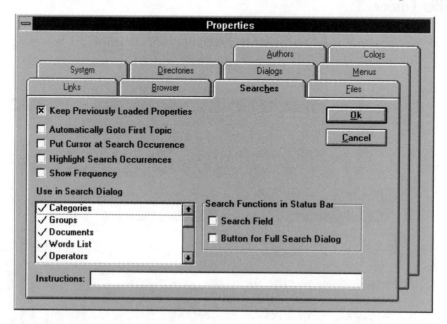

Figure 16.14 The **Searches** folder of options.

Commonly used options on the **Searches** folder as listed in Table 16.8.

Table 16.8 Commonly Used Options on the **Searches** Folder

Option	Description
Use in Search Dialog	Set the features that HyperWriter is to use in its search dialog box.
Put Cursor at Search Occurrence	Place the cursor at the beginning of search occurrences that HyperWriter finds.
Highlight Search Occurrences	Tell HyperWriter to highlight any search occurrences that it finds.
Dialogs Folder	Set the options that apply to HyperWriter's dialog boxes. Selecting the **Dialogs** folder displays the dialog box shown in Figure 16.15.

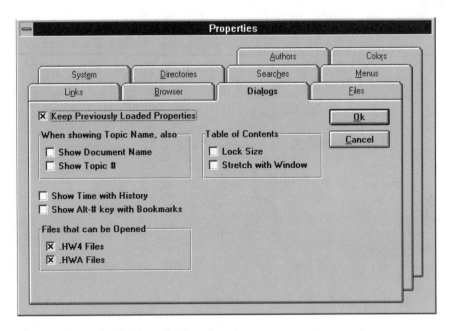

Figure 16.15 The **Dialogs** folder of options.

Commonly used options on the **Dialogs** folder are listed in Table 16.9.

Table 16.9 Commonly Used Options on the **Dialogs** Folder

Option	Description
Show Document Name	Display the document name in any dialog box where HyperWriter is displaying the topic name. For example, the **History** dialog box could display the topic name followed by the document name.
Stretch with Window	Set the table of contents browser to stretch with the window size.
Colors Folder	Set how HyperWriter's colors function. Selecting the **Colors** folder displays the dialog box shown in Figure 16.16.

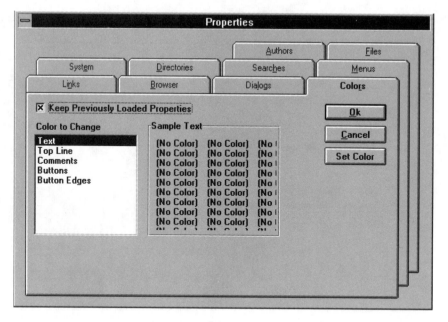

Figure 16.16 The **Colors** folder of options.

Commonly used options on the **Colors** folder are listed in Table 16.10.

Table 16.10 Commonly Used Options on the **Colors** Folder

Option	Description
Text	Set the default color for full screen topics. This is generally set by your background created with the Template Wizard.
Comments	Set the default color for popup or "comment" topics.
Authors Folder	Set the options that apply to a document's list of authors. This list is used for security purposes in the document. Selecting the **Authors** folder displays the dialog box shown in Figure 16.17.

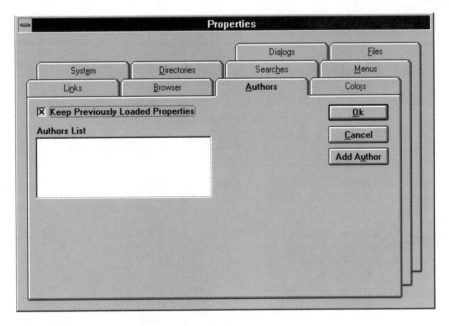

Figure 16.17 The **Authors** folder of options.

As with the **Browser** folder, the **Authors** folder simply isn't used that frequently. Consequently, there aren't particular commands that are more common than others. This concludes our discussion of HyperWriter document properties.

3

Applying Digital Publishing

While in Part I we covered the theory and issues found in digital publishing and in Part II we illustrated how to use HyperWriter, in Part III, we cover how to apply digital publishing. Specifically, we will be using the supplied digital publishing tool, HyperWriter, and tackling different types of digital publishing projects: Internet Web sites and interactive catalogs. When you have worked through Chapters 17 and 18, you will have created full-featured digital publications for each of these projects. Please bear in mind that like Part II, Part III is actually tutorial oriented and is best done with easy access to a personal computer.

C H A P T E R

17

Building an Interactive Catalog

In this tutorial, we will be building an interactive catalog, a digital publication designed for the purpose of selling something. The specific catalog that we will create is an electronic version of the John Wiley & Sons Computer Books catalog (John Wiley & Sons is the publisher of this book). When I approached John Wiley & Sons regarding this book, I wanted to include several powerful tutorials that illustrate common applications of digital publications. As catalogs are very common digital publications, it seemed natural to take the content for the John Wiley & Sons catalog and present a tutorial based on it. Not only would this approach satisfy the need for a substantial tutorial, but it also would also present a substantial real-world example.

Understanding the Content of the Catalog

Before we get into our tutorial, we first need to understand the content that we have for the catalog. The John Wiley & Sons catalog is organized by category with such topics as Artificial Intelligence, AS/400 Programming, Graphics Programming, and so on. Within each category are, of course, the books covered. As far as the data that we have for this catalog goes, it exists in two formats: Microsoft Word and .JPG. The Microsoft Word files contain the text for the catalog, with one file for each category of books. The .JPG files are scanned images that contain a picture of the cover for each book. There is a scanned picture for almost every book in the catalog.

Thinking of these scanned pictures gives us an idea as to how to present our interactive catalog. Consider a screen design where whenever you saw the catalog entry for a book, you also saw the book's cover as well. What this would accomplish is twofold. First, it would create a much more interesting, attractive application than a pure text-based application. The second benefit becomes apparent only when you consider how a book catalog is used. When people use a book catalog to find works, they then go to their bookstore to purchase the works they found through the catalog (mail order sales occur too, but book stores seem to dominate book sales). When they get to the book store, they have to try and find the book they want from the many different titles on the shelf. By presenting our catalog in such a fashion that they always see the cover of the book, users of the catalog will be able to more easily locate books at the bookstore by simply recognizing its cover. In case you are curious, HyperWriter does support a design feature called Topic Picture that we can use to create this type of design with both pictures and text simultaneously.

Within each Microsoft Word file is the data for the books in each category. This data is formatted using a standard set of styles that describe the type of data contained in the catalog. These styles are listed below.

- **HEADING1**
- **HEADING2**
- **AUTHOR**
- **KEYWORDS**
- **DESCRIPTION**
- **NORMAL** (converted to Body Text during import)
- **BULLET**
- **ISBN #** (this is a standard numbering scheme for identifying books)
- **PICTURE**
- **PRICE**

The styles listed are pretty standard for a catalog. The styles that we need to describe further are **HEADING1**, **HEADING2**, and **PICTURE**. The **HEADING1** and **HEADING2** styles are the standard Microsoft Word heading styles. In our data files, the **HEADING1** style is used at the top of each data file to identify the category of books contained in the data file. For example, in the file AI.DOC, the **HEADING1** style formats the text Artificial Intelligence. The **HEADING2** style is used to format the title of each book in the data file. In our data file AI.DOC, the **HEADING2** style is applied to the text Neural Networks in C++ (among other titles in the file). By working through the other tutorials in this book, you should recognize that HyperWriter's Import Text Wizard can be used to take these styles and create hypertext topics automatically if desired.

The **PICTURE** style is applied to text that has the name of the picture file needed for each book. For example, in the book *It's Alive*, the **PICTURE** style is applied to the name 0077.JPG. This picture file indicates the name of the scanned cover of the book. Please note that while I wouldn't agree with this type of sequential naming convention, as it is very hard to identify a particular image with a particular book. When a project has an existing naming convention, it is often better to use the existing naming scheme than to create a new naming approach.

If we were to examine a sample data file in Microsoft Word with the Word stylebar turned on so we can see the styles, we would see what is shown in Figure 17.1.

As shown, all of the data for our catalog shares a similar format and a similar order in which the styles are used. We will take advantage of this similar order later in this chapter.

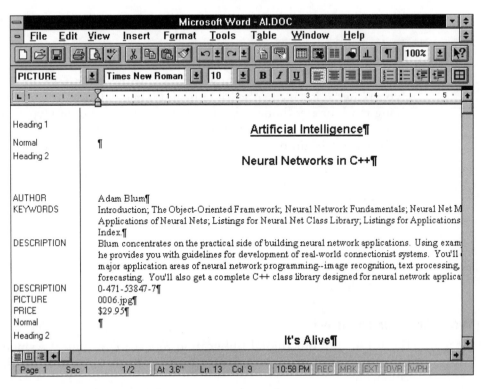

Figure 17.1 Viewing our data in Microsoft word.

Now that we understand the data that goes into our catalog, we are ready to begin our tutorial.

Understanding this Chapter

The tutorial sections in this chapter have four major parts:

- Getting Ready for Our Tutorial: Planning a Publication
- Tutorial Part 1: Building Our Publication
- Tutorial Part 2: Distributing Our Publication
- Tutorial Part 3: Publishing this Application on the World Wide Web

The first part, "Getting Ready…" covers how to plan a digital publication. Along with basic tips, it includes specific details for this chapter's tutorial. The following sections all cover how to build this chapter's application. If you don't want to read through the planning steps, feel free to move directly to "Tutorial Part 1: Building Our Publication."

Getting Ready for Our Tutorial: Planning a Publication

Like many tasks with a computer, when creating a digital publication with HyperWriter, it is easy to dive right in and immediately start working without giving much or any thought to planning or design. And, in HyperWriter as in many other tasks, this often doesn't work all that well.

Before we begin our tutorial, we need to start with some basic planning steps. These steps can be broken down along five guidelines, each of which will be covered.

- Features
- Goals
- Constraints
- Audience
- Architecture

What Are Our Features?

The features of our digital publication reflect the technical elements of our application, what we want our audience to be able to do with the final application.

For our electronic manual application, Table 17.1 lists the features needed.

Table 17.1 Features Needed for Our Electronic Manual

Feature	Why Do We Need It?
Attractive user interface and overall appearance	Just as print catalogs have high production values, so do electronic catalogs. In short, an attractive interface and appearance will help our catalog be more successful.
Easy to use	This brings us to an important point—people are currently deluged by catalogs. For our interactive catalog to succeed, it really must be truly easy to use or people simply won't use it.
Fully searchable	If our application is searchable, then it will be easier to find information. To make our application more useful, we will support searching in fields defined by the styles in the documents.
Table of contents	For users that don't like searching, a table of contents is useful for finding information.
Printing and exporting	To allow people to make records of the books they want to purchase, printing and exporting is a needed feature.
Categorical organization	By organizing the information into categories along the themes of the book, this will make it easy to use the catalog.

What Are Our Goals?

Digital publishing is a compelling, addictive technology. Because of this, when using digital publishing, it is easy to lose track of why you are using it, the specific goals or benefits that you hope to get from your electronic publication. For this reason, it is always good to address the issue of the goals that you want from your publication up front, before beginning work on it.

The goals or benefits we would like to receive from our digital publication are listed in Table 17.2.

Table 17.2 Goals From Our Digital Publication

Goal	Why Do We Need It?
Sell more books	When you come right down to it, the goal of any marketing piece (and this is a marketing piece) is to sell more product.
Easy to access	One of the objections people have to printed catalogs is that they are never as well indexed as they should be, so people can't find what they are looking for. For our catalog to succeed, it should have both a table of contents and be fully searchable.

What Are Our Constraints?

After working through the goals of your digital publication, the next step is to tackle the constraints on the publication. While not as apparent as the goals, understanding the constraints on a publication makes a big difference in planning the publication's architecture.

The limits affecting us for this project are:

- Easy authoring—John Wiley & Sons updates their computer book catalog frequently, so difficult authoring would make it hard to update frequently.

- Work with existing data without modifying it—We want to use the same data files for our interactive catalog as for our printed catalog. This will prevent errors or inaccuracies in our interactive catalog.

Who Is Our Audience?

When implementing any digital publication, one of the most important planning steps, if not the most important planning step, is to consider the audience. What considering the audience does is help to determine if your initial assumptions in planning the document are correct. This last question is really the most important question of all. Without knowing the audience of your electronic publication, you really can't even begin to implement an electronic publication (at least not successfully). Your audience should generally dictate everything from user interface to the publication to the features to the distribution media.

Given that the audience for this digital publication is a potential book customer, what does this imply for us? As noted earlier, the first implication is that our catalog needs to be easy to use. This reflects today's complicated marketing environment, where marketing efforts that aren't easy to use will simply be passed by. Another implication is that our digital publication needs to be essentially complete and bug free. Although errors in our digital publications are never desirable, in an internal application errors are not such a big deal. When you have an external application like a catalog, errors can really discourage its use, as people will see an error and then distrust the contents of the catalog.

What Is Our Architecture?

The final step in planning our digital publication is to determine how our digital publication fits in HyperWriter's internal architecture. You may recall this from Chapter 7, where we discussed planning your HyperWriter application. To determine our architecture, we need to answer the ten questions listed below.

What Is the Application?

The application that we have is an electronic catalog designed to publish the information found in the print catalog, although in an easier to use fashion.

What Documents Are Needed?

Our source documents are several files created with Microsoft Word. Despite the several source files, for ease of distribution we would like to create only a single HyperWriter document with all the content from our source files.

What Groups Are Needed?

This application is actually relatively small—the source files are under a half megabyte in size. Groups in HyperWriter are used both for searching and for printing. As our information is categorically organized, groups could be applied to searching as well. This would allow a reader to search only books about a particular topic (say, Artificial Intelligence). In a technical area like computer books, where the same terminology overlaps different categories, this would definitely help the reader find information. Additionally, groups would allow the different categories of books that are structured into multiple topics to be printed as a single entity. For these reasons, we will assign groups everywhere a section of the catalog exists. Each topic containing a book description will need to be assigned to a group.

Where Are the Topics?

When creating any HyperWriter application, a key question is where topics need to be created. Given the goal of our digital publication is to present a computer book catalog, a natural structure is to store each book description in a single topic. Not only would this tie right in with HyperWriter's search engine, which retrieves topics of information, but it would let us use the **HEADING2** styles found in our source data as a way to create these topics automatically with the Import Text Wizard. The **HEADING1** styles that appear at the top of each source file can also be used by the Import Text Wizard to create topics that contain the titles of all books in a particular category. In short, what we will do is create a topic everywhere a heading or subheading appears in our text.

Where Are the Links?

In a publication like this, the hypertext links that are needed are typically only those that would be considered table of contents links. In other words, they are the links that function to access information from a centralized table of contents. There really aren't the type of cross-referencing links that are found in a publication like a manual, where a *See XYZ* type of reference can be converted to a hypertext link.

What Properties Are Needed?

Properties provide a way for customizing the functionality of a link, topic, or document. For this application, our links will be pretty standard, without any need for properties. Our topics, however, will need a property called **Topic Picture**. What the **Topic Picture** property does is assign a picture as part of the topic so that a background can display it. Additionally, to configure our document, however, we will need several document properties. These properties will be covered later in this chapter.

What Action Lists Are Needed?

Action lists provide dynamic links. As this material is primarily text-based and static in nature, we won't need action lists for this application.

What Tags Are Needed?

Tags or styles provide elements to format the text in our documents. For an application like this where we have existing source data, we generally want to rely on the tags that are found in the data rather than new tags. As discussed earlier, our tags are already found in our data and seem appropriate for our needs.

What Backgrounds Are Needed?

HyperWriter's backgrounds provide the user interface for documents. Given that this is a catalog, it is pretty easy to guess what we need:

- The main user interface to the document
- A background for displaying the **Topic Picture** property
- A cover or splash screen

How Should the Application Be Indexed?

Indexing takes a HyperWriter application and makes it fully searchable. To make our application fully searchable, what we will do is index it at both the category (field) and group levels.

Summary

From the above planning steps, we found out the following information:

- What is the application? An electronic catalog aimed at selling more books.
- What documents are needed? A single HyperWriter document with the content of the catalog.
- What groups are needed? One group per category of books.
- Where are the topics? Topics are created where headings existed in the source documents. The general structure is one topic for every book description.
- Where are the links? Table of contents links are the primary links that are needed.
- What properties are needed? Only topic and document properties are needed. No link properties are needed.
- What action lists are needed? Action lists are not needed for this application.
- What tags are needed? Tags for each of the styles found in the source documents are needed.
- What backgrounds are needed? A main user interface background is needed. A cover screen background is needed as is a background for the topic picture.
- How should the application be indexed? Sophisticated indexing, including categories and groups, is needed.

With our planning stage completed, we are ready to begin our tutorial.

Tutorial Part 1: Building Our Publication

The following sections take you through our tutorial. To make this tutorial easier, we have broken it into three major sections, each arranged into discrete steps. For learning purposes, it is usually easier to work through a tutorial and complete a step in full than to leave a portion of it incomplete.

Step 1: Setting Our Directories

Before we can begin working through this tutorial, we need to run Hyper-Writer. HyperWriter is a standard MS-Windows application that is run from MS-Windows, as is any other Windows application. With HyperWriter running, we need to get started by setting our directories.

To make this tutorial easier, all the data files used for this tutorial have been organized into a separate directory. What we will do now is set Hyper-Writer's Preferences so that it uses this directory. This is an area of Hyper-

Writer that we really haven't covered yet—directories within HyperWriter. When you use HyperWriter, unlike many other software products, it is very important to understand where files are located, the directory where they are stored. The reason for this is that unlike a word processor or other productivity tool, with HyperWriter what you are doing is creating publications that will be given to someone else as files—not as printouts. Given that a HyperWriter publication can consist of literally hundreds of different files, HyperWriter takes advantage of directories to organize these files. HyperWriter uses four separate directory settings:

- Documents—where HyperWriter .HW4 files are stored
- Pictures—where picture files are stored
- Text Files—where text files (i.e., using the **Import Text** command) are stored
- Local Files—where temporary data files like bookmarks and searches are stored.

Although HyperWriter can look across directories to find files, these directory settings are where HyperWriter always looks first to find a particular file. Setting our directory options is covered below.

Setting Directories in HyperWriter

1. Select the **Preferences** command from the **File** menu.
2. Select the **Directories** folder. This displays the folder of options shown in Figure 17.2.
3. Enter \HW4\WCATALOG into the **Documents** field. If you installed HyperWriter into a directory other than \HW4, then substitute that directory.
4. Select the **All Directories Same As First** button to synchronize all directories with the **Documents** directory.
5. Select the **OK** button to close this dialog box.

With our directories set, we are ready to get started on our tutorial. You should be aware that a completed version of this tutorial has been supplied in \HW4\WCATALOG\DONE, in case you need to see how the tutorial functions when it is finished. To save disc space, we did not supply the picture files in this directory. When you open the completed version of this tutorial, you can leave your pictures directory set to \HW4\WCATALOG. You should also be aware that to save disc space, you can delete this directory if needed. Once you have worked through this tutorial, you can also delete the \HW4\WCAT-ALOG directory as well.

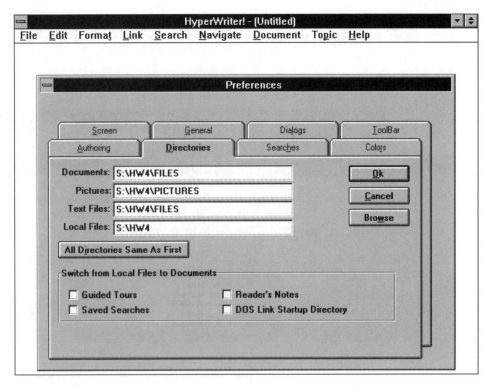

Figure 17.2 Setting directories with the **Preferences** command.

NOTE: The WCATALOG directory has over three megabytes of sample pictures (in JPEG format) in it. You probably want to delete these picture files to save disc space once you work through this tutorial.

Step 2: Using the Template Wizard

As described in Chapter 9, the Template Wizard allows you to define an initial template document for your HyperWriter applications, defining the appearance and functionality of your application. When using the Template Wizard, the key choice for your template is between text buttons and iconic buttons. While you might think that given our choice for an attractive interface we might choose iconic buttons; instead, we will choose text buttons. The reason is that text buttons are easier to extend for custom functionality. With text buttons, you just create a new button with the built-in Screen Painter instead of creating a whole new icon using an external graphics program and then bringing that icon into

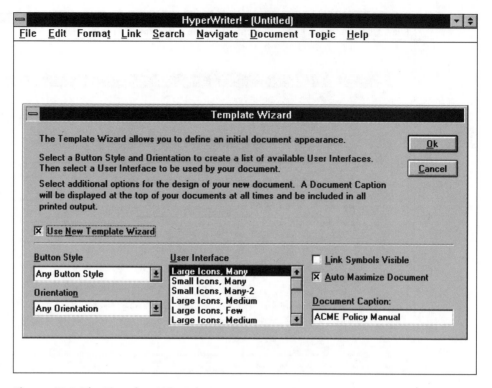

Figure 17.3 The Template Wizard.

HyperWriter. If we pick a good-looking set of text buttons, we can get the best of both worlds—attractive appearance along with easy extensions.

Using the Template Wizard

Select the **New** command from the **File** menu. This displays the Template Wizard shown in Figure 17.3.

The first step in using the Template Wizard is to select the style of buttons you want in the template document the Wizard will create. Select the button style that you want by selecting on the **Button Style** field. For this tutorial, select the **Text Buttons** option. If the **Use New Template Wizard** option is turned off, turn it on before continuing.

After selecting the style of button for your template document, we need to select the orientation for the buttons or icons. The available orientation options are **Along Top Side**, **Along Left Side**, **Along Right Side**, **Along Bottom Side**, and **Along Top and Bottom**. Select the **Orientation** option that you want by selecting on the **Orientation** field. Given that we want to have both a picture and the text of our application available at the same time, we will need a wide screen. This means that the **Along Left Side** and **Along Right Side** options shouldn't be used. With a choice between the top and bottom, it is easy to argue for the top option, as most Windows applications have toolbars along the top. For this tutorial, select the **Along Top Side** option. You have now set the Template Wizard to create a template document using icons along both the top and bottom of the screen.

Based on the choices we made, the list of different user interfaces shown in the **User Interface** list has been updated so that only user interface screens matching the options that you selected are displayed. To make using the Template Wizard easy, select the first user interface (**Win Help Modified**) from the list. This sets that user interface as the interface for the template document that will be created.

The **Link Symbols Visible** option sets whether links are displayed using HyperWriter's triangular link symbols or whether green, underlined text (like the Windows help system) indicate links. For our tutorial, leave this option off (green, underlined text is fine for our electronic publication, as our audience knows Windows and understands that text with this appearance is hypertext).

The **Auto Maximize Document** option sets the template document so that it automatically zooms the window to the maximum size that Windows supports when it is opened by a reader (it may not automatically maximize the first time as an author that you open it). For our tutorial, leave this option off as we don't want a maximized document (we will later lock our document's size).

The **Document Caption** option defines a title displayed at the top of the screen in HyperReader. Enter "John Wiley Electronic Catalog" into this field as the caption for our tutorial application.

We have now selected all the options needed for our template document. Select the **OK** button to create our template document. This creates a new HyperWriter template document with the specified user interface and options. The template document created is shown in Figure 17.4.

As you can see, the template document created has a series of buttons for common functions. It also has a screen of text that is inserted automatically by the Template Wizard to instruct you in what to do with the template document. To continue with our tutorial, we need to delete this text.

Deleting Text

1. Press **Shift+Ctrl+End** to mark all the text in the topic as a block. You can also use the mouse if this is easier for you.

2. Select the **Delete** command from the **Edit** menu and then select the **OK** button. This deletes the text.

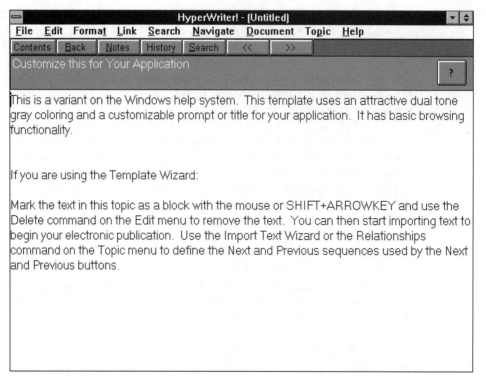

Figure 17.4 The template document that was created.

Before continuing with our tutorial, we should save our work. When you use HyperWriter, or whenever you use a computer, it is a good idea to save your work frequently. Saving your work in HyperWriter is shown below.

Saving Our Electronic Publication

1. Select the **Save** command from the **File** menu.
2. Type the name "WCATALOG" and press **Enter**. This saves your Hyper-Writer document.

Step 3: Using the Import Text Wizard

With the document template created, the next step is to use the Import Text Wizard to import our source document and automatically create hypertext links. Although HyperWriter has a very powerful manual linking system, the automatic linking features built into the Import Text Wizard create links very quickly, saving significant amounts of time in the development process. The

Import Text Wizard operates by using heading levels and table of contents marks to indicate hypertext topics (links are created to these topics). Page references are also converted to hypertext links.

If you don't have our tutorial application open, use the **Open** command to open it now.

Before we use the Import Text Wizard, we should think a little bit about our application. As noted earlier, we definitely need an attractive cover or splash screen for our catalog, so that when the user initially opens the catalog, he or she sees the cover screen and understands what they are looking at (the John Wiley & Sons catalog). As we want to ensure that this is seen, an easy way is to locate the cover screen in topic number 1 of our document. If we use the Import Text Wizard from topic number 1 then a table of contents will be placed in topic number 1, making it difficult to use it for a table of contents. The solution is actually quite easy—create a link from topic 1 to a new topic, topic 2. In topic 2, use the Import Text Wizard which will place the table of contents in topic 2. Creating this link is described in the next section.

NOTE: Technically, we don't have to create this. Our table of contents could always be moved from topic number 1, and HyperWriter has a feature called **Start At Topic** which allows using a topic other than number 1 for the cover screen. However, this approach is just simpler and, as we are starting a tutorial from scratch, there isn't a reason to follow the simpler approach. If we had already created our document and were looking to add a cover screen, then we would use the **Start At Topic** option.

Creating a Link

1. Type the text "Click Here to Start" on the first line in the topic.
2. Mark this text as a block.
3. Select the **Link to Text** command from the **Link** menu.
4. Select the **Jump Link** option.
5. Select the **New Topic** option. This creates a new topic and places you in it. As we started at topic number 1, this is now topic number 2.
6. Select the **Complete Link** command from the **Link** menu. This completes the link and places you back in the topic you started at. As we want to use the Import Text Wizard from this new topic, we need to activate the link we just created.
7. Select the link that you just created and activate it to move to the new topic.

   Now that we have created a new topic, we need to name it with the **Name** command on the **Topic** menu.

8. Select the **Name** command on the **Topic** menu. Enter the name Table of Contents, and press **Enter**. Having named the new topic we created, we realize that we didn't name the first topic we created. What we will do is return to the first topic, name it, and then go back to the second topic.

9. Press **Esc**.

10. Select the **Name** command on the **Topic** menu. Enter the name John Wiley Computer Book Catalog: Cover, and press **Enter**.

11. Select the **Click Here to Start** link and activate it to move to our new topic.

We have now created our new topic and are ready to use the Import Text Wizard to import our documents into HyperWriter. Before we do this, we should look at the documents we want to import:

- AI.DOC
- AS400PRO.DOC
- CCPPROG.DOC
- CLIENTSR.DOC
- DATABASE.DOC
- DOCUMEN.DOC
- GENERAL.DOC
- GRAPHPRO.DOC
- INFOENG.DOC
- INTELGSY.DOC
- MGMTOPER.DOC
- MVSPROG.DOC
- OBJTECH.DOC
- OS2PROG.DOC
- POWERBLD.DOC
- PROGRAM.DOC
- SOFTENG.DOC
- SYSDEV.DOC
- UIDESGN.DOC
- UNIXPRO.DOC
- WINPROG.DOC

As you might imagine, these Microsoft Word documents have filenames that reflect the category they cover. For example, the document AI.DOC contains the books that fit into the Artificial Intelligence category. As these categories can be organized alphabetically, this tells us that we want to select the files in their alphabetical order. By doing this, our next-and-previous browsing structure will support browsing in the correct order (this order is defined by the order documents are imported). To make importing all these documents easy, we will use HyperWriter's multiple document import facilities to import all documents with one command.

The first step in using the Import Text Wizard is to import your documents into HyperWriter.

Importing a Document into HyperWriter

1. Select the **Import Text** command from the **File** menu.

2. Select Word as the format to import.

3. Select the **Another** button. This expands HyperWriter's **Import** dialog box so that multiple documents can be selected. The documents to import are listed at the bottom of this dialog box.

4. Select the document AI.DOC and then select the **Another** button. This adds it to the list of documents to import.

5. Select the document AS400.DOC and then select the **Another** button.

6. Continue selecting each of the documents that make up our catalog in the following order: CCPPROG.DOC, CLIENTSR.DOC, DATABASE.-DOC, DOCUMEN.DOC, GENERAL.DOC, GRAPHPRO.DOC, INFO-ENG.DOC, INTELGSY.DOC, MGMTOPER.DOC, MVSPROG.DOC, OBJTECH.DOC, OS2PROG.DOC, POWERBLD.DOC, PROGRAM.DOC, SOFTENG.DOC, SYSDEV.DOC, UIDESGN.DOC, UNIXPRO.DOC, and WINPROG.DOC. Be careful not to select a document twice as this will import the document two times. When you are done selecting all the documents, you should see the dialog box shown in Figure 17.5.

7 Select the **Import All** command to begin the import process. This displays the **Import Text Wizard** dialog box shown in Figure 17.6.

8. Set the first option, the **Linking Method**, to **BASED ON HEADING1-HEADING?** tags. The documents we are importing are Microsoft Word documents using heading styles. This option creates a hypertext topic and link at every place a stylesheet tag named **HEADING#** is located. As we only want the first and second level of headings linked, we can set the **Last Used Heading or Level Number** field set to 2.

9. Enter a 1 in the **First** field of the **Assign Backgrounds** option. This assigns a HyperWriter user interface (a background screen) to each topic created in the import process. You entered a 1 in the **First** field as the only background screen in your document is background number 1.

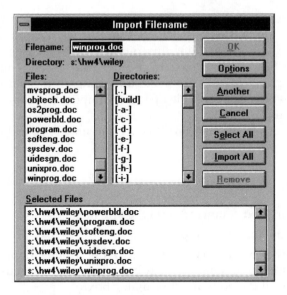

Figure 17.5 Importing multiple documents.

Whenever the Template Wizard creates a background for you, the background to assign is background number 1.

10. The **Global Table of Contents** option can be left in its off position, as we don't want a global table of contents created in this way.

11. Leave the **Link Cross References** option turned off, as we don't have any cross references in our documents.

12. Turn on the **Assign Next/Previous** option so that the document we are importing can be browsed sequentially. This accommodates the readers that want to read this work cover to cover.

13. Leave the **Text to Use for Page Ref's** option at its default setting as we aren't turning on the **Link Cross-References** option.

14. This completes setting the Import Text Wizard to function for our document. Select the **OK** button for it to begin importing your document. When it is complete, you will see the table of contents that the Import Text Wizard creates.

We have now imported our document into HyperWriter and created our links automatically. A picture of how your screen should appear is shown in Figure 17.7.

As you can see, the first topic in the document displays an automatically generated table of contents to the information that was imported. This table of contents is formatted with the stylesheet tags **HW_TOC_#** where # is a number

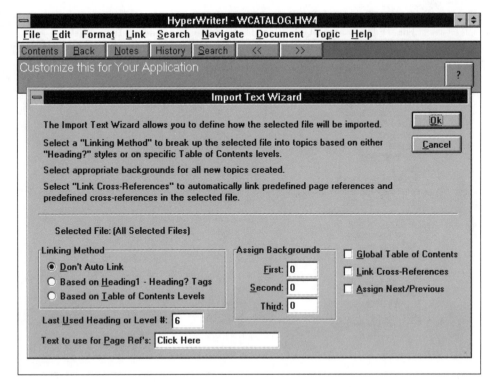

Figure 17.6 The Import Text Wizard.

from 1 to 9 indicating the level of the original information. In our next step, we will format our table of contents (and other elements in a document) using HyperWriter's **Tag...** commands on the **Format** menu.

As you can see, by importing documents in the correct order, our table of contents is alphabetically organized by category. Now that we have used the Template Wizard and the Import Text Wizard, it is easy to understand how the two Wizards function together to ease the development process for our electronic publication. The Template Wizard created a template document with a user interface taking advantage of **Next and Previous** buttons. The Import Text Wizard then brought a Word for Windows document into HyperWriter and established the necessary topic sequence so that we could browse it using the **Next and Previous** buttons.

If you were to activate any of the links created by the Import Text Wizard, what you would notice is that HyperWriter would be extremely slow. This is the result of using the Import Text Wizard where virtually every topic is open and a lot of memory is being used. By saving our document, we will increase performance dramatically.

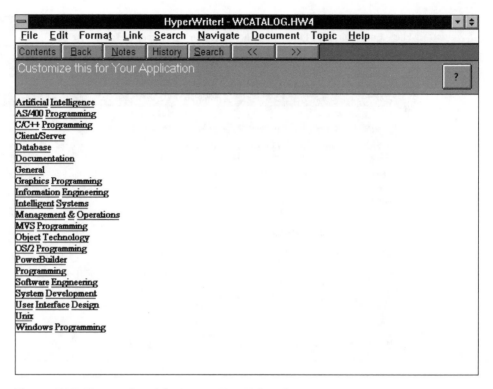

Figure 17.7 The results of the Import Text Wizard.

Saving Our Electronic Publication

Select the **Save** command from the **File** menu. This saves your document.

Step 4: Formatting Our Styles

In step 3, we imported the text of our application. The next step is to format the styles in our application so that our digital publication has a good appearance, similar to that of our print application. In HyperWriter, although you can find out what styles are part of your document by using the **Apply Tag** command, you can't format a style unless you have some text where that style is used. What this means for us is that we need to go to a topic that displays the text of a book for us to format the styles.

If you don't have our tutorial application open, use the **Open** command to open it now.

Depending on whether your document just opened the tutorial document (WCATALOG.HW4) or you had it open, you are looking at either the Click Here to Start text we initially typed in or the table of contents. Neither of these items really need to be formatted at this time. What we need to do is go to a book, format it in detail, and then format these items. A good book to format is *NetWarriors in C++*, which uses almost all of the styles in our documents.

Going to a Book

1. Select the **Goto** command from the **Navigate** menu.
2. Enter a 1 into the **New Topic** field and press **Enter**.
3. Select the link on **Click Here to Start** and activate it.
4. Select the **C/C++ Programming** link and activate it.
5. Select the **NetWarriors in C++** link and activate it. What you should see onscreen is shown in Figure 17.8.

As you can see, this book description has most of the tags used by our Microsoft Word documents. To start, let's format the book's title, the first para-

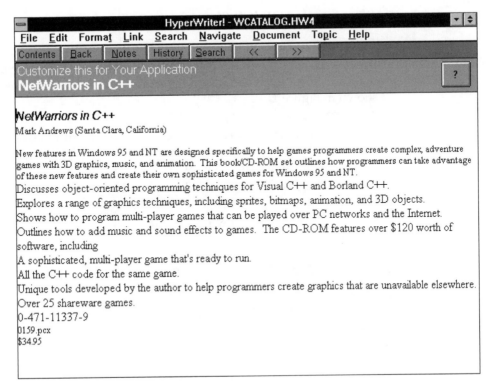

Figure 17.8 A sample book in HyperWriter.

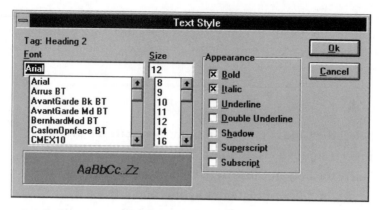

Figure 17.9 Using the **Tag Font** command.

graph of text in the document. As we know that a topic was created here, this must be a **HEADING2** style.

Formatting the HEADING2 Style

1. Select the **Tag Font** command from the **Format** menu.
2. Select Arial font, 18 point, as the format for the tag. Leave the bold and italic attributes imported from Microsoft Word alone. This dialog box is shown in Figure 17.9.
3. Select **OK** to close this dialog box.

   With the font set, we need to set the spacing with the **Tag Spacing** command. What we want is to add spacing below the paragraph so that the title stands apart from the text.
4. Select the **Tag Spacing** command from the **Format** menu.
5. Enter paragraph spacing below of 25 pixels. Set the spacing above value to 0. This dialog box is shown in Figure 17.10.

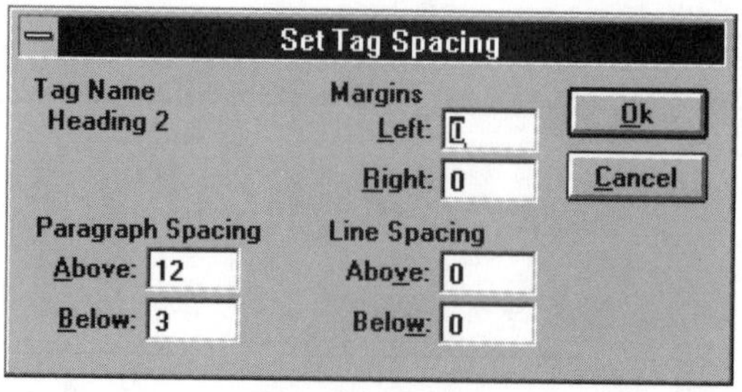

Figure 17.10 Using the **Tag Spacing** command.

Now that our spacing is set, we need to center the title on screen.

6. Select **OK** to close this dialog box.

7. Select the **Tag Justification** command from the **Format** menu. Select the **Centered** option. HyperWriter will tell you that tabs only work with left-justified text. Select **OK** to close this message.

After formatting the **HEADING2** tag, what you should see on screen is shown in Figure 17.11.

After formatting the **HEADING2** tag, we need to find another tag to format. To do this, just move to the next paragraph, which uses the **AUTHOR** tag. We will now format this tag.

Formatting the AUTHOR Tag

1. Place your cursor on the paragraph starting "Mark Andrews." This paragraph uses the **AUTHOR** tag (press **F5** if you want to make sure).

2. Select the **Tag Font** command from the **Format** menu.

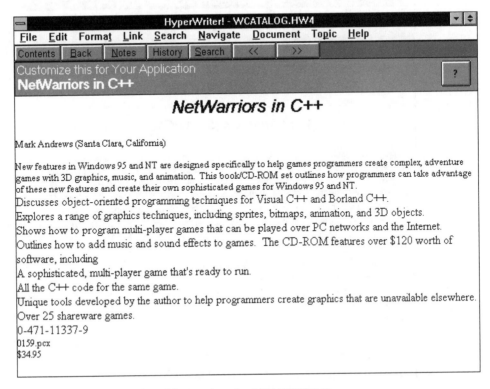

Figure 17.11 The results of formatting the **HEADING2** Tag.

3. Select Arial font, 14 point, italic as the format for the tag.

4. Select **OK** to close this dialog box.

5. Select the **Tag Spacing** command from the **Format** menu.

6. Enter paragraph spacing below of 10 pixels.

7. Select **OK** to close this dialog box.

8. Select the **Tag Justification** command from the **Format** menu. Select the **Centered** option. HyperWriter will tell you that tabs only work with left-justified text. Select **OK** to close this message.

After formatting the AUTHOR tag, your screen should appear as shown in Figure 17.12.

With the **AUTHOR** tag formatted, we need to move onto the **DESCRIPTION** tag (this will skip one tag that we'll come back to later). As the description tag is the body of our book descriptions, we want its font to be legible and easy to read.

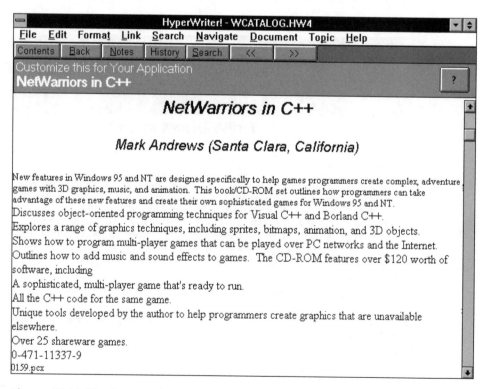

Figure 17.12 The formatted **AUTHOR** tag.

Formatting the DESCRIPTION Tag

1. Place your cursor on the paragraph starting "New features in Windows." This paragraph uses the **DESCRIPTION** tag (press **F5** if you want to make sure).
2. Select the **Tag Font** command from the **Format** menu.
3. Select Times New Roman, 12 as the format for the tag.
4. Select **OK** to close this dialog box.
5. Select the **Tag Spacing** command from the **Format** menu.
6. Enter left and right spacing of 25 pixels.
7. Enter line spacing below of 5 pixels.
8. Select **OK** to close this dialog box.

After formatting the **DESCRIPTION** tag, your screen should appear as shown in Figure 17.13.

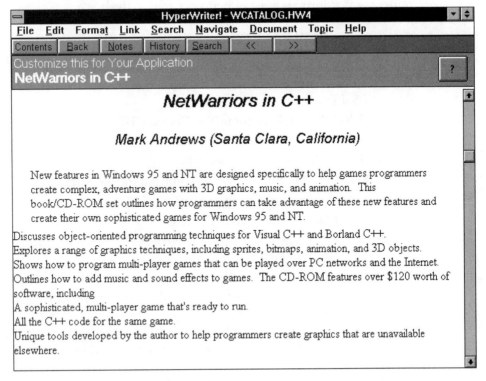

Figure 17.13 The formatted **CENTER** tag.

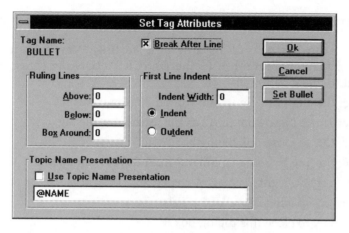

Figure 17.14 Using the **Tag Attributes** command.

With our **DESCRIPTION** tag formatted, the next tag used in our topic is a bullet tag that formats a list of items covered in the book.

Formatting the BULLET Tag

1. Place your cursor on the paragraph starting "Discusses object-oriented programming techniques." This paragraph uses the **BULLET** tag (press **F5** if you want to make sure).

2. Select the **Tag Font** command from the **Format** menu.

3. Select Arial, 10 as the font to use.

4. Select **OK** to close this dialog box.

5. Select the **Tag Spacing** command from the **Format** menu.

6. Enter left margins 50, right margins of 25.

7. Select **OK** to close this dialog box.

8. Select **Tag Attributes** from the **Format** menu. This displays the dialog box shown in Figure 17.14.

9. Set the indent width value to 25.

10. Select the **Set Bullet** button. This displays the dialog box shown in Figure 17.15.

11. Set the bullet field to **Character**. This tells HyperWriter to format the bullet from the same font as that currently used for the text of the paragraph.

12. Enter an "*" into the **Bullet Text** field as the character to use for the bullet.

13. Select the **Set Color** button and set the color of the bullet character to be blue on a white background.

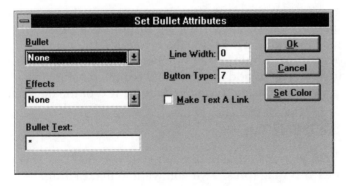

Figure 17.15 The **Set Bullet Attributes** dialog box.

14. Select **OK** to close this dialog box.

15. Select **OK** to close the **Tag Attributes** dialog box.

After formatting the **BULLET** tag, your screen should appear as shown in Figure 17.16.

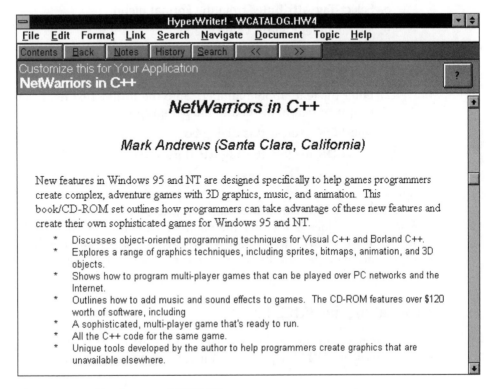

Figure 17.16 The formatted **BULLET** tag.

The next tag in our document after the group of **BULLET** tags is the one for the ISBN number of the book. This tag brings up a potential problem—many readers of the catalog who would recognize the term ISBN Number wouldn't recognize the format of the number itself. To address this, we will use a tag feature that lets us add the text ISBN Number: before the actual number. This will provide a constant prompt about the text of the number.

Formatting the ISBN# Tag

1. Place your cursor on the paragraph starting "0-471-." This paragraph uses the **ISBN#** tag (press **F5** if you want to make sure).
2. Select the **Tag Font** command from the **Format** menu.
3. Select Arial, 12 as the font to use.
4. Select **OK** to close this dialog box.
5. Select the **Tag Spacing** command from the **Format** menu.
6. Enter left margins of 25 and set the paragraph spacing above to 10.
7. Select **OK** to close this dialog box.
8. Select **Tag Attributes** from the **Format** menu.
9. Set the indent width value to 100.
10. Select the **Set Bullet** button.
11. Set the bullet field to **Character**.
12. Enter the text "ISBN Number:" into the **Bullet Text** field as the prompt to appear before the text of the paragraph.
13. Select **OK** to close this dialog box.
14. Select **OK** to close the **Tag Attributes** dialog box.

After formatting the **ISBN#** tag, your screen should appear as shown in Figure 17.17.

After formatting our **ISBN#** tag, the next tag to format is the **PICTURE** tag. What this tag does is identify the name of a picture file that needs to be displayed. What we will do for now is leave this tag alone and handle the remaining tag in this topic, the **PRICE** tag. For the **PRICE** tag, we will format it in a bold font and center it.

Formatting the PRICE Tag

1. Place your cursor on the paragraph starting "$34.95." This paragraph uses the **PRICE** tag (press **F5** if you want to make sure).

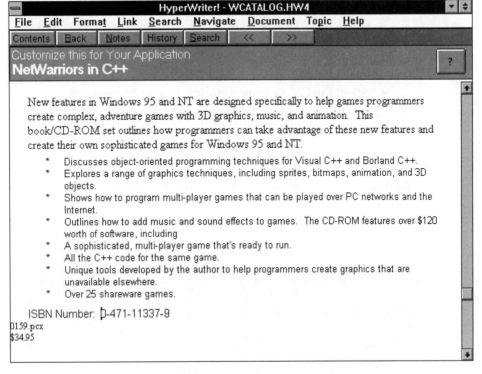

Figure 17.17 The formatted **ISBN#** tag.

2. Select the **Tag Font** command from the **Format** menu.

3. Select Arial, 12, Bold as the font to use.

4. Select **OK** to close this dialog box.

5. Select the **Tag Spacing** command from the **Format** menu.

6. Enter right margins of 25.

7. Select **OK** to close this dialog box.

8. Select the **Tag Justification** command from the **Format** menu. Select the **Centered** option. HyperWriter will tell you that tabs only work with left-justified text. Select **OK** to close this message.

After formatting the **PRICE** tag, your screen should appear as shown in Figure 17.18.

Having formatted our tags, you might think that this is the end of our formatting. Actually, we aren't done yet, but we need to go to another topic to see this.

Going to a Book

1. Select the **Goto** command from the **Navigate** menu.
2. Enter a "1" into the **New Topic** field and press **Enter**.
3. Select the link on **Click Here to Start** and activate it.
4. Select the **C/C++ Programming** link and activate it.
5. Select the **Object-Oriented Development** link and activate it. What you should see onscreen is shown in Figure 17.19.

As you can see, there is a large block of text near the beginning of the topic that isn't really formatted at all. This text has a KEYWORDS tag that indicates the topics covered in this book. What we need to do is format this text similarly to our **ISBN#** tag so that the reader of the catalog understands what these items are.

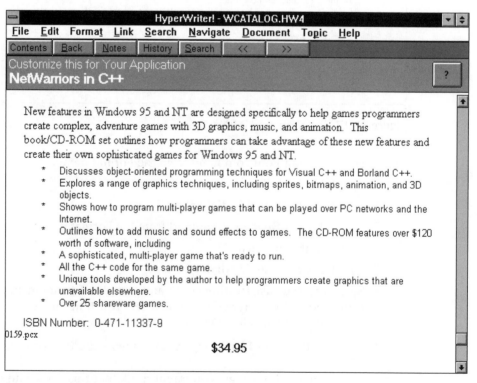

Figure 17.18 The formatted **PRICE** tag.

Formatting the KEYWORDS Tag

1. Place your cursor on the paragraph starting "The Fundamentals of Object." This paragraph uses the **KEYWORDS** tag (press **F5** if you want to make sure).
2. Select the **Tag Font** command from the **Format** menu.
3. Select Times New Roman, 8 as the font to use.
4. Select **OK** to close this dialog box.
5. Select the **Tag Spacing** command from the **Format** menu.
6. Enter left margins of 25, right margins of 25, paragraph spacing above of 10 and paragraph spacing below of 15.
7. Select **OK** to close this dialog box.
8. Select **Tag Attributes** from the **Format** menu.

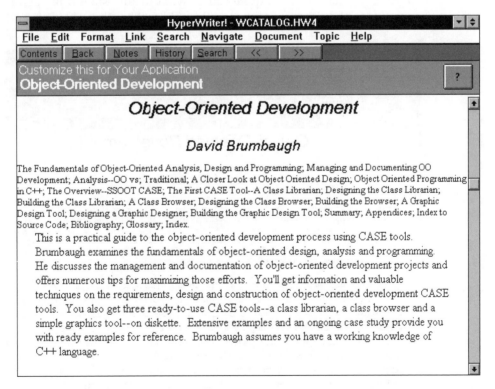

Figure 17.19 A sample book in HyperWriter.

9. Set the indent width value to 60.

10. Select the **Set Bullet** button.

11. Set the **Bullet** field to **Character**.

12. Enter the text "Concepts:" into the **Bullet Text** field as the prompt to appear before the text of the paragraph.

13. Select **OK** to close this dialog box.

14. Select **OK** to close the **Tag Attributes** dialog box.

After formatting the **KEYWORDS** tag, your screen should appear as shown in Figure 17.20.

With our **KEYWORDS** tag formatted, one thing to be aware of is the original book we formatted now has the prompt Concepts: with nothing following it. This occurs because there simply wasn't any text for that book that described the book's concepts, but there was a tag named **KEYWORDS** that was blank (there was no text that the tag formatted). This is a case where the source files really weren't quite right—what ideally should happen is that the source files should have said something like "Not Available" when the **KEY-**

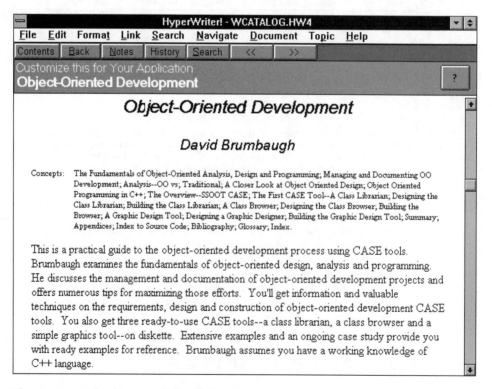

Figure 17.20 The formatted **KEYWORDS** tag.

WORDS tag would otherwise have been blank. If we wanted to, we could fix this ourselves by creating a new keywords tag (**KEYWORDS_BLANK**) that had this text as part of it. While we are not going to fix this in the tutorial, it does a good job of illustrating that in digital publishing, the source documents really drive the final application.

With our **KEYWORDS** tag formatted, we need to format our table of contents tags that the Import Text Wizard created for us. We need to start with the **HW_TOC_1** tag, which formats the categories of books available in our catalog. Like all tags, we need to start by moving to these tags. As we know our table of contents starts in topic number 2, we can just backtrack to the table of contents. By backtracking, I am referring to moving backward in our documents, backing up past the links that we activated.

Moving to the Table of Contents

Press **Esc** until you move to the table of contents shown in Figure 17.21. You will probably have to press it twice.

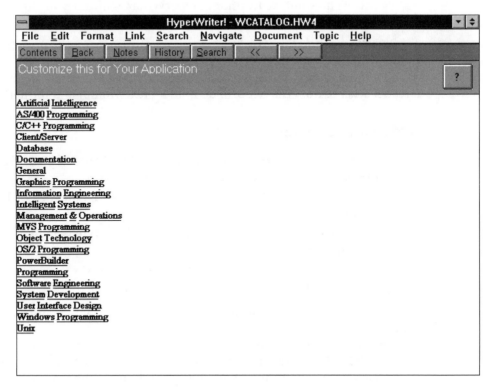

Figure 17.21 The table of contents of book categories.

Given that our table of contents is just a simple alphabetical list, there is only so much we can do to format it. We will make it a larger font and centered.

Formatting the HW_TOC_1 Tag

1. Place your cursor on the paragraph starting "Artificial Intelligence" at the beginning of the topic. This paragraph uses the **HW_TOC_1** tag (press **F5** if you want to make sure).
2. Select the **Tag Font** command from the **Format** menu.
3. Select Arial, 14 as the font to use.
4. Select **OK** to close this dialog box.
5. Select the **Tag Spacing** command from the **Format** menu.
6. Enter paragraph spacing below of 3.
7. Select **OK** to close this dialog box.
8. Select the **Tag Justification** command from the **Format** menu.
9. Select the **Centered** option. HyperWriter will tell you that tabs only work with left-justified text. Select **OK** to close this message.

After formatting the **HW_TOC_1** tag, your screen should appear as shown in Figure 17.22.

One thing that our table of contents doesn't have is any instructions telling a reader what to do. What we will do is add a text prompt and format it.

Adding a Text Prompt

1. Place your cursor on the paragraph starting "Artificial Intelligence" at the beginning of the topic and press **Enter** twice.
2. Move up two lines and type the text "Select a Category of Books by Clicking on It."
3. Mark this text as a block and select the **Text Style** command from the **Format** menu.
4. Select Arial, 18, Bold as the appearance for the text.
5. Select the **OK** button to close this dialog box.

After adding the text prompt, your table of contents should appear as shown in Figure 17.23.

One thing you might notice about our text prompt is that it is centered, like the **HW_TOC_1** tag. This happened because HyperWriter automatically continues tags from line to line when you press **Enter**. When we pressed **Enter** twice, we actually created two blank paragraphs, each formatted with the tag name **HW_TOC_1**.

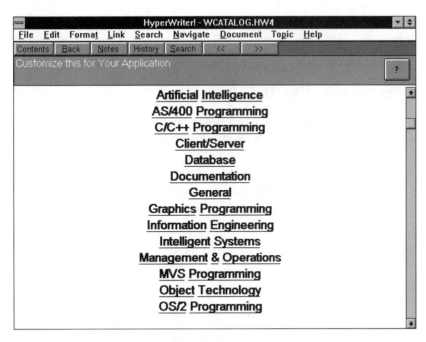

Figure 17.22 The formatted **HW_TOC_1** tag.

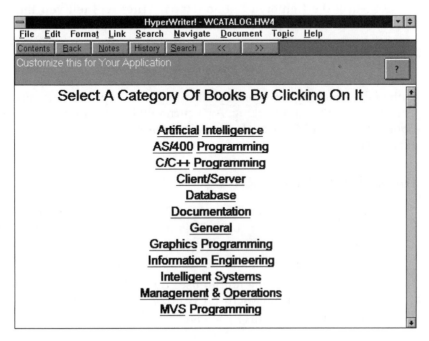

Figure 17.23 The formatted table of contents.

With the **HW_TOC_1** tag formatted and our prompt added, we need to format the HW_TOC_2 tag. We'll use a similar approach to the **HW_TOC_1** tag although with a smaller font.

Formatting the HW_TOC_2 Tag

1. Select the **Artificial Intelligence** link from the table of contents so that we have a tag to format. This brings you to the table of contents for books on Artificial Intelligence.

2. Place your cursor on the paragraph starting "Neural Networks in C++" near the beginning of the topic. This paragraph uses the **HW_TOC_2** tag (press **F5** if you want to make sure).

3. Select the **Tag Font** command from the **Format** menu.

4. Select Arial, 12 as the font to use.

5. Select **OK** to close this dialog box.

6. Select the **Tag Spacing** command from the **Format** menu.

7. Enter paragraph spacing below of 3.

8. Select **OK** to close this dialog box.

9. Select the **Tag Justification** command from the **Format** menu.

10. Select the **Centered** option. HyperWriter will tell you that tabs only work with left-justified text. Select **OK** to close this message.

After formatting the **HW_TOC_2** tag, your screen should appear as shown in Figure 17.24.

With our table of contents formatted, it is apparent that we need to do a better job formatting the heading at the top of the topic that identifies the category to which the books belong. As it currently looks very much like one of the books, a user could get confused. What we need to do format this tag (the **HEADING1** tag).

Formatting the HEADING1 Tag

1. Place your cursor on the paragraph starting "Artificial Intelligence" at the beginning of the topic. This paragraph uses the **HEADING1** tag (press **F5** if you want to make sure).

2. Select the **Tag Font** command from the **Format** menu.

3. Select Arial, 14 as the font to use. Turn off the **Underline** attribute that was imported from Microsoft Word.

4. Select **OK** to close this dialog box.

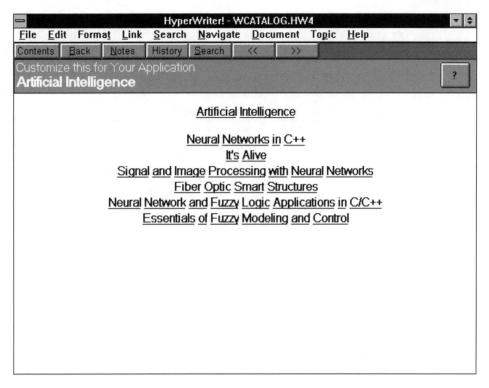

Figure 17.24 The formatted **HW_TOC_1** tag.

5. Select the **Tag Attributes** command from the **Format** menu.

6. Set the **Ruling Line Below** option to 2. This adds a two-pixel ruling line running beneath the text to the edges of the screen.

7. Select the **OK** button to close this dialog box.

After formatting the **HEADING1** tag, your screen should appear as shown in Figure 17.25.

This completes the formatting of our tags. At this point, we have formatted all of our tags and are ready to move on in our tutorial. What we need to do now is save our work.

Saving Our Electronic Publication

Select the **Save** command from the **File** menu. This saves your document.

What I recommend you do now is navigate through some of the different books to view the effect of the formatting commands. When you are done with this, then please continue to step 5.

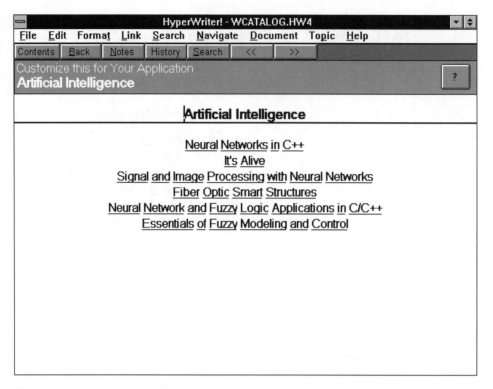

Figure 17.25 The formatted **HEADING2** tag.

Step 5: Handling the Topic Picture

With our text formatted, the next step in our application is to display our book covers. This requires understanding HyperWriter's Topic Picture concept. In HyperWriter, every topic can have a picture associated with it. This picture is called the *topic picture* and is set using the **Topic Properties** command. The way the topic picture is displayed is by a picture object in a background that does not have a particular picture file defined for it. By leaving the name of the picture file undefined, when HyperWriter displays the topic, if the **Topic Picture** property is set, then HyperWriter displays the picture using the picture object in the background. The benefit of this approach is that you get the flexibility of using a background object along without having to create a unique background object for every picture in your document.

Now that we understand the topic picture concept, consider the issue of the background object that we need to display the picture. Although we could add a picture object into our existing user interface background, not all of our books have pictures. Additionally, as our table of contents certainly doesn't have pictures, we probably don't want to add a picture object into our user interface background. What we will do instead is add another background to our document and then assign both of those backgrounds to books that have pictures.

What we need to do first is set our **Topic Picture** property for one of our books. We will do this by cutting the text that identifies the picture file to display and then pasting it into HyperWriter's **Topic Picture** field.

Going to a Book

1. Select the **Goto** command from the **Navigate** menu.
2. Enter a "1" into the **New Topic** field and press **Enter**.
3. Select the link on **Click Here to Start** and activate it.
4. Select the **Artificial Intelligence** link and activate it.
5. Select **the Neural Networks in C++** link and activate it.
6. Place your cursor on the text "0006.JPG."
7. Press **Home** and then **Shift+End**.
8. Select the **Cut** command from the **Edit** menu.
9. Select the **Properties** command from the **Topic** menu. This displays the dialog box shown in Figure 17.26.
10. Select the **Set File** button.
11. Select .JPG as the format to display.
12. Press **Ctrl+V** to paste in the name of the file to display.
13. Select the **OK** button to close the dialog box.
14. Select the **OK** button to close the **Topic Properties** dialog box.

This completes setting the **Topic Picture** property. However, you will notice that no picture is displayed, because we haven't yet created the back-

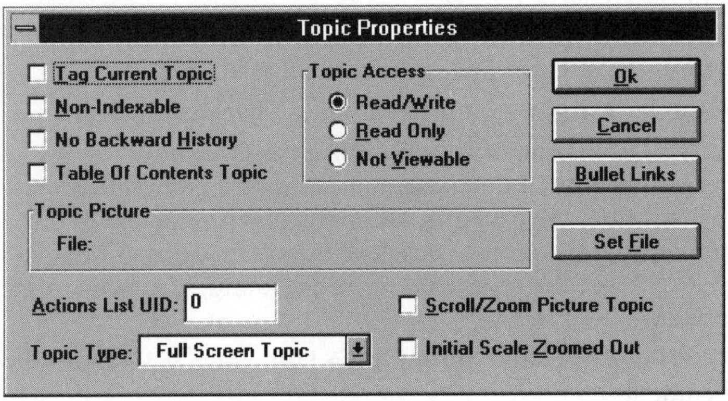

Figure 17.26 The **Topic Picture** dialog box.

ground objects that we need. If you recall our earlier discussion, we want the picture side by side with the text. Because people tend to look at computer screens from left to right, we will place our picture on the left, so it is first thing people see when they enter a topic. As all of our picture objects are the same size, what we will do is first create a picture using a filename, so we can easily determine the right size to create and then replace it with one the correct size but no filename.

Creating a Background for the Topic Picture

1. Select the **Add Background** command from the **Edit** menu.

2. Select the **Picture** command from the **Objects** menu to create a picture object. The picture object will be represented by four handles at the corners of the picture.

3. Move the picture object down approximately 1¼" so that the picture object doesn't overlap the user interface. We are now ready to determine the correct size that we need to create for our picture object by creating an object that we will later delete.

4. Select the **Properties** command from the **Objects** menu.

5. Select the **Set File** button.

6. Select .JPG as the format to display.

7. Select any picture file (the file "0001.JPG" is fine) and then select the **OK** button. What you should see is something similar to that shown in Figure 17.27.

    This displays our picture onscreen. The first thing that we notice is that we need to move the picture slightly to the right as it is currently running into the edge of the screen.

8. Press the right arrow key twice to nudge the picture slightly to the right.

    With our picture object created, we need to add a margin to our topic or our picture will overlap the text in our topic.

9. Select the **Margins** command from the **Background** menu.

10. Enter a left margin of 260 and select the **OK** button.

    At this point, our background is almost complete. What we need to do is see how the background interacts with the text of our catalog and then replace the picture object with one that doesn't display a particular file. To see the results of our background, we need to exit the Screen Painter.

11. Select the **Exit** command from the **File** menu. This returns you to your document.

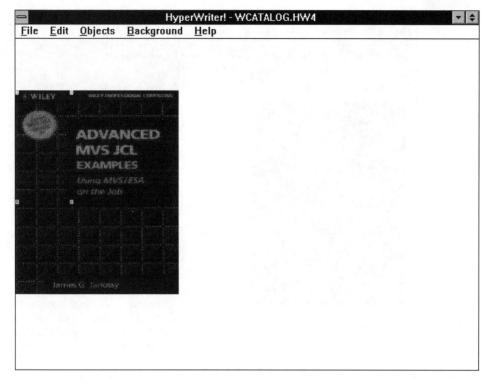

Figure 17.27 Creating a background with a picture.

When you exit the Screen Painter, you immediately notice that your picture isn't displayed. This is because the background hasn't been applied to the topic yet.

Applying the Background We Created

1. Select the **Apply Background** command from the **Edit** menu.
2. Enter a "2" into the **Second** field.
3. Select the **OK** button. This displays the picture shown in Figure 17.28.

Depending on where you placed your picture object, what you should see onscreen is shown in Figure 17.28. You may need to adjust the position of the picture object so that it doesn't conflict with your user interface background. If so, a quick key for jumping in and out of the background screen is **Alt+F7**. Do this now if necessary. When you are ready to continue, our next step is to replace our picture object with one that doesn't have a picture file defined.

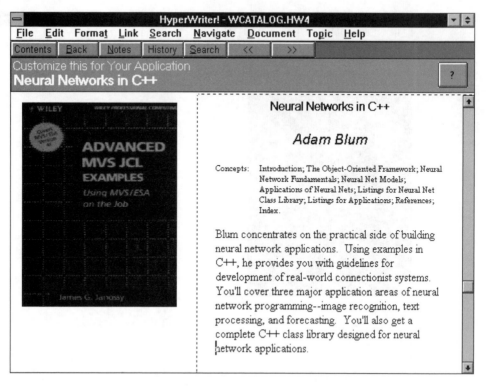

Figure 17.28 A book with its picture.

Replacing Our Picture Object

1. Select the **Edit Last** command from the **Edit** menu. This jumps you into the Screen Painter with the last background that you edited.

2. Select the **Picture** command from the **Objects** menu.

3. Use the mouse to drag the object onto the top left corner of the existing picture object. Remember that we are trying to replace the existing picture object with a new picture object of the same size.

4. Drag the lower right corner over to the lower right edge of the existing picture object.

5. Press **Shift+Tab** to select the picture object that we created earlier.

6. Press the **Del** key to delete the picture object. At this point, you should see the picture of the book cover disappear from the background and the second picture object will be selected.

7. Select the **Properties** command from the **Objects** menu.

Figure 17.29 A book with its picture set via topic picture.

8. Turn on the **In A Window** option, which constrains all picture files to fit within the size that made our picture object. Given that all of our picture files are supposed to be the same size, we shouldn't have to do this, but this will protect us in case one of our picture files turns out not to be the correct size. Without this option set, a picture file could extend out of the margin region and interfere with our text.

9. Select the **Exit** command from the **File** menu to exit the Screen Painter. Upon exiting the Screen Painter, what you should see is the screen shown in Figure 17.29.

As you can see, the correct book cover is now displayed with the book description indicating that the **Topic Picture** property is working correctly. Before we can continue, we need to turn on one of HyperWriter's document properties, the **Backgrounds to Keep** property. At the heart of HyperWriter are several very sophisticated routines that identify how the screen is to be redrawn as HyperWriter navigates from topic to topic. The key issue at hand is always how HyperWriter redraws background screens as the user navigates.

To enhance the speed at which HyperWriter redraws the screen, it lets you keep backgrounds from screen to screen. This is called the **Backgrounds to Keep** option and it literally sets what backgrounds are kept from screen to screen. When you use the Template Wizard, it sets the **Backgrounds to Keep** option so that the first background is kept. While this generally works correctly, it will not work correctly for our document as we have both a first and second background. Our first background is the main user interface for our publication while our second background is the one we just created to display our picture. If we leave the **Backgrounds to Keep** document property set to first, then we will find that our second background doesn't get drawn properly as we navigate between topics, as HyperWriter's doesn't know to keep the background. The solution is to set the **Backgrounds to Keep** document property to First and Second as shown.

Setting the Backgrounds to Keep Document Property

1. Select the **Properties** command from the **Document** menu.
2. Set the **Backgrounds to Keep** option to First and Second.
3. Select the **OK** button to close the **Document Properties** dialog box.

With our background created and our **Backgrounds to Keep** property set, it is now time to consider how we can assign our **Topic Picture** property effectively across the majority of topics in our document. While we could obviously use the same approach that we did earlier, clearly this is not an efficient solution. Given that we have over 250 books, even a small increase in our productivity could make a difference. What we will do is turn to the Windows Macro Recorder. This component of Windows 3.1 only records keystrokes and then plays them back using just a single keystroke. Using the Macro Recorder allows a macro to be recorded that can take the topic picture process from the point where the name of the picture file is cut to the clipboard to the end of the process where the second background is assigned to the topic. To make it easy to continue using the macro, this can even advance you to the next topic so that it is easy to run the macro again. Using the Macro Recorder is often key to large digital publishing projects as it can greatly reduce the effort needed for repetitive actions.

NOTE: If you are using Windows 95 the Macro Recorder isn't available and you will have to assign the topic picture by hand.

One characteristic of the Macro Recorder is that using it is unforgiving—macros cannot be edited, nor are mistakes allowed while macros are being recorded. What this means is that when you use the Macro Recorder, you must be very precise. If you aren't precise, then you will find that you need several tries to record the macro correctly. To make recording the macro easier, we will start by listing the steps that will go into the macro. A key concept when using the Macro Recorder is the idea of setting of the necessary conditions or prerequisites before recording the macro. The only prerequisites for recording our macro are that we need to be in a topic where the macro needs to be run and that the name of the picture file be already cut to the clipboard. The steps that will go into our macro are listed below.

1. Select the **Properties** command from the **Topic** menu.
2. Select the **Set File** button.
3. Select .JPG as the format.
4. Paste in the name of the picture file.
5. Select the **OK** button.
6. Select the **OK** button.
7. Select the **Apply Background** command from the **Edit** menu.
8. Enter a "2" in the **Second** field.
9. Select the **OK** button.
10. Select the **Goto** command from the **Navigate** menu.
11. Select the **Next** button to go to the next topic.
12. Press **Ctrl+End** to move to the end of the topic.
13. Press **Uparrow** to move up one line.
14. Press **Uparrow** to move up one line.
15. Press **Home** to move to the beginning of the line.
16. Press **Shift+End** to mark the name of the picture file as a block.

As you may have noted when looking through the topics after formatting your tags, not every book has a picture. What this does to our macro is make it less of an automatic process. Instead of always taking the second-to-last paragraph of text (which is the name of our picture file) and assigning it as the topic picture, it must instead rely on our choosing whether to run the macro. If we don't choose to run the macro, what we have to do is advance to the next topic and, if there is a picture file, cut the name of the picture file to the clipboard and run the macro. Although our macro can make this process easier, as reflected in the list by the steps regarding marking a block that should be the name of the picture file, it can't make it automatic. With these restrictions, you might wonder why we still choose to use the Macro Recorder. The answer is simple—it will save us a lot of time. With over 16 separate steps that go into assigning our **Topic Picture** property and 250-plus topics, over 4,000 separate steps can be reduced to approximately 250 steps (our goal is for one step per topic).

Before we begin recording our macro, a final note about using the Macro Recorder is that recording mouse actions is generally unreliable. While I doubt that Microsoft would agree with this, I have generally found it to be quite true. For this reason, the steps below will indicate the keystrokes to use as key sequences. For example, selecting the **Properties** command from the **Topic** menu will be followed by (**F10 P O**) which is the exact sequence of keystrokes that you need to press. If a function key equivalent exists for a command then it will be used in place of the menu commands. In the steps below, we will first set up the prerequisites for the macro and then turn on the Macro Recorder and begin recording.

Recording our Macro–Prerequisites

1. Select the **Goto** command from the **Navigate** menu.
2. Enter a "5" into the **New Topic** field and select the **Goto Topic** button.
3. This will take you to the next topic, where we need to use set our topic properties.
4. Move to the end of the topic by pressing **Ctrl+End**.
5. Mark the text "0077.JPG" as a block and select the **Cut** command from the **Edit** menu.

With our prerequisites set, we are ready to start recording our macro. Although the Macro Recorder is a standard part of Windows, it can be deleted by the user. If you find that the program RECORDER.EXE isn't available for you then you may need to go back to your Windows system disks.

NOTE: Although we will use the Macro Recorder for this tutorial, this book isn't intended to be documentation for the Macro Recorder itself. If you find that you have problems using the Macro Recorder, you may need to see its online help.

Recording our Macro with the Macro Recorder

1. Press **Alt+Tab** until you move back to the Program Manager.
2. Select the **Run** command on the **File** menu and enter the program name RECORDER.EXE into the **Command Line** field. Select the **OK** button to run the Macro Recorder. If you have the macro recorder installed on your system, what you should see is shown in Figure 17.30.

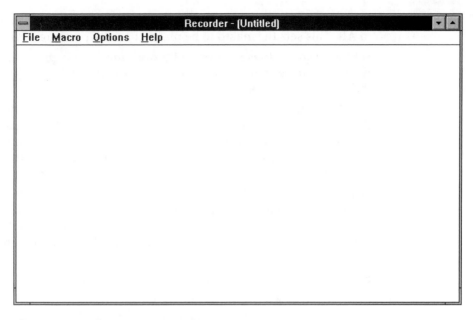

Figure 17.30 The Macro Recorder.

3. Select the **Record** command on the **Macro** menu. This displays the dialog box shown in Figure 17.31.

4. Enter the name "Assign Topic Properties" in the **Record Macro Name** field.

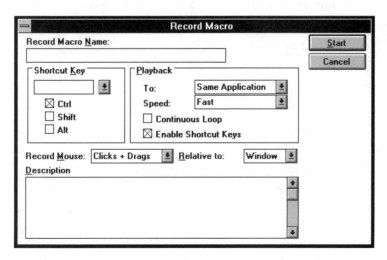

Figure 17.31 Recording a macro.

5. Enter a "Z" into the **Shortcut Key** field and switch the option from **Ctrl** to **Alt**. This sets the macro to be played back by pressing **Alt+Z**.

6. Set the **Record Mouse** option to **Ignore Mouse**. This prevents conflicts with the mouse (which as noted above doesn't really work well with the Macro Recorder).

7. Select the **Start** button. This starts the Macro Recorder recording. From this point on, everything you do will be recorded, so be careful and follow the instructions to the letter. If you don't follow the instructions exactly, you can press **Alt+Tab** until you return to the Macro Recorder, where you can select an option to cancel recording the macro.

8. Depending on how you ran the Macro Recorder software, you may not return immediately to HyperWriter when you select the **Start** button above. If you don't return to HyperWriter, then press **Alt+Tab** to move back through your Windows applications until you get back to Hyper-Writer.

9. Select the **Properties** command from the **Topic** menu.

10. Press **Alt+F** to select the **Set File** button.

11. Press **Enter** to select .JPG as the format to display.

12. Press **Ctrl+V** to paste in the name of the file to display.

13. Press **Alt+O** to select the **OK** button.

14. Press **Alt+O** to select the **OK** button to close the **Topic Properties** dialog box.

15. Press **Ctrl+B** to display the **Apply Background** dialog box.

16. Press **Tab** and then **Tab** again to move to the **Second** field.

17. Enter a "2" into the **Second** field.

18. Press **Alt+O** to select the **OK** button.

19. Press **Shift+F2** to display the **Goto** dialog box.

20. Press **Alt+N** to select the **Next** button.

21. Press **Ctrl+End** to move to the end of the topic.

22. Press **Uparrow** to move up one line.

23. Press **Uparrow** to move up one line.

24. Press **Home** to move to the beginning of the line.

25. Press **Shift+End** to mark the name of the picture file as a block.

26. Press **Alt+Tab** to move back through your Windows applications until you get back to the Macro Recorder.

27. The Macro Recorder will display a dialog box where you can save your macro. If you think you created the macro correctly, then choose to

save your macro. If you don't think you did, you can always choose to cancel recording and then redo it.

28. After selecting to save the macro, you will be returned to HyperWriter.

From the above list of steps, it is easy to see that a macro is very powerful. This is both good and bad. It is good that a macro can save you a considerable amount of work. It is bad in that a macro recorded incorrectly can actually damage your application. For this reason, always save your application before running a macro.

Saving Your Work

Select the **Save** command from the **File** menu.

As noted earlier, not all books have pictures available for them. As you can see, this book does not have a picture specified. What we need to do is skip past this book.

Skipping a Book

1. Select the **Goto** command from the **Topic** menu.
2. Select the **Next** button to navigate to the next topic.

If we scroll down to the end of this topic then we will see that it also doesn't have a picture. Skip this book as well.

1. Select the **Goto** command from the **Topic** menu.
2. Select the **Next** button to navigate to the next topic.

If we scroll down to the end of this topic, we will see that it *does* have a picture. This allows us to try our macro. Whenever we want to use our macro, the first step is to set up the prerequisites.

Running our Macro—Prerequisites

1. Move to the end of the topic by pressing **Ctrl+End**.
2. Mark the text that indicates the name of the picture file as a block, and select the **Cut** command from the **Edit** menu.

With the text for the name of our picture file cut to the clipboard, we can run our macro.

Running our Macro

Press **Alt+Z** to run our macro. What you should see onscreen is HyperWriter running through all the steps that you recorded into the macro. At the end of the macro, HyperWriter will advance to the next topic and mark what it thinks is the name of the picture file as a block. It will not select the **Cut** command, as the text it marks might not be the name of a picture file.

Having used our macro correctly, this completes recording the macro. What remains now is to use the macro for the rest of the topics in this document. When using the macro, you will have to choose between skipping past topics that don't have picture files and using the macro when they do have picture files (before you run the macro, remember to cut the name of the picture file first). If you want to go through the process of assigning the **Topic Picture** property for every topic in this document, you should allow an hour or two for this. One thing that would make this much easier and quicker is to record another macro, one that skips past topics and also marks a block on the paragraph of text that should be the name of the picture file. To record this macro, follow the process above and adapt it to the specifics of this new macro.

With the topic picture taken care of, we are ready to move on to step 6. Before we do this, we need to save our work.

Saving Our Electronic Publication

Select the **Save** command from the **File** menu. This saves your document.

Before you move on to Step 6, you should probably read the following sections, which covers automation for building digital publications and an alternative to assigning the **Topic Picture** property.

Automation

As you might tell from the discussion of using the Macro Recorder, when building a large digital publication there can be an awful lot of labor involved. One of the things that distinguishes digital publishing tools is their support for automating the building process. The tool set that John Wiley & Sons actually uses for their computer book catalog is HyperWriter Professional, a more advanced toolset which supports full automation of even powerful concepts like **Topic Picture**. When selecting a digital publishing tool, one of the key factors is looking at the amount of automation needed for your projects.

An Alternative to Assigning the Topic Picture Property

One thing that you might realize is that assigning the **Topic Picture** property for all topics in our document is a lot of work. To get around this, one option is to "hide" the contents of the **PICTURE** tag and not assign the **Topic Picture** property at all. To hide the contents of the **PICTURE** tag, set the color of the text to white text on a white background. This will prevent the text from appearing in your document (the reader can't see white text on a white background). Although this will prevent our pictures from being displayed, it will let us develop our catalog in a considerably easier fashion. If you do this and you also want to make sure that the names of the picture files don't appear in the search dialog's word wheel, then assign the **PICTURE** tag to the NULL category which prevents text from being indexed.

Step 6: Customizing our Background

As noted earlier in this chapter, among the features that we want in our application are **Print** and **Export** buttons. As long as we are going into the Screen Painter, we should consider several changes which are listed in Table 17.3.

Now that we have identified the goals for our background, we can start editing our background. The first step is to open the application we are creating. If you don't have our tutorial application open, use the **Open** command to open it now.

Adding Print, Export, and Titles Buttons

Although we have to make several changes to our background, the primary change is to add the three buttons for **Print**, **Export**, and **Titles**. The way we'll do this is to first move the << and >> buttons to make space for the new buttons. We will then copy an existing button so that our new buttons have a similar appearance. First, we need to edit our background.

Table 17.3 Changes to Our Background Screen

Change	Description
A **Print** button	Add a print button to our application.
An **Export** button	Add an export button to our application.
A **Titles** button	Add a button to view all titles in our application. This will be a good navigational tool for our readers.
Use the **View TOC** function	Our current **Contents** button is linked to topic number 1. We will replace this **Contents** button with one linked to the **View TOC** menu action link, which displays the table of contents created by HyperIndexer.
Customize the text object	Our application has a text object with the text "Customize this for Your Application." We will customize this text object to indicate the date our catalog was released. This will help reassure readers that the catalog they received was current.

Editing Our Background

1. Select the **Edit Background** command.
2. Enter a "1" into the **Background to Edit** field.
3. Select the **OK** button to edit the background.

By editing the background, we are now in HyperWriter's Screen Painter, where we can edit the objects in our background. The first step is to move the existing buttons to make space for our new buttons and then create the three buttons.

Creating the Three Buttons

1. Select the >> button and drag it to the right edge of the screen.
2. Select the << button and drag it next to the >> button. This makes enough space for adding our three buttons.
3. Select the **Copy** command from the **Edit** menu to copy the << button so that it can be pasted in for editing.
4. Select the **Paste** command to paste in the button.
5. As you can see, the button we pasted in appears behind the text object in our background. Because the button is behind the text object, we need to use the **Bring to Front** command so we can select the button with the mouse. Select the **Bring to Front** command from the **Edit** menu.
6. Use the mouse to drag the << button we pasted in so that it is located to the right of the **Search** button. With our button pasted in, we need to do this twice more to create our three buttons.
7. Select the **Paste** command to paste in the button.
8. Select the **Bring to Front** command from the **Edit** menu.
9. Use the mouse to drag the << button we pasted in so that it is located to the right of the other << button.
10. Select the **Paste** command to paste in the button.
11. Select the **Bring to Front** command from the **Edit** menu.
12. Use the mouse to drag the << button we pasted in so that it is located to the right of the other << button.

With our three buttons created, we are ready to link the buttons to their respective functions.

Creating the Print Button

1. Select the first >> button.
2. Select the **Properties** command from the **Objects** menu.

3. Enter the text "&Print" into the **Text** field. The "&" character underlines the character it precedes in the **Text** field and indicates that the button should respond to the reader pressing the **Alt** key with the underlined character. For example, this button would respond to **Alt+P**.

4. Select the **Set Link** button.

5. Select the **Make New Link** button.

6. Select the **Action** link type.

7. Select **Link to Action–Menu Action**.

8. Scroll through the list of menu actions and choose the **Print** menu action link.

9. Select the **OK** button to close the **Button Object Properties** dialog box.

With the **Print** button created, our next task is creating the **Export** button.

Creating the Export Button

1. Select the second **>>** button.

2. Select the **Properties** command from the **Objects** menu.

3. Enter the text "&Export" into the **Text** field.

4. Select the **Set Link** button.

5. Select the **Make New Link** button.

6. Select the **Action** link type.

7. Select **Link to Action–Menu Action**.

8. Scroll through the list of menu actions and choose the **Export Text** menu action link.

9. Select the **OK** button to close the **Button Object Properties** dialog box.

With the **Export** button created, we need to create the **Titles** button. Before we create the **Titles** button, we need to discuss how this button is to function. What we want this button to do is display a list of all titles in our catalog. By providing a list of all titles in one location, this will give the reader a valuable navigational tool, as the reader currently has to navigate between multiple topics to look at all the titles in our catalog. To make our **Titles** button work, we will link the **Titles** button to a popup comment topic. To make our list of titles, we will go to each table of contents in our document and copy each of the titles to our clipboard. By using the **Append w/Copy** command, we can gather together all of the titles in our catalog and place them in the clipboard. Once all our titles are in the clipboard, we can paste them into the comment topic linked to the **Titles** button. The final step is to alphabetize the list of titles in our comment topic. This is done by cutting and pasting the titles into the correct order.

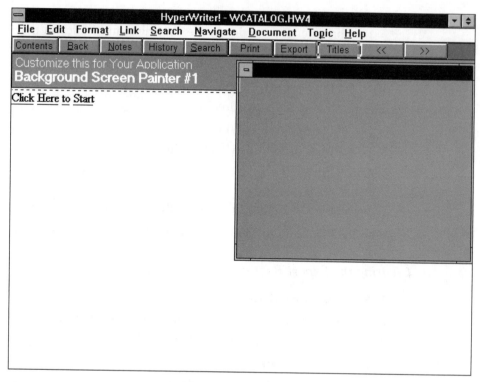

Figure 17.32 Creating the **Titles** button.

Creating the Titles Button

1. Select the third >> button.
2. Select the **Properties** command from the **Objects** menu.
3. Enter the text "&Titles" into the **Text** field.
4. Select the **Set Link** button.
5. Select the **Make New Link** button.
6. Select the **Text** link type.
7. Select **Link to Text–Comment Link**. This will create a comment topic as shown in Figure 17.32.
8. Select the **Name** command from the **Topic** menu.
9. Enter the name "Index of All Titles" and press **Enter**.
10. Select the **Complete Link** command from the **Link** menu. This returns you to the Screen Painter.

11. Select the **OK** button to close the **Button Object Properties** dialog box.

12. Use the mouse to drag the **<<** and **>>** buttons next to the **Titles** button.

With the **Titles** button created, we need to add the different titles into the comment topic. This will be done later in this section after we exit the Screen Painter.

Buttons in HyperWriter are selected in the order they were created. By using the **Bring to Front** command, we modified this order so that our buttons won't be selected in the correct order using the keyboard. The solution is to select each of the buttons in order and then use the **Bring to Front** command.

Setting the Correct Order for Button Selection

1. Select the **Contents** button and then select the **Bring to Front** command from the **Edit** menu.

2. Select the **Back** button and then select the **Bring to Front** command from the **Edit** menu.

3. Select the **Notes** button and then select the **Bring to Front** command from the **Edit** menu.

4. Select the **History** button and then select the **Bring to Front** command from the **Edit** menu.

5. Select the **Print** button and then select the **Bring to Front** command from the **Edit** menu.

6. Select the **Export** button and then select the **Bring to Front** command from the **Edit** menu.

7. Select the **Titles** button and then select the **Bring to Front** command from the **Edit** menu.

8. Select the **<<** button and then select the **Bring to Front** command from the **Edit** menu.

9. Select the **>>** button and then select the **Bring to Front** command from the **Edit** menu.

This completes our editing of the **Print**, **Export**, and **Titles** button. Our next task is to edit the **Contents** button.

Editing the Contents Button

Our application currently uses a **Table of Contents** button created by the Template Wizard. What this button does is jump to topic number 1, where it assumes a table of contents is located. As you may recall, we moved our table of contents to topic number 2, which would require us to change our button to jump to topic 2. Instead of doing this, we will link it to call up the **Table of**

Contents browser generated by HyperIndexer. While this won't work until our publication is indexed, this will provide a better table of contents than simply linking to topic number 2.

Editing the Contents Button

1. Select the **Contents** button by clicking on it with the mouse.
2. Select the **Properties** command from the **Objects** menu. This displays the **Button Object Properties** dialog box.
3. Select the **Set Link** button.
4. Select the **Make New Link** button.
5. Select the **Action** link type.
6. Select **Link to Action–Menu Action**.
7. Scroll to the end of the list of menu action links and choose the **View TOC** menu action link.
8. Select the **OK** button to close the **Button Object Properties** dialog box.

With our table of contents button updated to the **View TOC** menu action link, we are ready to customize our text object.

Customizing the Text Object

With our buttons completed, our next task is to customize the text object to indicate the date of our application.

1. Select the text object with the text "Customize this for Your Application."
2. Select the **Properties** command from the **Objects** menu.
3. Enter the text "Current Release: October, 1995" (or whatever is the current date) into the **Text** field.
4. Select the **OK** button to close the dialog box.

This is the last change that we need to make to our background. If your background doesn't appear as shown in Figure 17.33 then you may need to correct it.

Customizing this text object brings up an interesting point with respect to digital publications. Unlike a print publication which always shows at least some physical signs of age, it is generally impossible to tell how current a digital publication is. For this reason, it is generally quite important to ensure that your digital publication indicates when it was published. What this does is reassure readers that would otherwise doubt the publication due to concerns about its timeliness. Although this is important for all types of digital publications, this is particularly important for catalogs or other marketing types of

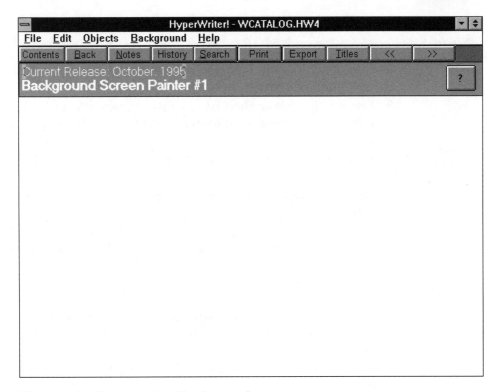

Figure 17.33 The completed background.

digital publications where the date of a publication really indicates how relevant it is.

Making the Titles Button Work

Earlier in this section, we created a **Titles** button for listing all titles in our catalog. When selected, this button will display a popup window (actually a comment topic) that lists all titles. What we didn't do was add the actual titles into the comment topic. We will now add these titles into our comment topic. First, we need to exit the Screen Painter.

Exiting the Screen Painter

Select the **Exit** command from the **File** menu. Having exited the Screen Painter, we need to start gathering together the different titles in our catalog so we can add them into our **Titles** topic. We will do this by navigating to the different tables of contents in our document, copy all the titles to our clipboard, and then paste them into our **Titles** topic.

Gathering Together All Titles

1. Select the **Goto** command from the **Navigate** menu.

2. Enter a "2" into the **New Topic** field and press **Enter**. This takes us to topic number 2 where our table of contents is stored.

3. Activate the link on the first category of books, Artificial Intelligence. This takes you to a topic listing all book titles about Artificial Intelligence.

4. Mark all titles as a block and select the **Copy** command from the **Edit** menu.

5. Move back to topic number 2 by pressing **Esc** or selecting the **Back** button.

6. Activate the link on the second category of books, AS/400 Programming. This takes you to a topic listing all book titles about AS/400 Programming.

7. Mark all titles as a block and select the **Append w/Copy** command from the **Edit** menu. This will copy all the titles to the clipboard, appending them to the titles that are already there. The **Append w/Copy** command is ideally suited to gathering together information stored in different topics.

8. Move back to topic number 2 by pressing **Esc** or selecting the **Back** button.

9. Select the next category of books and use **Append w/Copy** to copy all titles to the clipboard. Continue doing this until you have copied all titles to the clipboard. Always remember to use **Append w/Copy**, as the normal **Copy** command will overwrite the information in your clipboard setting you back to the beginning of this process.

10. Click on the **Titles** button to display the **Titles** topic.

11. Select the **Paste** command from the **Edit** menu to paste all titles into the topic. What you should see is shown in Figure 17.34.

As you can see, we have created a list of all titles. This list, however, is not quite what we want, as it has the following problems:

• The list isn't sorted.

• Titles in the list are centered—we want a left justification.

• The topic is too small.

• The topic lacks a name, so the user can't tell what it is.

The first problem, the list not being sorted, needs to be fixed simply by cutting and pasting the different titles into a sorted order. HyperWriter does not

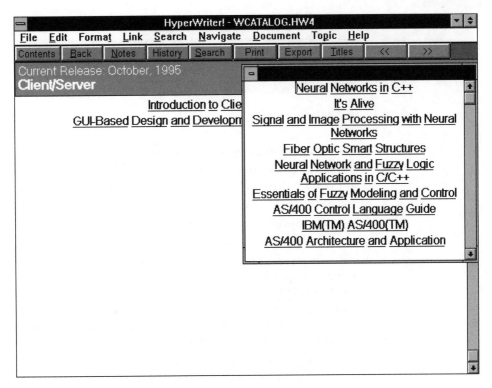

Figure 17.34 The **Titles** topic with all titles.

have any type of sort function for sorting text, so this must be a purely manual process. As this just requires editing text (cutting text out and then pasting it back in), we won't cover this. The items that we can easily address are the formatting of the titles, the size of the topic, and the topic's name. Addressing the formatting of the titles is best done by creating a **TITLES** style and then applying it to the titles. The other items can be handled by sizing the topic and using the **Name** command.

Fixing the Titles Topic

1. Select the **Create Tag** command from the **Format** menu.
2. Enter the name "TITLES" and select the **OK** button.
3. Select the **Tag Justification** command from the **Format** menu.
4. Set the justification to left.
5. Select the **Tag Spacing** command from the **Format** menu.
6. Set left and right margins of 25 pixels.

Figure 17.35 Naming a topic.

7. Select the **OK** button to close this dialog box.

   This completes our formatting of the **TITLES** tag. Our next step is to apply the tag to all topics in the document.

8. Mark all the text in the topic as a block.

9. Select the **Apply Tag** command from the **Format** menu.

10. Select the **TITLES** tag from the list of tags. HyperWriter asks if you want to apply the tag to selected block or selected paragraph. Choose selected paragraph. This formats all the titles with the same tag.

   With our titles formatted, the remaining task is to size and name the topic. Given that our topic is really just a long list of book titles, we want to size this topic so that it is basically tall and wide enough for the largest title (if this is feasible).

11. Select the lower right-hand corner of the **Titles** topic with the mouse and size the topic to meet our description.

12. Select the **Name** command from the **Topic** menu. This displays the **Set Topic Name** dialog box shown in Figure 17.35.

13. Enter the name "Index of All Books by Title" into the dialog box and select the **OK** button. With our topic named, our **Titles** topic is completed. Your topic should appear as shown in Figure 17.36.

14. Press **Esc** to close our **Titles** topic.

With our **Titles** topic completed, we are ready to move onto the next section of the tutorial. First, we need to save our work.

Saving Our Electronic Publication

Select the **Save** command from the **File** menu. This saves your document.

Step 7: Name Your Document

Having built the structure of our document and customized its background, we are ready to begin the finishing-up stages of our document. The first of these is to name the document for better navigation and searching.

If you don't have our tutorial application open, use the **Open** command to open it now.

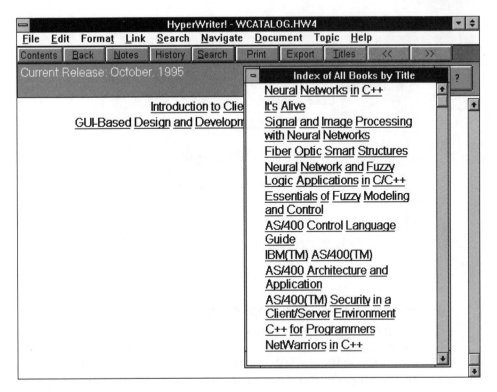

Figure 17.36 The completed **Titles** topic.

Naming a document is done with the **Abstract** command, which supports a document name, author, subject, and abstract (a description of the document).

Using the Abstract Command

1. Select the **Abstract** command from the **Document** menu. This displays the dialog box shown in Figure 17.37.
2. In the **Document Name** field, type "John Wiley & Sons Computer Book Catalog." For our tutorial application, you can leave the other fields blank (remember to fill them out for your own work).
3. Select the **OK** button to close the **Abstract** dialog box.

With our document abstract complete, we need to save our work.

Saving Our Electronic Publication

Select the **Save** command from the **File** menu.

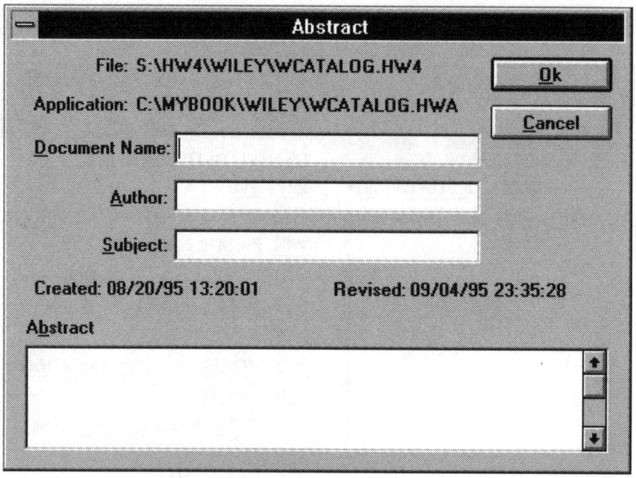

Figure 17.37 The **Abstract** command.

Step 8: Define a HyperWriter Application

In building our application, we have created a single HyperWriter .HW4 document file that contains the content for our catalog. We have not, however, created a HyperWriter .HWA application file. An *application file* is a file that lists all the HyperWriter documents that make up your entire application. This application file is used by HyperIndexer to define the document files to index, and by the HyperWriter Publisher to define the document files used to create a disc set. The application file is also part of defining groups in HyperWriter (which is our next task). The application file can also be used by HyperReader. The benefit of this is that when your application is built from multiple Hyper-Writer .HW4 files, HyperReader can be set to open only application files so that your reader doesn't ever have to understand the different filenames used in your application.

If you don't have our tutorial application open, use the **Open** command to open it now.

Defining a HyperWriter application file is done with the **Application** command on the **Document** menu.

Defining a HyperWriter Application File

1. Select the **Application** command from the **Document** menu. This displays the **Application** dialog box shown in Figure 17.38.
2. Select the **New Applic** button. This displays a dialog box for entering the name of a new application file to create or for overwriting an existing application file.

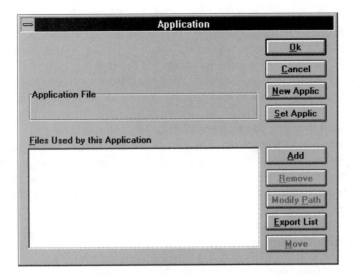

Figure 17.38 The **Application** dialog box.

3. Enter "WCATALOG" as the name of your application file and select the **OK** button. Any DOS filename can be specified here; it does not have to agree with the name of a .HW4 document file. This returns you to the main **Application** dialog box.

4. You should now see that your document file, WCATALOG.HW4, has been added to the application. Select the **OK** button to close the **Application** dialog box.

We now need to save our work so that the application file we defined is stored for the next step.

Saving Our Electronic Publication

Select the **Save** command from the **File** menu. This saves your document.

Step 9: Grouping Topics

With our application file defined, we can now use the **Groups** feature for our catalog. Groups are a key HyperWriter feature for working with information stored in multiple topics. What groups let you do is search and print across ranges of topics. For example, a reader could perform a search and restrict it to only searching books on Artificial Intelligence. Similarly, a reader could print only books on Artificial Intelligence.

A HyperWriter application can store multiple groups, and every topic in a HyperWriter document can belong to one or more groups. Using **Groups** is a two-step process. The first step is to create the group or groups that you need. After the group is created, the next step is to assign topics to the group. Assigning topics to the group is done by going to the topic and then using the **Groups** command and picking the group(s) for the topic.

In this step of our tutorial, we will show you how to create the groups we need and then assign topics to the groups. We need to begin by opening our application.

The first step in using the **Groups** command is to navigate to the first topic that you want to put in the group. The reason for this is that when you create a group in HyperWriter, the topic you are in is also assigned to that group. While you can always remove a topic from a group, it is easiest to use groups this way. Given that we want to create groups that mimic our table of contents, we will start by going there.

Navigating to a Group

1. Select the **Goto** command from the **Navigate** menu.
2. Enter a "2" into the **New Topic** field and press **Enter**. This takes us to topic number 2, where our table of contents is stored.
3. Activate the link on the first category of books, Artificial Intelligence. This takes you to a topic listing all book titles about Artificial Intelligence.

   As we are at the table of contents covering the Artificial Intelligence category, you might think that we want to create a group here. This is actually a debatable point: Should a table of contents that lists the books belonging to a group be part of the group itself? Given that a key use of groups is searching, the downside to making the table of contents part of the group is that any book will be found twice—first in the table of contents and then in the actual book description. While this too could be debated, it is more likely that people would prefer to have a search result in only the book description being found, not in the table of contents being found as well. For this reason, we will not include our table of contents in the group.

4. Activate the first link, "Neural Networks in C++."
5. Select the **Groups** command from the **Topic** menu.
6. Enter the group name "Artificial Intelligence" and select the **Add** button.
7. Select the **OK** button to close the **Groups** dialog box.

NOTE: Groups cannot be deleted or renamed once they are created, be careful when you create groups.

With our first topic added to the group, we need to move to the next topic we want to add to the group. The **Next** button can be used for this.

8. Select the **Next** button to advance one topic forward in the document.

9. Select the **Groups** command from the **Topic** menu.

10. Select the **Artificial Intelligence** group. This will place a checkmark next to the group name to indicate that the current topic belongs to the group.

11. Select the **OK** button to close the **Groups** dialog box.

With our group created, please continue using the **Next** button to navigate through the rest of the topics in the Artificial Intelligence category, assigning each topic to this group. When you reach the end of the Artificial Intelligence books, you will arrive at the AS/400 Programming books. What you want to do here is go to the first book, create a group titled "AS/400 Programming" and then continue navigating through the different books, assigning each book to the AS/400 Programming group. Continue this process through the remaining categories of books and assign each book to a group. If you feel adventurous, you could create a macro to help you assign topics to groups.

Step 10: Index Your Application

With our application basically complete, the application file created, and the **Groups** assigned, we are ready to index our application using HyperIndexer. HyperIndexer indexes every word in every document to make the application fully searchable. HyperWriter's full-text searching is powerful enough to search even hundreds of megabytes without a problem. HyperIndexer can also create a browsable table of contents based on a hierarchical outline of the application. Although we already have a basic table of contents, the table of contents created by HyperIndexer is more detailed. It also can be onscreen simultaneously with your documents in a separate window—a feature that many people really like.

NOTE: HyperIndexer takes advantage of groups, so you should always create your groups before using HyperIndexer.

HyperIndexer is a separate application from HyperWriter itself. To index an application, exit HyperWriter and then use HyperIndexer. Please note that while you don't have to exit HyperWriter, you generally don't want to be editing your document at the same time it is being indexed, as this could cause problems while indexing.

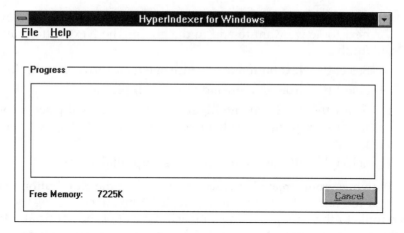

Figure 17.39 The HyperIndexer indexing application.

Exiting HyperWriter

Select the **Exit** command from HyperWriter's **File** menu. This should return you to the Program Manager.

From the Program Manager, we can run HyperIndexer.

Using HyperIndexer

1. Select the HyperIndexer Icon from the HyperWriter program group. This runs HyperIndexer and displays it onscreen as shown in Figure 17.39.

2. Select the **Set Application File** command from the **File** menu. This displays a **File** dialog box for selecting the drive, directory and file to compress. Select the \HW4\FILES directory (or the \FILES subdirectory from the directory where you installed HyperWriter) and then select the application WCATALOG.HWA. Select the **OK** button to close the dialog box.

3. With the application file specified, we need to set our indexing options. Select the **Options** command from the **File** menu. This displays the HyperIndexer **Options** dialog box shown in Figure 17.40.

Unlike the application that we covered in the previous chapter, which had only simple searching, this application will have very sophisticated searching. Specifically, we will index this application using HyperWriter's **Categories** feature which lets you define searchable fields to be indexed based on the styles in your document. For our application, we want to define searchable fields for the **HEAD2**, **AUTHOR**, **KEYWORDS**, **DESCRIPTION**, and **ISBN#** styles.

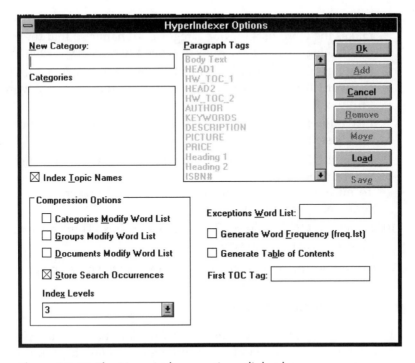

Figure 17.40 The HyperIndexer options dialog box.

1. Our first step is to define a searchable category or field. Type the name "Title" into the **New Category** field and select the **Add** button. This adds a category named "Title" to the list of categories.

2. Select the **Title** category from the list of categories by clicking on it with the mouse. When the **Title** category is selected, the list of paragraph tags to its right will become enabled so that they can be selected.

3. Select the **HEAD2** style or tag from the list of paragraph tags and click on it with the mouse. What this does is to map the **Titles** category to **HEAD2** style so that any searches in the **Title** category search information are formatted with the **HEAD2** style.

4. Follow the same process for the **AUTHOR, KEYWORDS, DESCRIPTION**, and **ISBN#** styles (first defining a category and then defining the style that it maps to). As you can tell from step 3, the name of the category doesn't need to be the same as the style it maps to. This lets us describe a book in terms of its "Title," when the actual style is **HEAD2**. When you are done with this, move on to step 5.

5. Select the **Index Topic Names** option and turn it off.

6. Select the **Categories Modify Word List** option and turn it on. This makes the word lists for our categories dynamic so that the only words in the category will be displayed when the category is selected.

7. Select the **Groups Modify Word List** option and turn it on. This makes the word lists for our groups dynamic so that the only words in the group will be displayed when the category is selected.

8. Leave the **Store Search Occurrences** option turned on and the **Index Levels** set to 3.

9. Select the **Generate Table of Contents** option so that a table of contents will be generated.
   To make sure that you have set the HyperIndexer options correctly, compare your screen with Figure 17.41.

10. Select the **OK** button to close the dialog box. This will return you to HyperIndexer's main screen.

With our indexing options set, we need to start the indexing process.

Starting the Indexing Process

1. Select the **Create Index** command from the **File** menu. HyperIndexer will begin indexing your application and display its progress onscreen. A picture of HyperIndexer illustrating its progress is shown in Figure 17.42.

2. When HyperIndexer has completed indexing your application, it will display an **Index Complete** dialog box. Until this additional dialog box comes up onscreen, your index is not completed (I state this because you can misread the HyperIndexer dialog box and accidentally cancel its indexing). When this additional dialog box comes up onscreen, select the **OK** button.

Saving Our Work

Unlike working in HyperWriter itself, HyperIndexer doesn't require any work to be saved, as it automatically saves the index file it creates. Your only option to save what you did in HyperIndexer is to save the categories that you defined. This is done from the HyperIndexer **Options** dialog box. As we don't need to do this, we'll continue by exiting HyperIndexer.

Exiting HyperIndexer

With our tutorial finished and our index file created, you can now exit Hyper-Indexer if desired. This is done with the **Exit** command on the **File** menu. This returns you to the Program Manager.

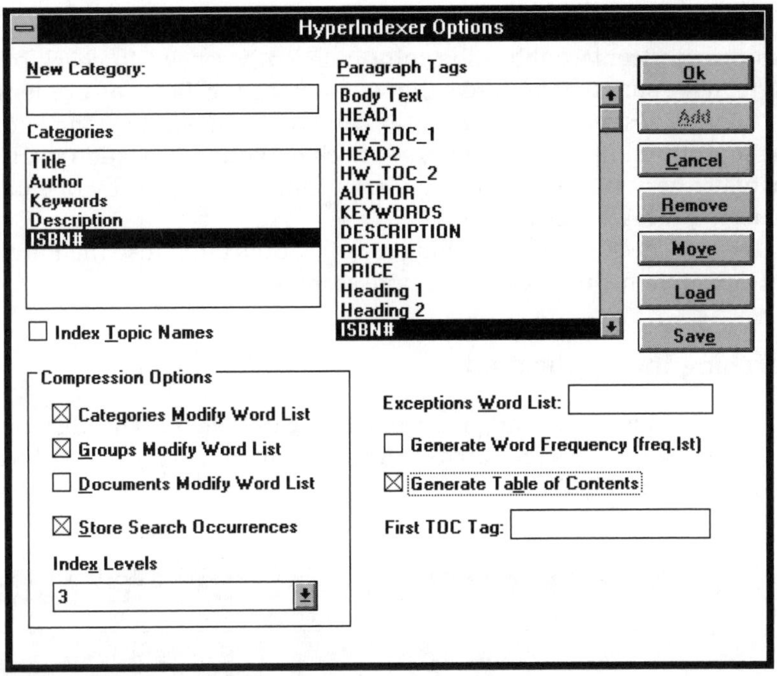

Figure 17.41 All the HyperIndexer options correctly set.

With our application indexed, we need to check that our application functions correctly. Checking your application is a key task that you should always do before your application is released.

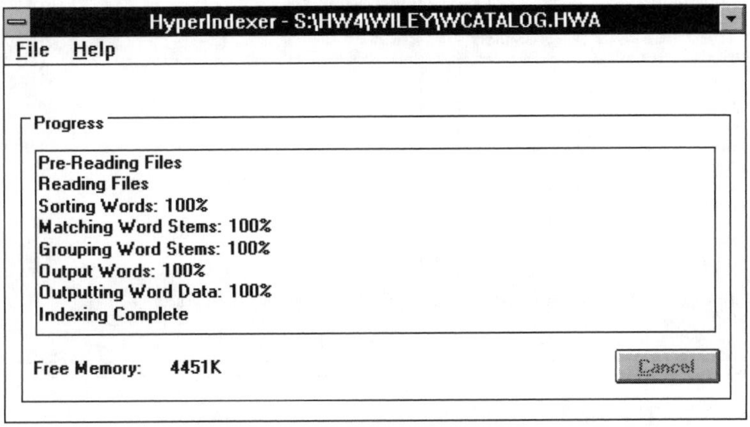

Figure 17.42 HyperIndexer showing its progress.

Step 11: Check Your Application

With our electronic publication fully indexed, we need to check our publication to make sure that both searching and using the **Table of Contents** browser functions as desired. HyperWriter has all the document viewing and searching functions found in HyperReader, so checking your application in HyperWriter is actually very simple. Checking your application begins by opening the document file WCATALOG.HW4.

To start checking the searching for our application, use the **Find** command on the **Search** menu to specify sample searches.

Searching the Application

1. Select the **Find** command from the **Search** menu. This displays the **Find** dialog box where search queries are entered. This dialog box is shown in Figure 17.43.

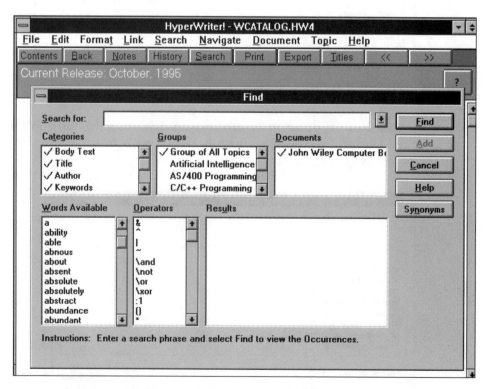

Figure 17.43 The **Find** dialog box.

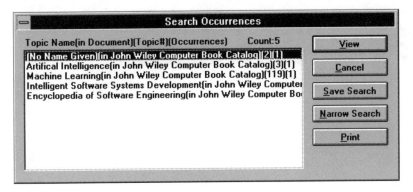

Figure 17.44 Sample search results.

2. Type the search term "Artificial Intelligence" in the **Find** dialog box and select the **OK** button. This displays the results of the search as shown in Figure 17.44.

3. Select any of the search results that you wish to check.

After entering the search query, you should try several additional searches to make sure that the searching is functioning correctly. A list of good searches to try is shown here:

- Fuzzy
- Fuzzy logic
- C++
- Hypertext
- Multimedia

NOTE: You should also check that the different search options like categories and groups function.

With our search engine checked, we need to check the **Table of Contents** browser. Calling up the **Table of Contents** browser is done with the **View TOC** command on the **Navigate** menu.

Using the Table of Contents Browser

1. Select the **View TOC** command from the **Navigate** menu. This displays the table of contents shown in Figure 17.45.

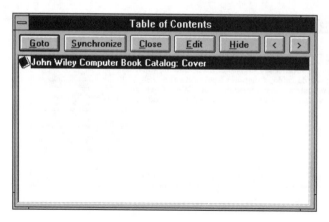

Figure 17.45 The **Table of Contents** browser.

2. Double-click on the first entry, "Table of Contents." This will expand the view of the table of contents to that shown in Figure 17.46.

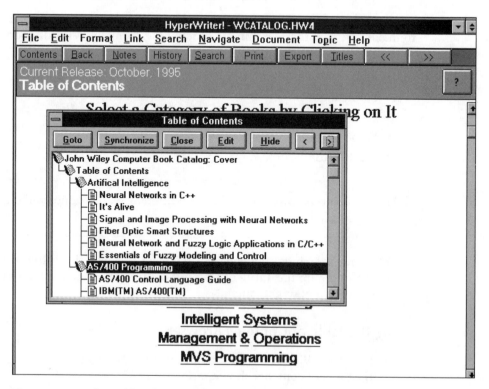

Figure 17.46 The **Table of Contents** browser—expanded view.

3. By clicking on different entries in the table of contents, HyperWriter will take you to the topic in the document that corresponds to those entries.

As you can see, the **Table of Contents** browser offers a powerful tool for navigating your document. One of the real benefits of using the **Table of Contents** browser is that it operates in a separate window, allowing you to keep a table of contents always available when the reader is browsing the document.

After checking the search functions and the **Table of Contents** browser, we need to save our work if we made any changes.

Saving Our Electronic Publication

Select the **Save** command from the **File** menu.

Step 12: Configure Document Properties

One of the final steps in finishing our publication is setting the document properties for our application. Document properties provide a way to configure our application by setting the properties of the documents in our application. As our application has only a single document, these properties need to be set only in this one file. Document properties include colors, how searching functions, and many other options. Although the Template Wizard automatically sets some of the basic document properties that are needed for an application, you generally need to set other properties as well. For our application, we need to set several properties including:

- Making our search user interface simpler.
- A copyright message when information is printed from our document.
- Locking our document size to a fixed window size.

If you recall from planning our document, we originally stated that we wanted powerful search features. While we do want this, we don't want search features that we aren't using. Take a look at our current **Search** dialog box shown in Figure 17.47.

As you can see, this is a powerful **Search** dialog box that supports one feature we don't need—the **Documents** list used for selecting between documents. As our application is only a single document, we don't need to select between documents. By setting the document properties for searching, we can remove this item and simplify the dialog box.

The second property we want to set will add a copyright message that appears whenever anyone prints from our manual, indicating that our interactive catalog has a copyright owned by John Wiley & Sons. This helps to prevent people from misusing our information. Our final document property to set locks our document size. By locking our document size to a fixed-window size, we can prevent any possible errors due to a reader sizing our document

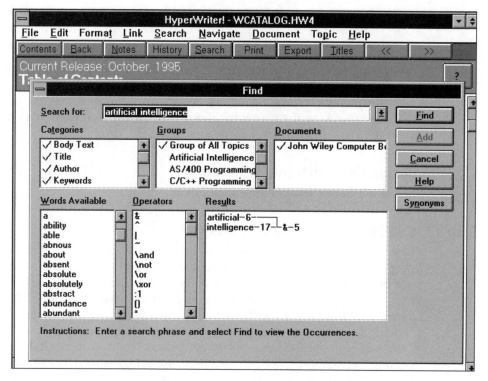

Figure 17.47 The **Search** dialog box.

incorrectly. While you normally don't have to set this option in HyperWriter, displaying the cover of the book next to the text for the book really demands that you set this option.

If you don't have our tutorial application open, use the **Open** command to open it now.

Setting document properties is done with the **Properties** command on the **Document** menu. Our first task is to configure how searching functions.

Setting Document Properties for Searching

1. Select the **Properties** command from the **Document** menu. This displays the dialog box shown in Figure 17.48.

2. Select the **Searches** folder. This displays the folder of options shown in Figure 17.49.

3. Turn off the **Keep Previously Loaded Properties** option. This option allows HyperWriter to "inherit" properties from previous documents. As we do not want to inherit properties for this folder of options, we need to turn this option off.

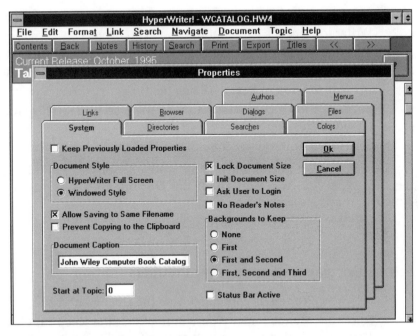

Figure 17.48 The **Document Properties** dialog box.

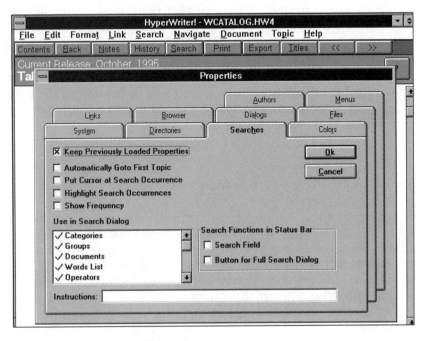

Figure 17.49 The **Searches** folder.

4. Turn on the **Put Cursor at Search Occurrence** option. This tells Hyper-Writer to place the cursor at the search occurrence.

5. Turn on the **Highlight Search Occurrences** option. This tells Hyper-Writer to highlight all occurrences of the search terms that it finds.

6. Move to the **Use in Search** dialog field.

7. Turn off the **Documents** option in the **Use in Search** dialog field to eliminate this option.

8. Select the **OK** button to close the dialog box.

To see the effect of configuring our search options, call up the **Search** dialog box. What you will see is that the **Documents** selection list has been removed from the search dialog box.

Our next task is to set the properties for printing, adding a custom header and footer.

Setting Document Properties for Printing

1. Select the **Properties** command from the **Document** menu.

2. Select the **Menus** folder. You will note that **the Keep Previous Loaded Properties** option is already turned off, as the Template Wizard modified these properties when it created your document.

3. Press **Tab** to move to the **Header** field. Add to the end of this field "Printed on @DATE." This causes HyperWriter to replace the "@DATE" with the actual date the document was printed, thus date stamping every printout.

4. Press **Tab** to move to the **Footer** field. This field allows you to set a default print header that will always be printed at the bottom of the page when information is printed. Enter "Copyright (C) John Wiley & Sons, 1995." in the **Footer** field.

5. Select the **OK** button to close the **Document Properties** dialog box.

If you have a printer hooked up, you may want to print out a sample section of this document so that you can check whether your document properties are functioning correctly.

Our final document property to set locks the size of our document. What we want to do is lock the size of the document to be exactly 640x480 (the minimum size for a standard Windows graphics system), so that the reader of the document can't resize the document and inadvertently cause a problem with our side-by-side graphics. Given that your computer system may not be running in 640x480 resolution, this can be tricky to accomplish. To make this easier, we can use a sample application, SIZE_640.HW4, to set the size of your application.

Setting Document Properties for Printing

1. Select the **Save** command from the **File** menu to save your work.

2. Select the **Open** command from the **File** menu to open the document SIZE_640.HW4. When this document is opened, it will set the size of your current HyperWriter Window to exactly 640x480.

3. Select the **Open** command from the **File** menu to open the document we're working on, WCATALOG.HW4. When this document is opened, you will notice that the window size has been changed to exactly 640x480.

4. Select the **Properties** command from the **Document** menu.

5. Select the **Lock Document Size** option. This will set HyperWriter so that it remembers the size of the document and locks it.

6. Select the **Init Document Size** option. This option works with **Lock Document Size** so that HyperWriter remembers the correct size.

7. Select the **OK** button to close the **Document Properties** dialog box.

At the end of this step, we need to save our work.

Saving Our Electronic Publication

Select the **Save** command from the **File** menu. This saves your document.

Step 13: Getting Our Document Ready for a Reader

We have now created an electronic publication that a reader can view with HyperReader. Using HyperWriter or HyperReader, the electronic publication that we created can be viewed by using the **Open** command on the **File** menu. If we want to make this electronic document automatically open in the Hyper-Reader or HyperWriter program, we can handle this with a HyperWriter startup document. A *startup document* is a HyperWriter document named _STARTUP.HW4. _STARTUP.HW4 is a special filename that both HyperWriter and HyperReader understand to automatically open when they are first executed. Creating a startup document can be done by either saving our electronic publication (WCATALOG.HW4) out to a file named _STARTUP.HW4, or by creating a new HyperWriter document named _STARTUP.HW4, then linking it to our WCATALOG.HW4 document using a **Jump Link to Another File**. Both of these approaches will accomplish our goal—that our sample electronic publication be automatically opened by HyperWriter/HyperReader so that a reader does not have to use the **Open** command in HyperWriter (please note that documents can be specified from a Windows icon at the Program Manager level).

The goal of a startup document should be to create an attractive and functional cover page for your application. HyperWriter's Screen Painter, **Import**

Picture, and **Insert Object** commands make creating startup documents easy. If you choose the approach of just saving the document WCATALOG.HW4 out to the file _STARTUP.HW4 then HyperWriter's **Start At Topic** document property can be used to define a topic that is shown initially when the document is first opened. In this topic that is shown only initially, you can place an attractive cover page. As there are several different approaches to creating a startup document, we won't go into them in this tutorial. If you do want to simply save our tutorial application WCATALOG.HW4 out to the file _STARTUP.HW4 to see how a startup document functions, you should first move it to another directory as your standard HyperWriter example files are supplied with a startup document.

NOTE: If you create a file for your application named _STARTUP.HW4 then you generally want to add this file to your HyperWriter application file so that it is part of the actual .HWA application file.

As this isn't a real application that we intend to give to anyone else, we won't actually create a _STARTUP file for this tutorial. What we will do is add an attractive cover screen to our application. HyperWriter's Screen Painter allows you to compose attractive screens that take advantage of pictures, text, lines, and buttons, among other elements. While you can use almost any design for an attractive cover screen, one common approach is to use content elements that you already have. If you think about our application, one content element that we have in abundance are the scanned covers of our books. As many of these covers are well designed and attractive, we can use these to put together an attractive cover screen. Beyond simply being attractive, a cover screen must also be functional, allowing the reader of the document to get started using the digital publication without difficulty. For this publication, two simple buttons, **Search** and **Contents**, make it easy for a reader to start viewing our catalog. To make it even easier, we can also include in our cover screen a text prompt that explicitly tells the reader what to do. While the technical aspects of creating a cover screen like this aren't difficult, the design process can be lengthy as you try to come up with an attractive, creative design. To make creating this cover screen simple, we will use a sample background file that fulfills our goals for a cover screen. A picture of our sample background is shown in Figure 17.50.

You will note that this cover screen requires the user to click past the entire cover screen for access to the information needed. This is common in applications that are marketing oriented, rather than those for internal productivity. In short, the visual effect that this attractive cover screen brings to the digital publication more than makes up for the effect of its click-past design.

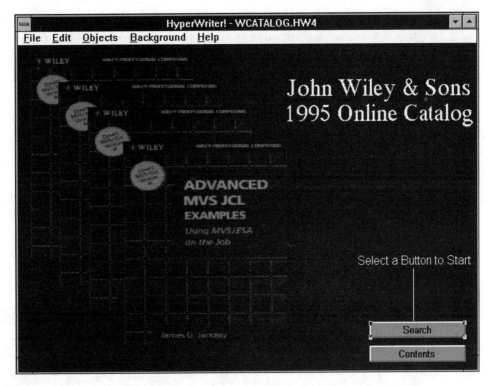

Figure 17.50 A cover screen for our catalog.

To add a cover screen to our application, we need to use the Screen Painter. If you don't have our tutorial application open, use the **Open** command to open it now.

To create our attractive cover screen, we need to start by going to topic number 1, where we will add our cover screen. If you just opened the WCATA-LOG.HW4 document then you should be at topic number 1. If not, use the following command.

Going to Topic Number 1

1. Select the **Goto** command from the **Navigate** menu.
2. Enter a "1" into the **New Topic** field and press **Enter**. This takes you to topic number 1.

As you can see, topic number 1 has just the link **Click Here to Start** and our user interface background. If you recall from the beginning of this chapter, we added this link to move to our table of contents. What we can do is reuse this existing link in our **Contents** button by examining it with the **Link Properties** command. Among other options, the **Link Properties** command displays a link's unique identifier (UID). What a link UID lets you do is reuse an existing link. To reuse an existing link, the first step is to find out its link UID.

Finding Out a Link UID

1. Place the cursor within the text of the link "Click Here to Start."

2. Select the **Properties** command from the **Link** menu. This displays the dialog box shown in Figure 17.51.

3. Take note of the number shown in the field for **Link Unique Identifier**. You may want to write it down as you will need it later in this section. Select the **OK** button to close the **Link Properties** dialog box.

Now that we have our link UID, we are ready to add our cover screen. The first step is adding a background to our document.

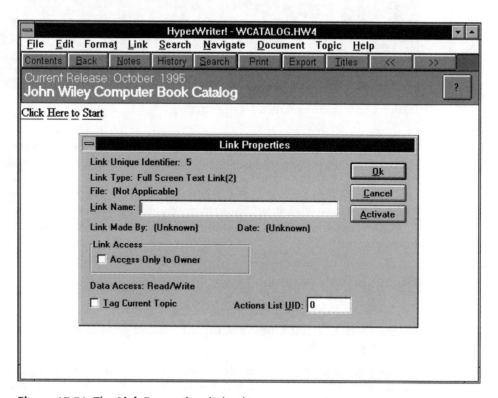

Figure 17.51 The **Link Properties** dialog box.

Adding the Cover Screen

1. Select the **Add Background** command from the **Edit** menu.

2. Select the **Import Background** command from the **File** menu.

3. Select the file WCATALOG.BKG from the dialog box. What you should see onscreen is shown in Figure 17.52.

With our background screen imported, the next step is linking the buttons for **Search** and **Contents**.

Linking the Search Button

1. Select the **Search** button by clicking on it with the **Left Mouse** button.

2. Select the **Properties** command from the **Edit** menu.

3. Select the **Set Link** button.

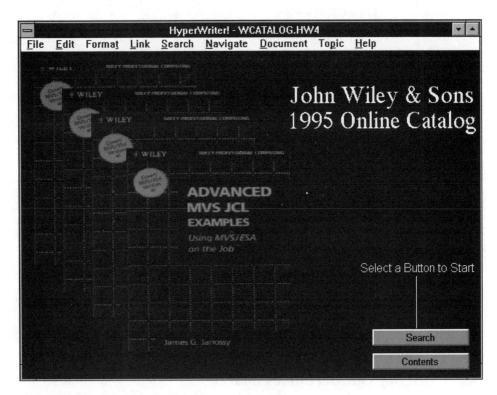

Figure 17.52 The imported background screen.

4. Select the **Make New Link** button.

5. Select the **Action** link type.

6. Select **Link to Action–Menu Action**.

7. Scroll through the list of menu actions and choose the **Find** menu action link.

8. Select the **OK** button to close the **Button Object Properties** dialog box.

To link our **Contents** button, we will use the link UID that we determined earlier in this section.

Linking the Contents Button

1. Select the **Contents** button by clicking on it with the **Left Mouse** button.

2. Select the **Properties** command from the **Edit** menu.

3. Select the **Set Link** button.

4. Enter the link UID value from the "Click Here to Start" link into the **Link UID** field.

With our **Contents** button linked, we are ready to exit the Screen Painter and apply the background for our cover screen to topic number 1.

Exiting the Screen Painter and Applying the Background

1. Select the **Exit** command from the **File** menu. This exits the Screen Painter and returns you to topic number 1.

2. Select the **Apply Backgrounds** command from the **Edit** menu.

3. Enter the number 3 into the **First** field, replacing the "1" that was there, and select the **OK** button. This applies the background to the topic as shown in Figure 17.53.

   As you can see from the picture above, our attractive cover screen is almost complete. The one exception is that our text link, "Click Here to Start." is still part of the topic. We need to delete this link to finish our cover screen.

4. Place the cursor at the beginning of the link "Click Here to Start."

5. Press **Ctrl+D** to delete the link.

At the end of this step, we need to save our work.

Saving Our Electronic Publication

Select the **Save** command from the **File** menu.

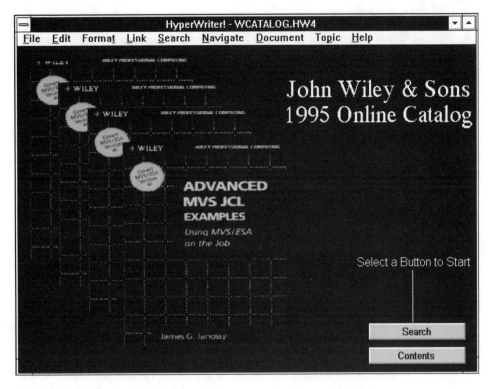

Figure 17.53 The cover screen.

Tutorial Part 2: Distributing Our Publication

We have now completed our electronic catalog and are ready to distribute it. This requires using the HyperReader program and the HyperWriter Publisher tool.

Step 14: Using the HyperWriter Publisher Tool

The HyperWriter Publisher tool is used to create disc sets to distribute your HyperWriter applications or to copy them to a network drive for distribution using a network server. For our tutorial, we will create a set of floppy discs so that we can distribute your HyperWriter applications easily. You should have two blank floppies ready before we begin.

Using the HyperWriter Publisher

1. Run the HyperWriter Publisher by clicking on its icon on the Hyper-Writer Program Group. This displays the program shown in Figure 17.54.

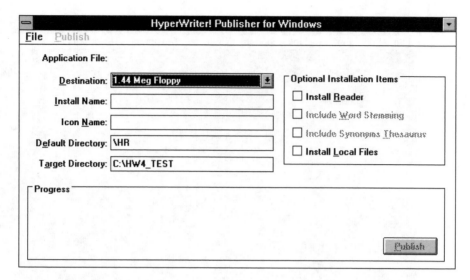

Figure 17.54 The HyperWriter Publisher.

2. Select the **Application** file to publish with the **Set Application** command on the **File** menu. The file to select is WCATALOG.HWA.

3. Select the **Preferences** command on the **File** menu and set the directories to where your information is stored. This should be C:\HW4\WCATALOG for the documents path and C:\HW4\WCATALOG for the picture path. If you originally installed HyperWriter into a different directory then substitute this one. You can leave the text and local files paths at their default settings, as we aren't using these options.

4. Set where you want to publish the application to by using the **Destination** options. The options include different disc sizes and a network (or other local drive) where the files can be copied. Select the 1.44 meg option (or another option if you don't have 1.44 meg floppies).

5. Enter "John Wiley & Sons Catalog" in the **Install Name** field. This name will be displayed at the top of the installation dialog box.

6. Enter "Wiley & Sons Computer Book Catalog" in the **Icon Name** field. This is the name of the icon that will be displayed when your application is installed.

7. Enter "\WCATALOG" as the default directory where your application will be installed.

8. Select the **Reader** option to install only the reader software and none of the supporting files.

9. Select the **Publish** button to begin the publishing process.

10. When the publishing process is complete, use the Windows File Manager to drag the contents of the directories created by the publisher, \HW4\DISC_1, \HW4\DISC_2, and so on, to a floppy disc.

NOTE: You don't want to drag the actual directories themselves onto the floppy, but the contents of the directories. This is a common error when using the Publisher. What you need to do is go to the directory \HW4\DISC_1 in File Manager and double-click it so that you can drag the contents of the directory onto the floppy.

This completes the steps of publishing our application on floppy disc. What you should certainly try is to install that application using the disc set that the HyperWriter Publisher created. To do this, run the SETUP.EXE program located on disc 1.

Tutorial Part 3: Publishing this Application on the World Wide Web

With our tutorial for building our electronic publication complete, we have successfully used HyperWriter to create an interactive catalog, which can be easily published on floppy disc or via network server. To gain additional distribution for our digital publication, we can take advantage of HyperWriter's Save As HTML Wizard, which allows us to convert our HyperWriter application to an HTML document suitable for use on the Internet-based World Wide Web hypertext system. This allows our document to be distributed to the approximately 20 million people, on all types of computing hardware, who take advantage of the Internet. Given that John Wiley & Sons publishes books about the Macintosh, UNIX, and other computer platforms that can't view our Windows-based catalog, this is something we definitely want to do.

In this section of our tutorial, we will convert our electronic publication to HTML format for Internet distribution. If you aren't using the Internet or simply aren't concerned with this option, please move on to the next section of this chapter.

Using the Save As HTML Wizard

Converting your electronic publication to an HTML format requires using the **Save As HTML** command on the **File** menu. However, before we can do this, we must first open our application (if it isn't still open).

We now need to select the **Save As HTML** command on the **File** menu. This command will allow us to convert our existing HyperWriter application to an HTML format.

Saving Your Document to HTML

1. Select the **Save As HTML** command on the **File** menu. This displays a **File** dialog box for setting the name of the HTML file that will be created. The name that you are entering is a *base filename* for your HTML document, up to four characters in length. As each topic in your Hyper-Writer document will be converted to an HTML format, at the end of the process you will end up with many HTML documents. For our application, we want to use the name WCATALOG. By entering WCAT-ALOG name, then files such as WCAT0001.HTM, WCAT0002.HTM, and so on, will be created. Type this name and press **Enter**. This displays the Save As HTML Wizard shown in Figure 17.55.

2. The HyperWriter Tag and HTML Tag fields are used to map the different HyperWriter tags to their HTML equivalent. To start, we want to select that the **HEAD1** tag in the HyperWriter Tag field is mapped to the **H1** tag in the HTML Tag field. Do this now by first selecting on the **HEAD1** tag and then on the **H1** tag.

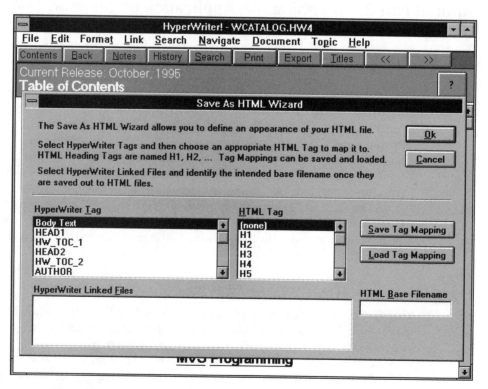

Figure 17.55 The Save As HTML Wizard.

3. After mapping the **HEAD1** tag, we need to map the **HEAD2** tag. Do this now by first selecting on the **HEAD2** tag and then on the **H2** tag.

4. Map the **HEADING1** tag to **H1** by first selecting on the **HEADING1** tag and then on the **H1** tag.

5. Map the **HEADING2** tag to **H2** by first selecting on the **HEADING2** tag and then on the **H2** tag.

6. Map the **BULLET** tag to the HTML tag **UL LI** by first selecting on **BULLET** and then on **UL LI**.

7. Select the **OK** button to begin saving your application to HTML. When HyperWriter finishes exporting to HTML, this dialog box will be removed from the screen and you can continue working with your HyperWriter application.

One thing you should have noted is that we didn't map all of our tags to HTML. Among the tags that we didn't map were the **PRICE, ISBN#**, and **KEYWORDS** tags. This reflects a key difference between HyperWriter and HTML-based systems. HyperWriter allows creating arbitrary tags as needed for an application, whereas HTML has a fixed set of tags. When you don't map tags in HyperWriter to specific HTML tags, then they are mapped to HTML's equivalent of Body Text (just normal text).

As you can see, converting your HyperWriter applications to World Wide Web format is really quite simple. Once you have converted your HyperWriter applications to World Wide Web format, the next step would be to move them to a Web Server so that they could be accessed through the Internet. This, however, is beyond the scope of this book.

Viewing Our Catalog in a Web Browser

After having published our interactive catalog to HTML format using the **Save As HTML** command, your natural reaction is probably to open those files in your Web Browser and take a look at them. If you do this, the file you want to start with is WCAT0001.HTM, the Home Page for this application. This would be the equivalent to topic number 1, the attractive cover screen that we created. However, when you look at this page in your Web Browser, what you will see is actually nothing at all—simply a blank page with no content. To understand this, we need to remember back to how we created this cover screen. Our cover screen was created with a background which displayed several book covers and two buttons, **Search** and **Contents**. The problem we are encountering is that the Web has no equivalent to backgrounds. Thus, when HyperWriter generates the HTML pages, as there is no content in the topic except for the background itself, no content is placed in the HTML pages.

To get past the blank page into which our cover screen was transformed, open the page WCAT0002.HTM. This page is the equivalent to topic number 2, our main table of contents. From this table of contents, select the category MVS Programming and then the book *Advanced MVS JCL Examples*. If you did this in HyperWriter, what you would see is the cover of the book on the left and the text for the book on the right. What you see, however, is just the text for the book; the cover is not shown at all. The reason for this is that HyperWriter's Topic Picture has no equivalent on the Web. Consequently, when HyperWriter generates the HTML pages, the Topic Picture is not moved out to the Web.

Now that we have observed what seems to be two semiserious problems with respect to the HTML version of our catalog, we need to consider what can be done about this. One thing we could do is to simply load our HTML pages into an HTML editor and make the needed fixes manually. While this would make developing our cover screen rather simple, it would require lots of manual labor to implement displaying the covers of our books. This brings us to an interesting point regarding the covers of our books. While on a CD-ROM–based application, the system is fast enough so that the covers of our books can be displayed simultaneously with the text for each book, this is not the case with an HTML-based application. As the average size for our covers is about 100K, this would dramatically slow down response time on our catalog in HTML form. This leads us to the fact that what we develop for a CD-ROM platform may not always be the same as what we develop for an HTML-based application. In an HTML-based application, we would generally use one of two options for the covers. The first is simply to omit them for reasons of performance. If we follow this option, then HyperWriter not moving them out to HTML format really doesn't matter. The second option is to use a hypertext link to display each picture. This would entail adding a "Click Here to See Book Cover" link to the text of each book. If we wanted to use HyperWriter for developing these links, but still use Topic Pictures for displaying the picture, we could create these links in HyperWriter and then use a special tag to hide the links by setting the color of the text to white on white. As this special tag would not be supported by HTML, generating the HTML pages would leave these links visible.

Beyond hand-creating our cover screen in an HTML editor, we could also create our cover screen not using a background, but using the **Import Picture** command and a text link to topic number 2. While this would probably not be as attractive as our custom-designed background screen, it *would* be supported by the **Save As HTML** command. Now that we have looked at some of the issues regarding the HTML version of our publication, some facts about cross-platform development have become quite obvious. The first of these is that when you are planning your application, consider the HTML version of the publication from the start. As HTML is generally more limited than Hyper-Writer, understanding this makes it much easier to figure out what may cause problems in the HTML versions of your digital publications. The second point is that the more you take advantage of product-specific features (such as Topic

Picture), the less portable your final application will be. This is not to say that you shouldn't use these features, only that you need to be aware of the trade-offs. For example, given the very nice results in our application from using Topic Picture, I would still make the decision to use Topic Picture for our inter-active catalog. An alternative to the tradeoffs with respect to taking advantage of product specific features is covered next.

Automation: A Shortcut to Portability

As discussed in Chapter 3, automation features are a key aspect of high-end digital publishing tools. Automation features can also provide a much needed short cut with respect to portability. Consider building this interactive catalog using the automation features, the HyperWriter AutoLinker, in NTERGAID's HyperWriter Professional product. The HyperWriter AutoLinker allows us to automatically create even complex digital publications like our interactive cat-alog through a scripting language. The way the AutoLinker allows us to address portability is that it would allow us to generate different versions of our publications for different platforms. For example, we could generate a CD-ROM version of our publication that took advantage of Topic Picture and an HTML version that replaced the Topic Picture with a link to the picture. Although not a perfect solution, automation features can go a long way toward addressing portability.

Tutorial Part 4: Resetting Directories

Now that we have completed our tutorial, the final step is to reset our directo-ries to their defaults so that we have access to the normal HyperWriter tutorial files. Use the **Preferences** command on the **File** menu for this.

Setting Directories in HyperWriter

1. Select the **Preferences** command from the **File** menu.
2. Select the **Directories** folder.
3. Enter "\HW4\FILES" into the **Documents** field. If you installed Hyper-Writer into a directory other than \HW4 then substitute that directory.
4. Enter "\HW4\PICTURES" into the **Pictures** field. If you installed HyperWriter into a directory other than \HW4 then substitute that directory.
5. Enter "\HW4\FILES" into the **Text Files** and **Local Files** fields. If you installed HyperWriter into a directory other than \HW4 then substitute that directory.
6. Select the **OK** button to close this dialog box.

CHAPTER

Building a Web Site

18

In this tutorial, we will be building an Internet World Wide Web site using HyperWriter. For people unfamiliar with the World Wide Web, the Web provides a distributed hypertext environment based on Internet protocols where you can publish electronic documents using hypertext links. For more details on the Web, please see Chapter 4. The Web site we will be building in this chapter is a version of NTERGAID's own Web site (it will actually be a subset of our Web site). The NTERGAID Web site is fairly standard as far as sites go, featuring a wealth of product information, technical details, and company background information. HyperWriter allows any digital publication you create to be saved out to HTML format for easy distribution on the World Wide Web. While we did not originally design HyperWriter for creating an entire Web site, it lends itself nicely to the task, thanks to its underlying hypertext-based architecture. In fact, using HyperWriter can actually be easier than dedicated HTML tools for certain types of Web sites.

In this chapter we will start by describing HyperWriter's **Save As HTML** Feature, continue with a description of the content for our Web site, move into planning our Web site, and then begin the step-by-step discussion of how we created our Web site. At the end of this chapter, you should have a good feel for using HyperWriter to create a Web site.

There are two elements you should be aware of before continuing. The first is that if you haven't read Chapter 4 yet, or you don't have a good understanding of the World Wide Web, you should probably read Chapter 4 before continuing. While this chapter will educate you in how to build a Web site, it won't teach all about the Web. The second note is that in this chapter, the term *page* is used interchangeably with the term *topic*. A HyperWriter topic is equivalent to a Web page. For readers familiar with the World Wide Web, this chapter uses both the terms page and topic, as while we are authoring HyperWriter topics in this chapter, their ultimate form is that of a Web page.

Understanding HyperWriter and Web Sites

Before we move into our tutorial and start building our Web site, we need to first go over some of the basics of HyperWriter's **Save As HTML** command, which tags your HyperWriter document and converts it to a series of linked HTML files. To start, the Save As HTML Wizard exports your HyperWriter .HW4 document files to the HTML 1.2 specification. If you are solely interested in development for the World Wide Web, the Save As HTML Wizard allows you to quickly and easily develop your application using HyperWriter and then publish it to the World Wide Web. This approach to using HyperWriter as a World Wide Web development tool has a number of powerful benefits:

- Support for importing ASCII, WordPerfect, Word, Ventura Publisher, Lotus Ami Pro, and .RTF format documents.
- Automatic hypertext linking through the Import Text Wizard.
- Easy hypertext linking that takes advantage of HyperWriter's many hypertext features.
- A default stylesheet, HTML1_2.HWT, that can be used to define a default set of paragraph tags for your document that match the HTML 1.2 specification.

Understanding How HyperWriter Exports to HTML

The HTML specification is a fairly simple ASCII-based format that is a subset of the SGML standard. The HTML specification outlines a simple convention using tags that begin and end with angle characters (< and >) that indicate hypertext links and topics, tags for lists, and tags for other elements in your document. What in HyperWriter terminology is a *topic* is to the HTML specification a *page*. Each topic in a HyperWriter document is exported to a separate HTML file. These files are numbered in the order in which they exist in the original HyperWriter document. Hypertext links in HyperWriter are converted to HTML links that reference the different HTML pages that HyperWriter exports. When you are finished exporting your HyperWriter document to HTML, you have a number of different HTML files, often hundreds of them. This results from the lack in the HTML specification of a way for a single HTML file to contain multiple topics.

What Exports from HyperWriter to HTML Format

The following document elements are exported from HyperWriter to HTML format:

- Hypertext topics are converted to individual HTML pages. Topic names are converted to the **<TITLE></TITLE> HTML** tag.
- Hypertext links are converted to HTML format links.
- Formatting tags can be mapped from their name in HyperWriter to their equivalent in the HTML specification.
- Inline text formatting such as bold, italics, and underlining.
- Imported and linked graphics. As HyperWriter supports more graphics formats than are standard for HTML files, you may want to standardize your HyperWriter application to use only .GIF graphics files which are commonly used for World Wide Web applications.
- Links to next-and-previous topics are converted to hypertext links to the next topic as it was exported from HyperWriter.

What Doesn't Export from HyperWriter to HTML Format

The following items in your HyperWriter document do not export to HTML, as they do not have an equivalent in the HTML specification. Please note that this is due to the richness of the tools that HyperWriter provides (the HTML specification is very basic).

- Link Properties
- Action Lists
- Links to Actions
- Links to ASCII files
- Topic Properties including Topic Pictures
- Document Properties
- Stylesheet attributes. Although you can map formatting tags in Hyper-Writer to their HTML equivalent, the formatting codes themselves are not converted. Formatting in HTML is handled with the World Wide Web browser program.
- Character Styles (styles applied to a marked block, rather than an entire paragraph)
- Background Screens
- Links from Regions of Pictures
- Next-and-Previous Relationships

- Tables. The HTML specification currently lacks a good way to handle tables. When this is available and widely used, HyperWriter will be updated to handle this.

- Tab settings. The HTML specification does not really address tab settings. The tab characters in your HyperWriter document will be exported to five spaces.

Using the Save As HTML Wizard

When your HyperWriter documents are ready to be saved to an HTML format, use the **Save As HTML** command on the **File** menu.

Saving Your Document to HTML

1. Before you use the Save As HTML Wizard, you should always save your HyperWriter document. Select the **Save** command on the **File** menu to save your document.

2. Select the **Save As HTML** command on the **File** menu. This displays a **File** dialog box for setting the name of the HTML file that will be created. Type a base filename for your HTML document up to four characters in length. As each topic in your HyperWriter document will be converted to an HTML format, at the end of the process you will end up with many HTML documents. For example, if the filename you enter is "MANU" (for a file originally named MANUAL) then files such as MANU0001.HTM, MANU0002.HTM, etc., will be created. Type a filename name and press **Enter**. This displays the Save As HTML Wizard shown in Figure 18.1.

3. Use the HyperWriter Tag and HTML Tag lists to map the different HyperWriter tags to their HTML equivalent. For example, you might choose that a **HEADING1** tag in HyperWriter is mapped to an **H1** tag in HTML. Using the mouse, select the tags to be mapped as needed for your document. For a reference to the different HTML tags and their meanings, please see the electronic HTML tutorials shipped with HyperWriter.

4. If you have previously defined a tag mapping, use the **Load Tag Mapping** button to load that tag mapping. Similarly, use the **Save Tag Mapping** button to save your tag mapping.

5. Use the list of HyperWriter **Linked Files** and the HTML **Base Filename** field to specify how links to external HyperWriter .HW4 documents are handled. This item is covered later.

6. Select the **OK** button to save your HyperWriter document to HTML. If your document is large, this may take some time.

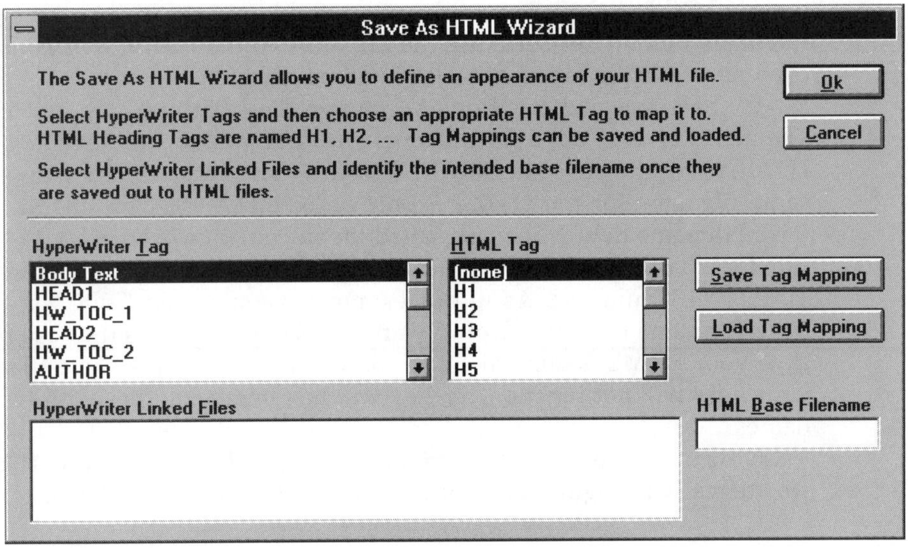

Figure 18.1 The Save As HTML Wizard.

As you can see, converting your HyperWriter applications to World Wide Web format is really quite simple. Once you have converted your HyperWriter applications to World Wide Web format, the next step would be to move them to a Web server so that they could be accessed through the Internet. This, however, is beyond the scope of this manual.

Understanding Multiple Files and HTML

The Save As HTML Wizard processes individual HyperWriter documents, not HyperWriter application files. When exporting a HyperWriter document that references other HyperWriter documents, you are required to use the Save As HTML Wizard once for each of the HyperWriter documents, as you need to save each HyperWriter document to a HTML format. To handle hypertext links to these external files, the HyperWriter **Linked Files** and HTML **Base Filename** options on the **Save As HTML Wizard** dialog box are used. The HyperWriter **Linked Files** field lists all linked files in your document and the **HTML Base Filename** field allows you to map the filename used for links to this document.

Consider a HyperWriter document, MANUAL.HW4, that is linked to one other HyperWriter document, TOC.HW4. When the Save As HTML Wizard is used, the document TOC.HW4 will be displayed in the HyperWriter **Linked Files** field. By first selecting on the document TOC.HW4 listed in this field and then clicking the mouse in the field HTML **Base Filename** field, you can specify the filename to be used for links to this file (for links to the information in the file TOC.HW4). For example, you would enter "TOC" in the HTML **Base Filename** field. After selecting the **OK** button, the HTML files containing the contents of the file MANUAL.HW4 will be created.

We have now exported one of the two files that make up our application. The next step is to open the document TOC.HW4 and export this document to HTML using the Save As HTML Wizard. What is *crucial* here is to specify the same filename for the HTML export of TOC.HW4 as you did in the HTML **Base Filename** field when you saved the document MANUAL.HW4, and indicated the base filename that links to the information stored in the original file TOC.HW4 would use. As in our example we specified "TOC" in the HTML **Base Filename** field, you would want to specify "TOC" as the base filename to save your HTML document to. If you do not specify the same filename then your links will not function, as they will be referencing files with two different names.

Now that we have a good understanding of the **Save As HTML** command, we are ready to begin understanding the content for our Web site.

Understanding the Content for the Web Site

One of the rules for building an Internet Web site is that you shouldn't just rehash your existing print content. This is a rule that, to some extent, we broke in building our own Web site, as we did use a considerable amount of our existing content to build our Web site. Before discussing our content, I would like to clarify this point. Many people are reusing existing content, taking the position that a Web site should have unique, engaging content. This is a point that in theory I agree with, however, in practice I often find isn't such a hard and fast rule. The reasons are threefold. From a practical standpoint, creating this type of unique and engaging content is difficult and expensive. Second, for some areas, creating content that is "unique and engaging" just isn't all that viable. Consider HyperWriter, for example. While, with nine-plus years of experience with HyperWriter, I might argue that HyperWriter is unique and engaging, I doubt that you would agree with me. Unlike a consumer-oriented Web site such as the Batman Forever Web site, for many business-to-business–oriented Web sites, the content is more functional than unique and engaging. The final reason that I disagree with this is that many people often overlook one of the key benefits of the Web: The Web brings all of a company's information resources to a single point and makes those resources available to anyone at any time. Even when simply republishing existing print content on the Web, these advantages can make the Web truly compelling. This is best illustrated with the example that follows.

Consider the process of researching a software company's products both without and with the Web. Without the Web, you call the company and request information. They may or may not send it to you and when you receive it, you don't really know if you are getting everything you should or if the company has additional information that might benefit you. Take our HyperWriter product, for example. While we have a standard product literature pack, we also have optional literature that we add for specific clients, such as a white paper on creating help systems using HyperWriter. If you didn't specifically ask for this, or if one of our salespeople didn't realize that you needed this, then you wouldn't even be aware that this information existed. Now, consider the process of researching a software company's products with the Web. While I would definitely agree with the need to speak with a company representative, I would also turn to the Web as well. If a company has a well-constructed Web site, it can distribute all of their printed materials (of course, subject to the restrictions of HTML formatting) and, more important, let me choose what information I want to see. By allowing free user navigation, the Web lets a reader choose and select only the information on the Web that he or she needs. In addition, the reader can do this literally at any time they choose, whenever they need this information. This navigation and selection ability, coupled with the time independence of the Web, lets even Web sites that do nothing more than present existing print information still provide a real benefit to the user.

Now that you understand some of the rationale that goes into reusing existing content for the Web, we need to consider the actual content that we have available for the NTERGAID Web site. The first aspect of our content to consider is that we want to place both technical reports and product literature on our Web site. The technical reports we want to place on the Web site were created with a word processor (WordPerfect), and really don't pose a problem at all. Our product literature is another story. Like many organizations, we choose to use a desktop publishing package to put together our product literature. Unlike a word processor which is document oriented, a desktop publishing package is page oriented. One of the characteristics of page-oriented software is that it lets you publish information in a fashion suited to the page. Shown in Figure 18.2 is a picture of one of our product literature sheets.

As you can see, a page of our product literature has an introductory section in the top left-hand corner of the page with a screen shot to its right and two columns of text below these elements. The two columns of text constitute the body of the page. The problem arises with the introductory section, which is placed in a separate frame from the body of the page itself. The reason this is a problem is that our desktop publishing package wouldn't allow us to export the introductory section of text along with the body of the page to give us a single word-processing file to use with our Web pages. What we had to do instead was manually take the contents of the introductory section, paste it into the body of the page, and then export this combined text to a word processing file. When trying to export information from page-layout software this is a fairly common problem, and you should definitely be aware of it. In case

Your One Solution for Electronic Documents and Interactive Training
Version 4.2

TODAY'S NEED

The Information Age has created a critical need for simple, efficient, accessible ways to reach all the information that's available. Traditionally, more information generates more paper -- so much paper, in fact, that finding specific items is frustrating and time consuming. Everything from internal reports, news bulletins, technical documentation, policy and procedures manuals and training courses -- TOO MUCH PAPER!

Also there are times when information on paper alone can not present the whole picture. A graphic, video, animation or audio clip could be more effective. Is there a way to integrate all media types and make it easier to find only the information that *you* need?

An Electronic Document in HyperWriter!

THE SOLUTION

Enter HyperWriter!. An advanced hypermedia based information management system, this is *the* toolkit for creating interactive, electronic documents. Now text, graphics, video, audio and animation can be combined to create an informative electronic document. Using hypertext links, instant *connections* between related information, HyperWriter makes information more accessible by removing paper's artificial boundaries. Using HyperWriter, you can jump between a word and its definition, follow cross references and even jump across documents. This hypertext linking, combined with HyperWriter's full text searching, makes finding the information you need almost instantaneous.

Why HyperWriter!

Creating electronic documents begins in the authoring system, HyperWriter! itself. To make getting started easier, HyperWriter functions much like a graphical word processor. It allows you to import existing documents, build hypertext links, reformat text, insert multimedia objects and even create custom user interface screens for your electronic documents. Its powerful navigation tools easily search, collapse, retrace and map with a simple click of a mouse or keyboard. The electronic documents that you create can be distributed via disk, notebook computer, CD-ROM, BBS or local area network -- saving expensive paper and distribution costs. Just one of NTERGAID's customers cut their documentation costs from $18.00 per copy for paper documentation to under $4.00 per copy for electronic documentation distributed on floppy disc.

With HyperWriter!'s **indexed search** capabilities for your electronic documents, searches across even hundreds of megabytes of information happen almost immediately.

HyperWriter! includes advanced search constructs such as fields, groups, fuzzy search, boolean operators, proximity searches and more.

After you have built your electronic documents, you can reduce their size by up to **50%** with built-in tools. Even better, compressed documents don't require a separate decompression step. Compressed documents are read transparently by HyperWriter or HyperReader and decompressed on the fly.

When your application is complete, HyperReader allows you to distribute it **royalty-free**. That's right -- whether one copy or one million, commercial or non-commercial -- HyperReader provides a royalty-free environment for distributing your application. And, like HyperWriter, HyperReader provides the same powerful searching, navigating, printing and exporting found in HyperWriter itself.

HyperWriter! All the Features You Need	HyperWriter 4.0
Powerful Hypertext Linking	YES
Full Text Retrieval	YES
Dynamic Word Lists Show All Indexed Words	YES
Results Map for Viewing Query Results	YES
Screen Painter for Custom Applications	YES
Action Lists for Adding Actions to Objects	YES
Multimedia -- Audio, Video, Animation	YES
WYSIWYG Import (Fonts, Tables, ...)	YES
Integrated Word Processor with Table Editor	YES
Spell Checker and Thesaurus	YES
Bookmarks, Annotation, Printing, Exporting	YES
ROYALTY-FREE RUNTIME	YES

Figure 18.2 A sample product literature page built in a desktop publishing package.

you are curious, we used Corel's Ventura Publisher as our page layout software, but this problem is found in virtually all page layout packages. When we actually start building the Web site, you will find that I have provided word-processing files for each of the documents we want to place on the Web (I already handled the export from the page-layout software).

Another aspect of our content to understand is our graphics. Our print marketing literature contains many different graphics, primarily screen shots illustrating functions within HyperWriter. When we first started building our Web site and experimenting with graphics, we quickly realized that the graphics would be problematic. The reason is that all of our graphics were screen shots taken at 800x600 high resolution. Not only did this translate to large-size images (> 150K per image), but it also translated to images that were just as large as or larger than the average viewer's screen. The implication of graphics this large was that they were very difficult to use effectively, as the user could never view them concurrently with text that referenced them (they always filled the screen). The final problem with the graphics came from the fact that although they started as 256 color .PCX files, the final format we had available was 256 gray scale .TIF files. As our page layout software couldn't properly print out the color images, we had to convert the colors to gray scale for type-setting purposes. And, in this process we managed to lose the original 256 color images. With all these projects with respect to graphics, we made an initial decision to put our Web site together with only minimal graphics, primarily as part of the user interface to identify the area of the Web site currently being viewed.

Now that we understand the different content elements that we have available for the site, we need to actually plan the elements of the site we want to construct. When you plan a Web site, you need to think about the type of information you want to publish and how it should be organized. As covered in Chapter 4, Web information is organized into pages that correspond to Hyper-Writer topics. When thinking about how to plan and organize the site, it is easiest to start by thinking about your organization. NTERGAID is a computer software and services company. This makes two topics easy choices: products and services. These topics would cover NTERGAID products and NTERGAID services. Another topic that we would want to offer is News, current news regarding our product line. Given that our software can be used to produce Internet Web sites, a nice enhancement to the site would be creating links to different sites built using HyperWriter. These sites would be organized on a topic of their own. To provide future extensibility, a **Miscellaneous** topic makes it easy to add future topics. A key use of the Web is that it provides an easy way to provide feedback. Generally you want to dedicate a page in your site to covering how to contact your organization. Two additional pages we would want are a Quick News Flash page and a Job Opportunities page. Although we have a News page already, a Quick News page is designed for news flashes, short bits of news that are constantly kept current. This area of a site typically summarizes any changes to the site as well as offering short news items. The Job Opportunities page advertises job opportunities as they become available. To summarize, we want to have the following topics available in our Internet Web site:

- Products
- Services
- News
- Sites
- Miscellaneous
- Feedback
- Quick News
- Job Opportunities

Is this list of pages complete? Not really, there is also a first page for the site, the Home Page, which serves a central table of contents. There are also various subpages that cover different elements within the major categories listed above; but these are the primary categories of information we want to post on our Web site.

Now that we understand the content that we have for our Web site, we are ready to begin our tutorial.

Understanding this Chapter

This tutorial is broken into five basic parts:

- Getting Ready for Our Tutorial: Planning a Publication
- Tutorial Part 1: Building Our Publication
- Tutorial Part 2: Publishing this Application on the World Wide Web
- Future Enhancements to Our Web Site
- Notes on Authoring Web Sites with HyperWriter

The first part, "Getting Ready…" covers how to plan a digital publication. Along with basic tips, it includes specific details for this chapter's tutorial. The following tutorial sections all cover how to build this chapter's application. The "Future Enhancements" section discusses several ways this Web site could be enhanced. The "Notes on Authoring Web Sites with HyperWriter" section covers some points on Web authoring that didn't come up in the course of the tutorial. If you don't want to read through the planning steps, then please feel free to move directly to "Tutorial Part 1: Building Our Publication."

Now that you understand how this chapter is structured, we'll move on to planning our publication.

Getting Ready for Our Tutorial: Planning a Publication

Like many tasks with a computer, when creating a digital publication with HyperWriter it is easy to dive right in and immediately start working without giving much or any thought to planning or design. However, in HyperWriter, as in many other tasks, this often doesn't work all that well.

Before we begin our tutorial, we need to start with some basic planning steps. These steps can be broken down along five guidelines:

- Features
- Goals
- Constraints
- Audience
- Architecture

Each of these will be covered.

What Are Our Features?

The features of our digital publication reflect the technical elements of our application, what we want our audience to be able to do with the final application. Unlike a HyperWriter application, the features of a Web site are really determined by the content on the Web site, not by specific technical features such as full text searching.

NOTE: The above statement about the features of a Web site being determined by its content is only true for Web sites that don't take advantage of special programming

For our Web site, the features listed in Table 18.1 are needed.

What Are Our Goals?

Digital publishing is a compelling, addictive technology. Because of this, when using digital publishing, it is easy to lose track of why you are using it, the specific goals or benefits that you hope to get from your electronic publication. For this reason, it is always good to address the issue of the goals that you want from your publication up front, before beginning work on it. The goals or benefits we would like to receive from our Web site are as listed in Table 18.2.

Table 18.1 Features Needed for Our Electronic Manual

Feature	*Why Do We Need It?*
Attractive overall appearance	A Web site has really become a reflection of the organization building the site. Given that an attractive appearance reflects well on an organization, this is generally a much desired goal.
Powerful user interface	Unlike a HyperWriter document, which readily provides many different access tools for fast navigation, such as a table of contents browser and full-text searching, a Web page only has a table of contents. By building a user interface that encompasses elements of the table of contents, the user of the Web site doesn't have to always navigate back to the table of contents to choose what to see next.
Good performance	Users of the Web have become increasingly intolerant of slow sites. One key to producing a site with good performance is minimizing the amount of graphics that make up the site. Another key element is not providing text pages that are too long, as an entire text page is transmitted in one shot. A normal Web page generally isn't more than 10k to 15k in size.
Table of Contents	A table of contents will allow easy access to the information that makes up our Web site.

What Are Our Constraints?

After working through the goals for your digital publication, the next step is to tackle the constraints on the publication. While not as apparent as the goals, understanding the constraints on a publication makes a big difference in planning the publication's architecture.

The limits affecting us for this project are:

- **Reuse Existing Content**. As noted, we needed to reuse existing content.
- **Quick Development**. We initially had only one weekend, between several other projects, to get our Web site up and running.
- **Graphics**. Use only a handful of graphics to get the site up and running.

Who Is Our Audience?

When implementing any digital publication, one of the most important planning steps, if not the most important planning step, is to consider the audience.

Table 18.2 Goals of Our Digital Publication

Goal	*Why Do We Need It?*
Sell more NTERGAID software	When you come right down to it, the goal of any marketing piece (and this is a marketing piece) is to sell more product. Our goal was that by providing information to our customers through the Web, we could ultimately sell more product.
Easy to use	When you build a Web site, you really want people to be able to treat it as an effective information resource—they can come in, quickly get information, and then get out. To achieve this goal, your Web site must be easy to use.
Be easily updatable	Whenever you build a digital publication, an important consideration is making it easy to update. If something isn't easy to update, then the general rule is that it simply won't be updated. Given that a key rule with Web sites is keeping them current, designing your Web site so it can be easily updated is important.

What considering the audience does is help to determine if your initial assumptions in planning the document are correct. This last question is really the most important question of all. Without knowing the audience for your electronic publication, you really can't even begin to implement it (at least not successfully). Your audience should generally dictate everything from user interface to the publication to the features to the distribution media.

Given who we are, the audience for our Web site is pretty easy to understand—it is someone who is interested in HyperWriter and a possible product sales or consulting sales opportunity. As HyperWriter is a technical product, aimed at a sophisticated audience, what this tells us is that our target audience is also quite technical. The implication is that we can gear our Web site to a technical audience rather than a nontechnical one.

What Is Our Architecture?

The final step in planning your digital publication is to determine how your digital publication fits in HyperWriter's internal architecture. You may recall this from Chapter 7 where we discussed planning your HyperWriter application. To determine our architecture, we need to answer the ten questions listed below.

What Is the Application?

The application that we have is an Internet Web site designed to promote HyperWriter and NTERGAID.

What Documents Are Needed?

Our source documents are many different files in WordPerfect format. Despite the several source files, for ease of development we would like to create only a single HyperWriter document with all the content from our source files. This single HyperWriter document will serve as a repository for all of our Web pages, with the **Save As HTML** command actually creating the different Web pages.

NOTE: A Web site can also be developed from many different HyperWriter documents.

What Groups Are Needed?

The Web lacks a concept of groups entirely, so we won't create any groups. Groups could be useful, however, for checking the content of the Web site as you could use HyperWriter's **Group Printing** facilities to print out copies of everything in a particular group for quality-checking tasks.

Where Are the Topics?

When creating any HyperWriter application, a key question is where topics (pages for a Web site) need to be created. In our section on understanding the content, we covered the seven major topics for our Web site: Products, Services, News, Sites, Feedback, Quick News, and Job Opportunities. Within each of these topics there will also be additional topics containing more information. As a general rule, these additional topics will correspond to individual documents. For example, a product overview document in the Products topic would correspond to our printed marketing information covering this. As most of our information is organized into short, individual document files, rather than long documents, we probably won't use the Import Text Wizard often—we will simply create links by hand and import files.

Where Are the Links?

A Web site, like a HyperWriter document, is constructed from topics interconnected by hypertext links. The links we will create will primarily serve to offer table-of-contents–like access to individual documents as well as cross-references between related information.

What Properties Are Needed?

Web sites do not have the concept of properties at all. Hence, there will not be any properties used in our application.

What Action Lists Are Needed?

Web sites do not have the concept of action lists at all. Hence, there will not be any action lists used in our application.

What Tags Are Needed?

Tags (or styles) provide elements to format the text in our documents. For an application like this where we have existing source data, we generally want to rely on the tags that are found in the data rather than new tags. What we will do for our Web site is map the tags in our data to the HTML tags when we use the **Save As HTML** command.

What Backgrounds Are Needed?

HyperWriter's backgrounds provide the user interface for documents. Although our Web site will have a user interface, it won't be built from backgrounds, as our backgrounds don't have an equivalent in the Web. Our Web site will instead be constructed from standard HyperWriter links. The user interface for our Web site will be covered in depth when we move into the tutorial on building our site.

How Should the Application Be Indexed?

HyperWriter's indexing facilities don't extend to the Web, so we don't need to index our Web site using HyperIndexer. Bear in mind that indexing our Web site could make some tasks like document maintenance and creating cross-references much easier.

Summary

From the above planning steps, we found out the following information:

- What is the application? An Internet Web site to promote NTERGAID and HyperWriter.
- What documents are needed? A single HyperWriter document to serve as the repository for all information that makes up the Web site.
- What groups are needed? No groups are needed.
- Where are the topics? Seven main topics are needed, along with individual topics for each document added to the Web site.

- Where are the links? Table of contents links are the primary links that are needed. Cross-referencing links may also be added.
- What properties are needed? No properties are needed.
- What action lists are needed? No actions lists are needed.
- What tags are needed? The tags found in the source documents will be mapped to HTML documents.
- What backgrounds are needed? No backgrounds will be needed.
- How should the application be indexed? No indexing is needed.

With our planning stage completed, we are ready to begin building our Web site.

Tutorial Part 1: Building Our Web Site

The following sections take you through our tutorial. To make this easier, we have broken it into two major sections, each arranged into discrete steps. For learning purposes, it is usually easier to work through a tutorial and complete a step in full than to leave a portion of it incomplete.

Step 1: Setting Our Directories

Before we can begin working through this tutorial, we need to run Hyper-Writer. HyperWriter is a standard MS-Windows application that is run from MS-Windows, as is any other Windows application. With HyperWriter running, we need to get started by setting our directories.

To make this tutorial easier, all the data files used for this tutorial have been organized into a separate directory. What we will do now is set Hyper-Writer's Preferences so that it uses this directory. This is an area of Hyper-Writer that we really haven't covered yet—directories within HyperWriter. When you use HyperWriter, unlike many other software products, it is very important to understand where files are located, the directory where they are stored. The reason for this is that unlike a word processor or other productivity tool, with HyperWriter what you are doing is creating publications that will be given to someone else as files not as printouts. Given that a HyperWriter publication can consist of literally hundreds of different files, HyperWriter takes advantage of directories to organize these files. HyperWriter uses four separate directory settings:

- **Documents.** Where HyperWriter .HW4 files are stored
- **Pictures.** Where picture files are stored
- **Text Files.** Where text files (i.e., using the **Import Text** command) are stored

- **Local Files.** Where temporary data files like bookmarks and searches are stored

Although HyperWriter can look across directories to find files, these directory settings are where HyperWriter always looks first to find a particular file. Setting our directory options is covered next.

Setting Directories in HyperWriter

1. Select the **Preferences** command from the **File** menu.
2. Select the **Directories** folder. This displays the folder of options shown in Figure 18.3.
3. Enter "\HW4\NTWEB" into the **Documents** field. If you installed HyperWriter into a directory other than \HW4, then substitute that directory.
4. Select the **All Directories Same As First** button to synchronize all directories with the Documents directory.
5. Select the **OK** button to close this dialog box.

With our directories set, we are ready to get started on our tutorial. You should be aware that a completed version of this tutorial has been supplied in

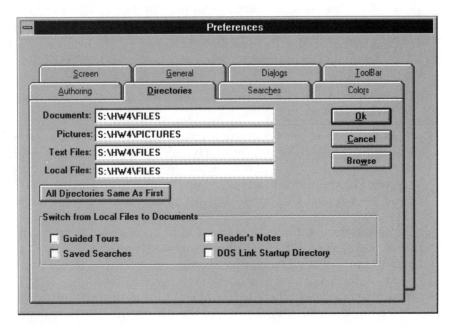

Figure 18.3 Setting directories with the **Preferences** command.

\HW4\NTWEB\DONE in case you need to see how the tutorial functions when it is finished. To save disc space, we did not supply the picture files in this directory. When you open the completed version of this tutorial, you can leave your pictures directory set to \HW4\NTWEB. You should also be aware that to save disc space, you can delete this directory if needed. Once you have worked through this tutorial, you can also delete the \HW4\NTWEB directory as well.

Step 2: Designing the Home Page

Building our Web site begins by defining our Home page. For a Web site, the Home page is the first screen that someone viewing the site sees. This places particular burdens on the Home page, as it must not only organize all of the information on the Web site, but also have an attractive appearance and provide acceptable performance. Building our Home page begins by creating a new HyperWriter document using the **New** command. Unlike most of the times we have used the **New** command, we won't use the Template Wizard at all, as our application won't use any backgrounds (which the Template Wizard creates).

The Template Wizard

1. Select the **New** command from the **File** menu. This displays the **Template Wizard** dialog box that we have seen before.

2. What we need to do is turn off the Template Wizard using the **Use New Template Wizard** option. Select this option so that no "x" is shown for this option.

3. Select the **OK** button to create our new document. The document created is shown in Figure 18.4.

As you can see, this document is completely blank—it has no user interface or content. This is the nature of HyperWriter's giving you a blank-slate approach to authoring applications. As you can see, when you don't use the Template Wizard, creating a HyperWriter application can be a little bit intimidating. To get past this, we'll start by quickly adding some content to our Home page.

If you think about our Home page in terms of how the user of the site will experience it, one of the first things that a user of the site should see is the name of the site or organization sponsoring it. This is important because it quickly assures the user that they have come to the right place. If the user typed http://WWW.NTERGAID.COM into their browser (this represents a direct jump to a site), they don't need this assurance, but many people come to a Web site through a search engine or hyperlink from a different Web site. By

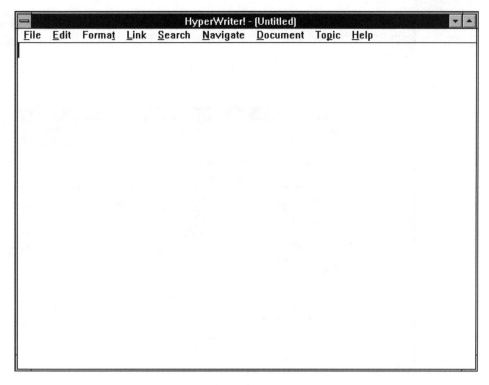

Figure 18.4 The document that was created.

providing this assurance, the person visiting the site can quickly decide whether or not to stay at the site or return to their previous location. In addition, presenting the name of the site or organization when the user first enters the Home page helps to reinforce the name of the site. If we want to present the name of our organization so that people see it when they first enter the site, we need to locate the name at the top of our page. This can be done using text, or a picture such as a logo. Given that we want to present an attractive site, we'll use a picture containing a version of the NTERGAID logo.

As you may recall from Chapter 13, a picture can be inserted into a Hyper-Writer document several different ways, including backgrounds, links to pictures, the **Import Picture** command and the **Insert Object** command. Given that backgrounds aren't supported on the Web, this obviously knocks out using backgrounds to insert a picture. Our second option, links to pictures, isn't really applicable because this would create a link to our logo, rather than inserting the picture at the top of our page. The next two options, **Import Picture** and **Insert Object**, could both be used to add our logo. The command we want to use is **Insert Object**, as this command functions like the Web itself in

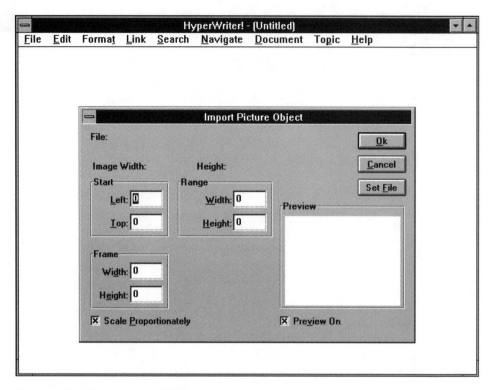

Figure 18.5 The Template Wizard.

terms of treating pictures like objects. For this reason, we'll use the **Insert Object** command throughout the rest of this chapter whenever we need to insert a picture into our Web site. Using the **Insert Object** command is covered in the next step where we insert a picture at the top of our Home page.

Inserting Our Logo at the Top of the Home Page

1. Select the **Insert Object** command from the **Edit** menu. This displays the **Import Picture Object** dialog box shown in Figure 18.5.
2. Select the **Set File** button.
3. Select .PCX as the format to import.
4. Select the file NTLOGO1.PCX as the picture to insert.
5. Select the **OK** button to insert our picture. This inserts the picture at the top of our Home page. The picture is shown in Figure 18.6.

Inserting this picture brings up two issues. The first is the size of the picture file. As you can see, this picture file is about one-inch high and three-

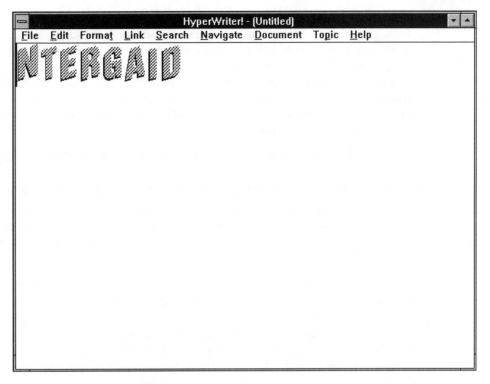

Figure 18.6 The picture we inserted.

inches wide. This picture was created at 72 dpi (dots per inch) or what is called *screen resolution*. This differs from what is called *printer resolution*, which is 300 dpi. Very often when you are reusing content from existing materials, your picture files turn out to be 300 dpi, leading to the effect that your picture files turn out to be too large (a 300 dpi file being four times larger than a 72 dpi file). If when you are reusing picture files, you find your pictures are too large, then you need to resize them.

People that are experienced with the Web, or who have read Chapter 4, are probably surprised that we used .PCX as our graphics format for our Home page, as the native graphics format for the Web is .GIF. Due to Unisys's position on demanding royalties for use of the .GIF graphics format, (see note), HyperWriter no longer includes support for .GIF format graphics. As .GIF format graphics are essential for Web development, when HyperWriter saves a document to HTML format, it automatically converts references to image formats other than .GIF, to .GIF. For example, if we saved our current Home page to HTML, it would transform the reference to the file NTL-OGO1.PCX to be a reference to NTLOGO1.GIF. Although HyperWriter handles converting the references to files to .GIF, it doesn't actually convert the .PCX graphics to .GIF graphics. This can be done through an external converter such as Graphics Workshop, which can batch convert multiple files directly to .GIF. Graphics Workshop is a shareware program, a copy of which is supplied on the CD-ROM disc accompanying this book (it is in the \GWS directory). Please note that GWS is shareware, and we do recommend registering it if you find it of use. To summarize, the procedure for using graphics in Web pages is as follows:

1. Embed graphics in formats other than .GIF using the **Insert Object** command.

2. Save your document to HTML using the **Save As HTML** command.

3. Use conversion software Graphics Workshop to convert all graphics to .GIF format (for this tutorial, we have included .GIF versions of these graphics so you don't have to use the conversion software if you don't want to).

NOTE: Although NTERGAID supported the .GIF format for a number of years, HyperWriter version 4.2 has had support for the .GIF graphics format removed. The reason for this is that although the .GIF format was originally developed by CompuServe, the underlying compression format makes use of a patented technology by Unisys—the LZW algorithm. Now, seven years after the .GIF format was released, Unisys has decided that they want to require royalty-based licensing from all software that makes use of .GIF technology. Although NTERGAID does not agree with the actions of Unisys, nor with their legal basis, because our software always includes a royalty-free runtime module, we simply cannot afford to license the LZW technology from Unisys. To avoid a potential lawsuit, NTERGAID has removed support for .GIF graphics from HyperWriter. We apologize for the inconvenience that this causes our customers, but we hope that you recognize that NTERGAID was merely a victim in this incident.

With our picture inserted at the top of our Home page, the next step is to add a basic text message below our logo, welcoming people to the site. The text for our message can be inserted using the **Import Text** command.

Adding a Welcome Message

1. Press **End** to move the end of the picture.

2. Press **Enter** to add a blank line.

3. Press **Enter** to add a second blank line.

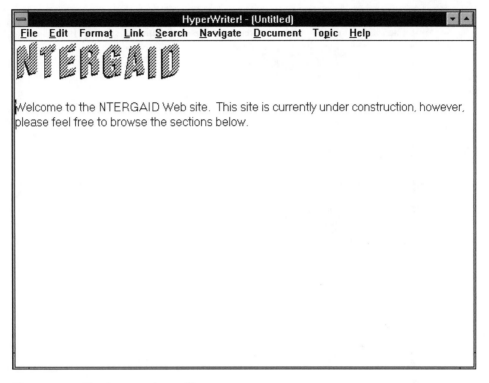

Figure 18.7 The imported text file.

4. Select the **Import Text** command from the **File** menu.
5. Select ASCII as the format to insert.
6. Select the file WEBMSG.TXT. This displays the Import Text Wizard.
7. Select **OK** to import the WEBMSG.TXT file without creating any links automatically. This imports the WEBMSG.TXT file into your Home page. A picture of how your Home page should appear is shown in Figure 18.7.

With our logo file inserted and our text message added to our Home page, we have a good start on our Home page. But for us to continue creating our Home page, we need to think back to the list of topics that we previously identified as being part of our Web site. To review, these topics are listed here:

- Products
- Services
- News
- Sites

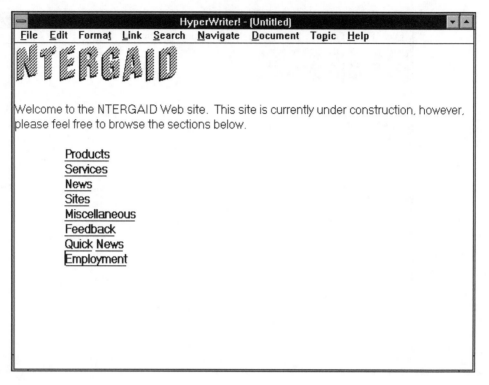

Figure 18.8 A Web page using text links.

- Miscellaneous
- Feedback
- Quick News
- Job Opportunities

This brings us to the question of how to present these topics to the person accessing the Web site. One option is a simple set of text links like those shown in Figure 18.8.

While text links make it very simple to create a Web page, they don't create a particularly attractive page. Given that attractiveness was one of the criteria for our Web site, this brings us to the idea of using icons to access different topics in our Web site. By using icons designed to represent the different topics in our Web site, we can present a much more attractive interface to our site. Keeping in mind our goal of good performance, we should use icons that are relatively small, about one inch square in size. This translates to a byte size of about 1,000 bytes per icon, an acceptable size for good performance. With the decision to use icons and the physical size of the icons determined, the next step is to consider how those icons could be visually laid out in our Home page. There are really two basic options: a vertical layout and a horizontal layout. In a vertical layout, the icons are stacked one on top of one another. In a horizontal layout, the icons are stacked next to one another. The advantage to a Home page for the number of icons that we will have, is that someone viewing the site can see all the icons at once. This lets them make a choice without having to scroll down. Given that users may not always take the time to scroll down, if you can build your initial Home page without requiring scrolling for most users, this is a nice benefit (not required, but nice).

Now that we know what we want visually for our Home page, we are ready to start designing icons we can use. As designing good icons can be quite a bit of work, you should always consider exactly which icons you need. This brings us back to the list of topics we want to cover on our Web page. If we look at this list, we see that the Quick News and Job Opportunities topics really aren't as important to the site as are the remaining ones. They really are ancillary or subsidiary topics, not primary topics. Because of this, we will use text links to represent these two topics and icons for the remaining topics. This will nicely focus the reader's attention on the topics that are important to the site as only the important topics are represented with a graphical icon. This leaves us with six icons that we need to design:

- Products
- Services
- News
- Sites
- Miscellaneous
- Feedback

Designing icons is not really a process I can talk you through and this book simply doesn't. To some extent designing icons is artistic, and it really comes down to an either you can or can't do it situation. With that said, you really need to use a graphics package and design icons for your site or have someone else do it. As far as tools go, any type of basic graphics package can be used to design icons, although sophisticated tools obviously have advantages. After designing our icons, we have six graphics files:

- Products (PRODS.PCX)
- Services (SVCS.PCX)
- News (NEWS.PCX)
- Sites (SITES.PCX)
- Miscellaneous (MISC.PCX)
- Feedback (FEEDBACK.PCX)

With our six icons designed, we are now ready to start putting together our Home page. This does bring up the question of the order in which our icons will be displayed. For now, we will just use the order in the list (this order is actually already structured from most important to least important). Our first task is inserting an icon and then linking it to a new page. Given that we want our icon to start just below our text message, we can continue authoring our page where we left off.

Inserting Our First Icon

1. Press **Enter** to add a blank line.
2. Select the **Insert Object** command from the **Edit** menu.
3. Select the **Set File** button.
4. Select .PCX as the format to import.
5. Select the file PRODS.PCX as the picture to insert.
6. Select the **OK** button to insert our picture. This inserts the picture at the top of our Home page, shown in Figure 18.9.

With our first icon inserted, we need to link it to a new page that will contain the content associated with that topic. Given that we are linking the **Products** icon, this new page will contain product-specific information. Linking our icons can be done in two fashions, using the **Mark Region** command or linking across the icon. As you may recall from Chapter 12, HyperWriter can create links from regions of pictures using the **Mark Region** command, which allows you to mark a region of a picture and then add a link to another location. While this seems ideally suited to what we want to do (which is making a picture into a link), the nature of Web servers actually makes it less than perfect. A Web server is the server program that makes Web pages available to the Internet. When a Web server works with a link on a region of a picture, this is called an *image map*. Not all Web servers support image maps and those that do often require special configurations to do so. You should note that if you know how to use image maps with your Web server, you will be happy to know that HyperWriter directly generates the needed image map files from images marked with the **Mark Region** command. Due to the difficulties in using image maps, we will link our icon by using a link made across the entire picture. What this means is using the picture as the anchor for the link, by marking the picture object as the object to link (instead of a text object that you would normally link). This makes the entire picture a hypertext link and is a common technique used on the Web.

You should be aware that in making this link and the links to follow, what we will be doing is really creating a skeleton or framework for our site. This framework will be a series of blank pages that we will add content to later in

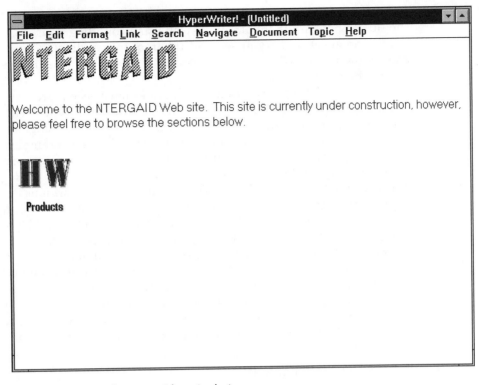

Figure 18.9 A Web page with a single icon.

this chapter. For example, linking our **Products** icon will create one blank page attached to our Home page, that we will later add content to. Linking our icon is covered below.

Linking Our First Icon

1. Press **Home** to move to the beginning of the line.
2. Press **Shift+End** to mark a block to the end of the picture.
3. Select the **Link to Text** command from the **Link** menu.
4. Select the **Jump Link** option.
5. Select the **New Topic** option. This creates a new topic and places you in the topic.
6. Select the **Complete Link** command from the **Link** menu. If Hyper-Writer asks whether to create a bidirectional link, choose No as bidirectional links aren't exported to the Web.

This completes the link and returns you to our Home page. What you should see now are triangular link symbols surrounding your icon. This may not be, however, what you see and this requires understanding a little bit about how HyperWriter works. If you don't see triangular link symbols on screen, then please read on.

In the tutorials we have used thus far, links have been represented with the standard Windows method of green, underlined text. HyperWriter also has another way, its default, for representing links—as green, triangular link symbols that surround the beginning and end of a link. For example, <this text might be a link>. The reason that HyperWriter has these symbols is that there are times when underlining is not a perfect solution and can cause problems. This is one of those times. HyperWriter's underlining algorithms do not allow underlining a graphical object, therefore our icon isn't underlined, and the link we created can't be activated. The solution is for us to turn on HyperWriter's link symbols so we can see and activate our links. As I stated that these link symbols are actually HyperWriter's defaults, why don't they appear on our screen? When you have used a document that has link symbols as green, underlined text and then create a new file, HyperWriter doesn't reset all of its document properties—including the document property for link symbols. If you exit, however, then HyperWriter reverts to its defaults. What we need to do is use the **Document Properties** command to turn them back on.

Turning on Link Symbols

1. (This step can be skipped if you currently have link symbols visible.) Select the **Properties** command from the **Document** menu.
2. Select the **Links** folder.
3. Turn on the **Link Symbols** visible and **Link Symbols** colored options.
4. Turn off the **Color Link Anchor Text** option.
5. Select the **Set Font** button.
6. Turn off the **Underline** option.
7. Select the **OK** button to close the **Document Properties** dialog box. A picture of how your Home page should now appear is shown in Figure 18.10.

When you look at our Home page, you see triangular symbols surrounding the icon. These symbols are HyperWriter's native method for representing links. They are equivalent to the green, underlined links that you have seen previously using HyperWriter. Given that we are linking across the icon, we need to use this method of representing links, as HyperWriter requires that some visible sign of the link be displayed onscreen (if we used green, underlined text then this wouldn't be visible when linking across the icon and the

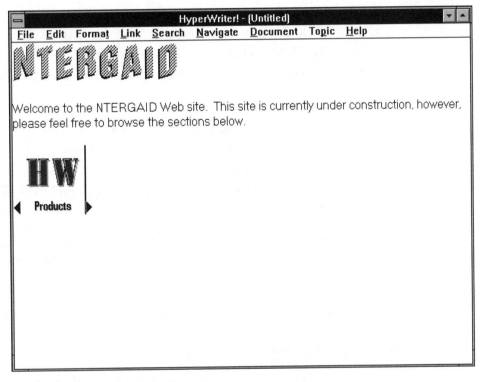

Figure 18.10 Our Home page with a single icon.

link couldn't be activated). By not using the Template Wizard to create our document, HyperWriter uses its default triangular link symbols.

NOTE: These triangular link symbols will only be seen in HyperWriter and won't be visible at all on the Web.

With our first icon inserted and linked, the next task is to insert each of the remaining icons and link them. When we have completed linking each of the icons, the majority of the structure of our Web site will be completed. The first icon we want to insert is the **Services** icon.

Inserting and Linking the Services Icon

1. Press **End** to move to the end of the line (next to the **Products** icon).
2. Select the **Insert Object** command from the **Edit** menu.

3. Select the **Set File** button.

4. Select .PCX as the format to import.

5. Select the file SVCS.PCX as the picture to insert.

6. Select the **OK** button to insert our picture. This inserts the picture into our Home page.

7. Press **Leftarrow** to move to the start of the **Services** icon.

8. Press **Shift+End** to mark a block to the end of the picture.

9. Select the **Link to Text** command from the **Link** menu.

10. Select the **Jump Link** option.

11. Select the **New Topic** option. This creates a new topic and places you in the topic.

12. Select the **Complete Link** command from the **Link** menu. If Hyper-Writer asks whether to create a bidirectional link, choose No as bidirectional links aren't exported to the Web. This completes the link and returns you to our Home page. A picture of how your Home page should now appear is shown in Figure 18.11.

After the **Services** icon is inserted, the **News** icon is the next one to insert.

Inserting and Linking the News Icon

1. Press **End** to move to the end of the line (next to the **Services** icon).

2. Select the **Insert Object** command from the **Edit** menu.

3. Select the **Set File** button.

4. Select .PCX as the format to import.

5. Select the file NEWS.PCX as the picture to insert.

6. Select the **OK** button to insert our picture. This inserts the picture into our Home page.

7. Press **Leftarrow** to move to the start of the **News** icon.

8. Press **Shift+End** to mark a block to the end of the picture.

9. Select the **Link to Text** command from the **Link** menu.

10. Select the **Jump Link** option.

11. Select the **New Topic** option. This creates a new topic and places you in the topic.

12. Select the **Complete Link** command from the **Link** menu. If Hyper-Writer asks whether to create a bidirectional link, choose No, as bidirectional links aren't exported to the Web. This completes the link and returns you to our Home page.

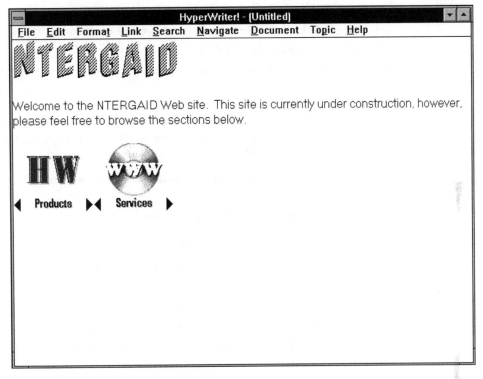

Figure 18.11 Our Home page with two icons.

After inserting our **News** icon, we have three icons running across the screen. As we have six icons in total, we will only place three icons on each line so the display is balanced. Because of this, we will press **Enter** at the beginning of the next step when we insert the **Sites** icon.

Inserting and Linking the Sites Icon

1. Press **Enter** to move to the next line so we have only three icons per line.
2. Select the **Insert Object** command from the **Edit** menu.
3. Select the **Set File** button.
4. Select .PCX as the format to import.
5. Select the file SITES.PCX as the picture to insert.
6. Select the **OK** button to insert our picture. This inserts the picture into our Home page.
7. Press **Leftarrow** to move to the start of the **Sites** icon.

8. Press **Shift+End** to mark a block to the end of the picture.

9. Select the **Link to Text** command from the **Link** menu.

10. Select the **Jump Link** option.

11. Select the **New Topic** option. This creates a new topic and places you in the topic.

12. Select the **Complete Link** command from the **Link** menu. If Hyper-Writer asks whether to create a bidirectional link, choose No, as bidirectional links aren't exported to the Web. This completes the link and returns you to our Home page.

The next icon we want to insert is the **Miscellaneous** icon.

Inserting and Linking the Miscellaneous Icon

1. Press **End** to move to the end of the line (next to the **Sites** icon).

2. Select the **Insert Object** command from the **Edit** menu.

3. Select the **Set File** button.

4. Select .PCX as the format to import.

5. Select the file MISC.PCX as the picture to insert.

6. Select the **OK** button to insert our picture. This inserts the picture into our Home page.

7. Press **Leftarrow** to move to the start of the **Miscellaneous** icon.

8. Press **Shift+End** to mark a block to the end of the picture.

9. Select the **Link to Text** command from the **Link** menu.

10. Select the **Jump Link** option.

11. Select the **New Topic** option. This creates a new topic and places you in the topic.

12. Select the **Complete Link** command from the **Link** menu. If Hyper-Writer asks whether to create a bidirectional link, choose No, as bidirectional links aren't exported to the Web. This completes the link and returns you to our Home page.

Our final icon to insert and link is the **Feedback** icon.

Inserting and Linking the Feedback Icon

1. Press **End** to move to the end of the line (next to the **Miscellaneous** icon).

2. Select the **Insert Object** command from the **Edit** menu.

3. Select the **Set File** button.

4. Select .PCX as the format to import.

5. Select the file FEEDBACK.PCX as the picture to insert.

6. Select the **OK** button to insert our picture. This inserts the picture into our Home page.

7. Press **Leftarrow** to move to the start of the **Feedback** icon.

8. Press **Shift+End** to mark a block to the end of the picture.

9. Select the **Link to Text** command from the **Link** menu.

10. Select the **Jump Link** option.

11. Select the **New Topic** option. This creates a new topic and places you in the topic.

12. Select the **Complete Link** command from the **Link** menu. If Hyper-Writer asks whether to create a bidirectional link, choose No, as bidirectional links aren't exported to the Web. This completes the link and returns you to our Home page.

A picture of how your Home page should now appear is shown in Figure 18.12.

With all our icons inserted, the next step is to insert the links to our News Flash and Job Opportunity pages. As noted earlier, we want to insert these using text links so they don't distract from our primary topics, which are represented by the icons we just finished inserting.

Inserting Links to News Flash and Job Opportunity

1. Press **Enter** to move to the next line.

2. Press **Enter** again so that a blank line separates our text from the icons.

3. Type the text "Other Topics:" and press **Enter**. This adds a subtitle to our Home page which will be displayed above the links.

4. Type the text "Click Here for Important News Flash" and press **Enter**.

5. Type the text "Job Opportunity" and press **Enter**.

6. Mark the text "Click Here for Important News Flash" as a block.

7. Select the **Link to Text** command from the **Link** menu.

8. Select the **Jump Link** option.

9. Select the **New Topic** option. This creates a new topic and places you in the topic.

10. Select the **Complete Link** command from the **Link** menu. If Hyper-Writer asks whether to create a bidirectional link, choose No, as bidirectional links aren't exported to the Web. This completes the link and returns you to our Home page.

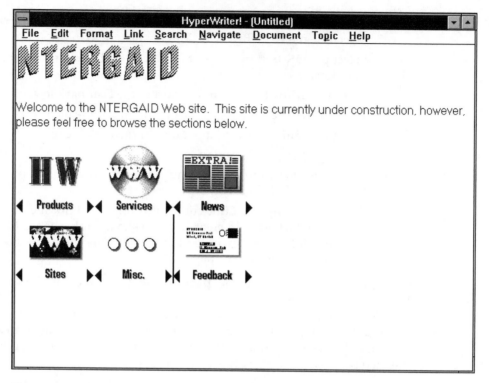

Figure 18.12 Our Home page with all six icons.

11. Mark the text "Job Opportunity" as a block.

12. Select the **Link to Text** command from the **Link** menu.

13. Select the **Jump Link** option.

14. Select the **New Topic option**. This creates a new topic and places you in the topic.

15. Select the **Complete Link** command from the **Link** menu. If Hyper-Writer asks whether to create a bidirectional link, choose No, as bidirectional links aren't exported to the Web. This completes the link and returns you to our Home page.

A picture of how your Home page should now appear is shown in Figure 18.13.

At this point, we have almost completed our Home page. There are two remaining tasks for us:

• Formatting the two text links as a list (In the future, we might add more items to these, so a list is a good format to use.)

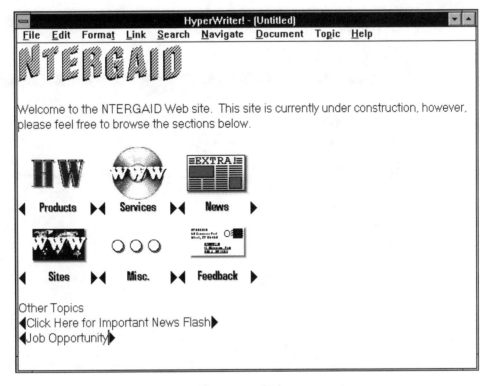

Figure 18.13 Our Home page with two text links.

- Adding a thank you message and a copyright statement to the bottom of our site

Formatting our text links as a list can be handled in three fashions. One way is by creating a style or tag to format them. Another approach is literal text formatting, such as using a "*" character before the text of the link. As you should recall from Chapter 4, Web pages are formatted using tags, so generally literal formatting is not used. Given that we want to create powerful Web pages, we want to use a tag, not literal text formatting. Although we could create our own tag, HyperWriter includes a standard stylesheet called HTML1_2.HWT, which contains all of the standard HTML tags supported by HyperWriter. The first step is to attach the stylesheet to your HyperWriter document.

Attaching a Stylesheet to Your HyperWriter Document

1. Select the **Properties** command from the **Document** menu.
2. Select the **Files** folder. This folder of options is shown in Figure 18.14.

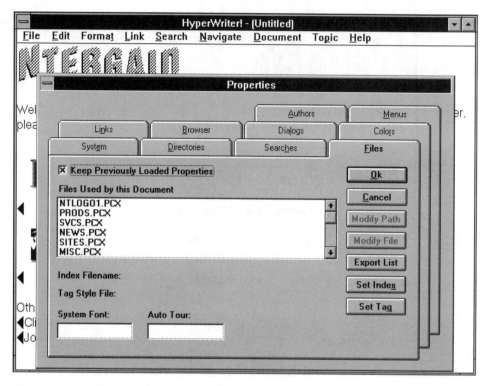

Figure 18.14 The **Document Properties Files** folder.

3. Select the **Set Tag** button.
4. Select the file HTML1_2.HWT.
5. Turn off the **Keep Previously Loaded Properties** option.
6. Select the **OK** button to close the **Document Properties** dialog box.

NOTE: Although attaching our stylesheet was very simple, it is important to understand a key restriction regarding using existing stylesheets with your existing HyperWriter documents. When a document already has existing styles or tags, attaching an existing stylesheet causes a conflict. Although Hyper-Writer will let you do this, generally speaking you don't want to attach a stylesheet to an existing document that already has styles of its own.

After attaching a stylesheet to your document, your document must be saved and reopened for the styles to be available for use.

Saving and Reopening a Document

1. Select the **Save** command from the **File** menu. Enter the name NTWEB and press **Enter**.

2. Select the **Open** command from the **File** menu. If HyperWriter asks you to leave a bookmark, select **Yes** as you want to continue authoring from your present location (a bookmark saves your location).

3. Select the document NTWEB to open. This opens your document.

Now that we have attached a stylesheet to our document, we are ready to apply a tag to the two links we created earlier. As we want to format these links as a list, the tag we'll apply is an UL LI tag. This tag indicates an unordered list (UL), such as the bulleted list that we want to be created. When you look at the stylesheet that we attached to our document, you will see that all the tags begin with the text "HTML_". As this is a stylesheet that was designed for use with documents being published to HTML format, you would probably think this is redundant. The reason for starting the tags with "HTML_" is that as you import documents with existing styles, these will be added to the stylesheet. The "HTML_" text allows you to distinguish between the supplied tags and tags that were created by importing documents with styles. You should note that when we refer to a specific HTML tag like an **H2** tag, we may not always use the "HTML_" prefix (as the name of the actual HTML tag is really just **H2**).

Formatting the News Flash and Job Opportunity Links

1. Mark a block covering the **News Flash** and **Job Opportunity** links. As these items are linked, using the mouse to mark the block will cause the links to be activated. Using **Shift+Arrowkey** prevents this.

2. Select the **Apply Tag** command from the **Format** menu.

3. Select the tag HTML_UL LI.

4. When HyperWriter asks you whether to apply the tag to the selected block or to the selected paragraphs, choose Selected Paragraphs. After formatting the two links with the unordered list tag, you should see a list like that shown in Figure 18.15.

With our text links formatted, we need to add our thank you message and copyright statement. These are pretty standard elements that appear at the bottom of many Home pages. Essentially they just thank the reader for visiting and state that all contents are copywritten. These can be added by typing them in at the bottom of the page.

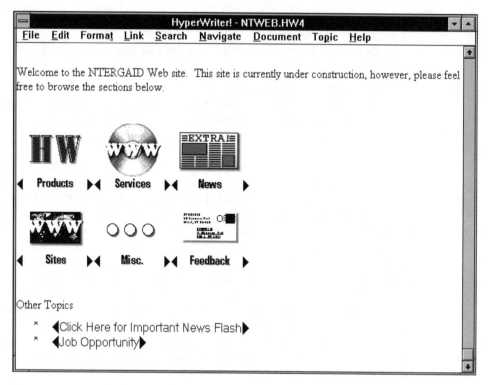

Figure 18.15 Links formatted as an unordered list.

Adding a Thank You Message and Copyright Statement

1. Press **Enter** to move to the next line after the **Job Opportunity** link.
2. Use the **Apply Tag** command on the **Format** menu to change the tag from the HTML_OL LI tag to the **Body Text** tag.
3. Type in the text "Thank you for visiting WWW.NTERGAID.COM. Please come again soon." and press **Enter**.
4. Type in the text "All information Copyright (C) NTERGAID, Inc., 1995." and press **Enter**. After typing in this information, your completed Home page should appear as shown in Figure 18.16.

The final step is for us to save our work as a HyperWriter .HW4 file. We don't want to save to HTML format yet, as we still have a lot of work to do.

Saving Our Work

Select the **Save** command on the **File** menu.

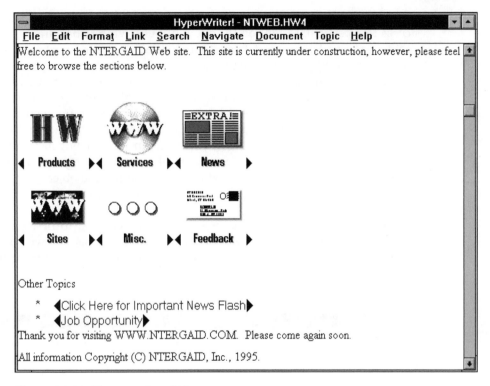

Figure 18.16 The completed Home page.

With our work saved and the initial appearance for our Home page completed, the next step is to design the user interface for our **Home** page.

Step 3: Designing the User Interface

As you may recall from the different tutorials that we have worked through, one of the first steps that generally begins a HyperWriter application is creating the user interface to the application. The user interface constitutes the buttons, icons, and other objects that the reader of the application uses to control his or her navigation throughout the application. This is done at the beginning of the application, as this interface needs to be consistent throughout the entire application and starting from the beginning makes this much easier. Although we are authoring a Web site, not a native HyperWriter application, the concept of a user interface still applies. Given that a Web browser used to view a site always provides a user interface, you may wonder if a user interface is needed for a Web site. While this depends on the particular site, many Web sites provide a user interface in the form of a button or icon bar that appears either at the top or bottom of each page. This user interface generally provides one-click access to a particular point on the site without having to backtrack to the site's Home page and then start from there. Thus, the user interface for the site streamlines navigation, making it more efficient for readers to browse the site.

From working through Chapter 14, you probably recognize that Hyper-Writer has a powerful user interface facility called *backgrounds* (the Screen Painter). While HyperWriter's backgrounds facility is powerful and well-suited to user interface design, interfaces designed with backgrounds aren't exported to the Web, as HyperWriter's Screen Painter is considerably more advanced than the Web is currently capable of supporting. To make the user interface for our publication, we will simply use picture objects that are hand linked. This type of user interface is simple to construct and easily moves to the Web.

Before we can construct our user interface, we need to first decide what style of interface we want to have. There are three choices that we have for the style of our interface: **Text Links**, **Buttons**, and **Icons**. A picture of the three types of interfaces is shown in Figure 18.17.

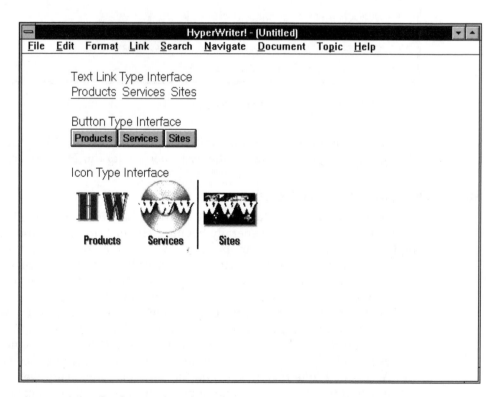

Figure 18.17 The three styles of interfaces.

As you can see, our interface can be composed of any of these three styles of objects. Generally speaking, you want to use a consistent style throughout, rather than creating a user interface from multiple styles. Given that one of the criteria of our Web site was that we wanted it to be attractive, we can quickly rule out **Text Links** for our interface. Although the icons shown in Figure 18.16 are attractive, we have already used these in our application once in our application, so we will instead use an interface of text buttons. You should note that the term *text buttons* is used loosely—the buttons are actually small picture files that are shaped like buttons, and actually aren't text. By using buttons for our interface, not only can we have an attractive site, but it will also slightly differentiate it from sites with a simpler interface using text buttons.

A key difference between the user interface that we will create for our Web site and the user interface found in the HyperWriter documents you have viewed to date can be summed up in three words: places versus actions. In a HyperWriter document, the user interface is dynamic, generally consisting of buttons that execute an action such as a search function, viewing a table of contents, or printing information. In a Web user interface, the buttons almost always jump to places within the Web site. This reflects the nature of the Web itself, where when actions exist they have to be specially programmed using CGI scripting. You should note that this is not a criticism of the Web, it is really just something that you should know. From a historical perspective, you may be interested to learn that when NTERGAID first got started, the types of user interfaces that we created in our early documents were actually very similar to those being built for Web today. I suspect that as the Web becomes more advanced, its capabilities will evolve towards the type of user interfaces that HyperWriter is already capable of.

As noted in the previous few paragraphs, the type of interface that we will be creating is one using text buttons that are linked to different places in the Web site. Given that we have stated that the goal of this user interface is to facilitate rapid navigation of the Web site, so that a reader doesn't have to return to the table of contents, figuring out where the text buttons will be linked to becomes quite simple. What we will do is link the text buttons to each of the main topics that make up our Web site. Returning to our list of main topics gives us the following list of buttons and the filename that we'll use for each button.

- Products (BTPROD.PCX)
- Services (BTSVCS.PCX)
- News (BTNEWS.PCX)
- Sites (BTSITES.PCX)
- Miscellaneous (BTMISC.PCX)
- Feedback (BTFEEDBK.PCX)

As you can see, we will have one button for each of the main topics in our Web site. A useful point to note is the naming conventions that we used for the buttons. To help distinguish the picture files for the buttons from the picture files for the icons, we used the prefix "BT" as part of the button name. This is the type of very simple, common-sense authoring technique that can make digital publishing much easier. If we hadn't already created our icons, we would probably rename them using the prefix "IC" to indicate that they are icons.

Although we haven't yet created our user interface, let's take a quick look at how it should appear. This is shown in Figure 18.18.

To add our user interface to our Web site, we need to add this user interface to each page or topic. One choice facing us is where to add the interface. The two options we have are adding it at the top or at the bottom of each topic. The answer to this question really depends on the type of Web site you want to create. As this site is really oriented to learning about HyperWriter in depth, we will add this user interface to the bottom of each topic, so that after someone has read a page in full, he or she then arrives at the user interface and can make a choice as to what to read next. If our site was more oriented towards rapid browsing, then we might choose to add this user interface at the top of

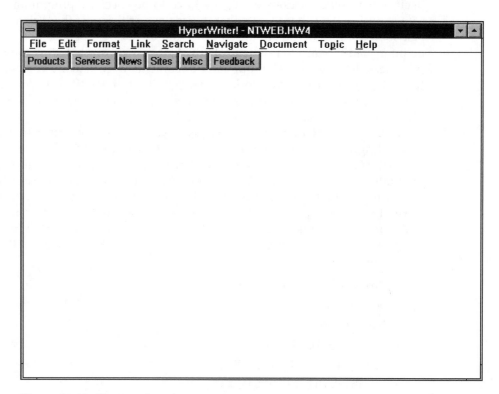

Figure 18.18 The user interface we want to create.

each topic so that a reader could access the user interface without having to go to the end of the topic.

Another issue facing us with respect to this user interface is whether the interface we create should be a static interface or an adaptive interface. Under a static interface, the interface remains fixed wherever it is used. With an adaptive interface, the interface adapts to what you are reading. Consider the interface shown in Figure 18.17. The first button is a **Products** button, which lets you navigate to the **Products** page. With an adaptive interface approach, when the reader is viewing the **Products** page, the **Products** button isn't there. The logic here is that if the user is at a particular page, there is no reason to present the user with a button to jump to that page. This is a point that while I agree with intellectually, my many years of practical experience argue quite strongly against it. The first reason is that a reader becomes comfortable with a user interface and when that user interface changes (even subtly), this disorients the user and makes browsing the material more difficult. Along with this is that an adaptive interface defeats the user's natural tendency to get used to clicking on a button located in a particular location. For example, frequent visitors to a site become used to clicking of the button located furthest to the left to jump to **Products**. With an **Adaptive** interface, sometimes this works and sometimes it doesn't, leading again to disorientation.

NOTE: A practical note about using adaptive interfaces is that from the perspective of the person creating the user interface they are significantly more difficult as you have to create what amounts to a custom interface everywhere the interface is used.

A final note about adaptive interfaces is really a more general note about interface design for digital publications. When designing an interface, the temptation as a designer is to implement something that is very subtle, if not tricky. Adaptive interfaces are a good example of this type of subtlety. To a designer this is the type of wonderful thing that all of feel makes our work unique and different. And I will agree that it can certainly make one's work unique. However, making ones work unique doesn't necessarily make it good. The problem with this type of subtlety is really quite simple—readers often just don't get it. When you are a reader of a digital publication, your focus is very often just to get into the publication, retrieve some information, and get out again. You often aren't concerned with these subtleties. I don't mean this statement as a criticism of using subtle features in design, it is more an observation derived from seeing a tremendous number of digital publications, only to find that I, too, "didn't get it." Given that you are a designer and that you probably do like to build subtlety into your publications, can this be done effectively to add value to your digital publications? The answer is definitely yes—with some guidelines. The first guideline is to test your digital publications on your audience to make sure that they understand what you are trying to do. This alone goes a long way to helping you detect this type of problem in your publications. The second guideline is simple and obvious—include a section in your documents that explains the subtleties. If you are going to use an adaptive interface then make sure that people understand this (or at least have the opportunity to find out why).

Although we have had to cover quite a bit of background information about user interfaces for the Web, we are now ready to begin creating the interface for our site. The first step is for us to navigate to a section of the site where the user interface is needed. As this user interface provides navigation between the different topics in the site, it isn't needed as part of the actual Home page—the icons there provide navigation already. What we'll do is go to the **Products** topic and create our user interface there.

Navigating to the Products Topic

Select the **Products** icon. This takes you to the **Products** topic, which is blank.

As you probably remember, all that we have created to date is the framework for our Web site. We haven't actually added any content to our pages. This is why our **Products** topic is blank. Now that we are at our **Products** topic, how do we go about creating this user interface? As we think about it, we realize that this interface really isn't any different from the interface that we already created for Home page. The only difference is the icons that are displayed. Although we could create this interface again from scratch using our text buttons instead of our icons, we can also just copy the existing interface and then change the buttons. This would be significantly easier, as we wouldn't have to create the links a second time and this is the approach we will use.

The first step is for us to go back to the Home page (topic 1) and copy the interface.

Copying the Existing Interface

1. Select the **Goto** command from the **Navigate** menu.
2. Enter a 1 into the **New Topic** field and select the **Goto Topic** button.
3. Mark the icons and the links surrounding them as a block, and select the **Copy** command from the **Edit** menu. Given that you are copying hypertext links, using **Shift+Arrowkey** is easier than using the mouse. Make sure that you copy both lines of icons, as we will need all of them.
4. Press **Esc** or **Right Mouse** button to move back to the **Products** topic.

With our original icon-based interface copied, we need to paste our interface in and then customize it by replacing the icons with the text buttons.

Customizing the User Interface—1

1. Select the **Paste** command from the **Edit** menu. This pastes in the links and icons that you just copied.

2. Move your cursor after the first link symbol on the left of the **Products** icon. This changes the **Insert Object** command on the **Edit** menu to an **Edit Object** command.

3. Select the **Edit Object** command from the **Edit** menu.

4. Select the **Set File** button.

5. Select .PCX as the format for the object.

6. Select BTPROD.PCX as the object to display.

7. Select the **OK** button to close the **Import Picture Object** dialog box. This inserts the picture object shown in Figure 18.19 (after you have edited the object, you may have to press **Alt+R** to redraw the screen).

As you can see, the **Products** icon has been replaced with a text button titled "Products." This button will initially be lined up with the top edge of the

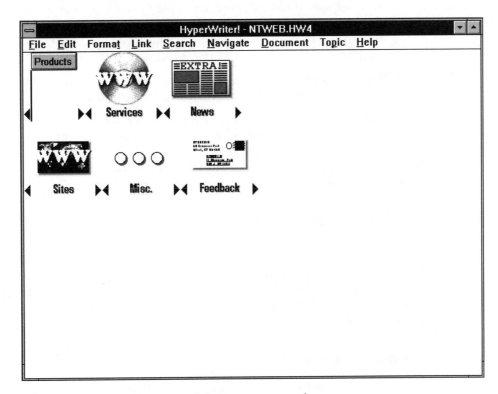

Figure 18.19 Converting one of the icons to a text button.

other icons. When all the icons have been changed to a text-button format, they all will line up. Customizing the rest of the user interface is covered below.

Customizing the User Interface—2

1. Position your cursor as described above and change the **Services** icon to the file BTSVCS.PCX.

2. Position your cursor as described above and change the **News** icon to the file BTNEWS.PCX.

3. Position your cursor as described above and change the **Sites** icon to the file BTSITES.PCX.

4. Position your cursor as described above and change the **Miscellaneous** icon to the file BTMISC.PCX.

5. Position your cursor as described above and change the **Feedback** icon to the file TFEEDBK.PCX. After you have edited the objects, you may have to press **Alt+R** to redraw the screen to see the edits.

   After changing the **Feedback** icon to a text button, we need to convert the user interface from two screen lines to one screen line. This is done by just deleting the carriage return separating the two lines.

6. Press **Home** to move to the beginning of the line with the **Feedback** icon.

7. Press **Backspace** to delete the carriage return separating the two lines. This creates the user interface shown in Figure 18.20.

We have now completed the user interface we want to use throughout the body of our Web site. The next step is for us to copy the interface, and then paste it into the different main topics that make up our site. As we add additional pages within each of those topics then we will also need to paste it into those topics as well. The first step is to copy the interface.

Copying the Existing Interface

Mark the text buttons and the links surrounding them as a block and select the **Copy** command from the **Edit** menu. Given that you are copying hypertext links, using **Shift+Arrowkey** is easier than using the mouse.

Now that we have a copy of our user interface, we want to paste it into the topics that are needed. The easiest way to do this is to actually use the interface itself to navigate to those topics.

Pasting in the Interface

1. Click on the **Services** button to jump to that page.

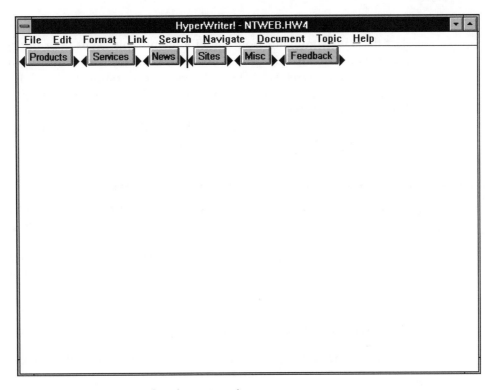

Figure 18.20 Our completed user interface.

2. Select the **Paste** command from the **Edit** menu. This pastes in the interface.

3. Click on the **News** button to jump to that page.

4. Select the **Paste** command from the **Edit** menu. This pastes in the interface.

5. Click on the **Sites** button to jump to that page.

6. Select the **Paste** command from the **Edit** menu. This pastes in the interface.

7. Click on the **Misc** button to jump to that page.

8. Select the **Paste** command from the **Edit** menu. This pastes in the interface.

9. Click on the **Feedback** button to jump to that page.

10. Select the **Paste** command from the **Edit** menu. This pastes in the interface.

At the end of this step, we need to save our work.

Saving Our Electronic Publication

Select the **Save** command from the **File** menu. This saves your document and completes the task of designing our interface and then inserting it into the main topics of our Web site. The tasks we have accomplished to date are really those that can be considered defining the architecture of the Web site, its over-all structure and its basic presentation to the user. At this point, we are ready to start working with the content that makes up the body of our Web site and the additional topics that will contain this content.

Step 4: Adding Content to Our Web Site Products Page

The Products page describes NTERGAID's HyperWriter product line. This page is going to contain a number of different hypertext links, each covering a different aspect of the HyperWriter product line.

The first step in authoring our Products page is adding a title at the top of the page that indicates that the reader is currently viewing the Products section of the Web site.

Authoring the Products Page: Adding a Title

1. From the Home page or the user interface at the bottom of every topic, click on the icon/button for the Products page.
2. Press **Enter** to move the user interface down one line.
3. Move up to the blank line you just added.
4. Enter the title "Information on HyperWriter Products."
5. Select the **Apply Tag** command from the **Format** menu. Select the HTML tag **HTML_H1**. This formats your Products page as shown in Figure 18.21.

As we look at our Web page for Products, the first thing that comes to mind is that it is quite plain and not really very attractive. If you recall that one of our initial goals was to produce an attractive Web site, we clearly have a problem. In thinking about what could be done to address this problem, we see one constraint—we don't really want to create any more graphics to improve the look of the site. As we look at the site, it comes to mind that we could insert the icon for each area of the site at the top of each page in the site, reinforcing where the user is. Not only would this improve the look of the site, but it also would help users navigate because adding this icon would provide constant, visual reinforcement regarding the user's position in the Web site. To add this icon, we'll use the **Insert Object** command on the **Edit** menu.

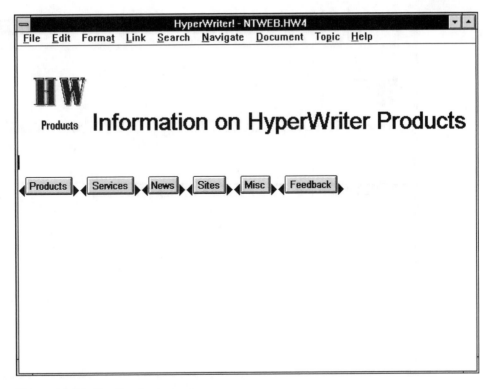

Figure 18.21 The Products page.

Authoring the Products Page: Adding an Icon

1. Place the cursor at the beginning of the first line on the screen (the line where the title is located).
2. Select the **Insert Object** command from the **Edit** menu.
3. Select the **Set File** button.
4. Select .PCX as the format to insert.
5. Select PRODS.PCX as the picture to insert.
6. Select the **OK** button to close the **Import Picture Object** dialog box.
7. Press **End** and then **Enter** after inserting the picture object to add a blank line.
8. Select the **Apply Tag** command from the **Format** menu and format the current paragraph as **Body Text**. This step has just added a blank line to our Products page where we'll import our content. This formats your Products page as shown in Figure 18.22.

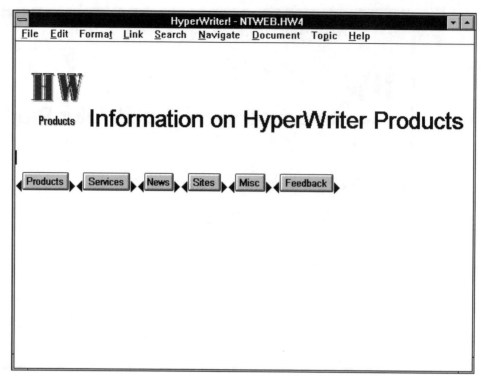

Figure 18.22 The Products page with title and icon.

As you can see, adding the icon has nicely enhanced the appearance of our Products page. We'll use this technique throughout our Web site to improve the appearance of pages. Adding the title and icon, as well as our user interface, to a page will generally be the first step in authoring all our Web pages from this point on. This could be referred to as establishing the *framework* for our Web pages, as this provides the required structure we want every page to follow.

With the basic structure of the Products page created, we need to add the content page. This content is going to be based on information imported from a number of different word-processing files we have that we want to publish on the Web. The approach that we are going to take with these files is very simple—we'll import all of them using HyperWriter's multiple file import and then determine how to handle them. As we have a company standard that each file start with a first-level heading style, the Import Text Wizard should be able to convert all of them to hypertext links and topics. Once they are converted to links and topics, it will be easier for us to manipulate them and organize them into a good Web page. You should note that this approach of simply importing all our word-processing files, without concern to their logical order, is very different from what we did in Chapter 17, where we used the multiple file import. In Chapter 17 we wanted to import the contents of our book catalog so that the next and previous order followed the original alphabetical order of the catalog itself. To do this, we had to import the files in alphabetical order or Hyper-Writer would incorrectly create the next-and-previous order. As the Web lacks the next-and-previous concept entirely, we can import our word processing files in any order and then organize them as needed.

The first task is to import our product literature files.

Authoring the Products Page—Importing Content

1. Select the **Import Text** command from the **File** menu.

2. Select WordPerfect as the format to import.

3. Select the **Another** button. This expands HyperWriter's **Import** dialog box so that multiple documents can be selected. The documents to import are listed at the bottom of this dialog box.

4. Select the document APP_PRO.WP and then select the **Another** button. This adds it to the list of documents to import.

5. Select the document CATALOG.WP and then select the **Another** button.

6. Continue selecting each of the documents that make up our catalog in the following order: CDROMPRO.WP, CHOOSEPRO.WP, COBUYALL. WP, COPIESHW.WP, HELPDESK.WP, HR2.WP, HW40FEA1.WP, HW40SPEC.WP, HW42_WEB.WP, HWCOPYWR.WP, HWCOURSE.WP, HWPRO_1.WP, HWPROFI1.WP, HWTSPEC.WP, PRICING.WP, SEARCH.WP, UNIQUE.WP, and WINHELP.WP. Be careful not to select a document twice as this will import the document two times. When you are done selecting all the documents, you should see the dialog box as shown in Figure 18.23.

7. Select the **Import All** command to begin the import process. This displays the **Import Text Wizard** dialog box shown in Figure 18.24.

8. Set the first option, the **Linking Method**, to Based on **HEADING1-HEADING?** tags. The documents we are importing are WordPerfect documents using heading styles. This option creates a hypertext topic and link at every place a stylesheet tag named **HEADING#** is located. Leave the **Last Used Heading or Level Number** field set to 6, as we want all levels of headings linked.

9. Leave all other options set to their default positions. This completes setting the Import Text Wizard to function for our document. Select the **OK** button for it to begin importing your document. When it is complete, you will see the table of contents that the Import Text Wizard creates.

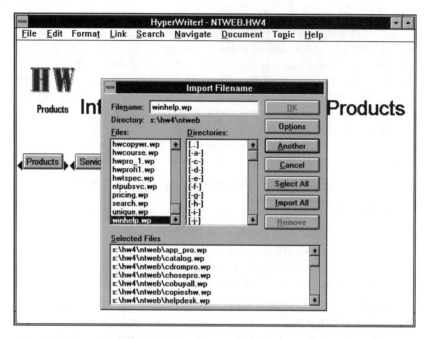

Figure 18.23 Importing multiple documents.

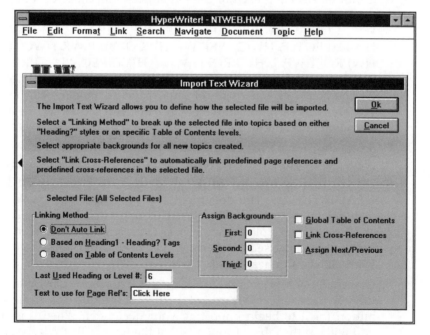

Figure 18.24 The Import Text Wizard.

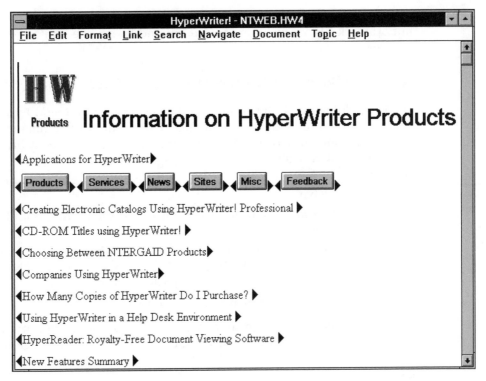

Figure 18.25 The results of the Import Text Wizard.

We have now imported our document into HyperWriter and created our links automatically. A picture of how your screen should appear is shown in Figure 18.25.

As you can see from Figure 18.25, our Products page now contains a series of links, our user interface (which is, oddly enough, now in the middle of our links), and a text message regarding the copyright status of this information.

If you were to activate any of the links created by the Import Text Wizard, what you would notice is that HyperWriter would be extremely slow. This is the result of using the Import Text Wizard where virtually every topic is open and a lot of memory is being used. By saving our document, we will increase performance dramatically.

Saving Our Electronic Publication

Select the **Save** command from the **File** menu. This saves your document.

With all our content imported, what we need to do is convert it all to an organized, usable, and attractive Web page. The first task we want to tackle is moving our user interface back to the bottom of this page. It is located in the middle of our links due to an anomaly in how HyperWriter's multiple file import works. What we'll do is cut it out and then paste it into the bottom of the page.

Authoring the Products Page—Moving the User Interface

1. Mark the text buttons (and the links surrounding them) located in the middle of our links as a block and select the **Cut** command from the **Edit** menu. Given that you are copying hypertext links, using **Shift+Arrowkey** is easier than using the mouse.

2. Move to the end of the current topic by pressing **Ctrl+End** or by using the scroll bar.

3. Press **End** and then **Enter** after inserting the picture object to add a blank line.

4. Select the **Apply Tag** command from the **Format** menu and format the current paragraph as **Body Text**. This step has just added a blank line to our Products page where we can paste in our user interface.

5. Select the **Paste** command from the **Edit** menu.

After pasting in our user interface, we need to move the copyright statement from the middle of our links to the end of this page, just before the user interface.

Authoring the Products Page—Moving the Copyright Statement

1. Move to the top of the Products page using **Ctrl+Home** or the scroll bar.

2. Mark the copyright statement, the text starting "TM HyperWriter," as a block.

3. Select the **Cut** command from the **Edit** menu.

4. Move to the end of the current topic by pressing **Ctrl+End** or by using the scroll bar.

5. Press **Enter** at the beginning of the user interface to insert a blank line where the copyright statement can be pasted in.

6. Select the **Paste** command from the **Edit** menu. This places our copyright statement at the bottom of the page before the user interface, as shown in Figure 18.26.

Now that we have moved the copyright statement and our user interface, what we have left is a series of hypertext links that we need to organize into our Products page. The way we'll organize these hypertext links is to use the **Cut-and-Paste** commands to group related information together. The first step

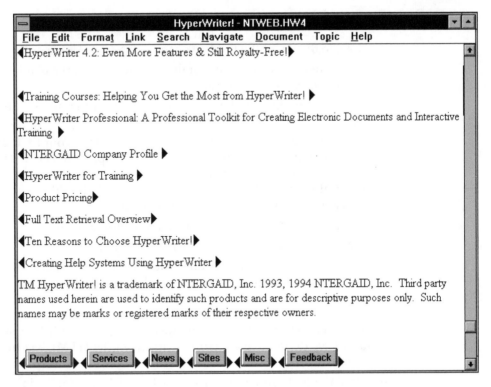

Figure 18.26 The copyright statement and user interface.

in doing this is to decide how this information is related. By looking at the different links, I can see that there are really four basic categories of information here.

- HyperWriter
- HyperWriter for Training
- HyperWriter Professional
- Other topics

This information is all about our HyperWriter products, some of it specifically related to HyperWriter and some of it only generally related (such as technical white papers). What we will do is group our information into these four categories along the structure of an outline. Although not a perfect approach to Web authoring, an outline offers a good, organized structure for people to use in accessing information. The first step in this is adding these four categories to the beginning of our Products page.

Authoring the Products Page—Adding Categories

1. Move to the top of the Products page using **Ctrl+Home** or the scroll bar.

2. Press **Enter** at the beginning of the first link to insert a blank line where we can place our categories.

3. Move up one line so the cursor is located on the blank line you just inserted.

4. Enter the text "Information About HyperWriter" as our first category.

   After entering our first tag, we need to apply an HTML tag so that it has the correct appearance when we save our document to HTML. As we already used an **H1** tag in this topic, we should use an **H2** tag as this category is really a second-level heading.

5. Select the **Apply Tag** command from the **Format** menu.

6. Select the **HTML_H2** tag and then the **OK** button.

7. Press **Enter** to add a blank line where we can add entries in the category. Press **Enter** to add another blank line where we can add another category.

   When you press **Enter** at the end of text with a particular tag or style, HyperWriter formats the next paragraph with that style. This means we don't have to continue applying the **HTML_H2** to our categories.

8. Enter the text "Information About HyperWriter for Training" as our second category and press **Enter** twice (once for adding items in the category and once for the blank line for the next category).

9. Enter the text "Information About HyperWriter Professional" as our third category and press **Enter** twice.

10. Enter the text "Other Topics" as our fourth category and press **Enter**. After entering our four categories, your screen should appear as shown in Figure 18.27.

With our categories established, we need to move our links so they are located within the different categories at the blank lines we inserted. The first category where we'll put information is the Other Topics category, as it is pretty easy to decide what information falls into this category.

Putting Information into Categories—Other Topics

1. Mark the link "Applications for HyperWriter" as a block using **Shift+Arrowkey**.

2. Select the **Cut** command from the **Edit** menu command to cut this link to the clipboard.

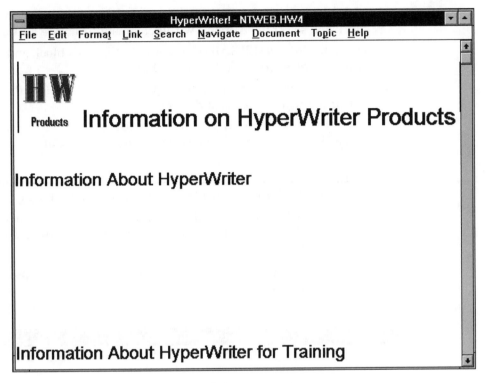

Figure 18.27 The Products page with four categories.

3. Mark the link "Creating Electronic Catalogs Using HyperWriter! Professional" as a block.

4. Select the **Append w/Cut** command from the **Edit** menu.

   The **Append w/Cut** command is very useful for gathering information. It takes the link we selected and adds it to the link we already cut. This lets us use a single **Paste** command to paste in all the links under the **Other Topics** category.

5. Mark the link "CD-ROM Titles using HyperWriter!" as a block and select the **Append w/Cut** command from the **Edit** menu.

6. Mark the link "Choosing Between NTERGAID Products" as a block and select the **Append w/Cut** command from the **Edit** menu.

7. Mark the link "Companies Using HyperWriter" as a block and select the **Append w/Cut** command from the **Edit** menu.

8. Mark the link "How Many Copies of HyperWriter Do I Purchase?" as a block and select the **Append w/Cut** command from the **Edit** menu.

9. Mark the link "Using HyperWriter in a Help Desk Environment" as a block and select the **Append w/Cut** command from the **Edit** menu.

10. Mark the link "NTERGAID Company Profile" as a block and select the **Append w/Cut** command from the **Edit** menu.

11. Mark the link "Product Pricing" as a block and select the **Append w/Cut** command from the **Edit** menu.

12. Mark the link "Training Courses: Helping You Get the Most from HyperWriter!" as a block and select the **Append w/Cut** command from the **Edit** menu.

13. Mark the link "Creating Help Systems Using HyperWriter" as a block and select the **Append w/Cut** command from the **Edit** menu.

14. Move under the category Other Topics and select the **Paste** command from the **Edit** menu. After doing this, your screen should appear as shown in Figure 18.28.

With our Other Topics category created, we are ready to start putting items into the HyperWriter Professional category.

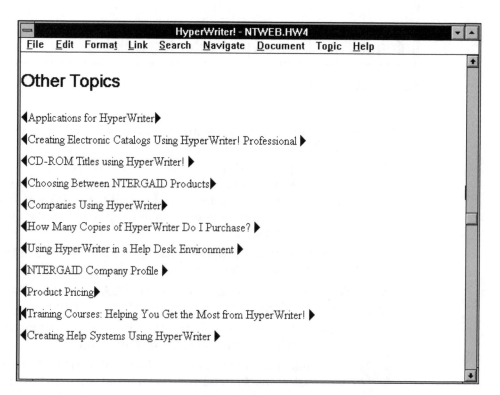

Figure 18.28 Items in the Other Topics category.

Putting Information into Categories—HyperWriter Professional

1. Mark the link "HyperWriter Professional:..." as a block using **Shift+ Arrowkey**.
2. Select the **Cut** command from the **Edit** menu command to cut this link to the clipboard.
3. Move under the category HyperWriter Professional and select the **Paste** command from the **Edit** menu.

With the HyperWriter Professional category created, the next category we want to put information in is the HyperWriter for Training category.

Putting Information into Categories—HyperWriter for Training

1. Mark the link "HyperWriter for Training" as a block using **Shift+ Arrowkey**.
2. Select the **Cut** command from the **Edit** menu command to cut this link to the clipboard.
3. Move under the category HyperWriter for Training and select the **Paste** command from the **Edit** menu.

The final category we need to organize is the HyperWriter category. We'll add the remaining links to this category.

Putting Information into Categories—HyperWriter

1. Mark the link "HyperWriter 4.2: Even More Features & Still Royalty-Free!" as a block using **Shift+Arrowkey**.
2. Select the **Cut** command from the **Edit** menu command to cut this link to the clipboard.
3. Mark the link "HyperWriter 4: Product Specifications" as a block and select the **Append w/Cut** command from the **Edit** menu.
4. Mark the link "Full Text Retrieval Overview" as a block and select the **Append w/Cut** command from the **Edit** menu.
5. Mark the link "Ten Reasons to Choose HyperWriter!" as a block and select the **Append w/Cut** command from the **Edit** menu.
6. Mark the link "HyperReader: Royalty-Free Document Viewing Software" as a block and select the **Append w/Cut** command from the **Edit** menu.
7. Mark the link "New Features Summary" as a block and select the **Append w/Cut** command from the **Edit** menu.
8. Move under the category HyperWriter and select the **Paste** command from the **Edit** menu.

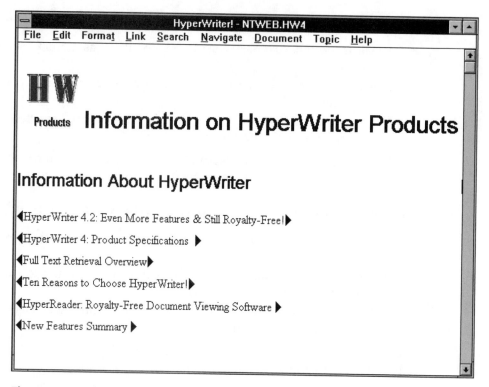

Figure 18.29 The Products page with links in all categories.

This completes organizing our information into categories. Your screen should now appear as shown in Figure 18.29.

As we look at the content in the Products page, we realize that the appearance of our different links is not really very good. Each link appears simply as unformatted text. If you have ever done any Web authoring or read Chapter 4, you probably realize that the way these links would normally be formatted is using a list item tag which produces a nicely formatted, bulleted list in a Web browser. What we could do is mark a block covering the links in each category and apply our **HTML_UL LI** tag (unordered list, list item) to the block. What this would do is nicely format each of these links with the correct **HTML** tag. Before we do this, let's see what tag these links currently use.

Examining the Tags on a Link

Place your cursor on any of the links in any of the categories and select the **Apply Tag** command from the **Format** menu. This displays the **Apply Tag** dialog box, which shows what tag is currently in use for a paragraph. This dialog box is shown in Figure 18.30.

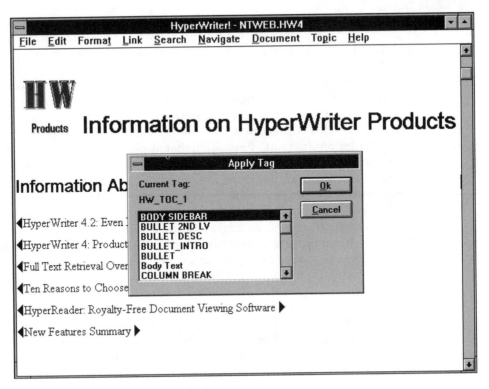

Figure 18.30 The **Apply Tag** dialog box.

As we look at the **Apply Tag** dialog box, we see that our link has the tag **HW_TOC_1**. As we know we didn't apply this tag to our link, how was this tag applied? When the Import Text Wizard brings text into HyperWriter, it automatically applies a tag in the format **HW_TOC_#** where "#" is a number from 1 to 9 indicating the level of the original information to any links it creates. Given that we have a tag applied to all our links, do we need to retag the links so they can have the appearance of the bulleted list we want? Fortunately, the answer is no. When you use the **Save As HTML** command, it allows you to map the different tags in your document to their HTML equivalent. Thus, we can map all tags with the name **HW_TOC_1** to a **UL LI** tag. This makes our authoring a Web site very easy when we are working with tagged data.

As you can see, with this approach to authoring a Web page, we are not operating in a very WYSIWYG (what you see is what you get) fashion in that there is nothing that visually distinguishes text formatted with a **HW_TOC_1** tag from any other text. If we wanted to, we could set up a HyperWriter stylesheet tag that had the appearance of the **HTML UL LI** tag that we ultimately will map this tag to. While we aren't going to do this now, it is a useful technique to make authoring your Web pages easier. Later in this chapter, as we start applying more of the built-in **HTML_** tags, you will notice that our standard HTML_12.HWT stylesheet has the standard Web browser formatting built in.

Now that we understand how our links are tagged, as we look further at our categories of information it becomes clear that some of our categories (HyperWriter for Training and HyperWriter Professional) don't have enough information. This is because both these products share features with the basic HyperWriter product but information that applies to all three products is available only under the HyperWriter category. This is something that we're not going to address now, but if we were going to do so, we would probably add some of the information to both the HyperWriter for Training and HyperWriter Professional categories. To indicate that the same information was being referenced in both categories, we might add the text "See Also: " at the beginning of the link. This is one great strength of using hypertext that many people don't always take advantage of—information can exist in one place (with only one copy to maintain and update), but pointers to that information can exist in many places.

In addition to making some of the HyperWriter information available from the HyperWriter Professional and HyperWriter for Training categories, another technique to make the Products page better would be to cross-reference related information. For example, when you view the NTERGAID Company Profile, you will realize that it could be cross-referenced to the Services Web page. These cross-referencing links can be created using the **Link to Text** command on the **Link** menu. Although we won't create any of these links now, it should be kept in mind when you author your own Web pages.

With the content for the Products page imported, linked, and organized, the next step is to add the user interface to each page that is linked from this topic. The first step in doing this is copying the existing interface.

Copying the Existing Interface

Mark the text buttons across the bottom of the current page and the links surrounding them as a block and select the **Copy** command from the **Edit** menu. Given that you are copying hypertext links, using **Shift+Arrowkey** is easier than using the mouse.

With our interface copied to the clipboard, we can now paste it into each topic that is linked to this page.

Adding the User Interface to Topics

1. Activate the first link in the Products page by clicking on it with **Left Mouse** button.

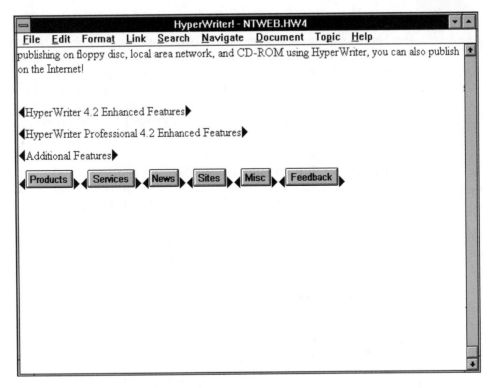

Figure 18.31 Pasting in the interface.

2. Move to the end of the topic by pressing **Ctrl+End**.

3. Press **Enter** to add a blank line where our user interface can be located.

4. Select the Apply Tag command from the Format menu and change the tag for the current paragraph to **BODY TEXT** if it isn't that already.

5. Select the **Paste** command from the **Edit** menu to paste in the interface. A picture of how your screen should appear is shown in Figure 18.31.

6. Press the **Esc** key to return to the Products page.

7. Continue activating the links from the Products page and paste in the user interface as needed. When you are done, press **Esc** to move back to the Products page. At the end of this step, we need to save our work.

With our Products page completed, the next page to author is the Services page.

Saving Our Electronic Publication

Select the **Save** command from the **File** menu. This saves your document.

Step 5: Adding Content to Our Web Site—Services Page

The Services page describes NTERGAID's electronic publishing service; as a full-service organization, NTERGAID also provides electronic publishing services. This describes our services and also covers some of the sample projects we have been involved with. Unlike the Products page which offers a number of different links, the Services page is very simple, offering only a few links.

The first step in authoring our Services page is to add the Services title and the **Services** icon.

Authoring the Services Page—Adding an Icon and Title

1. From the Home page or the user interface at the bottom of every topic, click on the icon/button for the Services page.
2. Press **Enter** to move the user interface down one line.
3. Move up to the blank line you just added.
4. Select the **Insert Object** command from the **Edit** menu.
5. Select the **Set File** button.
6. Select .PCX as the format to insert.
7. Select SERVICES.PCX as the picture to insert.
8. Select the **OK** button to close the **Import Picture Object** dialog box.
9. Move to the end of the picture object by pressing **End**.
10. Enter the title "NTERGAID Publishing Services."
11. Select the **Apply Tag** command from the **Format** menu. Select the HTML tag **HTML_H1**. This formats your Services page as shown in Figure 18.32.

With the basic structure of the Services page created, we need to add the content for this page. This content is fairly simple, based on a single sheet of product literature that describes our publishing services. The first task is to import this product literature file.

Authoring the Services Page—Importing Content

1. Select the **Import Text** command from the **File** menu.
2. Select WordPerfect as the format to import.
3. Select the **Options** button and make sure the **Use Tag Names** option is turned on. Select the **OK** button to close the **Options** dialog box.
4. Select the document NTPUBSVC.WP from the list of documents to import.
5. The Import Text Wizard is now displayed.

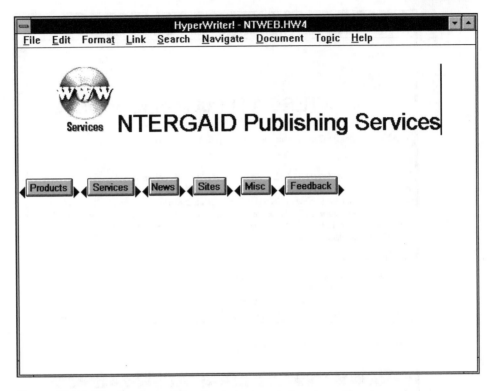

Figure 18.32 The Services page.

6. Set the first option, the Linking Method, to Based on **HEADING1-HEADING?** tags so that we create a topic at every first-level heading style.

7. This completes setting the Import Text Wizard to function for our document. Select the **OK** button for it to begin importing your document. When it is complete, you will see the document shown in Figure 18.33.

The text in the Services page is actually quite long. If we scroll down to the bottom of the topic, we can see the hypertext links created by the Import Text Wizard as shown in Figure 18.34.

Now that you have seen this document, I have to admit that for this tutorial I actually "cheated" a bit. In the original version of the NTPUBSVC.WP file, there was not a **CENTER** tag. Instead, each of the items that were tagged as **CENTER** were actually a **HEAD2** tag. As I knew when we would be building this page, I didn't want the items currently tagged as **CENTER** to be broken into topics, so I went into the WordPerfect file and changed the style of these items from a **HEAD2** style to a **CENTER** style. By leaving the last few items in the document as **HEAD2**, I ensured that they would be broken into separate

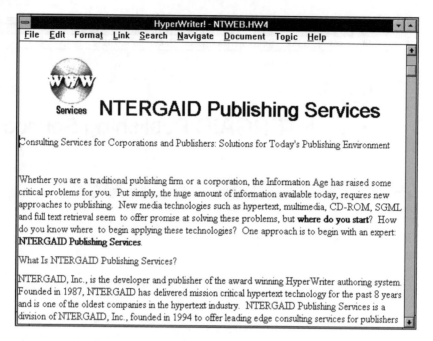

Figure 18.33 The Services page (top).

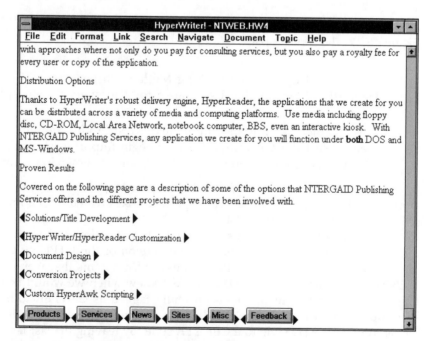

Figure 18.34 The Services page (bottom).

pages as I desired. This is a good example of how a simple modification to the word-processing source file can make creating a digital publication much easier.

When you scrolled through this page, you probably noted that it is longer than many of the pages that we have created that are directly from the Home page. Unlike the Products page, which is really composed solely of links with a little bit of text, this page is primarily text with only a few links. The reasons that I chose this approach for the Services page are threefold. The first reason was that I wanted to maintain the continuity of this information. If you actually read the content in this page then you will note that the section that is broken up is actually specific examples of publishing projects we have been involved in. By formatting this information as I did, the reader views this page as a continuous block of information rather than as bits and pieces where they choose what they want to read. The second reason that I kept this information primarily as a single, scrolling page was that I suspected that people would print out this page fairly regularly as they considered using our publishing services. By formatting it as a single scrolling page, someone can print all the information rather than going to several different pages and using the **Print** command in their Web browser from each page. The third and final reason that I chose this approach was actually much more pragmatic—I wanted to illustrate a different style of authoring a Web page than we have used thus far.

As noted in the previous section on authoring the Products page, we don't need to retag our content using **HTML** tags when our content already has tags (the **Save As HTML** command can map these tags to **HTML** format). To save you the effort of looking, I can confirm that our content does have tags. You should note that this is hard to see right now as our tags are unformatted and there is little, if anything, to distinguish one tag from another.

With the content for the Services page imported, the next step is to add the user interface to each page that is linked from this topic. The first step in doing this is copying the existing interface.

Copying the Existing Interface

Mark the text buttons across the bottom of the current page and the links surrounding them as a block and select the **Copy** command from the **Edit** menu. Given that you are copying hypertext links, using **Shift+Arrowkey** is easier than using the mouse.

With our interface copied to the clipboard, we can now paste it into each topic that is linked to this page.

Adding the User Interface to Topics

1. Activate the first link, "Solutions/Title Development" by clicking on it with **Left Mouse** button.
2. Move to the end of the topic by pressing **Ctrl+End**.

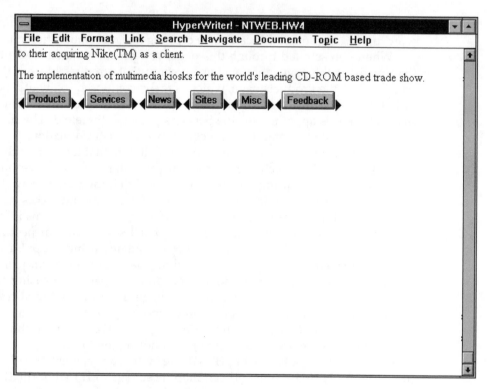

Figure 18.35 Pasting in the interface.

3. Press **Enter** to add a blank line where our user interface can be located.

4. Select the **Apply Tag** command from the **Format** menu and change the tag for the current paragraph to **BODY TEXT** if it isn't that already.

5. Select the **Paste** command from the **Edit** menu to paste in the interface. A picture of how your screen should appear is shown in Figure 18.35.

6. Press the **Esc** key to return to the Services page.

7. Continue activating the links from the Services page and paste in the user interface as needed. When you are done, press **Esc** to move back to the Services page.

With our Services page completed, the next page to author is the News page.

At the end of this step, we need to save our work.

Saving Our Electronic Publication

Select the **Save** command from the **File** menu. This saves your document.

Step 6: Adding Content to Our Home Page—News Page

The News page offers an archive of News about NTERGAID. This page contains all of the press releases that NTERGAID has ever released, dating back to 1987 when NTERGAID was founded. This body of information lets a reader of our Web site research almost any aspect of NTERGAID's HyperWriter product line including how the product has evolved over time.

The first step in authoring our News page is to add the News title and the **News** icon.

Authoring the News Page—Adding an Icon and Title

1. From the Home page or the user interface at the bottom of every topic, click on the icon/button for the News page.
2. Press **Enter** to move the user interface down one line.
3. Move up to the blank line you just added.
4. Select the **Insert Object** command from the **Edit** menu.
5. Select the **Set File** button.
6. Select .PCX as the format to insert.
7. Select NEWS.PCX as the picture to insert.
8. Select the **OK** button to close the **Import Picture Object** dialog box.
9. Move to the end of the picture object by pressing **End**.
10. Enter the title "News About HyperWriter."
11. Select the **Apply Tag** command from the **Format** menu. Select the HTML tag **HTML_H1**. This formats your Miscellaneous page as we formatted our other pages.
12. Press **Enter** to add a blank line.
13. Select the **Apply Tag** command from the **Format** menu and select the **BODY TEXT** tag for this paragraph.

With the basic structure of the News page created, we need to add the content for this page. Over the years that NTERGAID has been publishing press releases, we used a very simple approach for writing these. Every press release was written and then stored in a single Microsoft Word document, organized with the most current press release at the beginning of the file and the oldest at the end of the file. The beginning of each press release is formatted with a **HEAD1** style. This approach lets us use the Import Text Wizard to automatically bring our press releases into our News page, converting them into individual Web pages as they are imported.

Authoring the News Page—Importing Content

1. Select the **Import Text** command from the **File** menu.

2. Select Word as the format to import.

3. Select the **Options** button and make sure the **Use Tag Names** option is turned on. Select the **OK** button to close the **Options** dialog box.

4. Select the document NTPRESS.DOC from the list of documents to import.

5. The Import Text Wizard is now displayed.

6. Set the first option, the **Linking Method**, to Based on **HEADING1-HEADING?** tags so that we create a topic at every first-level heading style. Enter a "1" in the **Last Used Heading or Level Number** field as our press releases only have one level of heading.

7. Turn on the **Link Cross-References** option to convert any word-processor cross-references to hypertext links.

NOTE: At this point we don't know if there are any word processor cross-references in our documents, but it is better to link them if they exist than not link them at all.

---

8. Leave the **Text to Use for Page Ref's** option at its default setting. This option lets you specify a text string to use when a converted hypertext link has no text (i.e., the link was originally around a page number).

9. This completes setting the Import Text Wizard to function for our document. Select the **OK** button for it to begin importing your document. When it is complete, you will see the table of contents that the Import Text Wizard creates.

We have now imported our press releases into HyperWriter and created our links automatically. A picture of how your screen should appear is shown in Figure 18.36.

As you can see, our News page is now basically a table of contents of links to different press releases. Your first thought is probably that we need to improve the appearance of the table of contents because as you can see, it is currently unformatted text—or is it? As you look at the table of contents, I will agree that it appears unformatted. However, if you were to place the cursor on an entry in the table of contents, you would find out that when HyperWriter created these links, it also applied a style, **HW_TOC_1**, to each of these links. Although this style may not have an appearance that we like, with respect to the Web this is really irrelevant. When we create our HTML files using the

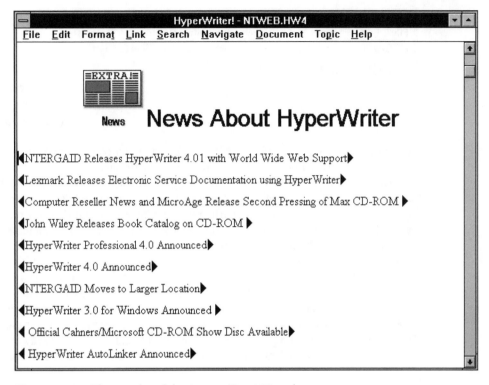

Figure 18.36 The results of the Import Text Wizard.

Save As HTML command, we can simply map this tag to an HTML tag that will create the appearance that we want (probably a list item tag).

As we have now imported our press releases and created (and formatted) a table of contents to all the press releases, you might think we are done with this section of our Web site. Before continuing, we should take a look at the contents of one of these press releases to see if we need to format it any further.

Examining a Sample Press Release

1. Activate the first link in the list of press releases. This displays the press release shown in Figure 18.37.

   As you can see, this press release comes in partially formatted, with a title that is left justified and actually smaller than the body text font, and the text of the press release has paragraphs that are both left and right justified. What we need to do is look at the tags that are used for these elements.

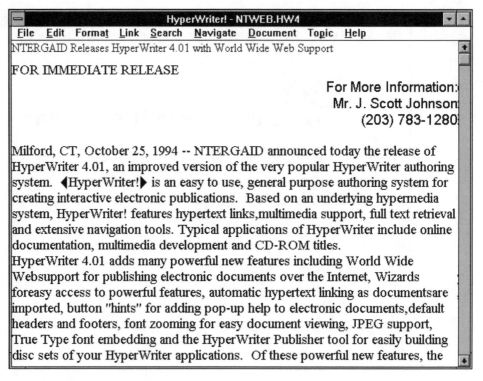

Figure 18.37 A sample press release.

2. Place the cursor on the text starting "For More Information" and select the **Apply Tag** command from the **Format** menu. This shows you that the tag **CONTACT** is used for this paragraph. Select the **Cancel** button to close this dialog box.

3. Press **Esc** to move back to the beginning of the News page.

By looking at the tags that format our press release (there are other tags as well), we can see that these tags are not standard HTML. As this content came from a word processor, this really isn't surprising. Given that the tags aren't HTML format, the question arises whether we need to change the tags that are used for this text. Although we could do this, it isn't really necessary. What we will do, instead, is map these tags to HTML format when we save this document using the **Save As HTML** command.

By looking at the sample press release, you may have noticed that we hadn't added the user interface to each press release. This is the final task for authoring the News page. The first step in doing this is copying the existing interface.

Copying the Existing Interface

Mark the text buttons across the bottom of the current page and the links surrounding them as a block, and select the **Copy** command from the **Edit** menu. Given that you are copying hypertext links, using **Shift+Arrowkey** is easier than using the mouse.

With our interface copied to the clipboard, we can now paste it into each topic that is linked to this page.

Adding the User Interface to Topics

1. Activate the link to the first press release by clicking on it with the **Left Mouse** button.
2. Move to the end of the topic by pressing **Ctrl+End**.
3. Press **Enter** to add a blank line where our user interface can be located.
4. Select the **Apply Tag** command from the **Format** menu and change the tag for the current paragraph to **BODY TEXT** if it isn't that already.
5. Select the **Paste** command from the **Edit** menu to paste in the interface.
6. Press the **Esc** key to return to the News page.
7. Continue activating the links from the News page and paste in the user interface as needed. When you are done, press **Esc** to move back to the News page.

NOTE: You can record a macro using the Windows macro recorder as described in Chapter 17 to make this task of pasting in each user interface easier.

At the end of this step, we need to save our work.

Saving Our Electronic Publication

Select the **Save** command from the **File** menu. This saves your document.

With our News page completed, we are ready to move on to the Sites page.

Step 7: Adding Content to Our Web Site—Sites Page

The Sites page offers a list of Internet Web sites that were constructed by users of HyperWriter. We are offering this page for two reasons. The first is that it allows people interested in HyperWriter to find other sites created using HyperWriter and see its capabilities. The second reason we are offering this page is to help expose the users of our site to other applications of Hyper-Writer. By doing this we not only help ourselves, we also help the authors of these other sites by directing more users to them. This nicely aids both parties and fits in with the Internet spirit of community among related users.

The first step in authoring our Sites page is to add the Sites title and the **Sites** icon.

Authoring the Sites Page—Adding an Icon and Title

1. From the Home page or the user interface at the bottom of every topic, click on the icon/button for the Sites page.
2. Press **Enter** to move the user interface down one line.
3. Move up to the blank line you just added.
4. Select the **Insert Object** command from the **Edit** menu.
5. Select the **Set File** button.
6. Select .PCX as the format to insert.
7. Select SITES.PCX as the picture to insert.
8. Select the **OK** button to close the **Import Picture Object** dialog box.
9. Move to the end of the picture object by pressing **End**.
10. Enter the title "Sites Created With HyperWriter."
11. Select the **Apply Tag** command from the **Format** menu. Select the HTML tag **HTML_H1**.

With the basic structure of the Sites page created, we need to add the content for this page. We have provided a simple ASCII file that lists the sites built with HyperWriter.

Authoring the Sites Page—Adding Text

1. Press **Enter** to add a blank line where we can enter some content. This tags this paragraph as **H1**, so we need to tag it as **BODY TEXT**.
2. Select the **Apply Tag** command from the **Format** menu.
3. Select the **BODY TEXT** tag.
4. Select the **Import Text** command from the **File** menu.
5. Select ASCII as the format to import.
6. Select the file NTSITES.TXT as the file to import.
7. Select the **OK** button to skip using the Import Text Wizard and import the file.

By selecting the file to import, HyperWriter imports this file into the Sites page. As there weren't any tags in this file, HyperWriter has imported it as just plain text. In order to improve the look of the Sites page, we can tag the list of sites as list items.

Authoring the Sites Page—Tagging the List of Sites

1. Mark a block starting on the first site down to the last site (including the last site).
2. Select the **Apply Tag** command from the **Format** menu.
3. Select the tag **HTML_UL LI**.
4. When HyperWriter asks you whether to apply the tag to the selected block or to the selected paragraphs, choose "Selected Paragraphs," formatting the paragraphs as an unordered list. This should format your Sites page as shown in Figure 18.38.

At the end of this step, we need to save our work.

Saving Our Electronic Publication

Select the **Save** command from the **File** menu. This saves your document.

With our Sites page completed, the next step is creating the Miscellaneous Page.

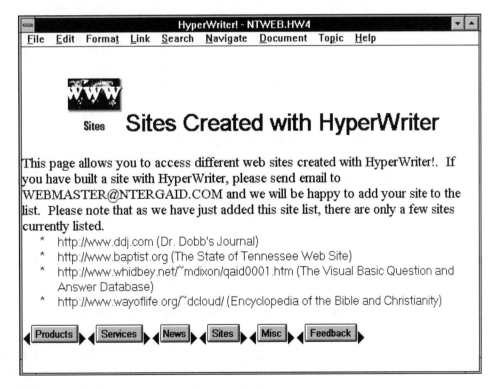

Figure 18.38 The formatted table of contents.

Step 8: Adding Content to Our Web Site—Miscellaneous Page

The Miscellaneous page is actually one of the simplest pages that we're going to construct. When building a Home page, even a very structured one, you will often find that you want to place content on your Web site that simply doesn't seem to belong with your other content. The way to tackle this is with a Miscellaneous page which gives you a general catch-all page where almost any content can be posted. The reason that our Miscellaneous page will be one of the simplest pages to construct is that currently we don't have any content for it. This page is purely for purposes of future expansion of our Web site. Among other purposes, we ultimately may use it for allowing our staff members to host their own personal Home pages.

Given that this page is for future expansion, to author this page we need to place a notice stating that it is currently under construction and will be completed shortly. Of course, we also need to insert our **Miscellaneous** icon at the top of the page and add a title tagged with the **H1** tag.

Authoring the Miscellaneous Page—Adding an Icon and Title

1. From the Home page or the user interface at the bottom of every topic, click on the icon/button for the Miscellaneous page.
2. Press **Enter** to move the user interface down one line.
3. Move up to the blank line you just added.
4. Select the **Insert Object** command from the **Edit** menu.
5. Select the **Set File** button.
6. Select .PCX as the format to insert.
7. Select MISC.PCX as the picture to insert.
8. Select the **OK** button to close the **Import Picture Object** dialog box.
9. Move to the end of the picture object by pressing **End**.
10. Enter the title "Miscellaneous Topics."
11. Select the **Apply Tag** command from the **Format** menu. Select the HTML tag **HTML_H1**.

With the basic structure of the Miscellaneous page created, we need to add the message that this section is under construction.

Authoring the Miscellaneous Page—Tagging Our Title

1. Press **Enter** to add a blank line where we can enter some content.
   By pressing **Enter** from a paragraph that was tagged **HTML_H1**, HyperWriter has continued the tag to the next paragraph. As this paragraph should be Body Text, we need to change the tag from **HTML_H1** to **BODY TEXT**.

2. Select the **Apply Tag** command from the **Format** menu.

3. Select the **BODY TEXT** tag.

4. Enter the text "This section is for future expansion. It is currently blank by design." Your Miscellaneous page should appear as shown in Figure 18.39.

At the end of this step, we need to save our work.

Saving Our Electronic Publication

Select the **Save** command from the **File** menu. This saves your document.

This completes authoring our Miscellaneous page. The next page we need to create is our Feedback page.

Step 9: Adding Content to Our Web Site—Feedback Page

The Feedback page provides a central area that indicates how to contact NTER-GAID. Along with listing our e-mail addresses, we also should list our physi-

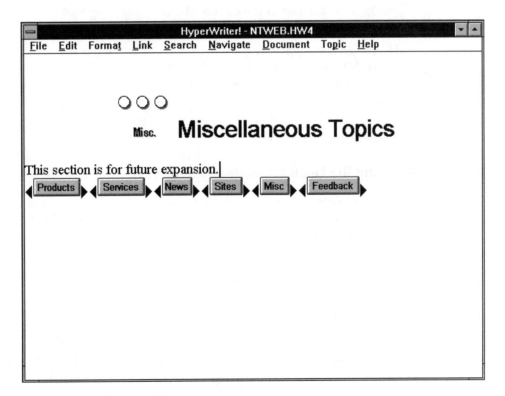

Figure 18.39 The Miscellaneous page.

cal address, phone and fax numbers, and even directions to our offices in case someone needs this information as well.

Authoring this page will be very simple, like the Miscellaneous page, with only slightly more detailed content. The first step is to add the **Feedback** icon at the top of the page and a title tagged with the **H1** tag.

Authoring the Feedback Page—Adding an Icon and Title

1. From the Home page or the user interface at the bottom of every topic, click on the icon/button for the Miscellaneous page.
2. Press **Enter** to move the user interface down one line.
3. Move up to the blank line you just added.
4. Select the **Insert Object** command from the **Edit** menu.
5. Select the **Set File** button.
6. Select .PCX as the format to insert.
7. Select FEEDBACK.PCX as the picture to insert.
8. Select the **OK** button to close the **Import Picture Object** dialog box.
9. Move to the end of the picture object by pressing **End**.
10. Enter the title "Contacting NTERGAID."
11. Select the **Apply Tag** command from the **Format** menu. Select the HTML tag **HTML_H1**. This formats your Feedback page in the same fashion as the other pages we formatted.

With the basic structure of the Feedback page created, we need to add the text of this page. Given that this is fairly detailed, we have supplied it in an ASCII file that can be imported.

Authoring the Feedback Page—Adding Text

1. Press **Enter** to add a blank line where we can enter some content. This tags this paragraph as H1 so we need to tag it as **Body Text**.
2. Select the **Apply Tag** command from the **Format** menu.
3. Select the **BODY TEXT** tag.
4. Select the **Import Text** command from the **File** menu.
5. Select ASCII as the format to import.
6. Select the file WEBFEEDB.TXT as the file to import.
7. Select the **OK** button to skip using the Import Text Wizard.

By selecting the file to import, HyperWriter imports this file into the Feedback page. As there weren't any tags in this file, HyperWriter has imported it

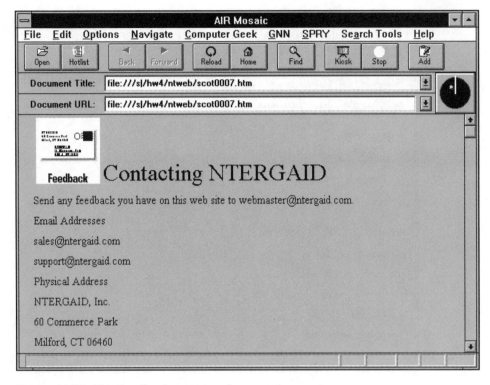

Figure 18.40 The Feedback page in a browser (no tags).

as just plain text. The only notable points in this text are the e-mail addresses we want to convert to hypertext links. Given that our text doesn't have any tags, is there anything we can do to improve its appearance and make it more usable for the reader? Without any tags, there really isn't much we can do. However, tagging this text will greatly improve its appearance. This offers us a good opportunity to look at how tagging the text affects its appearance in a Web browser. Before we tag it, let's look at what it currently looks like in a Web browser. Shown in Figure 18.40 is this page as it would appear in a Web browser without any tags.

As you can see, this screen is basically just text and is very difficult to read due to the lack of tags. To tag this text, we will use an **HTML_H2** tag to format our subheadings, and an **HTML_UL LI** tag to format our individual address elements. By tagging these elements, our Feedback page will appear in a Web browser as shown in Figure 18.41.

Now that we understand the goals of tagging our text, we need to actually tag the text of the page. We'll start by tagging just the headings on the page. This is done with the **Apply Tag** command on the **Format** menu.

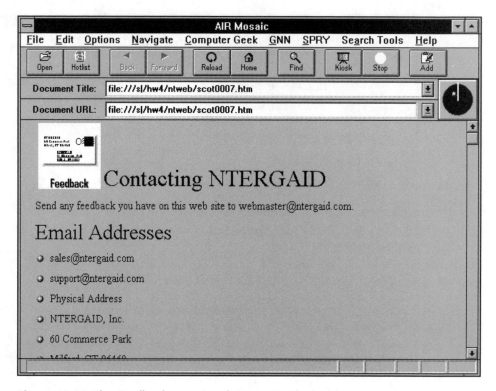

Figure 18.41 The Feedback page in a browser (with tags).

Authoring the Feedback Page—Tagging Headings

1. Place the cursor on the line starting "Email Addresses."
2. Select the **Apply Tag** command from the **Format** menu.
3. Select the tag **HTML_H2**, formatting the paragraph as a second-level heading.
4. Place the cursor on the line starting "Physical Address."
5. Select the **Apply Tag** command from the **Format** menu.
6. Select the tag **HTML_H2**.
7. Place the cursor on the line starting "Phone Numbers."
8. Select the **Apply Tag** command from the **Format** menu.
9. Select the tag **HTML_H2**, formatting the paragraph as a second-level heading.
10. Place the cursor on the line starting "Directions to Our Offices."

11. Select the **Apply Tag** command from the **Format** menu.

12. Select the tag **HTML_H2**.

With our headings tagged, we need to tag the elements below the headings as list items.

Authoring the Feedback Page—Tagging Lists

1. Mark a block starting on the line below the heading "Email Addresses" to the last line before the next heading (this should include this last line).

2. Select the **Apply Tag** command from the **Format** menu.

3. Select the tag **HTML_UL LI**.

4. When HyperWriter asks you whether to apply the tag to the selected block or to the selected paragraphs, choose "Selected Paragraphs," formatting the paragraphs as an unordered list.

5. Repeat this process for the remaining address items under each of these headings: Physical Address, Phone Numbers, and Directions to Our Offices. After tagging all of the elements in the Feedback page, your screen should appear as shown in Figure 18.42.

As you can see, the text has an appearance that is similar to that shown in the Web browser. It isn't identical as HyperWriter's tags aren't exactly the same as a Web browser, but the **HTML1_2.HWT** tag file offers an appearance basically similar to that of a Web browser.

By tagging the text in our Feedback page, we have greatly improved its appearance. But as we read this text, we see that some additional hypertext links are needed. If you read the text underneath the heading "Directions to Our Offices," you will notice that it doesn't clarify how to get to our offices. This is the type of very detailed information that you wouldn't normally include on a sheet of directions. This type of detail, however, is an excellent candidate for a hypertext link. When faced with this type of detail, a hypertext link lets you do a nice job of allowing the reader to drill down only to the content that he or she needs to retrieve without having to bother the reader with information that isn't relevant to them. Using a link in this fashion can be referred to as *Details on Demand*. You should also note that, unlike a print publication, a digital publication allows you to present the exact level of detail that is needed. Rather than give a general set of directions just from Interstate 95, we give two very specific sets of instructions, one from I-95 North and one from I-95 South. We also include a picture of our building to help people find it within the office complex in which we are located. A second point to note is that when creating a digital publication, don't second-guess the information

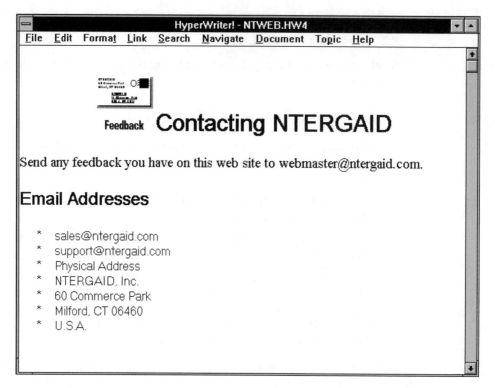

Figure 18.42 The Feedback page (with tags) in HyperWriter.

the user needs. Be complete and let the user pick and choose what he or she needs to retrieve.

We'll use the **Link to Text** and **Link to Picture** commands on the **Link** menu to add the links to our directions and our pictures. The first step in doing this is copying our user interface so we can paste it into the bottom of these pages.

Authoring the Feedback Page—Linking the Directions

1. Move to the end of the Feedback page where the user interface for the page begins.
2. Mark this user interface as a block using **Shift+End**.
3. Select the **Copy** command from the **Edit** menu.
4. Mark a block starting from the beginning of the text "From I-95 South" to the end of this text.
5. Select the **Link to Text** command from the **Link** menu.
6. Select the **Jump Link** option.

7. Select the **New Topic** option. This creates a new topic and places you in it.

8. Select the **Import Text** command from the **File** menu.

9. Select ASCII as the format to import.

10. Select the file DIR_I95S.TXT.

11. Select the **OK** button to skip using the Import Text Wizard and import the text.

12. Move to the end of the imported text and press **Enter**. Select the **Paste** command to paste in our user interface. This creates our first directions page. As this text is really very simple, we won't worry about formatting it with any tags at this time.

13. Select the **Complete Link** command from the **Link** menu. If Hyper-Writer asks whether to create a bidirectional link, then choose No, as bidirectional links aren't exported to the Web. This completes the link and places you back in the Feedback topic.

14. Use the same process to mark a block around the text "From I-95 North," create a link and import the file DIR_195N.TXT. When you have completed this page, use the **Complete Link** command to return to the Feedback topic.

15. Mark a block around the text "Click Here To See The Building We're Located In."

16. Select the **Link to Picture** command from the **Link** menu.

17. Select .PCX File as the format of picture to link to.

18. Select the file NTSITE.PCX as the picture to link to.

19. Select the **OK** button to finish linking the picture. The settings on the Picture Linking Wizard don't matter as they aren't used when Hyper-Writer saves to HTML format.

20. Select the **Complete Link** command to finish linking the picture.

At the end of this step, we need to save our work.

Saving Our Electronic Publication

Select the **Save** command from the **File** menu. This saves your document.

With our directions pages created, this completes our Feedback page. The next pages we need to create are our Additional Topics pages that we created using text links from our Home page.

Step 10: Adding Content to Our Web Site—Additional Topics

The Additional Topics section of our Home page offers two links, one to a news flash and one for job opportunities. These links were created earlier in this chapter as part of authoring the basic structure of our Web site. What we need to do now is add content to these two pages. We'll start with the News Flash. Our first task is to return to the Home page, topic number 1, where these links are located so we can access the New Flash topic.

Going to the News Flash Page

1. Select the **Goto** command from the **Navigate** menu.
2. Enter a "1" into the **New Topic** field and select the **Goto Topic** button. This takes us to our Home page.
3. Activate the "Click Here for Important News Flash" link by clicking on it with **Left Mouse** button.

Now that we are at our News Flash page, we need to author the basic framework of our page. This consists of the title of the page and the page's user interface.

Authoring the News Flash Page—Adding a Title and a User Interface

1. Enter the title "News Flash!"
2. Select the **Apply Tag** command from the **Format** menu. Select the HTML tag **HTML_H1**. This formats the title of the News Flash page. To add the user interface to our page, we need to go somewhere in our Web site where the user interface exists and copy it so we can paste it into this page.
3. Select the **Goto** command from the **Navigate** menu.
4. Enter a "1" into the **New Topic** field and select the **Goto Topic** button. This takes us to our Home page.
5. Activate any of the icons in this topic such as the **Products** icon.
6. Move to the end of this page where the user interface for the page begins.
7. Mark this user interface as a block using **Shift+End**.
8. Select the **Copy** command from the **Edit** menu.
9. Press **Esc** to backtrack through the path of pages you visited until you return to the News Flash page. You should have to press it twice.
10. Press **Enter** to add a blank line to this topic.
11. Select the **Paste** command from the **Edit** menu to paste in the user interface.
12. Select the **Apply Tag** command from the **Format** menu. Select the tag **BODY TEXT** as we don't want our user interface to be tagged as a heading. At this point, your News Flash page should appear as shown in Figure 18.43.

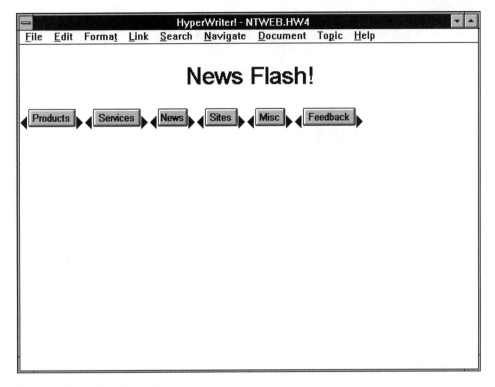

Figure 18.43 The News Flash page.

We have now completed the basic structure of our News Flash page. The next task is to add content. Like many items in this Web site, we'll do this using a list of items.

Adding Content to the News Flash Page

1. Place your cursor at the beginning of the user interface and press **Enter** to insert a blank line.
2. Move up one line to the blank line we just inserted.
3. Select the **Import Text** command from the **File** menu.
4. Select ASCII as the format to insert.
5. Select the file NEWSFLAS.TXT. This displays the Import Text Wizard.
6. Select **OK** to import the NEWSFLAS.TXT file without creating any links automatically. This imports the NEWSFLAS.TXT file into your News Flash page.

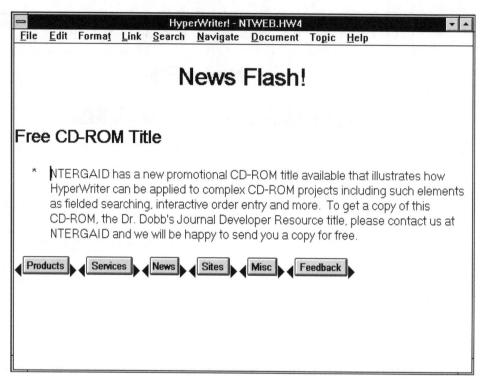

Figure 18.44 The News Flash page with List Tags.

As you should recall, whenever we import ASCII text into one of our Web pages it comes in without any tags. The next step is to tag each of the items that we imported as a list item.

Tagging the News Flash Content

1. Place the cursor on the paragraph after the item title.
2. Select the **Apply Tag** command from the **Format** menu.
3. Select the tag **HTML_UL LI**. A picture of how your News Flash page should appear is shown in Figure 18.44.

As you can see, our News Flash page consists of one title and one item. What we will do is just format our title as an **H2** tag.

Tagging the Title as an H2 Tag

1. Place the cursor on the title paragraph before the item we tagged.

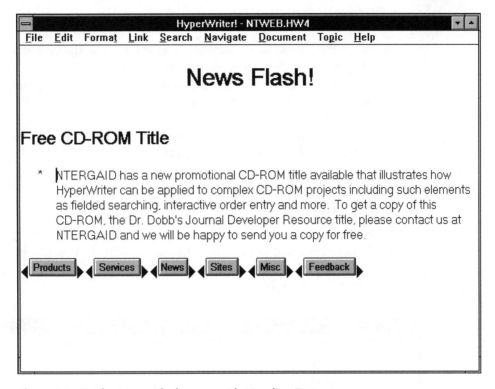

Figure 18.45 The News Flash page with Heading Tags.

2. Select the **Apply Tag** command from the **Format** menu.

3. Select the **HTML_H2** tag. A picture of how your News Flash page should appear is shown in Figure 18.45.

Given that the Web is based on a hypertext model, whenever you have information in multiple pages that is related it is often a good idea to create a hypertext link tying the two items together. A good example of this is our News page, which is related to our News Flash page. What we will do now is create a link so that readers can easily jump from the News page directly to the News Flash page. We won't create a link from the News Flash page to the News page, as the News page is a primary topic in our Web site that is easy to locate and access and the News Flash page is not. This means that while readers of our site generally wouldn't miss the News page, they might overlook the News Flash page. This link makes it much harder to do this. Creating this cross-reference is done with the **Link to Text** command on the **Link** menu and begins by going to the News page, as this is the location where our link needs to start.

Creating a Cross-reference

1. Select the **News** button from the user interface at the bottom of the current page. This takes you to the News page.

2. Press **Enter** after the title and add the text "If you are interested in news about HyperWriter, you might also want to check out Quick News Flash."

3. Select the **Apply Tag** command from the **Format** menu and tag this text as **BODY TEXT** (it was **HTML_H1**).

4. Mark the cross-reference we just typed in as a block.

5. Select the **Link to Text** command from the **Link** menu.

6. Select **Jump Link**.

7. Select **Existing Topic**.

8. HyperWriter will tell you how to complete the link. Select the **OK** button to close the dialog box. At this point, your screen should appear as shown in Figure 18.46.

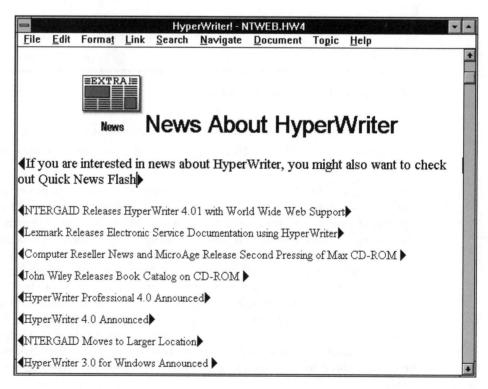

Figure 18.46 The completed link.

As you can see, HyperWriter has inserted link symbols around the anchor of the link (the text you marked). If you clicked on these link symbols, HyperWriter wouldn't be able to activate the link as you haven't specified the link's destination yet. To do this, we need to navigate to the destination of the link and select the **Complete Link** command.

9. Select the **Goto** command from the **Navigate** menu.

10. Enter a "1" into the **New Topic** field and select the **Goto Topic** button. This takes us to our Home page.

11. Activate the **Quick News Flash** link by clicking on it with the **Left Mouse** button.

12. Select the **Complete Link** command from the **Link** menu. If Hyper-Writer asks whether to create a bidirectional link, choose No, as bidirectional links aren't exported to the Web. This completes the link and returns you to the News page where you started making this link.

We have now completed the authoring of our News Flash topic. The next topic we need to author is the Job Opportunities topic where we'll add a job listing. As our job listing will just be straight text, authoring this will be very simple—just setting up the framework of the page (the title and user interface) and using the **Import Text** command. The first step is to go to this page.

Going to the Job Opportunities Page

1. Select the **Goto** command from the **Navigate** menu.

2. Enter a "1" into the **New Topic** field and select the **Goto Topic** button. This takes us to our Home page.

3. Activate the **Job Opportunities** link by clicking on it with **Left Mouse** button.

Now that we are in the **Job Opportunities** topic, we need to set up the page's framework and import our content.

Authoring the Job Opportunities Topic

1. Enter the title "Job Opportunities!"

2. Select the **Apply Tag** command from the **Format** menu. Select the HTML tag **HTML_H1**. This formats the title of the Job Opportunities page.
   To add the user interface to our page, we need to go somewhere in our Web site where the user interface exists and copy it so we can paste it into this page.

3. Select the **Goto** command from the **Navigate** menu.

4. Enter a "1" into the **New Topic** field and select the **Goto Topic** button. This takes us to our Home page.

5. Activate any of the icons in this topic, such as the **Products** icon.

6. Move to the end of this page where the user interface for the page begins.

7. Mark this user interface as a block using **Shift+End**.

8. Select the **Copy** command from the **Edit** menu.

9. Press **Esc** to backtrack through the path of pages you visited until you return to the Job Opportunities page. You should have to press it twice.

10. Press **Enter** to add a blank line to this topic.

11. Select the **Paste** command from the **Edit** menu to paste in the user interface.

12. Select the **Apply Tag** command from the **Format** menu. Select the tag **BODY TEXT** as we don't want our user interface to be tagged as a heading.

13. Place your cursor at the beginning of the user interface and press **Enter** to insert a blank line.

14. Move up one line to the blank line we just inserted.

15. Select the **Import Text** command from the **File** menu.

16. Select ASCII as the format to insert.

17. Select the file EMPLOY.TXT. This displays the Import Text Wizard.

18. Select **OK** to import the EMPLOY.TXT file without creating any links automatically. This imports the file into the current page. Your Job Opportunities page should now appear as shown in Figure 18.47.

At the end of this step, we need to save our work.

Saving Our Electronic Publication

Select the **Save** command from the **File** menu. This saves your document.

This completes the authoring of our Additional Topics section of the Home page. With this page completed, we have finished the content that makes up our Web site. The next step is to save our Web site out to HTML format so it can be opened in a Web browser.

Tutorial Part 2: Publishing this Application on the World Wide Web

With our tutorial for building our electronic publication complete, we have successfully used HyperWriter to create an interactive catalog. As described earlier,

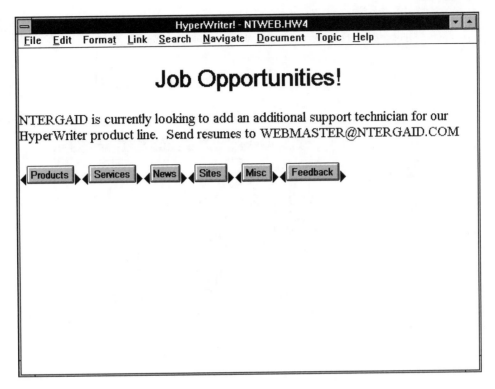

Figure 18.47 The Job Opportunities page.

this can be easily published on floppy disc or via network server. To gain additional distribution for our digital publication, we can take advantage of HyperWriter's Save As HTML Wizard, which allows us to convert our HyperWriter application to an HTML document suitable for use on the Internet-based World Wide Web hypertext system. This allows our document to be distributed to the approximately 20 million people on all types of computing hardware who take advantage of the Internet. Given that John Wiley & Sons publishes books about the Macintosh, UNIX, and other computer platforms, that can't view our Windows-based catalog, this is something we definitely want to do.

In this section of our tutorial, we will convert our electronic publication to HTML format for Internet distribution. If you aren't using the Internet or simply aren't concerned with this option, please move on to the next section of this chapter.

Step 11: Saving to HTML Format

This is the point where we take our HyperWriter application and save it to HTML format, converting every HyperWriter topic we authored to an HTML

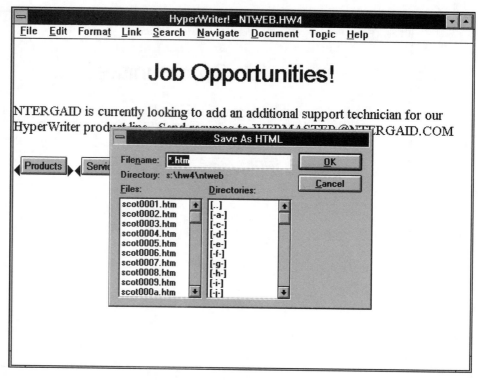

Figure 18.48 The **Save As HTML** File dialog box.

page. Converting our Web site to HTML requires using the **Save As HTML** command on the **File** menu.

Saving Your Document to HTML

1. Select the **Save As HTML** command on the **File** menu. This displays a file dialog box shown in Figure 18.48.

    This dialog box is used for setting the name of the HTML file that will be created. The name that you are entering is a base filename for your HTML document, up to four characters in length (if you enter more characters, they will be truncated to four characters). As each topic in your HyperWriter document will be converted to an HTML format, at the end of the process you will end up with many HTML documents. For our application, we want to use the name "NTWB." By entering "NTWB," then files such as NTWB0001.HTM, NTWB0002.HTM, and so on, will be created.

2. Type the name "NTWB" and press **Enter**. This displays the Save As HTML Wizard shown in Figure 18.49.

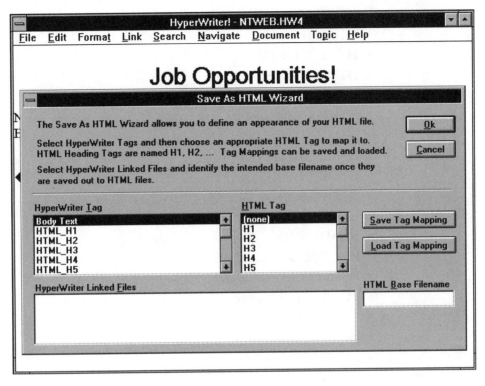

Figure 18.49 The Save As HTML Wizard.

3. The HyperWriter Tag and HTML Tag fields are used to map the different HyperWriter tags to their HTML equivalent. To start, we want to select and be certain that the **HTML_H1** tag in the HyperWriter Tag field is mapped to the **H1** tag in the HTML Tag field. Do this now by first selecting on the **HTML_H1** tag and then on the **H1** tag.

4. After mapping the **HTML_H1** tag, we need to map the **HTML_H2** tag. Do this now by first selecting on the **HTML_H2** tag and then on the **H2** tag.

5. As we have several tags to map, a list of all HTML tags and how they are to be mapped is shown here. The first tags listed are the built-in HTML_ tags, and the remaining tags are imported from our word-processing documents. Select each of the tags on the left and then the corresponding HTML tag on the right. When the list below indicates (none) then the tag shouldn't be mapped (this will cause it to be treated as BODY TEXT).

   - HTML_H1 -> H1
   - HTML_H2 -> H2

- HTML_H3 -> H3
- HTML_H4 -> H4
- HTML_H5 -> H5
- HTML_H6 -> H6
- HTML_OL LI -> OL LI
- HTML_UL LI -> UL LI
- HTML_MENU LI -> MENU LI
- HTML_DIR LI -> DIR LI
- HTML_DL DT -> DL DT
- HTML_DL DD -> DL DD
- HTML_PRE -> PRE
- HEAD1 -> H1
- HW_TOC_1 -> UL LI
- FOR RELEASE -> (none)
- CONTACT -> (center)
- HEAD -> H1
- HEAD2 -> H2
- HW_TOC_2 -> UL LI
- BULLET -> UL LI
- BULLET_INTRO -> UL LI
- DLDT -> DL DT
- DLDD -> DL DD
- HEAD3 -> H3
- HW_TOC_3 -> UL LI
- DESCRIPTION -> (none)
- QUOTE -> PRE
- QUOTE SOURCE -> PRE
- BULLET 2ND LV -> UL LI
- DL -> DL DD
- DT -> DL DT
- TABLE1 -> DL DD
- TABLE2 -> DL DT
- COLUMN BREAK -> (none)
- SPACER -> (none)

- BULLET DESC -> (none)
- DESCRIPTION2 -> (none)
- NUM_LIST -> OL LI
- BODY SIDEBAR -> (none)
- SOURCE -> (none)
- SYSTEM -> PRE

Given the number of tags that we have in our application, we should really save our tag mapping so we don't have to go through this again. You should note that you have to save your tag mapping before you select the **OK** button to save the HTML files. If you don't do this before saving the HTML files then you can't do it at all.

6. Select the **Save Tag Mapping** button. Enter the name "TAGMAP.TXT," and press **Enter** to save the tag mapping.

7. Select the **OK** button to begin saving your application to HTML. When HyperWriter finishes exporting to HTML, this dialog box will be removed from the screen and you can continue working with your HyperWriter application.

Going through the process of mapping our HTML tags brings up a key point: Standardize your stylesheets if at all possible. As you can see from mapping the tags, we had a large number of tags that all appeared to have the same function. For example, we had both **BULLET** and **BULLET_INTRO** tags when both are pretty clearly tags for simple bulleted lists. Although you can't always standardize your tag names as much as you would like, it is something you should try to work toward. In situations where you can't standardize on a single tag name, try to use descriptive names. It was clearly easier to understand what the tags **BULLET** and **BULLET_INTRO** are used for, but much harder to understand what a **DESCRIPTION** tag is for. This brings us to the next point, which is that sometimes even we, the people who authored the site, didn't know what all the tags were. You may find that you need to go back into your document and locate or create text with a particular tag (such as **DESCRIPTION**) to determine what HTML tag it should be mapped to.

With our HTML files generated, we are ready to move to the next step, which is converting all our graphics files from .PCX to .GIF.

Step 12: Converting .PCX Files to .GIF

As we discussed earlier in this chapter, when you author Web pages using HyperWriter, what you do is use graphics in a format other than the standard .GIF files used by the Web (such as .PCX), and then convert these files to .GIF. What I am going to do now is walk you through the process using the supplied

Graphics Workshop software to convert your .PCX files to .GIF format. You should know that you don't have to work through this section as I have supplied .GIF versions of the .PCX files used in this chapter. Feel free to move on to Step 12 if you want to.

Installing Graphics Workshop

Graphics Workshop can be installed by copying the file GWSWIN.EXE from the \GWS directory on the CD-ROM into a subdirectory on your hard disc, and then running the GWSWIN.EXE program. This starts an installation process which sets up Graphics Workshop on your system.

Converting Files Using Graphics Workshop

Graphics Workshop is a standard Windows application that is run by double-clicking its icon from the Windows Program Manager. When Graphics Workshop runs, you should see a Windows application like that shown in Figure 18.50.

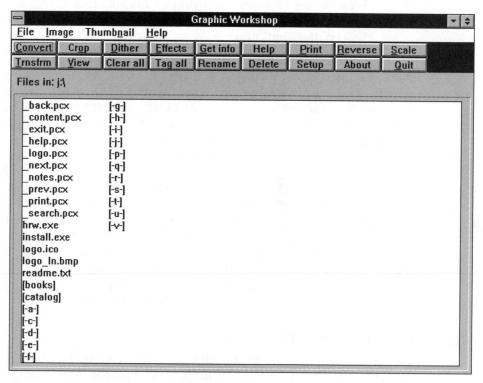

Figure 18.50 Running Graphics Workshop.

As you can see, the basic interface to Graphics Workshop is really one of selecting files. Convert your files using Graphics Workshop as covered below.

1. Navigate to the directory where the graphics files for this tutorial are located by selecting from the drives and directories displayed by Graphics Workshop. You can also use the **Change Directory** command on the **File** menu if this is easier for you.

2. Select the files: NTLOGO1.PCX, PRODS.PCX, SVCS.PCX, NEWS.PCX, SITES.PCX, MISC.PCX, FEEDBACK.PCX, BTPROD.PCX, BTSVCS.PCX, BTNEWS.PCX, BTSITES.PCX, BTMISC.PCX, BTFEEDBK.PCX, and NTSITE.PCX by clicking on them with the mouse. Graphics Workshop will leave them selected when you click on them.

3. Select the **Convert** button. This displays a list of the formats you can convert the graphics files to.

4. Select the .GIF format as the destination format the files should be converted to. This converts all the graphics files to .GIF.

There are two closing notes about Graphics Workshop. The first is that this is a very powerful program and well worth learning. It is very well suited to digital publishing. The second is that this package is distributed via shareware. If you are going to use it, then please register it with its author and pay the registration fee.

Step 13: Viewing in a Web Browser

With our Web site saved to HTML format, our next task is to test our HTML files by viewing them in a Web browser. As you may recall from Chapter 7, one of the guidelines for developing in HyperWriter is to always test your digital publications before they are published. A Web site is a digital publication just like a HyperWriter application. Consequently, your Web site must be tested before it is released (i.e., posted to a Web server). Although you can check the Web site inside HyperWriter, you still need to check it using a Web browser to make sure that all HyperWriter tags are properly mapped to HTML tags and that the Web site appears as you expected from developing it inside HyperWriter. Given that I don't know what Web browser you have, I can't tell you how to go about viewing these files in your Web browser. Two popular Web browsers are Spry Mosaic and Netscape Navigator. If you are using Spry Mosaic, use the **Open Local File** command to view the Web files we created. If you are using Netscape Navigator to view our Web files, use the **Open File** command.

Shown in Figures 18.51 through 18.55 are pictures of our Web site as displayed by Spry Air Mosaic.

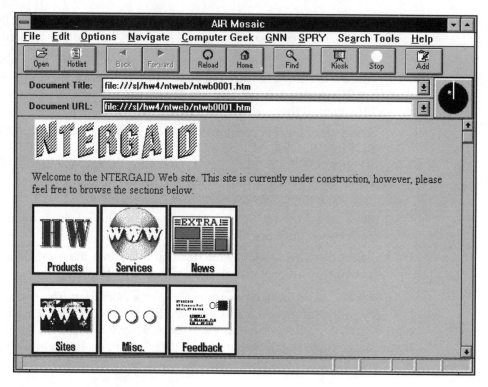

Figure 18.51 Our Home page.

Viewing our Web pages begins with the file NTWB0001.HTM, our Home page, as shown in Figure 18.51.

From the Home page, we select on the **Products** icon to jump to this page, as shown in Figure 18.52.

From the Products page, we might select on the HyperWriter Professional link to view information on this product as shown in Figure 18.53.

As we're through looking at the HyperWriter Professional page, we might select on the **News** button at the bottom of the page to jump into our News page, shown in Figure 18.54.

From the News page, it is just a quick hyperlink into the News Flash page as shown in Figure 18.55.

This completes our looking at some of the different pages that make up our Web site. As we now have a large number of pages, I don't want to take up space in this book with more pictures of Web pages that you can readily view on your own machine. It is probably a good idea for you to browse these Web pages further before continuing on to the next section which cover how to post these Web pages onto a Web server.

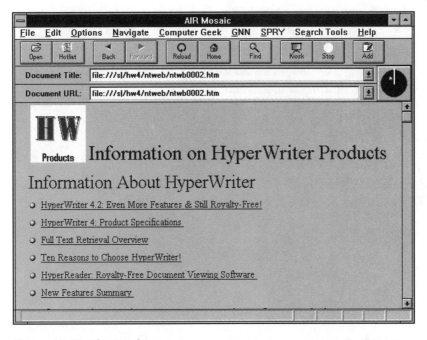

Figure 18.52 The Products page.

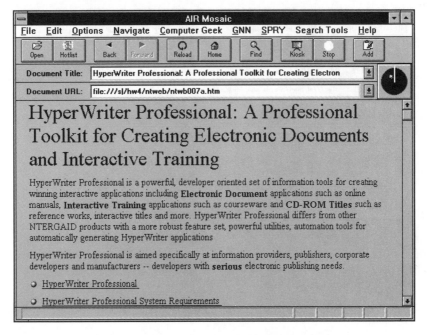

Figure 18.53 Looking at the HyperWriter Professional page.

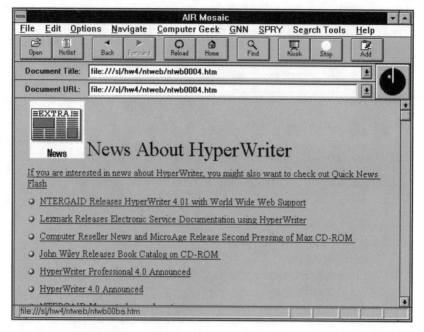

Figure 18.54 Looking at the News page.

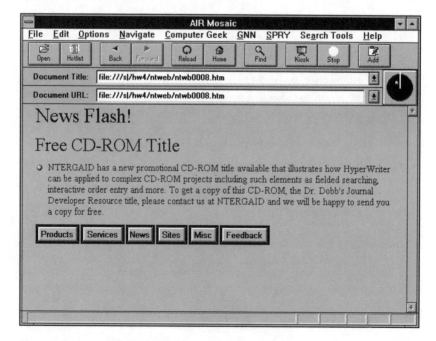

Figure 18.55 Looking at the News Flash page.

Step 14: Posting Files on a Web Server

The final step in authoring our Web site is to post our finished HTML files on a Web server. I can't tell you the exact procedure for this, because it will differ depending on the server software you are using, the type of server you are using, and the Web hosting service provider you are using (if you use a hosting service). What I can tell you is how we were required to post these files using our Web hosting service. After we completed the files, we told the hosting service what the name of the first file was (INDE0001.HTM). They granted us access to a set of directories on their UNIX system so we could place our files there. We then used an FTP (File Transfer Protocol) tool to upload the files onto their UNIX system. We deliberately kept the site simple and left all files in one directory. If our site were larger, we would have split it into multiple directories. When we got ready to FTP our files to the hosting service, we realized that the Web access software we were running, Netcom's NetCruiser, couldn't actually FTP files up to the Net—it could only retrieve files from the Net. This forced us to update our Internet software to Spry's Internet In A Box, a package that supports FTP both to and from the net. After installing Internet In A Box, we were able to easily FTP files up to the hosting service, and our Home page was available on the Web. In general, while the details will vary, this is the type of process you'll use to post your files on a Web server.

NOTE: If you have an internal Web server that is accessible through your local area network, this process might be a little simpler for you.

Tutorial Part 3: Resetting Directories

Now that we have completed our tutorial, the final step is to reset our directories to their defaults so that we have access to the normal HyperWriter tutorial files. Use the **Preferences** command on the **File** menu for this.

Setting Directories in HyperWriter

1. Select the **Preferences** command from the **File** menu.
2. Select the **Directories** folder.
3. Enter "\HW4\FILES" into the **Documents** field. If you installed Hyper-Writer into a directory other than \HW4 then substitute that directory.
4. Enter "\HW4\PICTURES" into the **Pictures** field. If you installed HyperWriter into a directory other than \HW4 then substitute that directory.

5. Enter "\HW4\FILES" into the **Text Files** and **Local Files** fields. If you installed HyperWriter into a directory other than \HW4 then substitute that directory.

6. Select the **OK** button to close this dialog box.

Future Enhancements to Our Web Site

If you have ever browsed the Web in depth, you know one of the most exciting things about the Web is that it is constantly evolving and improving. When you author a Web site, you should be aware that you need to constantly keep Web sites updated and make ongoing improvements. Although we aren't going to actually improve the Web site we just created, you should be aware that it can be improved. Listed below are some of the basic improvements we could make to our Web page.

- **Convert the references to e-mail addresses in our Feedback page to be hypertext links**. People can then more easily send us e-mail.

- **Convert the references to sites to hypertext links**. People can then jump directly to the sites mentioned in this page.

- **Add a button to our user interface**. People can thus directly return to our Home page. Currently they can jump to other pages within our Web site, but cannot get back to our Home page easily.

- **Add a link to each of the icons displayed at the top of each page**. This would allow someone to easily jump to the beginning of a particular section in our site from a lower level page in that section. Although our user interface also supports this type of jump, this saves the reader from having to scroll down to the user interface. This navigational technique is most useful when you have readers that will be accessing a site through random access techniques like a Web search engine.

- **Add a history of changes**. A reader will be aware of what has changed.

- **Add more content**. Among the content we might add would be a full set of HyperWriter's documentation so prospective customers could research HyperWriter's capabilities.

- **Make the content more engaging and interactive**. As an example of this, we could make this chapter part of our content of the Web site with links and figures that illustrate how the Web site was created.

- **Add additional organization to the Web site**. For example, we could organize the press releases along a time-line metaphor, a product metaphor, and so on. By providing additional organization, it makes it easier for readers to locate information in our Web site.

- **Index the Web site**. This doesn't refer to indexing the Web site using a search engine; what I mean is constructing an alphabetical index to the information in the Web site.

- **Be more consistent with our icons**. When we created each Web page, we made sure to put a copy of the icon for that section of the Web site at the top of each page linked from the table of contents. However, we weren't consistent with this and generally didn't place it on child pages that were linked from a page linked from the table of contents. Doing this more consistently would improve the appearance and usability of our Web site as a whole.

- **Better formatting and presentation**. We currently have used a very minimalist style of formatting this Web site. By taking advantage of different HTML tags, we could greatly improve the appearance of the text in this site.

- **Add additional cross-references between related information**.

- **Add more graphics**. Currently this site has very few graphics; more graphics would improve its appearance and make it more attractive.

- **Add interactivity through hypertext links**. One example of this is the product literature page that contains a question-and-answer driven approach to choosing among the HyperWriter, HyperWriter for Training, and HyperWriter Professional products. This page could be reimplemented from a single text page to an interactive application, where following links helped you decide which product to buy. For people looking to print out a copy of this information, a copy of the content as a scrolling text page could be retaining

From this list of enhancements, you can tell that there is a lot of room to expand on a basic Web site. You should bear in mind that there is nothing wrong with the Web site we have authored—it simply has room for improvement. This is the type of flexibility that you will often find with respect to the Web.

Notes on Authoring Web Sites with HyperWriter

The following sections offer some brief notes on using HyperWriter for Web authoring.

In this chapter we used HyperWriter to create a Web site. As you can tell from Chapter 17, while the process used was not totally different from authoring an application designed solely for use with HyperWriter (an application distributed with the HyperReader runtime), it certainly wasn't the same. A chief difference was at the user interface level where an application intended for use with HyperReader makes use of backgrounds, whereas an application aimed at a Web site uses a much simpler user interface, created from text, links, and pictures. One approach is to use this type of user interface in all your HyperWriter publications, even those aimed for use with HyperReader. While this is possible, it isn't optimal and really isn't a good idea. Unfortunately, in our base HyperWriter product, we don't have a perfect solution yet. You should note that this cross platform development is facilitated with Hyper-Writer Professional, as the HyperWriter AutoLinker toolkit can automatically modify Web pages saved by HyperWriter. For example, the HyperWriter AutoLinker could add an HTML-based user interface to an application automatically, allowing backgrounds to be used throughout the application for the best possible presentation in HyperReader.

Linking Into a HyperWriter-Created Web Site

A common technique when working with Web pages is to create links from one Web site to another. For example, a user of HyperWriter might want to create a link directly from his Web site to, say, the News Flash page so his users could see what is happening with HyperWriter. This offers an area of concern because HyperWriter automatically generates Web pages with a unique name. If this name changes, links to a particular page can be thrown off, leaving the reader at a spot in your Web site that isn't where he or she expected to be. When HyperWriter generates its Web pages, it takes the first four characters of the filename that you give it to use for the Web pages, generates a hexadecimal version of the current topic number, and then combines this number with the first four characters to create the unique filename for each page. You should know that HyperWriter topic numbers don't change. Once a topic is created, it is assigned a unique number and this is never altered. The implication of this is that as long as you don't radically change the contents of the basic structure of your Web page, links created to particular pages within the Web site will generally continue to work.

Creating FTP, Mail, and Other Internet Links

As you may recall from earlier in this chapter, our Web site included text such as e-mail addresses and the Web addresses of other sites created with Hyper-Writer. A very popular technique for Web pages is to make them more interactive by converting these references to hypertext links. The syntax for hypertext links that access these Internet resources is very simple. A sample e-mail link is shown here: **<a href="mailto:Webmaster@ntergaid.com">Webmaster@ntergaid.com</a>**.

You should be aware that while you can type in a link in this form, when you save your HTML pages, the link won't work. The reason is that when HyperWriter exports "<" character used to indicate this link, it automatically converts this character to "**&lt**" **and** "**&gt**," as it doesn't recognize this as a link, and thinks it is text (the way to actually embed a "<" character in your HTML documents is to place "**&lt**", no quotes, in your document). If you are authoring your own Web pages using HyperWriter and you want to fix your links, you just need to open them in a text editor and edit out the "**&lt**" and "**&gt**" characters, converting them back to "<" and ">."

NOTE: The HyperWriter AutoLinker module in HyperWriter Professional can address this limitation in HyperWriter by processing your Web pages to automatically convert these to links by converting the "**&lt**" and "**&gt**" characters to "<" and ">." We hope to fix this in a future release of HyperWriter through a special Internet Link feature.

Using an HTML Editor to Modify Documents Created with HyperWriter

Once you have created your Web pages using HyperWriter, you may find that you need to modify them. HyperWriter produces standard HTML pages that can be opened into any Web-editing software. Among the Web editors that we have tried ourselves are HotMetal and HTMLEdit.

Making Web Authoring Easier

Authoring Web pages with HyperWriter is not hard. However, there are several basic techniques that actually can make Web authoring easier. I didn't bring up these techniques earlier in this chapter, as these techniques are entirely optional and I didn't want them confused with features in Hyper-Writer. Also, as HyperWriter's HTML authoring features become more sophisticated, the need for these features will go away.

- **Using a background to emulate a Web browser**. When you author Web pages using HyperWriter (or another tool), it is often a task of going back and forth between HyperWriter and the Web browser to see if you have the right appearance. Although this isn't a perfect solution, you can set up a HyperWriter background with the same basic appearance as a Web browser. What this lets you do is view your Web application in much the same visual context as it will be viewed in a Web browser. You should note that this is definitely crude (HyperWriter isn't a Web browser), but it is useful.

- **Using a background button to access a Glossary**. A constant task that we did in this chapter was to copy repeated elements such as icons, titles, and user interfaces so we could paste them into a topic. This process can be greatly simplified by taking advantage of a background. Consider authoring a Web site using HyperWriter where on every page there is a background button titled "**Glossary**," located at the top of the screen. This button is linked to nothing more than a topic that contains different elements that we want to use repeatedly. As we can very quickly and easily copy elements from this Glossary, we can more easily add them to our Web page (no more navigating to particular topics to copy a user interface). Even better, as HyperWriter backgrounds don't move out to Web, this background button won't affect our Web pages at all. To make sure that our background is added to every page we create, set the **Default Backgrounds** option on the **Authoring** folder of the **Preferences** command to the number of the background you want assigned to each page.

- **Work in a batch-oriented fashion**. Often in this chapter we had to accomplish the same task for different pages. An example of this is assigning the user interface to the bottom of each topic. One thing that can make this easier is working in a more batch-oriented fashion where instead of adding the user interface as you develop each topic, you add it all at once. The benefit to this is you skip the repeated steps of copying the user interface before you have to paste it in.

- **Use the Macro Recorder**. As noted in this chapter, the Windows Macro Recorder can be a useful tool for Web authoring when you have repetitive tasks.

- **Supporting the ADDRESS tag**. As you may have noticed from using the **Save As HTML** command, HyperWriter doesn't support all HTML tags. For example, the **ADDRESS** tag isn't supported. When you use the **Save Tag Mapping** function to save your HTML tag mapping to a file so you can use it again in the future, this creates a very simple ASCII file which contains the name of a tag in HyperWriter and the name of the HTML tag it should be mapped to. This ASCII file can be loaded into a programming editor and additional HTML tags can be specified. While this isn't perfect, it provides an easy to extend HyperWriter's HTML support.

Reusing the HTML_12.HWT Stylesheet

As you may recall, one of the first tasks we did was attach the stylesheet HTML_12.HWT to our HyperWriter document. A HyperWriter stylesheet contains all of the styles used in an application. By importing word-processing documents into our HyperWriter document where we authored the Web pages, we caused any styles in these documents to be added to our HTML_12.HWT stylesheet. If you find this hampers your authoring, you might want to copy the HTML_12.HWT stylesheet off the CD-ROM disc so you have a fresh copy to work with.

A HyperWriter Glossary

The following terms are used in this book and are generally specific to Hyper-Writer. A second glossary aimed at the World Wide Web appears at the end of this appendix.

.BKG File. A HyperWriter file of screen backgrounds.

.DCP File. A HyperWriter file of document properties.

.HW File. A HyperWriter 2.0 or 2.5 hypermedia document file.

.HW3 File. A HyperWriter 3.x hypermedia document file.

.HW4 File. HyperWriter 4.x hypermedia document file.

.HWA File. A file that defines a HyperWriter application.

.HWB File. A HyperWriter bookmark on exit file.

.HWF File. A HyperLinker data file.

.HWG File. A HyperWriter group file.

.HWI File. A HyperWriter Boolean index file.

.HWL File. A HyperLinker data file.

.HWM File. A HyperWriter file of named bookmarks.

.HWN File. The topic names used by each HyperWriter .HW4 file. There is always one .HWN file for every .HW4 file.

.HWP File. A HyperWriter guided tour file.

.HWR File. A HyperWriter file of annotations created with the **Add/Read Notes** command.

.HWS File. A HyperWriter file of saved search queries.

.HWT File. HyperWriter formatting file of different paragraph tags.

.HWY File. A HyperWriter file of search synonyms.

.INI File. A HyperWriter configuration file.

.MAC File. A HyperWriter macro file.

.VDR File. A HyperWriter videodisc player configuration file.

.WDL File. A HyperWriter word link file.

Action Link. A link whose destination is an action that is executed when the link is activated. Action links can be created to DOS programs (DOS links), HyperWriter menu functions (Menu Action links), and to activate properties (Action List links).

Auto Tour. An Auto Tour is a tour that runs automatically when a document starts up.

Background Color. The background color of a block of text is the color of the screen behind the text.

Bidirectional Link. A link that can be activated from either end of the link allowing navigation both from the link anchor to the link end and from the link end back to the link anchor.

Comment Link. A Comment link displays a popup comment window containing either text or graphics when activated.

Digitized Sound. A sound that has been recorded by a computer into a digital format.

Document Properties. Options that configure the appearance and functioning of individual documents.

DOS Link. A link that contains a DOS batch file that is activated when the link is run.

Englebart, Doug. A hypertext pioneer. The inventor of the mouse, multiwindow editors, and cooperative work software.

Foreground Color. The foreground color of a block of text is the color of the actual text characters.

Grand Author. The first author to be added to a document. The grand author can modify all links in a document, even those created by other authors.

Graphic Link. A link to either a popup graphic image or a full-screen .PCX graphic image.

High-Intensity Color. A color with a color number from 8 to 15. High-intensity colors are displayed more brightly than low-intensity colors.

History Trail. The current path of links that have been activated. A history trail contains the record of link activations and is what is followed backwards when | ATTR 6 | ESC | ATTR 6 | is pressed.

Jump Link. A cross-referencing link between topics or documents.

Link Anchor. The text that a link is created from.

Link End. The destination of a link.

Low-Intensity Color. A color with a color number of 0 to 7. Low-intensity colors are displayed less brightly on screen than high-intensity colors.

Nelson, Ted. The coiner of the term hypertext, and its greatest supporter. Ted Nelson is also the visionary behind the Xanadu™ system and now Xanadu Lite™—the first global hypertext system.

Subauthor. Any author of a document below the Grand Author. That is, a sub-author is anyone who has added his or her name to a document after the Grand Author.

Link with Replacement Text. A Link with Replacement Text swaps its link anchor on screen with its link end. This occurs within the context of the currently displayed window.

Tour Point. A tour point is any spot in a tour where the tour stops briefly or pauses for reader input.

Topic. The basic data element in a HyperWriter document is the topic. Topics are also often called nodes, cards, or windows by other applications.

Videodisc. A twelve-inch optical disk that contains analog video images and sound.

A World Wide Web Glossary

Anchor. The location of a hypertext link in a document. Anchors can be placed on text or graphics.

Andreessen, Marc. One of the authors of the original Mosaic software which first brought the Web to wide usage.

Berners-Lee, Tim. The inventor of the World Wide Web.

Browser. A program used to view HTML documents. Also referred to as *Web browser*.

CERN. The European research organization where the Web was first developed.

CGI. Common Gateway Interface. A popular, though difficult to use, protocol for connecting a Web server to another type of computer software, typically a database engine.

GIF. The standard 8-bit image format for use on the Web.

Home Page. The first page of a Web site, often designed to be graphical and attractive.

Hotlist. A collection of references to web sites you want to return to.

HTML. Hypertext Markup Language. The basic text-formatting language that makes information available on the Web.

HTML Editor. A program for authoring HTML pages.

HTML v2. A revision to the HTML 1.2 specification. You should note that HTML v2, while in use by some people, is not yet officially ratified.

HTML v3. A revision to the HTML 2.0 specification. Like HTML v2, you should note that HTML v3, while in use by some people, is not yet officially ratified.

HTTP. Hypertext Transport Protocol. The networking protocol by which a Web browser requests and receives information from a Web server.

Hypertext. A technology for creating relationships between documents that allow navigation from one document to another.

Image map. A text file that defines a series of hot spots overlaid on an image in an HTML document.

JPEG. The standard 24-bit image format for use on the Web.

Link. A connection between HTML documents that allows navigation.

Mosaic. The original Web browser that led to the vast popularity of the Web (the Web was originally developed on computers from NeXT, an obscure maker of UNIX workstations, but did not come to wide usage until the release of the Mosaic browser).

Netscape. One of the leading firms in the World Wide Web community, Netscape was founded by one of the developers of the original Mosaic browser along with the founder of Silicon Graphics, a leading developer of UNIX workstations. Netscape is also the provider of a leading Web browser, Netscape Navigator.

Netscape HTML. A set of HTML tags that are originated by the Netscape Web browser as opposed to an official Internet standard.

Page. The basic building block of a Web site, a page is a single HTML file and generally represents a single chunk of information.

SGML. Standard Generalized Markup Language. A high-end, complex, text-formatting language often used for applications such as publishing volumes of technical documentation. While HTML can be viewed as an SGML derivative, HTML is actually considerably simpler than SGML and, from a purely technical perspective, is not true SGML.

SLIP/PPP/CSLIP. A popular method for connecting a personal computer to the Internet to use a Web browser.

Tags. The basic HTML formatting element. Tags are the codes that determine the structure and presentation of information in an HTML page. Tags are generally enclosed in "<" and ">" characters.

TCP/IP. The underlying communications protocol the Internet is based on.

UNIX. An operating system typically used on the workstations and minicomputers that act as Web servers for the Internet.

URL. Uniform Resource Locator. The core addressing method for indicating a unique address for an HTML document.

Web Form. An HTML document that contains a form used to enter or request information. An HTML form is connected through a CGI link to a Web server.

Webmaster. The person within an organization who administrates a Web site.

Web Server. The program that physically makes an HTML document available over the Internet.

Web Site. A site on the Internet where a Home page exists.

WWW or W3. Shorthand for World Wide Web.

Digital Publishing Resources

Company Addresses

Listed below are addresses for each of the companies mentioned in Chapter 3.

Product: HyperWriter and HyperWriter Professional

NTERGAID, Inc.
60 Commerce Park
Milford, CT 06460
(203) 783-1280
(800) 25 HYPER (9737)
Fax: (203) 882-0850
BBS: (203) 882-0848
E-mail: 75160.3357@compuserve.com or sales@ntergaid.com
Web: http://www.ntergaid.com

Product: Adobe Acrobat

Adobe Systems, Inc.
1585 Charleston Road
P.O. Box 7900
Mountain View, CA 94039-7900
(415) 961-4400
(800) 422-3623

Product: Book Manager
IBM
P.O. Box 12195
Research Triangle Park, NC 27709
(919) 469-7763
Fax: (919) 469-7423

Product: Doc-2-Help
WexTech Systems
310 Madison Avenue
Suite 905
New York, NY 10017
(212) 949-9595
Fax: (212) 949-4007
E-mail: 71333.1400@COMPUSERVE.COM

Product: Dynatext
Electronic Book Technologies
One Richmond Square
Providence, RI 02906
(401) 421-9550
Fax: (401) 421-9551
E-mail: info@ebt.com

Product: Folio Views
Folio Corporation
2155 North Freedom Boulevard
Suite 150
Provo, UT 84064
(801) 229-6700
Fax: (801) 229-6787
E-mail: sales@folio.com

Product: ForeHelp
ForeFront
5171 Eldorado Springs Drive
Boulder, CO 80303
(303) 499-9181
Fax: (303) 494-5446

Product: Guide
InfoAccess
2800 156th Avenue SE
Bellevue, WA 98007
(206) 747-3203
Fax: (206) 641-9367

Product: HyperCard

Apple Computer / Claris Division
5201 Patrick Henry Drive
PO Box 58168
Santa Clara, CA 95052-8168
(408) 987-7000
Fax: (408) 987-7440

Product: KMS

Knowledge Systems
RD 2
213A Evans Rd
Export, PA 15632
(412) 327-5022
rma@centro.soar.cs.cmu.edu

Product: Multimedia View/MediaView/Windows Help

Microsoft Corporation
One Microsoft Way
Redmond, WA 98052-6399
(800) 426-9400

Product: SmarText

Lotus Development Corporation
1000 Abernathy Road
Suite 1700
Atlanta, GA 30328
(404) 391-0011

Product: StorySpace

Eastgate Systems, Inc.
134 Main Street
Watertown MA 02172 USA
(800) 562-1638
(617) 924-9044
Fax: (617) 924-9051
Bernstein@eastgate.com or info@eastgate.com
http://www.eastgate.com/

Product: Toolbook

Asymetrix Corporation
110 110th Avenue NE
Bellevue, WA 98004
(206) 426-0501
Fax: (206) 455-3071

Table B.1 News Groups for Digital Publishers

Newsgroup	Comment
alt.hypertext	The best newsgroup dedicated to hypertext.
comp.text.sgml	The definitive place for answers on SGML.
comp.infosystems.www.authoring.cgi	Discussions on using Common Gateway Interface (CGI) scripts with Web pages.
comp.infosystems.www.authoring.html	Discussions on HTML authoring.
comp.infosystems.www.authoring.images	Discussions on authoring images for use on the Web.
comp.infosystems.www.authoring.misc	Miscellaneous authoring issues.
comp.infosystems.www.servers.ms-windows	Discussions on Windows-based Web servers.
comp.infosystems.www.servers.unix	Discussions on UNIX-based Web servers.
comp.infosystems.www.misc	General discussions about the Web.
comp.infosystems.www.announce	Announcements of Web sites.
comp.os.ms-windows.programmer.winhelp	Discussions on using Windows help.
comp.publish.cdrom.software	Discussions on CD-ROM publishing.

Usenet News Groups

Usenet (Internet) news groups are a great tool for learning about digital publishing, as they provide a place where you can ask a knowledgeable user and get an answer, often in very short order. Although news groups often have a lot of noise compared to signal, they provide a valuable tool for learning about digital publishing. Table B.1 lists the news groups which are of interest to digital publishers. You should note that there are more World Wide Web-specific news groups than I have listed here, as I only listed the authoring-specific ones.

Good Internet Sites

Listed below are a number of very useful Internet Web sites focusing on different aspects of digital publishing. I should note that many of these sites were discovered through Eastgate Systems' Home page, http://www.eastgate.com.

NTERGAID, Inc. Home Page—http://www.ntergaid.com

John Wiley & Sons Home Page—http://www.wiley.com

Eastgate Systems—http://www.eastgate.com

World Wide Web FAQ (Frequently Asked Questions)—
http://sunsite.unc.edu/boutell/faq/

SGML Open Home Page (SGML Open is an SGML trade organization)—
http://www.sgmlopen.org.

This site offers a searchable index of all the Web specific news groups—it
is a great tool for finding Web-specific information—
http://www.criticalmass.com/concord/index.htm

The World Wide Web organization that guides development of the Web—
http://www.w3.org

Netscape's home page (running the Netscape browser is advised)—
http://www.netscape.com

The current status of Ted Nelson's Xanadu—
http://www.aus.xanadu.com/xanadu

Brown University's current hypertext research—
http:/www.stg.brown.edu/projects/hypertext/hypertext_ov.html

ACM Special Interest Group for Hypertext—http://info.acm.org/siglink/

The Hypertext '96 Conference—http://acm.org/siglink/ht96-call.html

The Texas A&M Hypermedia Laboratory—http://bush.cs.tamu.edu/

Steve Pepper's Whirlwind Guide to SGML Tools. One of the best
references to SGML tools—http://www.falch.no/

The OpenText searchable index to the Web—http://www.opentext.com

An HTML validation service to make sure your HTML documents are
correct—http://www.stg.brown.edu/service/validate_form.html

Other Resources

Listed below are references to some additional resources for the digital publisher. Phil Murray, the author of the book *From Ventura to Hypertext*, and someone who has been involved in digital publishing and hypertext for a very long
time is now the publisher of the *Electronic Document Report*, a regular newsletter focusing on digital publishing. This is a truly excellent publication. Contact
Electronic Document Report at:

Electronic Information Age
462 Washington Street
Portsmouth, VA 23704
(804) 397-4644
Fax: (804) 397-4635
Internet: pmurray@infi.net

The Delphi group is a professional research firm specializing in detailed analysis of digital publishing, workflow, and text-management tools.

Delphi Consulting Group
266 Beacon Street
Boston, MA 02116-1224
(617) 247-1511
Fax: (617) 247-4957

The Seybold group publishes a very well-regarded series of newsletters covering publishing technology in general with regular coverage of digital publishing tools. Look into their *Seybold Report on Publishing Systems*, *Seybold Report on Desktop Publishing*, and *Digital World newsletter*.

Seybold Publications
PO Box 644
Media, PA 19063
(610) 565-2480

SGML Open is an industry trade group that exists to promote the use of SGML. If you are interested in learning more about SGML, SGML Open is a great place to start.

SGML Open
910 Beaver Grade Road #3008
Coraopolis, PA 15108
Voice: (412) 264-4258
Fax: (412) 264-6598
E-mail: laplante@sgmlopen.org

The *Gilbane Report* is a good newsletter that covers document centric technology such as SGML.

The Gilbane Report
CAPV/Publishing Technology Management
One Snow Road
Marshfield, MA 02050
(617) 837-7200
Fax: (617) 837-8856
ptm@world.std.com
fgilbane@tiac.net

C

The Version of HyperWriter Included with This Book

Included with this book on the CD-ROM is a special version of HyperWriter that was created just for this book (see Appendix D for more details). Our goal in bundling HyperWriter with this book was to provide you with one of today's most powerful digital publishing tools in such a fashion that it allowed you to not only understand digital publishing, but also get a real handle on how to best apply HyperWriter. We also hope that you will like using HyperWriter and consider upgrading to the most recent commercial version that we offer for $695. The version of HyperWriter packaged with this book is limited in the following ways:

- It displays a dialog box indicating that you are using an evaluation version of HyperWriter when you run the software and when you exit the software

- The standard data compression tool, HyperCompress, is not included

- It does not include the HyperReader document viewing software used for distributing documents.

- It uses a different file format from the standard HyperWriter documents, which the HyperReader software cannot read. If you upgrade to the full version of HyperWriter then the standard HyperWriter software can open your existing files created with the evaluation version, and save them so they can be used with the reader. This allows you to take anything you have developed in the version of HyperWriter shipped with this book and publish it with HyperReader.

- The indexing software, HyperIndexer, only indexes the first 100 topics in your .HW4 documents.
- When you create HTML documents for use on the Web, only the first 100 topics are saved out to HTML pages.
- Printing is not supported in the evaluation version.

As you can see, none of these limitations prevent you from learning about digital publishing, creating electronic documents for the Web, and evaluating HyperWriter. We hope that eventually you will contact NTERGAID and get information on purchasing the latest version of HyperWriter. You should be aware that NTERGAID offers a discount coupon in the back of this book for readers to get HyperWriter.

APPENDIX

Understanding the CD-ROM

Accompanying this book is a CD-ROM disc containing the following items:

- An evaluation version of HyperWriter (see Appendix C for the limits on this version)
- The standard HyperWriter demonstration applications
- Additional HyperWriter demonstration applications that illustrate many additional applications for HyperWriter
- Multimedia drivers for video and animation
- A copy of the John Wiley & Sons CD-ROM book catalog

To get started using this CD-ROM disc, just run the installation software on the CD-ROM disc (SETUP.EXE) and follow the prompts from there. A standard Program Manager group and set of icons will be installed.

APPENDIX

Installing Multimedia Drivers

E

Shipped along with this disc are a series of multimedia drivers for AutoDesk Animator animation files, Video for Windows, and drivers for importing Microsoft Word version 6.0 files (this requires the OLE 2.0 library software). To install this software, run the SETUP program in the \DRIVERS directory on the CD-ROM disc and follow the prompts it displays.

You should note that if you have Windows 95 then you shouldn't need to install any of these drivers, with the possible exception of the AutoDesk Animator driver (which can be installed separately from the other drivers).

How I Wrote this Book

Building the Print Version

This manual was written in HyperWriter version HyperWriter 4.2 using a custom HyperWriter template document, EDITOR.HW4, that allowed instant access to useful features such as text glossary, multiple versions of each chapter, an outline of each chapter, a checklist for tracking completion, as well as topics that served as note pad and an extra editor window. Overall, the functionality that this template provided let me be dramatically more productive than I could have been in a traditional word processor. Text from this manual was processed through several HyperWriter AutoLinker HyperAwk scripts for tasks as varied as consistency checking, document correction, and automatic figure numbering. Proofing copies were printed with Ventura Publisher v3.0 running under the GEM environment on a Hewlett Packard LaserJet 4M at 600dpi. All screen shots were captured with the Freeze Frame screen capture program as 256 color .PCX files and converted to gray-scale .TIF images using the Graphics Workshop program. To produce the typeset version, all text was exported from HyperWriter to a WordPerfect format, and then loaded into Microsoft Word where a WordBasic script was used to convert styles exported from HyperWriter into Microsoft Word styles. These Microsoft Word documents were then used by John Wiley & Sons to produce the final typeset work.

Building the CD-ROM Version

After John Wiley & Sons and I produced a final set of edited Microsoft Word documents, those were returned to me where I used the HyperWriter AutoLinker module from HyperWriter Professional to automatically convert the Microsoft Word documents to a HyperWriter document organized around a hierarchical table of contents. Although I could have used the Microsoft Word files with the Import Text Wizard, the AutoLinker gave me additional control and let me generate cross-referencing links automatically. Given that I originally authored this book using HyperWriter, you may be curious as to why I used this approach instead of using the original HyperWriter document as the CD-ROM version. The reason was the fashion in which I wrote this book treated each chapter as a linear scroll of text—the sections were not broken into hypertext chunks. The reason for this was not a particular desire to work in a linear fashion (I prefer working in a true hypertext environment), but that HyperWriter does not have any features for automatically linearizing a hypertext. Had I not used a basically linear approach, I would have had to manually export hundreds of individual topics.

Index

CUSTOMER NO **OFTWARE,**
PLEASE READ TH **CKAGE.**

DATE DUE

JUL 1 5 1996

APR 2 6 2001

FEB 1 3 2002

This software con bed in the
accompanying bo o be bound
by the following

This software proc e reserved
by the author and e this
software on a sing medium or
format for use on pyright
Law. Copying the f the U.S.
Copyright Law.

This software proc either
expressed or impli rranty of
merchantability ar ey nor its
dealers or distribu ual
damages arising fr re. (Some
states do not allow :lusion
may not apply to y

WILEY

DEMCO, INC. 38-2931